Rhetoric through Media

Gary Thompson
Saginaw Valley State University

Allyn and Bacon
Boston   London   Toronto   Sydney   Tokyo   Singapore

Executive Editor: Eben Ludlow
Editorial Assistant: Liz Egan
Executive Marketing Manager: Lisa Kimball
Editorial-Production Administrator: Rob Lawson
Editorial-Production Service: Colophon
Composition Buyer: Linda Cox
Manufacturing Buyer: Suzanne Lareau
Cover Administrator: Linda Knowles

Copyright © 1997 by Allyn & Bacon
A Viacom Company
Needham Heights, MA 02194

Internet: www.abacon.com
America Online: keyword: College Online

All rights reserved. No part of the material protected by this copyright notice may be reproduced or utilized in any form or by any means, electronic or mechanical, including photocopying, recording, or by any information storage and retrieval system, without written permission from the copyright holder.

Library of Congress Cataloging-in-Publication Data

Thompson, Gary
    Rhetoric through media / Gary Thompson.
      p. cm.
    Includes bibliographical references and index.
    ISBN 0-205-18918-0
    1. Mass media—Authorship. 2. Rhetoric. 3. Mass media criticism.
I. Title.
P96.A86T48   1996
808'.042—dc20   96-43263
                                                                 CIP

Printed in the United States of America

10 9 8 7 6 5 4 3 2 1   00 99 98 97 96

Contents

Preface ix

I EXPLORING CONCEPTS

Chapter 1: Seeing Rhetoric through Media 3

OVERVIEW 3
    Key Terms: Rhetoric, Media, Text 4
ISSUES 7
    Media Genres 7
    Reading Some Sample Texts 14
    Keeping a Journal 21
    Media Texts As Myths 21
    Reading News and Popular Texts 24
CONCLUSION 27

Chapter 2: Reading Media 29

OVERVIEW 29
ISSUES 30
    What's a Medium? 30
    Learning from the Media 37

Being a "Consumer" 39
Doing Without Media 43
Clutter and Context 50
Strategies for Reading Media 52
Conventions 58
Conventions in Writing and Writing Classes 67
CONCLUSION 73

II MEDIA AND PURPOSES FOR WRITING

Chapter 3: Making Use of Observations— from Prewriting to Drafting 79

OVERVIEW 79
ISSUES 82
Writing As Your Medium 82
Writing Essays As a Conventional Act 89
How Writers Write 100
Prewriting 108
Drafting 117
Readers' Roles 121
CONCLUSION 136

Chapter 4: Gathering and Evaluating News and Information 139

OVERVIEW 139
ISSUES 142
Stories in the News 142
How to Search for Information 150
What Counts As News? 157
News As Rhetorical 165
News and Entertainment 174
Reading the News Comparatively 177
PROBLEMS 191
Keeping Informed 192
Propaganda 197
Objectivity and Fairness 201
CONCLUSION 205

APPENDIXES
 4.1: CNN Prime Time 208
 4.2: CBS Evening News 213
 4.3: All Things Considered 218
 4.4: NPR Morning Edition 221

Chapter 5: Close Attention to Detail: Regarding the Commercial 225

OVERVIEW 225
ISSUES 229
 Why Ads? 229
 Collecting Ads 235
 How to Read an Ad 239
 Analyzing a TV Commercial 246
 Categorizing Commercials 254
PROBLEMS 260
 Ads As Propaganda 260
 Ads and Effects 262
 Dirt 264
CONCLUSION 271
APPENDIX 5.1: PRINT ADS 274

Chapter 6: Reading Pictures 291

OVERVIEW 291
ISSUES 294
 The Appeal of Seeing 294
 Pictures and Narratives 303
 How to Read a Picture 315
 Signs, Codes, and Conventions 322
 Visual Images and Descriptive Writing 330
PROBLEM 335
 The Gaze 335
CONCLUSION 340

Chapter 7: Entertainment As Information 344

OVERVIEW 344
ISSUES 347
 What's Entertainment? 347
 Entertainment As Play 353

More Dirt   361
Why Do They Want You to Play?   372
The Audience's View   386
PROBLEMS   391
Taste   391
Popular Music   397
Violence   401
Children's Entertainment   410
Science Fiction   415
Race and Entertainment Media   416
Stereotypes   418

III RECONSIDERATIONS

Chapter 8: Discovering Contexts and Deeper Purposes   427

OVERVIEW   427
ISSUES   430
Representation and the Natural   430
Labeling   438
Appellation and Ideology   446
Ideology: Definitions and Illustrations   453
Reading Die Hard   465
Reading Media Texts for Ideology   471
Ideology and Metaphor   475
PROBLEMS   476
The Example of "PC"   476
Nostalgia   484
CONCLUSION   490

Chapter 9: Revision: Bringing Drafts to Completion   492

OVERVIEW   492
ISSUES   494
Why Revise?   494
Writing As Conversation   497
Strategies and Tactics for Revising   502
Sample Revision: "Media in the Courts"   510

Collections of Writing 525
CONCLUSION 531

Chapter 10: Developing Style and Audience Awareness 533

OVERVIEW 533
ISSUES 535
Some Bad Advice about Style 535
Reducing Unnecessary Difficulty 546
Style As Constitutive: Or Would You Rather Be a Dog? 555
Hegemony and Style 559
Style and Audience 569
Words, Words, Words 572
Bad Rhetoric 575

Chapter 11: Expanding Media Resources 592

OVERVIEW 592
ISSUES 595
Collections As a Basis for Your Own System 595
What to Expect 598
Electronic Media 600
Search Procedures 606
Hypertext 610
Internet As Source of Information: A Test Case 612
Cyberporn 623
Library Material 629
Some Reservations about the Internet 635
CONCLUSION 642

Works Cited 643

Index 651

Preface

The title *Rhetoric through Media* expresses this book's central idea: Paying critical attention to the multiple forms and contexts of contemporary media can serve as the basis for understanding rhetoric. Understanding rhetoric, in turn, is crucial to improving the success of writing done in various contexts, including college. And we can best come to understand media critically by writing our way to comprehension on our terms.

There was a time when, in a college setting, *texts* meant books like this one. You carried your text to class, the instructor lectured and assigned problems from the text, and if you were fortunate you could find the answers in the back of the text.

What counts for a text has expanded considerably in recent decades, however. In some writing classes, the principal text is not so much a book as the students' own writing. Texts in communications include much that literally cannot fit into a book—broadcast media (radio and television programs) and other nonprint forms (films, electronic documents)—as well as print forms lacking the permanence of books. And in cultural studies, the sense of a text has expanded to include virtually any group of phenomena that can be associated for purposes of analysis—holiday activities, youth cultures, or the body language of men and women in photographs. Thinking of a *text* as *whatever is appropriate to study,* then, means widening the scope of what is available for academic work.

What counts for a text has grown because the number of ways in which we communicate has grown. Computer and video games, newspapers and other documents on line, movies in videotape or CD format, CD-ROM disks, and up to one hundred cable TV channels, along with more specialized magazines, World Wide Web, and bulletin board systems on the Internet—how many of these do you use at least occasionally? Texts in these media are available with no corresponding increase in leisure time. As a result, media are much more segmented than a generation ago; broadcasting has become "narrowcasting." The technologies providing entertainment and information through media will continue to multiply these options. It becomes increasingly important, then, to understand how to "read" such texts—what the texts' conventions are, what sort of roles they offer us as readers, what the costs will be to us in accepting these roles, and how we can write better roles for ourselves.

The model of one person consuming one text needs revision. We may believe that we encounter texts one by one, but that is true only in a sense. We read through everything else that we have read, and particularly through our social practices of reading: Single media texts exist within systems of communication. The devices by which texts reach audiences can be called *rhetoric*. It is important to understand rhetoric, both on its own terms and for what it can tell us about reaching audiences on our own terms. Rhetoric is not confined to dead texts; it's alive and more influential than ever, and its study can help us manage the clutter of messages which are thrown at us.

The idea of a text, then, should be developed beyond a specific television program or magazine article to include the con-text, or everything that comes with the text. How a text is produced and distributed, how audiences respond to it, and what the conventions are through which this happens—these are crucial to our reading of media texts. The goal may be thought of as media literacy: the ability to use a range of texts with full understanding of their presence and effects within the culture.

You may not have time in a normal college semester to make use of all of the materials presented here. *Rhetoric through Media* is set up so as to be used selectively, and instructors will choose chapters and assignments to fit whatever emphasis is appropriate. Materials from this book should be supplemented by the observations of those in the class and by accounts of events having recent or local interest. Study of some areas treated lightly here, such as film or popular music, may be expanded as interest and time allow.

Some chapters of *Rhetoric through Media* are directed toward tasks basic to writing: making observations, looking for associations, analyzing and classifying texts, developing insights, gathering further information, and shaping what is written for a more formal audience and purpose. These activities do not occur in neat stages: They are recursive, and they are signaled throughout the book in ways that are connected to the topics under discussion. Other chapters are oriented more toward forms of media and the ways they correspond to purposes for writing: news and information as our basis for collecting and evaluating what we need to know, advertising texts as material for close reading and analysis, photographs as the basis of visual media that resemble and to some extent supplant description, and forms of entertainment as simultaneously diverting and instructing the audience. But it is part of the purpose here to allow readers to discover the interconnectedness of reading and writing throughout, and not simply in alternation. Each chapter encourages readers to analyze and respond to a variety of texts, both popular and academic.

In addition to discussing a variety of media and media texts, *Rhetoric through Media* encourages its readers to examine ideology as the basis for more thorough analysis. Ideology is considered not in terms of conspiracies or others' "false consciousness," but as the set of values or ideas that animate a text and within which we read. When the concept of ideology is connected to familiar media, it loses some of its abstract, academic character. Chapter 8, "Discovering Contexts and Deeper Purposes," furnishes most of the discussion of how media connect to ideology; but related points are explored throughout the text in discussions of concepts such as *myths, stories,* and *signs.*

Textual features of *Rhetoric through Media* help to make it not just a book to be read, but a guide for observation and critical reflection. Each chapter moves back and forth between general issues and particular illustrations, and readers are invited to draw their own connections through Pauses for Reflection and Facts. Assignments are suggested to allow readers to discover the force of certain points for themselves; for example, we can appreciate the extent of our reliance on all forms of media by doing without media for a short period. Media logs establish early the importance of observation and record keeping to enable us to judge from data and not impressions or preconceptions. Readings from both students and professional writers are provided both as commentary on issues under discussion and as texts whose rhetoric is to be examined. Textbooks are media too, and the rhetoric of this book becomes material for analysis as well as part of its subject.

Advertisements, because they are both short and familiar, are used as texts for analysis. Chapter 5 provides some terminology for looking at technical features of both print and video advertisements. Transcripts and analysis of three video ads are provided, along with sixteen print ads. Students working through this section of the book may profit from collecting their own print and video ads as a basis for class discussion of the rhetoric of these texts. Such collections can serve as a model of collaborative research.

Most contemporary writing texts adopt a process approach to writing, and this book does so as well. Journals and other forms of informal writing are discussed and integrated into the book as valuable work in themselves; and two chapters deal with the movement from informal writing to draft and from draft to finished work, culminating in portfolios that involve writers in gathering and assessing their own work. But this discussion of process is grounded in texts that students already know, at least implicitly, and it connects to issues familiar from discussions in popular and academic publications, and in the political arena.

This book stresses the usefulness of writing in contexts beyond a writing class or even academic study, so that writing becomes connected with the making of meaning going on all the time. Many people in the United States are now skeptical or even cynical about media; but *Rhetoric through Media* reinforces the idea that writing, one's own writing, is a medium, and that we all necessarily take part in rhetoric. Writing not only functions as self-expression, but connects that self to concerns in the larger culture. In a sense, then, this text is unfinished: It remains for you, the reader, to complete it, with more recent examples and with the ones that affect you and that you care about.

The study of rhetoric as effective communication cannot ignore media as the predominant means of communication in contemporary culture. Media texts are widely available to serve as models, positive and negative, for rhetoric. We have rich resources of texts about which we have implicit knowledge; examining these texts to see how they work can enable us to put that rhetoric to our own purposes, in academic contexts as well as others. We can best attain this awareness of how rhetoric works, and how to apply it to our own circumstances, not in opposition to but through media.

This book, then, has a dual purpose. It should help develop your ability to read media and media texts critically, in order to understand how media texts connect with us (and connect us) as readers and writers through their rhetoric. And it should enable you to use that knowledge about rhetoric to improve your ability to write other sorts of texts, particularly those required in college courses. Rather than isolating writing, *Rhetoric through Media* emphasizes the connectedness of reading and writing and thinking critically about the materials of everyday life.

Acknowledgments

In the future, some multimedia version of this book may have a representation of the author smiling and telling you whom to thank and blame for having made it possible. In this earlier, printed version, you have the medium of print to suggest that you imagine such thanks. Print has its strong points.

My many more general debts will be obvious throughout this book. I would like at the outset to offer particular acknowledgments to friends, colleagues, and others who gave advice or incentive at just the right moment. First among these is Allyn & Bacon editor Eban Ludlow, who supplied just the right level of tactful restraint. Thanks to Donald McQuade, for encouragement early on and at key moments in the conception and writing. Thanks also to Susan Miller for timely and cogent suggestions on initial versions of three chapters. And I owe a good deal to the reviewers of the manuscript:

William A. Covino
University of Illinois

Kathy Evertz
University of Wyoming

Michael Keller
South Dakota State University

Kathleen O'Fallon
University of Oregon

James J. Sosnowski
University of Illinois at Chicago

Conversations with my colleagues at Saginaw Valley State University have been important in helping me develop this text. Andy Tessler (also of the *Saginaw News*) tried to correct my misapprehensions about newspapers. Basil Clark, Lynne Graft, Mary Harmon, and Sally Cannon offered comments on chapters; and more extensive help was generously supplied by Janice Wolff, Drew Hinderer, and Marianne Barnett. SVSU has supported this work through a research grant and through copying, postage, printing, telephone, and fax services.

I would like to express my gratitude to the many with whom I spoke about permissions to use advertisements and other texts. Even those who turned down requests were courteous and professional.

The importance of contributions and other work from my students cannot be overstated. I would like to thank the students in my classes all the way back to 1990, before I had any idea of producing this book, for keeping me anchored in a solid sense of the practical.

Last, my gratitude to Pam, Andy, and Ian for their support and willingness to listen while I talked through innumerable problems in the writing. I am indebted to B. J., our golden retriever, for also being a faithful listener and for bringing back whatever I threw. And a considerable debt is owed as well to Juan Valdez.

November 1996

Exploring Concepts

1

Seeing Rhetoric through Media

OVERVIEW

Writing classes are sometimes called "rhetoric" and sometimes "composition." But rhetoric is far older and far more widespread than the custom of requiring first-year writing classes in college—older, in fact, than college. This book is in part an attempt to help you see rhetoric as a far more consequential matter than a semester or two's practice in writing essays: You will be invited to examine your own rhetoric in connection with the most widely distributed and influential uses of rhetoric in contemporary culture, those to be found through media.

In this introductory chapter we will be concerned primarily with defining terms to be used throughout *Rhetoric through Media.* What is a text? How do texts acquire meaning? What is rhetoric? What are media? How do we learn to use rhetoric through media? And more pragmatically, what can critical reading of media contribute to your writing?

In order to get some sense of what it means to read critically a text such as a film or television program, we will look at excerpts from several short texts. Our critical readings will begin with attention to roles scripted by and for the authors and audiences of those texts.

Almost all readers of this book have been engaged by media and media texts for their entire lives. But most of that engagement has been for relaxation on the part of what might be called media consumers. Beginning to reflect on media means developing and extending your powers of observation, as a first step to critical attention. Not all your observation will be pointed to media texts that provide information and entertainment; some will be directed at systems of belief or myths that provide meaning for these texts.

Key Terms: Rhetoric, Media, Text

Rhetoric has become something of a dirty word in recent years. When a public figure makes doubtful claims about a position or attacks an opponent, that's denounced as "rhetoric." When an organization tries to put a positive spin on events or engages in damage control, that's "rhetoric." The term has often been used to mean exaggerated praise for oneself and one's cause, or unnecessarily negative comments about others. This connotation of political or financial interest is unfortunate, because rhetoric is by no means always fraudulent. In fact, all of us use rhetoric—in the sense of effective communication—many times daily.

Rhetorical skill is nothing to be ashamed of or to apologize for. In fact, it's one of the most important job qualifications you can have. In order to develop skill in communicating your ideas effectively, the first step is to realize that that is a worthwhile goal—that rhetorical ability is worth prizing and even enjoying.

Rhetoric may be thought of as *speech, writing, or generally any form of communication directed toward others.* The systematic study of how to make ideas more persuasive began thousands of years ago, with early and still influential thoughts about rhetoric originating in ancient Greece. Each of us begins our attempts to reach others even before we can speak, when as infants we call out for food or attention. We are continually trying to improve at this task, developing language, practicing at analyzing its contexts, and extending the forms of rhetoric we use to fit changing purposes.

Not all writing is directed to others. Much of what you write is for yourself: notes taken in class, shopping lists, diaries, poems (if you don't intend to show them off or send them out for publication), and the like. In these cases your writing does not need to satisfy anyone but yourself. But most of what you write is directed, at least in part, to other readers: parents, friends, teachers, those you work for, the general public, a very close friend. In these cases the writing needs to satisfy yourself *and* to reach another person or other people. When you direct your writing to others, your written voice changes; and this book is meant to help you reach others more effectively through your writing.

Writing for others involves knowing who they are, what they know and believe about the subject(s) of your writing, what they want of you, and who you are to them. When you write for others, you project a **persona,** an image of yourself—as someone who knows little about the subject of your writing, or as an expert; as a careful and impartial speaker, or as someone who articulates strongly held opinions. At the same time, you project an image of those you are writing for, casting them in roles which they may accept or reject (resisting readers, eager listeners, informed and careful thinkers, complete fools, etc.). And when you write for others, you make use of techniques and devices for persuading your readers to consider your views, whether these techniques have been learned in classes like this one or absorbed from your own reading and listening and conversing.

The key difference between this and other books that direct writers' attention to rhetoric is the importance given to media. Commonly, the word **media** refers to the principal sources of information and entertainment—newspapers and magazines among print media; television, radio, films, and popular music among nonprint forms. Many would argue that the most influential forms of rhetoric in our century are those transmitted through media. Rhetoric also can be found in conversations, one on one or in groups—and this use is not mediated by any technological devices. But beginning with the invention of the printing press, it became possible to project thoughts and ideas well beyond the circle of those physically present to hear them, especially in relatively permanent forms such as books. And in the later nineteenth century, with the invention of the telegraph and telephone, such projection could be done instantaneously. The invention of photography and cinema expanded the possibilities for visual representation, adding new and powerful devices to what could be done through the alphabet and speech. The development of radio and television combined the capacity for addressing thousands or millions of people, as was possible through newspapers and books, with the speed available through electronic forms of communication; now a diplomat, preacher, general, or public official could speak with a greatly amplified voice. The intensified commercialization of media, particularly in the United States, brought about the development of modern advertising as a dominant influence on the rhetoric of these texts. Computers and other technological developments promise to change how "readers" respond to/through media. And, finally, the multiplication of forms of media and media texts means that we must sort through a great deal of clutter in order to get the information we need and desire.

What is needed, more and more, is a developed ability to *read* these highly various forms of rhetoric: to read them critically, to notice their devices, and to think analytically about how they work. Media texts are sometimes read as though they just happened—but this book will stress the point that these texts are all **addressed,** or directed, by their authors or producers, who have particular purposes or interests to be communicated through a variety of means; that they are all addressed to particular audiences; and that they all exist within systems of conventions specific to their media.

Text in this book means any set of features that can be grouped for analysis. We'll use *text* as a common term for newspaper and magazine articles, television or radio commercials, films, billboards, CDs, or video games—all of which are recognizable as single units of commercial or other distribution. The term also allows us to consider related phenomena as a text—for example, Robert Dole's presidential campaign, fashion advertisements in magazines such as *Cosmopolitan* and *GQ,* media coverage of O. J. Simpson's trial in several forms, the 1996 Summer Olympics, or the relation between Nathaniel Hawthorne's novel *The Scarlet Letter* and the 1995 film version starring Gary Oldman and Demi Moore (if there is any relation beyond the title).

When we are thoroughly experienced in using specific forms of media, whether in creating or consuming them, their **conventions,** or the rules by which they work, seem like laws of nature. Thinking about a soap opera or a rock song, for those who are deeply familiar with these kinds of texts, means taking so much for granted that it may be impossible to imagine alternatives. Taking an analytical stance toward something with which you are very familiar may be difficult at first, but there are gains to doing so: Once you understand how a favorite text has built your loyalty and interest, you may be better able to use comparable devices to reach others in your own writing.

PAUSE FOR REFLECTION
Just for your own use, jot down a few examples of characters or programs or performers or publications or talk show hosts toward which you have developed a feeling of loyalty. What is responsible for that feeling on your part? Has your feeling changed over time? Were there earlier instances in which you used to feel such a sense of loyalty, but it passed? What was responsible for that change?

We communicate through language, both spoken and written, and we receive other forms of communication, such as music and visual images. This communication goes on practically nonstop. Our awareness of these forms of communication and their uses comes to us through our culture, and media texts are an increasingly large part of that culture. In order to become a more practiced reader of media texts, then, you need to know *how they work.* Being persuaded by a media text is not cost-free: It exposes you to some risks, such as the risk of wasting money and time on a bad investment or of lending your support to a political candidate who may not represent your interests. In observing rhetoric as applied through newspapers, magazines, films, radio, popular music, television, and other media, you will be able to become a more self-conscious participant in those media. Knowing how media work may not be the end of the story. Such knowledge doesn't guarantee immunity from manipulation, any more than knowing how colds are transmitted keeps you from getting sick. But it's a start. And understanding how media texts work should make more choices available to you as a writer.

ISSUES

Media Genres

Though you may not be accustomed to thinking about it in these terms, you already participate in media, not only as audience but as producer of texts. You write. Letters, essays, reports, examinations, notes, entries on computer bulletin boards, résumés and job applications are media, some of which you have been using for years. You may not write for pay, and you may reject the label of "writer"—but it is still valuable to know how to write well so as to reach others in the ways that are most to your advantage.

In addition to participating as a writer, you participate as a reader or audience member for media. Not all readers use media texts in the same way, and not all of us encounter the same texts or media. As you exchange views with others, you will find similarities and differences; and rather than trying to make your responses agree with theirs, you should take these differences as a starting point for understanding how diverse responses are possible.

We don't commonly refer to television programs or movies as *texts,* but there is some point to doing so. Naming something as a text makes it available for critical attention. If we want to understand a phenomenon, as opposed to simply experiencing it, we have to use or develop terminology to allow us to work with the phenomenon conceptually.

In the early 1980s doctors in various countries observed certain patients to have a set of wildly different but associated symptoms, which often led to exotic infections which the patients' immune systems were unable to fight off. As word of these situations spread through the medical community, they were described as a syndrome involving a failure of the immune system. Initially most cases in the Western Hemisphere were found among intravenous drug users, gays, and Haitians, and the syndrome came to be associated with either sexual contact or infection by blood. These phenomena were then labeled as

Acquired Immune Deficiency Syndrome, now familiarly known as AIDS. But at first, there was nothing that brought these several hundred patients into association with each other, nothing that made them a text. That came first through statistics, then through a theory of transmission, then through isolation of HIV, the virus that causes AIDS.

We understand texts not only by themselves, but also in relation to other texts that we have encountered. If you think of, say, the TV show *Friends,* not only do you consider a single episode or all the episodes you have seen; you also consider programs of similar types that seem to play by the same rules. Texts that follow the same conventions can be grouped together into a **genre.** Genres for literary texts include lyric poetry, the short story, and the novel; among genres for films are action–adventure films, romantic comedies, musicals, and documentaries.

Developing a list of texts that fit together is a start toward understanding how they work and how you interact with them. This book will offer some suggestions about media texts, how they have shaped our culture, and what is to be gained from analyzing them. It will also offer a look at how you might think about writing differently after thinking about some of these texts. But the first and most important step is for *you* to begin to notice things about media and your interactions with them.

It's not possible to have a one-size-fits-all approach to media, because the diversity of media and audience choices means that there are necessarily wide variations. When you ask others in your class, you will find that some people watch little or no television, while others may average thirty hours or more per week; some use the radio primarily for music—alternative or top forty rock, country, or R&B—while others attend to radio as a primary source of information or the mixture of information and entertainment provided by talk shows; some will engage with "high cultural" programming such as classical music, documentaries, and PBS programs, while others prefer more "blue-collar" offerings such as country music, stock car races, and Fox network dramas. The television programs members of your class watch may vary according to who has cable, satellite dishes, "rabbit ears," VCRs, or CD systems, or who hasn't troubled to acquire any of this technology. Habits of viewing television and film may be greatly affected by VCR ownership. Those who own VCRs may substitute recent or classic feature films for broadcast television programs, and may record favorite programs for later viewing (fast-forwarding through commercials) or for a private collection. There are bound to be regional variations as well, and contrasts between large metropolitan markets and rural areas. Finally, matters of taste and belief will shape importantly the ways in which we use media. So a first step for learning more about media is to watch carefully what you do, first individually and then across your class.

Chapter 1: Seeing Rhetoric through Media

ASSIGNMENT

Keep a log of your interactions with media. Impressions and memories are sometimes selective; in order to get a reliable picture of what and how you read, watch, and listen to in the media, you need to begin to keep records and to compare your records with those of others.

In order to confirm what sort of media consumer you are, you should keep a log for at least three weeks. Keep the log in tabular form for easy reference. At this point you don't need to write too much about any entry; the log is to be simply a list for reference, not a place for extended commentary or reactions. List in columns the date and time, the form of medium, the specific media text, something about the kind of attention you gave it, and other comments, as shown in Exhibits 1.1 and 1.2.

Some sample questions you might address in the log: Newspapers read? Which? Which sections? With what sort of attention? Magazine articles read? Which? What sort of audience does each magazine cultivate? How can you tell? Does the magazine divide into sections? Which catch your interest? Radio? What sort of programming? What characterizes that program or that channel? Television? Which channels, which programs, which genres of program? Films? In theaters or on video? Other media to be considered? Do these interactions take place in the company of others? If so, with whom, and what sort of discussions go on?

Exhibit 1.1 Media log by Kristina Salcedo. Used by permission. *continues*

Media	Media Text	Date	Times	Content & Form	Reaction & Viewing
TV	"Real World" —MTV	6–30	10–10:30 pm	Show where 7 strangers live together & try to get along, real people, not actors	Glued to the TV, reacted to their reactions of each other
Radio	"Late Night Joe Show"–WTLZ	–	10:30 pm– 7:30 am	Has slow songs through the night then picks up at 6 am	Had good sleep, gets me going in the morning
Radio	"Top 5 at 5"– WTLZ	7–1	5–5:30 pm	Top 5 requested songs of the week	Jammed, they were my favorites too
Tapes	*Drop* songs, Mexican music	–	5:30–3 am	Selena & party rap	Just relaxed with friends

Exhibit 1.1 *Continued*

Media	Media Text	Date	Times	Content & Form	Reaction & Viewing
Radio	Hype play	7–2	5–6:30 pm	Saturday songs	Was riding with cousin having fun, enjoyed music
Theater	*Speed*	–	9:30–11:30 pm	Action film with a lot of explosions and fast-paced activity	Liked it, got into the movie, sat uncomfortably till it was all over
CDs	Love Songs	7–3	12:30 am–5:30 am	Friend played love songs for all his company	Made me want to dance, put me in a happy mood
Tapes	Mexican music	7–4	10 am–2:30 pm	Bernado Martinez, Ranchera	Made me welcome my Grandma more for the holiday
Tapes	Old School Rap	–	8–12 am	Run-DMC, Afrika Bambaata	Reminded me of the old days watching Saginaw's fireworks
Radio	"Late Night Joe Show"	7–5	12 am–7:30 am	Has slow songs, then picks up at 6 am	Felt irritated about getting up early
Tapes	Hard Core Rap	–	7:30 am–8 am	Mack the Jacka, Doctor Dre	Fit my mood, I was getting angrier & angrier as I went to work
Tapes	Loud rap	–	9:55 pm–10:25 pm	Bass music, DJ Laz, Masta Ace, X-Clan	Cruised home tired with the beat, gave me inspiration to make something for me to eat when I got home
Radio	Afternoon music	7–6	10 am–3 pm	Adult songs, Luther Vandross, Toni Braxton	Was lounging heavy
Tapes	Loud Rap	–	9:45 pm–10:20 pm	Bass music, Preachas, Run-DMC	Trying not to fa'l asleep at the wheel on the way home

Exhibit 1.1 *Continued*

Media	Media Text	Date	Times	Content & Form	Reaction & Viewing
Radio	"Late Night Joe Show"	—	11:30 pm–7:30 am	Love songs & pick-up songs in morning	Was happy because my friend who likes music as much as I do was riding with me
Tapes	Real Rap	7–7	7:30–8 am	Gangstarr, Grand Puba, includes real thoughts about the way things are	Listened closely to the lyrics, had my friend explain what they meant about some things
Tapes	Hard Core Rap	—	10 pm–10:30 pm	Mack the Jacka	Was scared of the lightning so I turned the music up so I would not think about it
TV	News	—	11–11:30 pm	Watched the news for the weather conditions	Was tired and wondering about the weather
Radio	Morning music	—	7:30 am–8:00 am	Regular get-up-n-go music	Felt refreshed, relaxed and ready to work hard because I had two friends riding with me
Radio	Weekend party music	—	7 pm–8 pm	Music that is supposed to get you hyped for the weekend	Told myself to get a lot of rest
Video	*Mrs. Doubtfire*	7–10	7:30 pm–9:30 pm	Was a good movie on video about a family that was going through a divorce	Made me think about my parents, and my sisters and brothers
Radio	Slow songs	7–11	7:30 am–8 am	Listened to R Kelly	It reminded me that I missed his concert on June 30th because of class

Exhibit 1.2 Media log by Barb Hamilton. Used by permission.

Date	Time	Type of Media	Media Text	What It Was About	Other Comments (Attention)
8/29	2:45–4:45	Theater	Something to Talk About	Julia Roberts stars as a wife who finds out her husband is having an affair	it was a pretty good movie. Not as funny as I thought it was going to be. Full attention.
8/30	7:00–7:30	TV	Jeopardy		Full attention during the show, none during commercials
8/31	2:00–2:45	Newspaper	Tuscola County Advertiser	Local paper about news in Tuscola County	Gave the articles I read my full attention. Only read the articles that got my interest or were about towns near me.
8/31	8:00–8:30	TV	Friends	Poker episode	Gave it most of my attention, was a rerun.
9/1	9:00–10:00 a.m.	TV	Live with Regis and Kathie Lee	Morning talk show	Little attention, watched, but didn't really see it.
9/2	3:30–3:40	Newspaper	USA Today—Life section	What's going on with the entertainment world	Little attention, was on break at work, needed something to do.
9/3	8:00–9:00	TV	The Adventures of Lois and Clark	Clark's parents were kidnapped and he had to commit crimes so they wouldn't be killed.	Little attention, talking on the phone for most of the time.
9/4	9:30–10:00 p.m.	TV	Cybill	Marianne goes to Las Vegas and tries to marry a lounge magician	Moderate attention—was working on homework somewhat.
9/6	9:00–10:00 p.m.	TV	Dateline	Last story was about how you can get ripped off if you have a checking account.	Full attention, found it scary how easily people could get your money.

Exhibit 1.2 *Continued*   *continues*

Date	Time	Type of Media	Media Text	What It Was About	Other Comments (Attention)
9/7	8:45–9:15 a.m.	Radio	various	Various stations on my way to school	Very little, concentrated more on driving, changed when commercials.
9/7	8:00–8:30 p.m.	TV	Friends	Ross' ex-wife has his baby	Moderate, had seen it before, watched it anyway.
9/7	10:00–11:00 p.m.	TV	ER	Mother's Day—Susan Lewis' mom refuses to take her sister, Chloe, and the baby to their house.	Moderate attention—had not seen this episode before.
9/8	10:00–11:00	TV	Picket Fences	Euthanasia—the chief of police's wife is on trial for killing a terminal cancer patient	Full attention, found the topic and how they dealt with it interesting, especially with Dr. Death.
9/9		CD	Jeff Foxworthy—Games Rednecks Play	Stand-up comedy	Moderate, was cleaning my room while it was on, parts were very funny.
9/10	8:00–11:00 p.m.	TV	The Emmys	47th annual prime-time Emmy awards	Very little attention—depended on what award was given out, did homework during most of it.
9/10	1:30–2:00 p.m.	Newspaper	Tuscola County Advertiser	Local newspaper	Read the articles pertaining to Reese and anything else of interest.
9/11	7:00–7:30	TV	Jeopardy		Full attention while it was on—flipped through channels during commercials.

Exhibit 1.2 *Continued*

Date	Time	Type of Media	Media Text	What It Was About	Other Comments (Attention)
9/11	8:00–9:00	TV	Melrose Place	Season premiere—the apartments are blown up by Kimberly	Full attention, was not as interesting as I thought it was going to be. I knew mostly what was going to happen.

This book (and this class) will focus attention on what *you do with media* (as well as on what media do with you). TV watching is only physically passive, if that: Even "couch potatoes" are listening, viewing, comparing what is seen and heard with experiences and with other texts—and, often, thumbing the channel changer to see what else is on. No one's relationship with media texts is ever completely passive, because texts require viewers/listeners/readers to complete their meanings, and those who produce and distribute media texts have devised careful measurements to determine who is watching and why.

Reading Some Sample Texts

As we consider several sorts of texts and what they have in common, it may help to have some examples at hand. What Exhibits 1.3 through 1.7 all have in common is that all five texts are *addressed* by their authors or producers, who have particular purposes or interests to be communicated through a variety of means; all five are addressed to particular audiences; and all five exist within systems of conventions specific to their media. In other words, they all employ *rhetoric*.

> This is the second English course I've taken in my first year of college, and between the two I would have to say "Reading the Media" has been far more challenging and productive. The most interesting aspect was we were able to pick our own field of studies and develop those throughout the course of the semester. I've always considered myself to be an average writer, and English 114 reemphasized the fact that there is still room for improvement. Since the first class I believe I have steadily increased my writing skills.

Exhibit 1.3 Portfolio cover letter by Seth Yon. Used by permission.

Exhibit 1.4 "Floppy-Eared Friends" advertisement published in *Detroit Free Press* Magazine. Reprinted by permission.

As you read Exhibits 1.3 through 1.7, look for clues about what these texts' writers or producers assume about readers, and vice versa.

The texts in Exhibits 1.3 through 1.7 are drawn from a variety of media: a cover essay for a student portfolio, an advertisement from a Sunday newspaper supplement, the opening of a film, the opening to a television drama, and a brochure for a university. You have probably encountered similar texts (except for the student essay) without finding them especially worth noticing, much less analyzing. Some such texts consist entirely of words, while others mix words with visual or musical elements. Some are print texts, while others are broadcast.

We are routinely surrounded by texts, so much so that it may seem pointless or impossible to pay close attention to any of them. But each of these texts, in effect, writes a part for us to play as we read them. Noticing what those parts are and how they are written for us offers us more choice as to whether or not we want to play along.

Despite their many differences, there are commonalities among various kinds of texts, whether "mass media" or privately produced. Some texts are directed to hundreds of thousands of viewers at once; others are typed on a word processor for one reader, perhaps an instructor. But both kinds make use of language and other symbol systems for communication. In Exhibit 1.3, Seth Yon is writing a cover essay for his portfolio at the conclusion of the semester's work. He has produced a rhetorically sophisticated and complex response to the assignment, balancing the task of assessing his progress through the semester with his desire to get an acceptable grade for his writing. The essay is *interested*—that is, it's being written to achieve a certain end, and he and I and other readers of his essay know this and read from within these assumptions.

The other texts shown are also interested in this sense. The company producing "Floppy-Eared Friends" (Exhibit 1.4) hopes to sell their readers dolls that resemble those seen at craft fairs, either through the mail or at the shop in Underwood, Iowa. Commercials are among the most common media texts in this country, and you are probably thoroughly familiar with the assumptions they make and the roles they offer you as audience. Advertisers have something to sell, and their language and images are carefully chosen in order to achieve that end. Even relatively inexperienced readers and viewers, such as small children, understand that advertisers sometimes make exaggerated claims for how good a cereal tastes or how much fun a toy may be to play with. Presumably readers of this print ad do not expect to buy real "friends" but to acquire cute objects to set on a shelf or give to a niece or nephew. We play, or refuse to play, the role of consumers with specific preferences and tastes.

College brochures (Exhibit 1.5) are carefully assembled to make their colleges seem as attractive as possible. Frequently these brochures combine claims about the social and economic value of a college education with suggestions that college life will be personally rewarding and enjoyable. Our society does not ordinarily stress education as a service or product, but competition between universities often results in appeals that look very much like advertisements.

Though you may not be accustomed to thinking in these terms, films and television programs—entertainment texts—also have something to sell. Like advertisements, college brochures, and end-of-semester essays, the first thing that they "sell" is themselves. They convey the message that they are valuable and intriguing texts, worth paying further attention to. Without this message, any further content might be lost, because audiences would stop watching or listening to them.

Films and television programs also sell an idea of the "consumer" of the text. Our agreement to play the consumer's role tells us what to do with the

It's your move.

From the first day you step on campus, you'll experience a strong balance of academics and extracurricular activities while building lifelong friendships. At Ohio Northern, future engineers play on the NCAA Division III champion basketball team, pharmacists choreograph musical theatre productions, accountants perform in the jazz ensemble, and artists lead campus organizations.

While at Northern, you will be surrounded by others whose ambition to excel will complement your own. One of every ten undergraduate students here ranked first or second in his/her high school class. Northern students have received national recognition for professional accomplishments, scholastic achievement, and athletic prowess.

Your college search is not a roll of the dice. It is a strategic move.

College of Arts and Sciences
Art
  • Ceramics
  • Graphic Design
  • Painting
  • Printmaking
  • Sculpture
Biochemistry
Biology
Chemistry
Communication Arts
  • Musical Theatre
  • Public Relations
  • Speech Communications
  • Telecommunications
  • Theatre
Computer Science
Criminal Justice
Elementary Education
English
Environmental Studies
French
Health (nonteaching)
Health Education
History
International Studies

• concentrations

Mathematics
Medical Technology
Music
Music Composition
Music Education
Music Performance
Philosophy
Philosophy and Religion
Physical Education
Physics
Political Science
Psychology
Religion
Secondary Education
  Certification
Sociology
Spanish
Sports Management
Sports Medicine
Technology
  Co-op Program
Writing
  (second major only)

College of Business Administration
Accounting
International Business & Economics
Management

College of Engineering
Civil
Electrical
Mechanical
  Co-op Program

College of Pharmacy
Pharmacy
Pharmacy/Law Joint
  Degrees Program

College of Law
(Graduate school)

Preprofessional Programs
Predentistry
Prelaw
Premedicine
Pretheology

Exhibit 1.5   Cover and a page from recruitment brochure of Ohio Northern University. Used by permission.

information being provided. As with other texts, the most crucial part of the message is to *keep watching.*

From the opening of the film *Pretty Woman* (Exhibit 1.6), we watch the effects that money has on people's lives, and this combines the potential for moral condemnation with a glimpse of Lifestyles of the Rich and Famous.

---

1. A blue line with a rounded end moves across lower part of screen, R to L; closes off until it forms a circle. Next to it is the label TOUCHSTONE PICTURES.
2. White letters on black screen: TOUCHSTONE PICTURES / PRESENTS.
3. IN ASSOCIATION WITH / SILVER SCREEN PARTNERS IV.

Sound: Low buzz of conversation at a party.

4. Extreme close-up of the midsection and hands of a man in a tux. To the left, the hands of a woman wearing a red dress; to the right, a woman wearing a yellow dress. There are four oversized gold-colored coins, with which the man is doing a magic trick.
5. Superimposition: AN ARNON MILCHAN / PRODUCTION
6. Camera pulls back slowly.

Sound: Magician's voice emerging from the party noise:

No matter what they say, it's all about money. So, let's imagine, ladies, that you're a savings and loan officer. Watch. One, two, three. See? You've got it all. And we've got nothing. And you have all four. Take a look.

7. Superimposition: A / GARRY MARSHALL / FILM

Woman's voice:

Oh!

Magician again:

But I wouldn't trust you with real gold. That's why this one's only worth about a penny. You wonder where the other one went? Watch.

8. Camera pans up and right to the head of the woman in yellow, who is an attractive blonde; the magician pulls a coin from her right ear. Laughter.

Philip:

A penny from the ear, how much for the rest? (More laughter) *Have you seen Edward?*

Camera follows Philip through crowd....

Exhibit 1.6 Excerpt from script of film *Pretty Woman.* Used by permission from Touchstone Pictures.

Vivian sells herself ("We say who, we say when, we say how much") and carries a veritable rainbow of condoms, but refuses to kiss her customers on the lips. Edward buys and breaks up companies, without regard for what this means to "family" corporations—but he cannot maintain a consistent love relationship until Vivian teaches him to walk barefoot in the grass. By the end of the film, Edward's money has been put to more constructive purposes: He has transformed Vivian into a woman he can consider living with in the long term (with her own hair, her good clothes, her appreciation for opera, and her desire to educate herself above her background), as well as being transformed himself. And the two of them have dropped out of the competitive worlds of high finance and prostitution.

This ending is offered to the viewers, however, only as fantasy. (The street person's call at the close invites us to think of the film as fantasy—"This is Hollywood. What's your dream?") In the case of *Pretty Woman*, then, the dominant role written for us is escape. We watch attractive surfaces—the (supposed) gold coins, the pretty people at the party, eventually the characters played by Richard Gere and Julia Roberts—and we are shown that what's on the surfaces may mask uncertainty, deviousness, or unhappiness. "A penny from the ear, how much for the rest?" says Philip, the film's greediest character—and it's "the rest" that titillates in addition to providing the film's Cinderella-like resolution.

A common form that "dreaming" in entertainment takes is *identification* with the characters. How important to you is a specific star in a film or television role? Or a specific TV reporter or anchor on a news program? For many viewers, identifying with individual performers is very important: Particularly in television, an actor's favorability ratings are one of the most crucial factors determining how much money the actor makes. (One critic notes that an agreeable actor is the most vital ingredient for the success of a TV show.) Something like this identification is at work in how we react to politicians as well. A clean-cut face and likable voice and, often, race and class backgrounds like our own are almost job requirements for statewide or national office.

PAUSE FOR REFLECTION
Think back over a film or television program in which it was important to your reaction that you liked the way an actor/actress looked. Have there been instances in which you disliked a program or film because of the absence of this essential liking? Do you react to political figures in comparable ways?

Largely through identification, then, texts such as *Pretty Woman* "sell" **ideologies**—values or assumptions or ideas of how the world is and should be. Such texts do not generally originate these ideologies, but draw from those in circulation and offer them for audiences to adopt, or not. They lead us to want to participate in the world shown. *Pretty Woman* is in some respects critical of its world—greedy businessmen and women tempted into selling themselves and others for money. But at the same time, the movie communicates powerfully about how money can transform a woman who has it from a vulnerable streetwalker to someone who has the power to do what she wants to do. (It is money, after all, that allows a man like Edward to hire a desirable woman as his "beck-and-call girl.")

In contrast to *Pretty Woman,* the opening to *Law & Order* (Exhibit 1.7) deals not with money but with the U.S. justice system, inviting the show's audience to play the role of *the people* who are "represented" by investigative police and prosecuting attorneys. Characters who are caught up in the series's narratives sometimes receive careful and sympathetic treatment, but in the end it is our connection with the regular characters of the series, the police and prosecutors, that defines us as "the people." In addition to entertaining us, then, this and other police shows invite us to see the justice system as legitimate and fair, and to regard our watching a fictional program as participation in the governmental system. We vote with our remotes.

---

1. Black screen with an assortment of white marks, as though very large letters were being lit from the left; while the narration continues, these recede as though the camera were pulling back; simultaneously, the light comes around more to the front, and eventually the letters emerge as LAW & ORDER.

Narration

In the criminal justice system, the people are represented by two separate yet equally important groups: the police, who investigate crime, and the district attorneys, who prosecute offenders. These are their stories.

2. A few seconds after the lettering becomes full, the colors modulate so that the top line is white fringed by blue, the bottom white fringed by red.
3. Cut to vignette introducing that episode's story.

Exhibit 1.7 Excerpt from TV drama series *Law & Order.* Copyright © by Universal City Studios, Inc. Courtesy of MCA Publishing Rights, a Division of MCA Inc. All rights reserved.

We'll return to media texts such as these in the chapter on entertainment, and it will be important to consider the ways in which these texts encourage or confirm our systems of belief. But this textbook is not written primarily to describe or analyze media. It's up to you to do that, singly and with your class. As you continue to interact with texts, you should begin to watch for specific ways in which they reach you. These may range from language, to visual images, to music, to the kinds of people texts include and leave out. The most important task at the beginning is to become a better observer of what you already do with texts and what they do with you.

Keeping a Journal

At this point you need to begin writing down your ideas and observations in a journal (or other form recommended by your instructor). While there may be benefit to reading this book, just as there is to casual engagement with other sorts of texts, attentive and critical reading requires that you also work out your thoughts and observations in some informal kind of writing.

Writing serves not only to communicate to others: Since its invention, writing has been a useful device for paying attention to the world around us. Your journal will be important for that purpose. In other words, the journal will serve as a space in which you may discover what you think about experiences in connection with media. Journals should serve as raw material for essays to be written later in the course. For now, don't worry too much about issues that may concern you in formal writing, such as spelling, punctuation, mechanics, organization, or even knowing where a particular piece of writing is going. Those aspects can be improved when you edit. The most important thing is to get into the habit of putting your thoughts down in writing, so that you can come back to them later for further development.

Media Texts As Myths

Media texts are interesting objects of study in themselves. Certainly they are colorful and attractive, and they are everywhere, presenting themselves to us for our notice and use. What we notice about our world, and how we notice it, come from our culture; and as media become more plentiful, they begin to play roles formerly filled by the family and by religious and educational institutions. We may approve or disapprove, but media increasingly offer us *myths* through which we understand our roles in society and even predict our personal futures.

This meaning of *myth* may be unfamiliar to you. Usually the term is used to refer either to a past culture's religious belief, as with "Greek and Roman myths," or to a lie or self-deception, as in claims that the Holocaust was faked or the superstition that cats are harmful to babies. But a **myth** can be seen more generally as *any story that helps to explain to us why things are as they are,* and in this sense the term can be applied to many concepts strongly held by people in the contemporary United States. The man should be the breadwinner of a house; women are better parents for young children than men; a family should be defined as a woman and man in their first marriage having at least one child; a young adult driver is at a high risk of accidents—these are beliefs held strongly by many in the United States, and they are equally strongly disputed by others as not applicable in some or even most cases.

We usually think of myths as systems of belief that *others* are subject to, not ourselves. What *I* believe is not myth but the truth. But in a pluralistic society such as the United States, claims to absolute truth are usually scoffed at. Belief, from the inside, may seem absolute—but a democracy based on freedom of religion and tolerance of opposing views means that, in the field of public discourse at least, myths have to stand some scrutiny. (Tolerance of others' worldviews is, of course, one of the central myths of our culture.) Many disputes about media are grounded in conflicts between two or more myths: For example, the debate over censoring or at least labeling rap music comes from a conflict between the principle of free speech and artistic freedom of expression and the public interest in polite discourse and orderly behavior, not to mention the desire to control what teenagers do with their time and money. The argument over Channel 1, which provides twelve minutes of news and two minutes of commercial advertising in public schools, reflects differing views about education as a noncommercial activity and about the legitimacy of doing business in the schools. Part of education is learning how to interact with others whose views differ from your own, and understanding where both their and your systems of belief come from. And such an inquiry may be important to your consideration of media and their effects in your life.

Media make important use of myths. If a media text contradicts a widely held public belief, odds are good that it will be of very little influence. The most successful media texts are those that connect with public beliefs, reinforcing and being reinforced by them. Many of the most popular films and television programs of the last decade have reached their audiences in part through providing stories that resonate with one of our favorite myths, the success of an isolated individual who bucks the system and triumphs in the end. In a variant of this myth, many such programs show us a character who initially seems weird or even deviant, but who grows on us as we come to understand his or her true qualities.

The widest and perhaps most significant use of myths by media comes in advertising. Advertising texts are much shorter and more intense than other narratives: Having only a part of a page, only a few seconds of air time, or only a billboard to be read at sixty-five miles per hour, advertisements have to use shortcuts to get our attention. Catchphrases that connect to myths in public circulation are crucial to their workings. ("Just Do It.") In this way, advertisements draw from beliefs already present in the culture—but by their repetition and wider distribution, they help to reinforce and even help create these beliefs.

As you discuss texts mentioned in this book and, more important, those brought into your class, you will be learning to read myths. Most of the time, myths are left unstated, present beneath the visible surface of what is around us. It is probably not possible to live without myths—the idea that any of us can be completely free and independent is one of our most cherished illusions. But recognition that myths are present around us in the contemporary world, and not something that only others are subject to, is a key step toward the ability to participate sensibly in public discourse. The following essay focuses on one contemporary myth.

JENNIFER DITRI

Cheerleaders Are Athletes Too!
When I think of myths, I think of Hercules slaying monsters, Achilles dying only if he got sliced in the back of the ankles, or Aphrodite as the goddess of love. In actuality we encounter myths in our everyday lives: at work, in the classroom, or at home. Many myths are tied into our television, newspaper, and radio programming.

The general definition of myth is a set of assumptions or beliefs that disregard the truth. Watching commercials on television or reading advertisements in magazines or newspapers you can find many. There are so many lotions and creams that are supposed to clear up acne or wrinkles, cologne that makes you more attractive to the opposite sex, shoes that make you a better athlete, and toothpaste that gives you prettier teeth. But beauty and skill come from the inside; physical products can only accentuate the beauty and skill you already possess.

Other than myths in the media, there are myths in society that are inbred, in a way. Most people have heard that athletes are dumb jocks, cheerleaders are bimbos, rock and roll is satanic, or after you hit fifty years you are too old. Whether or not one believes these myths is a whole different topic.

There are so many ridiculous myths about cheerleaders. A few examples are *cheerleaders are dumb; cheerleaders are promiscuous;* and *cheerleaders are not athletes.* If you watch a film that focuses on high school or college social life, the filmmaker usually depicts the average cheerleader as a "blonde bimbo." She is usually well endowed in the chest and hip areas, wears too much makeup, and giggles a lot. She is naive and does anything to gain the attention of others.

I have been involved in cheerleading from Little League to college, and I have never done anything to deserve the "blonde bimbo" title, yet I was always called one. I worked very hard to become what I am now, a college student coaching a high school varsity cheerleading team.

Being a cheerleader did not make me any more promiscuous than anyone else. If the smartest, most respected girl in school joined cheerleading, would that automatically make her promiscuous? No. I do not see how it could. Cheerleading does not change your beliefs and morals for the worse. I do not believe in grouping people together and giving them a title, especially when it is not true.

While I was cheering in high school I was always told by my peers that cheerleaders are not athletes. My team and I worked very hard and eventually became the Michigan Class B State Champs. We worked harder and longer hours than any football player. To prove this, my senior year of high school, my teammates and I invited some of the varsity football players to practice with us to see if they could keep up. The results were disastrous, but hilarious. The next day the football players were whining about how sore they were—most of them anyway. Some were too proud to admit they had had the workout of their lives.

My theory is that everyday myths in our society arise from jealousy and ignorance, and they serve no purpose other than to hurt people's feelings. Other myths, like legends, tall tales, and Greek/Roman myths, formed to explain the unexplainable and to teach lessons to those who needed them.

[Used by permission.]

PAUSE FOR REFLECTION
Have you ever encountered myths about some aspect of how you think of yourself? Do you recognize some of the myths pointed out in this essay? How would you reply to this essay?

Reading News and Popular Texts

One reason commonly given why we should not waste our time on media texts is that they are not important enough to pay attention to. Those that are popular or entertaining are often dismissed as too lightweight for critical attention.

And texts that provide information, news media, are also not treated seriously, because they are thought of as giving us invisible and objective windows on reality. What we get on page 1 is "just the facts," rather than instruction about how to think about those "facts."

Both these perspectives are based on commonly held beliefs or myths, and they may prevent us from understanding how media work rhetorically: In fact, these myths are fundamental to the rhetoric of texts providing entertainment and information.

News is far more than just "facts": The category of what counts for facts is itself created by the genre of news. News is presented through forms of transmission and distribution that select just a few items from the thousands available; these items are given in such a way as to show a dramatic difference in their importance, ranging from the "lead story" or page 1 headlines down to human interest stories or fillers at the close of the broadcast or in the inside pages. It is comparatively rare, however, for the audience to pick up on what is not in the news or what is underplayed—only well after the issues in question came to public notice did we understand about matters such as the savings and loan crisis, the Watergate break-in, the United States' role in selling armaments to third world countries, and so on. Because these and other stories did not initially match up to what news reporters and organizations were featuring as news that the public was paying attention to, they did not come to us as important issues, and therefore they were not "news."

TV news is heavily oriented toward the visual, toward stories that can be filmed. Exotic locales, scenes of disaster, appealing people in moments of crisis all make for good television coverage; they rivet viewers to their seats. Stories that are not easily filmable, however—those that depend on reporters' sniffing out contradictions between public officials' stories, or those that depend on complex phenomena—very often do not get coverage. It is possible that the set of events known as Watergate, which involved surreptitious political activity on behalf of President Richard Nixon, followed by a long series of denials and cover-ups, would not have come to light in our present, visually oriented news system.

The slow emergence of the AIDS crisis gives us an illustration of how poor the news system may be at giving the public vital information: Only after some celebrities began to contract HIV infections and develop AIDS—Rock Hudson, Liberace, Arthur Ashe—did word begin to circulate about the virus's transmission and presence as a health menace. (You can't film a virus.) And when AIDS did come to public awareness, it did so in conjunction with myths—about homosexuality as an affront to morality, about the desirability of keeping the seriously ill out of sight and out of mind even when there is very little risk of contagion, and about the relative unimportance of deaths among the poor and lower class. AIDS began to emerge as a public health crisis when it began to cross over from drug users and gays to a point of visibility for the middle class in, for example, Magic Johnson's retirement from basketball after his infection with HIV. In short, we hear and understand news that we are prepared to hear and understand, and myths are a vital and little-recognized part of this process.

We can find strongly held beliefs about the media's invisibility in how we consider popular texts. Most people claim that their principal use of media is for entertainment—as in watching television at the end of a day of work, seeing films on the weekend, or listening to music while commuting. We do not routinely analyze these texts: Thinking about *Married with Children, Home Alone,* or songs by Alice in Chains is considered to be a waste of time. And offering analytical comments during a program or a song is generally not encouraged or appreciated. (Try it.)

You may find curiosity or confusion among your acquaintances and family when doing some of the assignments this book will suggest. Doing without media for a period of time, watching commercials closely, or counting ethnic references may strike others as much effort spent on something of little importance. But one contention of this course is that these matters are *not* of little importance, because they tell us a great deal about ourselves and our culture's systems of belief. Most media organizations have no interest in calling attention to their power and influence. They make a great deal of money under the present system and do not wish to disrupt that. Furthermore, most people who work in the various activities that come under the heading "media" see their work in narrow professional terms: "I just write about the news, I don't make it," or "It's just a story, there's nothing more to it." News, entertainment, and other categories of media come with their own belief systems, and an important tenet of those systems is the insignificance of individuals' own roles in shaping and confirming public belief.

Popular media are important in part because of their popularity and in part because of their invisibility. Rush Limbaugh may reach three million people daily on his radio broadcast, and many of them write and call congresspeople, independently, with Limbaugh's message of the day. MTV videos communicate powerful messages about what it is to be a woman or a man in contemporary youth culture. And while MTV broadcasts may not ordinarily lead to directly visible political action, the Rock The Vote series in 1992 had some influence in increasing the vote among people under twenty-five. The sheer numbers of people reading the *National Enquirer* (1994 circulation 3,066,032) or watching Oprah and Ricki and Phil means that these "tabloid media" must be providing something that should be noticed.

Popular media tend to be beneath critical notice partly because people in universities and foundations prefer to deal with phenomena that stand still a little longer. This week's hot news becomes next week's old news and, the week after that, a trivia question. But the academic prejudice against critically inspecting media texts is itself the product of a myth—that it is the *texts* that are the object of inspection. If we think of the phenomenon of media rather than the texts themselves, media are not at all rapidly changing—they are remarkably consistent in their methods and goals, as an inspection of early print ads or tapes of old radio broadcasts will illustrate. The rhetorical devices in use in media texts are consistent and continuous, and your study of these devices will repay you in enabling you to respond adequately to the new forms through which rhetoric will be reaching audiences in the twenty-first century.

ASSIGNMENT

Write an informal essay describing yourself or another person as interacting with media. You need not attempt to include all or even most media—but work with media that show the person most characteristically as an audience for a media text. What are this person's concerns, interests, uses of media? How does she or he look to other people? Is the person typical of others, or rather different?

CONCLUSION

No one learns rhetoric in isolation. Take such opportunities as are available to you to learn from others—in your class and outside of it—about their experiences with media. This semester's work will depend in large part on the texts that you observe, bring in, react to, and talk and think about—texts that are around us more or less as water is around fish. Learning to pay attention to what may be seen as background noise, and to find significance in it, may be a new activity for you. But it should be a rewarding one.

FURTHER ASSIGNMENTS

Assignment
Extend the lists of genres on page 8 to other media: Add other TV and film genres, and form your own lists for magazines, newspapers, popular music, and radio programs.

How does it help you understand a text to put it into association with others of similar type? What defines a text as being of a certain genre? What are the conventions or rules by which that text must play, and what happens when one or more of these are violated?

Assignment
Examine a copy of your college or university's recruitment materials and college catalog. How do the photographs, graphic design, and printed text portray your institution? What elements do they emphasize? Are there aspects of college life that are not mentioned or stressed in the brochures? If you could make some changes to represent more accurately your own experience at your institution, what would these be?

2

Reading Media

OVERVIEW

In the words of Stanley Fish, "If at this moment someone were to ask, 'What are you doing?' you might reply, 'I am reading,' and thereby acknowledge the fact that reading is an activity, something you do." If you were asked the same question at another time, your reply might follow the same pattern, but in a different medium: "I'm watching television." Both reading a book and watching television are things you *do,* not things that are done to you. But *how?* How do we learn to make sense of texts?

We have defined rhetoric very inclusively as any form of communication primarily directed towards others. Traditionally, studying rhetoric has meant first analyzing the kinds of appeals used in speech or writing to influence or persuade, and then using that analysis to extend one's own abilities. This chapter builds on that tradition by inviting you to extend this analysis to other media. Later chapters of *Rhetoric through Media* will go into some detail in examining specific forms of media that may be regarded rhetorically. But first it may be important to consider how we as audience form our understandings in connection with conventions or rules through which these texts have their meanings.

This chapter will discuss *reading media* as an activity, focusing attention on models for how audiences make use of media. The most common model offered is that of *consumer,* implying a relatively passive reception of media texts. An alternative involves an audience that is active in engaging with selected texts. Without necessarily planning very coherently or consistently, we pick and choose from media, according to our understanding of appropriate *conventions,* and we use what we gather in such a way as to fit it into contexts provided by previously existing myths and stories. Understanding conventions and how they allow texts to fit into these contexts is an important element of what might be called media literacy.

The previous chapter, "Seeing Rhetoric through Media," asked you to begin observing your own interactions with media. This chapter, "Reading Media," will invite you to think about your role as an audience member for media—that is, to reflect on yourself as an observer. We draw connections with other texts ourselves, in ways that are permitted but not required, by working through systems of conventions that have developed around and through media.

Examining conventions in media will allow you to draw connections with writing. Writing also takes place through conventions—you have spent years in school learning what these are. Becoming a more skillful writer means developing your ability to move within the rhetorical conventions established by the context for your writing. Seeing conventions as chosen, rather than as rules to be followed without question, may give you greater freedom as a writer. Understanding how conventions both limit communication and make it possible is essential to making the best use of rhetoric.

Our subject is more than just reading, as we usually understand it. The sense of what counts for a text is extended not only to popular media, in broadcast as well as printed forms, but also to the reader's activity. To be complete, reading requires writing and vice versa. Reading and writing are different phases of a common action: When you write, it is because you first have "read" others' texts, both written and spoken. All of us have absorbed the conventions through which language works. And as we read, we bring others' texts (spoken and written) into a story we are continually writing, and one that is being written for us—the story of who we are in our culture.

ISSUES

What's a Medium?

Conventional definitions of *media* include, among those using print, newspapers and magazines; among broadcast media, radio and television; and among forms of entertainment, film, popular music, and perhaps others such as electronic media. For this chapter, it may be useful to expand slightly the account of how media develop over time.

It may help to think of these media as assembled from other forms. Radio, television, and film include speech; television and film use photography (itself evolved from drawing and painting); music is important to radio, television, and film. Printing is integral to newspapers, magazines, and some genres of television (for example, advertising and news). And writing is itself a medium, one which can be found throughout all the other media. Almost all texts in the conventional media mentioned above began with a script, storyboard, or other written document. Looking at these texts may in turn give us resources for our own writing.

Writing is made of words—*thinking* is made of words—and it might be a good idea at the outset of this chapter to look more closely at the word *media* and some of its close cousins. Exploring the origins and associations of key words is a useful device for expanding our sense of their context.

Media is not just one thing. We sometimes refer to media as though it were singular—*the media*—but the word is the plural form of *medium*. There are many media with overlapping functions, and many media texts that do not speak with one voice. During your work with this course you will want to investigate for yourself the extent of their overlapping, and the reasons behind it.

It may help us to start with the word itself. A *medium* is something that comes between two other things. You may like your coffee *medium* hot; that is, between hot and warm. A *medium* as "spiritual reader and advisor" may claim to go between or *mediate* between the spirit world and the customers attending a seance. A good political solution may be thought of as a *medium* between extremes. A related word used in negotiation is *mediation:* Mediators help opposing sides reach a compromise or middle ground. For example, mediators may split the difference between what labor wants and what management is willing to pay. So in this sense, media move between us, the audience, and something else. They *re-present* that something else to us. If we can, we should think of the television screen as what it literally is, a flat surface onto which patterns of light are projected, rather than as our window on the world.

The term *medium* also has meaning in physics. A medium is whatever material provides the substance through which waves move. AM or FM radio waves serve as the medium to carry talk or music, and television is also broadcast over FM frequencies. Medium in this meaning is a device for carrying something else; it becomes noticeable only when there's a problem in transmission.

We find *medium* in use in biology as well. A medium is a substance, such as agar, that allows a bacterial or other culture to be grown on it. If the medium is prepared correctly, it will sustain, not interfere with, the culture.

Here, as in physics, a medium carries something else; but it is not ordinarily something to be paid attention to. Rather, the medium is a means to facilitate something else—it directs attention elsewhere. The medium is self-effacing, invisible, neutral. Perhaps we might think about media in communications as anything that carries and sustains contemporary culture. This use should remind us that *culture* is something that is grown, as in *agriculture*, not something that happens all by itself.

But if we think of the sort of media with which this book is concerned as being like ideal transmission waves, nutrient agar, or channels from the spirit world, we may be misled by our metaphors. What our sort of media supply are elements of a culture that has shaped us, a culture in which we participate. Human beings do not receive messages as unproblematically as radio sets receive broadcast signals—and the "messages" we receive are much more ambiguous and complicated than FM signals received by a portable radio. We are not machines but primates, and we often take pleasure in playing with our messages rather than receiving them straightforwardly.

PAUSE FOR REFLECTION

Another important word whose history is important to examine is **culture**.

> Culture is one of the two or three most complicated words in the English language. This is so partly because of its intricate historical development, in several European languages, but mainly because it has now come to be used for important concepts in several distinct intellectual disciplines and in several distinct and incompatible systems of thought....
>
> The word is only available, in its modern sense, when the independent noun, in the artistic and intellectual or anthropological senses, has become familiar. Hostility to the word *culture* in English appears to date from the controversy around [Matthew] Arnold's views.... It is significant that virtually all the hostility...has been connected with uses involving claims to superior knowledge (cf. the noun "intellectual"), refinement (*culchah*) and distinctions between "high" art (culture) and popular art and entertainment. It thus records a real social history and a very difficult and confused phase of social and cultural development. (Williams pp. 87, 92)

Media in the cultural sense, the sense that concerns us here, communicate through symbol systems. The most important and most highly developed of these is language. Language has a way of carrying its own content rather than simply submitting to what we might intend. Some ambiguity will occur under the best of circumstances; and many of those on the "producing" side of media make use of ambiguities and other features of media to reach (influence) their audiences.

There's nothing evil about influence, in itself. All of us use language—journalists, editors, publishers, film and TV producers, anchorpersons, reporters, experts, government officials, the professional middle class, writers of textbooks, and professors and students in university classes. And in using language, we all put our own particular spins on what is said. Neither "their" communications nor "yours" are completely innocent. This is an old complaint about rhetoric, as old as Plato—but it's one that suffuses our world, one we have to work within. The difficulty is to recognize, and make use of, devices that influence readers and listeners, but to do so fairly, so as to build and sustain confidence.

We might do well to think of media as ways to amplify our voices. The first technological breakthrough that made a fundamental shift in media, extending the possibility of communication beyond conversation, was the alphabet—or, more generally, all forms of graphic communication, including cave paintings. By that means one person could "speak" to another distant in space and in time; an absent author could be "present" by means of recorded messages.

But the very process of transcription alters the nature of the message. The earliest surviving literature is a transcription of oral narratives, such as the Greek epics *The Iliad* and *The Odyssey*. These were necessarily different when chanted from the way they exist for us as written texts. What did Homer look like? With what gestures were his lines accompanied? The features of oral interpretation largely disappear in transcription. Some of these features may be recreated by a reader of the poet's lines, but necessarily with some change from their previous existence. And most of us do not chant poetry aloud, but read silently.

Commonly we assume that understanding will be more complete with face-to-face communication. If we have questions or need information, we can ask the person we are talking with. We generally do not have this possibility with writing or contemporary media (although call-in shows and letters to the editor are gestures in this direction, and some feedback is available through book reviews and sales figures). If we cannot ask for clarification, it falls on us to interpret what is said and written.

In other words, dialogue is a common part of personal encounters; but dialogue with media is, at best, occasional and imprecise. The invention of the alphabet and of writing, then, provided some possibilities and precluded others, but fundamentally multiplied the avenues of persuasion. With photography, film, and especially television, there is the appearance of face-to-face communication—but it is only the appearance, almost a parody of a conversation.

PAUSE FOR REFLECTION

Many people prefer to have news read to them by someone who is on camera, rather than reading the same words in a newspaper or hearing them from a voice on the radio.

What is important about seeing someone's face in presentation of a news report, an endorsement of a product, or a photo accompanying a news story? You may test your reaction to this by watching an unfamiliar television news broadcast with the picture darkened. How does this change your response to what is said? What happens if you watch a television interview with the picture darkened?

Returning to the normal use of the television, what details mark differences among the faces that you watch—for example, age, race, facial hair, glasses, expression—and how do these details figure into your reading of the faces and the messages they deliver? What changes if you read these media as using people's faces as another element of their meaning? Speculate on what led the producers of those texts to select those specific faces.

You may wish to look at some photographs of faces, such as those in Chapter 6, as examples. What uses could be made of those faces on television? In films? In connection with print advertising? For another example, see Exhibit 2.1.

After the development of writing, the next fundamental technological change was *mass* communication, made possible by the invention of the printing press. Now texts, rather than being reproduced only through handwriting, could be mass produced. This took communication farther away from the face-to-face model—you can't talk face-to-face with 10,000 people.

Over time, printed materials began to address as audiences not only the educated upper and professional classes, but the middle and lower classes as well. Wider distribution of printed material depended on increasing literacy, and the ability to read became increasingly important for functioning in society.

We pride ourselves, at the end of the twentieth century, on technological innovations such as computers, electronic mail, and interactive video. But we sometimes overlook the innovations that preceded these—writing, the printing press, the popular newspaper—because we live inside of a world that they made possible. Electronic media may be seen as extensions of the potential already present with the printing press; as amplifications of what was already possible with typewriter and carbon paper, with telephone, with printing press, or with quill pen and parchment. A crucial distinction, however, is that there are *many more* media now than formerly. Our verbal world is far more crowded than it was a few centuries ago.

Clutter is the term used to describe how crowded the world of information has become. The problem is evident when we look at television commercials, in which information (visual, auditory, and verbal combined) may be pre-

"Friends, do you suffer from hemorrhoids?"

Exhibit 2.1 The Image Works Archives.

sented very rapidly. A thirty-second commercial may have fifty or more cuts, camera movements, sounds, and other technical events. These occur too quickly for us to register their content consciously except after repeated viewing and analysis. And when one commercial is finished, three or four more follow.

Analyzing media texts, whether in advertising or other forms, depends on decoding symbols through which they communicate. Media exist within—through—symbol systems: not only language but also conventions for understanding photographs, drawings, film, color, and other elements of media texts. Symbols change when they are used—and after accumulated uses, they can wear out. If you doubt that a symbol can be worn out, measure the thrill of pride at seeing the national flag flying in the breeze above a lighthouse or patriotic building against the experience of seeing the flag over and over, in front of libraries, post offices, and houses, over car dealers' lots, in classrooms and in patriotic street decorations, on postage stamps, as patches on jackets, in art museums, on bumper stickers and decals, in political advertisements, and in other locations.

The more a symbol is repeated, the more natural and less symbolic it appears. This naturalized appearance is part of the difficulty of analyzing media texts: They persistently direct our attention away from themselves and toward something else, some message, that they are communicating. Many media downplay symbols' existence and rhetorical functions. And clutter complicates the task of sorting out this symbolic function of media texts.

Media have shaped our way of understanding the world. More than 2,000 years ago, Plato argued that the invention of writing would impair the human memory—that instead of developing a facility for remembering things, as was necessary during the time when rhetoric meant the art of *speaking* persuasively, people would grow lazy because words could be written down rather than committed to memory. Whatever the virtues of that argument, writing did occur and did take hold, and as a technology it changed human culture. Similarly, the printing press, photography, telegraph, telephone, and typewriter brought other changes; and closer to our own time the list should be extended to radio, film, television, and computer media. Some people question the effects of these technologies in themselves, along lines that resemble Plato's; others consider the technologies good or neutral in themselves, but express doubts about the material they convey. But whether you are inclined to worry about or celebrate the increasing diversity of media now available, they are a fact of contemporary culture. What is needed is greater ability to analyze and interpret media—**media literacy,** beyond the "consumer" phase.

ASSIGNMENT: ATTENTIVE TV VIEWING

Some of your television watching as you read this textbook needs to be attentive TV viewing. This phrase is used for watching in an alert state of mind, with scratch pad at the ready—because it greatly helps us recall details of any sort if we write down just a phrase. When doing attentive TV viewing, you should be writing things. Write down the starting time, finishing time, times taken for snack or bathroom breaks. Write down who else is present and what sort of interactions are going on during TV viewing. Write the program being watched, key phrases to help you recall scenes, good lines, reactions, impressions. Write what sort of signals let you know that a commercial break is coming and how things resume. Write what commercials and promos are aired, along with your reactions. Write brief reminders of others' comments during the program.

Finally, you should do some reflective writing about this attentive TV viewing, at least three or four times, in an informal style. Do so both immediately after attentive TV watching, and after a day or so has passed. What difference does that passage of time make in your ability to make use of your notes to recall what you saw and experienced? How do the notes help you assess the importance of the TV viewing?

Learning from the Media

Cartoons and stereotypes about television illustrate one of the most common myths about media—that their flow is all one way, that they provide mainly nourishment for couch potatoes. This view of media consumers as vegetables tends to be about *other* consumers, not ourselves. (Cartoon characters tend to have names that are different from most of ours, such as Dagwood or Opus.) We sometimes play along with this way of thinking about media, by saying that we are going to "veg out" this weekend, by imagining newspaper reading as an armchair activity, or by using the radio as background noise. But while there are many apparently passive ways of engaging with media, we are more active than this myth suggests.

Even in passively absorbing media texts, we learn things. For starters, we learn about language. New language learners are advised to immerse themselves in the language they are studying, because by watching television, listening to radio and tapes, and paying attention to conversations—even before being able to sort out the words and phrases involved—they absorb the sounds and rhythms of the language they are studying. We learn our first language the same way as infants, and we continue to learn English as adults, by absorption as well as by conscious effort.

Media continue to shape language use for adults as well as for children. Broadcast media have contributed substantially to a homogenizing of speech and language use in the United States. Radio and television have helped establish one regional accent, Midwestern American English, as standard. Generations ago, American English was characterized by diversity, with more pronounced regional accents.

You might confirm this homogenizing tendency by observing how those with accents are portrayed in entertainment media. Notice how rare it is to find someone on television with an accent—and notice how that person is frequently subordinate to other characters or speakers, either socially or in terms of importance to the plot. In a variant of this phenomenon, villains are sometimes marked by accents—especially a Southern or Eastern American or a foreign accent. Especially with recent immigration, a foreign accent has changed from a comic but essentially harmless trait to a serious, sometimes even threatening marker of difference from the majority culture. For another illustration, keep track of those interviewed for national news programs over a period of a week or two—how many speak with anything besides Midwestern accents?

PAUSE FOR REFLECTION

Search out media texts in which a person or a fictional character appears who is marked as different from what might be called mainstream or majority American culture. This might occur, for example, in a travel brochure that advertises trips to other countries or regions; in *National Geographic* magazines (current or old); in a feature film such as *Black Rain*, *Native Son*, or *The Joy Luck Club*; or in reports about Iraq, South Africa, Somalia, Haiti, or other areas in the news. What initial impressions do you have about the figures portrayed in these texts? What features in the texts help to create or reinforce those impressions?

Language learning extends from pronunciation to the selection of words and phrases to be used. It's possible to follow the flow of terms and phrases from newspaper and magazine and from television and radio and film into everyday use. During the Watergate hearings in 1973, John Dean and others appearing before the congressional special committee on Watergate made use of the phrase *at that point in time* (a wordier way to say *then*), and the term began to echo here and there in common use—in newspaper and radio columns about the Watergate testimonies, in conversations, in books, and in other texts. Other terms have come into use in part because of their distribution through the media; for example, the use of *-gate* as a general suffix for a scandal (Irangate, Travelgate). In 1987, President Reagan's partial admission of guilt in the Iran-Contra scandal—"Mistakes were made"—became a very useful term for accepting official but not personal responsibility. In addition to these relatively trivial examples, media are important devices for conveying general knowledge about technical terms, geographical locations, legal phrases—and, necessarily, the concepts and values that underlie these terms.

Media can affect not only our language but our general outlook and demeanor. You probably have a selection of books or magazines you read or music you listen to in order to cheer up or get into a desirable mood. Program music, or Muzak, is often provided to put grocery shoppers into a buying frame of mind, to relax patients in dentists' or doctors' offices, or to relieve travelers' anxieties in airports. Negative influences can be traced as well: It has been observed that spouse abuse reaches its peak on the evening of football playoffs and the night of the Super Bowl (Cohen and Solomon p. 59).

In addition to serving as a source of language or a personal sound track, media tell us all sorts of things about how people like ourselves are placed within our culture. Major factors such as race and gender, and minor and changeable ones such as appearance, weight, and style of dress have a great deal to do with how we are "read" by others in society—and it is media, in large part, that teach us how to "read" these things. A substantial number of readers of magazines like *Cosmopolitan, Harper's Bazaar,* and *GQ* are looking at articles and advertisements for advice about how to dress and style themselves.

Concern with appearances may be far more than superficial. In November 1994, ABC's *20/20* aired a report about a study in which two sets of identically well-qualified applicants (two men, two women) were sent to interview for jobs. Within each pair, one was relatively plain-looking and one noticeably more attractive. The less attractive candidate routinely was told to "Call back next week, we may have something for you," while the more attractive candidate (who followed the first) was usually offered a job on the spot. In the follow-up interviews the prospective employers explained their preference by things other than appearance—she had a nicer voice, or he seemed better able to relate to customers; and in most cases they did not even acknowledge the extent to which appearance had influenced their judgment. It may be that decades of seeing the attractive lead actor get the girl while the slightly overweight sidekick gets to be best man have inclined us to accept this basis for preference as natural.

PAUSE FOR REFLECTION

Write informally about ways in which your personal appearance has affected the way in which you have been treated by others. Does this effect change with time and deeper acquaintance? Are there ways in which you try to shape your appearance to meet others' expectations of you?

How has the personal appearance of someone you know affected how you think about that person? For instance, did you form a first impression that later was either confirmed or changed? What was it about the person's appearance that struck you? Why?

It's no use, then, to say that media are strictly sources of entertainment: We do use media texts, consciously or not, as ways to confirm our understanding of what is considered appropriate speech and behavior. Sometimes we may intend to imitate what we see, and sometimes to reject it—but positive or negative, media have an influence.

Being a "Consumer"

Because a common model for describing us as users of media is that of relatively passive viewers or consumers, it may be useful to look more closely at the concept of consumption—as Raymond Williams does below.

RAYMOND WILLIAMS

Keyword: Consumer

In modern English **consumer** and **consumption** are the predominant descriptive nouns of all kinds of use of goods and services. The predominance is significant in that it relates to a particular version of economic activity, derived from the character of a particular economic system, as the history of the word shows.

Consume has been in English since C14 (the 14th century), from [the French word] *consumer*, and the variant *consommer*,... [from Latin] *consumere*—to take up completely, devour, waste, spend. In almost all its early English uses, **consume** had an unfavourable sense; it meant to destroy, to use up, to waste, to exhaust....

It was from mC18 that **consumer** began to emerge in a neutral sense in descriptions of bourgeois political economy. In the new predominance of an organized market, the acts of making and of using goods and services were newly defined in the increasingly abstract pairings of *producer* and **consumer**, *production* and **consumption**.... [I]t was really only in mC20 that the word passed from specialized use in political economy to general and popular use. The relative decline of *customer*, used from C15 to describe a buyer or purchaser, is significant here, in that *customer* had always implied some degree of regular and continuing relationship to a supplier, whereas **consumer** indicates the more abstract figure in a more abstract market.

The modern development has been primarily American but has spread very quickly.... The development relates primarily to the planning and attempted control of markets which is inherent in large-scale industrial capitalist (and state-capitalist) production.... The development of modern commercial *advertising*...is related to the same stage of capitalism: the creation of needs and wants and of particular ways of satisfying them, as distinct from...the notification of available supply which had been the main earlier function of *advertising*.... **Consumer** as a predominant term was the creation of such manufacturers and their agents.

[From Raymond Williams, *Keywords: A Vocabulary of Culture and Society*, 2 ed. New York: Oxford University Press, 1983. Reprinted by permission of Oxford University Press.]

QUESTIONS

1. Do you ordinarily think of *consuming* as related to destruction or waste? Is it significant that that is the root sense of the English word?
2. What story or myth about economic development underlies Williams's account of the history of the word *consumer*?
3. If this account seems jarring to you, what in your own assumptions about being a consumer does it conflict with? That is, from within what story or myth do you read Williams's account?

The word *consumer* has some effect on how we have come to think about our uses of media. We know about consuming things: Our modern economy is built on the concept. Consuming takes place in exchange for money. We exchange money (usually, though not always, the product of our time and labor) for tangible items, which we eat or wear or play on the CD player or otherwise make use of. These uses vary considerably between individuals, as a little time watching the contents of shopping carts in grocery stores will illustrate: Diversity in shopping preferences is one of the markers by which we consumers display our individuality. But regardless of whether we dine steadily on snack foods, frozen dinners, red meat, or green vegetables, we do all eat; and we do all interact with the culture verbally.

But the term "consumer" may not apply very well to our use of media. Usually, consumers use and discard food, clothing, or other products. But "using" a text—whether playing a piece of music on a CD, listening to a football game on the radio, watching CNN World News, reading the *Star*, or doing problems from a mathematics textbook—does not physically destroy it. And, more significantly, it means taking the text into your mind and, to some degree, thereby changing your consciousness. Some critics of media argue that, rather than our using media, it might be said that media use us; this class is in part an invitation to think about whether that is true for you; and, if so, how you should feel about it.

You may have discovered in observing other media consumers, such as television watchers, that we may not be all that passive. Some subjects may be observed to talk back, hit the remote button to mute the sound, change channels during a commercial, or talk with others in the room during the program (Exhibit 2.2). As newspaper readers, we don't just glance over the newspaper: We sort through the sections to find information in which we are interested, information to be used in some manner, on the job or in conversation. In engaging with media texts, we select materials according to several purposes: to confirm who we are or want to be, to glean illustrations of what's wrong with the world, or to keep tabs on what everyone else is talking about. From our selections we draw language that we use in writing to shape a persona for our readers or listeners.

PAUSE FOR REFLECTION
Look back over your media log and journal entries to date, and draw some conclusions about your own typical uses of media. If the log entries are typical, what uses do you make of media?

Exhibit 2.2 Cartoon by Ed Stein, reprinted courtesy of *Rocky Mountain News*.

If you are an "average" American consumer of media, statistically you spend around four hours daily watching TV and devote somewhat less time to reading newspapers and magazines and to listening to radio. But averages can homogenize and conceal wide variances. Besides obvious exceptions—many people who work or study full-time do not have time for sustained television watching—there are those who have chosen to watch little or no television, who may not own a television set or who leave it in the attic. Others participate selectively in television, viewing some programs (news, documentaries, "high culture") or some networks (PBS, the Discovery Channel, Nickelodeon, the Family Channel). Still others view selectively by time, watching soaps or game shows in the daytime while doing household chores, or watching late-night television just before going to sleep (Exhibit 2.3).

The television audience is segmented demographically. Children select along networks and hours that offer programs directed to them (a mix dominated by syndicated offerings and cartoons from the last sixty years, along with some recent programming). Some of the rowdier talk shows draw audiences heavily from the fourteen- to twenty-four-year-old age group; older viewers are driven away by some of the topics and style of interaction.

Locality and availability further segment television audiences. Some viewers' access to television is limited to the broadcast channels in their area—

Exhibit 2.3 Calvin and Hobbes © 1990 Waterson. Reprinted with permission of Universal Press Syndicate. All rights reserved.

usually the major networks, a public TV channel, and an independent or two. Slightly more than half the households in the United States have cable TV, with its improved reception and access to many more channels—40-some is common, and in some major metropolitan centers there are 100 or more. Still more channels are available by satellite dish, and there are plans to improve the technology to open up as many as 500 channels to viewer access. Television, the principal mass medium in the United States, which has itself diversified since the so-called Golden Age of the 1950s and early 1960s, now faces increased competition from feature films and other programming available on videotape. If just the number of choices available were the main factor, today would have to be considered television's Golden Age.

But despite the growth in the number of choices, there has been little if any change over several decades in the amount of time people spend with media. Television viewing has remained roughly constant since television sets became part of most households, and any slight increase there is perhaps offset by a reduction in time spent reading the newspaper or going to films. This should be no surprise. The average work week in the United States has lengthened since the 1950s, and there are many more two-career families than there were forty years ago. It would follow that there isn't much more leisure time to be found. Between TV broadcasts, cable, and satellite dishes, consumers of media have more options, but no more time—and the competition for time and therefore for money has intensified.

Doing Without Media

Developing an analytical stance toward media may be difficult at first, because we take our uses of media so much for granted. Our involvement illustrates how much contemporary culture is saturated with media. In order to help you measure how much you depend on media, this section of the text will ask you to go without for a while.

The pattern for this assignment is drawn from a nineteenth-century writer and critic of his times, Henry David Thoreau. Thoreau criticized his New England contemporaries for failing to look consistently and deeply into the nature of things around them because these things had become routine. Determined to show that the routine manner of life was not the only one possible, Thoreau decided to live as simply and frugally as possible for an extended period. He kept a journal at the time, which (after much revision) became *Walden*.

For slightly more than two years, Thoreau managed without spending much on housing, clothing, food, or other "necessaries of life." Along with expensive luxuries (for the time) such as tea and coffee, he did without newspapers or telegraph accounts about political developments, the war with Mexico, and so on. (His comment was that it was wonderful that Maine could now talk to Texas, but that it would be more appropriate to consider *what* was being said across the wires.) Doing without the news was no very great struggle for Thoreau, as he could engage in his preferred media, reading classic texts and taking extended walks in the woods. By raising questions about the railroad and other forms of technological progress that people took for granted, Thoreau encouraged his fellow townspeople to question the customs and practices of everyday living.

A contemporary book that follows some of the lines of inquiry set out by Thoreau is *The Age of Missing Information* by Bill McKibben. In order to get a point of departure for assessing the quantity and quality of information available through television, McKibben arranged to record *every minute* of television broadcast over one twenty-four-hour period, on May 3, 1990, in what was at the time the largest cable television system in the United States (that of suburban Washington, D.C.). McKibben collected and viewed all these tapes, requiring more than 1,000 hours of watching. The book draws a contrast with a less rigorously defined period spent backpacking in upstate New York, away from television and other technological distractions. McKibben contends that our reliance on media such as television is costing us in ways that we do not recognize.

For most people in Europe and North America and in many other parts of the world since World War II, our way of knowing the world has been formed to a large extent within the frame of the television screen, so that it becomes difficult to conceive of any other possibilities. But television, like other media, tends to rely on what it does best—specifically, presenting news stories that are visual, presented in uncomplicated and clearly understood terms, and narratives that fit conveniently into a consumer-oriented way of looking at the world. There are other ways of interaction—which we may forget or overlook if we are tied to our routines. As saturated with media as we are, it takes an effort of will to ask what it would be like not to have that presence always available.

Living in the woods for two years or taping and watching 1,000 hours of television may not fit your immediate plans, but it may be useful for you to engage in a more modest sort of examination of the media's overall effects on you. People sometimes comment, playfully or not, that reliance on television and other media has effects like those of a drug. The next assignment in this chapter asks you to go cold turkey for a brief period. You should sign off on all avoidable forms of media for the specified period, making necessary arrangements with friends, roommates, and family so as to minimize your exposure to media texts. This project will encourage you to examine media not by paying attention to it, but by doing without it and taking note of what you are missing.

ASSIGNMENT: MEDIA DEPRIVATION

In order to gain some perspective on how your interactions with media affect you, choose some period of time—forty-eight hours might be a reasonable start; extend it to a week if possible—during which you will do *entirely* without mass media. (One-on-one media such as telephone conversations or e-mail are permissible.) Leave the television off; play no video cassettes (favorite programs may be recorded for later); drive to school and work without turning on the radio or playing tapes; don't read the newspaper or magazines; and so forth. You may need to make some compromises for this assignment—billboards or signs on the subway may be unavoidable; other classes may assign you to read something; and those who live nearby may have to be persuaded to cooperate. You should discuss with your instructor what to do about borderline events such as live concerts, e-mail, or novels. But give it a good-faith effort.

Most important for this experiment is that you *observe* and *pay attention to* your thoughts and perceptions. Keep an extensive journal during this time, and write informally on what difference it makes not having your ordinary media at hand.

The following readings, Exhibits 2.4 through 2.9, are journal entries from students who did without all forms of media for forty-eight hours.

After your own media deprivation, compare your reactions to those given in Exhibits 2.4 through 2.9. What other sorts of comments came up among students in your class?

> I chose this past weekend to do my media deprivation assignment. I had to work both Friday and Saturday night, so it wasn't quite as bad as I thought it would be. All I had to do was keep myself media-free during the day.
>
> Media is such a part of my life, that I had to actually concentrate on not doing anything to involve myself in it. It made me realize how many habits I had. One habit I noticed is that whenever I get home I automatically turn on the television, whether I plan on watching it or not. Not watching television was the hardest part of all.
>
> I also like to fall asleep with the radio on, or have it on while I'm doing my homework. It was really difficult going on with these things without being able to use my radio.
>
> I also got a new magazine in the mail. It was torture letting it sit there without reading it.
>
> I've come to the conclusion that I can't go on with my day as usual without participating in the media. I don't think I could ever get used to not watching TV, listening to the radio, or reading magazines. I've done all these things all my life.

Exhibit 2.4 Media deprivation journal by Marci Nowak. Used by permission.

> Forty-eight hours with no television, radio, or video games?!! Are you crazy? I guess it would not be so bad if I did not have three roommates. I told them about my assignment and they all laughed in my face. They told me to lie and pretend I was deprived of media, but I know I would not have gotten the full effect. I did my best and decided to do it on Thursday and Friday. I chose these days because Thursday I have class all day, then work, and then I go out at night until very late. Fridays I sleep in late, do homework, and go to work. Don't get me wrong, it is still very hard for me to do, I am a die-hard soap opera fan, video game freak, and country music fan. Even if my day is very busy I still find time to do all of the above.
>
> * * *
>
> I began this assignment hoping I would study more, read more novels, and relax, but all I did was sleep! I chose Thursday and Friday to do this project. I have three other roommates, so it is hard to find a room in the house that is media-less. When I woke up in the morning on Thursday and had to keep myself from turning on the radio during my shower—I just sang to myself instead. To my dismay our VCR broke, so I could not record my soap opera and I could not watch it either! That was the worst part of the day. I was coming and going most of the day, so the rest of the day was in the car, so again I resorted to singing to myself. In the evening I became very frustrated because my roommates would not help me out at all; they had the radio blaring and the television on. I was forced to become a hermit in the basement. Later, it was time to get ready to go to the

Exhibit 2.5 Media deprivation journal by Jennifer Ditri. Used by permission.

bar—wrong! Music—I was not allowed to hear music! The rest of the evening I sat in my basement smoking cigarettes, playing solitaire, and sleeping.

* * *

Friday, to put it bluntly, sucked! I was crabby from Thursday and I just wanted to lay on the ground to kick and scream like a two-year-old! I guess I didn't want to—I did it! My little temper tantrum relieved me *slightly* and I continued my day. You must understand that Fridays are my day to lay in bed and watch television all day until I have to go to work at 4:00 p.m. Needless to say I was very unhappy getting up and actually starting my day! I kept myself occupied by doing *some* homework (too frustrated to do a lot), running errands, and going back to sleep. Friday after work wasn't so bad because my friends and I talk and play cards. I think I was the most overjoyed person in Saginaw at midnight—I watched TV until 4:00 a.m.!

My 48 hours turned into nothing more than smoking too much and sleeping too much. I cannot handle media deprivation now, but if I was raised that way, little to no media I mean, then I think I would be a much more productive person.

Exhibit 2.5 *Continued*

When I first read the title for this journal assignment in the course syllabus, I wasn't sure what it would be about. I could have guessed from the title, but I thought there might be more to it. Purposely blocking out all forms of media for 48 hours. What could you possibly write about that would explain the feeling you have from a lack of media? Furthermore, how could you completely avoid all forms of media without driving your family nuts? Well, lucky for me, I had a camping trip planned. My family and I would be out of the house from Friday afternoon until Sunday afternoon. The only form of media I would have to worry about would be the radio. This wasn't too much of a problem, since I usually preach abstinence from radio when we're up north. "I came up here to get away from civilization and the rat race," I tell my oldest son when he tries to play his favorite station or CD. I didn't even tell them I had this assignment. We made it all the way there and back without a single radio being turned on, or any form of printed media being read.

What did I think about it? It was great! I didn't even miss the world. Although I must admit, I was quite curious as to whether the U.S. had invaded Haiti yet. This falls back to the fact that I consider myself a news freak. When I'm away from my normal forms of news media, I'm afraid something big will happen and I'll miss out. Why do I need to know about it as it's happening? I'm not sure. I like to believe I'm well informed. If I don't know about something,

continues

Exhibit 2.6 Media deprivation journal by Mark Maxson. Used by permission.

and I hear it from a friend or family member, I feel like I've let myself down. "How could you not know this," I tell myself. Or even worse. Someone who knows I'm into news will wonder what kind of news freak am I anyways. I hate it when someone rubs it in. "Mark, you didn't know that?"

I'm making more out of this than there really is. News is important to me, and I do like to stay on top of the current events. But it's not something I'm going to skip a vacation or excursion over. I've gone longer than 48 hours without the media before. This past summer I spent five and a half days on Isle Royale backpacking. In a place like that you not only have no contact with any form of media, but you also can go days without running across another person outside your group. Even if someone wanted to reach you, they couldn't. Not without tracking you down. The ranger stations at each end of the island don't even have phones.

Now that's a funny feeling. I remember the first time I took a trip like this. You try to think of every possible precaution. If I'm cut off from the world for a week, what do I need? Food, shelter, clothing and a first aid kit.

What comes to mind after the first couple days? I wonder how my family is doing. I wonder what's new in the world. Are we at war with anyone, or is all well with the world? It's very easy to imagine a happy peaceful world when you're gazing across a small lake surrounded by thick woods. The sun is no longer visible over the far ridge, but it's still very light. Loons are swimming across the lake calling to one another through the light mist that's settled on the water. I wonder what it was like in the past. Before television. Before radio. Before telegraph. People didn't hear about news events until they were days or weeks old. Go back further. How long did it take for the King of England to find out about the Boston Tea Party? I think it's good to get away completely. It allows us to reflect on life without the constant interruptions of mass instantaneous media.

Exhibit 2.6 *Continued*

No media for 48 hours! Well, I was able to do the assignment to some degree. Because I work as a nursing assistant in geriatrics, I watch TV a lot and listen to the radio because my patients don't have much else to do or want to do; therefore, I really couldn't get away from media. I did, however, turn off the radio when I drove on Saturday and Sunday—which was very hard to do because the silence drives me crazy. I absolutely *love* music and when you first announced the assignment, I thought you were crazy—I could go w/o TV because I've done that before. I lived in Zaire, Africa for 3 months in '91 and didn't watch TV even once and after the first month I went w/o radio also—the funny thing is, when I came back to civilization, I found out that Gorbachev had been ousted and then back in—all this happened and I didn't know. That experience really changed my view on TV/radio... yes, media is necessary, but for a short amount of time, you can go w/o it... or for a long time.

Exhibit 2.7 Media deprivation journal by Stacey McAfee. Used by permission.

> In the first day of my media deprivation I have already noticed that it takes more effort to avoid the media than it does to interact w/ it. I can hardly enter a room w/out the television or radio being on. In absence of both, I find myself bombarded w/ conversation about the media. Everyone wants to talk about O. J. or Haiti or any number of other things.
>
> This brings me to another point. What is media? Is it considered media when someone tells you about something they heard from the media? Discussion of current events? It's interesting to try and decide how far to go in an attempt to avoid the media. A better understanding of the concept would help.
>
> * * *
>
> In absence of media, I finally started a book I have been interested in reading for some time. I am enjoying the book and wish I could read more often. With all the homework I do I can never find the time for books. However, I seem to have time to receive media on the other hand. It's funny to sit back and to realize that I "take the time" to watch T. V. and read magazines and newspaper, but I often am sorry I don't have time for other things. Perhaps media deprivation is something that would be good to practice from time to time. Then again, too little media for someone who is concerned about the world around him may not be a good thing either.
>
> * * *
>
> After two days of media deprivation I find several differences in the way I interact with it as a result.
>
> First off I find myself feeling somewhat guilty every time I turn the television or radio on because I've spent two days training myself not to. This is good in the sense that simply turning on the television is not as automatic as it once was and now actually requires a conscious decision on my part.
>
> Secondly, the selective media interaction I've had since depriving myself has been more enjoyable than normal. The feeling I get is that I'm normally so saturated w/ media that I've grown somewhat numb to it. The two days off has given me a new appreciation for media.
>
> Last, but not least, I've found more time to do things that I normally don't think I can fit into my schedule. The novel I've wanted to read for such a long time only took me two days.
>
> Overall, the new appreciation I've acquired convinces me that interaction w/ media is worthwhile. At the same time, thoughtfully limiting the time involved w/ such interaction not only allows more time for other things but leads to a better appreciation for media itself as a result of its absence.

Exhibit 2.8 Media deprivation journal by Michael Halstead. Used by permission.

What you may find as one result of this experiment is that, like other people, you use media for more than sources of information. Television in particular has taken on a role as leisure entertainer, babysitter, companion for those not in the workplace, source of background noise during routine household

> I chose to begin my media deprivation at 3:00 p.m. last Monday because my work schedule made that time period easiest to be faithful. I started work at 4 p.m. and went to midnight. During this time I was fairly busy but had empty minutes which I generally would have filled by reading parts of the newspaper, which is readily available to read. And I even instinctively picked up the paper, but realized just in time what I was doing and replaced it on the counter. It was strange to see how media had become such a habit.
>
> I returned to my dorm room about 12:15, and got ready for bed, no TV or anything. The next morning I had a necessary cheat. My alarm works by radio, so at 7:15 I rushed to shut off the tunes before I could enjoy them.
>
> Then at 8:25 I went to class which lasts until 11:20 (art). Then to my English class until 12:50. Then I chose to at 1:00 indulge in a 5 minute cheat. I had to find out the conclusion to the OJ soap opera. I could definitely have just listened to the reactions from my roommates and known what the outcome was but I wanted to see history first hand, not hear it second hand. So after hearing the verdict, I retreated to my room until my next class began at 2:30. When it got done, at 4:00 I had another class until 7:00 and then after getting something to eat, I played cards for a while with my roommates. Then some friends came out and we went to a coffee house and drove around for a while.
>
> So anyway the point of all these ramblings is that I kept busy and that made it a lot easier to deprive myself of media. But you can't get away from hearing about it anyway. Someone's always talking about something in the news or about something they saw on TV.

Exhibit 2.9 Media deprivation journal by Meredith Roedel. Used by permission.

tasks, supplier of conversational material at the workplace, and so on. In later chapters we will consider some of the functions attributed to television—specifically, as entertainment and as provider of news and information—as well as TV's economic function of providing audiences for advertisers.

Clutter and Context

As Bill McKibben's experiment showed, one of the essential things about media is that there is far more material available than any one person can make use of. As a result, we have clutter. There are more kinds of media available now than a generation ago—not only newspapers, magazines, radio, television, and film, but related forms such as handbills, bumper stickers, T-shirts, sermons, lectures, computer information services, microfiche systems, CD-ROM indexes, virtual reality, popular music, publicity blurbs, buyers' guides, specialty publications, real estate brochures, talk shows, radio commercials, television commercials, "infomercials," tabloids, rock videos, documentaries, cartoons, promos.... Anything that communicates, verbally or visually or auditorily, or for that matter tactilely or olfactorily, can be considered a medium. (Smell-o-vision is at present a joke or a promotional device; but if dogs were paying customers, things might be different.)

Because of the sheer profusion of media texts, much of the news we receive through media does not have sufficient context for us to feel confident about our understanding. Newspapers and magazines often strive to provide some context—but the limits on space mean they cannot supply enough in any one issue, and there is no guarantee that readers will have read previous discussions. Television news reports are even thinner: More specifics can be conveyed in a column of newsprint than in two minutes of broadcast time (the average length of major network news stories). Of course, television can communicate some matters visually, an ability largely unavailable to print media. Most radio news coverage is limited to the "headline" services that take up five minutes at the top of the hour; in addition, there are selective, anecdotal, mostly politically conservative commentaries offered by radio figures such as Paul Harvey. When we consider as well the partisan atmosphere that surrounds discussion of political matters—election news, discussions about the president and Congress, and complex and controversial public issues such as health care—the problem of context is multiplied. We hear contradictory charges and, unable to examine the issues thoroughly, choose a "pro" or "con" stance instead of looking at more complex responses.

Clutter is most visible as a problem in connection with advertising. Advertising is the most obviously rhetorical medium: Advertisers are usually quite open about who they are, who their desired audience is, and what the purposes of their communications are. And we've all seen ads, probably more than we like or need. Commercial messages are everywhere in media, and therefore practically everywhere in contemporary culture. Up to 30 percent of prime-time television is given over to commercials and promotions for other TV broadcasts. Commercial radio strings together many fifteen- and thirty-second ads between their "much more music." Public radio and television channels do not run advertising (they do, of course, have promos); but many programs are sponsored by corporations, which receive prominent mention at the beginning and ending of the programs. A high percentage of space in newspapers and magazines is given to advertisements, and commercial messages are present in our means of transportation—ads in buses and trains, and billboards on streets and highways. According to the American Association of Advertising Agencies, 1,600 commercial messages are aimed at the average consumer daily. If audiences are hostile toward advertising, the reason may be that it's inescapable.

Faced with such a degree of clutter, all of us develop some tactics for dealing with the conceptual overload. One tactic may be hostile or cynical indifference. People often say that they don't even notice the ads, and statistics bear them out: Studies show that out of the 1,600 commercial messages encountered daily, we notice 80 of these momentarily, and only 12 make a conscious impression (Bagdikian p. 185). Remote controls for television and seek buttons on car radios are most often used to look for alternatives during the ad cycles—often a futile tactic, since broadcasters carefully sequence their programming units to counter this tactic. VCRs, however, do allow TV programs to be recorded for later viewing, when commercials can be fast-forwarded past, or even edited out.

Another means of dealing with clutter might be to select among (or within) media. Many newspaper readers look at only a few sections—front page, editorials, selected columns, and sports—and turn past the ads in these sections. Limits on the time allocated for media often imposes another sort of selection. And the fact that TVs and radios will generally play only one channel at a time dictates selection in these media. You may select media for ideological reasons or reasons of taste: "I never watch programs like that"; "I don't listen to rap music"; "...country music"; "Soap operas are too unrealistic"; "Rush is right"; "We don't have cable because of MTV"; and so on. Or financial limitations may play a role: "Going to movies costs too much now"; "We don't have cable because it costs too much"; "I don't want to pay that much for a newspaper when I don't read it anyway."

People's encounters with media are more diverse and more selective than formerly because of the general problem with clutter. You may have noticed that you differ significantly from others in your class in what you do with media. These differences may be important in our examination of the media in the contemporary United States—it would be unwise to draw conclusions too soon about what people read and watch, and what the consequences of that might be.

Strategies for Reading Media

As noted above, this book is built on the idea that reading and writing are connected activities; we write through our reading, and we read through our writing. So the most important strategy for reading media is to write about it. Writing about media gives you a way to engage with media texts more on your own terms. You are already under way with this to some extent, in keeping a log and a journal about your contacts with media. And this activity will be sustained throughout your use of this book.

PAUSE FOR REFLECTION
In your academic experience so far, how are reading and writing connected? Are there courses in which you do mostly or exclusively reading with little writing? Mostly or exclusively writing with little reading? When both reading and writing take place, how are these connected?

What to write? Start with what you care about most. List those issues that move you, that you would like to work with. List ideas or events you strongly oppose. Work from what these are to reasons why these are important to you. You might, for example, write as a fundamentalist Christian, and concentrate on media treatment of matters such as sex outside of marriage, abortion, or religion in public life. Or you might write as someone concerned with how women and men are portrayed in media, or with how few women occupy positions of authority in news organizations. Or you might focus on the negativity and cynicism reflected in some news stories and dramas.

Another place to start might be journalists' stock questions: who, what, when, where, how, and especially why. Who are *you* in relation to this text, this story, this medium? How does it speak to you? What image of its audience is presented? What are we assumed to know and to be unaware of, to think about the text from the outset? Who is presenting this text to you—both in terms of an author (reporter, director, producer, corporate voice or sponsor) and in terms of the institution(s) responsible for the text? What is being presented in the text and through the text? What is there in the text to concern you? When and in what circumstances did you encounter this text? What did those circumstances do to affect how you responded or thought about it? Why is a given text important to you personally, or to some aspect of the culture?

Another strategy might be to write back to someone connected to the text. If the text is a story of some sort, write back in your own persona to a character or to the author or producers of the story. Or you might write how events look to someone who is not a leading character. You might write an explanation of what it is about the story that interests or concerns you—or bores you and turns your attention away. You could write a letter to the producer, to an actor, to a character; you could play the role of someone within the text, taking occasion to talk back from that perspective.

Do you have a consistent set of questions or issues that color your responses to media? One such issue might serve as a "lens" through which to view media; for example, you might be concerned with how people whose position in society resembles your own (based on class, race, age, and so on) are represented, or not, in news stories and comedies. Organizing your responses to media texts through this "lens" may help to, well, focus your thinking.

Whatever your entry point into dialogue with a media text, you need to take note of details. Your overall impression of a message is constructed of accumulated details—words, pictures, style of delivery, music, color, type fonts, and many more. Noticing details is important to confirming your initial judgment about a text; and when you begin to write for others, your grasp of details will be important in convincing them that your reading is well founded.

Register details as soon as possible after reading or watching a text: Relying on memory can be tricky. If you read three or four news accounts relating to a subject, these can sometimes get mixed up with each other, so that an overall impression can be created that doesn't exist in any one text. (Test this out by watching a video of a film or a television program simultaneously with a sharply contrasting piece of music.) If you watch a film that resembles one you've seen previously, matter from the earlier text may get confused with the later. Writing a few phrases while watching a program, or writing briefly for a few minutes after its conclusion, will help you hold the details in mind.

One last consideration for reading media texts: You must keep in mind the interests of those who produce such texts. Media, in the United States and many other countries, are commercial entities. They fulfill the function of keeping us informed and entertained, to be sure—but they also exist to turn a profit. Media that do not make money must either function as nonprofit organizations (as with public television and radio and some university publications), operate at a loss for a while, or go out of business. The drive for profit means keeping advertisers as well as subscribers happy. In the case of magazines and newspapers, this means attracting and holding a readership that will pay attention to featured products. Usually it means downplaying or avoiding altogether subjects or treatments that advertisers, or sometimes readers, will find objectionable. In some cases, too, the perspectives of the publishers and editorial staff will have a considerable effect on the content, tone, and style of articles published. The United States unquestionably has one of the freest presses in the world—there is no government board of censorship to review publications or broadcasts, before or after the fact—but we sometimes overlook the fact that systems of ownership and commercial support function effectively to prevent some viewpoints from appearing or from getting an equal hearing. In order to be a fully informed reader or viewer of media, then, it is necessary to understand something about how the media function both economically and in terms of editorial perspective. The readings that follow explore aspects of this issue.

PAUSE FOR REFLECTION

Find out what you can about who owns the major media in your area—the local newspaper, the chief statewide newspapers, any local or state magazines, television and radio stations. How many of these are independent, and how many are connected in some way to larger conglomerates? Is this information easy to find?

S. ROBERT LICHTER, STANLEY ROTHMAN, AND LINDA S. LICHTER

Who Are the Media Elite?

Paradoxically, the advent of television increased the influence of a few East Coast newspapers and magazines. What television had done, of course, was to nationalize and standardize communication to an extent never before achieved in the United States. New York and Washington styles and modes now became national styles and modes. The *New York Times* was read by the New York and the Washington elites, and by those who produced the news for the television networks. Thanks to their amplification via television, the issues the *Times* considered important and the approach it took to them would become national currency.

Most studies agree that the key national news media today consist of national television, the *New York Times,* the *Washington Post,* the *Wall Street Journal, Time, Newsweek,* and possibly *U.S. News and World Report....*

No other magazine or newspapers came close to these six outlets in their access to America's leaders. These media are read by various leadership groups because they are perceived as influential and important, and they are influential and important because they are read by such groups.

Are the media biased?...[T]he question is wrongly phrased. Between overt bias and pristine objectivity exist infinite shadings, subtle colorations, and elective affinities between personal outlook and news product. The trail that leads from journalists' perspectives to the news they report is often poorly marked. It winds through conscious attitudes, unquestioned assumptions, and inner motivations.

[S]ubstantial numbers of the media elite grew up at a distance from the social and cultural traditions of small-town middle America. Instead, they came from big cities in the northeast and north central states. Their parents were mostly well off, highly educated members of the upper middle class, especially the educated professions. In short, they are a highly cosmopolitan group, with differentially eastern, urban, ethnic, upper-status, and secular roots.

[N]ews judgments are no more "value free" than social science judgments. A majority of the journalists surveyed believe their work should be a force for social reform. It is hardly surprising that people in this profession should hope that their work might, in some way, help bring about a better world. But the kind of world one desires, and how to attain it, underlie all ideological divisions.

The media uphold two conflicting ideals that cannot always be reconciled. The reformer's social commitment coexists uneasily with the cool nonpartisanship of the objective observer. This is a dilemma that even the best journalists rarely face head-on....

We all reconstruct reality for ourselves, but journalists are especially important because they help depict reality for the rest of society. They do so through the everyday decisions of their craft: What story is worth covering? How much play should it get? What angle should it be given? What sources are trustworthy and informative? The unavoidable preconceptions journalists bring to such decisions help determine what images of society are available to their audience....

Social perspectives may unconsciously color the very way journalists perceive the news itself. This might strike psychologists as a very mild hypothesis, almost an axiomatic principle. Why should journalists be any less prone to selective perception than anyone else? Yet the way they perceive the news is tremendously important, because it determines the kind of stories they transmit to the rest of us.

The organizational perspective encompasses two lines of argument. The first stresses the importance of constraints like those of time, money, and competition in shaping the news product. The second holds that editorial control overrides any bias by reporters, or that conservative editors, acting as agents of management, provide a check on liberal reporters....

By emphasizing the social context of newsmaking, organizational perspectives provide a needed corrective to crude conspiracy theories of the news. However, they also contain some limitations. First, social control in the newsroom is not what it used to be. Dramatic changes in the journalistic profession have significantly weakened the ability of senior management to reshape reportage, especially at national media outlets....

Second, organizational theorists lean heavily on the method of participant observation to prove their case.... Participant observation can show how news values commonly attributed to personal perspective might instead reflect organizational imperatives. But it cannot preclude the impact of personal values.

[From S. Robert Lichter, Stanley Rothman, and Linda S. Lichter, *The Media Elite.* Bethesda, Md.: Adler & Adler, 1986. Used by permission.]

JEFF COHEN AND NORMAN SOLOMON

The Real Media Elite

Dan Quayle is on the warpath, denouncing a "media elite" which has nothing but "scorn" for people who uphold "basic moral values." From newsrooms and sitcom studios, says Quayle, this elite looks down on "average Americans."

When Dan Quayle attacks the "media elite," it's like Arnold Schwarzenegger decrying the evils of body-building.

Quayle is much closer to the media elite than he lets on. His family owns a chain of newspapers, including the most powerful papers in Indiana and Arizona. He personally owns $400,000 worth of stock in Central Newspapers Inc.

Vice President Quayle would have you believe that the media elite is biased against conservative politicians like him. But this claim doesn't square with the fact that of the daily newspapers making presidential endorsements in 1988, about 70 percent backed the Bush–Quayle ticket.

Far from being the liberal chorus that Quayle describes, the media's loudest voices are conservative—some so far right they think Quayle is too liberal.

On radio, for example, no one has more opinion-shaping power than extreme conservative Rush Limbaugh. On national TV, only two political pundits—both conservative—have become ubiquitous enough to appear every day of the week: John McLaughlin and Patrick Buchanan. Among the most widely published political columnists, four of the top seven write from the right: George Will, James Kilpatrick, William Safire and William F. Buckley, Jr.

There is a media elite in this country. But that elite is corporate establishment. After a decade of mergers, takeovers and newspaper closings, media power has concentrated into fewer—and more conservative—hands. Look at the managers of companies such as Time Warner, General Electric, Dow Jones, Cap Cities/ABC, and you'll have a good idea who is in the media elite.

Also, take a look at the media's biggest advertisers—General Motors, Philip Morris, Procter & Gamble, DuPont, etc.—companies with the power to muzzle viewpoints that offend them.

Imagine, for example, that Rush Limbaugh had a change of heart one day about how to use his pulpit of 500 radio stations. Imagine that instead of scapegoating "environmental extremists," gays and "feminazis" as the forces ruining our country, he began attacking by name the "greedy corporations" that "pollute the earth, rip off consumers and export good American jobs to slave laborers in the Third World." How many weeks would it take before his sponsors pulled the plug?

When Dan Quayle castigates the media elite, he certainly does not mean the media owners or sponsors (most of whom are Republicans) or the political pundits (most of whom are fairly conservative).

Like the "media criticism" of Vice President Spiro Agnew more than two decades ago, Quayle has political goals in mind: intimidating media professionals into softer coverage of the White House, and corralling the votes of social and religious conservatives who are offended by the media.

Quayle's speeches echo Agnew's. In 1969, Agnew denounced "liberal" media snobs who "do not represent the views of America." Lately, Vice President Quayle has denounced the media in these words: "It sometimes seems we have two cultures—the cultural elite, and the rest of us.... They're embarrassed about the views of the average American—because moral values are what the American people care most about."

There *is* a serious critique to be made of the media elite and its moral values. This elite values one thing above all else—maximizing profit. Worship of the "bottom line" seems to take precedence over family, community and country.

That's why the TV industry insists on bombarding our kids with ads for candy and sugar-coated cereal every Saturday morning; why so many magazines advertise cigarettes while avoiding tough coverage of the tobacco industry; why TV ratings periods are endless parades of sexual titillation; and why TV stations serve up such edifying programs as "Studs," "Geraldo" and "Gorgeous Ladies of Wrestling."

Dan Quayle can't seriously address the elite's moral bankruptcy because he is ideologically committed to the one value these media corporations revere: profiteering. Of course Quayle—and the media managers—have a prettier-sounding name for it. They call it "free enterprise."

[Epilogue: Three months after leaving the vice presidency, Dan Quayle joined the board of Central Newspapers Inc.]

[From Jeff Cohen and Norman Solomon, *Adventures in Medialand*. Monroe, Maine: Common Courage Press, 1993.]

QUESTIONS
1. Do the two readings above agree on what is meant by "media elite"? If not, what are the differences in how they use the term?
2. What are some of the stories about social and cultural difference in the United States that the readings draw on for context?
3. Lichter, Rothman, and Lichter's work was published in 1986, and Cohen and Solomon's article first appeared in mid-1992. Do you think subsequent public events and changes in the political climate have affected how readers would respond to their arguments?

Conventions

One of the key concepts for understanding media as rhetorical is that of *conventions*. When you "read" any form of media, you do so from within an understanding of what conventions apply to that medium. It's easy to forget about conventions in discussing media, because, once you are "inside" conventions, they appear to be both natural and necessary, so that it's impossible to conceive of any other way of proceeding.

A long-running dispute in public discussions about "cultural literacy" focuses on which texts are taught, at all levels. E. D. Hirsch argued in a 1987 book, *Cultural Literacy,* that certain core texts are necessary in order for conversations to take place; and other, less rigorous writers sometimes lament that the general public, or students, do not know about X (whatever X might happen to be). But it might be argued that *real* cultural literacy, or media literacy, means more than quick recognition of references and allusions—it means knowing something about the systems through which such information is provided, and about the tacit rules or conventions that govern the providing.

All of us grow up inside of our cultures, and move inside of sets of conventions, many of which we do not recognize because they are thoroughly natural to us. Such conventions help hold society together, by establishing relationships between its members; conventions can be great time-savers, because they offer us codes of behavior for dealing with others. Conventions also serve to reinforce the status quo, however, and those who do not like or accept some aspects of contemporary culture are interested in asking why, if conventions are largely arbitrary, they should be continued.

The root of the modern word *convention* has to do with *coming together*. Political parties come together literally, every four years, to hold conventions to nominate presidential candidates, while other groups convene more frequently for their purposes. The sense of the word *convention* is transferred from those who have to agree upon rules and procedures to the rules and procedures themselves. It's a convention, in many bodies such as Congress or the English Parliament, to follow a formal agreement (such as *Robert's Rules of Order*) governing who may speak and when. But there are many conventions established more informally, as customs if not as official rules.

Convention governs how we represent things, to a considerable degree. Some conventions are built into media themselves and are relatively inflexible—these might be called codes. Others are variable from text to text, reflecting matters such as personal and institutional style (Mitchell p. 13). These conventions grow out of the habits of a culture, or its practices, and—especially since the development of electronic media and easier, faster transportation—out of the practices of other cultures as well.

We may not know conventions consciously, but a few questions about practice can make them available for discussion. We might compare this problem to the distinction between competence and recognition in language. Native speakers of a language demonstrate through usage their knowledge of grammar. While there may be points of contention, there are others on which there's absolute agreement: Speakers may argue over splitting infinitives, ending sentences with prepositions, or using a plural pronoun to refer back to an indefinite pronoun (e.g., "Everyone should remember to carry their umbrellas to the game"). But there's no argument over other matters, such as when to use or omit articles, or how to arrange sequences of adjectives. Consider the following phrase:

The two young French acrobats

No native speaker would transpose the adjectives into "The young two French acrobats," "The French two young acrobats," or "The French young two acrobats." But native speakers of English do not have to learn rules to govern such phrases. The rules come with the conventions of the language; and every language has such matters, which, from the outside, seem impossibly complex. (Only when you learn a second language do you come to understand this aspect of your own.)

Like language, hand gestures are culturally specific. In the United States, extending index and middle fingers with the back of the hand toward the person addressed might be a request for two more beers; in Britain it's an insulting gesture. Extending your fist with the thumb out might mean "Good luck," "Up yours," or "I want a ride." There may be different gestures for roughly the same meanings (American "shooting the bird," European hand-inside-elbow, raised fist). In the United States people count "one, two, three..." starting with the index finger, while in Europe the sequence begins with the thumb. In Poland one may refer to money or a bribe by passing the thumb quickly over the first two fingers, as if counting quickly a stack of bills; and holding the outside edge of the hand against one's neck indicates that someone (not oneself) is drunk. These gestures change over time, as indicated by their literary traces—a street fight between the Montagues and the Capulets in *Romeo and Juliet* is initiated when a group of young men "bite their thumbs" at the others, an Elizabethan gesture of contempt that no longer signifies. But if you are within a conventional system that recognizes gestures, you do not need instruction about them.

ASSIGNMENT: HAND GESTURES

In this assignment, you should compile a glossary for hand gestures. (Their representation in drawing or writing may present a challenge.) Your glossary has for its audience someone from a different culture who wants to learn our customs, right down to the apparently insignificant things done with the hands. Work on your own to come up with a list, then compare with other students in groups in order to extend and compare items. Finally, do some writing in your journal or as an informal essay on the possibilities and limitations of hand gestures as a medium.

If your class has someone who knows American Sign Language, have her/him discuss what it is like to communicate in a language of gestures.

If the class includes someone who has spent a significant amount of time outside your region of the United States, determine if the person knows gestures that are different from those you understand to be standard in your area. Are there particular gestures to do the following in your experience, perhaps in your family?

- Call animals
- Insult someone (strongly; or mildly)
- Refer to someone being drunk
- Refer to sex or the sex act
- Comment on someone who is attractive
- Refer to money
- Celebrate or express triumph
- Wish someone good luck
- Wish someone bad luck; jinx someone
- Communicate other, specific information about someone (e.g., the cuckold gesture)

Newspaper articles may serve to illustrate how closely connected conventions are to meanings of texts. One of the crucial conventions in a newspaper is *where* the text appears: Front-page stories are understood to be of greater importance than stories inside the paper. Some sections of the newspaper are strictly for "factual" material judged to be of importance internationally, nationally, or within the newspaper's area of distribution. The front page and inside pages of "news" sections, excluding the editorial page, op ed page, and anything clearly labeled as a column, would be sites for these stories. The editorial page presents the opinions of the publisher and the editorial staff. Usually (though not always) the editorial and opposite page carry a range of opinions, and scattered throughout the paper may be columns offering the writers' personal observations. The sports, entertainment, arts, business, and other sections will carry news about their respective subject areas.

All these sections carry advertisements, and by convention there is a sharp distinction between the news stories and what is said in space paid for by advertisers. Minor scandals result when this distinction is breached; as, for example, when stories in the real estate section are written by the advertising department or, worse still, by a real estate company's public relations department.

The news is supposed to be *objective*, giving factual statements about events and allowing readers to determine how to interpret them. This convention is of relatively recent date: In the nineteenth century and well into the twentieth, newspapers were openly partisan. If you didn't like what the *Evening Banner* had to say on matters—which you knew from past experience and the conventions of the time—you could buy the *Herald-Tribune* or *Clarion*. However, it is now rare for even large cities to have more than one local newspaper. And in some cities where two or more newspapers do exist, the papers may be jointly owned or have operating agreements to cut expenses.

Conventions govern how news reports are written. While news articles frequently have bylines, the reporter is expected to avoid using the first person: Even though the presence of the press generally changes how those being interviewed will express themselves, the convention of the news article is that the reporter is an invisible observer, a fly on the wall.

PAUSE FOR REFLECTION
To what extent do conventions affect your use of the first person in writing essays? Do you believe that your audience for essays permits you to speak personally, or that you must avoid saying "I"? Does the choice of subject affect your adherence to this stylistic convention? Under what circumstances can a textbook use the first person?

Television is probably the medium most familiar to you, and its conventions may be the most naturalized of all. There are, first, conventions carried over from photography: Patterns of light on a two-dimensional surface are read as though they exist in three dimensions. There are few if any broadcasts comparable to nonrepresentational painting—all television is either pictorial or graphic (combined or in alternation). Faces of people looking into the camera—in effect, through it—work roughly as do portraits, and we expect to be able to read a person's character in his or her face.

Television broadcasts are divided into units of time—a development carried over from radio. Broadcasts proceed through "programs," except when there is an extraordinary event such as a presidential assassination or a breaking news story of great interest. There are breaks at definite intervals for the station to announce its call letters and channel number—most often with a logo placed inconspicuously somewhere on the screen, or else with a sign shown for this purpose at the hour or half-hour. If it's a commercial station, there are advertisements at frequent and more or less regular intervals.

Conventionally, time segments are entirely separate from each other. A program broadcast at 8:30 P.M., for example, reflects no connection with what preceded it at 8:00. (Network programmers, however, are very concerned with "program flow," and work very hard to set up an evening's programming so as to attract and keep viewers.) There is also no explicit connection between commercials and the program sponsored. *Sponsor* may strike us as a curious, old-fashioned word. It derives from the Latin term "to make a solemn pledge," and a sponsor "assumes responsibility for a person or group during a period of instruction, apprenticeship, or probation." Sponsorship had more significance when the convention was for a single company to buy exclusive airtime to showcase both its chosen programming and its product, as with early radio and the so-called Golden Age of television. (Something similar goes on with college football bowls; e.g., the Thrifty Car Rental Holiday Bowl, the Doritos Fiesta Bowl, or the Poulan Weed Eater Independence Bowl.) But the drive for increased advertising revenues soon brought an end to explicit ties between program and a single corporation—though the connection lives on in the phrase *soap opera*.

Procter & Gamble is the largest manufacturer of detergent and other related products in the United States, and the largest sponsor of television programs, especially daytime programs oriented mostly toward women at home. Daytime dramas are called "soap operas," derisively, because of their sponsorship. Procter & Gamble began inconspicuously in 1837 selling a product called White Soap. But as Ben Bagdikian notes in *The Media Monopoly* (p. 155), the product was renamed as the result of the company president's reading of a biblical passage: "[I]n 1879 Harley Procter, a descendant of the founder, read in the Forty-fifth Psalm, 'All thy garments smell of myrrh and aloes and cassia out of the ivory palaces.'" Thus White Soap was rechristened Ivory Soap, and the Procter & Gamble domain of sweet-smelling products for clothing and bodies was born from a fundamentalist religious interpretation of the Old Testament.

Given that commercial television divides into segments for advertisements, narrative portions between commercials function as equivalents to chapters in books or acts and scenes in drama. (Some relatively high-prestige television shows of the 1950s and 1960s, such as *The Fugitive*, introduced segments with act divisions.) Scriptwriters signal these divisions by moving toward some plot turn, so as to hold the audience, precisely as did writers of serial fiction in the nineteenth century or of serial films in the 1930s and 1940s. That is why these shows came to be called "cliffhangers."

One principle that can be applied to the reading of several sorts of media is separation into hierarchies: No matter how "popular" or "trivial" or "low" the medium or the genre, within that medium or genre there will be some segments more deserving of attention and some you can take or leave. For example, the hours between 7:00 and 11:00 P.M. Eastern are designated as "prime time," carrying higher advertising rates and enjoying stronger audience shares than any other hours during the week (except for special events such as the Super Bowl). Hours of the day, like locations in the newspaper, are part of the rhetoric by which those media signify importance.

PAUSE FOR REFLECTION
Television is often considered a low-prestige medium; that is, one of low social and intellectual value. Do you agree? What are some television offerings with which you are familiar that seem to aspire to higher-than-usual prestige? What are some low-prestige programs or kinds of programs? Where does this valuing come from?

Program integrity is another convention that most television programs observe. Under normal circumstances, events in one broadcast do not carry over to another. Sequels or multipart broadcasts are exceptions, clearly labeled as such by the tag line "TO BE CONTINUED." Multipart dramas on public television are sometimes introduced by a host, who reminds viewers about what happened in the previous week's broadcast and helps establish the cultural value of that offering. Characters conventionally do not recall what they were doing in the preceding week's episode. (A different convention is followed by some evening dramas, such as *NYPD Blue* or *ER*, which open with a summary of the previous week's episode.) Plot events are generally worked through to an acceptable or desirable resolution by the end of the program, so as to leave viewers feeling satisfied with how things have turned out. Aristotle described the effect of tragic drama as catharsis, a purgation of pity and fear. Contemporary television offers its own brand of catharsis, one consistent with a settled frame of mind, so as to avoid disturbing viewers or sponsors.

In addition to conventions that apply to all television, there are some conventions specific to kinds of programs or genres. Sitcoms, like other programs, begin with a standard introductory segment and end with a conclusion. Introductory segments have changed over time, from the "introduce the players" concept in 1950s and 1960s standards such as *The Donna Reed Show* and *My Three Sons* to the theme song opening used by *The Flintstones* and still in use (parodically) in *The Simpsons*. This convention was seen in adapted form in the production numbers that opened *The Cosby Show*. Another introductory possibility put to use in some sitcoms and in dramas is the opening vignette, which may or may not be connected to the main story line (*Murphy Brown* and *Home Entertainment*). In *Seinfeld*, the opening vignette for years was

Jerry's comedy act. Opening vignettes are useful for capturing channel surfers before they drift on to something else.

Conventionally, conclusions are shorter than introductions. They function principally for two purposes: to give the credits—producer, director, actors, technicians, and generally everyone who had a hand in the program, as required by contract; and to serve as transition either to next week's program or, more commonly, to the network's or the station's upcoming offerings.

Television respects the conventions of the modern stage in establishing a separation between stage and audience. This separation extends to the compression of time: Twenty-two minutes on screen usually represents a much longer but indistinct period. Some sitcoms make use of canned laughter to simulate the reaction of a live audience; at least through the 1960s, broadcasts were still using laugh tracks recorded from 1930s radio shows, providing those long-departed audiences a curious form of immortality. As these laugh tracks have begun to feel old-fashioned, more sitcoms are being taped before live audiences. In no case, however, do the actors respond to audiences (or, for that matter, to music or other sounds provided).

There are exceptions to these adaptations from stage practice, of course—but not usually within the genre of the sitcom. The exceptions come in the comic/variety broadcast such as *Saturday Night Live, Monty Python,* or David Letterman—in some of these segments, actors walk offstage, followed by the camera, in order to break the frame established and maintained in sitcoms and other drama. But these exceptions help to establish a principle: Strictly speaking, there is no breaking of conventions. Rather, in breaking a convention, a program crosses into another convention or genre. Conventions are what define a genre—conventions constitute an implicit contract between "author" (or what functions as an author for collectively produced media such as films and television) and audience as to how they will mutually play the game of whatever text is being experienced.

Conventions may be thought of as rules, then—but "rules" is an ambiguous term. In games there are some rules that it is possible to break, and others that one literally cannot break. In football, for example, it's against the rules to move across the line of scrimmage before the ball is snapped, or to start play with twelve men on the field—but infractions occur frequently and are penalized. There are other rules that cannot be broken, because if they are, you aren't playing football. A touchdown has to be worth six points, a field goal three; the referee cannot take part in the game; players are not permitted to fly; and so on. A game could be devised in which all these rules or conventions could be broken—but it would not be football. Similarly, in a given genre of television there are some conventions that can be broken, such as that which says that in sitcoms or dramas actors do not speak directly to the audience through the camera, so long as one works within that genre. Modifications do occur—as in some episodes of *Moonlighting,* for example. And in other TV genres—political speeches, news broadcasts, or commercials—direct address happens routinely. (Direct address that does not speak to individual viewers, however, but to potentially millions across the glass divide of the screen.)

TV conventions come about through a kind of negotiation, as has been the case between writers and readers—but in television there are more participating parties. No television program is created by one person; just to produce the telecast requires a team of writers, directors, technicians, producers, managing companies, and actors. Cooperation of broadcasters at the local level is also necessary, along with the financial system that has grown up around television. And the entire medium creates a context within which any one of its texts exists. Understanding the most successful sitcom of the 1980s, *The Cosby Show,* means knowing that it existed in contiguity with, and in competition with, other sitcoms on at the same time or before it. Other parts of *Cosby*'s context would be the show's success, Bill Cosby's prominence, and his functioning as an educator as well as someone concerned with providing positive role models for African Americans. And, in turn, understanding that program now would require us to reflect on other programs that followed it.

By convention, official institutions—corporate and governmental—play a role in broadcast media, though in the United States this role is usually a quiet one. The United States is unusual in this regard. In most countries, broadcasting is seen as a public resource and monitored or carried on exclusively by the government. The BBC (British Broadcasting Corporation) is probably the most familiar model worldwide; people in areas of the northern United States can listen in on CBC (Canadian) broadcasts, and those with shortwave radios can listen to offerings in English from Moscow, Australia, Germany, the Netherlands, and many other points—including our own Voice of America.

In the United States, however, we generally rely on corporate structures to provide broadcast information and entertainment, with very little governmental oversight. (Since 1967 the Corporation for Public Broadcasting has had a significant but minor role in radio and television.) The Federal Communications Commission (FCC) allocates frequencies and issues licenses and periodically monitors broadcasters for how they address the public interest, but it rarely deals with program content. Most of those who own radio or television stations, and their employees, approve of this absence of governmental censorship. However, not having an Information Czar does not necessarily mean that all ideas receive full and fair discussion. Large corporations have the same potential for bureaucratic regulations and the silencing of opposing views as governments.

Looking seriously at conventions may be useful for several reasons. With regard to television, a tremendous amount of effort and money goes into making a half-hour television program (including commercials) that is as easily *consumed* as possible. Observing conventions means seeing that there are alternatives. A full understanding of any text—visual, print, handwritten, or spoken—requires some knowledge about factors that are not out there on the surface to be observed. The apparent naturalness of a media text is a convention, one that it may be in your interest to inspect. Learning to be an adequate reader of an instance of any genre requires that you at least occasionally denature the conventions within which it is working.

Just as with televisual and other media texts, there are conventions involved in writing to address readers. Some of these apply in writing for college composition courses; conventions may change slightly or substantially in other college courses, and they may be radically different for writing done in various other settings. Rather than learning to stay within one convention, thought of as The Way to Write, what you should concentrate on is learning to discover what the conventions are in the writing task you are facing at the moment. You may have learned such conventions for essays in other classes, such as placing a one-sentence thesis statement at the end of an introductory paragraph, or treating subjects in divisible groups of threes. There are some rhetorical contexts in which these conventions should be observed, but there are others in which they should be closely examined or cast aside entirely.

PAUSE FOR REFLECTION
Write down as many conventions as you can recall about writing done for course assignments. When you have twenty to thirty items, go through and categorize these: How many are rules that cannot be broken (or else you are not writing at all)? How many are conventions specific to any reading situation? How many were specific to writing classes? How many to one particular class?

Conventions in Writing and Writing Classes

What are some of the conventions that apply in college writing assignments? It might be helpful to think of these conventions as a series of larger and larger circles. In discussing conventions in TV sitcoms, we saw that some were derived from fictional television, some from television generally, and some from pictorial or dramatic representation. Similarly, there are writing conventions such as those discussed in the Pause for Reflection above. Usually you have to sort out these distinctions for yourself. An instructor may insist that your assignments be typed, or written in ink on one side of the page, or folded in half lengthwise—and it will be understood that these are matters that apply only to that instructor's class. On the other hand, a requirement that you write in upper and lower case, rather than all caps, will apply to almost all writing done for others.

In other words, all writing is done from within a context. Writing for others means that you assume others will read from within a given context. And figuring out what the context is, and how it is to be reflected in the texts you write, might be said to be the *real* assignment in any course. If you are unclear about a particular piece of advice or an instruction, it's usually an important step to ask your instructor (tactfully) whether, in her or his judgment, it's something that all readers of college writing look for, or something with a more limited application.

It sometimes happens that an expectation in one class is in apparent or real conflict with what you learned from another writing class, or from your understanding based on other writing. One instructor, for example, may be very severe about sentence-boundary errors—sentence fragments, comma splices, and fused sentences—on the assumption that, if you can't recognize what constitutes a sentence, then there's no basis for taking seriously other things you say. Another instructor may be less severe about the same errors, on the assumption that these are surface-level problems you can edit out of your work at a later stage. The conflict between these positions may be based on pragmatic considerations: How can a class of writers be taught most effectively to meet readers' expectations? By quick and consistent reminders, or by a sequence of revisions that address content and development before mechanics? Or the conflict may be based in deeply held convictions about how we acquire language.

When there is a conflict about the quality of writing, rather than about pedagogy, you should take it as a reflection of reality: Readers, even college writing instructors, do often disagree about what constitutes good writing. It is better to understand that there are such disagreements, and to look for their sources, than to pretend that they don't exist or complain about contradictions.

One convention that holds for any written text is that it has to fit the capabilities and concerns of its presumed audience. Words used have to be primarily within the readers' vocabulary, or be comprehensible from the context; the syntax must be neither too complex for readers' understanding nor too simple to articulate the subject. One problem with this fairly standard advice is the difficulty of gaining any hard information about audiences. Writers tend to base their conception of "the audience" on experience and guesswork rather than on an actual notion of who is reading that text. Getting information about how a text is received is a problem for any author. Whether the text is a college essay, a newspaper article, a rock song, or a television program, there simply are no adequate means of knowing what the reactions are. Surveys of readers' or viewers' opinions and sales provide some rough guidance. But most media texts are part of a market that is limited and controlled by what else is available.

Advice to *consider the audience* doesn't help us very much, because the audience is usually simply implied by the meanings and connotations of words, syntax, style, level of detail, and other choices made while writing. In other words, we should separate the audience implied by these choices from the actual audience receiving a text. The *fictive* audience is constructed by the text, and the *real* audience is persuaded by that text, to a greater or lesser extent, to play along with it. "Playing along" is another way of saying that we read according to conventions of the form. When we read a newspaper article, for example, we are playing a role as part of the general public so addressed, accepting provisionally the importance implied by the appearance of an article on the front page, the emphasis on who–what–where–when–how of contemporary journalism, the willingness to label people and simplify events that is necessary to the level of treatment provided.

So as you write an essay for a college class, you are in effect inviting the instructor to play a role. The instructor's role may be to accept you as having done the thorough and detailed work necessary to be an authority on the subject, or perhaps to regard you as a bright apprentice making an entry into an area of specialization, or as someone who is giving it an earnest effort deserving of encouragement rather than harsh criticism. If you are persuasive enough, the instructor will accept this role and read the work favorably, perhaps making some suggestions for revision or for the next essay. If not—for example, if you claim a level of expertise that your treatment of materials or issues in the essay doesn't back up—then the instructor will decline to play along.

In other words, one convention that should be acknowledged is that writing takes place within the context of a class. The class might be designated English or Writing or Rhetoric, or it might be designated Biology or Marketing or Political Science, and that designation is an important factor in determining the context. There are rarely any institutional means by which what is developed in one class is systematically carried over and applied within another. It is often left to you to do that—to apply the advice about writing given in a first-semester writing class, for example, to second-semester courses.

Other conventions could be mentioned explicitly as well. Often, the starting point for an assignment is a prompt from the instructor, given orally or in writing, rather than an impulse from the writer or a standing body of material to be analyzed and written about. Key words in the prompt are important in establishing the purpose and genre of essay to be written; these may be explicit in the prompt or implied by the assignment or the class. The length of the assignment is an important determinant of what you say. Length will often determine the magnitude of the subject chosen and extent of the substantiating detail you must provide. In most first-year writing courses, there is little or no source material to be gathered, except in a research paper, summary, or assignment specifically for this purpose. In many subsequent writing assignments, it is assumed that you will look for supporting source material related to the assignment.

The voice used in student essays is a feature unique to student writing. That is, in many cases you are writing for an instructor, although you do not address that person directly; rather, you pretend that you are addressing the world generally, or at least your classmates. In almost all student writing, no one except the instructor is going to read the work. The response provided for the writing varies with the instructor: Sometimes there will be a conference to go over a draft, sometimes there will be written feedback in greater or lesser detail, and sometimes hardly more than a grade. But probably the most important consideration is that your work is seen as *student work*. Your writing has to prove its merit; its merit is not assumed. This may be unfair or unfortunate, but it's fact. Texts do not come from a vacuum; they come from institutions and individuals that give them important parts of their meaning. A new novel will be read differently if it comes from an established writer rather than an unknown; a news story draws its credibility from the reputation established over decades by the news organization producing it. Students are labeled as students. Bill McKibben, however (see reading below), is a highly regarded author.

ASSIGNMENT

Think back over a previous semester's writing class, if possible inspecting what you wrote in that class and what comments your instructor made in response. What were some of the conventions that held in that class? How did you "construct" your audience in your texts? Which of the conventions seem to you to have been based on that instructor's own preferences within that class, and which integral to writing of the kind you were doing?

Now consider writing you have been required to do for a class not labeled as a writing class (e.g., history, philosophy, business). What are some of the conventions that hold in that class? In what ways do these resemble those of the writing class previously described? In what ways are they different?

BILL MCKIBBEN

7:00 A.M.
"If you have a cold, you do not need to worry about reinfecting yourself with your lip balm." That's Beverly, who leads Christian calisthenics on Channel 116, Family Net. "If you used someone else's lip balm, I could see that. But not your own." *So much happens* between seven and eight in the morning on the ninety-three stations of the Fairfax, Virginia, cable system, until recently the largest in the world. On *Good Morning America,* Joel, the movie critic, says, "I learned something about England. For sore throats, the actors of Shakespeare's time used to take a live frog and lower the frog by its foot into their mouths. They figured that would keep the juices going. That's where the expression 'a frog in your throat' comes from." Since seaweed grows "in the nutrient-rich ocean," it comes as no surprise to anyone in the Annushka cosmetics organization that it attacks and destroys cellulite. An Amtrak train has gone off the rails in Iowa, according to CNN, and American companies will now be allowed to sell laptop computers in Eastern Europe. Kevin Johnson of the Phoenix Suns, so racked with the flu he had to be fed intravenously, nonetheless tallied 29 points and 12 assists in last night's game. Meanwhile, a robot surgeon has successfully replaced a dog's arthritic hip with an artificial joint. On the Fox affiliate, a cartoon Mr. Wilson is *sure* that's Dennis (the Menace) in the gorilla suit, so he uses a pair of pliers on the snout; entertainingly, however, it's an actual gorilla escaped from the zoo. The Infiniti Q-45 goes 0–60 in 6.9 seconds—"Wow' is an involuntary response of pure pleasure." Type A personalities are five times as likely to have a *second* heart attack, according to Otto Wahl, the psychiatry professor at George Mason University. Following vertical roasting on the Spanik Vertical Roaster, a chicken can be—is—carved with a carrot. In Czechoslovakia, Ambassador Rita Klimova tells C-SPAN, the newly emerging democracy has spawned dozens of political parties, including one for beer drinkers. Sesame Street is brought to you this morning by L, S, and 6. Only 11 percent of Americans feel the penny should be banned. Mr. Wizard is ripping apart fireworks to get at the chemicals inside. "Finally one of my favorites—strontium chloride," he exults. In Japan an exchange has opened to trade memberships in golf clubs as if they were stocks—they are already accepted as collateral by banks. Margie Grant now uses Dove soap: "I had this revelation. It's about time for me to start paying more attention to my skin, my face. Because you just don't realize how fast time passes." The Travel Channel provides the Lisbon forecast (high of 77) and then a documentary about Austria, a country you "may encounter on the far shores of the world, wherever humanity is striving to improve life." For instance, "airport passengers in Los Angeles may be driven to the terminal by airport buses made in Austria." The Hobel, a machine from nearby West Germany, is featured on *Breakthroughs.* It transforms food preparation from a tedious routine into an exciting event, and is top-rack-dishwasher-safe. Precision-minted pewter medallions celebrating former President Reagan are available for $10 on the Nashville Network. "Tums tastes like chalk," proclaims

an ex–Tums user. On *McHale's Navy*, all leaves have been canceled until annoying enemy pilot Washing Machine Charlie can be silenced, much to McHale's disgust. ("If he's a menace, I'm a ring-tailed goony bird," he declares.) Hans, a Dutch national, prepares a creamy Gouda sauce to drizzle over cauliflower for the A&E audience. A harrowing documentary on the Howard University station documents the British genocide of Tasmanian aborigines, right down to the last man, whose skeleton hangs in the Oxford Museum. Richard Simmons introduces his brother, who used to weigh 205 pounds: "Here I was only forty-two and I felt fifty-two, maybe sixty-two." There's terrible flooding in Texas—on the *Today* show, a woman is plucked off the roof of her submerged car by a helicopter. Richard Nixon tells Bryant Gumbel that while it's true his resignation from the presidency may continue to cloud his record, "the main point is to live life to the hilt, all the time you possibly can, and to continue to give it your best shot to the end." Owning a firearm is a deeply personal decision, says a young woman in a checkered suit appearing on behalf of the NRA. "Whistle at me, will you, you shirt-tail cousin to a piccolo!" declares Wally Gator, "the swinging navigator in the swamp." A preacher is explaining something on the Inspirational Network—"As long as you're holding on to cash, you can't do anything with it. And if God tries to give you more, what happens?" He demonstrates—the bills bounce off your closed fist and fall to the floor. On the CBS morning news a "controversial Milwaukee alderman" says that unless a hundred-million-dollar minority jobs program is created soon, "revolutionary violence will be committed against the city of Milwaukee." Newly released hostage Frank Reed declares from his hospital balcony that he is looking forward to a three-pound Maine lobster. A man named Delvin Miller has been harness racing for eight decades, not including a stretch in World War II where he trained mules to deliver medicine in Burma for General "Vinegar Joe" Stilwell. The members of singing group Wilson Phillips remark that people tell them their name makes them sound like a law firm or a type of screwdriver. Fairfax County residents are encouraged to burlap-band their trees for gypsy-moth detection and control. "The reason I'll always make a big deal about three-quarters sleeves is that you always used to have to push up your sleeves," says an announcer on the J. C. Penney Channel. Hamstrings work in opposition to quadriceps, according to an exercise instructor on the Lifetime Channel, who adds, "the adductor muscles are too tight in most of the population." More CEOs of Fortune 500 companies were born under Taurus than any other sign; also, age-based sizing for children's clothing is out-of-date because children are larger than they were when the sizing was devised. A National Family Opinion Research survey discussed on Channel 34 found that most consumers "aren't shy about testing out beds in retail showrooms." On MTV, Bruce Dickinson of Iron Maiden describes his new solo album, which has songs about how there are "all those people at the cocktail party with their little masks on, and all the businessmen in their suits and ties and they're just stabbing each other in the back all the time." (Adds Dickinson, "We've got a real rip-your-head-off direction in Maiden, and we're very proud of that direction. But with the solo stuff I can do stuff that's a little more varied.") Research from the University of Wisconsin indicates that hamburger may contain certain substances that inhibit skin cancer. Congressman Donald "Buz" Lukens, who was convicted of having sex with a sixteen-year-old, said he had made a "dumb mistake" but that he would run for reelection anyway.

By now it's nearly eight.

[From *The Age of Missing Information* by Bill McKibben. Copyright © 1992 by Bill McKibben. Reprinted by permission of Random House, Inc.]

QUESTIONS

1. A convention frequently cited in writing classes is that every paragraph should have a topic sentence and should be moderate in length, with clear connections between sentences. Would you say that the first paragraph in the McKibben excerpt above follows this convention? If not, why not? What effect does the paragraph's structure (or lack of structure) have on you as you read it?
2. What sentence or phrase in the paragraph functions like a topic sentence?
3. Is the sort of information provided by the paragraph (originally provided by the television) valuable information? What determines its value?

CONCLUSION

Rhetoric through Media encourages you to think about reading and writing not as separate activities, but as done together. Your own writing depends on what you have read or observed in and about your life, and how that connects to your culture. The conventions through which you understand pretty much anything have to be inferred through reading. And it is by writing that you have your best mode of participation, putting what you have read through media to good use. The next chapter will present at some length a discussion of writing as a medium.

A contemporary philosopher and critic, Jacques Derrida, has said that there is no getting outside of texts: What might be called *textuality* is a condition of our lives. This means not only that texts (especially media texts) are everywhere, as they generally seem to be—but also that we cannot but make meaning, that we are always creating the text of our lives and our thoughts, and reading texts from inside of our own text. The trick is how to shape that text into something that will please us more and work effectively for us, and media texts have a role to play in teaching us how to do that.

The issue, in other words, is what might be called *intertextuality:* We live our lives, in contemporary culture, between, among, and through texts. Some of these texts we write ourselves; the overwhelming number, however, have been written by others, from such substantial texts as the Old Testament, the New Testament, and various theological commentaries on these, to cultural presences such as Shakespeare and Poe and Melville, to nonliterary texts such as *Time* magazine and *Reader's Digest* and *TV Guide* and *The Plain Truth*, to the sports pages and the personal columns of newspapers, to MTV and *Beverly Hills 90210*, and on and on. Your task is to write yourself into a relationship with these and other texts, classical and literary and popular and transitory.

FURTHER ASSIGNMENTS

Assignment
Look at a TV magazine for your area, in order to relate programs broadcast at certain times to their likely audiences. Can you draw any conclusions about who the target audiences are for given shows? Which viewers predominate on particular days and times?

Assignment
Consider, first individually and then in discussion groups, what use might be made of specific media texts by the following: *(a)* the owner of a broadcasting station; *(b)* a corporate advertiser; *(c)* an advertising agency; *(d)* an actress; *(e)* a producer; *(f)* a screenwriter; *(g)* a reporter; *(h)* an athletic director at a university; *(i)* the information officer at the university; *(j)* a city councilman; *(k)* the governor of your state; *(l)* a parent of school-age children; *(m)* a researcher for a political campaign; *(n)* a Sierra Club member; *(o)* an unemployed person considering relocating; *(p)* the owner of a travel bureau; *(q)* a waitress in a resort area; *(r)* a trial lawyer; *(s)* a satirist; *(t)* an employee of a trucking firm; *(u)* a member of an antiabortion group; *(v)* a retired person who plays golf and gardens; *(w)* an investment broker who sails competitively; *(x)* a high school science teacher; *(y)* a real estate agent; *(z)* a single person looking for companionship.

In what ways are the individuals in these different roles "consumers" and in what ways are they "producers" of texts? Can these be kept separate?

Assignment
Write a news report of one of your classes. Try to recount what happened in the class, leaving out explicit statements of opinion and judgment. Make your news report comparable in length to a newspaper article—approximately 150 words. Write or type the story in a column, as would be an appropriate format for newsprint (this will require shorter paragraphs than usual). Keep in mind that newspaper writers often lose the last several paragraphs of their work in the cutting room, so don't plan to build up to a conclusion. Last, come up with a good newspapery headline for the class.

When your work is completed, write another account of the same class, as you would express it in writing to a classmate who has asked what went on that day. Try for approximately the same length and level of detail, but for a different audience.

Assuming that there are differences between the two accounts, where do these come from? What are the conventions that are at work when you describe a class to another member of that class?

Assignment

Choose another genre of media with which you are familiar and outline some of the conventions that apply to it. Possibilities: action films; hunting and fishing programs; rap music; "coming-of-age" stories; quest narratives; soap operas; alternative rock videos; country music ballads. Can you think of an example within that genre in which a convention is broken? If so, what is the result?

Assignment: Answering-machine announcements

One form of media that may be little noticed but is highly conventional is the "announcement" composed for an answering machine. In order to get some feel for conventions, first jot down some ideas about conventional announcements: What these should include, what they should not say, usual organization, tone and style, and so on. Then compose two announcements—one that respects these conventions, and one that in some way breaks the conventions. If you have access to a cassette recorder (or telephone answering machine), record these. Then bring drafts and tapes to class and discuss your work with other students.

From the group should emerge some sense of what is conventionally appropriate, what is not conventionally done, and what some reasons are for either respecting or departing from conventions.

Media and Purposes for Writing

3

Making Use of Observations—from Prewriting to Drafting

OVERVIEW

The first two chapters of *Rhetoric through Media* introduced the concepts of *rhetoric* and *media*. This chapter might be said to be about the middle term in the title, *through*. Here we will be dealing with *drawing connections*—between media texts and the texts that you write; and between your initial notes, journal writings, and the eventual drafts you give to others to read. What happens to your writing, in practical terms, if you begin to think of it seriously as a medium?

To see writing as your medium, you may have to get past a stubborn fact: If you are like most readers of this book, you are not a professional writer. The journalist with a byline in a magazine or newspaper, the screenwriter credited for a film or television script, and the producer of a CD or a children's program all do work that is regarded as *finished*. They are professionals not only because they are paid for their work, not only because they have credentials and experience that qualify them, but because their "readers," including colleagues and employers as well as audience, automatically *read* their work as finished.

Students do not have these advantages. An important convention of reading student work is that it's seen as still in progress, still not good enough, still *to be graded*. In addition to having to learn what you are capable of as a writer, then, you also have to convince others (particularly instructors) that your ideas should be taken seriously. This means you have to find ways to get your observations into their best possible form for first reading. Developing some procedures to do that is the subject of this chapter.

Drafts of the writing done by professionals are more like your drafts than you might think—often rough, messy, and incomplete. But we don't see professionals' work at draft stages, and so we are likely to assume that it always existed in its perfect state. The difference between professionals' writing practices and those of most students is that the professionals have developed some strategies to bring their drafts to completion.

Having good ideas, by itself, isn't enough. Observation and reflection about media, or more generally about writing or language, are valuable in themselves; but you also want to make your observations work for you. This means matching them up with expectations of real readers in specific institutional contexts, such as the workplace, a publication, or your college classroom. The issue, then, is how to adapt your writing to others' expectations while making sure that it pleases you as well.

To reach both of these goals, you will need to look carefully not only at what you write but at *how* you write. Writing considered as a process is commonly divided into three stages: *prewriting, drafting,* and *revision*. Rather than focusing on these phases in distinct chapters, we will be looking for links between them. This chapter's purpose is to suggest some ways of moving from observation and preparation to the point at which you have a complete and reasonably coherent draft of a piece of writing. You should then apply these transitional strategies as you work through Chapters 4 through 7, which are specifically focused on genres of media texts as these reflect purposes for writing. The other link, between draft and finished work, will be the subject of Chapter 9.

When you are thinking through an issue, it is important to be able to come up with ideas on a topic, produce a body of text, develop your ideas, and group them effectively. Those who teach writing have given careful thought to techniques for prewriting. Some of the material here may be familiar from previous writing classes; this book borrows several prewriting techniques from others' practices. What may be new about the techniques here is their integration into a discussion of rhetoric in contemporary culture.

It would be misleading, however, to think of the movement from observation to sustained draft as purely a matter of technique. Thought takes place in language—so when you gather, examine, and select from a group of tentative and incomplete statements those that you want to develop before others, you are not just assembling knowledge but *creating* it. The way you select, order, and develop your materials shows what you value—and will determine how well your values speak to others who read your text.

Some ideas about adapting your work for others' eyes can be gleaned from media texts. Media are used in this book not only to provide subjects for writing, but to help you conceptualize the work of writing. As we have seen, media texts and college writing assignments are rhetorical: They are directed to others, for discoverable purposes. These purposes are not solely those of the creators of those texts—they come in part from the institutional context, the genre or type of writing, and the conventions or agreed-upon ways of reading that derive from these. (If you write a song, you provide melody, chords, and lyrics, but you don't invent the idea of music.)

What media can provide us, then, is a valuable guide for examining conventions in writing, particularly when we are in the phase of producing a draft we want others to read. Whether we like it or not, media offer models for writing. Taking media texts as models does not mean these texts are something to imitate. It's not that your writing should aspire to mimic the *National Enquirer,* but that media texts remind us that our writing is rhetorical and has to address both our purposes and those of readers.

A piece of writing can be said to be satisfactory if it suits these purposes. But as practical advice, that doesn't take us very far. What are your purposes? To get an A? To express or define yourself? To establish a reputation? To become rich? To reform the world? For that matter, what are your readers' purposes? And how do you connect their purposes with your own?

It may help us establish these purposes for readers and writers if we take a step back. Why is there communication at all? The answer starts with the fact that human beings are fundamentally social. We have to reach out to others in some way, to participate in a community. (You may have come to feel this with greater force when giving up media for a period.) Writing is a way of extending your voice beyond the range it has in speech, so that you can reach more people, or reach people differently. Media are extensions of that "reaching out" principle. And rhetoric, in both media and writing, is the approach used to reach others effectively. So one important consideration for making the shift between insights and finished draft is to begin to see things from the audience's perspective.

To analyze your writing process, you have to look at conventions in the forms of writing you are practicing, in order to see which must be observed, which may be followed or not, and which might usefully be violated in order to give a subject your own imprint, to make it in some sense your own. No matter how original a writer you are, you have to use language and concepts that come from others. It's necessary to know what is conventionally done, in writing or in other contexts, in order to follow or to meaningfully violate conventions.

ISSUES

Writing As Your Medium

We saw in Chapter 1 how important media and media texts are as sources of information, language, and even values in contemporary culture. And in Chapter 2 we began to explore the interplay between textual conventions and our role as the audience. Now we need to turn attention to ways in which thinking about media can help with our own writing. The starting point is a change in concept: You need to try out the notion that writing can be not only a medium, but *your* medium.

Claiming writing as your medium may strike you initially as presumptuous or just flat-out wrong. Many in writing classes believe (initially, at least) that people either are born writers, or they are not. As with other articles of faith, no one invents such a black-and-white idea: It's a myth we have absorbed along with the rest of our culture. Like other myths, this one helps us to explain things. It may be flattering to think of yourself as a born writer; or, on the other hand, you may get some consolation for difficulty in writing from the belief that you are just not naturally a writer. But neither position is finally very helpful for improving your writing. One starting point might be to come to regard writing not as a task or as an art, but as a medium. If you think of your writing as a medium, you can work more in intermediary stages on ways to establish closer communication with those reading your texts.

The very existence of writing classes implies that it is possible (or at least that someone believes it is possible) to *learn* how to write. We may be discouraged by comparing our texts with those we encounter through media. But this comparison is misleading, because we always see others' texts as finished work, as products, whereas our own work we see in process. What we need is to develop a double vision: We need not only to see our work as in process, but also to have an anticipation of what it might become. That means we need to develop an awareness not only of conventions of media texts, but of conventions of the texts we write as well.

And we should apply appropriate conventions to both the process and product phases. In other words, we may create problems for ourselves by rushing too quickly to apply the conventions that are appropriate to a completed work, while the text is still under construction. When we move from rough notes exploring insights and testing potential organization to unified work for others to see, there has to be a crossover point. But if we move too quickly to thinking of our work as finished product, we skip one of the most valuable and productive phases, discovery. Writing in the discovery mode allows you to explore the potential in a subject without being too concerned about *using* what you come up with: The conventions of discovery are not restrictive but liberating. One important convention for the early phases of working through an idea, then, is that discovering ideas is more important than getting them down at first in exactly the right form.

You may feel more comfortable with your ability to write when you are able to think of "rules," "grammar," "good style," and the other features of writing classes as conventions for a later phase. Set these aside as less important, for the time being: They are part of what you will use to communicate your ideas to others. As we work through the process of writing, we need to follow the convention of keeping an eye out for what may be useful later on.

One difficulty in seeing writing as your medium may be that we often think of media as *others'* media. Relatively few of us in the United States write for, talk for, sing for, or otherwise participate in the production or ownership of texts to be broadcast over television or radio, shown in theaters or on video screens, or read in magazines, newspapers, or other publications. The world of discourse may seem to be divided into two sections: a private, nonprofessional sphere, which largely receives information; and a public, professional one, which largely distributes it. Seeing these as separate areas may prevent you from thinking about what they have in common.

An important connection between these areas is that both public and private forms of communication depend on conventions to guide both writers and readers. As we have seen, texts reach us by making use of the implicit knowledge we have gained from reading other texts. These have been built into systems of conventions or rules for understanding. But what links texts with *some* other texts, but not all?

The answer lies, once again, in the existence of *genres*. We depend on textual cues to help us sort, say, *Caroline in the City* in with *Ellen* and *Friends*, but not *Days of our Lives* or *The Ricki Lake Show* or *Sportscenter*. Textual cues help us place television programs, films, magazine articles, and other texts into genres. *Genre* is a French word meaning *kind*—we can relate it to English words such as general and generic. Both your texts and media texts are always encountered as specific *kinds* of writing, which are understood in comparison with other, similar texts; readers make sense of your work by slotting it into established sets of conventions. This interplay between genre and text is important for how we make sense of things, and it goes on all the time.

Even what you say to others fits into genres. Words and phrases like *hello, good morning, good afternoon, glad to see you,* and *how's it going?* signal that you are within the genre of greetings. Greetings in English vary individually, regionally, and within subcultures; for example, *Howdy* works well in many areas of Texas but would be thought odd in New York (not to mention London). And conventional ways of greeting people (or not) in Manhattan transplanted to, say, Tyler or Bryan would be downright rude. The opposite genre would be farewell: *Goodbye, my best to the family, have a nice day, see you later, take care of yourself,* and other, more individualized phrases indicate that you are taking leave on good terms. Other speech genres might include congratulations, exchanges of information, talk about matters such as weather or sports, romantic interchanges, and gossip.

PAUSE FOR REFLECTION
Do you have characteristic ways of expressing greeting and farewell? Are there phrases that you avoid for these purposes (e.g., "Have a nice day")? Why do you make these choices? Can you add to the examples of speech genres given above?

Knowledge about the appropriate genre is part of any conversation. That is, you know the type of conversation you are having, even if you haven't taken the trouble to label it. You may notice this knowledge when, in the middle of a conversation dominated by one speech genre, a participant tries to shift to another. For example, one person may want to talk about last night's playoff game, while another wants to talk politics or religion. Either there is some persuasion, silent or open—"Oh, let's not talk about that now; I can't stand thinking about my soul before ten in the morning!"; "How can you waste your time thinking about the Cubs with the country falling apart the way it is?"—or one participant dominates the conversation and sets the agenda (usually with some resistance from the others). In either case, the conversation usually breaks off, at least for the moment.

In order to be real, then, conversation has to meet the needs and interests of all participants. You can't just grab people by the collar and talk *at* them; you have to talk *with* them. This principle has to be kept in mind when you write for an audience: Readers do not have the same opportunities to respond immediately as do those in a conversation, but they do have expectations that you must address if the readers are to be kept interested. Otherwise, they will do the equivalent of walking away, which is to stop reading—or, if they must read, will read resentfully.

Like speech genres, writing falls into specific patterns or types. Some of these are initiated by the writer, in the equivalent of "Let me tell you what I heard last night" (gossip) or "Do you know why Cheerios is different from Notre Dame?" (joke). The possibilities within any genre—spoken or written—are supplied by the context. Writing for a composition class depends on a certain level of formality and a tone that writers transgress at some risk. You will have to feel your way toward understanding what this level of formality is in any given class. What are some of the signals by which you can find this out? (Consider dress, style of speech, arrangement of desks, etc.)

PAUSE FOR REFLECTION

List some genres of media texts (those mentioned in previous chapters included sitcoms, news, talk shows, rock music, among others). Make a separate list for genres of writing expected of you in writing courses. Do these lists have areas in common? As you look at an item in one list, can you think of something that corresponds on the other?

Every text, public or private, presumes an audience—even if the audience is the writer reading the text at some later time—and is written with that audience's expectations in mind. Over time, such expectations are formulated into conventions: academic genres of writing such as essays, research reports, and argumentative papers are as much subject to conventions (gathered into handbooks and guides for style) as are interviews, news reports, or sitcoms. What counts for a pleasing style or correct format has developed, finally, because readers became accustomed to certain ways of doing things. Similarly, conventions in various media have evolved from usage. The differences between what we commonly mean by *the media,* and the media you yourself have used most often (writing and speech) come from the particular means of communication, the size of the audience, the institutional authority for communication, and the rhetorical conventions used to reach others. In your writing, these considerations are typically built into the assignment, so that you take them for granted. But reexamining your writing process means finding a way to reflect on them.

Audience and genre, then, are important factors in what you do with your draft; and the movement from prewriting to draft might be thought of as a shift in audience and genre. Writing in early stages is mostly for yourself, whereas writing in later stages is directed toward others—an instructor certainly, others possibly. Genres are marked by textual cues, and some of these for early-stage writing include relative messiness on the page, talking to yourself about work in progress, easy use of first person, informal choice of words and style, and relative lack of concern for organization, introduction, or conclusion. Informal writing is likely to be less concerned with boundaries: If you need to stop and come back, you can, and if you want to return to an earlier topic, your reader will not object—because usually you are your only reader. Textual cues for more formal genres of writing would include an introduction that in some way initiates your subject for a reader, words and phrases more carefully chosen for effect, clean copy, transitions, and a conclusion that in some way points to the significance of the topic. These textual conventions derive, in turn, from the purposes for both kinds of writing.

When doing exploratory writing, you are still finding out things. What you say to yourself can be incomplete, based on what you know at the moment. You can write without concern about characteristic writing problems, because you expect to come back later and modify what you write. But what you say to others in your draft has to be informed by their concerns. You have to be responsible about choosing examples fairly, using appropriate logic, and making connections between points, as well as editing your work. It doesn't matter if exploratory writing is fragmentary (see the journal entries about media deprivation in Chapter 2 to get a feel for how fragmentary these can conventionally be) but most writing for others needs to be developed and connected through transitions.

To make writing your medium, then, you need to work back and forth: forward from your ideas and observations, expressed as exploratory writing, and backward from some sense of where you want to go, based on your understanding of the appropriate genre of writing and the rhetorical conventions it entails. The following essay by William Stafford may give you some help in relaxing into writing to discover what you think.

WILLIAM STAFFORD

A Way of Writing

A writer is not so much someone who has something to say as he is someone who has found a process that will bring about new things he would not have thought of if he had not started to say them. That is, he does not draw on a reservoir; instead, he engages in an activity that brings to him a whole succession of unforeseen stories, poems, essays, plays, laws, philosophies, religions, or—but wait!

Back in school, from the first when I began to try to write things, I felt this richness. One thing would lead to another; the world would give and give. Now, after twenty years or so of trying, I live by that certain richness, an idea hard to pin, difficult to say, and perhaps offensive to some. For there are strange implications in it.

One implication is the importance of just plain receptivity. When I write, I like to have an interval before me when I am not likely to be interrupted. For me, this means usually the early morning, before others are awake. I get pen and paper, take a glance out of the window (often it is dark out there), and wait. It is like fishing. But I do not wait very long, for there is always a nibble—and this is where receptivity comes in. To get started I will accept anything that occurs to me. Something always occurs, of course, to any of us. We can't keep from thinking. Maybe I have to settle for an immediate impression: it's cold, or hot, or dark, or bright, or in between! Or—well, the possibilities are endless. If I put down something, that thing will help the next thing come, and I'm off. If I let the process go on, things will occur to me that were not at all in my mind when I started. These things, odd or trivial as they may be, are somehow connected. And if I let them string out, surprising things will happen.

If I let them string out.... Along with initial receptivity, then, there is another readiness: I must be willing to fail. If I am to keep on writing, I cannot bother to insist on high standards. I must get into action and not let anything stop me, or even slow me much. By "standards" I do not mean "correctness"—spelling, punctuation, and so on. These details become mechanical for anyone who writes for a while. I am thinking about such matters as social significance, positive values, consistency, etc. I resolutely disregard these. Something better, greater, is happening! I am following a process that leads so wildly and originally into new territory that no judgment can at the moment be made about values, significance, and so on. I am making something new, something that has not been judged before. Later others—and maybe I myself—will make judgments. Now, I am headlong to discover. Any distraction may harm the creating.

So, receptive, careless of failure, I spin out things on the page. And a wonderful freedom comes. If something occurs to me, it is all right to accept it. It has one justification: it occurs to me. No one else can guide me. I must follow my own weak, wandering, diffident impulses.

A strange bonus happens. At times, without my insisting on it, my writings become coherent: the successive elements that occur to me are clearly related. They lead by themselves to new connections. Sometimes the language, even the syllables that happen along, may start a trend. Sometimes the materials alert me to something waiting in my mind, ready for sustained attention. At such times, I allow myself to be eloquent, or intentional, or for great swoops (Treacherous! Not to be trusted!) reasonable. But I do not insist on any of that; for I know that back of my activity there will be the coherence of my self, and that indulgence of my impulses will bring recurrent patterns and meanings again.

This attitude toward the process of writing creatively suggests a problem for me, in terms of what others say. They talk about "skills" in writing. Without denying that I do have experience, wide reading, automatic orthodoxies and maneuvers of various kinds, I still must insist that I am often baffled about what "skill" has to do with the precious little area of confusion when I do not know what I am going to say and then I find out what I am going to say. That precious interval I am unable to bridge by skill. What can I witness about it? It remains mysterious, just as all of us must feel puzzled about how we are so inventive as to be able to talk along through complexities with our friends, not needing to plan what we are going to say, but never stalled for long in our confident forward progress. Skill? If so, it is the skill we all have, something we must have learned before the age of three or four.

A writer is one who has become accustomed to trusting that grace, or luck, or—skill.

Yet another attitude I find necessary: most of what I write, like most of what I say in casual conversation, will not amount to much. Even I will realize, and even at the time, that it is not negotiable. It will be like practice. In conversation I allow myself random remarks—in fact, as I recall, that is the way I learned to talk—so in writing I launch many expendable efforts. A result of this free way of writing is that I am not writing for others, mostly; they will not see the product at all unless the activity eventuates in something that later appears to be worthy. My guide is the self, and its adventuring in the language brings about communication.

This process-rather-than-substance view of writing invites a final, dual reflection:

1. Writers may not be special—sensitive or talented in any usual sense. They are simply engaged in sustained use of a language skill we all have. Their "creations" come about through confident reliance on stray impulses that will, with trust, find occasional patterns that are satisfying.

2. But writing itself is one of the great, free human activities. There is scope for individuality, and elation, and discovery, in writing. For the person who follows with trust and forgiveness what occurs to him, the world remains always ready and deep, an inexhaustible environment, with the combined vividness of an actuality and flexibility of a dream. Working back and forth between experience and thought, writers have more than space and time can offer. They have the whole unexplored realm of human vision.

[From William Stafford, *Writing the Australian Crawl.* Ann Arbor: The University of Michigan Press, 1978. Used by permission.]

QUESTIONS

1. Do Stafford's comments about writing surprise you at times? What in his description of writing differs from your prior assumptions about what writers do?
2. Does it matter that Stafford does not show his initial explorations to others?
3. Write a brief account of your own writing process, explaining how it resembles or differs from Stafford's as described here.
4. How do you think the writing process might be different in a more social or collaborative medium (for example, working with other screenwriters on a film or television program; working with reporters and editors on a newspaper or magazine)?

5. Are there reasons why some students, and perhaps you yourself, might find some of Stafford's (implied) advice difficult? (For example, his words about getting up early, being receptive, being willing to fail.)

Thinking about your process of writing, about the various sorts of prewriting you do or might do, is looking at writing from what might be thought of as the entry side. Thinking about writing in terms of conventions or genres or the audience is looking at it from the exit side. Like the two ends of a tunnel, both views are necessary.

Writing Essays As a Conventional Act

In one fundamental sense, everything we do from a very early age is governed by conventions. Preschools help to create and reinforce conventions of how to behave in groups (lining up for walks by twos, addressing adults respectfully, picking up after oneself, not hitting). The conventions continue in elementary school (asking permission to talk or get a drink, printing neatly, not hitting) and throughout the rest of our schooling (turning in homework on time, taking care of textbooks, not hitting). But in some contexts we are encouraged not to follow conventions—to think for ourselves, resist peer pressure, stand out from the crowd. Still, the devices by which we can break conventions are themselves conventional.

This paradox has everything to do with succeeding as a writer, whether on college assignments or in other contexts. For example, newspaper columnists follow closely requirements of length, format, appropriate word choice, and audience address. They work at achieving a personal style built on consistency from column to column; but imitation, whether based on someone else's writing or the columnist's own past work, is not allowed.

Conventions are matters of common agreement—and one area of common agreement is that we should not be too closely bound by trying to do what others expect of us. This means that writers' relations to convention involve a kind of interplay between convention and personal insight.

PAUSE FOR REFLECTION

Choose a newspaper columnist with whom you are familiar—Ann Landers, Dave Barry, Miss Manners, Art Buchwald, William Raspberry—and look at several columns to determine what characterizes that writer's style. Distinguish as best you can the features that may be required in all newspaper writing; those that may be common to all column writing (as opposed to news reporting); and those that separate this particular columnist from others working in the same genre.

It may be useful to look at how some conventions in media function, because both media texts and writing have to work within conventions. For example, one very powerful convention in news programming is that the anchor or reporter on television news looks straight into the camera while reading the news. This is a successful convention, because we believe someone's sincerity more easily if the person is looking us directly in the eyes. The television image is a technological imitation of that look. Some of the pragmatic side of the rhetoric of news on television can be seen in the dialogue from the 1987 film *Broadcast News* in Exhibit 3.1.

Tom Gives Aaron Some Tips on Reading the News

In the film, Tom (William Hurt) has been hired from a local station where he has been the TV sports reporter to a job with national network news. Tom is handsome and has good screen presence but is inexperienced as a journalist and not well informed about public affairs. Aaron (Albert Brooks) is a news reporter who writes brilliantly but doesn't come across on camera very well. The network is rumored to be making some personnel cuts soon, and in an effort to position himself to keep his job, Aaron has gotten permission to anchor the news the next weekend. Somewhat against his principles, he's asking Tom for some help in improving his style of news delivery.

Scene: A studio at the network's office. Shot of TV camera and monitor.

Aaron: This is very uncomfortable for me—because, and I don't mean this as a knock, but we approach these things so differently.

Tom: We sure do. And I don't mean that as a knock, either. OK, go ahead. I'll just tell you what I think, and you can disregard it if you want.

Tom walks from off-camera at front to behind the camera and back.

Aaron: All right. I just don't know how effective this is going to be because of our different approaches.

Tom: OK.

Exhibit 3.1 Excerpt from the screenplay of *Broadcast News*, written by James L. Brooks. *Broadcast News* © 1987 Twentieth Century Fox Film Corporation. All rights reserved.

Aaron: Reports tonight...

Tom: Wait.

Aaron: What?

Tom: Your coat jacket is rising up in back.

Aaron: OK.

Tom: When you sit, sit on your coat jacket a little. That'll give you a good line.

Aaron: Reports tonight...

Tom: *Don't* look at the monitor!

Aaron: Reports tonight from far down on the Arabian peninsula indicate that heavy fighting continues...

Last few words simultaneous with Tom's; Tom rises from chair, goes behind Aaron.

Tom: Your jacket, Aaron.

Aaron: ...for a second... What are you doing? Don't touch me!

Tom: Sit on it.

Aaron: No, but just don't handle me...

Tom: *Sit* on it!

Aaron: I'm sitting on it.

Tom: Now look.

Aaron: Don't fit...(*admiring*) Fantastic tip! That's great.

Tom sits down.

...continues for a second day between government and rebel forces in pro-Soviet South...

Tom: No, no.

Aaron: No?

Tom: Don't let your eyes move from the beginning of a sentence to the end of it like that. You don't want to look shifty, do you?

Aaron looks at him.

Aaron: No.

Tom: And the right side of your face is the good one. OK—go ahead.

continues

Exhibit 3.1 Continued

Aaron turns his head to show that side to the camera. It looks very awkward.

Aaron: They're going to let me do the news like this?

Tom laughs.

Aaron: Heavy fighting continues for a second day between government and rebel...

Tom: (*interrupting*) Try to punch one word or phrase in every sentence, one idea per story. Punch.

Cut to hallway. Tom and Aaron are walking.

Tom: You were smokin' there toward the end.

Aaron: The pointers were great. I'll study the tape.

Tom: I go this way. (*Stops; face-to-face*) Just remember that you're not just reading the news, you're narrating it. Everybody has to sell a little. You're selling them this idea of you, you know, you're sort of saying, "Trust me, I'm, um, credible." So when you feel yourself just reading... Stop! Start selling a little. OK. So long.

Music. Aaron looks about him a bit.

Exhibit 3.1 *Continued*

PAUSE FOR REFLECTION

What do you think about "selling yourself," as Tom advocates in Exhibit 3.1? What are the ethical implications of concentrating on the style of delivery so much, as opposed to the content of the news being presented? Are there ways in which you sell yourself in writing done for college classes? For other purposes?

Television, an electronic medium, has adapted the cultural conventions of face-to-face contact. This should not be surprising, since the size of most television screens brings the image of a close-up to approximately the scale of another person sitting across the room. Our responses to television, and consequently the conventions through which TV "speaks" to us, would be very different if television had developed on wall-sized screens, or on wristwatch-sized ones. While the newscast genre of television programming is an imitation of conversation, obviously the news anchor does not address *us* directly. Such direct address, if technologically possible, might strike viewers as intrusive or threatening, in a way similar to what happens in George

Orwell's *Nineteen Eighty-Four,* when Winston Smith slacks off in doing his morning calisthenics and is shouted at. But even without the advantage of being able to call us by name, television anchorpersons try to communicate a kind of warmth—to resemble a friendly visitor. Something analogous happens in the tone used in writing some essays; that is, many writing situations call for a direct and sincere tone to the writing, as though the words on the page came from a voice as straightforward as that cultivated by a television news reader. But it's also a convention that in a college essay you do not address the reader directly, even when you are sure that only your instructor will read your work. (Some instructors may encourage or allow direct address in highly informal kinds of writing such as journals, but most find it intrusive there as well. On the other hand, it's OK conventionally for a textbook to address you directly, even though the author doesn't know you personally. Go figure.)

Something comparable happened earlier in the medium of radio. Early on, radio developed a conversational, intimate tone, as though the person whose voice was being broadcast to hundreds of thousands of sets were everyone's close acquaintance or confidant. This tone was supplanted to some extent when music, especially rock, became dominant in radio programming. But the conversational tone has made something of a comeback in genres such as Christian broadcasting, talk radio, and the monologues of Garrison Keillor's *Prairie Home Companion* broadcasts. The return of such intimate voices, after a relative absence, gives them additional rhetorical force.

Prose writing has also adapted conventions from spoken forms: conversation, sermons, speeches, and other public discourse as carried out centuries ago were taken into essays when these developed in the eighteenth century and later. What you are now able to write has been shaped by modes of writing that in turn developed from earlier written as well as spoken genres (newspapers and other print journalism, advertising, fiction, academic writing, and many other sources). Very little in any genre is invented *for* that genre; most of the form is appropriated from something else.

The difficulty, then, comes in deciding which conventions will work for you in your circumstances. Complaints about "writer's block" sometimes are phrased as though the writer has nothing to say—when the problem is more likely that there's too much to say, and no procedures to help the person decide where to start. What should *you* appropriate? You *can* write virtually anything; what *should* you write? What will make your writing effective? Here the usefulness of a textbook breaks down: This book can no more tell you that, directly, than your TV screen can criticize your dress or hair style in the morning. What is needed is for you to become a better reader of your own local and institutional needs. But there are some conventions that are very widely held. Academic readers may differ somewhat on expectations of style, format, and genre; but most will agree that good writing is unified, coherent, and clear, with logical reasoning and sufficient illustration for its points. If you work toward these things, you will have a good start.

Writing for academic or other purposes is not a proposition in which one size fits all. Some conventions may differ between academic disciplines as well as between individuals. For example, sentence length and directness may vary a great deal. Some disciplines permit the use of the passive voice, which allows them to emphasize the *what* as opposed to the *who*. Something like the following might be found in the sciences:

> After having been infected with the AIDS virus, the chimpanzees are observed until they develop symptoms, then they are euthanized and their lymph nodes are analyzed.

Notice how such a sentence avoids stating who carried out the actions. But passive voice is widely misused, concealing those who act in order to pretend that an unfavorable event or decision just happened all by itself:

> After careful review of your application, it was decided not to continue your candidacy for the position.

Such a sentence is bad both syntactically and ethically. If you receive such a response to an application, you don't know who carried out a supposedly careful review or who decided you weren't a good choice.

Other academic disciplines follow more closely the model of the daily newspaper in preferring active voice:

> On Saturday, the Lions spanked the Minnesota Vikings 41–19 at the Silverdome, lifting them into a first-place tie with the Vikings. (Eric Pate, "Just Win to Get In," *Saginaw News*, Dec. 19, 1994, D1.)

Here the conventions of sports reporting encourage the writer to use active verbs (what could be more active than spanking?) and thereby indicate clearly who does what to whom.

Thinking about writing in terms of conventions may help us past a problem left over from English classes of former generations, in which "bad" (i.e., "nonstandard" or nonconventional) grammar had to be eradicated *before* people moved on to writing essays or anything more interesting. There's no right or wrong about writing apart from the context within which your stylistic choices are made: Effective writing means the ability to work within the appropriate conventions. (Of course, grammatical choices are rigorously policed in some contexts—you would be well advised to find out what readers expect as "standard English" and be prepared to work within those expectations.) Writing has to meet others' expectations, including what counts for appropriate grammar—but the sequence doesn't have to be *first* grammatical correctness, *then* development and coherence.

Particularly in early stages of writing, you should avoid thinking of what you write as "right" or "wrong" or "good" or "bad." There is only the way in which your writing meets or fails to meet your own and others' expectations, which in turn are set by the conventions that you are working within. The trick is to become more adept at finding ways to assess these conventions for yourself, and ways to reflect usefully on what conventions are for you. The problem to take up, then, is how to make the turn, in your writing, from observations as notes, journal entries, and other informal writings to a continuous draft.

Some illustration of how one student moved from initial reflections in her journal to a draft may be seen in Teri Hurst's journal entries and drafts below (used by permission).

Journal entry—8/31
My relationship with the media involves mostly TV and radio. I am currently working full-time and attending school three nights a week. I like to watch the 6:00 news when I come home from work prior to leaving for school. I like to know what's going on in the community as well as the world. I also have the radio on all day at work. Mostly, I listen to it for enjoyment. I also listen to it for the weather and any news bulletins that may be of importance to our community and/or world. I would say these are my main two media sources to which I tune in seven days a week.... Without these media sources available to me, I believe I would be greatly less informed about current events.

Comment

Hurst's journal entry mentions media's combined functions of news and entertainment; her concluding sentence, and the space and detail given to staying informed about events in the community, suggest that she wants to concentrate on the "useful" functions rather than those devoted to leisure.

Journal entry #2 (approximately a week later)
I get my news and information from watching the local news on television at 6:00 when I am not attending class, followed by watching the national news at 6:30 p.m. [*Specifics added to further divide "community" and "world" information.*] I like to watch the 6:00 news prior to leaving for class that evening. The radio station I listen to does not carry much news, and I do not have much time to sit down and read the newspaper. [*Rationale for watching news on TV, as opposed to getting it through radio or print media.*]

I find watching the news on television, at least catching the headline stories, gives me some knowledge of the day's events. Usually Monday evenings I am able to watch the full news broadcast at 6:00 p.m. and 6:30 p.m. This lets me know the latest stories from the past weekend, gives me a general idea of the weather forecast for the week and lets me know the winners of the sports events that took place during the weekend. [*Here sports is added to weather as a functional concern.*]

If there should happen to be a breaking story or a story I want to hear more about I will stay up and watch the 11:00 evening news, but I usually go to bed at that time because I have to get up for work early the next day. [*This journal entry stresses the importance of how a news source fits into her schedule.*]

Watching the 6:00 evening news, at least the local news, is very important to me. I turn it on every night when I get home from work. Sometimes I only get to see the first fifteen minutes, but this is the part where they tell you about the headline stories, the most important stories from the day, so at least I am aware of what is going on. I like to be informed and kept up to date regarding issues in my community and the world in which I live. [*Some repetition from paragraph 2 on catching the headlines; further emphasis on usefulness of keeping up with events.*]

I feel that turning on the television and watching the news is a very easy way for me to get my news information. It takes no effort to turn on the television set and sit down in a chair. For me and my schedule it's the way I feel I can get a general idea of the current events. I know there is a lot of information and news that the television won't cover which I could find by reading a newspaper, and there are times, mostly on the weekends, when I will look through the Saginaw news. But if it were not for me taking an interest in making an effort to watch the news on television, there are many stories I would not hear about until after the fact. In addition, I like to know what people around me are talking about when they refer to an event that was broadcast either on the local news or the national news. I think it's important to get other people's views about news issues, and when you know what they are talking about you can contribute to the conversation. I think it's important to get opinions on these issues from the people around you, and without knowledge of these issues they would mean nothing. So for now, I will continue to get my news information, hopefully on a daily basis, by turning on the TV, sitting back, listening and watching about the community and nation. [*Further exploration of convenience and schedule, and the uses of staying informed, at the headline level, in order to be able to take part in conversations.*]

First draft of essay—Portrait of a Media Consumer

1) My relationship as a media consumer consists primarily of television. I would say that television is, to say the least, my main form of seeking information about the community and world. It is also my main form of entertainment. [*Casting journal material into essay form means giving more nearly equal weight to the motifs of information and entertainment. Both were present in journal entries, but the motif of entertainment was downplayed.*]

2) Although I currently am working full-time and attending evening classes three nights a week, I still manage to get absorbed into television. When I come home for my lunch hour I find myself turning on the television while grabbing a bite to eat. If I have early lunch I will watch the game shows, and if I have late lunch I will watch my soap opera. These programs are strictly for entertainment. When I am watching these shows I forget about my morning at work whether it was good or bad and just relax while preparing to go back to work for the afternoon. [*More specific exposition about her daily schedule, with emphasis on the function of entertainment programming.*]

3) When I get out of work, I come home and immediately turn on the television to watch the news. I try and catch the 6:00 evening news every night. This is how I become aware of what happened in the community today and what happened in the city last night. This is also where I get my information on the weather for the next day and the forecast for the week, although it has usually changed the next day. I also watch the sports to find out if my favorite teams won or lost. [*This paragraph recreates the generic division of local news programming into news, weather, and sports.*]

4) If I am not attending class that night I watch the world news to see what is going on in the country and world in which I live. I like to be kept up to date on current events, and I find myself watching it on television rather than reading it in the newspaper. [*World news here is separated out from local news.*]

5) For me personally, I find it more informing to watch things as they are actually happening or have happened. Television also can give you news flashes as current events happen and weather flashes if the need arises, whereas you could not obtain this information from a newspaper until after the fact. I also find it more informing as you get the interviews with the actual people or witnesses involved in the news stories. If you were to get this from a newspaper or magazine, you would just get a quote. This way you can put a face with the events of a news story whether it be a pleasant event or a sad event. [*New material not in journal entries, developing reasons for preferring television news over print—face-to-face interviews are important to her for the personal connection, and television can provide breaking news and announce the weather more quickly.*]

6) If I happen to get some time off from work and I am home, I find myself watching the talk shows during the day. To me, these are entertaining and informative. There are, of course, some stories that seem far-fetched. These I would be watching for entertainment. Some of the people they have on these talk shows you can't help but laugh at. Then there are others that you can learn a lot from. The stories of abuse, crime or medical issues. And, again, you can put a face with the actual story. It's not often I get to see these kind of shows, but I do enjoy them.

7) In the evening, when I'm not at school, I will watch a sitcom or two just for relaxation and a few laughs. I think it's important to laugh every day, life is serious enough and you just need to kick back every now and then and have a good laugh. After the sitcoms, I will watch more news shows, like *48 Hours, Dateline, 20/20, Prime Time*, etc. I also find these types of shows very informative and at the same time entertaining. I like the hosts of these shows, I find them very appealing and I like the stories these shows have on them. Sometimes they have light story lines and sometimes they are very heartwarming and informative. I would have to say that these news story shows are my favorite.

8) I also enjoy watching some sporting events on television. I like *Monday Night Football* and I like to watch football on the weekends, college and pro. I also enjoy watching college basketball and the play-offs in pro basketball. I think it's the fast-paced action and competitive feeling from these sports that I enjoy.

9) I don't watch many television movies. There are very few movies that I can actually say sounds like a good one to me. I like the true story movies of actual events, I don't like the movies that contain a lot violence and sex. I see enough of this on the news and I don't enjoy watching a two-hour movie about it. In addition, there are a lot of movies that are made into a miniseries, and that's too many hours watching one program for me; I like a variety.

10) Television has always been a part of my life from childhood to adulthood and probably always will be. I enjoy television as a consumer and would be lost without it, not only for entertainment but also for new information purposes. [*Concluding paragraph repeats the news/entertainment motif. Additional material may be there in the interests of completing the portrait; much of it isn't brought into an organized framework.*]

Revision of Essay

I would say that television is, to say the least, my main form of seeking information about the community and world. It is also my main form of entertainment.

[*Paragraphs 2–4 are kept as they were on the first draft.*]

I believe seeing the actual people involved in the story gives you more of a feeling for that story. You can tell a lot by looking at a person. I think by seeing pictures of the people involved you can get a good sensation of what they are feeling whether they were involved directly or indirectly in the story. Usually the news interviews people right after the incident in question, and the people they interview are generally truthful. I think you get that feeling from actually seeing these interviews in process, and some stories, especially when young children are involved, really tug at your heart. I think that people are affected by this and if help should be needed for a family the community will respond. I think that's why seeing these people is important to me.

[Paragraphs 6–9 are kept as they were.]

I think there is a sharp distinction between entertainment and news on television. I don't watch the local news or world news to be entertained, but to be informed. I feel that whenever a news/entertainment show is on, you have to be careful not to confuse the two. Most of these shows contain very informative information. Some of them have informative information and a story or two that you would consider entertaining. For example, if they interview an actor or show you how certain scenes were made in a motion picture. I would consider this kind of information to be entertaining; it's something you could live with if you hadn't seen or heard about, but just fun to watch. Then there are other instances in which you will consider the information they provide very informative. For example, the shows they have had on lately about the bacteria found in beef and in the water system. I found these shows to contain vital information that everyone should be informed about. So, you can get a combination of the two, entertainment and news, but they are very different categories which I take into consideration as I watch these shows on television.

Comment

The underlying question about the difference between entertainment and news/information has received some response, but not definitive discussion. The discussion of "news shows" such as 48 Hours *and the others listed illustrates how these blur the genres: Hurst's response to these shows is to read them as like the entertainment programs she enjoys rather than the news programs she uses to stay informed and brings into conversations.*

PAUSE FOR REFLECTION

The idea that television news anchors and readers are modeled on conversation might lead to other comparisons. Are there ways of speaking with people face-to-face that resemble in tone the following?

a. sports commentators doing play-by-play during a football, baseball, or basketball game
b. a talk show hosted by Oprah Winfrey, Sally Jessy Raphael, or other familiar host
c. a TV column by Andy Rooney
d. a religious broadcast (not televised church service or mass)
e. a fishing or hunting show (locally, this is called *Michigan Outdoors*)

f. stand-up comedy
g. *Roger and Me* (film by Michael Moore)
h. a news conference with the president or a prominent congressional leader
h. opening monologues such as those of David Letterman or Jay Leno
i. other presentations on camera

How many of these genres are open to women primarily? To men primarily? To either gender?

How Writers Write

Now that we've looked at one writer's movement from journal entry to draft, it may be useful to return to the myth of the born writer. This myth transfers some of the prestige of the finished work (especially a work of literature) to the author—which would be harmless except that such elevation occurs at a cost. It gives a few writers a bit more cultural clout, but it may keep others from a source of pleasure and expression.

Writing can be demystified if we adopt an alternative model, one divided into several distinct phases, with different purposes and techniques. The model or myth proposed here considers writing as taking place within three phases, which pivot on the point at which a single, more or less unified draft is prepared. Work that leads up to this draft is termed *prewriting* (even though most of it is writing in some form), and work that follows this draft is called *revision* (in some cases, editing). These phases apply regardless of the length and complexity of the writing being done. That is, preparation for an impromptu essay of the sort required for an essay exam might amount to a few minutes' quick jotting down of key phrases, and the revision might be a quick read-through to insert a few sentences for clarity and check for misspelled words or missing punctuation. Preparation for a major essay might involve weeks of reading, making notecards, typing a formal outline, and writing to explore the topic, while revision could involve transcription from longhand to word processor, extensive rewriting of passages, and composition of notes and a formal bibliography.

Contrary to the myth of inspiration, writing well is never easy. If your hope has been that instruction will make writing easier, you are in for some disappointment. Becoming good at one set of tasks enables you to see how much more is needed to get to the next level—it's the problem of the receding horizon. Writing may sometimes *look* easy, in part because everything before the finished text is generally done in private, off-stage or off-camera. In texts ranging from newspaper articles to films to works having the status of great literature, we rarely if ever see them in the process of being created: Creation takes place as if by magic.

Media texts are easily accessible to us, for the most part, and do not show themselves as created. They are there, just as the light is there when we flip the switch. It's important to their power of interpretation that it not be seen as an *interpretation,* but *reality.* Many contemporary media conceal or at least downplay the fact that they are representations of reality, by making it a convention that what you get through these media is reality itself. The claim to reality can be noted in the close of the CBS News through the 1960s and 1970s: *"And that's the way it was,"* stated in the sonorous tones of Walter Cronkite. This statement stressed the idea implied throughout the news broadcast, one that is carried over from the conventions of print journalism: that the TV news is a window on reality, rather than a carefully selected and prepared version of reality. There would be some harm to the credibility of news broadcasts if viewers could see the processes of selection and preparation, and could understand what does *not* get onto the news. Other media texts follow comparable practices. When we watch an entertainment program or film, for example, it might break the spell if we were reminded that we are watching Dennis Franz pretending to be Officer Andy Sipowicz on a set, rather than in a police station, in a carefully chosen representation of New York City. These media texts are products whose effectiveness depends, to some degree, on concealment of the means of their production.

There are occasional exceptions to art that conceals art. Some TV shows, such as *COPS* or *NYPD Blue,* have taken on a "rough" quality, particularly in transitions, as though to suggest that these parts are more "real." Several commercials have adopted comparable visual styles. And we do see some part of the process in films and television programs about productions, such as *The Making of* Star Wars, Terminator II, Jurassic Park, and so on. Other entertainment can be gotten from mistakes and bloopers sometimes gleaned from outtakes and shown on television. But these outtakes are carefully separated from the programs themselves and serve more as advertising for the programs than as any sort of interference with the spells they create. *Home Improvement* often closes with an outtake or two from that program. These, however, are run under the credits; they do not interfere with the finished quality of the evening's program, but serve to remind viewers of what they've just watched. In sum, the myth that writers create whole works through some mysterious quality that sets them apart from ordinary human beings is reinforced by the fact that we see only finished works—not only texts produced by writers, but texts that are broadcast, shown, printed, or otherwise distributed in final form.

So being asked to show the steps in your writing process may go against the grain of your experience of other texts. When media texts are received as though they have always existed in their present form, while *your* texts are defined as works in progress even when you consider yourself to have finished them, the implicit message is that *your* work is essentially inferior to professional texts. In fact, these other texts are produced through long and difficult labor, just as yours are. Habitual and practiced writers know their writing processes well, and are perhaps able to relax a bit more in early stages because they know they can finish their work over a period of time. So an important first stage for you is understanding how you work, knowing ways to do that work better, and developing patterns that serve you well in getting your texts ready for others to read. For some ideas, consider Ernest Hemingway's methods.

GEORGE PLIMPTON

Interview with Ernest Hemingway
Ernest Hemingway writes in the bedroom of his house in the Havana suburb of San Francisco de Paula. He has a special workroom prepared for him in a square tower at the southwest corner of the house, but prefers to work in his bedroom, climbing to the tower room only when "characters" drive him up there.

The bedroom is on the ground floor and connects with the main room of the house. The door between the two is kept ajar by a heavy volume listing and describing *The World's Aircraft Engines.* The bedroom is large, sunny, the windows facing east and south letting in the day's light on white walls and a yellow-tinged tile floor.

The room is divided into two alcoves by a pair of chest-high bookcases that stand out into the room at right angles from opposite walls. A large and low double bed dominates one section, oversized slippers and loafers neatly arranged at the foot, the two bedside tables at the head piled seven-high with books. In the other alcove stands a massive flat-top desk with a chair at either side, its surface an ordered clutter of papers and mementos. Beyond it, at the far end of the room, is an armoire with a leopard skin draped across the top. The other walls are lined with white-painted bookcases from which books overflow to the floor, and are piled on top among old newspapers, bullfight journals, and stacks of letters bound together by rubber bands.

It is on the top of one of these cluttered bookcases—the one against the wall by the east window and three feet or so from his bed—that Hemingway has his "work desk"—a square foot of cramped area hemmed in by books on one side and on the other by a newspaper-covered heap of papers, manuscripts, and pamphlets. There is just enough space left on top of the bookcase for a typewriter, surmounted by a wooden reading board, five or six pencils, and a chunk of copper ore to weight down papers when the wind blows in from the east window.

Chapter 3: Making Use of Observations—from Prewriting to Drafting

A working habit he has had from the beginning, Hemingway stands when he writes. He stands in a pair of his oversized loafers on the worn skin of a Lesser Kudu—the typewriter and the reading board chest-high opposite him.

When Hemingway starts on a project he always begins with a pencil, using the reading board to write on onionskin typewriter paper. He keeps a sheaf of the blank paper on a clipboard to the left of the typewriter, extracting the paper a sheet at a time from under a metal clip which reads "These Must Be Paid." He places the paper slantwise on the reading board, leans against the board with his left arm, steadying the paper with his hand, and fills the paper with handwriting which through the years has become larger, more boyish, with a paucity of punctuation, very few capitals, and often the period marked with an *x*. The page completed, he clips it face-down on another clipboard which he places off to the right of the typewriter.

Hemingway shifts to the typewriter, lifting off the reading board, only when the writing is going fast and well, or when the writing is, for him at least, simple: dialogue, for instance.

He keeps track of his daily progress—"so as not to kid myself"—on a large chart made out of the side of a cardboard packing case and set up against the wall under the nose of a mounted gazelle head. The numbers on the chart showing the daily output of words differ from 450, 575, 462, 1250, back to 512, the higher figures on days Hemingway puts in extra work so he won't feel guilty spending the following day fishing on the Gulf Stream.

A man of habit, Hemingway does not use the perfectly suitable desk in the other alcove. Though it allows more space for writing, it too has its miscellany: stacks of letters, a stuffed toy lion of the type sold in Broadway nighteries, a small burlap bag full of carnivore teeth, shotgun shells, a shoehorn, wood carvings of lion, rhino, two zebras, and a wart-hog—these last set in a neat row across the surface of the desk—and, of course, books: piled on the desk, beside tables, jamming the shelves in indiscriminate order—novels, histories, collections of poetry, drama, essays. A look at their titles shows their variety. On the shelf opposite Hemingway's knee as he stands up to his "work desk" are Virginia Woolf's *The Common Reader,* Ben Ames Williams' *House Divided, The Partisan Review,* Charles A. Beard's *The Republic,* Tarle's *Napoleon's Invasion of Russia, How Young You Look* by Peggy Wood, Alden Brooks' *Will Shakespeare and the Dyer's Hand,* Baldwin's *African Hunting,* T. S. Eliot's *Collected Poems,* and two books on General Custer's fall at the battle of the Little Big Horn.

The room, however, for all the disorder sensed at first sight, indicates on inspection an owner who is basically neat but cannot bear to throw anything away—especially if sentimental value is attached. One bookcase top has an odd assortment of mementos: a giraffe made of wood beads, a little cast-iron turtle, tiny models of a locomotive, two jeeps and a Venetian gondola, a toy bear with a key in its back, a monkey carrying a pair of cymbals, a miniature guitar, and a little tin model of a U.S. Navy biplane (one wheel missing) resting awry on a circular straw place mat—the quality of the collection that of the odds-and-ends which turn up in a shoe-box at the back of a small boy's closet. It is evident, though, that these tokens have their value, just as three buffalo horns Hemingway keeps in his bedroom have a value dependent not on size but because during the acquiring of them things went badly in the bush which ultimately turned out well. "It cheers me up to look at them," he says.

Hemingway may admit superstitions of this sort, but he prefers not to talk about them, feeling that whatever value they may have can be talked away. He has much the same attitude about writing. Many times during the making of this interview he stressed that the craft of writing should not be tampered with by an excess of scrutiny—"that though there is one part of writing that is solid and you do it no harm by talking about it, the other is fragile, and if you talk about it, the structure cracks and you have nothing."

As a result, though a wonderful raconteur, a man of rich humor, and possessed of an amazing fund of knowledge on subjects which interest him, Hemingway finds it difficult to talk about writing—not because he has few ideas on the subject, but rather that he feels so strongly that such ideas should remain unexpressed, that to be asked questions on them "spooks" him (to use one of his favorite expressions) to the point where he is almost inarticulate. Many of the replies in this interview he preferred to work out on his reading board. The occasional waspish tone of the answers is also part of this strong feeling that writing is a private, lonely occupation with no need for witnesses until the final work is done.

This dedication to his art may suggest a personality at odds with the rambunctious, carefree, world-wheeling Hemingway-at-play of popular conception. The fact is that Hemingway, while obviously enjoying life, brings an equivalent dedication to everything he does—an outlook that is essentially serious, with a horror of the inaccurate, the fraudulent, the deceptive, the half-baked.

Nowhere is the dedication he gives his art more evident than in the yellow-tiled bedroom—where early in the morning Hemingway gets up to stand in absolute concentration in front of his reading board, moving only to shift weight from one foot to another, perspiring heavily when the work is going well, excited as a boy, fretful, miserable when the artistic touch momentarily vanishes—slave of a self-imposed discipline which lasts until about noon when he takes a knotted walking stick and leaves the house for the swimming pool where he takes his daily half-mile swim.

Interviewer: Are these hours during the actual process of writing pleasurable?

Hemingway: Very.

Interviewer: Could you say something of this process? When do you work? Do you keep to a strict schedule?

Hemingway: When I am working on a book or a story I write every morning as soon after first light as possible. There is no one to disturb you and it is cool or cold and you come to your work and warm as you write. You read what you have written and, as you always stop when you know what is going to happen next, you go on from there. You write until you come to a place where you still have your juice and know what will happen next and you stop and try to live through until the next day when you hit it again. You have started at six in the morning, say, and may go on until noon or be through before that. When you stop you are as empty, and at the same time never empty but filling, as when you have made love to someone you love. Nothing can hurt you, nothing can happen, nothing means anything until the next day when you do it again. It is the wait until the next day that is hard to get through.

Interviewer: Can you dismiss from your mind whatever project you're on when you're away from the typewriter?

Hemingway: Of course. But it takes discipline to do it and this discipline is acquired. It has to be.

Interviewer: Do you do any rewriting as you read up to the place you left off the day before? Or does that come later, when the whole is finished?

Hemingway: I always rewrite each day up to the point where I stopped. When it is all finished, naturally you go over it. You get another chance to correct and rewrite when someone else types it, and you see it clean in type. The last chance is in the proofs. You're grateful for these different chances.

Interviewer: How much rewriting do you do?

Hemingway: It depends. I rewrote the ending to *Farewell to Arms,* the last page of it, thirty-nine times before I was satisfied.

Interviewer: Was there some technical problem there? What was it that had stumped you?

Hemingway: Getting the words right.

Interviewer: Is it the rereading that gets the "juice" up?

Hemingway: Rereading places you at the point where it *has* to go on, knowing it is as good as you can get it up to there. There is always juice somewhere.

Interviewer: But are there times when the inspiration isn't there at all?

Hemingway: Naturally. But if you stopped when you knew what would happen next, you can go on. As long as you can start, you are all right. The juice will come.

Interviewer: Thornton Wilder speaks of mnemonic devices that get the writer going on his day's work. He says you once told him you sharpened twenty pencils.

Hemingway: I don't think I ever owned twenty pencils at one time. Wearing down seven number two pencils is a good day's work.

Interviewer: Where are some of the places you have found most advantageous to work? The Ambos Mundos hotel must have been one, judging from the number of books you did there. Or do surroundings have little effect on the work?

Hemingway: The Ambos Mundos in Havana was a very good place to work in. This Finca is a splendid place, or was. But I have worked well everywhere. I mean I have been able to work as well as I can under varied circumstances. The telephone and visitors are the work destroyers.

Interviewer: Is emotional stability necessary to write well? You told me once that you could only write well when you were in love. Could you expound on that a bit more?

Hemingway: What a question. But full marks for trying. You can write any time people will leave you alone and not interrupt you. Or rather you can if you will be ruthless enough about it. But the best writing is certainly when you are in love. If it is all the same to you I would rather not expound on that.

Interviewer: How about financial security? Can that be a detriment to good writing?

Hemingway: If it came early enough and you loved life as much as you loved your work it would take much character to resist the temptations. Once writing has become your major vice and greatest pleasure only death can stop it. Financial security then is a great help as it keeps you from worrying. Worry destroys the ability to write. Ill health is bad in the ratio that it produces worry which attacks your subconscious and destroys your reserves.

Interviewer: Can you recall an exact moment when you decided to become a writer?

Hemingway: No, I always wanted to be a writer.

* * *

Interviewer: These questions which inquire into craftsmanship really are an annoyance.

Hemingway: A sensible question is neither a delight nor an annoyance. I still believe, though, that it is very bad for a writer to talk about how he writes. He writes to be read by the eye and no explanations or dissertations should be necessary. You can be sure that there is much more there than will be read at any first reading and having made this it is not the writer's province to explain it or to run guided tours through the more difficult country of his work.

* * *

Interviewer: So when you're not writing, you remain constantly the observer, looking for something which can be of use.

Hemingway: Surely. If a writer stops observing he is finished. But he does not have to observe consciously nor think how it will be useful. Perhaps that would be true at the beginning. But later everything he sees goes into the great reserve of things he knows or has seen. If it is any use to know it, I always try to write on the principle of the iceberg. There is seven-eights of it underwater for every part that shows. Anything you know you can eliminate and it only strengthens your iceberg. It is the part that doesn't show. If a writer omits something because he does not know it then there is a hole in the story.

["Ernest Hemingway" by George Plimpton, from *Writers at Work, Second Series* by George A. Plimpton, editor, introduced by Van Wyck Brooks. Copyright © 1963 by *The Paris Review*. Used by permission of Viking Penguin, a division of Penguin Books USA Inc.]

QUESTIONS
1. What do you think is the purpose of all the details Plimpton gives about the environment in which Hemingway works (some were cut from the excerpt above)—the books, the animal skins, the positioning of the desks, and so on?
2. How would you describe the roles played by Hemingway and the interviewer (Plimpton)?

3. Based on the interview, what aspects of Hemingway's writing correspond to prewriting? To drafting? To revision?
4. Compare Hemingway's reluctance to talk about elements of his writing process with the ease shown by William Stafford on pages 86–88. What explains the contrast?
5. What did you know about Hemingway before reading this excerpt? Are there ways in which that knowledge is reinforced or contradicted by the interview?
6. How would you describe the genre of text called the interview? What are its distinguishing textual features? What can you not do, conventionally, in an interview? What, conventionally, must you do?

Prewriting

You've been doing prewriting all your life. That is, if **prewriting** is defined broadly as preparation for writing, everything goes into the mix. Previous education, acquisition of language (from media sources as well as from your family and others whose discourse has surrounded you since birth), life experiences, words on paper—all can be included. Defining prewriting so broadly risks making the term of no practical use—but it may serve as a reminder that what you are prepared to write comes directly out of who you are in relation to your culture and local circumstances.

Perhaps a more particular definition of prewriting would involve preparation for writing a specific text. You have an assignment due next Tuesday, or a longer paper just before the midterm recess, or a report to be given at a sales meeting in January, or an annual report due in two months—exactly where does preparation begin? While it might be said to begin when you take your job or become a student, perhaps we can consider prewriting for a text to be anything directed consciously toward that text or incorporated into it. The *conscious* part is iffy—as seen in the essay by Stafford, with some professional writers the habit of reflection is so developed that they may not consider journal entries as directed toward a specific text until well along in the process.

Some common forms of prewriting have already been incorporated into your work with this book, as you have been taking note of your observations about media in (mostly) informal kinds of writing, through journals, media logs, and informal assignments. These have helped to establish a routine, which is important to your success as a writer. You should cultivate a sense of when and how you work best. Some writers like late-night hours; others (such as myself) do their most valuable work early in the morning; and still others may work equally well at any time. The mode of writing is equally variable—writing in longhand is important to some writers, while others swear by (and occasionally at) computers.

There are greater and lesser capacities for carrying material in one's head. As you are in a writing class, your might consider trying a variety of practices for writing to see which work well for you. Whatever you try needs to allow you to accumulate and review thoughts and bits of draft material. (Recall Hemingway's comment about the iceberg: You will necessarily observe and record more than you eventually use in draft form.)

One habit to cultivate is that of "metacommentary." That is, as you write in your journal, save a wide margin so you can go back and comment on what you've written. (This may require a separate file if your journal is kept on word processor.) Your metacommentary serves several purposes: It can help you think of ways to use passages, either as you are writing them or after you look back over what you have written; and it can help you see how to use your strengths as a writer, and think about traps to avoid. One possible format: a double-entry journal, with a line down the middle of the page, separating initial entries from reflections about them.

Prewriting can be further separated into two phases—looking for a subject, and developing the subject once your work is under way. There are times when a subject may seem to come to you and all you have to do is get started; other times you have to search about a bit for an idea, or evaluate one that has occurred to you in order to see if it's a good choice. Neither phase is quite as open to intention as we might wish to believe. Sometimes it feels as though ideas come of their own accord and cannot be forced. It might be more appropriate to say that we have ideas continually—our mouths and our minds produce a stream of thought interrupted only by unconsciousness—but that most remain unrecorded and are quickly forgotten. The problem is not producing text, then, but recording and selecting from thoughts according to those we value and those that will be valued by readers, working within the established conventions and institutions that have shaped what we value to begin with. Exhibits 3.2 and 3.3 suggest two ways of thinking about the writing process.

Making a transition from notes and fragmentary writings to a draft may be the most important phase of your work on a piece of writing. It certainly is the point at which a wrong choice means a maximum of wasted effort. Much of what was written for this book became waste paper (or its computer equivalent, memory to be written over). However, making such wrong choices may be necessary to getting better ideas later. It may be helpful to think of your writing self as consisting of at least two beings—one concerned with generating lots of text, regardless of how it fits with anything else, and one whose responsibility is to tidy up afterwards and organize the lot, reserving or tossing out anything that doesn't fit readers' expectations of order and coherence. (We could introduce other selves—the copy-editing self who grumbles about phrasing, grammar, spelling, and other aspects of style; the cynical self who

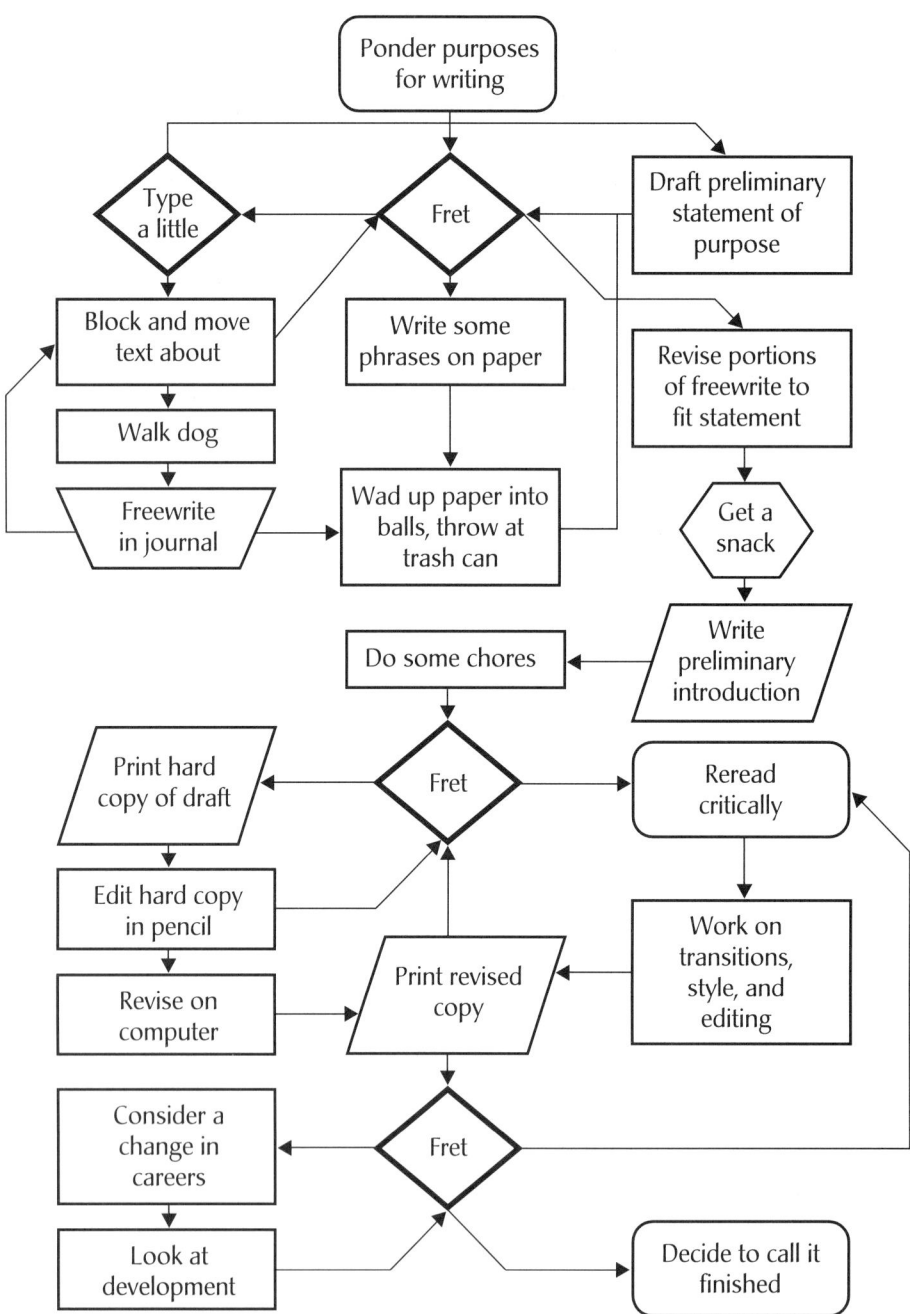

Exhibit 3.2 Flowchart for the writing process: one approach.

Chapter 3: Making Use of Observations—from Prewriting to Drafting 111

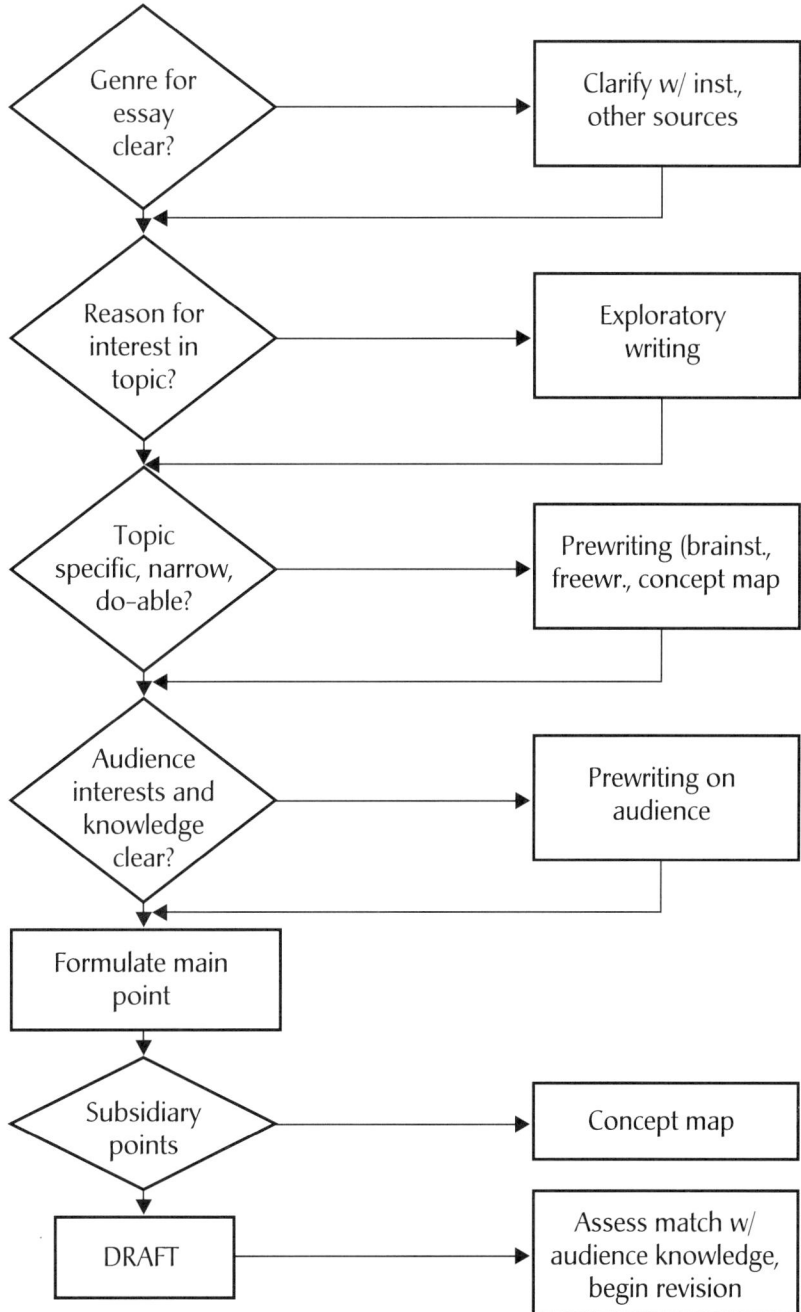

Exhibit 3.3 Flowchart for the writing process: a second approach.

advises you to chuck it all and become a professional hitchhiker, busker, or surfer; the celebratory self who exults in how something is said and wants to read it aloud to total strangers or submit it for a Nobel Prize; and so on.)

"Freewriting" and other devices discussed below will enable you to come up with a lot of text, and you may have a fair amount written in your journal by now. The difficulty comes in recognizing good material—in what you have written, what is of value, and for whom? It is, after all, your writing, and you may have insights in it that you prize for personal reasons; and yet you have to select and shape that writing for other readers. If rhetoric is writing directed toward others, it's necessary to recognize (or imagine) what these others will be interested in, and to understand the context sufficiently to see ways in which your writing can work for you.

Here are several prewriting devices you should try, along with a brief account of how and why each device is supposed to work.

BRAINSTORMING

The term *brainstorming* came into prominence in the 1950s, in association with the sort of corporate creativity expected from advertising agencies, film producers, and others dealing in marketable ideas. The popular image is that of a group of people sitting around a table or in an office talking off the top of their heads. (A negative spin on the word *brainstorm* also persists, as shown by the definition in the first *American Heritage Dictionary:* "A sudden and violent disturbance in the brain; a sudden clever, whimsical, or foolish idea" [p. 160].) "Brainstorming" here applies to idea gathering, whether done singly or in groups, orally or in writing. The suggestion is to take a sheet of paper (or computer screen) and list phrases in whatever order you think of them, in connection with a topic or not. Initially you might work with a preestablished time period. Don't worry about relevance, legibility, or writing in complete sentences. Once you generate a list of satisfactory length, go back through and mark any that seem to be of use, perhaps incorporating them into an outline or more formal arrangement.

FREEWRITING

The use of freewriting has been advocated by Peter Elbow:

> The idea is simply to write for ten minutes (later on, perhaps fifteen or twenty). Don't stop for anything. Go quickly without rushing. Never stop to look back, to cross something out, to wonder how to

spell something, to wonder what word or thought to use, or to think about what you are doing. If you can't think of a word or a spelling, just use a squiggle or else write, "I can't think of it." Just put down something. (p. 3)

There are several uses to freewriting in this mode: first, you show yourself that you can come up with a lot of text, quickly, which allows you to get past the feeling of being frozen in place that sometimes comes with a large or complex assignment. Second, it helps to divide a writing task into generation and selection, which minimizes the two phases' getting in each other's way. And you can use freewriting to develop a topic, by setting up loops: For example, you might do three ten-minute freewrites, taking as a starting point for the second a single sentence or concept from the first, and so on, and at the end of the last loop examining all three for usable developments.

A freewrite can be done with the topic entirely open, or it can start with a specified topic or sentence. You should not, however, force yourself to stay on a topic or to write toward a preset end, because the point of doing freewriting is to let discoveries emerge without conscious direction. Exhibits 3.4 and 3.5 offer additional perspectives on the loop process in freewriting.

HEURISTICS

Another exploratory device is asking what have been called heuristic questions. The term *heuristic* has to do with discovery, and any standard set of questions that serve to prompt your thinking about an issue can serve as a heuristic prewriting device. Some of these have been popularized in connection with a particular genre, newswriting—the reporter's list, *Who? What? When? Where? How?* and *Why?* These can serve as reminders, in the early stages of writing a news account, to cover specifics in a brief and orderly fashion. Though they don't provide any automatic guide to drafting, they do help round the narrative out. The reporter's heuristic works better for some purposes, such as informing, than others, such as analysis or persuasion. If these questions don't especially apply to your topic, you can construct your own list of heuristic questions that you want to make sure you address in prewriting.

OUTLINING

One of the prewriting devices students have often practiced before reaching college is outlining. Outlines don't work particularly well as devices to encourage invention: To make a successful outline, you have to know something

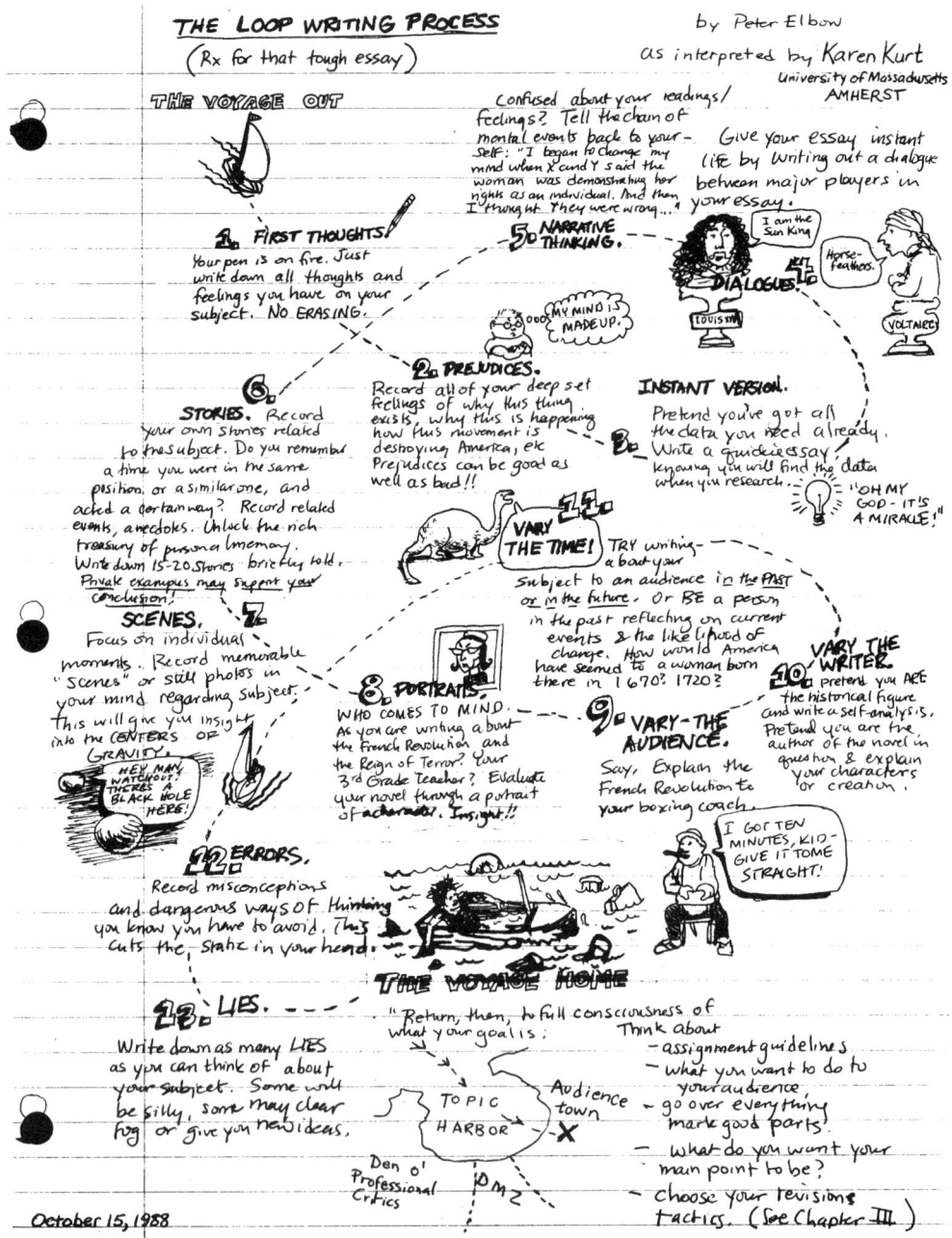

Exhibit 3.4 The loop writing process as envisioned by Peter Elbow, drawn by Karen Kurt Teal. From M. Elizabeth Wallace, ed., *What's Happening with Writing at Western Oregon State College?* Monmouth, Ore.: WOSC, 1991. Used by permission.

> While taking "The Teaching of Writing" with Peter Elbow at the University of Massachusetts in 1988, we had an unusual argument. Professor Elbow asked us to turn in our reading journal pages written while we were studying *Writing With Power*. He wanted to understand how we received his book. When I got to the chapter on the Loop Writing Process, I had become tired of writing pages of notes and felt the process could also be presented visually. On a page of pink notebook paper, I sketched and paraphrased his thinking, remaining strictly faithful to the book. Instead of asking me to do my homework again, Professor Elbow was satisfied by my little cartoon, and shared it with friends. Over the semesters, my own students have expressed bemusement over the cartoon, and then gotten down to the serious fun of producing material with the aid of Elbow's Loop. These writing practices have been, along with other Elbow strategies, the most valuable writing tools given to me in my long scholarly journey.

Exhibit 3.5 Reflection on the loop writing process by Karen Kurt Teal. Copyright 1997 by Karen Kurt Teal, University of Massachusetts.

about the hierarchy of topics you intend to address, and that knowledge usually isn't there in the early phases of prewriting. However, outlines work well as devices to organize once you have your material fairly well under way. It's advisable to make outlines in complete sentences if others will be reading them. If you are outlining for your own use, you may choose to work with phrases rather than sentences.

CONCEPT MAPS

A device that may be helpful earlier in the process of checking your organization is the concept map (sometimes called clustering or branching). To make a concept map, you need to have a topic to explore and a large surface (piece of paper, blackboard, sidewalk, etc.). Write the topic in the center, and circle it—then draw branches off as you think of associated topics, and continue to branch off from these as you think of subsidiary points connected to them. See Exhibit 3.6 for an example. As with the device of looping freewrites, you may need to do several versions of concept maps before relationships become clear. Concept maps give a spatial dimension not accessible in outlining or brainstorming. They are particularly useful for group work.

Prewriting devices are tools to be used, or not. You should make use of all these as you work through this book, so as to determine which might be useful for you later. They can help you think through a topic, and are therefore important for writing about complex matters. (Writing something for which you can draw strictly from your own experience, on the other hand, may require little more than a few phrases to get you started.)

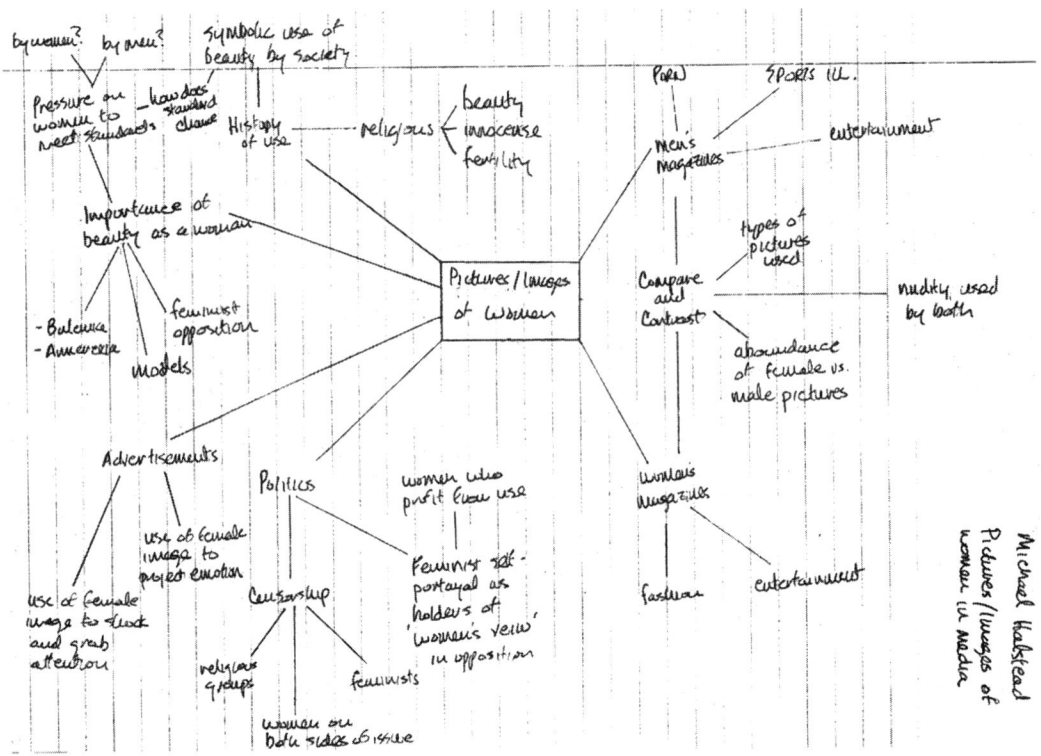

Exhibit 3.6 Concept map by Michael Halstead. Used by permission.

You should use prewriting devices not only to explore a topic, but to explore what *you* know and what *your readers* know about a topic. For example, a concept map can be very helpful for displaying in easily visible terms what your reader needs to be told on a subject. Suppose, for example, you are exploring the idea of writing about video games. Your audience is an instructor who is receptive to the topic but knows nothing about it beyond general cultural knowledge gained from having seen *Ms. Pac-Man* and *Pong* and *Space Invaders* played when video games were found only in arcades. You could use a concept map productively to explore not only what you know, but what you understand to be the range of your reader's knowledge about video games. Does he or she know about the growth of Nintendo, Sega, and other corporations? (Probably.) About some specific game titles? (Perhaps.) About what it's like to win through to the higher levels of a game, or what the attraction is? (Unlikely.) Can you get at the quality of the experience by analogy with some other activities? And if so, what would work? It is best to explore these questions by thinking them through before writing a draft, because then you have made less commitment than if you'd written a prose passage.

As you progress from earlier to later stages of prewriting, you might progressively use prewriting devices that more closely resemble drafting. If you move, for example, from brainstorming to concept maps to freewriting, you may find that you can take groups of sentences or even paragraphs over from the freewriting into your draft. (I've done some such in writing this and other chapters, moving from short brainstormed lists, to a journal permitting freewriting, to a typed draft.)

The goal of any prewriting is to improve your writing fluency by dividing the large task of writing into specific parts that can be carried out programmatically, so that you can deal with your thinking as writing, which is external and subject to what you see as improvement. Fluency is important, because you want to be able to write enough to throw some away. (At least half of what I have written for this chapter has not found its way into the finished text.) Prewriting may bring some awareness of contradictions in a subject or in how you perceive it—but rather than repressing or ignoring contradictions, it's important to explore them, even if they don't appear in your final material.

Finally, be sure to save some space—on the page, in a separate file, or in brackets—for metacommentary. It's important to get your raw material down to work with; but it's equally important to evaluate what you have, and metacommentary can help you keep focused on what's still ahead to be done, and on what you can use of the material you have written already. Remember, writing helps you think better than you can if you have to work in your head. Some things that you need to write about, for academic and other applications, cannot be done in your head, any more than you can (probably) multiply two six-digit numbers in your head, or keep a running balance of your checkbook, or memorize all the phone numbers you need to call, or do a box score for a baseball game.

Drafting

Before learning to break the process of writing into separate components, you may have used a different term for drafting—*writing*, as in "I've been getting some references together, but I haven't started writing yet." Calling your text a draft is a reminder that more can and perhaps should be done before calling it quits.

Drafting is the point at which you commit yourself to a writing task. You may have been committed, in a sense, at some earlier point—for example, an assignment might ask you to bring together several perspectives on a public issue, so you might gather materials with the writing task in mind. Drafting, however, is the stage at which you try to pull these materials together, not only in your own consciousness but in your prose. One goal in the drafting phase is to bring your materials, which may be in several different places and forms, into some kind of logical relation with each other, so that a reader can see how everything fits together.

"Pulling things together" may be an apt metaphor for drafting. The word *draft* applies to anything drawn (Indo-European root: **dhragh,** drag). Meanings include a current of air; something, such as a current of air, pulled in; the pulling power of a locomotive; how much water a ship draws; a "pulling" of resources, as at a bank; amount drunk or swallowed; liquid drawn from a keg; people drawn in for military service; a "preliminary outline of a plan, documentary, or picture." So a draft is something pulled together or pulled out of you, perhaps something compulsory; or a promissory note for a document to be produced later.

A draft is in between your preliminary explorations and the finished version of what you are doing. Being in between, it fits the meaning of the word *essay,* which at its root means *to try.* The essay, as a kind of writing, might be defined as occurring in between the public and the private, or occurring when one's private attention is focused on public matters. Writing an essay necessarily brings *you* into some relationship with *it,* whether the *it* turns out to be the place of the automobile in American culture, some principal causes of the Civil War, or ways in which media representations of gender have affected your self-image. Every issue can be conceived in terms of how to relate it to your understanding of yourself.

When you are setting out to do a draft, there may be times when everything is clear in your mind and ideas flow conveniently from mind to paper. If this happens, go with it, remembering to give your draft a careful look at the revision stage to make sure you aren't taking it too easy by ignoring your audience.

Remember that there will be time to improve what you do later. It may help to think of drafting through analogies: putting together a jigsaw puzzle, arranging a bouquet or a formal dinner, building a piece of furniture, composing a song, or skiing down a challenging hill. All these activities involve dealing with a potentially large number of component parts, finding some principle by which you can understand the parts and put them into a sequence that makes sense to you, and bringing them together into a single continuous act that gives satisfaction to you and to others. Once you become practiced at one of these activities, it's no longer necessary to give careful and conscious attention to analyzing the parts—and the same may be true of writing. But if you do undertake one of these activities before dealing with the parts in some fashion (that is, before you are sufficiently skilled), you may find yourself in a chaotic and panicky state—in effect, looking at puzzle parts that don't belong together; or holding bunches of flowers that somehow just don't look right; or having the main course and vegetables ready while the potatoes are just getting started; or staring at pieces of expensive wood that just don't fit together; or playing chords that don't fit into a pleasing sequence; or doing an eggbeater fall halfway down the hill.

In pulling material from notes and exploratory writing together for a draft, you are not only trying to make a unified piece of work; you are also constructing a representation of yourself as others will know you through your writing. In other chapters, we will be considering the concept of representation in media. Photography, film, and television require us to go along with the convention that a two-dimensional image is a representation of three dimensions. Viewing within conventions happens automatically: When we see a landscape painting, we do not have the impulse to remind ourselves that the cows in the foreground are not really larger than those trees in the background—because the conventions naturalize the images so that we see them as though we were looking at an actual landscape, in which objects closer to us appear larger than those far off. (Vision is also conventional.) Similarly, media represent to us a carefully selected version of reality: When their conventions of representation are in synch with ours, we accept this representation without raising objections—in fact, we may not even reflect on a difference between representation and reality.

In an essay—this is a source of anxiety for many writers—you are representing yourself to others, some of whom may have a degree of power over you. You are expected to show your command of the conventions involved in academic writing, your knowledge of a subject (about which your audience frequently knows more than you do), and something of your own personality and way of thinking about your culture. As you set out to become better at drafting, there's no substitute for experience: The more you write, the more familiar the component activities will become. But experience with language counts for something as well: Many excellent writers began as excellent talkers, growing up in households and in cultures where storytelling was valued and practiced. Most good writers are also good readers, who absorb material unconsciously from reading a great deal of material, good, bad, and indifferent. But good writers manage to stay with the process long enough to shape that material according to a previously internalized sense of what their audience needs.

Doing a draft will be easier if you use your awareness of your writing process. Much of the preparatory work (coming up with ideas, developing those that look promising, and grouping them into a sequence) has already been cleared away. Now you will be free to concentrate on the task of writing a draft, which is work enough in itself. Drafting requires you to put parts together; supply transitions between sections; make preliminary judgments about audience, tone, and style; and provide an introduction and a conclusion.

Word processors make some of the appropriation of prewriting for drafting easier. Notes that have initially been thought of as journal entries or freewrites can often be taken across into a draft in paragraph-length chunks. Many colleges provide computer labs, and if you do not already make use of these, you should begin to do so. At both prewriting and revision stages, computers can help a good deal in improving some features of writing, as well as ease, facility, and the appearance of copy. Pretty much all word-processing programs now have a spelling checker and a thesaurus, and several provide advice on style as well. (The program I use permits me to split the screen in order to keep a short list of topics in view, or to look at one short passage while it's being revised.) You can use a search function to look for key words or phrases, in order to cut down on repetitions. (I used this to hunt down overuse of the word *convention* in a draft of this chapter.) And the possibility of changing fonts and print sizes permits a nice variety in how your work looks.

A few words of warning about word processors, however. If you are accustomed to writing on a computer, you probably know the possibilities for disaster when you do not save files frequently and make backup files. But in addition to these problems, there are two difficulties inherent to writing on word processors that you will need to compensate for. First, most word-processing programs give you about twenty lines of text on screen at a time, or two to three paragraphs. If you are writing a short essay (say, 350 words), this may not be too confining—but if your document runs to several pages, it is easy to forget what you've written or how it connects to later passages. It's advisable, then, to print fairly often and work from "hard copy" rather than relying exclusively on memory. You should keep paper and/or electronic copies of successive versions, so you can follow the evolution of an essay through its various revisions.

The other danger in relying on word processors is that the printed versions may look better than they really are. Compared to the old, clumsy manual typewriters (not to mention handwriting), there's a world of improvement in format. Depending on your program, you may even be able to make your writing look as though it were professionally printed. But a pleasing appearance may distract you from attending to your words and sentences. If your computer makes professional-looking drafts, it is essential to leave them alone for a period of time in order to be able to criticize them with detachment. Of course, you may as well make your drafts as impressive as you can when turning them in for a grade. Appearance is part of the rhetoric by which your work will be received. But don't be fooled by a pretty format into thinking too early that your text is complete.

Readers' Roles

By now you've gotten an overview of what rhetoric is—communication that is directed to others—and how it can be important for influencing how we understand and act on ideas. We sometimes speak in such a way as to underscore this, in making statements about "the press" or "the media." What we usually mean is that writers, or publishers, or editors, or actors, or producers, or the corporate hierarchy of a network or film company, are producing texts that have influential effects on their audiences.

Unstated but still important is the fact that audiences play roles, too. Texts that address large audiences—most television programs, popular music, large-circulation magazines—are generous in providing easy roles for readers to play. Sometimes these texts even allow readers with contradictory perspectives to play along; for example, the TV version of *Batman* broadcast in the 1960s and shown now in syndication allows viewers at one level to consider the program as "serious" narrative, while other viewers can laugh at the campy aspects of the program as they did in 1965 (e.g., Batman's potbelly or Robin's "Holy..." exclamations). Other texts may inscribe roles that a smaller number of readers will wish to play, either because these roles are less "mainstream" or because they are more complex—although audiences may be more intensely interested in those roles, because they fit more specific interests. For example, viewers of the original *Star Trek* in the 1960s not only lobbied against its cancellation, but maintained an interest in the program sufficient to create a market for *Star Trek* films, syndication of the original programs, and eventually the sequels *The Next Generation* and *Deep Space Nine*.

PAUSE FOR REFLECTION

The various *Star Trek* programs invite readers to play roles in their viewing. What sort of role do you choose to play? That is, are you distanced? Contemptuous? Mildly interested? A Trekker? How much of this interest is popular response, how much the result of merchandising?

As readers we have the capacity to play roles, within the space of the text, because the conventions of those texts leave some latitude for us to do so. Some texts—those labeled as more literary, more imaginative, or more playful—may leave a great deal of the construction of the text to the reader. More precisely, these texts work according to expectations that their readers want the challenge of figuring out what is going on. Other texts still within the category of literature may leave the reader to imagine setting, physical description, tone of voice, and such, while working within strict conventions of plot, characterization, and style. Texts offer an entry to readers, an entry that we may choose to accept or reject according to our own needs and desires. Cassandra Amesley's essay, below, explores interactions between text and audience.

CASSANDRA AMESLEY

How to Watch Star Trek

Fan culture at science fiction conventions ("cons") is, for much of the United States, exotic. People's costumes are chosen more for the idealized possible than for the rules of fashion. Games played reflect the specialized knowledge available to fans.... An innocent bystander who is not oriented to science fiction could perhaps be forgiven for finding fans both esoteric and obsessive. Only years of living in proximity to fandom could explain why one feature at a con might be a "superfan" such as Jerry, who publishes a zine about other fanzines.

But most fans are invisible. Their enthusiasm only shows when their special subject is available for discussion. That enthusiasm makes *Star Trek* fans easy to find if you look for them.... Even casual conversations would yield fans. For example, at the library when I was checking out the *Star Trek Concordance*, the librarian and I began to discuss *Star Trek*, and the man next in line told a story concerning a fake button for his car dashboard that was supposed to "engage warp drive." He had taken the car to a mechanic, and on his bill was noted, "Warp drive could not be fixed; Scotty unavailable."...

Another time, I was reading a *Star Trek* comic book in an Iowa City café when the waitress engaged me in conversation about the book. When she found out that I was interviewing fans, she (without my solicitation) went on her break, sat down at my table, and told me what she thought in an extremely productive and entertaining interview. I have gotten free cable movies from talking about *Star Trek* to the man installing my cable, gotten astonishing turnouts from undergraduates to early morning convention papers on *Star Trek* theory, and had fans show up to my classes the day I lectured on their community. *Star Trek* fandom is much larger than its central group of convention goers, or even fanzine writers.

To understand *Star Trek* culture, then, it's first necessary to understand the periphery: those who would not call themselves "hard-core" fans (because I asked them if they would) but who include *Star Trek* as an important text in the construction and maintenance of their social world. I talked to fans intensively for six months, and have done follow-up interviews since then. Fans cheerfully spent hours talking to me about their viewing habits, sorting cards with characters' names on them into categories, watching episodes I selected to provide glosses on interactions, and writing letters with self-addressed stamped envelopes for me to ask them more questions. From these interviews and observations, I have developed an account of the evolved agreements on how one watches and interprets *Star Trek*.

I will call these viewers a "proprietary audience." I define proprietary audiences as those viewers—or readers—who appropriate the primary elements of a mass-mediated narrative and actively rewrite it. Such an audience acknowledges and responds to elements in a particular text or set of texts, but develops its own interpretive relationship to it. Proprietary audiences will have somewhat different ways of approaching the text than the overtly intended ones, and will grow to view the text not as external to their construction, but within it. So, for example, a *Star Trek* fan will without hesitation write the producers of a film and advise them what plot actions should be taken, viewing this act as part of a negotiated process rather than as a plea from an undeserving outsider.

Producers will often foster this myth of fan negotiation, as *The Making of Star Trek* amply demonstrates. This book, ostensibly a "factual" report on production of a particular television show, emphasizes and celebrates fan participation in the (limited) success of the series. It also rhetorically constructs the producers as allied with fans against the "big business" mentality of the networks, eliding [producer Gene] Roddenberry's own interest in making money. But the results of an appropriation myth are not especially controllable. The fans of *Star Trek* are particularly proprietary. And some—such as the "slash" writers described by Henry Jenkins—view the division as not between producers and network, but rather between legal owners and morally justified appropriators.

Most viewers are introduced to *Star Trek* through the episodes, or at least the films. The first line of appropriation tends to be the act of viewing. It thus seems appropriate to commence my ethnography at this level. I will give an account of an actual viewing event with three of my informants. This taped event will show the existence of a set of tacit rules concerning viewing and interpreting....

It's Friday night in Iowa City. Four people, three women and one man, gather around a large television screen. On the screen, a group of actors in bright colors anxiously watch yet another large screen, in which stars flicker. The round set occasionally trembles. Dialogue reveals that the characters are experiencing ripples in time.

"Aha!" says one of my companions. "It's the giant space doughnut."

"There's a yeoman we've never seen," another observer reports. One of the actors jerks backward from the instrument panel where he has been seated, now sparking and smoking. The woman in red hurries over and raises the actor's head from the floor. "That's what she's there for—to hold Sulu."

A man in a gold tunic orders medical aid. A watcher remarks, "I'm a captain, not a doctor."

"I've never understood why they don't buckle themselves in."

An accident occurs: the doctor injects himself with a drug identified as dangerous, throws off restraint, and leaps through doors that have swished open to receive him.

"He's suddenly stronger than Kirk and Spock together."

Music, and voiceover: —Space, the final frontier. These are the voyages of the Starship Enterprise. Her five year mission...—

Attention wanders in the room, then returns to the screen as several actors appear on a barren outdoor set in a shower of glitter.

"Count how many are beaming down."

"Six."

"Okay, just remember that."

The large, rounded prop begins to glow and pulse, and then speaks. The voice reverberates.

"Why does your voice echo?"

"It's a superior thing. Superior things have echoey voices."

"Why didn't they just get McCoy with a phaser?"

"They get him, but he wakes up."

The superior thing remarks upon the inferiority of the beings interrogating it. One, a tall man wearing a blue jersey and pointed ears, frowns. The shorter, blondish figure identified by the watchers as the captain, asks:

—Annoyed, Spock?—

"No, just a little pissed off, Captain."

The doctor leaps through the doughnut, and it develops that as a result the *Star Trek* past has been changed. As the guardian explains, the watchers recite along: —Everything you ever knew is gone.—

"Wow! Existential crisis!"

The scene shifts. "Accoutrements."

Gold shirt and blue shirt are on a 1930s set, attracting some attention from passersby. Gold shirt steals some clothes from a clothesline, and is brought up short by a man in the costume of a 1930s police officer.

—I recognize the traditional accoutrements,— says gold shirt.

"Nice word."

"They're not just accoutrements, they're traditional."

"That's the same music as in *Shore Leave*."

"It's surprising how well the clothes fit for stolen clothes."

"They stole them off their doubles."

An actress enters the room where the two men have changed.

"Cue the violins."

"It's Alexis."

"There's the love music."

More scenes. —I find her... most uncommon.—

"Yeah, we know, Kirk. Pick your tongue up off the floor."

"We have a flop." The character obligingly echoes:

—We have a flop.—

The story unfolds. The captain informs his pointed-ear friend that he believes he is falling in love with the young woman.

"So what else is new?"

The doctor is found, raving and paranoid. "I'm a doctor, not a psychiatrist."

"So how come he can give psychiatric reports then?"

In the end, history is saved. The three in the past return to the barren set, and all disappear in a shower of glitter. Credits.

"So how many are beaming up?"

"Seven."

"All at the same time. But there are only six transporter pads."

"They just keep one in transit."

The observers have been watching with some approval and much commentary: this is an episode of the show they consider "all right." The next is one they all dislike, agreed to be one of the worst *Star Trek* episodes ever shown: the captain of the Enterprise switches bodies with a woman he used to be involved with, against his will: she wants to be a starship captain....

We have by now uncovered two senses of the term "audience": that of an interpretive community which exists in time and over distance, and that of an interpretive community which is in direct and immediate contact with each other as the text is being viewed. There are agreements, of course: the historical development of *Star Trek* interpretation has created the myths through mass mediation. The texts develop a culture into which the fan moves, maintaining a set of tacit agreements on what *Star Trek* is and is not, and arguing over another set of not-so-tacit disagreements on *Star Trek* boundaries. Moreover, even when viewers are directly interacting with the original episodes, rather than producing written texts, the attraction of *Star Trek* does not lie wholly within the structure of the show itself. This is not surprising; watching a show fifty times must ultimately yield diminishing returns, if no other factors enter the picture. But viewers in this oral medium, while sometimes acting on the information from the rapidly expanding body of critical interpretation of the canon, have developed a particular approach....

[T]he viewing process recorded above [can be] analyze[d] ... as a textmaking event.... By focusing very narrowly on the actual interactive viewing process itself, it becomes possible to see that the audience develops a particular relation to the text and becomes a creative part of the communication process.... [W]hat *Star Trek* fans have is a subtle and sophisticated way of reading text as simultaneously constructed and real. They have developed a method of reading television which exploits the intense involvement in and commitment to *Star Trek* by maintaining affection and loyalty to events and people in the *Star Trek* universe, while providing ironic commentary on its creation.

The result appears to be a wealth of interpretation which makes every *Star Trek* text open to rewriting as it is aired. Thus, *Star Trek* cultural participants can enjoy new texts developed from familiar ones, favorite parts of the original, and the satisfaction of shared understanding and agreement from like-minded individuals all at once....

[Star Trek episodes feature] predictable plot lines. Most fans could find quite large groups of stories which belonged together, and all identify "good" and "bad" stories as appropriate differentiating categories. They generally agree that bad stories are those which can't be believed. Plot, for *Star Trek* fans, appears to be subordinate to character, for what makes a story unbelievable is almost always someone acting in a way he wouldn't ordinarily act....

There are occurrences, as well as characters, which mark a typical episode, fans agree: the arguments between Spock and McCoy, Kirk's romantic involvement with a woman, Scotty's attempts to maintain shields or other energy levels, and Spock's calmness under pressure. Equally part of typical episodes are a series of lines that fans readily recognize: some that are favorites in particular episodes (such as the "accoutrements" cited in the beginning commentary) and some which are closely identified with characters: Dr. McCoy says, "He's dead, Jim," and "I'm a doctor, not a —"; Spock remarks, "Fascinating" to occurrences which appear likely to kill or maim the crew; Scotty says things like "One more hit and the shields will be gone" (in Scottish dialect); Kirk advises, "Phasers on stun."

Not all of these "typical" occurrences are viewed with approval. Several fans objected to McCoy's constant baiting of Spock on the grounds of unacceptable xenophobia; all disapproved of what one fan from India referred to as Kirk's "constant smooching." "[These occurrences] get old," and another fan conceded, "But it wouldn't be *Star Trek* without them, I suppose."

In short, every plot has the potential of being "bad" *Star Trek* or "good" *Star Trek*, based primarily on how the characters act...although there are plots that seem to be bad simply because they are dull. However, that an episode is "bad" does not mean it will not be watched, or even enjoyed in places. In every episode, no matter how bad, there are favorite lines or scenes.

* * *

I call...discourse that opens the possibility of an ironic stance "double viewing." Double viewing suggests that it is possible to maintain and understand two divergent points of view at once, and use them to inform each other. In this way identification and distanciation may occur simultaneously. The double view explains and helps interpret the scene I described earlier.

"The space doughnut" comment is a typical phrase used to identify episodes, which are identified by particular indices to the scene rather than recaps of occurrences. So, for example, when I gave titles of episodes, fans would generally say, "the cloud thing," or "the spores," rather than "The one where Kirk goes crazy," or "The one where Spock falls in love." Moreover, it is a tradition of fans to attempt to identify the episode as soon as they can. "Hard-core fans," it is said, claim to be able to recognize the episode by the first word. While remembering the title may or may not be a point of honor, knowing the show somewhat better than the less initiated is a matter of pride.

"I'm a captain, not a doctor," is a direct reversal of McCoy's traditional comment, "I'm a doctor, not a —." Its humor as commentary obviously depends on the assumption that everyone knows the original, as is true for most of these comments.

"Count the number beaming down"... displays concern for a technical problem that will occur later. Fans are aware, or quickly become aware, of the number of pads in the transporter room, where people beam up to the *Enterprise* or down to the planet. There are no episode-acknowledged rules dictating that only so many people may beam in or out at a time, and so it is an interesting matter for debate: can the transporter room take more than six? And if not, what happens to the extra person? If so, why are never more than six shown beaming down or up? It would be inappropriate during a show to distract attention from an episode for the length of time necessary to debate this question fully, but it indexes discussions several fans in different cells had that week.

"Just a little pissed off, Captain" is the imposition of dialogue for a character reflecting his or her projected inner state, of a kind none of the scriptwriters would provide. It seems to function as a combination of entering into the dialogue and underlining a particular interpretation of a character perception....

"Wow! Existential crisis!" Here, a direct commentary on the problem of the occurrence satirically raises the tone of the show to a metaphysical one, rather higher than would be reasonable for the average television show. The result is to make fun of the problem at the same time it is agreed that the problem could not be a very pleasant one to have....

"Accoutrements" is again an index to a scene: the scene in which this word occurs. This is a kind of reverse echolalia, dependent on utterances within the text but so familiar that it can predict. It also occurs with the "We have a flop," spoken just before the character speaks it.

"Have we ever gotten a name for her?" (about the Joan Collins character) offers at least two points of interest. First, "we" refers to the viewing group, which has created itself, so that members presume that all information is shared; what one knows is available to all. The question concerning McCoy answered by another viewer demonstrates that this assumption is a valid one. Second, the question both refers to the viewing *past*—other times this episode was watched and known—and to the viewing *future*—later in the episode, when the giving of her name might/might not occur. The response, that Spock will be told her name, is given in the present tense, avoiding issues of both past and future, and placing the occurrence within the episode, rather than within viewer time.

"It's Alexis" refers to...Joan Collins, who twenty years later will be famous for portraying a conniving woman in *Dynasty*. Other comments on her sexual proclivities ensued when this conversation was being recorded, providing a strange conflation of her *Star Trek* missionary role with the *Dynasty* evil woman role.... Again, note that awareness of the actors as actors is built into the text and is a legitimate part of the commentary.

"That's the second time he's killed him" refers to another *Star Trek* episode, "Amok Time," where Spock "kills" Kirk (who, naturally, turns out to be alive). Comments are often intertextual, directly referring to other episodes.

In this way, *Star Trek* takes on a "once and future" aura where everything has happened, is happening, and will happen. At first it appears that in commentary, anything goes: comments *to* the character, *for* the character, and *about* the character. But, in fact, within each are appropriate and less appropriate things to say. All my informants agree that some commentary is entirely unacceptable. One said, "I hate people talking about what's going to happen." However, she had cited "This guy's dead meat," as an acceptable thing to say about security guards. (It is a fan tradition that all unfamiliar redshirted people will die quickly in an episode.) It developed that within the tradition of *Star Trek* "essence," one could predict certain reoccurrences. One could not, however, baldly state, "In this episode the Klingon kills that guy."

Others cited, with some disapproval, non–*Star Trek* fans who watched an episode, remarked that it looked like a submarine movie, and then began to discuss its similarities. "You just don't do that while it's happening," one fan explained. In this case, metacriticism of the *Star Trek* fiction was unwelcome.... What you *can't* say about an episode is anything that takes it out of its "always–already" existence and puts it into a point in time, which is what critiquing it must necessarily do.

For that reason, code words, indices to themes and images, and ironic commentaries are acceptable and in fact desirable, but a position that requires directly and propositionally distancing oneself from the action and recognizing it as narratively framed is suspect. Since saying "This guy's dead meat" fits into the shared agreements of what's likely to happen to security guards, it violates nothing. On the other hand, direct prediction in a particular episode is unacceptable. This probably explains why episode themes are indexed by image rather than occurrence: identification of an image does not give away the episode as inevitably moving to one end and no other. Hence the use of terms which index rather than identify: "space doughnut" rather than "time portal."...

What are the consequences of this rule? First, of course, the original text remains untouched by history; it is always occurring, unbroken by the imposition of commentary which directly states that it has happened before. Second, a new discourse emerges from the viewers which exists as counterpart to the original text, playing off it but providing creative pleasure for its participants, who are also its audience. This new text is regenerated with each episode, so that it doesn't repeat as the original does, although salient comments and particularly amusing ideas may be played with from viewing to viewing. Even the worst episodes contain points which may be enjoyed for their own sake. These points may be improved—and the duller moments rewritten—by audience participation, just as the best can be embroidered. In short, *Star Trek* provides a basic medium which the audience then uses to create its own metatext.

[From Cassandra Amesley, "How to Watch *Star Trek*," *Cultural Studies* 6(1992): 2. Used by permission.]

QUESTIONS
1. Do you yourself view or read texts interactively, solo or with others as described here? If so, which texts? Why those?
2. What is involved in being a "fan," "hard-core" or otherwise? Are you a "fan" of anything? What difference does "fanship" make for how you respond to Amesley's "ethnography"?
3. What sort of reader is implied by Amesley's text? What are the points in the text that help you decide how to answer this question?

As we read and interact with texts, we are somewhere between two extreme positions: The first would have us imagine ourselves as reading or receiving the text exactly as its producers or authors might wish, while the second would have us imagine ourselves with complete latitude to interpret it however we wished. Our actual roles are somewhere between these—specifically where is to be determined.

ASSIGNMENT
Write informally about a reading or viewing experience where you believe you were an agreeable reader, going along with the role implied for you by the text. Then write about such an experience in which you played the part of a resisting reader, moving against textual cues that you believe pushed you in a direction you did not want to go. What were the texts involved? Why did you respond as you did?

Now reflect on your own writing experiences and purposes for writing. To what extent do you want readers to go along with your intent in a text? To what extent do you want readers to go their own way?

Specific forms of media encourage you to make certain choices: to buy a car or brand of detergent, to vote according to a political program, to develop a cheery or determined attitude. Later chapters of this book will examine some discrete rhetorical purposes, such as representing reality through news or information, or communicating through the visual rhetoric of photography and other signs. But one way to think about your activity as a writer is that you are taking on the responsibility of *constructing a role that your readers will want to play.* This is done through language, of course, but language that you come up with in connection with kinds of writing, or genres, already established for you. The creativity in being a writer comes not so much in inventing new forms as in finding applications of existing forms for your own insights and experiences, which are in turn shaped by your understanding of (and through) genres.

Three essays follow—two published in magazines, one from a writing class—which illustrate how writers construct roles for their readers. In reading through the essays, notice specific references, phrases, metaphors, and other matters of language that nudge the reader in certain ways. You should give some thought as well to ways in which the context for each essay has constructed the reader, even before the writing itself appears.

LINDA WELTNER

The Joys of Mediocrity

My husband plays the tuba badly. No, wretchedly. Execrably. With unforgettable inexpertise. After my husband played "When Irish Eyes Are Smiling" at my older daughter's wedding as a way of welcoming our son-in-law's Irish family, his father created an award for Jack that read, in part, "for a spontaneous public performance which demonstrated an originality so stark that it stunned the audience, rendering them incapable of meaningful response."

This did not hurt my husband's feelings. He knows the impact his music has. This is a man for whom practice means playing all the notes, right or wrong, at least twice. His tuba, purchased at a yard sale for $100, looks as if it's been run over by a truck. His entire repertory consists of five songs that run the gamut from "Happy Birthday" to "So Long, It's Been Good to Know You."

Still, the phone rings and people ask him to play at some special event, an occurrence that happens more frequently than I might hope. He doesn't get nervous or decide to polish up his technique a bit. He glows. He basks. He's unabashedly delighted. And delightful.

At his first note, audiences burst into hysterical laughter, and the more earnestly he attempts to render a recognizable melody, the harder they laugh, until they leap to their feet, choking and cheering. I understand why he's in demand. What has been harder for me to accept is how he can be perfectly capable of enjoying his tuba solos without ever aiming at competence.

This is not the way I was brought up. Whether it was swimming, tennis, or ballroom dancing, my mother made sure I began with lessons. The pleasure in doing a thing, I was taught, is in doing it well, and so my whole life has been about mastery, whether I was skiing, sewing, or cooking. I never enjoyed trial and error. I wanted to do things as they should be done. I disliked looking awkward or amateurish, and to my way of thinking, mistakes took the pleasure out of things. If I felt I'd end up doing something badly, I politely declined the opportunity to begin.

That seemed a perfectly sensible way to operate until I started dancing for exercise a few months back. At the beginning, I gave myself time to learn the steps, but I'm no longer a novice. What's happened now is that newcomers to my class are catching on while I'm still struggling. I've come to the reluctant conclusion that these complex patterns of movement we do may never come to feel like my second nature.

You know what? I don't care.

I've learned that it's possible for me to tune in to how good it feels to move without having to submit my performance to my superego for approval. Oh, what bliss it is to slip my pleasure right by that little inner overachiever!

My dance class has helped me experience what Howard Gardner calls bodily–kinesthetic intelligence, the ability to use one's body in very different ways. In general, Gardner writes in *Frames of Mind: The Theory of Multiple Intelligences*, we respect those who rate high in language, logic, and math, but he contends that there are other equally important forms of intelligence having to do with movement, music, spatial ability, and personal and interpersonal skills.

These forms of intelligence are like packages under the tree, wondrous gifts given to our species by a generous creator. By opening only those at which we have been trained to excel, we diminish the ways in which we can express ourselves in the world. The culture colludes, teaching us reading, writing, and arithmetic at an early age and leaving us to discover our other talents in a hit-or-miss fashion.

My husband and I are proof of how rewarding it can be to sing or dance, to play a musical instrument or a sport, to study a foreign language, or calculus, or anything that doesn't come easily. All you have to do first is free yourself from the prison of excellence.

As Nike says, "Just do it."

Oops, add one more word. "Badly."

[From *New Age Journal*, Sept./Oct. 1993. Used by permission.]

QUESTIONS
1. How do you envision the writer of the article? (Age, gender, race, social position, etc.) What clues in the text of the essay help you form your impression? Are there points in the article at which your ideas about the writer change?
2. What does the writer's husband's tuba playing have to do with her exercise dancing? If there's a general point of which these are illustrations, why does the author present this point *through* the illustrations?

3. How would you describe readers who feel ready to "play along" with the article? What sort of role(s) are they offered? What would be some characteristics of readers who are not likely to read this essay favorably?
4. What do you know of the context in which this essay appears? How would knowledge of the context affect its reception?

KIRKPATRICK SALE

Fighting the Darkness

The darkness is all around us; it is called industrial civilization. And it is leading the world to the verge of ecocide, the final extinction of surface life as we know it. The darkness has been fashioned for us by an industrialization that is embedding us ever more deeply in a technosphere, an industrialization that is, in effect, declaring war on the biosphere. And in that war, the war of technology against nature, technology—modern, cybermad technology—is winning.

Herbert Read, the great British historian, once said, "Only a people serving an apprenticeship to nature can be trusted with machines. Only such people will so contrive and control those machines that their products are an enhancement of biological needs and not a denial of them." Our civilization has not served such an apprenticeship. That is why our machines are making war on the living world. If we let this continue, if we let the technosphere continue to dominate our lives and dictate our values, the biosphere will be destroyed and the human species along with it. This is a truth we must take to our hearts.

The only and necessary light, therefore, is the light we shed on the darkness of industrialism. George Grant, a Canadian philosopher, has said, "The darkness which envelops the Western world because of its long dedication to the overcoming of chance is just a fact. The job of thought in our time is to bring into the light that darkness as darkness." So the job is to shed that light, to act as starkly and as forthrightly as possible to resist the technosphere. To free ourselves and thus all of nature from the iron chains of an ecocidal industrialism. The Luddites tried this nearly 200 years ago. And they gave us a name, an image, a vision, and a means. The best we can do in shedding light is to use that means now.

[He then smashes a computer onstage.]

[From *The Utne Reader*, Jul.–Aug. 1995, p. 37. Used by permission.]

QUESTIONS

1. How do the metaphors of war and violence, light and darkness affect your response as a reader?
2. How does your reaction to the term "ecocide" shape your reaction to the essay?
3. Why does Sale quote other writers? How does that quoting help define his audience?

DANIELLE SMITH

Publishers' Clearing House
The "American Dream" has always consisted of a big beautiful house, with a white picket fence. In the "American Dream," there is no such thing as divorce. Everyone in this dream has a nuclear family with a wife, a husband, two children and a dog. The scene is set to where the father was working all day and comes home to his lovely family to sit down to a nice full-course meal, have a family discussion about each person's day and maybe watch the television for a couple of hours.

Although the "American Dream" at one time or another used to motivate people to want and strive for this dream, it is dying out and becoming more or less a fairy tale rather than a reality. The divorce rate in America itself is rising higher and higher each year. Families no longer have any spare quality time to spend together anymore. Both parents nowadays have to work just to make ends meet in America. So where does that leave the children? Probably at home cooking their own meals. It sounds to me that the "American Dream" has lost its luster and the dream of becoming rich in a short period of time is taking over.

Besides the lottery, the next best gamble for millions is the game of the sweepstakes. One of the more popular sweepstakes is the Publishers' Clearing House. The Publishers' Clearing House is thought to be one of the easier ways to fulfill whatever is left of the "American Dream." Many people dream of becoming millionaires and going from rags to riches in a moment's time. Of course this does not always happen; very few people become rich over a short period of time. In fact, becoming rich takes many years of hard work and saving unless it is inherited or born into.

Publishers' Clearing House in itself is a dream. The advertisement of this sweepstakes is televised quite often during soap operas, the *Star Search* show, and at other times in the afternoon. The commercials come on showing the award committee driving around in their van talking about how they are looking for their next winner in the sweepstakes. Then they suddenly appear at someone's home, knock on their door and award them their check for one million to ten million dollars. Next the award committee goes on to say that they will be on the road again at some certain date and you have so many days before the deadline to get your entry form in the mail or you might miss out on the money. Many viewers get to witness the (so-called) winners on television. Just viewing the many different commercials is strange. It was weird how all of the winners of the Publishers' Clearing House Sweepstakes were mainly middle-aged to elderly white people. On each commercial there were one or two blacks and no Mexicans at all. So does this mean that this sweepstakes can be won only by middle-aged or elderly white people? Not really. Maybe the fact is that these people are the ones who send off for the information more often than the others.

It was a surprise to receive a package from the Publishers' Clearing House. I have been receiving this stuff every year since I was eighteen. I still cannot figure out how my name got on their mailing lists. I had never sent off for anything in my life before. I can only guess that these advertisers somehow find out who is living within the household.

The envelope was filled with pictures of what I could (possibly) win, like cars, televisions, luggage, trips and of course the grand prize money. Along with this mind-boggling information was a typed letter congratulating me for picking the Publishers' Clearing House Sweepstakes (which I never did) and telling me all about how I could win wonderful prizes just by mailing back a response. Of course there is *no purchase necessary* to enter the drawings, but if you want your name to be placed higher upon the *winners list* it is advisable that you order from their magazine list. When ordering, your chances (of winning) increase with each order, but it has also been said that most of the people who have won never sent off for any of the merchandise.

They have a little system that has to be followed if you want to enter. There are all of these stickers and winning numbers that are to be stuck on the back and the inside of the envelope to be mailed. The purpose of this is to let them know for example what type of car you might like, which type of magazine you are ordering, or what your winning numbers are that they have assigned for you. After a few weeks, the order comes back along with a bill saying if the bill is paid right away, there might be chances of getting a $10,000 bonus in the near future. If the bill is not paid, the company will pay for the magazine but you will receive letter after letter as a reminder to pay your bill.

The discouraging part about this game is that consumers feel they are going in circles. There seems to be an abundance of mailing back and forth with *no real sign* of progress. There just seems to be more stickers and more talk about how closer and closer you are getting to the million dollar award. Some people give up on ever winning, while others become addicted to the fact that this might be "the one." They are so hooked on the million-dollar dream that they end up spending more money than they will ever get back.

Publishers' Clearing House may only be a scam to get money out of people. Of course a person is going to be suckered into the game, if only once. I never understood why my parents would not send for prizes, but now I do. The fact is that customers' hopes are built up to come crashing down. Before you know it, after P. C. H. has drained your pockets, here comes another money-winning sweepstakes to your door. Don't send for the information. [Used by permission.]

QUESTIONS

1. As with the Linda Weltner essay, how do you envision the writer of the article? (Age, gender, race, social position, etc.) What clues in the text of the essay help you form your impression?

2. Why does the writer open the essay by talking about the "American Dream"? What roles does this open up for readers, particularly when the essay's real subject becomes clear in paragraph 3?
3. Have you taken part in promotional devices such as the sweepstakes described here? How does your participation or nonparticipation affect your reaction to the essay?
4. Besides lotteries and sweepstakes, are there other aspects of contemporary culture that connect to the dream of getting rich quickly?

There's no requirement that you read texts as intended—and there is often pleasure in deliberately misreading a text (as happens with the films on *Mystery Science Theater 3000*). Entertainment texts sometimes assume a passive reader, the reader as consumer; but readers often derive amusement from examining the conventions of these texts critically, perhaps in a different context, as with the *Star Trek* audience described above. And if not amusement, then education: What entertains people in a culture or period is often very revealing about what those people take for granted, as can be seen when you watch programs or commercials from another time or place.

Later chapters will ask you to add to your repertoire of skills in reading texts—not only in what you read, but in how you read. In addition to more or less passive enjoyment, you will need to develop the capacity to read texts critically and analytically. You'll need to ask what specific roles texts ask readers to take on, and what the costs are of adopting those roles. What do we give up, and what are we encouraged to do, when we agree to read texts according to the roles envisioned for us?

It may be of more direct concern to try to see where you yourself fit into all the rhetoric that projects roles for you as audience. These roles vary from each other, and may even be contradictory: You may be addressed as a responsible parent or spouse or citizen in an insurance ad; then in the next commercial be invited to cut loose, driving a four-wheel vehicle through a birthday cake and into the woods; then metamorphose into someone whose hair makes you the passive object of others' gaze and desire thanks to the shampoo you use. Sitcoms and TV dramas, news and documentaries, rock music, magazine and newspaper articles all cast their audiences into roles that are more or less narrow, and we as audience members decide whether and how strongly to affiliate with these roles.

Accepting our intended role is generally assumed to be our choice: If a media text asks us to play a role that we reject, we resist. We change the channel, walk out of the theater, or make sarcastic remarks. These forms of reaction are usually not very effective, however, because almost all media are one-way. Talking back to the television is considered to be irrational behavior. If you are sufficiently motivated, you can write letters to the network, the producer of a film, a record company, and so on—but the chances are that your comment will have little result, because the rhetoric built into the situation doesn't open itself for you.

Most commercial media texts are fairly remote from our daily concerns. What happens on *Roseanne* isn't generally a matter of great moment for day-to-day life. Other forms of rhetoric, however, matter a great deal to us individually: How well you can write for your customers, your present or prospective employer, your instructors, your peers, or other parts of the public may have immediate and concrete effects on your life. And analyzing the readers' role in other texts should carry over into your work with your own texts. That is, from the earliest prewritings through the last drafts, you should cultivate the ability to ask what sort of role your text intends your reader to take on. Are your expectations too confining, so that they may be rejected out of hand? Do you leave room for disagreement, or do you require absolute agreement with your perspectives? Are there possibilities for amusement along with serious points to be grasped? In reading over your own initial observations and reflections, you need to think about the form that you want your writings to have, based on your assessment of your audience's expectations. Only very near to the essay's completion can you relax into the pleasure of reading for pleasure.

Rhetoric, in other words, is a way of involving the reader; and involving the reader can improve your communications and thereby give you greater power to do what you want. Whether it's getting and holding a job, doing effective writing in college courses and other circumstances, or participating in informal contacts with others, the ability to analyze and discover what will work is of immense practical importance. And effective writing is a source of personal satisfaction.

CONCLUSION

Writing is where you get to talk back to—analyze and understand—others' texts. You may not have broadcast time made available to you; letters to the editor are no match for newspaper articles; and commercials and popular songs can overwhelm any kind of countergesture you could come up with.

But understanding how these texts work, gain influence and power, and represent you and others like you is a necessary step to asserting some degree of authority for yourself. Writing can serve as the basis of a community of some sort; as you write for and about others, you may begin to treat writing as a medium in fact, not just in potential. Your class can serve as such a community—limited in size and time, but still a community in potential. To the extent that writing can help you shape your own view of the world, it may afford you a degree of independence from the versions of reality offered you by others.

FURTHER ASSIGNMENTS

Assignment
Contemporary media depend heavily on audience analysis. That is, television programmers have in mind a clear sense of those for whom a program is intended, in terms of factors such as age, gender, racial background, and income level. The situation is somewhat different for newspapers, because most newspapers enjoy a monopoly in their area of distribution and are not distributed nationally—but the demographics in their areas are important considerations as well. And other media are similarly audience-conscious.

What sort of audience are you writing academic essays for? If you conceive of your writing as being about a subject or area of content, does the audience even matter? Is your audience primarily or exclusively your instructor? If so, what does that mean for your style, choice of words, and other writing decisions? Are you writing for others besides your instructor (e.g., other members of your class)? How does thinking about the audience change the way that you write? Write informally in response to these questions. You may find it useful to examine a piece of writing done for a previous class as a guide, looking for specifics from that text for support.

Assignment
Drawing on the interview with Ernest Hemingway (pages 102–107) as a model, conduct an interview with a writer. You may choose as your subject another student in your class, or someone you know who has published. Try out some of the interviewing conventions found in the Hemingway interview: Do they seem artificial or dated?

Assignment
Take an essay (a piece previously written for another class, or a draft being prepared for this class) and read it closely to determine what aspects of that essay *represent* you to oth-

ers. What conception of your reader led you to make those specific choices? What are some other possible choices about yourself that you may have passed over or downplayed?

Assignment
Go to a library that keeps bound copies of old magazines—*Life, The Saturday Evening Post,* or *National Geographic,* for example. Browse through some of these from thirty years ago, or earlier, with an eye to matters such as advertisements, photographs, styles of dress, uses of language, and so on. What are some areas of continuity and some areas of difference between then and now?

4

Gathering and Evaluating News and Information

OVERVIEW

I have some news for you.... Jim Morrison and Elvis faked their deaths and are living happily in retirement. Ever since the first atom bombs exploded, flying saucers have been regularly sighted. The so-called moon landings were actually faked out in the desert someplace. Seven Elders of Zion rule the world. John F. Kennedy was shot by several assassins, and is now alive in a rest home. The moon on the Tide box is a Satanic symbol. And the Holocaust was all a historical fraud.

Some of *what I know* is true, and some is not. Before 1450 most Europeans "knew" the world to be flat; and when circling the globe, Magellan's sailors "knew" what day it was, even after they crossed what we now call the International Date Line and began holding Sunday mass on Saturday.

What we know is compiled from personal experience and from what others have told us since birth. This *telling* takes many forms: conversation and gossip; public address in speeches, lectures, and sermons; words printed in books and newspapers; and information broadcast to millions. Out of all that's available, we select (sometimes unconsciously) what to place our confidence in, according to the systems of belief we have grown up inside, which have shaped who we are. But it is often useful to check both individual items and aspects of those systems of belief—as illustrated by the rumors and false statements in the first paragraph above, which are believed by hundreds of thousands of people.

What's "the news" got to do with your writing? Perhaps nothing, directly. Your subjects for writing may have nothing to do with anything in the news. Many people now largely ignore news until it concerns them directly; others keep tabs mainly by scanning the front page, or listening to *Headline News* or updates on the radio. Just following newspaper coverage, much less evaluating it, takes time and concentration. It may be difficult to work up reasons for caring about news, since most of it seems to be in a remote part of the world, or about decisions in which most of us have little say.

But to reach others on any subject, you have to convince them that you know what you are writing about, that your perspective is valuable. And apart from establishing authority—the fact that you know enough to be an author—just knowing more about the world gives you more options. The reliability of what you hear and think about and know has a considerable effect on your life.

In the previous chapter we were considering ways to convert thoughts and observations into a coherent draft; this chapter will focus on what is sometimes called news and information and how that subject connects with writing in an academic context. How you gather, process, and evaluate information is crucial in writing for others. Writing in a classroom—or on the job—is hardly confined to self-expression: you have to link your writing to public concerns in some way in order to reach an audience. This means paying some attention to what you know and how you know it—which in turn means assessing the quality of your information, along with that of others' perspectives, and searching out more as needed.

To develop your capacity for rhetoric, then, you need not only to be able to shape your language to an audience, but to examine how your purposes are shaped by others' rhetoric, particularly the rhetoric of news and information. The problem, both for a student of media and for a writer reconsidering sources, is this: *How do we know what we know?* It's a crucial question to ask at any point in your writing, from prewriting to draft stages. For example, if you are planning an essay about supposed safety flaws in an automobile, and it turns out that the reports that caused you to want to write the essay in the first place were based on faulty or unrepresentative testing, then your argument would fall apart. We sometimes make decisions that may profoundly affect our lives on the basis of limited or faulty information—from votes in national elections, to the purchase of a house or a car, to a decision on a college major (and, by implication, possibly a career).

As seen from our present perspective, past centuries had problems getting *enough* information. Before modern transportation and communication, it might take weeks even to find out who had been elected president or whether war had been declared. With the development of contemporary systems of media, the problem is rather *too much* information. As Bill McKibben's book (see excerpt in Chapter 2) illustrates, there may be too much available for us to decide on our own whether any one item is any good. With all the clutter of competing voices and systems of interpretation, what sort of filters will help us make use of the information we have? Or are we filtering out some perspectives we had better consider?

This chapter will encourage you to look at how you gather and confirm information—how you bring in what you need to know and filter out what is irrelevant or without basis. In part, this means returning to Chapter 3's topic of observation. Getting good information may involve more of a conscious effort than is implied by the term *observation*, however, because you have to adopt or construct a working definition of what is "good" and check texts against that definition.

Looking at your basis for judgment should be an activity at several stages of writing. It's important at the outset, both while you feel your way toward a topic and while you make notes and reflect on what you are finding out. And such reconsideration is also important when you have completed a draft and are ready to start revision. Evaluating information you've gathered involves more than running through items on a checklist. The basis for evaluation can involve, at some level, questioning who you are in relation to the larger culture. What sources of information have helped form your view of the world? How reliable are they? What further sources do you trust to give the best picture of the world beyond your own senses? What stories help to shape your understanding of events? These questions, pursued seriously, connect to ideology, the subject matter of Chapter 8. But they have to be considered here as well, as part of how you think about news texts, how you use them, and in some cases how they use you.

"The news" is most commonly read as part of a story that says that *reality is largely public,* describable through clear and reasonably simple language, and capable of being made available and extracted at the reader's or viewer's convenience. The name of this story: *realism*. It's a good story, in the way we usually mean that—one that has had notable success at sustaining itself and contributing to satisfying lives for many people. It does, however, run into some problems and complications; and setting out some of the hazards of "realism" is the story of this chapter of *Rhetoric through Media.*

News and information, as a phrase, will be used in this chapter to describe the systems that gather, process, and deliver information. Much of this information has a long shelf life: Some books and articles can be relevant and influential for decades or longer. The news and information texts we call "the media" are not intended to last so long—but the *kinds* of texts have remained fairly stable since the development of the modern newspaper. (The *Oxford English Dictionary*'s earliest citation for the phrase *news-paper* is dated 1670, and another source dates the term from 1609.) These news and information texts do their work from within specific historical, social, political, and generic contexts—while implicitly encouraging the audience (us) to ignore or de-emphasize those contexts. But if we take a look at some of those contexts, we will be better equipped to understand how media address news and information to us in order to achieve certain goals—and to decide whether playing along with these goals is in our interest.

ISSUES

Stories in the News

Earlier I suggested that we think of media as extensions of conversation. Instead of being face-to-face with others, through media we can "talk" to people distant in space and time—and not just to a few, but to hundreds or thousands at once. But one crucial difference emerges between contemporary media and conversation: *Conversations are two-way.* In a conversation you can modify your comments according to your listener's reactions, and vice versa. You can ask for clarification or illustration. As a listener, you can express boredom or irritation or excitement, thereby influencing the direction of the conversation.

With a few exceptions, contemporary media are one-way systems. Even the exceptions are unequal, like conversations in which one participant dominates. Newspapers and many magazines carry letters, but these are far shorter than the articles to which they respond. Readers can "talk back" primarily by canceling subscriptions or just not buying the publication. It's even more difficult to give effective reactions to broadcast media. Most have no equivalent to the letters-to-the-editor column (exceptions include CBS's long-running *60 Minutes* and the public radio programs *All Things Considered* and

Morning Edition). Ratings and circulation figures provide the most important feedback for media producers. In most significant respects, important contemporary media, unlike conversation, deliver their texts to you but do not receive your texts in response.

At the beginning of our discussions about news media, then, it would be useful to consider this factor of one-way communication.

PAUSE FOR REFLECTION

Look back over your media log to get a sense of what proportion of the time you spend with media involves news and information. What issues have you paid attention to during this time? Why those?

Write briefly about what you want from news media. How well do the texts you use for information serve those purposes?

Also write about ways in which you characteristically think about news media. What stories have helped shape the way you think about the news and about the organizations that provide news and information? What are some of the narratives by which other people think about news?

As with other sorts of writing, you can best evaluate the category of news and information by starting with what you know already. Stories about the news furnish a good place to start. Some romanticized accounts are put in circulation through the news itself, while others are provided by films, television programs, novels, nonfiction books, and other texts. The story most often held up as an ideal to strive for is that of

1. *News as produced through a dedicated search for truth* unswayed by powerful governmental and corporate figures, the influence of money, or personal interests. This story is reinforced by narratives such as *All the President's Men,* which grew out of Watergate. Some older journalism texts echo this narrative—for example, the statement that the news reporter's "sole duty is to concentrate on discovering the truth" (MacDougall p. 17).

> He [sic] must resist all pressures from outside, whether they be from advertisers, government officials, businessmen, labor organizations, churches, ethnic groups, or any other source which has an effect on the circulation or revenue of his paper. This applies whether the newspaperman is a publisher, editor, reporter, reviewer, or columnist. Since the danger in many cases is that he will anticipate the pressures before they are exerted, and censor a news story, review, or opinion

which may hurt circulation or revenue, he has the obligation to resist the voice from within himself which tells him to play it safe. (Lerner, "A Newspaperman's Credo," from *Editor and Publisher*, reprinted in MacDougall p. 2)

Another story, somewhat at odds with this one, gives us

2. *The reporter as gritty professional* of the sort to be seen in *The Front Page* and, in 1995, in *The Paper* and *I Love Trouble.* The mythic figure in this case pecks out hard-boiled prose on an old manual with two fingers while holding a lit cigarette; keeps late hours; drinks hard; and turns in hard-hitting, Hemingwayesque copy.

Other stories may strike antiromantic stances—for example,

3. *News organizations as businesses that keep the public informed.* These serve an important public function, but always within the mandate to turn a profit. Related to this is yet another story,

4. *News organizations as suppliers of consumer products.* In this story news, information, entertainment, and many other texts are products to be delivered to essentially passive readers for a fee. Two more stories stress political components. The first is

5. *News as part of the system by which society is organized into ruling class, management, and workers.* In this story, news organizations work largely for those in power, who can thereby voice their opinions and persuade those of us not in power that it's in our best interests to go along. The other politically directed story fits a conspiracy model:

6. *News as written by liberals and leftists in order to misinform if not corrupt the general populace.*

These stories and others are important guides to how we receive the news. What is interesting is the currency of several contradictory stories and systems of interpretation, rather than one that predominates. The news, and accounts of those who produce it and who profit from it, do not in themselves prove or disprove any of these stories. At the outset of discussions about news, then, it's important to know what *your own* stories are, to the extent they can be described as your own. What are your typical judgments about news media? What are these based on? What keeps you working within those stories or systems of interpretation, and why are those stories satisfying to you?

The term *stories* here closely resembles what I called myths in Chapter 1. Stories or myths are satisfying to us to the extent that they give us explanations about our lives. If all we have are events, one after the other, having no connection or logic, the world does not reflect any satisfying humanness. Culture provides us with maps for reading the world—maps that come complete with guides for interpretation. One basic property of our maps for news is the desire for beginnings and middles and ends, for confirmation of events that are important to who we (collectively) are. We read the news from within a need for stories that provide some organization and sense of purpose. And in the process, we select from all the available stories those that fit most comfortably with our own subcultural and community and individual preferences—or, it might be said, we are who we are because of those selections, many of which have been made for us.

Each of stories 1 through 6 above has its satisfactions. The one about the "dedicated search for truth" gives us a sense of drama and the satisfactions of an image of grand ideals and virtues. Story number 2 humanizes its figures, making them ordinary citizens whose work is all the more interesting for its earthy origins. Stories 3 and 4 bring news into the more general narrative of the marketplace, with its translation of most human actions to abstract financial equivalents—which also has its satisfactions. Stories 5 and 6 appeal to those who like the drama of conspiracies and worldwide conflicts. In this case as in others, what we want to believe or what we expect to see strongly influences our perceptions of how things are.

Not only are these stories about the news business as a whole: A crucial convention for news articles is to have a central focus or theme, generally signaled by the headline and an early paragraph, that constitutes a larger story or narrative into which that article is inserted. For example, an account of a football game becomes part of that team's season—the progress toward a championship, another near miss, another mediocre season, rebuilding, or the story of the coach's incompetence. Such an account might fit into the story of a few individual heroes who manage to pull the game out, even though there are forty-five team members on the field. It might fit into stories about how athletes aren't what they used to be in the good old days, or about how athletes are better now than ever. Or it might portray sports as being about character, either positively or negatively. Stories about political figures are fitted into continuing narratives along these same lines—success, failure, characteristic problems, and so on.

These narratives help us understand the significance of any day's events as featured in the news, and equally important, they give a common perspective. But these larger narratives are also the subject of complaints by those so treated: No human being is as simple as these stories suggest, and they tend to bring to prominence moments that are less than flattering.

During the 1992 presidential campaign, for example, when President Bush was trying to get across the message of his experience and international expertise, in contrast with then Governor Clinton's more limited experience as governor of Arkansas, Bush had the misfortune to come down with flu in Japan and vomit during a state dinner. Anyone can become sick, and presidents have cameras trained on them far more often than most of us—but Bush's illness became a powerful message that undercut the image he would have preferred, that of a statesman in control.

Stories are often signaled by key words or phrases. Look for these signals in the following news item.

Barcia Joins Conservatives in Fight against Unfunded Mandates
WASHINGTON—Democratic Rep. James Barcia joined the conservative bandwagon Thursday by signing on as a co-sponsor of a far-reaching constitutional amendment to restrict unfunded federal mandates....

"I believe that states and local communities should have the responsibility of deciding what programs they can afford to fund.... The federal government should not be in the business of dictating to the states where they can spend their valuable resources.

"To think otherwise is, in my opinion, an inside-the-beltway mentality," said Barcia.

State and local governments have complained for years about Congress adopting legislation and federal agencies drafting regulations that cost them millions of dollars. Unfunded mandates are the orders Washington issues on everything from protecting spotted owls to making buildings wheelchair-accessible without providing the money to carry them out.

Although Democrats raised a string of technical objections during the first day of Senate debate on the proposal, key lawmakers of both parties said the power of the "no money, no mandate" message was so great that some kind of legislation is likely to pass.

Republicans hail it as their first landmark legislation of the session, but many Democrats question its consequences as they fear for environmental and health and safety requirements they maintain the public wants.

[From *Midland County Review*, Jan. 23, 1995, p. 1. Used by permission.]

QUESTIONS:

1. In the first paragraph, what is implied by "joined the conservative bandwagon"? Does this phrase suggest that the congressman has given careful thought to the proposal, or that he's just going along with the crowd? What is implied by the term "far-reaching"? Consider some alternative possibilities: extensive, sweeping, wholesale, indiscriminate, radical, extreme.
2. What is the effect of the phrase "inside-the-beltway mentality" in the third paragraph?

3. Why are the examples of federal regulations in the fourth paragraph spotted owls and wheelchair-accessible buildings rather than, say, school lunches, restrictions on hazardous materials in the workplace, or rules governing nursing homes? How do you respond to the allusion to wheelchair ramps if you use a wheelchair?

Narratives in the background of this and other articles might be thought of as stories made from the news (and other materials). They usually don't originate with the media, but pick up on themes and ideas present already; and their presence in media reinforces popular reaction. As with gossip or jokes, it's usually hopeless to look for the origins of these stories. They bounce back and forth between media and audience, or are passed around. They circulate, like coins. Just whose coin is that? It's yours now, until you spend it, and then it's someone else's.... Ideas and stories may carry an image, like the profile of Lincoln on the penny, but they aren't really anyone's property.

A familiar term for many of these common stories is **stereotypes.** A stereotype literally is the method of printing newspapers from cylindrical plates, a method developed in the mid-19th century, which greatly sped up the production of newspapers. The term became a useful metaphor for habitual ways of thinking that can be kept on the shelf for easy reference.

Stereotypes might be thought of as stories that serve as convenient guides for characterizing people and events. They wouldn't be used if they weren't useful; that is, we don't always want to know people and events in their full complexity. It's easier to start with something familiar and vary from that, rather than invent a new category.

Information, by definition, involves something new. If you know something already, information about it is not information for you, but confirmation. If information is sufficiently new, it will take some time to comprehend it. For example, late in World War II, reports about the systematic murder of the Jews in territory controlled by Nazi Germany were so new and horrifying that it was difficult for many on the Allied side to process that information. (Some in the United States and elsewhere were aware of mass deaths in the concentration camps, however, as is shown by documents in the U.S. Holocaust Museum in Washington, D.C.) Once the concept of the Holocaust was grasped and publicized, however, the term became available for extended use as an analogy—for example, to characterize murders by the Khmer Rouge in Cambodia, Hutus in Rwanda, or Serbs in Bosnia.

Stereotypes work to familiarize information so that it can be easily digested. However, they present a conflict with an ideology widely valued in the United States, that of the uniqueness of each individual. All of us can be labeled by race or age or religion or region or profession. But such labeling violates our belief in our uniqueness.

PAUSE FOR REFLECTION

Generate a list of stereotypes, using and adding to the categories just listed. Have you been stereotyped by others? By whom, on what basis, and with what appropriateness?

The following essay illustrates some effects of stereotypes, as seen by the author—and also shows her working through some of their implications.

SABRINA CANTU

It's O.K. to Make Fun of Jesus, If He's Black

It was a late Friday night when I went to a little get-together at an African-American friend's apartment. Most of the people were sitting around playing cards and drinking. I also had a couple of drinks. There were people playing cards in the dining room. It was when I entered this room that I noticed a painting hanging on the wall. It was a painting that looked so familiar, yet very peculiar. The background of the painting contained clouds of every color, mostly pastels. And the central image was of a man with a white cloth tied around his waist, which reminded me immediately of biblical times. But the man wearing the cloth was a black man. The color of his skin was not black but more of a coffee brown tone. It was a black man with a well-defined body and long dreadlocks that hung to his waist.

I must have been staring at the picture for a while, because a young man standing next to me asked, "What are you looking at?" To which I asked, "Is that painting supposed to be a black Jesus?" At first he couldn't hear me clearly because most of the people were in the dining room or the adjoining living room talking. I started to think back to the *Autobiography of Malcolm X* where I faintly remembered the theory that Jesus was a black man. So I asked in a louder tone, "Is that supposed to be a black Jesus?" To which the young man answered, "Yes." I looked back at the painting and said to myself out loud, "He looks like a gangster to me." I knew that I had said this loud enough for nearly everyone in the apartment to hear, and if it weren't for the sudden uproar of laughter in the apartment I would have been ashamed of myself for making such a comment.

At first I couldn't believe that everyone in the apartment was laughing, because except for me, everyone there was African-American. Some people were laughing so hard that they were literally rolling on the ground and holding their stomachs. So I began to laugh too, although I hadn't intended the comment to be funny. To my surprise, the owner of the portrait was laughing and another African-American male agreed with my statement, saying, "Yeah, he does look like a gangster or a dope dealer with all them dreadlocks." Another person exclaimed, "I thought the same thing when I seen it." Shortly after, the laughter died down and we all went back to drinking and playing cards. But throughout the night there were quick glimpses of the picture and tiny chuckles following.

After rereading books that challenge one's ideology such as *The Autobiography of Malcolm X*, and novels such as *The Color Purple* and *Temple of My Familiar*, both by Alice Walker, I've often thought back to that moment in my friend's dining room, and wondered why I and so many other young people, including African-Americans, have such a hard time imagining Jesus any color but white. Well, it's not too hard to see why, once you think about it. Since the time we are born we are presented with images, photographs, and portrayals in which Jesus is a white man. When I was one week old I was baptized at a Catholic church which displayed a most detailed icon of Jesus nailed to the cross. That Jesus was a white man. I remember going to religious services with my grandmother and trying to read her books that were all in Spanish, and yet Jesus in those books was not of Latin descent, but he was a white man. As I watched movies on television about Jesus and his disciples, I took the white men for being the actual characters they were portraying. And when someone finally did tell me that those were only actors, and Jesus didn't look exactly like the man on TV, I still took it as truth that Jesus was white, with dark hair, and he even had blue eyes.

I've been in the homes of white people and in idols and portraits they present Jesus as a white man. As I go into the homes of my Christian family, I see paintings of Jesus and he is always white. When I go into the homes of African-Americans, Jesus is always portrayed as a white man. So, when I went into the home of this young African-American who challenged the idea of Jesus being a white man by purchasing a painting that depicted Jesus as black, I couldn't accept it. The sad part about this whole ideology of Jesus being white is the opposite ideology of a gangster being black.

Why is it that I truly thought this painting of a black man with a well-defined body looked closer to a portrayal of a gangster than to an athlete, a bodybuilder, or a nutritionist? Why is it that a young African-American man thought the dreadlocks signified a dope dealer rather than a musician or a dancer? Well, doesn't the media portray those with dreadlocks to be Jamaicans? Most of the time. And aren't we simultaneously presented with the idea, through television media especially, that Jamaicans sell large amounts of marijuana?

It's no wonder now that all the young African-Americans at the party laughed when they heard my statement. They live in the same country I do. A country where the media has proved to be very influential at shaping people's thoughts. So, they grew up with the same ideologies as I did. They were taught that Jesus was white also. And when they saw that painting hanging on the dining room wall, in their minds they were probably making fun of the black Jesus. [Used by permission.]

QUESTIONS:
1. Based on the description of the painting, how does it work as a medium? What messages are communicated to Sabrina Cantu through the painting?
2. What difference do you think it would have made if she had encountered the painting in an art museum?
3. The reconsideration of stereotypes described in the essay is carefully framed as within the author's personal experience. What effect does this have, as contrasted with a more third-person approach?
4. Might there be some alternative explanations for the reactions of others at the party, besides those the author sets out?

News texts, like ads and entertainment texts, are sometimes criticized for furthering stereotypes already present in the culture. Senior citizens are frequently presented as crime victims, or as people who are feeble-minded, weak, or dying. Gang violence is sometimes treated in news stories in such a way as to contribute to the perception that gangs are exclusively African American, Spanish-speaking, or (rarely) Asian, and that young men of these ethnic backgrounds are likely to be violent. People in their twenties are labeled as "Generation X," directionless and cynical about their place in society. What astrologers say about the influence of the stars is true of stereotypes: They incline but do not compel. There are many exceptions to stereotypes in news media, and in other sorts of media. But it's much easier for producers of media texts to make use of stereotypes than to work against them in order to connect with audiences. Our own values appear to us to be natural and right, and others' values seem strange to the extent that they do not coincide with ours. The "naturalness" of looking at pictures makes stereotyping even more of a factor in television than in print media. And this stereotyping is a factor in far more than reading news: Local and national political leadership has been slow to open up to women and minorities, in part because of the tenacity of stereotypes suggesting that leaders should be "male, white, middle-aged, wealthy, physically attractive, healthy, intelligent, forceful, moderately religious, heterosexual, and monogamous" (Schwoch, White, and Reilly p. 45).

How to Search for Information

If you want to become more adept at recognizing and resisting stereotyping, you will have to broaden your usual ways of getting information. Both when you write and when you are a member of the audience, it's in your interest to examine your sources and how you organize them. News comes to us through existing stories, and news is also understood through these stories—not the same stories for everyone, of course. If everything comes to us through stories, whose stories are they? How does their origin affect our writing? How do *we* participate in stories, as writers as well as readers?

Sabrina Cantu's essay above is a narrative of discovery. Most of it is framed in terms of a moment of recognition—of seeing a painting of a black Jesus with the iconography of religious imagery transmuted to that of a crime story, or vice versa. But the discovery doesn't stop there, or with Cantu's unguarded comment at the party: It is extended to her reading of the texts mentioned in the fourth paragraph (*The Autobiography of Malcolm X, The Color Purple,* etc.) and to her rethinking and her shaping of encounters with stereotypes into the form of a story with a beginning, a middle, and an end.

Allowing your own news stories to fit familiar patterns can be comforting. Stories have plots (beginnings and middles and ends), and they have characters whose actions are connected with these plots. Like the narrative in Cantu's essay, the news comes to us through events with their own plots; but the events are gathered into larger stories as well—*metanarratives* or *master narratives.* The story of the painting told above connects to others about challenges to the writer's ideology, which are in turn part of a metanarrative about reaching maturity in a contemporary, ethnically diverse United States. Similarly, newspaper stories connect to master narratives. A Wal-Mart store opens in town, there's a burglary someplace, political leaders talk about the budget or a foreign conflict—these separate accounts may not belong together logically, but we make them fit regardless. The stories tease us by saying just so much and no more, and we plug them into other stories, as in a connect-the-dots puzzle.

The desire to know more and to have a coherent picture of reality keeps us reading and keeps us "writing," whether we literally write or not. Wanting to know more, to fill in more of the puzzle, can serve as a reason for finding out things. This desire can be useful to you in the practical matter of assignments. You have an idea for an essay, or even a complete draft setting out the idea: What next?

Start with curiosity: What do you want to know more about? If you are curious about something, perhaps your reader will be as well. Some questions you can answer by asking yourself, on the basis of your experience and imagination; answering other questions may require the collective experience of others.

Some of the impulse to find out more comes not from you but from your reader(s). Throughout your education teachers have been pressing you to find out more. While some of this may have been phrased in terms of a course requirement—*You have to do a research paper because it's a requirement for this course*—in most cases it's not the paper written in fulfillment of a given assignment, but the ability to do research, that is the real goal.

Many careers require the ability to solve problems, and part of that ability is being able to find and process information: to find things out from several sources and synthesize what you find into a coherent account (story). Teachers model information-gathering for their students, at all levels; and an investment counselor, banker, or manager in any number of business settings who couldn't do well at finding information needed to solve a problem would be without clients soon, and shortly without a paycheck.

Developing the ability to solve problems—whether those you take on for yourself, or those that others request or require you to deal with—means thinking in different terms about gathering information. It's not *going to the library to do some research.* There are specifics you need to find out, questions to answer, problems to be solved, and a search procedure to generate questions and get (limited) answers. Two opposing ways of thinking about using source material—that you first have an idea and then find what you need to support it, or that you first find the printed material required and then formulate a thesis—are both half true. That is, skillful use of others' work means it has to be integrated with your own, which requires that you work back and forth between your own perspectives, as you find them, and what you are finding out, in a kind of dialogue. You have to go with open time and an interest in discovering things. And discovery may mean more work at writing, not less—and perhaps even changing your opinions. What are the effects of environmental regulations on costs of products? On the other hand, what would be the costs of not having regulations, in areas such as health care and environmental damage? Responsible writing, in academic genres as well as in the media, means being fair to several possible positions—not just seizing on those that support your beliefs and ignoring those that raise objections (i.e., positions that belong in different stories). Unfortunately, that's exactly what happens sometimes, in media as in the law, politics, and advertising. You might think of research, too, as a conversation, between your sources and your eventual readers, in which you play the role of moderator.

The discussion about finding out things here will be very general. Most search procedures are discipline-related. The need to gather knowledge is common to innumerable professions, but the means of gathering—where you look and how you look—is very different for doctors and lawyers and ministers and mechanics and software salespersons and prison guards. There is undoubtedly an advantage to working within a discipline. You know the forms of inquiry, the questions to ask. Experienced reporters or writers of ad copy do their writing fairly routinely. But there is also a disadvantage to being part of a discipline, because its key questions may keep you thinking along predictable lines, rather than being able to step back and consider something new. For example, looking at media from the perspective of a college writing course may allow us to ask fundamental questions without concern for embarrassment. Those already working from inside media are not likely to ask such sweeping questions, because those questions never come up.

The point at which thinking about news can help you with your writing is in your evaluation of what you do have, particularly at the draft stage. Read through the student draft essay below, and make notes about points that raise your curiosity. Some such questions are already raised, in italics. (Note that this is a fairly early draft—there may be matters of style, development, or organization that might be improved.) Where would you like to know more? How would you go about looking?

STACEY COLE

Negativity in the Media
Why is it that when we open the newspaper, or when the radio or television is turned on, only the negative side of our world is seen and heard? [*True?*]

This also brings about another question, "What do we consider negative?" I feel negativity in the media could best be defined as "taking the worst of every situation and using it as a tool for viewer attraction." When we watch or hear of a crime, does the media include the survivors, or the people that risked their lives? Are we even aware of pure heroism, or are we just familiar with the accident? [*Test this by examples?*]

Returning to my definition of negativity in the media, I have found that negativity does not satisfy the customers to the extent of media belief. In fact, it's quite the opposite. I have heard many people make the comments, "another tragic story," or "only more bad news." I am a firm believer that positive attitudes and actions have a positive impact on the people affected by them. So what are all the murders, robberies, and political wars doing to our society's image? If we had more positive examples around us, I feel we could build a more structured positive building block for everyone. [*Are the examples representative of all the audience? How could you confirm the writer's conclusions?*]

I decided to watch and read the media for a week to see exactly how much negativity is displayed in comparison to the positive aspect. My references included: *ABC News*, drama series, *Bay City Times* news, and various radio stations. I found it difficult to find anything positive in a seven-day period. I couldn't find one inspiring story on the front page of the *Bay City Times*. Heroic acts, uplifting ideas, and pleasant stories were buried within the paper. Sometimes they weren't even there. The front page usually had a picture of a burning building, a murder trial, or a political issue. *ABC News* always started the evening highlights with the latest crime, war, or tragic story. Again, no survivors listed, political breakthroughs, or heroic acts were mentioned. The radio seemed to follow much of the same pattern. Television dramas such as *COPS, Unsolved Mysteries,* and various talk shows seemed to thrive on the downside of our environment. Radio, newspapers, and television news seem to display negativity in the same fashion. What is meant by this is that all seem to reflect on the negativity in our world. Topics seemed more broad and distant. Not much of this was close to home and personal. At the other end, talk shows seemed to hit closer to home. Most of these stories were personal, dealing with family or personal problems, topics that usually are considered to be none of anyone's business. [*Wide enough sample? List examples? Are political issues always negative? Establish that the TV dramas listed here are representative? Might it be considered positive to deal with family or personal problems?*]

I feel, as a society, we have grown to accept the negativity that is displayed day in and day out. It has come to the point that a positive, influential story would shock us as viewers. I think the media has become quite predictable. The only difference is variation in scene or time. People in our society have become very aware of the problems our world holds, we don't need it forced down our throats. I feel that in order to conquer a change, the media has to alter the focus of day-to-day issues that are presented. I understand that current issues must be brought to the attention of the public eye. I don't agree that the media should dig up as much dirt as possible and use it as a satisfaction to viewers. What does satisfy the viewers? Does watching every murder, robbery, war, and the reason and whereabouts of every jail sentence make us feel better as a society? Or would it satisfy us to see and hear of some good that our world actually holds? You as a reader decide.

The sitcom *Murphy Brown* aired a very interesting show a few weeks ago. The emphasis was the news station trying to find a heartfelt story to air for the viewers. The newscast found it almost to be impossible. This went side by side with my argument. [*Is a work of fiction really confirmation of the trend described?*]

I don't feel that it's difficult to find good news. I feel the media's priorities are elsewhere. To define this theory, I feel that the media is still hooked on the myth that violence, tragedy, and other forms of negativity attract the attention of the viewer. I feel that media tries to relate to cinema; that is, the idea that violence and danger thrill the viewer. Much of this holds true. But aren't fiction and real life two different ideas? Isn't fiction–fantasy viewed a lot different from true-life stories? I feel it's safe to answer "yes" to these questions. [*Examples from cinema? How would we be able to confirm that "fiction–fantasy" is different from "true-life stories"?*]

I realize that it would be impossible to avoid negativity completely in our media, it's part of life. I feel a mixture of good and bad would show promise. Wouldn't people welcome an uplifting story? It's these stories that linger in the minds of viewers longer than any tragic story. Instead of a robbery on the front page of the paper, let us see someone's life that was saved and the people that committed themselves to help. Let's put some inspiring details in the evening news highlights. We may be surprised to see who will stay up to watch the late-night news. We also may be surprised at the reviews that would come about. [*Aren't there some "uplifting" stories?*]

The theory that negativity is the onset of more negativity often holds true. I want the media to show us the good that's often buried beneath all the bad. The outcome would very likely be a positive one. Viewers may start looking forward to what will be presented, instead of dreading what the next day has in store for us. Let's give "good" a chance, we may find that the world isn't such a bad place to live. [*How could we test this theory?*] [Used by permission.]

ASSIGNMENT
Examine the essay above, or "Publishers' Clearing House" on pages 133–134 in Chapter 3, and write a brief set of recommendations to the author, outlining some points at which more information would be useful to you in reading the essay. What resources would be good starting points?

With your own writing, once you decide on some questions for further consideration, where do you go from there? That depends on what sort of information the genre and context require. You might be looking primarily for further illustrations or confirmation of a general media trend you've already observed, as with the example of negative news stories in Stacey Cole's essay. Or you might want to take the context deeper, looking to substantiate your theme by looking for articles and books that qualify or question the stories implied by the media cited. These aims require you to look in different places.

Several major newspapers (for example, the *New York Times* and the *Washington Post*) publish indexes to make it easier to find stories on particular topics. Print indexes have something of an old-fashioned flavor about them now that CD-ROM and databases can be found in most libraries—but they continue to work when the power is off. (Electronic search devices and search strategies are discussed in Chapter 11.)

PAUSE FOR REFLECTION
Look at one of the quarterly *New York Times Indexes* in a convenient library. Check the heading under "News and News Media": How much do the entries there have to do with each other? How are the entries under any single heading organized?

As an illustration, consider the possibility for using the July–September 1994 *New York Times Index* for a paper on minorities and news media. The following entries appear to be relevant:

Earl Caldwell, black journalist whose career as a columnist at New York Daily News was cut short in dispute over column about alleged sexual assault on five black men by a white New York police officer, sees a disturbing racial division in journalism; his recent problems in news business have had reverberations for many minority journalists; photo (M), Jl 18,D,6:1

Over 6,000 minority journalists meet in Atlanta, Ga, to advance what their leaders say is goal of making newsrooms and reporting more inclusive of all Americans; Paul DeMain, president of convention, Unity '94, comments (M), Jl 29,A,12:1

Issue of political correctness is addressed at convention of minority journalists in Atlanta, Ga; one view is that news media are paralyzed by political correctness and can no longer tell the truth; second view is that term 'political correctness' has become weapon used by those who want to squelch honest discussion and block people's demand for respect (M), Ag 1,D,6:4

Whether the entries are relevant might depend on the particular focus for your topic—you might have to read the article (in newspaper or microfilm format) to determine that.

Not all the work is done for you by indexes and databases. If you know the precise date you are looking for, one index may be enough—but if (as with the topic cited above) there's no special reason to concentrate on one three-month period, you may have to look through several volumes, even through several years. In addition to newspapers with a national scope, there's usually at least one state newspaper that is recognized as a valuable source for state-level events. As for local coverage, you will have to inquire about that with your reference librarian.

Indexes for magazines are organized differently—not by the specific publication, as with newspaper indexes, but by the kind of journal. Popular magazines are indexed in the *Reader's Guide to Periodical Literature,* whose thick green volumes are to be found in academic and public libraries. For publications more specialized than *Harper's* and *Esquire* and the *Atlantic* (not to mention *Cosmopolitan* and the *Reader's Digest*), you may need to look in indexes by discipline, such as the *Humanities Index,* the *Social Sciences Index,* the *Education Index,* the *Business Index,* and, for literature and language, the *Modern Language Association International Bibliography* (mostly in academic libraries). Several of these, as well as commercial research systems, are available in electronic form.

More complex topics may require work with books. One good strategy for research is to use fairly recent books or scholarly articles as bibliographic resources—because recent books and articles will generally include lists of works cited. (The extent and quality of the bibliography is a good clue to how "academic" a publication is, and how its citation will be regarded by a professional or college audience.) Sometimes a publication's bibliography will lead to sources that are of more use than the initial source. And if you are looking at several sources that mention the same work, that will give you a clue to its importance.

With subjects related to broadcast media, there are limitations to what you can find conveniently. Archives for nonprint texts are less generally available than the indexes given above. If you are looking for recent or classic films, libraries and video stores may be useful, provided the title isn't too obscure. Well-stocked academic libraries may carry indexes such as *Television Network Daytime and Late-Night Programming, 1959–1989* and *Television Network Prime-Time Programming, 1948–1988,* which give titles of programs, debuts, dates of cancellation, and so on. But archives of radio and television broadcasts—particularly commercials—are rare and difficult of access. (This in itself tells you something about how these texts are regarded culturally.) In order to gather information about a television or radio broadcast, you may have to draw on a secondary text such as a promotional article, a review, or critical articles or books (if any).

Often, too, the issue is not how to find material, but how to recognize what you need to find. This, in turn, is a function of knowing your audience and what you have to say on a subject. If you are working with a subject such as news and information, it may be a productive strategy to begin with your preconceptions on a subject, look for material that can confirm these or call them into question, and go from there. Generally, college writing requires more careful examination of preconceptions and statements about subjects than many of us are accustomed to. One set of such preconceptions may be the notion of what is considered to be news.

What Counts As News?

The category of "news" goes back a long way, even though news items generally do not include much history. (If it's *history,* it's not *news.*) Newspapers originated in the seventeenth century and developed especially during the nineteenth century, when print media were dominant. Newspapers allowed those with something to say to reach dozens or hundreds at once, and other than hiring the town hall and giving a speech, newspapers were the only choice. In some cases, the impulse was the same—the publisher/editor/ reporter (often the same person) had something to say. The challenging part was to persuade others that it might be worth their buying and reading the paper to see what this was. While operating a newspaper was never cheap, producing and distributing a newspaper was within the means of many, and even small towns often had several competing papers. Frequently these were associated with political parties, and they were much less dependent on advertising revenue than modern newspapers.

Over the last fifty years, the numbers of newspapers printed have declined, so that it's relatively rare now to live in a city served by more than one newspaper. This recent concentration of print (and other) media organizations is paradoxical, because ours is sometimes labeled "an information society." Think of all the forms in which information is presented to you in a typical day. You could start with your media log, but that probably covers the times when you were reading the newspaper or a magazine, watching a television program, listening to the radio, and so on—activities that *you* sought out. What about the other forms of information thrust in your face? Messages on a pad or Post-it, notes on the refrigerator, labels on dozens of products, billboards on the highway, Christmas card greetings, product guarantees, insurance policies, cash register receipts, bumper stickers, T-shirts.... My cat meows at me when I go to the basement, calling my attention to the empty food dish—that's information. The dog barks from the back porch—stranger (or strange dog) in the neighborhood. Information. A siren sounds, the doorbell rings, mail is put into the mailbox, horns honk. If your media log were extended to all forms of communication, verbal or nonverbal, you'd spend your days keeping track of your days. The task would be like making a map of the country on a 1:1 scale—a map as large as the country.

Maps are useful because they bring something that is large down to a manageable scale, and the same is true of information. Without even thinking about it, we sort information into categories and access items according to what we need at the moment. Maps and categories are necessary simplifications. If for some reason I need to think about international affairs, the notes on the refrigerator are of little use to me; and if I need a reminder about next Thursday night, I don't look in the *Wall Street Journal.* Some of this sorting we do ourselves, but most of it is done for us, according to systems that were in place long before we were born. What we need is a map for this sorting.

What is it that separates the category of information our culture calls **news** from other sorts of information? We are all confident in believing we know what is meant by news—until we try to define exactly what fits that title and what doesn't. Working from our internal sense will carry us a good way: We know implicitly that whatever is meant by *news,* it probably doesn't extend to a billboard for antiques, a guarantee for a camera, or a dog's bark. But what does it extend to?

We might start with the operational definition that news is what newspapers print. That seems to work until we start to ask questions about what is found in the newspaper. What about advertisements—at least 35 percent of any newspaper, on average, more than any other category (Bagdikian pp. 136–37)? Well, no. Ads aren't news. Letters to the editor? Not ordinarily, unless written by Elvis. Editorials? The comic page? The bridge column? Would a feature on aspiring songwriters in mid-Michigan count? (Perhaps.) Film, TV, and book reviews? League standings in professional and college sports? What about columnists' commentary—is that news? Saying that news is whatever goes in the newspaper is about as useful, or useless, as saying that literature is anything taught in classes about literature. Some portions of the newspaper are considered news, while other portions are not.

Etymologically the term *news* is tied to the new: to something recent, notable, or unusual. It suggests that we don't need to hear (as news) something we already know. There's a folk etymology connecting the word *news* to the points of the compass (North, East, West, South); the word antedates the familiar indicator of directions on maps, but the N-E-W-S idea does indicate that news directs our attention elsewhere, in directions other than looking at ourselves.

News is as slippery a term as *literature*—and in fact it is used the same way, as a way of claiming value. "Real news you can use" expresses more than the producer's hope that we will find it useful—it puts forward news (real news) as a category of approval, in the way that literature (real literature) is sometimes put forward in English classes. One critic, in discussing conflicting definitions for literature, argues that the term *literature* is like the term *weed*, but positive rather than negative: Any plant you don't want growing where it's growing is a weed, and literature is any kind of writing we (collectively) like. Perhaps news works like this—news is writing that tells us something we feel we should know, something of a more public and a more temporary kind than literature.

 The database "Nexis reports 24,142 newspaper articles mentioning O.J. in 1995, compared with 12,175 containing the word 'racism,' 7,288 touching on 'welfare reform,' and a mere 1,592 on the subject of global warming." (Barbara Ehrenreich, "Media Matters," *The Nation*, Nov. 6, 1995, p. 529.)

If news is information that we like or need because of its seriousness or importance, perhaps the definition can depend on the audience. However, that idea doesn't take us much farther, because audiences for news are highly various. As an audience, we may draw our news principally from one medium or from several; we may read news texts intensely or superficially; we may read so as to give equal or unequal weight to several categories of news (international, national, local, oriented to special concerns such as business or health). Not many readers read systematically. Most of us graze.

One book on writing for media gives as a definition for news "anything timely that interests a large number of persons, and the best news is that which has the greatest interest for the greatest number." (Rivers and Work p. 61) But this definition gives precedence to events or circumstances that are of some shallow interest to a great many people, such as the weather, and scants events that may be of intense interest to a smaller percentage, such as atomic tests in the South Pacific.

Readers read newspapers differently. A study done in 1960 indicated the following differences among readers.

50.4%	Proceed through most of the paper one page after another and read whatever is interesting
14.2%	Proceed through the paper page by page, but scanning quickly
20.0%	Turn first to some specific item (e.g., the stock market tables or a particular column) and then proceed through the paper one page after another
2.8%	Turn to a specific item but do not look at or read anything else

(Newsprint Information Committee, *A National Study of Newspaper Reading* [1961], vol. II, p. 17; rpt. Bush, p. 41)

A 1982 survey by Newspaper Readership Project asked what readers usually read or look at in the paper. The responses:

89%	News about the local community
86%	News about the economy
84%	World news
74%	News about local politics or government
61%	Calendar of local events
53%	Obituaries
51%	Sports news and news about local schools, colleges, or clubs

(Brian S. Brooks, George Kennedy, Daryl R. Moen, and Don Ranley. *News Reporting and Writing*, 3rd ed. New York: St. Martin's, 1988).

In most current news media, we are given an assortment of news items, and we select what to pay attention to. This selection, usually habitual and unconscious, takes place on several levels: through our choices of news sources—newspapers, magazines, television, radio, other media—and of segments of those sources. The modern newspaper is designed on the assumption that readers will skim, selecting sections and then headlines as guideposts for what to give further attention to. Remote controls make a version of this possible for television watchers—except that there's no convenient way to know what is being shown on another channel before changing to it. Another practice may be shifting attention between media, as in reading the evening paper while the radio or television is on.

Studies show that, on average, fewer than half the readers of a newspaper who begin a story finish it if it is seven paragraphs or more in length.

The assumption built into this system is that of the marketplace. If you found that the *Herald* didn't meet your needs, you could buy the *Tribune* instead—at least until they merged into the *Herald-Tribune*. Something like that assumption is carried over into any contemporary newspaper: headlines, lead paragraphs, graphics, and photographs allow you to see at a glance what any story is about, and you can either read it word for word or let your gaze pass over it and on to something else. It might be said that, because of this selectivity, no two people read the same newspaper.

Newspapers follow a strictly conventional scheme for signaling the importance of whatever is inside, and perhaps examining these conventions is our best hope for defining news. Page 1 is usually reserved for what is judged to be the most important news of the day, with clear lead stories at the top, and stories of lesser importance "below the fold." "Inside" stories rank farther down, in importance, and separate features such as sports and what used to be called "the women's section" (now usually given a title such as "lifestyles") still farther down the hierarchy. Because as readers we often skim through the newspaper, we can choose whether or not to take an interest in conventionally important news. News gives us a map for understanding the world, then, but it's a map whose accuracy we need to confirm from time to time.

The conventions of the front page combine an assessment of newsworthiness with the desire to attract audiences, by sensationalism or other means. The publisher of *USA Today*, Allen Neuharth, reportedly directed his editors to keep this principle in mind: "'When you run a picture of a nice clean-cut all-American girl like this, ...get her tits above the fold'" (Lee and Solomon p. 7).

PAUSE FOR REFLECTION

Test your acquired knowledge about the conventional importance of news stories. The following topics are drawn from an issue of the *Christian Science Monitor.* Which would you put where? Indicate order of importance as follows: A—page 1; B—back cover; C—pp. 2–3 or just inside back cover; D—deep inside pages. (Answers on page 165.)

Review of new book about Francisco Franco _____
President's speech fails to convince opposition _____
Home cities of Super Bowl teams prepare to party _____
Report on president's State of the Union address _____
Arts feature on early 20th-century painter, Thomas Eakins _____
Column from Jordan—Arabs object to Western stereotypes _____
Travel article on trip to Himalayas _____
Editorial commentary about "new covenant" theme in president's speech _____

What we consider news, then, is to a large extent defined by the conventions of news texts, through which we understand the news. Confusion about what counts for news may be the result of conflicts about the purposes of newspapers (and, by extension, of other organizations that collect and distribute information to the public). Most news organizations would probably agree that their purpose is to keep the public informed about events and decisions of importance; but that statement masks further questions. Is the singular form "the public" really so unitary? What are "events and decisions of importance"? Of importance to whom?

Operationally, these matters are left to professional judgment (that of editors, reporters, and other personnel), which keeps the news organization moving along smoothly, so long as there's no ruckus raised; sales or market share are acceptable; and the publisher, producer, and others of influence like the product. What counts as news is the result of a careful negotiation between producer and audience, which follows several sets of guidelines. Does an item fit local concerns? Can we cover it? Is it good TV/radio/print news? Does it offend people whose good opinion is important to maintain? If a newspaper misrepresents facts, the result could be a libel suit or governmental inquiry. If a story's interpretation is disputed by readers, there can be angry letters, phone calls, canceled subscriptions, critical accounts in other media, or other reaction. In sufficient numbers, these responses can affect what gets covered.

Profitability has become a larger concern of late, which has meant that newspapers have merged, and publishing organizations have bought each other out and sought corporate tie-ins. These trends present the possibility both of reduced competition and of increased borrowing from other media texts. How much of a concern this is depends on your view of the marketplace and ideas.

In the United States as of 1987 there were "1,700 daily newspapers, 11,000 magazines, 9,000 radio and 1,000 television stations, 2,500 book publishers, and 7 movie studios." But this did not make for so diverse a set of media as might appear: A majority of these were owned by fifty corporations, some concentrating in print media and publishing, some in broadcasting or film production, and some across all these media (Bagdikian pp. xxvii–xxviii).

In 1995 two networks were bought by corporations—ABC by Disney and CBS by Westinghouse. (General Electric had purchased NBC in the 1980s.) In addition to strengthened ties between major communications media and large corporations outside of media, the rules were being revised to permit other sorts of consolidation. Congress in late 1995 eased restrictions on ownership of media, so that (for example) a firm could own a TV station and a newspaper in the same area. But the increasing concentration of ownership, and the potential for conflict between news gathering and profit making, are not highly visible as problems, because news texts do not announce themselves as written by anyone in particular. Also, for most readers it's not evident that it matters very much who publishes and profits from the news, or whether Houston has one newspaper or two.

Shortly after the Disney Corporation took over ABC/Capital Cities, ABC Radio Networks stopped carrying Jim Hightower's radio talk show. Hightower's consistent theme—unlike most talk radio—was criticism of large corporations, not excluding his new employers. Disney, he pointed out, requires its contract workers to pay for uniforms and tools out of an hourly salary of $4.25, in contrast to CEO Michael Eisner's $78,000 per hour. Taking ABC News to task for settling a lawsuit with Philip Morris, Hightower observed that ABC "had just merged with the Mickey Mouse empire of Disney Inc." Coincidentally, he learned of his show's cancellation the next day (*EXTRA! Update*, Dec. 1995).

Professional journalism aspires to provide media texts that are neutral and objective accounts. (Bob Woodward, who was instrumental in uncovering Watergate, has used the phrase "the best obtainable version of the truth" [Brooks et al. p. 20].) Examining this implied claim will be the basis of the next section. The tricky part in thinking about news is figuring out whose interests it serves. This requires that we in some sense negotiate the space between *we* and *I*—that is, between the collective aspect of our lives addressed by newspapers and other media (ideally, at least), and the singular and individual. Somehow, mysteriously, each of us picks an individual path through the abundance of media texts offering us information (see Exhibit 4.1). In all this large quantity of information, are we getting what we need to know?

Exhibit 4.1 Tom Tomorrow (Dan Perkins). Used with permission.

In the Pause for Reflection on page 162 above, Franco, arts feature, and travel are deep inside the paper; opposition reaction and editorial commentary are inside front and inside back; the column from Jordan is on the back page; the report on the president's speech and lead-in to the Super Bowl are from page 1. If your judgment matched up with these stories' actual locations, you are pretty well attuned to how this newspaper decided on what was important. If not, you have a different sense of their conventional location. There's no particular virtue in being well trained in this way, unless you want to work for a newspaper.

News As Rhetorical

If you use the word *media* in casual conversation, most people assume you are talking about news. News can be thought of as our culture's system of gathering and evaluating information—not the only such system, of course, but perhaps the central one. This function is in contrast to what is probably the dominant use of media, entertainment; but during important events, news contributes to a cultural bonding, a sense that we are taking part in public events, even when they are far away. (You may recall such a mood from the period of the Gulf War in late 1990–early 1991.) Because of the importance of such moments, we need to look closely at news texts' rhetoric.

Much of this chapter's discussion has drawn examples from newspapers, rather than other media—news magazines, radio, electronic news sources, and especially television. Newspapers have a long tradition, and they are easily preserved. But other media have developed their own conventions and ways of reading. Reporting in newspapers differs to some extent from that in magazines, and both differ from television and radio. There are other genres besides reporting—the interview, the review, the editorial, the column, and so on. Print news shares some but not all conventions with news on radio and television; and these also break into genres (headline services or news in brief, interviews, reports from the scene, investigative reports, etc.). When television added a camera to the conventions of radio news, the visual grammars developed for film were adapted to the new medium.

In addition to reading news texts rhetorically through a recognition of their genres and the possibilities of their media, we have to consider their context. News organizations in the United States are defined by the tension between the carefully preserved canons of journalistic integrity and the commercial system within which the news is produced. With the exception of public radio and television—principally the Public Broadcasting System and National Public Radio—U.S. media are dependent on a combination of sales and advertising for their funding. Most U.S. media must turn a profit for continued survival; the exceptions are specialized or academic publications that are supported to some extent by universities and other groups, such as the League of Women Voters, corporations, unions, specific political groups, church groups, and so on. Public, noncommercial media are defined by their contrast with (or occasional similarity to) commercial media; but since the 1980s, publicly funded media have become more commercial, with corporate sponsorship playing a more significant role in funding specified programs. In early 1995 Congress even considered proposals for doing away with public funding for the Corporation for Public Broadcasting, which provides developmental money for many programs on public radio and television.

Despite the rigorous professional canons of ethics espoused by news organizations, those who produce the news have specific interests. Just as we need to know something about the conventions of news genres, so we need to know something about the individuals and organizations producing news texts—and the entire system within which they work. Popularly we tend to think of the interests behind the news as those of individuals—especially of reporters, as shown by attacks on Dan Rather or Peter Jennings. But the ownership of news organizations and the entire commercial system is at least as powerful in influencing the rhetoric of news, and must be considered. Let's begin by considering the formal or generic qualities of news texts, their conditions of production, and their reception as well.

Forms of News

Not everything found in a newspaper or aired on a network news broadcast is generically "hard news." Journalists and some in the public have long worried about the "softening" of news: One fear is that space given to human interest stories, astrology columns, sports reporting, cooking, advice, and so on will dilute or divert attention from material presented to keep the public informed about public events. (The same argument is more rarely voiced about advertising space.) The appeal of these genres threatens the privileged one of "hard news." Another way of thinking about the growth of these "soft" genres is as a response to audience demand. One journalism textbook describes "lifestyle journalism" in the 1970s as treating as significant news those matters that are closer to the common experience of most readers: the "how-to-cope story, intended to help readers with everything from buying a new car to handling stress"; the consumer story, "developments in health care, changes in tax laws and information about the quality of goods and services"; and other genres (Brooks et al. p. 17).

According to one journalism textbook, news that appeals to many is likely to have one or more of the following characteristics: *proximity* (i.e., it happened nearby); *consequence* (it affects readers fairly directly); *human interest* ("news focusing on the individual rather than just on an event or issue"); *prominence* (concerning celebrities); *novelty, conflict, sex,* or *fun* (Rivers and Work pp. 62–63).

ASSIGNMENT
Choose three newspapers available in a convenient library—say, one with a substantial national reputation (*New York Times, Washington Post, Chicago Tribune, Los Angeles Times*), one good but more regional newspaper, and one that does not have so high a reputation. For each, review a week's worth of stories in the first section (which usually has the highest proportion of news, in contrast to columns, features, sports, etc.), and see how all the stories fit the categories named above. Do any fall outside them? How do the categories listed compare with your own sense of what makes news important for you?

As you read newspapers from different localities, how much seems to be substantially different, and how much essentially the same?

Another way to test the adequacy of such a list of categories would be to consider how well it shows why stories receive widespread coverage. In the first half of the 1990s, some representative items might include the Amy Fisher/Joey Buttafuoco intrigue; U.S. military interventions in Somalia and Bosnia; the coverage of Tonya Harding and Nancy Kerrigan in winter 1994; and the O. J. Simpson arrest and trial. Was the coverage widespread because of previously existing audience interest, which it was the media's responsibility to satisfy? Because of media treatments that stimulated audience interest? Because these stories fit with the audience's established metanarratives? Because of hype that manufactured interest? Or some combinations of these?

The implication of such categories for news is that the question "what is news?" can be answered in terms of content. Another way to define news would have to do with format or style. Newspaper texts (news reports, not commentary) are generally very compact: Five double-spaced typed pages would be a long news article. At such a length, nothing can be wasted. In an essay one paragraph corresponds to one developed idea, but in a newspaper article one idea carries you through several paragraphs. Essays are expected to have an introduction, development through several paragraphs, and a conclusion; newspaper articles have to get the essentials into the first few paragraphs, and provide more material in such a way that a story can be literally cut at any point—in a usual article format (in contrast to a column) there can be no building to a conclusion. These aspects of newspaper writing should not usually be imitated in academic writing.

Broadcast news texts are farther still from conventions of essay writing. Stories presented on television are substantially shorter even than print news texts (see Appendixes 1 and 2 at the end of this chapter); and rather than paragraph breaks, there are introductory and transitional cues ranging from theme music and breaks for commercials to a change in expression or tone of voice, a shift in camera, or the anchor's lifted eyebrow. Visual elements to a story are as important as the news writer's prose, and the interplay between visual and verbal is an important formal element.

Despite these differences, however, learning to write in newspaper format may still be good practice for some academic prose. In order to fit a limited quantity of air time or newspaper space, writers for these media have to be practiced at listening to several sources (which may conflict with each other), extracting those elements that seem to be important according to the writer's estimation of the audience, and presenting them in summary form in as few words as possible. Writing concisely is good discipline for academic work.

Not all conventions in newswriting should be followed in college work. To begin with, newswriting favors a different style from much academic writing, with more declarative sentences—that is, sentences in familiar subject-verb order without clauses added to the sentence's core. Some academic writing encourages complex sentences, whose parts can be connected so as to suggest how concepts link up to each other in more complicated fashion than would be tolerated by those skimming a newspaper. In newswriting, complicated syntax would lose the audience: They would change channels or turn the page to another story. This fact about the form of newswriting suggests a problem with the news generally: We can be kept well informed about *events* through the news, but not so well about *processes*. Analysis of complex processes often requires a complex style. Plane crashes are pretty straightforward, a matter of date and time and place and number of fatalities. But the reasons for plane crashes may or may not be straightforward. There may be a thunderstorm or ice buildup on the wings, pilot error or misdirection from airport controllers, a collision with another aircraft, or more basic causes that require a level of analysis most readers will not have patience for. If an airline company has a worse safety record than others, as happened in 1996 with ValuJet, what's the explanation? Bad luck? Problems with maintenance? Faulty personnel policies? What was the long-term effect of the government's forced resolution of the air traffic controllers' strike in the early 1980s? Should the United States consider privatizing air traffic control? Discussing these processes doesn't allow simple, one-shot treatment. The format of news stories—particularly on television—doesn't often permit careful and cautious development of subtle issues. (Such development can be approximated to some extent through a series of stories.) It's hard to get good film of an abstract issue; and lacking that, TV news just may not be interested, because the competition may be doing something more visually attractive.

In addition to the characteristic restrictions imposed by style and format, newswriting has adopted a use of example and illustration that is different from the tradition in academic writing. Most news stories are connected to a specific statement of a general theme or position (sometimes explicit, sometimes implied), which needs illustration to be convincing. This illustration usually consists of an account of one person, perhaps two or three: These may or may not be typical, but the format leads us to assume that they are.

Academic writing connects assertions to illustrations just as newswriting does—but the connections are made differently. In academic writing, it's important to make sure that the examples are representative rather than dramatic, and they should be logically connected to the argument. Newswriting's restrictions in length and format mean that reports usually must be content with one illustration per point, and this illustration is frequently chosen with an eye to dramatic effect. Typically, what we have in newswriting is a set of anecdotes or examples, and it's left to the audience to test whether these are representative and fair. Both print and broadcast journalism have gravitated towards the dramatic event as illustration, in order for a story to make maximum impact and keep the audience's attention. But the problem with this tendency is that, as readers of the news, we are likely to assume that these events are representative, when they may actually be extreme cases of what might happen. When we read the news, then, it's important to recognize the possibility of misrepresentation of this kind, and to avoid it in our own writing.

PAUSE FOR REFLECTION

Take a draft of an essay you've been working on, and write in your journal about how you would recast it as "news." Would it be possible to use the essay for news in some form? In what form? What would have to change in order for it to be successful?

Both the content and the format of a piece of writing are closely connected to the image (or illusion) of the speaker implied by the writing—what is in literary writing called the persona. The persona or speaker in a text such as a poem is sometimes closely identified with the writer, as in some Robert Frost poems; sometimes the speaker is more distant from the author. The question of how much distance exists between speaker and author is part of the game you are playing in reading a literary text—you are expected to figure it out, and to enjoy the figuring out. The term *persona* is adapted from the Greek word for mask, particularly the oversized masks worn in Greek dramas, which provided a large image of comic or tragic expression for the guidance of those in the back rows of very large audiences. The masks also held megaphone-like devices to help project the actors' voices. Nonliterary writing also involves personae. The persona of the writer of this textbook is that of someone who explains things—similar in some ways to a teacher, but with some differences. But that persona isn't to be equated with the author, who like any writer has other personae or personalities that are part of different rhetorical occasions.

Think for a moment of the image of your self that comes through your writing: How does that self differ from other selves you project in personal letters or other forms of writing? In news genres the personae are supposed to remain fairly constant. News writers, unlike storytellers in fiction, are presumed not to be playing roles but simply telling events as they happened, without personal involvement. In other words, the persona is objective. But while the form presses us to interpret the news as objective, news organizations exist in a commercial context that sometimes calls this objectivity into question.

NEWS AS COMMERCIAL

It should come as no surprise that news organizations in the United States are run as businesses. However, we are not kept conscious of the news *business* precisely because of the borders between news and the most visible signs of the commercial context, advertisements. In newspapers and magazines there are normally clear divisions between news and ads, based on borders, size of type, format, presence and use of photography, and so on. (A rare exception is pseudonews, which sometimes runs in sections devoted to real estate, for example—and this is labeled in small type as advertising.) Radio news on commercial stations is separated from ads by pauses, by a change in announcer, and by different format. Television news has similar signals and differentiations. The implication of this change in format is that the news and other programming is somehow *not* commercial.

But news organizations in and of themselves are highly profitable. By one account, the newspaper industry by the 1980s was the third largest in the country, with profit margins around 17 percent (Bagdikian pp. 119, 265–66). It can be hard to find out about profits, however, partly because some newspapers are part of "vertical" corporations—organizations owning stock in lumber companies, which sell wood for paper to paper companies (also partially owned by the newspapers), which supply the newspaper, which at the other end buys old papers for recycling. Others are involved in "horizontal" corporations, either chains of newspapers like the Gannett Corporation or conglomerates involved in books, magazines, newpapers, television, and radio.

Newspapers rely heavily on advertising, which usually supplies around two-thirds of their revenue (the rest comes from subscriptions and newsstand sales.) Similarly, magazines derive a large portion of their income from ads (see Exhibit 4.2). Editors struggle to maintain some level of independence from the business office—usually with good success, because the publication's credibility is part of what it has to sell. In the somewhat old-fashioned phrasing of the "Newspaperman's Credo": "Beset as he inevitably will be by favor-seekers, special interests, press agents, public relations men, and operators of all kinds, he must keep himself scrupulously independent of their favors and pressures. This means that he must be strong enough to make himself unpopular with those who can smooth his path or make life pleasant for him" (MacDougall p. 2). Failures to live up to this credo are sometimes found

	Magazine	Total Revenue*	Ad Revenue*	Circulation	Parent Corp.
1	TV Guide	$1,036,903	$391,727	14,037,062	News Crp.
2	People	762,714	405,713	3,424,858	Time-Warner
3	Sports Ill.	653,789	385,254	3,252,641	Time-Warner
4	Time	638,616	372,189	4,063,146	Time-Warner
5	Reader's Dig.	477,817	134,166	15,126,664	RD Assoc.
6	Parade	447,650	447,650	37,610,000	Advance Pub.
7	Newsweek	427,730	278,948	3,158,617	Wash. Post Co.
8	Better H&G	353,462	220,966	7,613,661	Meredith Corp.
9	PC Mag	325,701	276,059	1,051,381	Ziff-Davis
10	Good Housek.	315,259	218,605	5,223,935	Hearst Corp.
11	US News & WR	315,023	221,148	2,240,710	Mortimer Zuckerman
12	Business Wk.	279,241	233,799	880,357	McGraw-Hill
13	Family Cir.	260,980	178,725	5,005,301	Bertelsmann
14	Woman's Day	245,187	167,274	4,724,500	Hachette Filipacchi
15	Ladies' HJ	242,484	138,763	5,048,081	Meredith
16	Forbes	235,901	189,219	777,353	Forbes, Inc.
17	Nat. Enq.	221,197	33,976	3,066,032	American Media
18	Cosmopolitan	220,404	147,987	2,527,928	Hearst Corp.
19	USA Weekend	218,095	218,095	19,026,254	Gannett
20	Nat. Geog	212,605	47,719	7,837,993	Nat. Geog. Soc.

*Revenue figures are in thousands of dollars.

Exhibit 4.2 Top 20 Magazines by Revenue.

out and pilloried in watchdog publications such as the *Columbia Journalism Review.*

> DART to *The Wall Street Journal,* for showing why the credibility of journalists isn't a whole lot higher than the credibility of car salesmen. At a March 9 [1995] breakfast held at Chicago's Hotel Inter-Continental and jointly sponsored, as the invitation to subscribers phrased it, "by *The Wall Street Journal* and Lincoln Mercury, a Division of Ford Motor Corporation," the featured guest was "Mr. Tim Schellhardt, Chicago Bureau Chief." Also "on display," as the invitation promised, was "the all-new 1995 Lincoln Continental," along with a company representative to answer questions about the car. (*Columbia Journalism Review,* July–Aug. 1995, p. 18)

Despite well-established professional expectations, there are always temptations to favor the interests of the parent company, one's friends, local public figures, and others. In contrast to the event that earned the *Columbia Journalism Review* "dart" above, these lapses are most likely to happen unconsciously through association.

> The main traditional sources of news are people who are close to the centers of power in society—government officials, business leaders and the advisers, aides and public-relations functionaries who surround them. Most reporters still spend most of their time dealing with people who hold and exercise power—whether governmental power, political power or business power. The sought-after assignments still are those requiring reporting on the power centers with direct impact on a widespread audience—the White House, the state capitol, city hall, the school board, business and labor. (Brooks et al. pp. 18–19)

Television news has gradually established its dominance as the primary source of information for the public, and its commercial nature makes occasional incursions on the journalistic ideal of objectivity. Even though there is still a strong separation between TV commercials and other programming, anchors, reporters, and other on-screen personnel are called on to promote the network's own news and news-magazine programs. The network's earnings vary directly with ratings, because the per-minute price of advertising is tied to estimates of the number of viewers watching. This means that, for any source of news in a competitive commercial system, decisions about content and about personnel who write and deliver the news are based partly on audience appeal.

Some of the effects of the emphasis on profit are described by Neil Postman and Steve Powers in *How to Watch TV News*. Emphasis on ratings has produced the increase in "tabloid" stories—great attention paid to Susan Smith, the South Carolina mother who drowned her children, for example, even though that story had no direct or indirect effect on viewers in other parts of the country. Another side effect of the drive for more profit is the absence of context for international stories. Those who live in a region presumably know the most about events there—but their English may not be very good; they may not be accessible; they might be biased in one direction or another; and, not being from the United States, they may not tell things along lines that the domestic audience is prepared to hear. The next best thing might be to have reporters who live in a region and know the language and culture and people—but with so many countries in the world, that would get expensive. The tendency, then, is to fly a reporter or even the anchor to the location to do a stand-up and perhaps an interview—but being physically present in a place does not in itself make you an expert.

The commercial context of news, particularly television news, has taken it in the direction of entertainment, which has resulted in blurring of those categories. Television news stories are likely to be selected on the basis of visual appeal rather than significance, so that (for example) the failure of savings and loans institutions is downplayed because there's nothing to film, while fires and floods and car wrecks predominate, particularly in local news. What gets onto the news may be decided in part on the basis of what there's film for. And in the treatment of "hard news," personal dimensions are emphasized: Individuals are interviewed on camera, and their versions of events are rarely questioned or placed into context. Some of the results of these dimensions to television news can be seen in the CBS and CNN treatments of a story under Reading the News Comparatively, later in this chapter.

The following essay is written by a student with a background in journalism. Look for places in which the essay indicates an interest in shaping the news to the purposes of entertaining readers.

JAMES AMEND

A Spicier, More Racy New Medium

As a former "member of the media," I continually find myself looking at conventions in the newspaper medium. I not only read newspaper articles for the facts, but I also like to see what conventions the writer used to deliver his story. Or perhaps I would be more correct saying that I tend to look for "unconventional" deliveries.

For years journalists stuck to one style of writing, the inverted pyramid. Picture if you will an upside-down pyramid, the most important material delivered at the top of the story and then, as the piece fades out, the incidentals thrown in at the end. I think we are seeing a trend now of hard news writers taking a feature-writer approach to their stories. Instead of "just the facts, ma'am," news writers are now trying to keep the reader through the entire story.

In conventional newswriting, of for example an auto fatality, the writer would deliver the who, what, when, where, why and how in the first paragraph, if not the first sentence. An example would be—A 24-year-old Caro man was killed yesterday after being struck by a motorist at the intersection of State St. and Monroe St. Meanwhile an unconventional delivery would go something like this—It was a walk John T. Smith had taken many times. He would leave his house early in the afternoon, head down Monroe St. to State St. and across to his mother's Madison St. residence for dinner. The day was also routine for Philip K. Walker. A few early morning beers on the porch and then off to the liquor store for the hard stuff. Then, according to police, it was downtown to a local pub for some serious late-afternoon drinking. Neither man had any clue their paths would fatally cross at 5:15 p.m. yesterday.

I like to think of the first example as *USA Today* journalism: delivering the facts quickly and allowing the reader to move on. The second, however, reaches out and pulls the reader in; keeps him or her looking for facts, picking up morsels of information one sentence at a time. I like to think of it as feeding them just enough so they'll stay hungry through the entire story.

The *USA Today* example is also what we commonly see in television news reporting. (Incidentally, I've heard interesting parallels drawn between *USA Today* and TV. *USA Today* coming in a newsstand that closely resembles a TV set, the amount of color and graphics used, and then of course the short, concise articles.) As in print news, however, if we examine it closely, we can see this trend of feature journalism developing on the nightly TV news.

It is common knowledge, and I practice it religiously, that the reader will hardly ever ingest an entire news article. In fact it is likely the reader will not go farther than the third or fourth paragraph and hardly, if ever, follow a jump from the front page to the second page. Therein lies the challenge of presenting a news article with spice: keeping the reader in the story long enough to achieve the purpose of news reporting. I am nearly 100 percent sure, however, that if a reader were asked which news story, or front page story, he or she read in its entirety this morning, it would have been the one with the feature-writer twist. [Used by permission.]

News and Entertainment

Our expectations as audience members have everything to do with how a news item is understood. We should look further at the mixing of news and entertainment. There was some discussion of these categories and their overlap in Chapter 3 (see, for example, the journal entries and essay by Teri Hurst starting on page 95). It might be useful here to start with your own media log.

ASSIGNMENT

Look back over your media log and journal entries to date, and estimate what percentage of your interactions with media were given to the purposes of gathering news and information. You should count under this category reading the newspaper or newsmagazines such as *Time* or *Newsweek*, but not entertainment publications such as *People* or *Cosmopolitan*. (If you consider tabloids such as the *National Enquirer* to be a source of news for you, count them; otherwise not. Stories on celebrities should usually count as entertainment.) On television, count CNN, Headline News, local and network news broadcasts, morning news shows such as *Today*, and news-oriented public affairs programs such as *The News Hour with Jim Lehrer*; but not the *Tonight Show*, documentaries, talk shows such as *Donahue* or *Oprah*, or programs that interpret the news from a specific ideological viewpoint, such as *Rush Limbaugh* or *The 700 Club*. Keep track of texts that present problems for these categories, and be prepared to consider why.

What other categories are there for your media interactions besides news? What are some other uses that you have for media besides keeping up with public events?

When you do actively seek out news (rather than getting it in the middle of something else, as with a news bulletin or headlines on the hour), what are your purposes? What forms of news do you consider, and how does your choice indicate what your purposes are?

You may have had some difficulty, when working through your interactions with media for the Assignment above, in separating out what is and what is not to be considered "news." As the list in the Assignment shows, "news" has become a "dirty" category: Many media texts combine the intent to inform with the intent to entertain, which makes them hard to classify. Morning news programs on television have done this since the 1950s, featuring engaging personalities in order to give these shows a more pleasing, less business-like atmosphere. One of the early draws for NBC's *Today* show was J. Fred Muggs, a chimpanzee (Exhibit 4.3).

PAUSE FOR REFLECTION

Watch a morning news show or local network broadcast, and take careful note of comments, stories, or segments that seem to you to be at least partially meant to entertain. When are these "entertainment" portions placed in the program—not only in relation to other segments, but in relation to commercials? How do the personnel on the program signal that they are coming? What sort of reactions, if any, do the program hosts give? What are your reactions? Are they identical to those of the hosts?

The combination of information and entertainment has been evident in newspapers for many decades, with the inclusion of comics, advice columns,

Exhibit 4.3
Two top *Today* show personalities, 1957: Dave Garroway and J. Fred Muggs. NBC. Corbis-Bettmann.

human interest stories, coverage of celebrities, and so on. This mixture has been blamed for the audience's lack of receptivity to "hard news"—readers' impatience with long or complex news events, in-depth coverage, or attempts to get beyond superficial accounts. Yet it's hard to blame news organizations for some combination of these purposes, because within a commercial framework they need to get and hold as large an audience as possible.

PAUSE FOR REFLECTION
The following are topics of talk shows for the week beginning Sunday, January 29, 1995. How do these topics fit with your understanding of what is considered news and information?

Ricki Lake:
(Mon) Pleading with former mates for another chance to make the relationship work
(Tue) A psychiatrist offers advice on how to end domestic violence
(Wed) How to get rid of unwelcome houseguests
(Thu) Women who say their mates are using them for sex
(Fri) Settling a score with a former mate

Susan Powter:
(Mon) What to do if you hate your body
(Tue) The difficulty of being a parent
(Wed) Overcoming panic attacks
(Thu) Inside scoop on the controversial Gulf War syndrome
(Fri) Combat stress with a club for burned-out parents

Oprah Winfrey:
(Tue) People who have had to turn in loved ones to the authorities; guests include the father of serial arsonist Paul Keller
(Wed) Why some women make bad relationship choices and how this affects their lives
(Thu) People whose weight loss cost them friends
(Fri) A self-defense instructor teaches a class on assault prevention techniques

Maury Povich:
(Mon) Women accused by members of their families of being unfit mothers
(Tue) People who hold Guinness world records
(Wed) People who use a sibling's identity to avoid arrest
(Thu) A man arrested for the murders of a family vacationing in Florida speaks from prison
(Fri) Unhappy reunions

Sally Jessy Raphael:
(Mon) Women who admit to using men
(Tue) People whose families are unsupportive of their interracial romances
(Wed) Parents who disapprove of their children's plans to get married
(Thu) Women claiming their mates left them after learning they were pregnant
(Fri) Women who had babies as teens and were forced to give them up

Reading the News Comparatively

Curiously, given the competitive nature of the news business, each of us tends to rely heavily on a single source for daily news. It may be the area's daily newspaper, a newspaper from another region, CNN or one of the other television networks, local news broadcasts, or NPR's *All Things Considered*. It's also fairly common to make use of single sources in several media, bringing in other sources such as weekly newsmagazines as we feel the urge.

But it's not so common to read news stories comparatively: to take two or more stories as told by competitors (in the same medium or in different media) and read them carefully, in order to see how they differ. Such an exercise can be instructive, not so much for what it tells us about any given news story as for what it tells us about the media that are presenting us with the news.

Later in this section we'll examine news texts from January 19-20, 1995, about the aftermath of the earthquake centered on Kobe, Japan. I analyzed this story because it happened to be the lead story in news media for the date chosen. On any given day, even the slowest news day, there is more happening than can possibly be presented on the evening news. A half-hour TV network news program spends eight minutes of the allotted time for advertisements and promos for other programs—and some portion of the remaining twenty-two minutes is taken up with the program's title and theme music, transitions, introductions, and (especially in local TV coverage) banter between members of the news team. Newspapers present the appearance of more space than network television, with the famous claim of having "All the news that's fit to print." But "all the news" comes in articles that generally range between 150 and 800 words. And because newspapers are divided into various segments, "hard news" actually takes up only a small portion of the newspaper, in order to make room for various features. As a result, editors carefully select any day's news so as to present what they judge will interest their audience.

What is selected for us as the news actually doesn't vary all that much from program to program. Commonly, a story will surface in one publication, such as a newspaper or magazine; then it will be commented on by other print media, picked up by television and radio—and kept alive when someone involved is asked for a response, there's reaction in Congress, and so on. An issue can be kept in circulation by this means for a long time, sometimes beyond the patience of some readers: As with sensationalized stories like the conflict between U.S. skaters Tonya Harding and Nancy Kerrigan or the preliminaries and trial of O. J. Simpson, which ran for nearly a year and a half, most people expressed irritation with finding coverage everywhere, even when nothing of significance appeared to be happening. If a story has a political dimension, it may be kept in the media through conferences, carefully planned "leaks," and so on, as was the case with the Whitewater affair. But the various media seem to be consistent in determining what are lead stories, which categories of stories can be moved into inside pages, and which are not worth much coverage.

Journalists are trained in deciding what to feature as news—just as the rest of us are trained to regard what we read in the newspaper as news. The difference is that journalists' training comes in formal programs at colleges and universities, in books written by those who have written for newspapers for years, and in apprentice programs responsible for much of the training of professionals in this field. Audiences for the news (including, of course, those who are to become reporters) are trained in reading news by the news itself, and by its reception in the culture generally.

Even if we see a version of the same story in several media—hearing about it on the radio, watching a report on two network broadcasts and a local news show, and reading about it in a newspaper and a magazine—we don't generally compare these closely. Perhaps there may be an event that concerns us specifically—something that happens at our place of work or to someone we know—and we take an interest in the treatment for that reason. But normally we wouldn't encounter a story in many different versions anyway, and if we do, we don't read them closely.

In the 1960s, President Johnson used to watch the three network news broadcasts simultaneously; because of VCRs, such comparison could be done fairly readily now. But it's not usual to compare coverage of television news in the way that we might compare front pages of newspapers. Let's consider two half-hour news broadcasts, from CBS and CNN. Average duration of items listed: about one minute.

CBS Evening News, January 19, 1995
Opening logo, theme music—CBS Evening News with Dan Rather and Connie Chung. Segments:

1. Report on death toll in Kobe—Bob Simon.
2. Associated story—"smoldering resentment" at slowness of Japanese government to provide relief—James Hattori.
3. Comparison with other devastating earthquakes.
4. Tease: Newt under fire.
5. Ads: Honda Odyssey
    Dimetapp
    Tums
6. Gingrich, a gripe, and gridlock—Bob Schieffer.
7. Chung—Representative Jim Leach threatens to delay support for the peso if Democrats keep attacking Gingrich.
8. Linda Douglass—Clinton tries for positive spin.
9. Headlines: Economic news—high exports, higher imports; Michigan strike; Dow Jones and Nasdaq numbers.
10. Ads: Just for Men hair color
    Aspercreme
    Velveeta
    Total
    Promos: *Eye-to-Eye, 48 Hours*
11. Headlines: Chechnya.
12. FBI agents suing for discrimination—Scott Pelley.
13. Headlines, with some footage: Winter storm news.

14. Ads: Arthritis Foundation (Julie Andrews)
    Mylanta
    Caltrate Plus
    Scalpicin
    Egg Beaters
    Promo: Tomorrow's CBS News
15. Christina Jeffrey, fired as House historian, fights back (Eye on America feature)—Bob McNamara. Context is not mid-1980s, Reaganite Department of Education attempt to control looking into history; rather, the context is the continuing partisan fights in Congress.
16. Ads: Theraflu
    Healthy Choice
    Ensure
    Royal Caribbean tours
17. Twins born in separate years—New Orleans couple.
18. Promo from Rather and Chung for *Eye-to-Eye* and *48 Hours*. Signoff.

CNN Prime Time News, January 19, 1995
1. Coverage of damage from Japan earthquake.
2. Headlines: Japanese government's lack of responsiveness.
3. Two Americans dead in Japan, English teachers.
4. Earthquake in Colombia.
5. Tease: Reaction in California, Smithsonian exhibit of *Enola Gay*.
6. Ads: Met Life (Peanuts kids)
    Tylenol
    Kiplinger retirement report
    Promo: "Clinton at the Crossroads"
7. Headlines: Chechnya—takeover of presidential palace; fighting in Bosnia; book about MIAs in Vietnam.
8. *Enola Gay* exhibit; protests by American Legion, saying that it's too pro-Japanese—Jeanne Meserve.
9. Ads: Promo: Coverage of debate about public broadcasting
    Promo: World News—"A Different Story"
    Local ad: Garber Buick
    Local ad: Rowleys
10. Headlines: O. J. news; trade deficit; Dow Jones numbers.
11. Clinton seeks credit where credit is due.
12. PBS report—Carl Rochelle.
13. George Burns unveils sign on street named after Gracie.

14. Headline—Flowers and cognac left on Poe's grave.
15. Ads: Promo
    GE-Japan ad—this is interesting in its timing
    Janus—mutual funds
    Lanier office supplies
    Sally Struthers for Save the Children
    Promo: "CNN at work" on line
16. Tease: Snow in Arkansas; earthquake news; anxiety on West Coast (Hayward fault); Red Cross.
17. Twins born 50-some days apart in New Orleans.
18. Ads: Promo: Crossfire
    Local ads: Ken's Office Systems
              Garber Buick (not same as above)
              Mr. Hot Dog
              Timm's TV
              Health Hut
19. Japan news: Swiss dogs used to hunt for bodies.
20. Earthquake news.
21. Report on spring training.

In addition to comparing choices and time allocations of news coverage, there is some value in examining different texts of the same news story, because they will tell us something about different forms (television, radio, print media) and what they are best equipped to do. Television gives us much less in the form of words but presents information visually: How do we process that information? Radio is mostly words, but these are spoken rather than printed—does that make a difference? And different print media employ type sizes, fonts, pictures, color, and other devices that characterize different publications' styles. But even among verbal texts, the actual words chosen, there are usually different emphases.

Appendixes 4.1 through 4.4 at the end of this chapter are transcripts of four accounts broadcast a few days after the January 1995 earthquake in and around Kobe, Japan. The transcripts are taken from CNN and CBS television news and from National Public Radio's *All Things Considered* and *Morning Edition*. (For comparison, you might also look at print media accounts, such as those to be found in the *New York Times* or *Washington Post* and/or in *Time* or *Newsweek*.) Looking at these accounts comparatively will indicate which narratives are presented in common, which are given specific emphasis by different forms and different organizations—and this in turn will tell us something about reading the news that we might not otherwise note.

To start with the television news reports, both are placed in the context of evening news—*CNN Prime Time* and the *CBS Evening News.* Both are surrounded by other texts—the introductory theme music with program logos, introductions by anchors, following stories that may or may not be related, and advertisements. News on commercial television exists in the context of the network's need to make profits. News divisions have at times been run at a loss, contributing primarily in prestige value. But particularly in the 1980s, local and network news began to face financial pressures, which meant sharp competition for ratings in order to get more revenue. If you pay careful attention to which advertisers sponsor television news, you get some clues about who the network and the advertisers *think* are watching news. Commercials on CNN on the Thursday in question included (in addition to local ads) one for an insurance company, two for investment firms, one for an over-the-counter drug (Tylenol), one for General Electric (ironically, an ad with a Japanese theme), one public service ad (Save the Children), and one for an office supply theme—a strong business orientation. CBS sponsors were more domestic and a little higher in the implied audience's apparent age: There were six ads for over-the-counter medicines (Dimetapp, Aspercreme, Caltrate Plus, Scalpicin, Arthritis Foundation, and Ensure), two for stomach remedies (Tums and Mylanta), four for food (two cereals, Total and Healthy Choice, plus Velveeta Cheese and Egg Beaters), one for hair coloring for men, one for Royal Caribbean Tours, and one for the then-new Honda minivan.

Other stories carried by both news programs included some comparison with other earthquakes (on CNN: Northridge, California, in 1994, and a small quake in Colombia; on CBS: comparison with other devastating earthquakes in history). Also present in the day's events were some treatments of difficulties between the new Republican Congress and President Clinton and the Democratic side. For CNN, the story was the president's attempt to put a positive spin on his first two years, perhaps connected with their promo for a special on the following Sunday, "Clinton at the Crossroads." For CBS, in addition to Clinton's accentuating the positive, the focus was more on Congress—Bob Schieffer reported on "Gingrich, a gripe, and gridlock"; Representative Leach threatened to delay consideration of loan guarantees for Mexico; and there was a long feature on Christina Jeffrey, the House historian and friend of Representative Gingrich who was fired after a week on the job because of prior statements (taken somewhat out of context) about the need to give the Nazis a fair hearing. Both programs carried brief stock market reports. And both closed with a story of twins born fifty-some days apart, in separate calendar years. Some short reports touched on the same material (for example, fighting in Chechnya). However, several stories were treated in one broadcast but not in the other. CNN mentioned two U.S. citizens killed in the Kobe earthquake, and had some film of another American returning from the Kobe area to New York; they covered the American Legion–sponsored protests over the May exhibit by the Smithsonian of the *Enola Gay,* the U.S. plane that dropped the atomic bomb on Hiroshima; they showed George Burns unveiling a sign on a street named after Gracie Allen; and they offered a feature on the use of Swiss dogs (not Saint Bernards) to hunt for those buried in the earthquake. CBS carried a story about Hispanic FBI agents suing the agency for discrimination, and had a report on the winter storm which hit Arkansas and Missouri.

In order to compare news stories, it's most useful to try to find the themes. Characteristically each theme is announced by the anchor, often reinforced by graphics at the opening of the report and signaled by recurrent key words or metaphors in the dialogue. These serve to direct viewers' attention toward a specific interpretation of the visual images and sounds provided on film or video, just as do captions in newspaper photos or dialogue, superimposition, and other text supplied by commercials. The CNN story emphasizes the prime minister's visit to Kobe in the context of people's frustration with the government's slowness to respond to the emergency and the failure of measures to prepare for earthquakes. Interviews feature people who are angry. One woman speaks on camera, saying, "Anyone can see how awful it must be, but the prime minister has to do something about it"; another observes that it's nice to have the prime minister there, but he should have brought some supplies. This is followed by an account of supplies in warehouses but insufficient means to distribute them. There is a later segment about "earthquake preparedness" day and the concerns of some people in Tokyo about the possibility of a major quake there.

Contrast this with the theme stressed in CBS's report: In addition to covering the widespread destruction, essentially the same as in the CNN report, Bob Simon's account stresses the cultural differences between Japan and the United States: "And there they were, serenaded by sirens, meeting disaster the Japanese way... with unflinching politeness." This statement is illustrated by a woman who tells about her injuries, then thanks him for coming. Later in the report there's a touching sequence of an old woman dug out of the rubble after two days, met by her husband, who had left the hospital himself to come look for her. The reporter's on-camera summary: "The earthquake, which shattered the homes and the lives of these people, didn't lay a finger on the depths of their dignity, their determination."

Both accounts are convincing. Watch the CNN report and you note the widespread destruction, the failure of construction to protect against a quake of that magnitude, the chaos caused by the disruption in communication and transportation; and you believe, in part because of the interviews provided, that people are angry at their government for not doing more, sooner. This message is reinforced by the later segment with its summary that "the earthquake in Kobe has brought home a sense of vulnerability to the forces of nature." If you watch the CBS report, you see the same shots of rubble and fires, the same "suburbanites transformed into scavengers, searching for what was left of their lives"—but the account is framed so as to stress the Japanese people's will to pull things back together again. The reporter here allows a man in the rubble to make his summary for him: "The Japanese are strong. We will rebuild." Both CNN's theme of calamity and CBS's theme of hope were reinforced by other media over the days that followed.

So which interpretation is *true*? Which presents a more objective picture of reality? There is no question about the reality of the stacks of supplies in the warehouse, the remains of buildings in the street, the people working to restore order, the traffic jams, and so on. But both CNN and CBS, and the other networks and NPR accounts and newspaper and magazine accounts, combine objective facts (more than 4,000 dead; 7.2 on the Richter scale; more than 250,000 homeless; prime minister visits Kobe) with stories that tell us what the facts mean (people angry at insufficient preparation and at construction that couldn't stand up in an earthquake—or people politely and purposefully restoring order in their lives). News organizations provide organized accounts of events, or stories, and we measure their adequacy by how well they hold together internally (and jibe with other stories), how well they match up with versions provided by different sources, and how well they match up with our own stories—which are in part constructed by our past experience with other media stories. In this context, an "objective" interpretation is one that doesn't cause us any conflict, one we already agree with.

Complaints about bias in the news, then, are misstated: The news is always an interpretation. The questions to be asked are these: What is the interpretation given in this news text, this source, this medium? Whose interpretation is it? What alternative interpretations does it supplant or leave out? Where does it match with and where does it conflict with my own interpretation? What effects does it achieve? Do I approve of these effects?

PAUSE FOR REFLECTION

Read the following paragraphs from *V.* by Thomas Pynchon:

> Twenty days before the Dog Star moved into conjunction with the sun, the dog days began. The world started to run more and more afoul of the inanimate. Fifteen were killed in a train wreck near Oaxaca, Mexico, on 1 July. The next day fifteen people died when an apartment house collapsed in Madrid. July 4 a bus fell into a river near Karachi and thirty-one passengers drowned. Thirty-nine more were drowned two days later in a tropical storm in the central Philippines.

9 July the Aegean Islands were hit by an earthquake and tidal waves, which killed forty-three. 14 July a MATS plane crashed after takeoff from McGuire Air Force Base in New Jersey, killing forty-five. An earthquake at Anjar, India, 21 July, killed 117. From 22 to 24 July floods rampaged in central and southern Iran, killing three hundred. 28 July a bus ran off a ferryboat at Kuopio, Finland, and fifteen were killed. Four petroleum tanks blew up near Dumas, Texas, 29 July, killing nineteen. 1 August, seventeen died in a train wreck near Rio de Janeiro. Fifteen more died the 4th and 5th, in floods in southwest Pennsylvania. 2161 people died the same week in a typhoon which hit Chekiang, Honan and Hopeh Provinces. 7 August six dynamite trucks blew up in Cali, Colombia, killing about 1100. The same day there was a train wreck at Přerov, Czechoslovakia, killing nine. The next day 262 miners, trapped by fire, died in a coal mine under Marcinelle, in Belgium. Ice avalanches on Mont Blanc swept fifteen mountain climbers into the kingdom of death in the week 12 to 18 August. The same week a gas explosion in Monticello, Utah, killed fifteen and a typhoon through Japan and Okinawa killed thirty. Twenty-nine more coal miners died of gas poisoning in a mine in Upper Silesia on 27 August. Also on the 27th a Navy bomber crashed among houses in Sanford, Florida, and killed four. Next day a gas explosion in Montreal killed seven and flash floods in Turkey killed 138.

These were the mass deaths. There were also the attendant maimed, malfunctioning, homeless, lorn. It happens every month in a succession of encounters between groups of living and a congruent world which simply doesn't care. Look in any yearly Almanac, under "Disasters"—which is where the figures above come from. The business is transacted month after month after month. (Pynchon pp. 270–71)

QUESTIONS:
1. Is there a theme in these paragraphs? Where is it stated?
2. How does the theme (if there is a theme) guide you in making sense of the long list of disasters?
3. What is there in these paragraphs that lets you know that they come from a genre of writing other than news? What genre(s) do you see as possibilities?

All the words spoken on a half-hour segment of TV news can be transcribed to half a page of newspaper. But as I've stressed before, TV news is not reducible to its words: Television communicates through visual images; through sounds besides words; and, perhaps most important, through their combination. Something of television's reliance on the visual can be seen when we contrast Appendixes 4.1 and 4.2 with the two National Public Radio reports in Appendixes 4.3 and 4.4: *All Things Considered* and *Morning Edition*. The *ATC* account, by contrast with the televised accounts, does more of what might be considered word painting: Together with sound events such as sirens or construction equipment, the language used renders an equivalent to what cameras can show:

> [V]ast stretches of the Japanese city of Kobe look like war zones, a testament to the power of nature.... Buildings have literally been shredded, and entire sections of walls flap in the wind like long oversized strips of paper.... The convoys of green trucks form long lines as they inch through the city.... Snaps line the walls, and sad statistics chronicle the life of the quake.

(See Appendix 4.3 for full text.) An interesting feature of some of the language here is that inanimate objects are described as if taking conscious actions—such descriptions lend to buildings and objects an imagined life, which is ironically what happens in an earthquake. The reporter here is using a poetic device in a radio news report. Poetic devices are of course available to verbal accounts on television, but tend not to be used because pictures are available.

Radio tells stories through the reporters' accounts and also through longer conversations with observers and experts. On *Morning Edition* Susan Stamberg's telephone conversation with Mary Kay Magistad is punctuated with conversational phrases, such as "gonna" for going to; there are also phrases such as "I mean" and "uh" and "you know," omitted in the transcript, which signal the offhand and informal mode of presentation. The discussion with Yoshio Hota, a Japanese journalist in the United States, brings in a point of cultural difference between the Japanese and ourselves, *shonunai*, a phrase meaning "it can't be helped." This concept is related to the "politeness" and "determination" mentioned in the CBS report, but here it's being discussed by someone from Japan, as opposed to a Western analyst. (Notice how little airtime goes to anyone except the reporter in the TV accounts: Television reports downplay most of the stories that might have been gathered, subsuming them into the story told by the visuals. The principal exception is the mini-narrative of the older woman dug from the rubble and joined by her husband, and their role in the drama is to give a human side to the desolation and an example of attempts to survive.) Explaining the cultural difference appears to be an important theme in the *Morning Edition* narrative; the *CBS Evening News* narrative collapses the cultural difference into "politeness," while the Japanese present in the CNN account appear to be as frustrated with their government's inability to respond quickly as U.S. citizens are alleged to be, at times, with our own government. Yoshio Hota's account on *Morning Edition* stresses the centrality of socially acceptable behavior—if someone complains or laments too much, that person may be ostracized, a concept that might appear strange to U.S. listeners. However, the idea that after such a disaster, personal effects will probably be looted, which we have come to take more or less for granted, is inconceivable to the Japanese reporter. The *Morning Edition* report at least notes cultural differences, while the other accounts tend to pass over these and to focus on recognizable sorts of reactions—reactions we would be likely to have ourselves.

One of the local newspapers in Michigan, the *Saginaw News,* drew its account of the earthquake from the *Washington Post,* placing that account alongside a photo, "quake facts," and "rescue steps" from the Associated Press, and a map of earthquake damage from the *Japan Times.* As with most local newspapers, news coverage from outside the state originates with a wire service, news agency, or other newspaper; unless there is a significant local tie-in, it's too expensive to send reporters around the world on assignment. It might be said that local newspapers furnish pretty much the same news, with variations concealed somewhat by the selection of different photographs, composition of different headlines, and placement within the newspaper.

As you read the transcripts in Appendixes 4.1 through 4.4, reflect on what else goes into our understanding of the news. No news report starts from scratch: There is always an assumption of some knowledge about the subject of the report. In addition to a working sense of conventions within the medium and some ability to understand English, the audience is assumed to start with knowledge about the basis of the report as well. To make sense of any of the transcripts at the end of this chapter, you need to know what an earthquake is, roughly where Japan is, and so on. Some of this knowledge has come from school, but much of it has come in other ways—from books you may have read, from films, from talking with other people, from previous media reports about earthquakes or about Japan. And this knowledge is accumulated in the form of "stories" that form more or less coherent accounts about Japan.

PAUSE FOR REFLECTION

Compile a short list of "stories" about Japan that have formed part of your context for these news broadcasts (World War II, cheap "Made in Japan" imports, economic development and competition, etc.). What can you recall about your first recollections of these stories? How many different stories about Japan are there? How do they reinforce or conflict with each other? What is your connection with these stories?

In evaluating news stories, sometimes we turn out to be evaluating ourselves, or some set of stories we have been telling ourselves about ourselves. I might approach a story about Japan from the experience of someone who identifies strongly with the economic competition of the 1980s, in which many thousands of laid-off auto workers blamed Japanese manufacturers for their situation. From that perspective, I might take a sour satisfaction in anything bad that happened to Japan. Or my experience might be that of someone who has lived in Japan; knowing the culture and having some friends and acquaintances there, I would have a stronger interest and concern in what took place. A third perspective might not focus specifically on Japanese culture, but might pick up on the differences between others' reactions to disaster and what I think would be my own; a fourth might stress the similarity of these reactions.

Spillovers from these Japan stories color two other parts of the half-hour *CNN Prime Time News* we looked at earlier. At the time of that broadcast, preparations were under way for an exhibit in the Smithsonian Institute in Washington, commemorating the fiftieth anniversary of the dropping of the atomic bombs at Hiroshima and Nagasaki. The commemoration became politically charged. The museum's account presented questions raised by historians

Exhibit 4.4 Kobe earthquake fires. *Newsweek.* January 30, 1995. Photo by Asahi Shimbun. Reprinted by permission.

Exhibit 4.5
Kobe rescue work. *Newsweek,*
January 30, 1995. Photo by Asahi
Shimbun. Reprinted by permission.

about the necessity for the bombs, in view of the likelihood that Japan would have negotiated a surrender shortly anyway; this account provoked controversy from veterans' groups in particular, who generally held to the point of view current at the war's end, that Japan had initiated the Pacific war at Pearl Harbor and pretty much deserved what it got. Other currents were flowing around the exhibition—the newly elected Republican Congress with strongly conservative members, trade disputes with Japan, and so on. These positions connected, in turn, with other ideological positions.

In sum, when we begin to look seriously at how to interpret the news, the questions lead directly to choosing among possible interpretations, and that in turn means seeing these as they connect to views of how culture is, and ought to be, organized. "The news" is always connected to an agenda of some sort, even if that agenda is a good-faith attempt to present facts and allow the reader to do the interpreting. "The facts" always come preinterpreted. It is therefore up to us as readers to take responsibility for the stories we hold to and pass along to others in our turn—to assess as best we can the accuracy of what we are witnessing, and in turn to be as fair as we can in constructing our own accounts.

PAUSE FOR REFLECTION
Watch a television newscast and take note of occasions on which those in other countries get to speak for themselves. How much of their speech is mediated by others—by reporters or anchors or by the context into which it is inserted?

PAUSE FOR REFLECTION
Exhibits 4.4 through 4.7 are four photos of Kobe quake damage and rescue attempts that were featured in earthquake coverage by *Newsweek*, January 30, 1995. Which of your own stories—about Japan, about disasters, about humanity—do they connect with? Write several statements, as they come to you, that are associated with these stories.

Exhibit 4.6 Kobe line for supplies. *Newsweek* January 30, 1995. Photo by Natsuko Utsumi. Used by permission.

Exhibit 4.7
Kobe aftermath. *Newsweek,* January 20, 1995. Photo by Natsuko Utsumi. Used by permission.

PROBLEMS

The U.S. system of providing news and information is highly developed. Word gets out about emergencies, weather alerts, current events, and other matters, quickly and efficiently. There's no office of censorship, and those with unpopular viewpoints face no restrictions preventing them from speaking or writing their piece—*if* they have enough money or prestige to get access and attention, and *if* their message fits the popular story called common sense. Despite all these advantages, however, there are some problems with news in the United States—problems with keeping informed, with propaganda, and with objectivity and fairness.

Keeping Informed

One problem with news and information lies with the audience end: We have become so accustomed to having our information provided for us in simple form that if the issue is complex or contested, we aren't able or don't bother to work through it on our own.

The Program on International Policy Attitudes at the University of Maryland conducted a survey in early 1995 that showed that 75 percent of Americans believe that the United States spends too much on foreign aid, and 64 percent want foreign aid cut. But when poll respondents asked how much of the federal budget the United States spends on foreign aid, the average answer was 18 percent; the correct answer is less than 1 percent. Comment on this poll by Michael Kinsley: "It's not just that Americans are scandalously ignorant. It's that they seem to believe they have a democratic right to their ignorance" (Kingsley pp. 4–5).

The protracted discussion of health care during 1993–94 can serve as a test case for how well the public was informed by media. (Note that this is different from how well we *could have been* informed.) The initiative for health care reform began with President Clinton's State of the Union speech in 1993 and was followed by committee meetings, hearings, open meetings, and many public and private meetings. The issue was highly contested: Health professionals such as physicians, nurses, health care administrators, and pharmaceutical companies have specific (and conflicting) interests; lawyers, insurance companies, and others affected by any change in the delivery and funding of health care also weighed in on the discussion. Members of Congress took more or less partisan positions, depending on their convictions, what they were hearing from constituents, and who had donated campaign money. Organized groups such as the American Association of Retired Persons, small business groups, and labor unions had their positions as well, speaking for (or in the place of) their constituencies. Much confusion was created by the wide circulation of conflicting claims.

Those with money spent it to get their positions heard. Millions were spent—$14 million on one advertising campaign alone, funded by the Health Insurance Association of America, featuring characters known as Harry and Louise. As became abundantly clear, however, those who were uninsured or underinsured had no access to airtime and, as a result, little voice in the public discussions about health care.

> Black screen, with what appears to be an EKG trace across the screen. Typing sound, followed by superimposition: throughout the ad, the superimposition is read by voice-over. Background sound: heartbeat, which gradually accelerates through the ad.
>
> **Superimposition (and voice-over [VO]):** Bill Clinton Wants to Socialize Health Care.
>
> **VO:** Bill Clinton wants to socialize health care. And many members of Congress support him.
>
> **Superimposition:** Small Business Will Pay The Bill.
>
> **VO:** Every small business in America will be forced to pay the bill.
>
> **Superimposition:** The Largest Government Bureaucracy In History.
>
> **VO:** His plan creates the largest government bureaucracy in history.
>
> **Superimposition:** The Bureaucracy Will Decide.
>
> **VO:** Your doctor won't decide what care is right for you. The bureaucracy will.
>
> **Superimposition:** The Bureaucracy Will Never Examine You.
>
> **VO:** (same)
>
> **Superimposition:** Never Talk To You.
>
> **VO:** (same)
>
> **Superimposition:** Never Even See You.
>
> **VO:** (same)
>
> **Superimposition:** Limit Your Choice Of Doctors.
>
> **VO:** It will severely limit your choice of doctors.
>
> **Superimposition:** The Bureaucracy Will Dictate.
>
> **VO:** The bureaucracy will dictate what treatments are necessary.
>
> **Superimposition:** The Bureaucracy Will Decide.
>
> **VO:** The bureaucracy will decide when and even if you can see a specialist.
>
> *About here, the tempo of the heartbeats and accompanying beep accelerates.*
>
> *(continues)*

Exhibit 4.8 Transcript of Empower America health care commercial aired in 1994. Used by permission.

> **Superimposition:** You Will Lose Choice And Control.
>
> **VO:** Under this plan, you will lose choice and control.
>
> *Camera moves in, enlarging the EKG trace, as the tempo accelerates greatly. Then the EKG line goes flat, and the beep continues nonstop.*
>
> **Superimposition:** It's Your Health Care They're Socializing.
>
> **VO:** Remember: It's your health care they're socializing.
>
> *Screen goes white, followed by an image of a waving American flag, close-up.*
>
> There is a better way.
>
> *The flag image zooms back a bit into the center of the screen, between the words EMPOWER above, and AMERICA below (a small five-pointed blue star above the capital I). Below, in gray, is "1-800-4-EMPOWER."*
>
> **VO (different voice):** Call Empower America. 1-800-4-empower.
>
> *Music comes up.*

Exhibit 4.8 *Continued*

Chapter 5 will present in more detail some of the problems with advertising as a source of information—in particular, the difficulties in processing symbolic (largely visual) information such as the oscilloscope trace and beep as connected with health care proposals, the confusion that results from viewing several misleading messages at different times; and the "leakage" between what we hear through commercials, "infomercials," partisan talk shows, statements by public figures, and news reports. The blurring of such texts, called "dirt," is an important consideration when we assess media texts and their reception.

Commentator and author Kathleen Hall Jamieson had this to say, in Bill Moyers's 1994 TV special *The Great Health Care Debate*, about the commercial in Exhibit 4.8:

> Bill Clinton, a new Democrat, deliberately moved away from a government-driven program, to preserve the private insurance industry in his plan. He thought in the process he was moderating towards the center. Of course, the right then moved from the center further to the right, and made the same claims against him they would have made had he sponsored a Canadian-style single-payer plan, for example. The problem with the [Empower America] ad is very straightforward. First, it continues to air after the mandatory purchasing alliances are gone, so a big piece of the bureaucracy described here is gone at the point at which this ad continues to air; but secondly, Clinton specifi-

cally made the choice to preserve fee-for-service medicine, which would guarantee choice of doctor, although at a higher cost, and so the ad is just simply deceptive. And at the end, when the EKG goes flat, it visually invites the inference either that you're going to die under the Clinton plan, or that the health care system is going to die, and that's just palpably false.

Jamieson estimates that approximately 60 percent of the advertising about health care was misleading or fraudulent.

Free speech, in media terms, depends on access. In the health care debate, in some cases, even those with money to advertise were shut out of the discussion, at least in some forms. A group backing a single-payer plan similar to that of Canada could not buy airtime because their advertising dollars were greatly outweighed by those of the insurance companies, which would lose from such a plan. And a group sponsored by labor, medical, and consumer groups, the Health Care Reform Project, found its ad prevented from airing in the Washington, D.C., area. Exhibit 4.9 describes the ad (but omits the ad's

---

Music—electric piano, up-tempo, a little dark. Several shots in succession: close-up of young man on telephone; cut to midsection of young man on a bicycle, balancing a Pizza Hut box on the bars; camera on midsection with pizza box, front view; pan up to head and shoulders. Camera, which has been moving around in previous shots, freezes on head with bicycle helmet.

The voice-over points out that Pizza Hut pays health insurance for its workers in Japan and Germany, as required, but not for many workers in the United States. Fade-in to Pizza Hut logo on sign. Camera zooms back and pans right to a Pizza Hut restaurant, then zooms in to the sign on the rooftop.

Cut to young man on bicycle, side view, riding on a street. He passes a parked car in front of a house. Camera pans back.

Cut to view of public buildings with pillars; shot is from bottom, with view of blue sky; Pizza Hut logo visible in upper left. Camera pans left to U.S. Capitol dome.

Voice-over then notes that Pizza Hut is lobbying against congressional proposals for health insurance. Cut to view along Washington boulevard, Capitol dome visible at the end. Young man with pizza rides past; camera zooms slightly to follow, then pans up slightly to Capitol dome. Telephone number on screen. Cut to shot of restaurant; zoom in on Pizza Hut sign on roof. Voice-over concludes with a plea to call Congress on behalf of American workers.

Exhibit 4.9 Description of ad prepared by Health Care Reform Project.

text, because the Health Care Reform Project is apparently no longer around to grant permission for reprinting of their words). Note that the ad's use of Pizza Hut, while perhaps offered as a concrete example, suggests that Pizza Hut bears some special responsibility.

Washington area television stations were concerned not only that they might lose Pizza Hut's advertising business, but that *they* might be sued if Pizza Hut took issue with the factual claims in the Health Care Reform Project ad. In this case, the threat of a lawsuit worked to suppress one position in the potential debate about health care. (As it happened, the censoring of the ad was picked up as news; the ad got national exposure—once—on network news, more widely than would have happened otherwise, but without the repetition available to other appeals.)

According to Kathleen Hall Jamieson, "Approximately 70 percent of the advertising dollar [in the debate] was spent against [health care] reform." Much of this was focused on one part of the proposals, but cumulatively the effect was to raise anxiety and eventually opposition to any health care reform.

Because of the uneven level of discussion about health care reform, the burden of proof fell heavily on those proposing reform to defend their proposals: No one was obligated to defend the status quo. The United States had thirty-eight million uninsured people at the time of the proposals, and many more whose insurance was (and remains) on an unsure basis; but all the ink was spilt decrying ideas like employer mandates, or making exaggerated charges about "socialized medicine."

Just as we may have difficulty discriminating between the categories of news and entertainment, so in the health care discussions there was difficulty distinguishing between news/information and propaganda.

ASSIGNMENT

Choose a public issue currently under discussion, and do an inventory of how you know what you know about it. (A concept map would be useful for this purpose—see Chapter 3, Exhibit 3.6) What are your channels of information? Where do they lead? You need to be more specific than "TV" or "radio" or "the newspaper": Which? Which reporters? Which experts? Which interests were expressed through them? What interests are left out of your inventory, and how would you go about discovering their perspectives?

Propaganda

Is it possible to define **propaganda** in such a way as to distinguish it from news and information? Or is propaganda ultimately only someone else's perspective on the news? If we cannot define propaganda as something distinct from news, does that mean we descend into the Swamps of Relativism?

The problem of distinguishing propaganda from news is one that rhetoric has been concerned with from its origins: the problem of how to get at the truth in spite of—or through—its many partial and sometimes self-interested representations. A look at the word's history takes us to propaganda's near relative, to *propagate,* or cause to spread, and to the division of the Catholic Church charged with preaching its doctrines in non-Christian countries. Religious beliefs sometimes do not admit the possibility of a plurality of viewpoints on *the truth.*

If we inhabited a society in which there was automatic and universal agreement on what truth is and what concrete actions and practices should follow from it, then propaganda and news would be identical. But the history of any religious group will illustrate that even official dogmas of infallibility do not prevent disagreement and even schism.

Modern concern with propaganda arises in the context of the totalitarian political systems that developed in Europe before World War II—and amid renewed worry about the effects of mass media on large numbers of people newly able to vote. The image of tens of thousands of Germans cheering Hitler at Nuremberg, captured and preserved on film in Leni Riefenstahl's *The Triumph of the Will,* provides a demonstration of the potential of media to establish political control and influence events up to and including war. Film was one medium of propaganda crucial to Germany (and other countries) before the war; even more influential were radio and print media. In the United States we have remained generally complacent about the influence of propaganda in our own society, assuming that if we avoid a centralized bureau of censorship, the free market system of information will allow us to avoid such means of controlling ideas.

ASSIGNMENT

View films of some World War II-era propaganda films—for example, *The Triumph of the Will,* and the *Why We Fight* series directed by Frank Capra. What are some of the devices by which these films presumably affected their audiences? How do these devices affect you now? Are there contemporary equivalents for these?

If possible, view some popular films from the same period or from the Cold War period to see how these merge entertainment with propaganda. Try war films featuring

John Wayne (*Back to Bataan, The Fighting Seabees, Sands of Iwo Jima, Flying Leathernecks*); compare these with more recent films involving war settings that had cooperation from the Pentagon (the *Rambo* films, *Red Dawn, Top Gun*), and with others that did not (*On the Beach, The Deer Hunter, Apocalypse Now*).

But propaganda has not ceased in the years since the end of World War II. During the early stages of the Cold War, concern with propaganda was focused not only on countries in the USSR's sphere of influence, but on means of communication and entertainment in the West as well. During the early 1950s this concern extended to blacklisting artists, actors, screenwriters, and others who were suspected not only of having been communists, but of any "leftist" tendencies. This was the period of the House Committee on Un-American Activities, with its public hearings into any manner of opposition to the U.S. government's activities here or abroad. The United States Information Agency was formed in this period, with its major agencies the Voice of America and Radio Free Europe, in order to counter communist propaganda with . . .

With what? With the Truth? With our own propaganda? How is it possible to distinguish objectively what was said by "our side" from what was said by "their side"? One test would be statements contrary to fact: If something is claimed contrary to fact, that should be a good indication that it's propaganda. (In that case, we would be guilty—though perhaps not equally guilty—as in our official denials of CIA activities, the faked North Vietnamese attack in the Gulf of Tonkin, denials of spying incidents such as the U2 shot down over the Soviet Union, and so on.) Another test: Propaganda slants evidence and tells only one side of things. (In that case, we should examine how Saddam Hussein was portrayed in American news accounts and official statements leading up to the Gulf War.) Propaganda is partial information used for a bad end, as opposed to balanced information that may be used for good ends. (In that case, we have to consider who judges good and bad.) Propaganda discourages the audience from seeking a diversity of opinion, whereas information encourages openness and confirmation.

The Cold War makes a good backdrop for a spy story. Whether your spy is named James Bond, Jack Ryan, or Maxwell Smart, it makes for a better story if contrasts are sharpened. Our side is for "truth, justice, and the American way" (as the opening to the 1950s *Superman* television series had it—recall that Clark Kent worked as a reporter for the *Daily Planet*), while their side is presumably opposed to these things. But the story loses some of its symmetry if we begin to ask about the free press in, say, Saudi Arabia, or in Central America, or in Chile after the CIA overthrew President Allende. In the East

European bloc, censorship was not as rigorous in Poland or Hungary as in Romania or China. So long as we recognize that conflicts between pure good and absolute evil belong to genres of popular fiction, we're OK. When we elect public officials, conduct public policy, and determine spending priorities on the basis of fiction, that's another matter.

The concept of propaganda depends on the classical "false consciousness" model of ideology (see Ideology: Definitions and Illustrations in Chapter 8). In that model, the world divides into (usually) two positions, *ours,* based on a correct understanding of the truth, and *theirs,* which is based either on delusion or on willful twisting of reality in order to suit an agenda. One problem with the false consciousness model is that it's ultimately nonconfirmable: You have to depend on a leap of faith in order to claim untranscendable truth, whether that truth is the word of Allah, or the Marxist understanding of history, or God as understood by one of the 150 Protestant religious denominations, or the "invisible hand" of the marketplace, or some other principle that gives you a leg up on the competition.

The idea of propaganda exists in contrast with something else—the truth, perhaps. It's propaganda if it's false, if it's an attempt to influence how you think, and so forth. But we've seen that media texts are always an attempt to influence how we think: "The truth" is always selected and arranged for us in a shape that conforms to our expectations of it, which in turn have been created for us by the culture at large. Seen in this way, all communication would be propaganda: You cannot get outside of interests—your own as well as those of a text's producers—in order to measure its degree of truth.

Judge a text by its effects: Whom is it meant to help? Whom is it meant to harm? You have to consider this for yourself—this is a textbook about media, not about ethics. But media do have ethical consequences, in themselves as well as in the messages they pass along. As a writer, you have a similar ethical responsibility.

Other stories about propaganda can be written (they often aren't) that depend not on the division of the world into two camps, black and white, along political lines, but on other structures. If we define propaganda as the effective creation and maintenance of an ideology, then Western societies (particularly the United States) are doing very effective propaganda—not so much through governmental controls but through the marketplace. Many texts in our culture reinforce and circulate the idea that happiness largely equals acquiring and consuming things. Advertising has advanced this view, collectively; the idea is often reinforced by entertainment texts that glamorize personal appearance and the benefits of having a good income; and news and information texts largely avoid messing the picture up too much. Given the total weight of commercial matters in U.S. culture, governmental promotion of this idea would be superfluous.

Susan Jeffords and Lauren Rabinovitz, in *Seeing Through the Media,* recount some devices by which U.S. support for intervention in the Persian Gulf was built. "In October 1990, testimony before the U.S. House of Representatives Human Rights Caucus told of Iraqi atrocities, particularly how Iraqi soldiers had removed babies from incubators in a Kuwait hospital and taken the incubators back to Iraq, leaving the infants to die on the hospital floor. The story was disseminated by the mainstream media and circulated quickly around the country. It became a justification cited by many people (including seven U.S. senators) for going to war against Iraq. The story was eventually revealed as a well-orchestrated propaganda campaign engineered by the public relations firm of Hill and Knowlton (a firm that was headed by former Vice President Bush's chief of staff, Craig Fuller). Hill and Knowlton made numerous videos (called 'video news releases') about Iraqi destruction of Kuwait and distributed these tapes to television news programs, many of which simply replayed them as 'news.' Although journalists eventually revealed that the incubator incident was propaganda, their articles did not appear until long [after] the war was over" (pp. 12–13). The same issue was raised in John McArthur's op-ed piece in the *New York Times,* January 6, 1992, and the ABC story on January 17, 1992.

Perhaps we should consider all attempts at persuasion as propaganda, and judge each (1) by how well it considers and represents opposing views, and (2) by what its aims are. If propaganda represents opposing arguments fairly and can tolerate dissent, that's different from propaganda that caricatures or silences opposing views in order to prevent its audience from thinking differently.

A discussion of advertising as propaganda will be part of Chapter 5. More relevant to this chapter is the question of how news media connect to those in power—specifically including corporations and what might be called culture leaders as well as governmental figures. What uses do media make of the powerful? What uses do those in power make of media? How does the system work to encourage certain interpretations and discourage others?

To start with, propaganda cannot be dismissed as brainwashing. Particularly during the 1950s, there was a fascination with the idea that people could be reprogrammed so as to value different things, to have different personalities, and so on. (There was much attention to GIs captured by the North Koreans and "brainwashed.") Popular media such as films and TV continued to consider the possibility, in a variety of forms—for example, in the 1956 film *Invasion of the Body Snatchers.* But propaganda is much more effective in working through seduction; that is, effective propaganda starts from beliefs and values already in circulation and flatters us into agreeing with it. Being told that "America is number one," for example, builds our confidence and self-esteem. We *want* to think so; and if news is carefully selected for us so as to build that impression, we will be pleased, and we'll continue to be an audience for that news. (Bad news can also be pleasing by confirming a negative viewpoint: Few sour pleasures are more gratifying than the opportunity to say "I told you so.") Effective propaganda works by telling us what we want to hear, quietly connecting that with what others want us to hear, and downplaying conflicting messages.

To dismiss a message as propaganda is a shortcut, a way to avoid considering the message's claims. But there are no good shortcuts—no substitutes for practice. You should practice distinguishing between fact, opinion, and inference, and practice seeing what ideological arguments are being used to advance. Is the effect of an argument to open up discussion, or to close it down?

Objectivity and Fairness

The professional ethic of objectivity in news is under attack from several directions. Those who are suspicious of the commercial side of news distrust the willingness and ability of reporters, editors, and producers to remain distant from powerful figures in government and business, from specific corporate interests in their area, from what might be called a general "free market" ideology, or from the understandable wish to write what people want to hear. Others note that objectivity is simply not possible: News is limited in time and space, which means there must be selection, and any selection must be done according to positions that are necessarily interested. Still others believe that objectivity is theoretically possible but that reporters and others in media have a political or social bias which is imposed through the news. Examining any of these or other attacks would require substantiation and evaluation of evidence.

Perhaps it would be more helpful if we adopted a different model. **Objectivity** requires perfection: To be completely objective implies a position outside of human weakness and interests, that of Mount Olympus or God on Judgment Day. The demand for objectivity directs our attention to the media product, to the text itself, measuring that against some ideal outside of history. It would be more useful to begin to think in terms not of being *objective*, but of being *fair*. **Fairness** directs attention not to the product but to the process. Have I considered other perspectives on this subject besides my own and those I agree with? What would opponents say of my point of view here? How have I gathered evidence? With an eye to supporting my position, which is already arrived at, and to weakening positions of others who don't agree with me? Or have I looked just as thoroughly, or even more thoroughly because it goes against my instincts, at the evidence for other interpretations? Have I looked at the possibility of flaws in my logic, such as drawing conclusions based on insufficient or nonrepresentative examples? Getting caught up in emotional appeals? Being swayed by analogies that don't really fit the case?

Being fair to opposing positions doesn't come naturally to us. It's hard work. It is easier to root with the home crowd at a football game, and boo at a referee's call against your team, than it is to maintain a point of reference that would be fair to the evidence. It's easier to listen to news for what will help your preferred side and hurt the other, rather than to hear everything out and weigh it impartially before or even after committing. So often we get appeals to our loyalty—calls to be patriotic, to be a team player at work, to "be true to your school"; and we may not observe that there's a cost to these appeals. Being fair requires discipline and ethical practices, but it will give you better credibility in the long run.

Within the limitations of deadlines and space, professional journalists try for accuracy and fairness. The standard of being fair admits to the existence of interests in an argument. Absolute standards of disinterest are hard to maintain, either in theory or in practice; but if you check your thinking through an issue at several stages to make sure you have given some energy to seeing what other perspectives might mean, that will be a considerable advance. And it gets at what is unconvincing in much contemporary rhetoric, its one-sidedness.

Much public discourse in the 1990s has been carried on with no attempt at fairness or balance, as with most of the texts in the health care debate. Many texts continue to be produced under the guidelines of responsible journalistic practice: The news parts of many newspapers and magazines, network news programs, *The News Hour With Jim Lehrer,* and public radio programs (among other texts) try to be scrupulous about making sure that several perspectives are presented and that reporters and anchors strike a tone of nonadvocacy. However, other texts make no such attempt at balance but take positions identified with specific perspectives. Most influential of these have been talk radio programs, which combine commentary by the host (in most cases, a political conservative) with phone calls from listeners. Not surprisingly, listeners are overwhelmingly in sympathy with the ideological positions of the hosts, so that little if any screening is necessary to bring phone calls into line with the agenda of the program. A common tactic on these shows is to present arguments on one side of an issue, largely devoted to showing that a specific initiative is foolish or harmful or hypocritical, with no attempt to air competing perspectives. Another rhetorical device is to claim the center—to say that the more traditional journalistic practices are "liberal," while those of the host's program are more in touch with "America," with the main evidence being the opinions of those who call into the program. The positions taken by hosts and listeners of such shows are overwhelmingly cynical toward governmental figures—but not usually toward conservative members of Congress, corporations, Ross Perot, or political figures such as Pat Buchanan or Pat Robertson. The callers are cynical toward "the media," but none of that cynicism is turned toward the medium they are listening to. The effects of uncritical listening can be illustrated by the news story excerpted below.

JEFFREY GOLD

Talk-Show Host Accused of Fraud
Endorsements by a radio talk-show host induced investors to spend $9.38 million on worthless shares of a would-be wireless cable system in Washington state, some of the angry buyers claim.

Harry I. "Sonny" Bloch, whose show is heard on 173 stations reaching 41 states, responded yesterday that the investors are "trying to extort money from me" because the cable company went bust.

Nearly all statements he made about the offering were during paid advertisements, Bloch said. The ads ran in February, March and April....

Lynne Berke of West Orange said she spent $20,000 on four units because she listened to Bloch for years and trusted him.

"We thought he was for the consumer, and whatever he said was gospel," Berke said. "It wasn't just an advertisement the way he did it."

The lawsuit contended the units were unregistered securities and illegal to sell in a public offering....

[The Sonny Bloch show] has aired for 15 years. Between 1.3 million and 1.6 million people listen to part of the four-hour show each day, Bloch said. It airs six days a week.

The broadcasters should have known listeners would be unable to distinguish between personal advice and advertising, the lawsuit said....

Bloch said his show runs more than 20,000 advertisements a year, and "If you're going to do that many commercials over that many years, you're bound to have sponsors who go bankrupt."...

He said he announces all commercials. If listeners cannot tell what is a commercial "they just aren't paying attention," he said. [Associated Press, December 1994. Used by permission.]

Less openly political are what might be called public affairs talk shows on television. Just as the call-in programs find radio a congenial medium, so these talk shows have gravitated to TV. Typically, producers for the show work with a theme, select participants to be interviewed (and often to dramatize a personal conflict), and look to the host to work with a live audience to interact with participants. These themes range from fairly responsible but personal treatments that arguably supplement more distanced public stances, to sensational and lurid topics. The more informal tones of these programs are signaled by the preponderance of first names among their hosts—*Oprah, Geraldo, Maury,* and the rest. The evening equivalents of these mostly daytime shows adopt less of their tabloid quality, but still involve the entertainment values of people shouting at each other. (See *The McLaughlin Group* or *CNN Crossfire.*)

The mixture of elements here does have its effect on how we gather news and information. Our expectations about the kind of program we are watching influence how we understand that information: If a program is mostly talking heads, we are inclined to think of what is presented as news. In the case of more traditional news programs, news copy is scrupulously checked by reporters, editors, and producers—not only to fit journalistic expectations of objectivity but, more pragmatically, to avoid the erosion of credibility and lawsuits. But if a program consists of clearly subjective and personal perspectives, expressed either by someone on the other end of the telephone or by people willing to come on camera to tell what they believe about what has happened to them, there are no facts to check, no one to sue. As audiences add more such shows to what counts as "information," more biased, incorrect, or distorted "facts" are added to the mix. People may become genuinely confused and unable to develop informed positions on matters such as health care or government spending.

The danger in the current state of information is not so much that government figures, corporate heads, and others in positions of authority are able to persuade the public to adopt views that reinforce the status quo—that goes on as usual—but that these voices are being supplemented by confusing and cynical attacks not only on "the left" (in terms of public discourse, there's no left left) but on centrist positions as well. Much of the public, presented with repeated claims that add up more or less to "they're all crooks," concludes that there's no point in voting for *anyone,* and as a result the United States has the lowest rate of participation in elections of any democracy. Decisions about public policy are being made in the sort of partisan discussions characteristic of election campaigns, rather than in a climate that would be fair to all positions.

Cynicism is a heady position to take. There can be a great sense of relief in being able to say "They're all crooks," "There's no difference between any of them," "The media are all in it for the money," and so on. It's a good story. But cynicism is paralyzing: Those who adopt it as a stance are most likely not to vote, not to consider supporting positive programs that might make a difference, and not to be able to persuade others of any value in their arguments. (How, logically, do you support an assertion that all politicians are corrupt?) Academic writing, like responsible journalism, requires that you support what you say. Healthy skepticism is a good stance to take toward what is offered you as fact—but without prejudging it as twisted or corrupt in advance.

CONCLUSION

This chapter began by encouraging you to evaluate your present means of gathering information, touched briefly on some strategies for adding to material already in draft form, and concluded with some problems in obtaining information through the system of news delivery that has evolved. Some of the problems are indirect consequences of our commercial system: Those with money and social position almost always have more chance to get their viewpoints heard, and the pursuit of wider audience shares can mean that the news provided is selected for dramatic impact.

However, the commercial system can be worked to your advantage, if you wish to be better informed. We in the United States are on average poorly informed about current events because staying informed seems like too much trouble; we resist going to the effort of gathering information in the first place or of evaluating the quality of what we do find (and ultimately the ideologies we bring to our information). But if you develop the capacity and habit for reading critically, our system can provide adequate information. Reading critically does not mean reading cynically: Dismissing everything because there's an interest behind its publication will leave you with no sources of information at all. Dismissing everything but one ideological viewpoint may be even worse, because it leaves you so vulnerable to manipulation. But if you develop the habit of checking competing sources—not just reading the *Times* and the *Post* and watching CNN and CBS, which may be working from the same wire service reports and corporate journalistic culture, but looking for positions by those who are really on opposing sides—then our system offers the possibility of good information for responsible choices.

The next three chapters will broaden issues of "information" beyond what is generally considered informative. Chapter 5 will look at commercials and test the extent to which these have developed techniques to influence our wishes and desires—techniques that have spilled over into information more generally. Chapter 6, on visual images, will invite a discussion about whether we get material through pictures equivalent to that previously delivered by print or by spoken language. And Chapter 7 will look at information that comes through entertainment media. These are important supplements to the notion that we learn important facts about contemporary life primarily through "the news."

FURTHER ASSIGNMENTS

Assignment
Look at "Labeling" in Chapter 8 for further discussion of how photographs and news stories contextualize each other. Drawing on this example as well as on the Barcia story on page 146, look for a comparable treatment in a newspaper or magazine of your choice.

Assignment
Write in your journal about stereotypical associations with the following: people who live on welfare; feminists; fundamentalist Christians; rock stars; straight-A students; politicians; college professors; students at your university; people who wear glasses; mechanics; Jews; Mexicans; athletes; blondes; working people; the French. Name other groups and provide their stereotypes. Can you come up with any groups about whom there are no stereotypes? If so, how do you account for this?

    Ask around in your class to see if anyone has been featured in a news story, has been interviewed on TV or in the newspaper, or knows well someone who has been. If so, how did they feel themselves represented?

    When you watch television news, keep tabs on everyone who is on camera. Make up categories as seems appropriate (anchor, reporter, expert, witness, victim, etc.). What groups—by race, age, gender, class, and so on—do the different categories fit into? What does the overall count tell you about how these groups are cumulatively viewed?

Assignment
Describe a news text that seemed to you to be biased. (If possible, work from a clipping or transcript or tape.) What is the interpretation being set forth by that text? Where do you perceive bias? What is the interpretation given in this news text, this source, this medium? Whose interpretation is it? What alternative interpretations does it supplant or leave out? Where does it match with and where does it conflict with your own interpretation? What effects does it achieve? Do you approve of these effects?

Assignment

Choose some recent event that has received reasonably wide coverage. Make video- and audiotapes so as to be able to repeat broadcast accounts, and collect two or three print accounts as well. Read these carefully to pick up on similarities and differences in the treatments in different media, and speculate on reasons behind these.

Assignment

Working collaboratively with other members of your class, choose some recent event that has affected students at your university and write a news report about it from at least three different perspectives, conceived of in terms of different media. For example, if there's a parking problem for students, you might write a news release from the college information office giving the administration's perspective (money's limited, we're doing all we can, at least it's better than the parking situation at Enormous State University, etc.); one for the student newspaper giving the students' view (we pay a lot of tuition, faculty and administration have privileges, dark parking lots are not only inconvenient but dangerous, etc.); and one from a group of taxpayers, pro or con (pro: parking's an important service, legislature should commit funds for improvement; con: projections are that enrollment will be going down soon, students should be encouraged to carpool, there are more important priorities than parking). Other possibilities might include lighting, buildings, or other capital improvements; class sizes; tuition increases; the campus bookstore; child-care facilities for working students.

As you discuss your drafts in groups, consider what larger frameworks or stories these accounts come from.

Assignment

If possible, view a videotape of news coverage of an earthquake or some similar disaster. Compare the visual dimensions of the coverage with the photographs in Exhibits 4.4 through 4.7 above. In what respects does print commentary plus photographs resemble, and in what differ from, television reporting on disasters?

APPENDIX 4.1: *CNN PRIME TIME* STORY ON EARTHQUAKE, 19 JANUARY 1995

Shot of smoke, attempts to put out fires.

May Lee: ...A more frustrating problem is access.

Shot along street in business district—smoke from fire in distance, people walking along street in foreground.

> Firefighters can't even get through the crowded and broken streets to help.

Shot of people in rubble; camera pivots right to a man in rubble.

> And this woman says rescue workers stood by helplessly when an old woman trapped under the rubble was burned alive.

Medium close-up of woman; she speaks in Japanese, crying as she talks. Translation:

> There was nothing they could do. They apologized to the old woman, saying, "I'm sorry," and came down from the debris.

Cut to shot of debris:

> We could still hear her calling out.

May Lee: On Thursday Japan's prime minister, Tomiichi Murayama,...

Cut to another shot of rubble; camera zooms back.

> ...surveyed the hardest-hit areas firsthand, and visited some of the 250,000 survivors...

Medium shot of five people talking in rubble.

> ...who are now homeless and angry.

Interior shot of two women sitting next to a wall, window above them. One woman speaks, in Japanese. Translation:

> Anyone can see how awful it must be...

Medium shot of prime minister in a crowd, surveying damage.

> ...but the prime minister has to do something about it.

Medium close-up of man, speaking in Japanese. Translation:

> Everyone is saying that it was good that Mr. Murayama came. But he should have brought some supplies with him.

Cut to interior shot—prime minister, with several other people, talking to earthquake refugees. Camera pulls back to show him bending over to talk to a woman seated on the floor.

Reporter: The prime minister promised more emergency assistance, including 13,000 self-defense forces.

Cut to shot of high stacks of boxes. Camera tracks forward, showing more boxes to right.

> Supplies are beginning to reach Kobe, but there is still no way to distribute them.

Cut to medium close-up of man in orange suit with hard hat, with black dog:

> Rescue efforts got a big boost Thursday, when a Swiss team arrived in Kobe...

Cut to another shot of a man in an orange suit with a dog—then cut to close-up of black dog barking.

> with dogs trained to search out survivors.

Cut to several men carrying a coffin.

> But here at this ancient temple turned into a temporary morgue, it is becoming all too clear—

Cut to shot of several coffins.

> time is quickly running out. May Lee, CNN, Tokyo.

Cut to CNN Anchor, Linden Soles: Over his head, a string of CNNs; below that, a row of monitors, a world map, other technical-looking equipment.

Soles: Prime Minister Murayama says the national government is doing its best to respond. It has set aside a billion dollars for relief. Still, criticism is growing that authorities were unprepared to respond to the disaster despite Japan's long experience with earthquakes. CNN's Mike Chinoy on that.

Cut to medium shot of red fire truck. Caption over photo, CNN logo and "Earthquake Preparedness." Lower right, caps CNN NEWS Update. Cut to telephoto shot of two men squatting, with rags over their faces.

Mike Chinoy: (Sirens, voice over bullhorn.) Every year, Japanese have an Earthquake Preparedness Day...

Cut to shot of a fireman on a cherry picker, followed by distant shot of a building with an emergency slide out a third-story window. Someone is sliding down the chute.

when people all across the country practice coping with the prospect of a major tremor.

Close-up of two children under a table, which is being shaken left to right. Camera zooms back to medium shot. Cut to videotape footage (black and white) of an office (?) with furniture being shaken by earthquake. A few seconds into the film, the lights go out.

But when the real thing happened, the Japanese found themselves overwhelmed, the best-laid plans collapsing like the buildings of downtown Kobe.

Cut to telephoto shot of a fire; cut to longer shot of the same fire, visible from down a street.

As the once elegant port city burned, rescue workers were unable to reach many of the worst-hit areas...

Cut to an aerial shot of another fire, followed by aerial shot of a freeway with two trucks and a car, tilted at a sharp angle. Camera pans up and along a long shot of the freeway.

...their movements blocked by the rubble of shattered buildings, highways, and railway lines supposedly designed to withstand such tremors.

Cut to shot of city intersection with hundreds of people crossing. Slow zoom in to medium shot.

To a people told for years that their earthquake preparations were second to none, it has been a considerable shock.

Cut to medium close-up of man outdoors, in front of building, wearing a suit and tie; other people walking past. After a few seconds, caption identifies him as Professor Motohiko Hakuno, School of Engineering, Tokyo University. Translation:

I don't think it was enough only to have construction merely earthquake-proof. We have to reconsider everything.

Mike Chinoy: The experts agree.

Cut to another man, medium close-up in interior shot, also wearing suit and tie. Translation:

> We felt buildings and bridges were strong enough that they wouldn't collapse. That's been our attitude for the past few years. Now I think the basic construction method against quakes should change.

Cut to shot along a section of freeway—shot looks down to a break in the road, another section inclines up.

Mike Chinoy: Already the transport ministry has announced an urgent review...

Cut to shot of wrecked train. Camera pans quickly left to show extent of this wreck.

> ...of antiquake construction standards...

Cut to collapsed section of building—now looks like a courtyard. Camera zooms slowly back and pans up and left to show several stories of a building fallen across a street.

> ...looking at ways to ensure structures have greater flexibility to withstand major tremors.

Cut to aerial shot of another collapsed building in an intersection.

> But the Japanese people have to be prepared to pay for any improvements.

Close-up of Western man in gray beard and glasses, in suit—background is same as for expert above. The man is identified as Professor Robert Geller, seismologist, Tokyo University.

> There are lots of things that can be done, but they all cost money. So everyone right now would be ready to pay the extra cost. But if you ask them in a month or two they might not be willing to any more.

Cut to telephoto of intersection, perhaps the one above—closer shot, with perhaps ten people at a time on screen. Camera zooms back and pans up.

Mike Chinoy: In the meantime, the Kobe disaster has set off a wave of anxiety here in Tokyo, where a major quake has long been predicted.

Cut to close-up of a box, white-on-red label in English, "Emergency Foods/Sanritsu." Camera pans back to show a display in a store.

> Stores report a run on emergency supplies like bottled water...

Cut to department-store shot; woman and man in foreground, backs to camera; before them is a display, with three hard hats on styrofoam heads visible.

... canned and dried food, protective helmets and flashlights.

Medium close-up of man in jacket, scarf; two men visible behind him; exterior shot, looks like a street or a shop. Translation:

> This quake has made us more aware that a big quake could hit Tokyo. I'm much more concerned now. It's become a problem very close to home.

Cut to young woman on street; traffic visible to right. Translation as voice over her comments:

> I'm always thinking about what to do when the quake actually hits. It's a very scary thing.

Cut to telephoto shot of crowded sidewalk, mostly of people facing camera.

Mike Chinoy: To people all across Japan, the earthquake in Kobe has brought home a sense of vulnerability to the forces of nature.

Cut to medium close-up of Mike Chinoy, speaking on camera: exterior shot, with city lights visible behind. Caption—Mike Chinoy, Tokyo:

> In the short term, though, there's little the residents of Tokyo can do, except to hope it doesn't happen here. Mike Chinoy, Tokyo.

Cut to medium close-up of anchor:

Soles: The U.S. embassy now says that two Americans are known to have died in Kobe's quake. Both were female English teachers. It estimates at least 8,000 Americans are in the Kobe area.

Segue to New Yorker who returned home after the quake.

(© 1995 Cable News Network, Inc. All Rights Reserved. Used by permission.)

APPENDIX 4.2: *CBS EVENING NEWS,* 19 JANUARY 1995

Connie Chung *(in medium close-up)*: Good evening. The death toll in Japan has passed 4,000, and it's still rising.

Voice-over, on top of film footage of workers digging in rubble, injured being carried on stretchers:

> By now, it's Friday morning in Kobe, three days since the earthquake struck. A few more survivors were pulled from the rubble in the last twenty-four hours, but now hope is fading for the missing, and those who did live through the quake are desperate for help.

Diagonal wipe to map of Japan, with Kobe labeled in white on red and concentric circles marking the earthquake.

> Correspondent Bob Simon is on the disaster scene.

Label for Kobe enlarges and becomes the top of a rectangle; beneath the label is a tracking shot of a street. Background: rubble. Foreground: mostly people walking, a stationary vehicle (truck with a bulldozer on it).

Bob Simon: The city of Kobe was hardest hit by this quake, but this isn't Kobe, it is the road to Kobe, ten miles out of town. (*Siren in background.*)

Cut to a building with the exterior wall missing; a bunk bed is visible in the foreground, along with some other household items.

> The cold, cruel sun shone today inside homes which look like dolls' houses now.

Cut to woman with a backpack on sidewalk with numerous household goods on display. Camera follows her a short distance.

> Suburbanites transformed into scavengers, searching for what was left of their lives. (*She picks up a desk lamp.*)

Cut to man carrying a box through some rubble; camera zooms back to a shot of a ruined building with what appears to be a power line tower down in the background.

> And there they were, serenaded by sirens, meeting disaster the Japanese way—

Cut to Bob Simon walking over some rubble; cut to a middle-aged woman with a rag over her head, in the middle of some rubble.

—with unflinching politeness.

Woman speaks in Japanese; voice-over gives translation. She's holding some papers.

Woman: I was here when it happened. I was hit in the face. My son's in the hospital.

Cut to medium close-up.

Thank you. Thank you for coming. (*She bows.*)

Cut to view of city street, with much traffic, cars on the right, pedestrians on the sidewalk, going and coming. Buildings are present on the right, rubble on the left. During voice-over below, there are several cuts to different street scenes; the first two are stationary shots of traffic, the last a tracking shot of a man with a bandage on his face, wearing a backpack.

Bob Simon: The sides of the road were clogged with Japan's new homeless, many of them walking wounded, walking out of town. Walking where? Very few seem to know.

Cut to another street: Truck visible in background, man in foreground wrapped in an orange blanket. Camera circles around him.

The men wrapped in orange aren't Buddhist monks. They're among the new refugees, just trying to keep warm.

Cut to four people standing between a car and a fence.

There's a man showing his wounds, speaking of his wife who cannot help him because she is dead.

Cut to tracking shot of a four-lane street, across a median. Building in background.

Ambulances heading towards Kobe were often paralyzed by gridlock,

Cut to telephoto shot of traffic cop waving bumper-to-bumper traffic along.

and this was the only way into town,

Cut to medium shot of pedestrians on crowded sidewalk. Cut to shot along rails, twisted into waves.

because this is the railroad,

Cut to collapsed overpass, on top of vans.

and this is the freeway.

Slow zoom in on broken overpass. Cut to surface of freeway, twisted up on the right. Two machines are at work picking up chunks of asphalt. Camera zooms back, reporter walks in at medium shot, dressed in trench coat. Superimposition: "Bob Simon/CBS News." CBS logo in lower right of screen.

Bob Simon: When Los Angeles loses a freeway like this, many Californians speak of hitting the road, going to another state. For the Japanese, there's no place to move to. No place is safe.

Cut to city street, with crushed car in foreground. Camera pans up and left to wrecked building.

Voice-over: In Kobe, the fires ignited by this quake were all out by this morning.

Cut to alley with burning building in background, two firemen in foreground.

There were ninety new ones by midday.

Camera pans up and right to the house's roof. Cut to tracking shot of fireman squatting in an alley, spraying water onto a fire; then to four firemen carrying heavy rubble in a tarp.

The firemen ran from putting out blazes to digging for the dead.

Cut to medium close-up of young man looking left (CBS logo at lower right). Pan up to young person crying.

They were still pulling them out today. The list of the missing grows shorter;

Cut to firemen in hard hats carrying a body; in foreground are the two young people from previous shot, their backs to the camera. One man in foreground is taking a picture.

the death toll keeps rising.

Cut to woman covering her face with a cloth, a girl next to her.

Every excavation brings a new onslaught of grief.

Cut to older woman lying on stretcher, in close-up.

But this old woman was alive after two days under the rubble.

Camera pulls back to show fireman at right, bending over her. Cut to same fireman, in medium close-up, wearing a helmet and chin strap. Microphone is in his face.

"Everything collapsed on her," the fireman says.

Cut back to woman on stretcher, in medium shot; two firemen are working with her. One of them touches her legs as he asks about them.

"Her legs were crushed. She says her husband is still inside." "Can you feel your legs?" "Yes." "Do they hurt?" "Yes."

Cut to medium close-up of old man with fur cap on; fire truck in background, right. Camera pivots as he kneels down beside the stretcher.

Then an old man runs up. It is her husband.

Camera circles to the right so as to get both his and her faces, then zooms in on him to extreme close-up. Camera zooms back, then up again.

He was rescued on Tuesday, ran away from the hospital, came back here. Now she doesn't recognize him. "Don't you know me?" he says.

Extreme close-up as he takes her hand; part of her face is visible in the shot.

"I've been shouting your name all day and all night."

Top view of man and woman on stretcher; camera moves in and down.

Yes, she recognizes him finally,

Cut to several firemen carrying the woman to the vehicle. They move off-camera while the man is shown watching, in close-up.

then she is taken away.

Camera pivots around to the right while she is loaded into what appears to be a station wagon.

The earthquake which shattered the homes and the lives of these people

Cut to street scene—less crowded now. Couple pushing a baby carriage, with many blankets strapped into it.

didn't lay a finger on the depths of their dignity, their determination.

Cut to medium shot of man in a house without an exterior wall; another person is next to him, foreground, and a third man in the background. The man in the center holds up two fingers in a V sign.

"The Japanese are strong," says the man in the rubble. "We will rebuild."

The man waves and walks back into the room.

Bob Simon, CBS News, Kobe.

(CBS News Archives. Used by permission.)

APPENDIX 4.3: *ALL THINGS CONSIDERED,* 19 JANUARY 1995

Robert Segal: The death toll from the earthquake that hit Japan this week has now climbed above 4,000. That makes it Japan's deadliest natural disaster since the 1923 Tokyo earthquake. Several hundred people remain missing, a handful are still being pulled alive from the wreckage.

In a rare public statement, Emperor Akito expressed his condolences; he said, "from the bottom of my heart." And he offered words of encouragement: "I truly hope everyone can overcome this unfortunate period," he said, "through strong solidarity and cooperation." The Japanese government is accepting technical assistance from the rest of the world, and is beginning the task of rebuilding the shattered city of Kobe, and the other areas worst hit by the quake. NPR's Julie McCarthy reports.

Julie McCarthy: *(in the background as she talks can be heard heavy moving equipment):*

Today, vast stretches of the Japanese city of Kobe look like war zones, a testament to the power of nature. Reconstruction crews don't know where to begin. Buildings have literally been shredded, and entire sections of walls flap in the wind like long oversized strips of paper. A hospital in one of the city's worst-hit wards had to be evacuated when two of its wings buckled. A surgeon at the hospital says he treated 500 patients since the quake struck Tuesday, but added, the seriousness of the injuries has subsided, and that most today are minor.

Surgeon's voice, in Japanese, followed by translation (woman's voice):

It was just like a mountain of dead people. One after the other, dead people were brought in to the hospital.

Sound of siren (continues in background as she talks):

This nonstop wailing punctuates the air everywhere here, a constant reminder that this was the worst natural disaster to hit a major urban area in Japan since Tokyo was leveled in 1923. Japan's self-defense forces have been mobilized to help cope. The convoys of green trucks form long lines as they inch through the city, delivering badly needed food, medical supplies, and blankets. Rescuing victims of the quake trapped under the debris of homes and apartment buildings is one of their chief tasks. And one officer described how inexact a science the excavations really were.

Officer's voice, in Japanese, followed by translation (man's voice):

> There is no clue where to find the missing people. If you have family members around, and have them pointing out where they might be buried, you might be able to do it. But if you don't have that, you have to take things one at a time, case by case, and there's no information about where they're buried.

Sound of many people conversing; continues in background:

Julie McCarthy: Back at City Hall, the war room has been set up. Snaps line the walls, and sad statistics chronicle the life of the quake. Sheets of paper, some tacked to bulletin boards, document the rising death toll, the number of fires, the number of people who have been forced to evacuate their homes. Rescue teams and utility crews are dispatched from here. A spokesman for the relief operation has been surveying the damage, and said that [in] areas where wooden homes were clustered closely together, there's nothing now but kindling.

Spokesman's voice, in Japanese, followed by translation (man's voice):

> I've been patrolling the city, and when I saw it, I almost cried.

Julie McCarthy: This kind of devastation wasn't supposed to happen here. The area is a rather quiet one, as quakes go in Japan, a country that prided itself on its technology to spare itself the worst when a big tremor struck. Those assumptions are now being challenged by the experts today, and, acknowledges the relief spokesman, the residents as well.

Spokesman's voice, in Japanese, followed by translation (man's voice):

> The people are holding their anger, and they don't know who they can be angry with. But we just accept that as part of the city government, and we want to restore the city.

Julie McCarthy: Those who were forced to leave their homes have taken up residence on the floor of City Hall. This forty-story building, which sustained only minor damage, has been turned into a huge homeless shelter. Residents crowd around phone banks in an attempt to reach family members in other cut-off areas, and as they fight for floor space for their futons, in the drafty halls and stairways, there's a remarkable spirit of optimism.

Woman's voice, in Japanese, followed by translation:

It is miraculous to be alive. Everybody in our family survived.

Julie McCarthy: Prime Minister Tomiichi Murayama paid a visit to the area today. He told a news conference that all the briefings he had had couldn't prepare him for what he saw.

Prime Minister Murayama, in Japanese, followed by translation:

This is a disaster so big, no one could have imagined it.

Julie McCarthy: By nightfall, it is evident that large sections of the city are still without electricity. The only lights illuminating any streets were searchlights, or fires set by those who were made refugees from their own homes. This is Julie McCarthy, reporting.

(© Copyright National Public Radio® 1995. This news report by NPR's Julie McCarthy was originally broadcast on National Public Radio's *All Things Considered* on January 19, 1995, and is used with the permission of National Public Radio. Any unauthorized duplication is strictly prohibited.)

APPENDIX 4.4: NPR *MORNING EDITION*, 20 JANUARY 1995

Susan Stamberg: The hundreds of thousands of residents of the Japanese city of Kobe who were left homeless by Tuesday's earthquake now face hunger, cold, and the threat of disease. Relief teams, many using trained dogs, continue to search the rubble that was Kobe. In the past twenty-four hours, close to fifty people have been found alive, including an eighty-five-year-old grandmother. NPR's Mary Kay Magistad spent the day touring the city, talking with survivors. She joins us now from Kobe, where it is evening.

Susan Stamberg: Mary Kay, how are people in Kobe dealing with this disaster and the aftermath of it?

Mary Kay Magistad: Well, very stoically, at the moment, for the most part. I mean, people are still obviously in shock about how much they have lost in terms of lives of people they care about, their homes, their cars, their livelihoods. In many cases, offices are completely destroyed, and people are wandering around, saying "you know, I don't know when I'll be going in to work again, it could be months, and I don't know what I'm going to do in the meantime." But, for all of that, you know, I'm in the middle of the Kobe City Hall at the moment, where there are hundreds of people camping out, and the attitude among many of them is, you know, we're just glad we have a roof over our heads, at the moment, we're getting food and water, and we're helping each other out here, and some people even say "We'd like to be able to dream about a time when life in Kobe is going to be normal again, but in the meantime, we're just gonna have to make do."

Susan Stamberg: Um-hmm. There have been almost continual aftershocks since the big quake struck on Tuesday. What kind of effect has that caused?

Mary Kay Magistad: Well, in fact, yeah, there have been many aftershocks, hundreds in fact, and one of the problems has been that in fact when people do go back to their homes, to their apartment buildings, to their offices, to try to pick through the rubble, sometimes they're there when an aftershock comes, and more rubble is dislodged, and they get injured. I was at one hospital today where two or three of the people being admitted were those kinds of injuries.

Susan Stamberg: Yeah. There have been warnings from some seismologists that the aftershocks could be as intense as the original earthquake. Are people prepared for that possibility?

Mary Kay Magistad: Oh, people are definitely scared. You know, whenever they feel another aftershock, of course, they start thinking about the original earthquake and wondering, you know, whether there's going to be a lot more damage from the aftershock they're feeling, and of course none of them has been anything close to the original earthquake. But these people are traumatized, and they definitely are nervous every time they feel the ground shake.

Susan Stamberg: Who's involved in helping the relief effort now?

Mary Kay Magistad: Well, there are the traditional groups, like the Japanese Red Cross, there's the Japanese self-defense forces, which have boosted their numbers here over the last day or so, the police, the fire departments, et cetera, but then there are also some rather unconventional groups that have joined in. There's the Yakuza, which is the Japanese version of the Mafia, they're distributing food and water. [Susan Stamberg laughs.] I was walking down the street today and saw this extreme right-wing group that had trailers emblazoned with slogans about the islands that are disputed by Russia, other sorts of extremely right-wing slogans about Japanese nationalism and pride, and they were handing out hot cups of noodles and drinks to anyone who passed by. So a lot of political groups are kind of getting their licks in, and hoping that people remember them afterward for having helped out at the right time.

Susan Stamberg: NPR's Mary Kay Magistad, speaking with us from Kobe, Japan. Natural disasters in this country are sometimes followed by hysteria, rage, and some pretty hearty finger-pointing, blaming. The stoicism in Kobe underscores some deep cultural differences between Japan and the United States. A number of observers say the attitude of the Kobe victims emerges from something called *shogunai*, a Japanese expression and philosophy that means literally, "cannot help it." On the line with us to help to explain it is Yoshio Hota. For seven years he's been a freelance journalist in this country, but he's lived here for twelve years. Talk to us a little bit more about that philosophy, the *shogunai*, "cannot help it." Is it what we could call "stoicism"?

Yoshio Hota: Yes, in the daily life we use *shonunai* pretty often. "It can't be helped," or it could be "destiny."

Susan Stamberg: And do you only apply it to natural disasters, storms, tsunamis, earthquakes?

Yoshio Hota: No. Someone beyond your power, beyond your ability, something's going on, that you really cannot touch, you could say, *shonunai*. Like someone, some thing, precious thing on the shelf, falls down, and it's broken, you could say *shonunai*.

Susan Stamberg: Is this, by the way, a survival skill that seems to work particularly well in Japan, where so many millions of people are crammed into such a small space? Is it just sort of a coping skill—there's so many of us, so little room, we've got to find ways to get along?

Yoshio Hota: Um-hmm, and so tight and dense, homogeneous society teaches us and the way we behave, and once we're in the train or the bus it's always so crowded. You might know the Japanese jump trains, in commuting time—

Susan Stamberg: Yes.

Yoshio Hota: Yeah. And nobody complains about that, unofficially. People can handle it. This is the way it is.

Susan Stamberg: And this is *shogunai*.

Yoshio Hota: *Shonunai.*

Susan Stamberg: What are you permitted then to express in public with a philosophy like that? I mean, is it seen as a disgrace to get hysterical, to tear your hair out when your house has collapsed in an earthquake?

Yoshio Hota: If somebody really complains and blaming someone, he might be dropped out from the society. Another phrase called *hachibu*. Now this means it's to let someone drop out of society, you're not in the village, this is the literal meaning, any more.

Susan Stamberg: So you're ostracized, really.

Yoshio Hota: Right. And you lose your face. You can't associate with us any more.

Susan Stamberg: I noticed, too, in the reports that there is no looting going on in Kobe.

Yoshio Hota: That's correct.

Susan Stamberg: And I wondered, too, would someone seen to take advantage of a situation like this, would that be seen as a loss of face, too?

Yoshio Hota: Yes, a reporter and I covered Hurricane Andrew... in 1992.

Susan Stamberg: Hurricane Andrew?

Yoshio Hota: At night I saw the many looters and burglars moving around in Homestead, Florida. But in Japan, after the earthquake, no one actually would do such a thing.

Susan Stamberg: It's really a very strong social contract about behavior.

Yoshio Hota: Exactly. I think so, and if you do that, the Japanese police might arrest these people, and they might lose their face, and in this kind of tragedy, you do such really worse things as a human being.

Susan Stamberg: What else has struck you as a reporter covering a natural disaster here as being different?

Yoshio Hota: When I covered Hurricane Andrew, I saw so many volunteers and the rescue team groups from other states. But I don't see that many volunteers in Kobe area at this moment.

Susan Stamberg: And what do you think the reason for that is?

Yoshio Hota: People tend to rely on the government and we might contribute some cash, money, but all the government people should take care of this.

Susan Stamberg: Very different, and very interesting. Thank you so much.

Yoshio Hota: You're welcome.

Susan Stamberg: Journalist Yoshio Hota.

(© Copyright National Public Radio® 1995. This news report by NPR's Mary Kay Magistad was originally broadcast on National Public Radio's *Morning Edition* on January 20, 1995, and is used with the permission of National Public Radio. Any unauthorized duplication is strictly prohibited.)

5

Close Attention to Detail: Regarding the Commercial

OVERVIEW

If you were asked to think of a kind of media text at the furthest extreme from what is usually studied in college classes, perhaps the first choice would be advertising. Ads are so foreign from usual assumptions about higher education that treating them as a serious topic requires some explaining, even in a text about the rhetoric of media. College is widely regarded as being about knowledge that is valued and probably difficult, not popular and accessible, and about knowledge that will last. Media texts are notorious for not lasting long—nothing is more useless than old news, except for wrapping fish and recycling. (You can't even wrap fish in old television news.) And ads get old faster than anything.

Of all the popular media, television is probably most removed from what people value in higher education. And of everything to be seen on television, the least valued texts are the ads. As viewers, we don't really count commercials as part of what we are watching. For most of us, the only positive aspect to ads is that they subsidize the costs of the media we want to have—print media or broadcast, information or entertainment.

But annoying or not, ads are important to study. Most of us, as consumers, are in denial about the persuasive power of advertising. Even when we admit that *some* people are swayed by the usual pitches for wheels and meals, soaps and suds, we may assert that ads have no hold on us personally. But businesses are not in the habit of spending money unnecessarily. At least fifty U.S. corporations have advertising budgets in excess of $200 million annually (Mayle p. 103); clearly they believe that advertising has results. If we want to understand media, we have to look at its commercial side: Nowhere in contemporary society is rhetoric more visible.

Advertising is the dark secret of media. The commercial—like slavery in the pre–Civil War South—makes the whole system work. Neither producers nor consumers want to acknowledge this, because we prefer to think that our entertainment and our information come to us as a free public service, used without obligation. But the commercial side of media moves the rest, as we can see by examining why television programs are canceled, why radio stations change formats, and how newspapers and magazines grow larger and smaller to accommodate advertising. The system works more smoothly if its money-making aspects are kept at a distance from the rest. In order to get a clear understanding of media in the United States, then, we have to look at the connections between commercials and everything else.

Ads are good texts for the examination of rhetoric. As we read or watch them, we are conscious that they are attempting to persuade us to adopt one point of view. News texts, by contrast, do not normally take sides so directly. Ads exist to sell things, and all but the youngest or most naive readers understand this. We may or may not easily agree that *Beverly Hills 90210,* the *Wall Street Journal,* CNN, or Casey Kasem adopt rhetorical positions. But we understand clearly that advertisers are interested parties, and we recognize that they will use their devices as means of persuasion. Watching ads, we are assumed to be on our guard. And in order to reach us despite our wariness, the advertisters' rhetoric must be effective indeed.

In addition to their rhetorical openness, other features of ads also make them good texts for analysis. First, they are short, so that it's possible to register *everything* that is there. (Television commercials can be somewhat more complex than print ads or radio commercials, but videotape makes it possible to analyze them as well.) Second, there are plenty of ads to analyze. For sheer number, they probably outnumber all other genres of texts: Ads are to the textual world what insect species are to the biological. With the high number of commercial messages most of us see every day, it's not surprising that most pass without our conscious notice. Third, because we take ads so much for granted, getting some meaning from them offers us the interest of discovery.

Understanding the rhetoric of advertisement will require you to look at the overall enterprise of advertising, drawing on what you already know and extending it through systematic observation. It will mean developing the capacity to classify and reclassify ads in order to defamiliarize them from their usual settings and bring out themes and relations that may normally be hidden. It will mean doing some close reading of ads in order to see how the smallest parts contribute to the whole message. In other words, studying the rhetoric of advertising means developing facility in **analysis.**

Analysis means breaking something down in order to examine the parts and their functions. Analysis is basic to all areas of study, and it is a practice that can be pointed in any direction. You *can* analyze anything. The question is, what *should* you analyze? The central issue in advertising is the combination of its pervasiveness in our culture and our persistent belief that ads have no effect on us. Getting at this issue will require that you look at your own responses as a starting point for what might be considered the story of *common sense,* about ads and more generally about media. What attitudes and values are taken for granted by media? If we can discover how attitudes and values are referenced by details in ads, we may find a basis for greater latitude of choice in deciding how we participate in media.

Analyzing rhetorical texts such as ads should offer some advantages for your own use of rhetoric. Successful rhetoric depends on skilled use of details to build a unified presentation in the smallest as well as the largest concerns. The capacity to read closely—whether advertisements, poems, or the fine print in contracts—is very useful to develop. Your writing style, and the self you project through your writing, is built of an accumulation of small choices. Seeing the small choices that go to creating effective ads should help you when you reconceive and rework your writing tasks.

In this chapter, then, we will be surveying the terrain of advertising (concentrating on print ads and television commercials) for the purpose of examining texts in detail. This book assumes a wide experience with advertising texts, but not necessarily any background in their analysis. Our ads will provide an illustration of the practice of close reading, a technique that allows us to move from the explicit to the implicit—from what is obviously *there* to what it implies or what we can conclude from it.

As we saw in our discussion of news, we don't simply read a text, but insert it into some other "stories." This is especially true of advertisements, because they work more by symbol and suggestion than do news texts. When we make inferences about a text, we participate in creating its meaning, not just receiving some previously existing meaning. Becoming a more skillful close reader of texts (ads and others) will extend your control over them.

Making inferences about texts has to start with literal observation, with paying attention to what ads are made of: images, words, stories. Your experience with words by now should tell you that not everything can be found in the dictionary. Dictionaries list specific meanings, but do not and cannot show all the associations. (For example, *bitch* is defined as a female dog, and there is some mention of its slang uses—but that doesn't convey very much about the term in use. See the essay "What a Bitch!" in Chapter 10.)

All texts, not just single words, have what might be considered both a denotative and a connotative function. There's a portion that is literal—say, a photograph of two men shaking hands while a third looks on (Exhibit 5.1)—and a portion that is figurative. The two men represent others: The late Yitzhak Rabin represents the government and people of Israel, Yasser Arafat represents the Palestinian people, and Bill Clinton the mediating presence of the United States. In other words, we cannot stay with the literal level, even if we want to; we always bring our previous experience into forming an interpretation along symbolic lines. Ads provide a useful terrain for observing this process.

And there's another use to analysis: It allows you to check the basis of ideas, your own and those which derive from others. Writing provides the

Exhibit 5.1 Yitzhak Rabin, Bill Clinton, and Yasser Arafat, 1994. AP/Wide World Photos.

opportunity, and the responsibility, of examining the basis of your and others' judgments. You need to look carefully, programmatically, and fairly at details (as at stories in Chapter 4) to get at the truth of your contentions. This practice will help you solidify your own logic and put across your ideas with greater authority. It's important to examine carefully the basis of what you think and argue—and it helps convince others if you can show that you have done so.

The discussion in this chapter, like your own examination of ads, will employ three basic approaches:

1. *Collecting and classifying advertisements:* It is useful to develop a base of information gotten together deliberately and programmatically, rather than just taking what comes to hand. Accumulating a large number of advertisements will allow you to group these so as to illustrate your contentions about advertising.
2. *Developing a grammar for discussing techniques in print ads and commercials:* No analysis can proceed very far until we can develop a language to account for what is going on in the text. This grammar will enable you to choose a short text and describe its literal surface so as to move from that to inferences about it.
3. *Gathering observations about how audiences respond to ads:* It's important that, rather than repeating conventional opinions, you do your best to confirm how ads are actually received, by you and by others you know.

ISSUES

Why Ads?

In the contemporary United States, more money, time, and professional expertise is devoted to advertising than to any other rhetorical line of work—possibly excepting law and politics. A significant part of the national economy goes into advertising—more than $30 billion annually. According to the Newsprint Information Committee, ads occupy 65 percent of the space of the daily newspaper (Bagdikian p. 135); this can be compared to around 30 percent of prime-time commercial television and a similar percentage of radio broadcasts. Advertising is also present in billboards, direct mail, World Wide Web postings, and many other venues. A good starting point might be considering how all these advertisements are received by their audiences. For this, it will be useful to assess your and others' attitudes toward advertising.

PAUSE FOR REFLECTION
Write in your journal briefly about advertising. What is your reaction to advertising as a practice? Do you believe it stimulates the economy? That it misleads people? Do you enjoy reading ads or watching commercials, or do you try to avoid them, or some of both? Do you see your attitude toward ads as typical? Do you talk with others about ads?

More than any other genre, advertisements provoke hostile reactions. Not all ads do so, and not everyone resents ads equally strongly. But you will probably find more resistance to advertising in general than to soap operas, sermons, porno films, sports programs, or other media texts you might name. One explanation for this resentment is ads' wide exposure. No one has to watch World Wrestling Federation matches, the Shopping Channel, or infomercials; no one has to listen to country music, talk radio, classical music, alternative rock, or Muzak (excepting those who work where it's played); no one has to read tabloids or the *Reader's Digest*. But everyone encounters advertising, in the middle of "free" TV or "free" radio, commuting in a bus or train, or driving along the road. Ads compete for our attention, divert us from our private thoughts, and insinuate their way into our conversation. Because we are saturated with commercial messages, in almost every medium, but particularly in television, the reaction is mostly resentful indifference and willed unconsciousness. As a student put it in a journal entry:

> In a thirty-second spot, you have almost a cut per second. That is too fast for you to pick up on or care about.... Most advertising is done because [advertisers] are afraid to find out what happens if they don't. Spending money, lots of money, on fear is ridiculous. People have become impervious to the constant bombardment of ads. I don't remember any of them unless someone brings it up specifically. Then I remember that I saw it. I don't remember them when I see the product either. Maybe this is my own defense system, but I'll go out on a limb and say everyone has this defense system. Some are more effective than others. (Gary Banks)

You may have found your own "defense system" penetrated by ads that stand out for some reason. An ad may be attractive because it's funny or touching or well made. You may notice a commercial if it's for a product you are thinking of buying or for a service you need. Or you may be struck by a situation portrayed in an ad that is either similar to your own experience, or so far from probability that you are amused or annoyed. Or you may simply indulge in staring at pretty pictures. Ads that conflict with your views about how men and women behave or should behave, ads that perpetuate or conflict with racial or ethnic stereotypes, ads that insult a region of the country with which you identify, all may catch your attention. The music or a slogan in an ad may stay in your head despite any conscious intention of yours. Just as in any situation where you want to get someone's attention, ads use a variety of devices, from shouting to taking you by the arm to telling you what you want to believe to backing you into a corner and offering you unbelievable prizes and "free gifts."

While there may be exceptions, most people have difficulty consciously recalling advertisements. Test this assertion: Can you recall the last ad you saw on television? Any ad you saw in yesterday's newspaper or in a magazine you read recently?

PAUSE FOR REFLECTION

Write for ten minutes or so, recalling as many television commercials as you can over the past week. When you run out of what you can recall, write about advertisements in other media—radio, billboards, newspapers, magazines, and so on. Rely solely on memory.

When you can no longer recall any advertisements seen or read over the past week, list *any* others that you recall.

Look back over what you've written, and take up a related topic: How much do television commercials, and advertising in other media, seem to stay in your mind? If you have little or no trouble recalling ads, why is this? If you have trouble remembering any ads, why? If you recall ads selectively, what is at work behind the selection? Do you remember ads for specific products or services? Do you recall one genre better than another? Do you remember ads for the techniques they use (for example, jingles or catchphrases)?

It's surprising we can't usually recall more ads, because we see so many. It's been estimated that by age seventeen the average child in the United States has seen (counting repetitions) 350,000 commercials (Bagdikian p. 185). But perhaps the reason is that exposure to that many commercials makes them into a complete blur—or, perhaps, so many commercials work to keep us generally interested in buying, apart from specific products.

According to the American Association of Advertising Agencies, cited in a 1969 article, "1,600 advertising messages are aimed at a consumer in an average day.... [T]he average consumer takes momentary notice of about eighty commercial messages. Only twelve make a conscious impression," which may not motivate the consumer to buy (Bagdikian pp. 185–86).

Perhaps our annoyance with ads is the result of their familiarity—as with an acquaintance we see too often, or school cafeteria food. And it's not surprising that annoyance has inspired guerrilla tactics. We turn the page quickly while reading a magazine; we toss aside entire sections of the newspaper when we notice that they are largely or exclusively made up of ads. We hit the mute button on the remote or change the channel on the car radio in an attempt to blank out or avoid the commercial message. In fact, one company is marketing a television set that will automatically reduce the volume on commercials—including their own. ("Smart. Very smart.") We tape programs and fast-forward past the ads, and we zip past the trailers on videos. We choose tapes or CDs over broadcasts in order to avoid interruptions, even when the station of our choice claims to broadcast ten hits in a row.

Another line of defense is denial: Ads have no effect on us, we say. When it's time to buy something, we make our decisions independently of commercials. But if ads have no effect on people, what explains the existence of an advertising industry? There are good reasons for the strong correlation between advertising and sales in soft drinks, cleaning products, and other consumer goods.

But there are plenty of exceptions to this resistance to ads. Think back over your conversations with friends, to recall instances in which a commercial provided material for a joke or comment. (Tag lines such as: "Just do it" or "Yes, I am" come from recent advertising campaigns. From the 1970s and 1980s, there's Alka-Seltzer's "I can't believe I ate the whole thing"; "Where's the beef" from Wendy's, which helped Walter Mondale to the 1984 Democratic presidential nomination; the "Tastes great"/"Less filling" chants from Miller beer ads.) Part of the hype around the Super Bowl draws attention to the new commercials to be "premiered" then. Advertising's Clio awards have been televised for years, and it's not unusual to find "favorite TV commercials" used as the basis of specials. Many commercials make skillful use of humor and other devices in order to counteract our resistance.

PAUSE FOR REFLECTION

Brainstorm a list of ads that use humor or whimsy to capture and hold your attention and lessen your irritation at the interruption. (1995 examples included Budweiser's frogs, Miller Lite's magical appeals to male fantasy, or Pepsi's boy sucked into the bottle.) Can you think of other devices that can be effective for these purposes?

Commercials are often the most carefully crafted texts on television. Careful testing procedures, including focus groups, ensure that advertisers foresee everything they can about audience reactions.

 One testing firm "uses infrared eye scans to record rapid eye movement in response to test images in television commercials, advising clients on elements of ads like the most effective juxtaposition of sex objects, for example, a woman in a bikini and the brand name of the advertised product" (Bagdikian p. 185).

But even if we admit that advertisements are significant enough to be studied, *how* should they be studied? Ads come to us in strictly defined contexts—from within magazines, radio and television programs, and so on. Is it legitimate to separate them from their contexts in the middle of other media texts? When we create other contexts for analyzing ads, does this violate their meaning?

That way of phrasing things requires us to pose other questions. Who determines meaning? What counts as a *violation*? The concept of violation comes from our culture's practice of assigning and policing property rights over texts. The author of a text (individual or corporate) has legal title over it for a number of years. But does the author get to determine what the text *means*? Some theories of meaning are built on this assumption: The text means whatever the author intended, no more and no less. But authorial intention is a difficult principle under the best of circumstances, because authors may have unclear or mixed intentions. And openly commercial texts, by intention, mean *buy this product*. It may not be in our interests as consumers to read these texts, or others, simply as intended.

Readers will make their own uses of texts despite what may have been the intention. I can produce a text, and retain the legal rights to its printing and distribution—but I can't tell anyone what to think of it. Its meaning is something established by others: by the culture, in smaller and larger groupings, face-to-face and through writing, through negotiation and interchange. Words do not automatically respond to intentions, despite what we may wish, as Lewis Carroll suggests:

> "[T]hat shows that there are three hundred and sixty-four days when you might get un-birthday presents—"
> "Certainly," said Alice.
> "And only *one* for birthday presents, you know. There's glory for you!"
> "I don't know what you mean by 'glory,'" Alice said.
> Humpty Dumpty smiled contemptuously. "Of course you don't—till I tell you. I meant 'there's a nice knock-down argument for you!'"
> "But 'glory' doesn't mean 'a nice knock-down argument,'" Alice objected.

> "When *I* use a word," Humpty Dumpty said, in rather a scornful tone, "it means just what I choose it to mean—neither more nor less."
>
> "The question is," said Alice, "whether you *can* make words mean so many different things."
>
> "The question is," said Humpty Dumpty, "which is to be master—that's all." (Carroll p. 79)

It's interesting to compare this dialogue with Carroll's comment about authority over language, written in a logic text:

> I maintain that any writer of a book is fully authorised in attaching any meaning he likes to any word or phrase he intends to use. If I find an author saying, at the beginning of his book, "Let it be understood that by the word '*black*' I shall always mean '*white*', and that by the word '*white*' I shall always mean '*black*,'" I meekly accept his ruling, however injudicious I may think it. (Carroll p. 269)

Humpty-Dumpty regards words as employees: He has contracted with *glory* to mean *a nice knock-down argument,* and he insists on staying with the terms of that contract. And Lewis Carroll argues that the author has the right to make *black* mean *white* if desired. Alice, however, believes that language doesn't work that way. Words (or language) refuse to be *mastered.* By its nature, language is shared rather than possessed; it's a means of communication, and therefore has to be spoken and heard, written and seen, in order to have any existence that matters. All parties assert some rights: those who write texts, those who read them, and those who share in the medium of language. (Interestingly, Carroll's comment in the logic text depends on a common view of language even as it attempts to deny it: A writer who says "by the word *black* I shall always mean *white*" depends on our prior understanding of what these terms refer to. What would be necessary, in order actually to mean what Humpty-Dumpty or Lewis Carroll's injudicious author says, would be to use the term *black* and *mean* white, to say *glory* and mean, without explanation, *a nice knock-down argument.*)

Authors and others who produce texts cannot compel our agreement on how to read them. That compulsion, or rather inclination, comes in other ways. We are always using texts in ways other than those anticipated. Whenever you sing a bit of a song (seriously admiring it or making fun of it), you are adapting it to your purposes rather than submitting to property rights. Sometimes this works to advertisers' benefit—advertising slogans can take on a currency well beyond the capacity of the advertisers to control or even foresee.

Audiences make their own meanings out of texts, then, and this popular aspect of making meaning is never entirely under others' control. Corporations have tried unsuccessfully for decades to keep trademarks like "Kleenex," "Xerox," and "Coke" from entering the public domain as generic terms. But what do you wipe your nose with? What kind of copies do you make? What do you order for something to drink at lunch with your cheeseburger and fries? Popular usage works its will. And individually you can have some input to making meaning. By taking ads out of their prepared context into contexts that *we* construct, we engage in making alternative meanings in addition to those provided by the consumer context, establishing some degree of control. And our meanings will last to the extent that we can persuade others that they are valid.

Ads have taken on tasks that make the equation of "glory" with "a nice knock-down argument" easy by comparison. Understanding the devices by which ads work is a first step to becoming able to define your own meanings out of those provided for you. One of the most powerful of the devices by which ads work their magic is the claim to "common sense": If common sense tells me, as it does, that I make my own choices in the marketplace, why then the need for a $30 billion industry to help me do that? Why the need for advertising at all, which adds as much as 15 percent to the price of goods and services?

In 1990 the average cost of a TV commercial without a lot of special effects was $250,000 for thirty seconds. Prime-time costs to run ads were approximately $100,000 per minute (with many repeats needed) (Mayle p. 60).

One device for checking your own investment in this "common sense" is to prepare a collection of ads—print, audio, or video, or all three—to serve as prompts for how you participate in the making of meaning through advertisements.

Collecting Ads

We can learn a lot from looking intensely at a single ad, as we'll do in the next section of this chapter. Before doing close analysis, however, it might be helpful to get an overview of ads as seen in association with others.

Advertisements never come to us singly. They come along with, in the middle of, and in conversation with, other texts. *Which* texts they are in the middle of depends on who makes the categories and for what purposes. The ads' means of production places them in various media (newspapers, magazines, television and radio programs, etc.). The manufacturer and type of product may serve as the basis for categorizing ads along different lines (ads for soft drinks, snacks, cars, airlines, etc.).

But we also construct our own associations along our own lines, first, out of the total of all the ads we have seen or read or heard, then second, according to some other lines that we may not fully understand—ads with actors who appeal to us sexually, ads with fast-paced presentation, or ads with singable music, for example. Whatever the bases for our groups may be, they are partly our own and partly formed from patterns provided for us by our culture.

Grouping or classifying things might be compared to forming stars into constellations. Many cultures have named sections of the sky after what looked to them like pictures recalling legends or myths (Leo the Lion, Orion the Hunter, or Cassiopeia and Perseus). But does Cassiopeia *really* look like a chair? Or Ursa Major like a bear, or a big dipper? No constellation has enough stars, exactly enough placed, to suggest even the degree of resemblance of a stick-figure drawing to a person. Rather, in looking at the sky, cultures have written the star patterns into available stories.

As we arrange ads into configurations, we may use the organizing systems or constellations provided for us—according to sequences made for us by the media doing the broadcasting and printing; according to sequences made by those who manufacture the products and provide the services; or according to other systems, provided by others or made up by ourselves. The test of any system's adequacy is what kind of sense it makes, to us and to others—and how persuasive we can be in arguing for its value.

Ads, like other media texts, are intertextual, presenting us with meanings constructed out of bright bits and pieces of other texts. Part of making meaning from ads is collecting them, and initially we have to note those aspects of meaning that come from the publication or agency providing the ad. As we ordinarily encounter them, ads are embedded in other texts: For print ads, these other texts are magazines and newspapers, while broadcast ads are presented in the context of radio or television programs and, outside of the programs themselves, the radio station or television network or cable channel.

Newspapers and magazines are addressed to specific groups of readers, defined by region, age, income, education, and other factors, and print ads have to be understood as part of the demographics of those publications.

PAUSE FOR REFLECTION

Next time you are in the periodicals section of your collegiate or public library, pick up issues of three or four magazines you do not customarily read, and see what you can infer about their readership from the advertisements alone. Suggestions: *Seventeen, Field and Stream, Yankee, Wired, Cosmopolitan, Family Circle, The New Yorker, Ebony, GQ, Tennis.*

Local newspapers necessarily reflect their region, so their advertisements often call attention to promotions and sales in the area. We can see a local emphasis in specific appeals linked to local events—for example, a tire ad might feature a tie-in to a winning sports team. Magazines, which are distributed over larger areas, tend to select along lines other than region—professional interests, education level, income, political preferences, male/female/mixed audiences, and other factors. Modern magazines don't start out with a certain body of readers and then find advertising to suit; rather, the readers' profile and advertising come together. It might be said that the magazine or newspaper is there to provide articles and other texts to convince potential advertisers that the publication would be a good place to run their ads.

In broadcast media, the nearest equivalents to such specialty publications would be programs and, at a more general level, networks or cable channels. Television networks generally reach a wider spectrum than some cable channels—compare, in this respect, Discovery or Family Channel to ABC, NBC, or CBS.

It's a little more difficult to take stock of the overall assortment of commercials in broadcasts than to do an inventory of ads in a magazine or newspaper. Print media hold still for us to look over them and make connections; broadcast media provide a *flow* of images and words, and it requires some effort to develop an overview.

One example of an analysis based on collecting advertisements in this fashion: Robert L. Schrag taped Saturday programming on ABC, NBC, and CBS from 7:00 to 12:00 A.M., a period of time that yielded a total of eighty-four commercials. Schrag grouped these into five categories on the basis of actors' genders and their relations.

1. Girls' ads: Featured girls or women, aimed at girls.
2. Boys' ads: Featured boys or men, aimed at boys.
3. Social ads: Featured girls and boys, aimed at girls and boys.
4. Romantic ads: Featured girls and boys, aimed at girls and boys, implying a girlfriend–boyfriend romantic relationship.
5. Segregated ads: Featured girls and boys, aimed at girls and boys, but edited so that girls and boys never appear in the same shot.

Some of Schrag's observations: (1) The largest proportion of girls' ads (61 percent) involved "grooming behavior" such as "brushing hair, applying makeup, and dressing up." (2) The largest proportion of boys' ads (44 percent) were devoted to sports—"young boys or adult males engaged in athletic activities, either organized or in a playground or backyard." This category also included three ads involving trucks and cars. (3) In the social ads, 30 percent followed gender stereotypes, 12.5 percent violated them, and 57.5 percent involved gender neutrality—in this last category, however, males filled most of the roles. (4) The romantic ads featured stereotypical behavior along gender lines: "The boys gave presents (candy) and were strong (a boy pulled two buildings together so he could share a Pop-Tart with the girl). The girls were passive recipients who batted their eyelashes and turned up the ends of most of their phrases." (5) Three of the four segregated ads projected gender stereotypes (Schrag pp. 226–30).

It should not be surprising that television commercials make use of stereotypes. After all, advertisers want commercials to reach a specific audience, and in the United States gender is a useful divider for the Saturday-morning audience of preteens. As we saw in Chapter 4, however, stereotypes are not merely used but also created and perpetuated by media. Gender in these commercials is associated with the exercise of power. This association draws from a realistic assessment of contemporary society; but, portrayed as part of the natural order through children's commercials, it also helps to sustain such a social hierarchy. Schrag could make that point only after collecting a reasonably large sample of commercials for support.

Collecting instances of advertisements, whether print ads, broadcast ads, or other species such as billboards or junk mail or brochures, places you in the position of seeing what your classification is based on. Doing a collection requires that you formulate something like a hypothesis, gather examples to illustrate it, and adjust your system of classification in order to accommodate necessary changes. (See Chapter 11 for further discussion of collections.)

ASSIGNMENT

Begin collecting some advertisements for further work. Your collection may feature instances from print media (newspapers, magazines, other possibilities such as brochures) or broadcast media (radio as well as television). You may have to rely on a description of a commercial rather than the actual text. Your collection will have to be limited in some fashion: Some possibilities for limitation might be by category of product, by time of broadcast, by publication, by devices used to attract and hold attention, or by some other means.

Before beginning your collection, you should freewrite about some of the possibilities. What are some of the issues through which ads can be associated with each other? What leads you to see connections in what might otherwise be considered disparate texts?

How to Read an Ad

Another sort of analysis depends not on the association of texts but on their close reading. This might be compared to the difference between looking at stagnant water and examining a drop under a microscope, or between flying over agricultural land and examining the chemical composition of the soil. Both are valuable ways of looking, but they tell you different things. In order to classify, not only do you have to devise overall categories, or accept and extend other categories and issues already present, but you have to make inferences based on details of texts. A useful skill to develop as part of analysis, then, is the ability to observe details present in a text and connect these to your inferences about it.

There's a name for moving from small details to generalizations based on experience—**induction.** Induction depends on the observation of patterns in repeated events. A typical example from logic texts: Suppose you have a truckload of green apples. You bite one; it's sour. You take another and bite it—sour, too. You repeat the process until you get through the entire truckload (or until your upset stomach forces you to stop). At some point you feel justified in concluding that green apples are sour (or at least that this truckload is). The movement from individual observations to general statement is induction. The reason this sounds obvious and even silly is that each of us does induction from the moment we first observe that the table in the delivery room is cold and a lot less pleasant than the womb. On the other hand, when you move from a general statement to a particular instance—green apples are sour; therefore this green apple will be sour—that is called **deduction.**

In practice, logic moves back and forth between these, rather than in one direction only. You may already have an idea that green apples are sour before taking your first bite, either because you've had a similar experience before (induction), or because you've heard from others that they are (deduction). In analyzing television commercials, you won't be starting from scratch but will be making use of presuppositions (or prejudgments or biases or hypotheses or stories), which you bring to your choice of commercials to analyze and to your guesses about what details are likely to be significant for your interpretation.

But in addition to being a habit of thought, induction is also a form of presentation. It can be rhetorically effective to lay your evidence out before the reader step by step, then draw conclusions—in order to put the reader in the (fictive) position of being a fellow investigator, following something like your reasoning process in moving through the essay.

Following are analyses of four print ads. First, the essay that follows illustrates ways of bringing details of ads forward as a means of moving from description to conclusions about their meanings.

TARA L. PRAINITO

Advertising's Enhancements
While thumbing through one of my magazines, I came across an ad for a Frigidaire stove that really made me laugh. I found it so comical because these advertisers had perfected the art of "presenting perfection." They used every angle and advertising effect they could to reach their audience.

This product's big line is that it is "Built for Generations." With this line in mind, they show you a perky happy little couple that will supposedly "last for generations." This everlasting couple has a perfectly clean kitchen, even after cooking a four-course meal. They also cook in their perfectly clean, very fashionable clothes. To further enhance this cozy image, Frigidaire dims the lights and adds a fuzzy effect to the picture. In this ad they also have the husband in an apron helping his wife cook. I guess we are supposed to assume he does this because he just likes his Frigidaire stove so much.

After Frigidaire catches our attention they try to appeal to your intellectual side. They have a small picture of the stove's heating element and then a wordy little technological description of the stove.

> New instant-response surface elements and a unique Dual-Radiant baking system give more consistent results, while our sealed, almost indestructible, smooth CERAN surface cleans up with a simple wipe.

(Notice how they conveniently use the term **almost indestructible**.)

After the technological pitch, they cap it off by telling you how fashionable your new Frigidaire stove will make you. Finally they tell you that "It's the kind of long lasting, intelligent craftsmanship that you can only find in the new Frigidaire." So what they're basically trying to tell you is that **intelligent** people buy their stove.

Therefore, if you buy Frigidaire's new stove, they want you to believe that you will be more happy, fashionable, and intelligent, not to mention that your marriage will "**last for generations.**"

As in the case of newspaper photographs with their captions, print advertisements juxtapose two parallel systems of signs. Newspaper photos commonly present a short label along with a sentence or two of further comment, which conventionally link the photograph to a story on that page; or sometimes the picture plus caption are run on their own, without an accompanying story. In addition to the printed verbal text, the photo itself works within a set of codes for reading newspaper photos. (Captioning is discussed under Labeling in Chapter 8; codes for visual images, in Chapter 6.) What we read in the newspaper photo is different from what would result with either the caption or the photograph in a different context: The two, verbal and visual image, work by juxtaposition. Captioning provides readers with signals about what codes to connect, and what general law the text is supposed to connect to.

A similar principle holds with print ads, though the symbolic systems are often less distinct than the image-and-caption structure of the news photo. Let's turn now to a close reading of Exhibit 5.2. To start with the visual image in the advertisement, most of the page is black. (The spatial ratio between image and text is approximately 4:1.) Dominating the upper half of the ad is a stylized representation of the front of a Jeep, mostly light blue, but with lines outlined in orange (the headlights are yellow). The way that the representation is cropped makes it resemble a face staring out at the reader—a little confrontational in tone; this is a vehicle with an attitude. The orange border suggests the frame of a painting. Because of the space it occupies and the bright colors, the image seizes and holds attention. The image includes two verbal components: the word "Jeep" on the stylized front of the vehicle, and the orange-on-black text "Accept Only Signed Originals." The juxtaposition of image and statement serve to create curiosity, which directs the reader's attention to the smaller printed black-on-white text below.

The text picks up on the "signed originals" concept with its first sentence: "In a world of fakes and forgeries, there's one original no one has been able to copy—Jeep." It goes on to claim that what gives the vehicle its authority is its status as a brand name; the text says *twice* that Jeep is a Chrysler trademark, which is a way of equating legal and corporate property rights with the authority granted artists in Western culture. (The term *jeep* is not an individual construction and did not originate with the corporation. It derives from armed forces usage during World War II, from "G.P." or general purpose.) The apparent inconsistency between "there's only one Jeep" and the existence of several models (Grand Cherokee, Cherokee, and Wrangler) mentioned in the text, or the idea that even with the tens of thousands of copies of each model, "there's only one Jeep," isn't addressed: Like many ads, the statement functions not logically but emotively.

Because this textbook is printed in black and white, you will need to look for examples on your own of ways in which color affects the reading of a print ad. Color is an important dimension of the Jeep advertisement. Exhibit 5.3, an ad for Laser sailboats, relies on color not so much to catch the eye by contrast, but to provide a realistic image of two women using the product. In this case, the entire space of the ad is filled with the image, and the text is superimposed onto the photo in yellow letters—one section as headline ("Wind is Free. Use It.") and one as commentary ("Rejuvenate your senses... Sail a Laser, the hot new Olympic watersport," etc.). The photo provides a diagonal from lower left

Exhibit 5.2 "Accept only signed originals." Used by permission of Chrysler Corporation.

Exhibit 5.3 "Wind is free." Used by permission of Sunfish/Laser Corp.

to upper right, as the women hike out to balance the wind's force across the boat.

A third illustration of how text and image are integrated in a print ad can be seen in a Phillips 66 ad, Exhibit 5.4. In this case the image is less dominant: The text appears both above and below the image, in a larger font—and the image comes in at midsentence, as though interrupting the words. In this case, the woman's body is halted in midair as she leaps into the water: The impression is overwhelmingly one of force (no leaning back in pursuit of pleasure, balancing the power of nature, as in the Laser ad).

Another point to consider in reading these and other print ads is the usual sequence of reading, left to right and top to bottom. This sequence allows

Exhibit 5.4 "She makes it look effortless." Used by permission of Phillips Petroleum Company.

advertisers to govern the order of presentation, even if not in so rigorously linear a fashion as in a broadcast ad. The Phillips Petroleum ad (Exhibit 5.4) may depart from that expectation: Because the accompanying text in its black-on-white type is so ordinary, the photograph (strategically located in the center of the page) keeps pulling us back to the image of grace and power it presents, so that the movement is more back and forth than top to bottom. In other words, it's too simple to regard text as commentary on image, or image as illustration of text: Both exist in a mutual relation which is different from either separately.

It may also be significant that the specific references to the individual woman photographed occur *above* the photo—"She makes it look effortless"; "she's practiced and honed her skills"—while the section *below* the photo takes us to what the photograph symbolizes, "the command for perfection" and the advertiser's equation of this with the corporation.

Additional print ads appear in Appendix 5.1 at the end of this chapter. Make use of some of the suggestions below as a basis for analyzing those texts. You should also apply these suggestions to your own collections of print ads. Consider the ads' use of the following: (1) visual image(s); (2) caption, if any; (3) text, with special attention given to key words; (4) use of logo or image of the product. Other aspects to analyze:

Audience: What signals do you have from the print ad about who the intended audience is? Who might be excluded, directly or indirectly, by the ad (as opposed to by the product)?

Picture–text relations: What are the connections between the printed text and photographic or other images in the ad? Are these read from left to right, top to bottom, or according to some other pattern? Which tends to dominate—the image, the text, or neither? What relation is there between the head (if any) and smaller-print text? How is the corporate logo (if any) brought into the ad? What would you say is the theme of the ad, and where is that theme signaled for you?

Focus on the photograph or other image(s): What would the image(s) convey apart from the text and other materials presented in the ad? What qualities do you suppose led the advertising agency to select that image or those images? What texts or experiences do you associate with the image(s)? What codes in the image(s) tell you something about the ad's audience?

Unconventional use of text: Search out some examples on your own for unusual placement of text. What would be changed if the texts appeared in more usual locations at the bottom or right side?

Narrative categories (1) Landscape, women, other symbols: In a sense, all these are part of the grammar of print ads. How is the landscape put at the service of the products mentioned? (What is the product in "North Carolina" [Exhibit 5.19]?) In what circumstances would you find a man posing as the woman does for Cover Girl (Exhibit 5.12)? What other products could such a pose sell? How would you put into language the message conveyed by symbols in ads?

(2) Characters, stories, prestige, humor: All these link products up with narratives in some way. What stories do these ads tell? What else is implied

by the image that the text does not explicitly say? In what ways do these stories recommend the products or services offered? How do the ads that make use of humor work to interest you in their product or service?

Analyzing a TV Commercial

Television commercials share with print advertisements the imperative of catching and holding the audience's attention. In order to make such texts available for analysis, we need to break from our routine way of reading them. One device for doing this is suggested by Jerry Mander: Concentrate on technical events as a way of breaking through what Mander considers television's hypnotic quality. Technical events on TV would correspond to factors such as image, text, caption, and logo in print; however, the potential number of such events is much higher because of differences in the medium.

Some of the principles are similar in both video and print media. Like print ads, television commercials frequently combine verbal with visual texts, and a reading of the ad has to take both into account. Text and image sometimes work in parallel, sometimes in opposition, and sometimes in ambiguous or paradoxical relation. Television images invite us to connect with the figures represented in numerous potential ways, just as photographs in ads do. Like print ads, commercials may make inventive use of graphic text in many different styles, sizes, and colors.

But television commercials add a crucial element: They move. Instead of being held in contemplation of a single visual image, we may follow it as it changes through time. The change may be a flow of animated drawings, someone's face as she talks directly to the camera (as though talking directly to us), or a photograph of a product prepared for use. The images may be connected to short narratives that give us a (very thin) slice of life, perhaps structured as problem + solution; or they may be simply a series of rapid cuts that hold us watching the screen to see what comes next. In addition to the analytical tasks of deciphering image and text, then, we have to account for the ways in which the image moves.

Another point of difference from print ads is a third area, that of sound. TV commercials may present us with three dimensions simultaneously, *visual* (photograph of an image), *textual* (words superimposed on or below the image), and *auditory* (music, environmental sounds, and voice-over). For example, a Budweiser campaign running in winter 1995 had for visual image an extreme close-up of a glass of beer being drawn from a tap, with a neon product logo above; for sound, there was laid-back, bluesy jazz such as might be found in a bar; and for text, a black rectangle in the middle of the image, with letters in white asserting that Budweiser used to be a microbrewery about 1860 but then got bigger and better (one of several such verbal texts in this campaign). Any tendency to question the truth value of the claims in the text is subverted by the visual image of the beer and the symbolic associations with the easy music.

In order to develop an understanding of how the rhetoric of television commercials works, we have to be able to separate these three elements—visual, textual, and auditory. And in order to do that, we have to be able to stop the flow of the ad (and the flow of the program around it) for purposes of analysis. Even the simplest contemporary TV ad moves too quickly for anyone to be able to detail the principal movements on the basis of one viewing. So in order to carry out this activity, you have to have access to a VCR—whether your own or someone else's—to record commercials. It will be necessary to prepare a description of the ad along the visual, textual, and auditory dimensions before you put together an account of the ad's effect. And you will have to view the commercial many more times than is usual. The ideal result would be a description that translates the commercial into print text, analogous to a transcription on paper of a piece of music. Articulating the parts of a commercial may also serve as good practice for articulating the parts of other texts—including essays by other writers and by yourself. The purpose of such repeated viewings and description is to *denature* the commercial in order to see it not as a flow but as a series of describable camera movements. Television is a technology which tends to present itself as natural; in order to understand its constructed nature, you have to conceive of it in uncustomary ways. Exhibits 5.5 and 5.6 provide glossaries of terminology you'll need for your analysis of commercials.

Getting accustomed to these terms can be difficult because we are not used to viewing television or film analytically. Some practice may be valuable for this purpose.

ASSIGNMENT

Select a five-minute segment of a program (preferably one that has no particular narrative unity, so that you aren't distracted by the story line) and compile a list of *all* the camera shots and movements. It's best to do this with the sound down, and you should make frequent use of the pause button on the VCR to compile the description.

After working with camera movements, you should go back through the segment and note sound events besides dialogue. What else is there? Environmental sound? Applause and other reactions by a studio audience or provided on a laugh track? Music? Sound effects? How do these affect your response to the segment?

Camera Positioning

close-up	Camera focused on head and shoulders, presenting (for example) the image of a person at a comfortable distance for intimate conversation. Close-ups and medium shots are normative for television.
extreme close-up	Same, but at a still more intimate distance.
medium shot	Camera gets image of a person roughly from waist up; commonly used with two or three on camera.
full-length	Image is shown head to feet.
distant shot	Image is shown farther off; can be medium distance to farther.
telephoto shot	Image is shot from far off, but through telephoto lens the image appears closer.

Camera Movement and Editing

fade in/out	Image comes up from or goes down to blackness.
cut	Shift to another image, done by editing.
pan	Camera holds on an image but moves (left, right, up, down, or two in combination).
wipe	Replacement of one image by another through a line or other movement across the screen.
tracking shot	Camera follows an image (on wheels, on a boom or vehicle, or hand-held).
zoom in/out	Through movement of the lens, the image is made to appear closer/farther.
focus	Camera isn't exactly at the point to make the image clear—this may direct attention to foreground or background, or may provide a gauzy halo effect.
matte	The superimposition of one image as foreground onto another background (e.g., portrait photo in a "natural" setting, or the U.S. Capitol's image behind a reporter).

Exhibit 5.5 Glossary: Camera movements in TV production.

Doing a test run with something besides ads is important for comparison. Jerry Mander notes that technical events are half as frequent in programs as in ads, which has the effect of making the ads more visually interesting so as to lead us to pay attention. His account was before MTV, which has increased the number of cuts in programs generally—the rapid cuts and camera movements in rock videos created audience expectations of similar movements in other programs and ads. (Compare camera movement in some contemporary

Chapter 5: Close Attention to Detail: Regarding the Commercial   249

Sound	
dialogue	Recorded conversation between actors; effect is usually to imitate our overhearing what they say "naturally."
voice-over	A narrator speaks on sound track (may be on black screen or over images).
soundtrack	Other sound provided to accompany image, such as environmental noises or music.
Graphics	
text	Here, any set of words on screen.
caption	Words that function as a label (e.g., to identify someone on camera).
superimposition	Words placed on top of an image.
scroll	Words that move across or up the screen (imitates eyes moving down a page).
logo	Word/image combination associated with a corporation or other group.
fine print	Text on screen so small as to make it unlikely that a viewer would succeed in reading it (may be present for legal purposes).
headline	Large text, which functions roughly as do headlines in newspapers—to get attention to one word or a short phrase (e.g., SALE! SALE! SALE!).

Exhibit 5.6 Glossary: Sound and graphics in TV production

telecasts—such as *NYPD Blue*—with the same aspect in some pre-1980 programs.) Most programs have raised the pace of their technical movements slightly, but have not nearly kept up with commercials in this respect: Where Mander described an average of fifteen technical events in a thirty-second ad, a more reasonable average now would be thirty, or one technical event per second.

An example of a description of a commercial may be useful. The description below is adapted from a television commercial broadcast in 1994; its duration is about twenty seconds.

Analysis of Technical Events in Midol Ad Aired July 1994
1. Black background. Woman in her 30s, leaning forward, close-up, at right of screen. She's wearing a beige dress and pearl necklace. Pained facial expression.
2. Music—low bass, regular quarter notes, violins; tense music.

3. Dialogue: *Oh, menstrual cramps. Bloating? Tylenol did nothing for my bloating.*
4. Across the background floats a blown-up logo in the typeface used for Extra-Strength Tylenol, but on a black background.
5. Simultaneous with that sentence is a superimposition at left of screen—"Tylenol did nothing for my bloating."
6. Cut to extreme close-up of Midol label, with words "Maximum Strength Multi-Symptom Formula" above the brand name MIDOL, and "Menstrual Formula" below.
7. Camera pans L. to R. across label.
8. Music changes—relieving theme: high notes on something like marimba (synthesizer?).
9. Voice-over (woman's voice): "Midol does help."
10. Cut to second woman, slightly older, left side of screen. Medium shot; she's sitting on a high stool. She's wearing a yellow blouse and jeans. As she speaks, she seems quite agitated.
11. Dialogue: *Headaches. Tired. Advil didn't keep me from feeling worn out.*
12. Music as #2 above.
13. Superimposition as #5 above—"Advil didn't keep me from feeling worn out."
14. Background is still black, but bears an Advil brand name on a graph, similar to #3 above.
15. Music as #8 above.
16. Pan of Midol label as #7 above. Visible this time is the print below "Menstrual Formula" on the label: "Maximum strength relief of cramps, bloating, water–weight gain, headaches, backaches, muscle aches and fatigue. Aspirin-Free."
17. Cut to second, slightly closer view of label.
18. Voice-over: "Tylenol and Advil only relieve pain. Maximum strength Midol relieves pain, but adds an ingredient to relieve fatigue and bloating."
19. Blended in with Midol label is another woman, blonde, younger than the other two, in close-up, wearing what appears to be a business suit. She's positioned to the right of the screen, but more central than the first.
20. Superimposition as #5 and #13 above, but on top of the label—"I felt like myself again."
21. Simultaneous with #18, in smaller typeface—"Use only as directed."
22. While third woman is on screen, label fades out to black background.
23. Camera pulls back from woman as she speaks her line.
24. Dialogue: *I felt like myself again.*
25. Cut to white background with several objects to suggest a dresser top—foreground left is what looks like a glass of colored beverage; center is the Midol package with two capsules in foreground; foreground right is a jewelry container with (fake) pearl necklace and other jewelry visible; behind package is a lamp and another bottle possibly holding flowers.

26. Large-typeface superimposition, black letters: "Midol helps it all go away."
27. Small-typeface superimposition, black letters: "Use only as directed."
28. Voice-over: "Midol helps it all go away." [Used by permission of Bayer Corporation.]

COMMENTS

This Midol ad seems to be one of the "anonymous testimonial" variety: that is, the product is endorsed by people of whom we have no prior knowledge, as opposed to a known actor or recognizable public figure. It is essential that the endorsers *be* unknown, because they are supposed to represent typical or characteristic users of the product, so as to convince viewers who are of comparable age, gender, and so on to identify with them and accept their valuation of the product. (Whatever we may think of Arnold Schwarzenegger, we probably do not identify with him.)

Ads for over-the-counter medicines often adopt the problem–solution plot, in order to suggest that their product will ease our pain. In the Midol commercial there are alternating codes for distress and relief: The "distress" is signaled by a painful expression or agitation on the part of the first two actresses, who are associated by their dialogue and by letters on the background with rival products. The distress portion is reinforced by the music, which is low and menacing when they are on screen. In the "relief" portion, the camera pans over the contrasting (mostly) blue and white lettering of the product box—here we see the significance of the fact that the Tylenol and Advil logos are abstracted from their packages and presented against the black screen—and while the Midol box is on screen, we hear pleasant, higher-pitched music (no bass), with a syrupy-voiced woman saying pleasant things about the product, by contrast with the complaints about the competitors.

The last woman looks directly at the camera, in contrast to the other two, who were looking left and right; she is definitely younger, blonder, and more attractive, perhaps to signal the message that if you use Midol you will attain these qualities. The screen is black for a much briefer period with her, because the camera lingers longer on the Midol box and moves more quickly to the mock-up dresser top, which is more colorful and pleasant looking than the black screen.

The three women in the ad are all early middle-aged or younger, all white, all blonde or near-blonde, suggesting a daytime television demographic largely female (which is reasonable, given the nature of the product). Like many ads for nonprescription medicines, the Midol ad assumes that you have to have *something* to solve the problem and suggests that it's a choice between Tylenol, Advil, and Midol. (As Michael Pertschuk has noted, we never see an ad for going upstairs and taking a nap—there's no product to be sold by doing so.)

A student analysis of a Chevrolet commercial follows. (You may also wish to look ahead to Reading Media Texts for Ideology in Chapter 8, where another analysis—of a Nike commercial—appears.)

AARON KUKLA

Analysis of Chevrolet Camaro Ad

1. Shot of Chevy Camaro speeding down the highway in the middle of the desert. Very fast-paced rock & roll music is playing in the background. The desert background and the music remain constant throughout the commercial.
2. The screen goes black. "We Invented The Telephone" is superimposed in big white letters on the middle of the screen.
3. View from above and to the front of the Camaro driving into the camera. The camera pans around the car as it comes into the screen. We end up with a close-up of the passenger side door.
4. Like before, the screen goes black. This time the words "We Invented The Light Bulb" are superimposed.
5. Shot of the driver side door. The camera moves from the rear to front until the car goes out of the picture.
6. The next scene is a view of two attractive ladies through the driver side window. The windows are rolled down. The driver is a brunette and the passenger is a blonde. Both of the women appear to be laughing and having a good time.
7. Again, the screen goes black. "We Invented Rock & Roll" is superimposed in white.
8. Cut to the rear of the car positioned diagonal to the screen. The shot then widens.
9. Medium distant shot of the car showing a full side view. A semi truck passes in front of the camera, blocking the view of the car for a second.
10. Close-up rear-side view of the car. Slowly the car moves off the picture.
11. As before, the screen blackens. "We Invented The New Camaro, $13,999" superimposed in big white letters in the middle of the screen. Also, some fine print at the bottom saying "M. S. R. P. including dealer prep. Tax, license, destination charge and optional equipment additional."
12. Long-distance shot of the Camaro driving away from the camera on a hilly highway toward the sun. There is a telephone line next to the highway adding to the distant effect.
13. Frontal view of the car heading directly into the screen.
14. Once again the picture goes black while "Is This A Great Country Or What?" is superimposed.

Chapter 5: Close Attention to Detail: Regarding the Commercial

15. Another shot of the women in the car having a ball. This time the sun is shining brighter.
16. Top view of the car diagonal to the screen. The car slowly moves out of the picture.
17. Normal shot of the car from the front-left. Voice-over begins during this shot and lasts to the end of the ad. It says, "The new Camaro—what else would you expect from the country that invented rock & roll?"
18. Shot of the girls in the car. The blonde is waving to the screen across the driver. They slowly move out of the picture.
19. Long-distance shot of the car from above driving away into the sunset. The words "Chevy Camaro" fade onto the bottom of the screen in big white letters. The Chevy logo then appears in red above the letters. The car keeps getting farther and farther from the camera. Voice-over ends here.

Comments: The invention of the television revolutionized the world. The lives of millions of people were changed by this new contraption. People switched from leisurely listening to the radio to spending hours zombified in front of that talking picture box. Many people do not know who pays for this programming. Most of this task falls upon businesses, which pay considerable amounts of money for airtime used to advertise their products. Businesses realized quickly that the profits gained from successful TV advertising outweigh the cost of the commercials by a landslide. During the hours individuals spend watching TV, they are bombarded by thousands of ads. The nature of these ads ranges from being very simple to very complex, but nevertheless, much hard work goes into the making of each commercial.

To illustrate this point I examined a commercial for Chevy Camaro. As shown in the technical analysis, there are many cuts among other things that go into that thirty-second ad. In all of the shots the car is depicted in motion. The car always moves out of the picture implying that it is so fast that the camera cannot even keep up with it. Along with the unique camera shots, the upbeat music and voice-over aid in conveying the fact that this is a very exciting automobile.

Every commercial appeals to a certain audience. I think that this ad is appealing more to the male audience as opposed to women. Fast cars and women are two of men's favorite things. However, the women driving also may show that women can enjoy a Camaro too. Even though this ad may appeal to some women, the idea of driving a sports car on the open road is more of a masculine fantasy.

After viewing the ad a few times in slow motion, I noticed how the background plays a big part in the commercial. The color scheme uses bright reds, oranges, and yellows. These are very upbeat colors. At the beginning the sun is high in the sky, but as the commercial goes on it gets lower and lower until it sets. This illustrates that a person can have hours of fun driving the Camaro.

The main persuasive element of this ad is patriotism. The messages printed on the screen during the blackout shots are bragging about the accomplishments of the United

States. Buying a Chevy is portrayed to be something you can do to benefit your country tremendously. Basically what these shots are saying is that America can build a sports car as good or better than any other country. I believe this patriotic effect is the main point that makes this a successful ad.

A great deal of thought and research is put into every television commercial. Advertising agencies spend countless hours researching new methods to manipulate people. Most people, when asked if they were influenced by TV commercials, said they were not affected by them. The bottom line is, commercials must have some influence on people or businesses would not spend such enormous amounts of money on television advertising. These ads are just as important as the programs that people watch on television. Television commercials can be viewed as minifilms in their own right. [Used by permission.]

Analysis of technical events provides a powerful tool for examining everything that is "there" in a television commercial, more or less as we can do with a print ad. One difficulty with television texts is that they come to us through several modes at once. Often we see a succession of pictures, hear voices and music, and see printed text, all at once, and it is as hard for us to halt the process and think about its parts and what they add up to as it would be for a six-month-old to make sense of the lights and sounds and colors while being carried through a shopping mall. It can be very useful to halt the movement and separate the strands, taking some degree of control in transcribing language and describing sound and picture. The experience of making commercials *alien* rather than familiar can make them vivid for us. However, doing so should not deceive us into thinking we are immune to their persuasions: Much of the work of commercials is done cumulatively rather than singly. And it is also important not to demonize ads: Their persuasions are fundamentally the same as those of other media texts.

Categorizing Commercials

"Advertising is the art of arresting the human intelligence just long enough to get money from it."

—*Chuck Blore*

Categorizing texts—putting texts into relation with other texts—is a basic activity in any study. Anthropologists put kinship systems or religious beliefs from one culture into relation with those from other cultures. Art historians juxtapose paintings with other paintings; literary critics do the same with poems and plays and novels, and musicologists with musical compositions. Developing such a basis of comparison for commercials or other popular texts strikes us as unusual only because popular culture does not occupy a prominent place in academic study. But those involved in studying media or rhetoric see such texts as important to the culture of the United States, and their study as legitimate.

Television does not compel any particular reading for its texts. Rather, as a medium addressed to millions simultaneously, it leads us to *want* to give its texts specific, desired meanings, and not others. This means that, particularly with commercials, TV has to address previously existing needs and desires, or ideologies, so as to connect the product or service with these, preferably in such a way that we will believe that we wished for these things spontaneously and on our own. If we wish to maintain our independence from such suggestions, it will help to recognize how they work, and defamiliarizing commercials by viewing them in different contexts can help with this end.

When you are working with a body of texts as numerous as television commercials, they can be grouped, like stars in constellations, so as to give meaning. Let's look at some of the many possible categories. You could, for example, associate products advertised by type. You could look at commercials by narrative strategies (person talking directly to the camera; person on screen with voice-over; dramatic scene acted out; symbolic object or action; etc.). You could work with genres of commercials (endorsement, demonstration, storytelling, fantasy, hard sell). You could consider the uses of music (in commercials having nothing to do with music). You could examine applications of the problem–product–solution structure that forms the plot of many commercials. Commercials can be linked up with how our culture thinks about people within groups: class (including, but not limited to, income level), race, ethnic background, gender, age, region, occupation, weight, and so on.

Grouping commercials according to categories gives them a meaning—but does it give them *the* meaning? Is there a single, definite meaning to an ad? The answer to this question varies depending on whom you talk to. Those who incline to think about ads and other texts in connection with the marketplace might say, Yes, and it's the meaning defined by whoever pays the bills. Buy this car. Use this service. However, consumers, and viewers, have free choice, and we may prefer our own meanings to those officially provided for us. It may be uncomfortable, but it's unavoidable: Texts such as ads have several meanings, depending on the context.

PAUSE FOR REFLECTION

What are some kinds of groupings that could serve to bring out meanings of television commercials? Two familiar systems for grouping are by *product* and by *target audience* (e.g., commercials for automobiles and those directed to children). What are some other possibilities in these categories? (Jeans, shampoos, beer, sweet snacks; elderly people, rich men, jocks, etc.) A third suggestion would be to categorize the *people present in ads* by race, by age, by appearance, and so on. Do we see people in ads as individuals, as couples, as members of families? Why so? What markers do you have in an ad as to the income group being represented?

Categories by product type are familiar enough not to need extensive discussion: These tend to show up in association with the same programming niches, so that ads for daytime television are dominated by household cleaners (the origin of the nickname *soap operas*), over-the-counter medicines (especially those marketed for retired persons, preschool children, and women), and other products marketed for the population at home during these hours. Saturday morning and preschool/after-school programs are the preferred context for toys, sweet snacks, and sweetened cereals. Sports broadcasts feature products and services oriented towards men: shaving products, beer, investments, salty snacks, computers, cars. Prime-time and news broadcasts tend to be more diverse, with wide-spectrum ads. (Check these generalizations out against your own ad logs.)

Narrative technique refers to the way a story is told. Advertisements have one story to tell—the value of the product or service being advertised. However, the essential similarity of the "message" has to be disguised by intriguing and innovative ways to get it across. Ingenuity is what keeps advertising agencies in business. Let's turn now to some categories of narrative techniques.

PAUSE FOR REFLECTION

Jerry Mander's comment on what drives advertisers to find something new and different:

> Advertising content has no inherent interest at all. The content is always the same. The image may be a seascape and the product is beer. Or it may be a landscape and the product is cars. Or it may be a home and the product is coffee. Whatever the setting, the content of advertising is always a sales pitch. There is nothing inherently interesting in this. It is worse than boring; it is annoying. So tricks *must* be used in every advertisement. Maxwell Arnold, a San Francisco advertising man who is one of the industry's few outspoken critics, once told a radio interviewer: "Who the hell would choose to watch ads if there wasn't something going on aside from the content?" (Mander p. 304)

No one ordinarily *wants* to be sold something. There's an initial resistance to be gotten past, and ads can be grouped into genres according to how they undertake to do so. *Endorsements* involve people on camera (or photographed in print ads) who say that the product is good and does what is claimed for it.

Sometimes those who do endorsements are celebrities, whose background may or may not be relevant to the product. Basketball players do spend a lot of time in basketball shoes, but they may not be the most knowledgeable authorities about how well shoes are made. Often celebrities' qualifications to speak about the quality of products are limited, as with Andre Agassi's endorsement of a camera or Shaquille O'Neal's of a soft drink.

Some endorsements come not from celebrities but from people in relevant occupations, or from actors associated with an occupation. These "endorsements" are on shaky ground logically. (See Bad Rhetoric in Chapter 10.) Some legendary signals for these: *I'm not a doctor, but I play one on television...; My husband's a doctor, and he recommends X for colds...; I was so impressed with the razor, I bought the company.* Other endorsements come from what might be called "users": These are usually cast so as to give the impression that those in the commercial are "real people" rather than actors, sometimes giving a name and city as a further claim to authenticity. But in a commercial "real people" become people on television. What may change is style and tone, which are rhetorical devices. They are necessarily actors, even if they are playing the role of nonactors. At any rate, real or fictitious identity doesn't affect the adequacy of the claim advanced in the endorsement.

PAUSE FOR REFLECTION

Have you ever bought something on another person's advice? If so, were you satisfied that you were given good advice? What difference did it make that you knew the person recommending the product or service, that you knew her/his basis of relevant experience, and that you knew the person was not being paid to make a recommendation?

Many ads will recommend a product or service not by means of someone telling you that it's worthwhile, but by *showing* it in use: *Demonstration* is the mode of many commercials. Laundry detergents often involve some form of comparison (before-and-after samples or comparison with another, usually unnamed "leading brand"), as do household cleaners, denture adhesives, and so on. Other demonstrations are not comparative, but show the effects of the product (antacids, pain relievers, mouthwashes, shampoos). Play with fairly ordinary toys is made to look as exciting as amusement park rides by this means. Car ads frequently show us the car on the road (or off it) in order to demonstrate its capacities and our chances for happiness, should we buy it. Some demonstrations are quite outlandish, as with the pyramid of champagne glasses on top of the car (running on a stationary platform) at 100 mph or the ORV driving through a gigantic pink birthday cake. Others draw less on fantasy than on familiarity.

There are several ways to sustain *visual interest* in an ad, in addition to dramatic and symbolic action. One tool that developed along with color television in the mid-1950s is color itself. Color is influential in establishing the "naturalness" and appeal of landscapes in sentimental or exotic landscapes in ads. It can either naturalize or stylize a face's or costume's attractiveness. Bright colors are particularly important in ads directed at children (such as the Ronald McDonald campaigns and ads for fruity soft drinks, candy and other sweet snacks). And there's a long tradition of bright colors in detergent ads, established by the orange-and-yellow swirls on the Tide box. Finally, now that color is established as the norm, some ads use black-and-white film for contrast. The black and white may suggest an artistic genre, or it may be used to refer to a past historical period. (This may be done in combination with music, as in diamond ads in recent years.) At times black and white is code for the distant past, and the same ad shifts to color in order to signal more comfortable and progressive modern times. Sometimes a single object or person in an ad is in color, focusing attention on that spot more or less as is done with a spotlight in the theater. (Compare Steven Spielberg's use of this device in *Schindler's List* to draw attention to a child's coat, shortly before a Gestapo raid on the ghetto in Cracow.)

The use of text on screen, like colors, can catch the eye and carry meaning. Some commercials in the 1990s use highly variegated print fonts, which, rather than being superimposed on the screen, scroll up from bottom to top, or appear from all sides in free-floating association with the screen images. (Unfamiliar, brightly colored, or freely moving letters and words and phrases tend to attract the eye more than forms of print that resemble what is found in the newspaper.) These often are accompanied by voice-over reading the same words, which not only reinforces the verbal content (allowing the audience to both hear and see it) but defeats to some extent any viewers' attempts to avoid the ad by using the mute button.

Another category of ad narratives is *storytelling.* The story usually takes the form of problem–product–solution, since nothing more complex is likely to be successful in thirty seconds. (An alternative is to do a series of ads with parts of a continuing story, as with the soap opera–like Taster's Choice ads, or the sports fans whose trip to the 1995 and 1996 Super Bowls is interrupted by their insatiable longing for McDonald's products.) Storytelling often depends on portrayal of a character—sometimes an attractive face and voice, other times a caricature, and occasionally these two in juxtaposition. Rold Gold pretzels ran an ad in 1996 with Jason Alexander showing up in the wrong airplane and bailing out with his dog and bag of pretzels. Lee's jeans featured a narrative in 1994 of a 1950-ish guy coming to pick up his date, who can't get into her jeans, and who manages to cast a silhouette on the shade that her date finds discouraging....

Storytelling can be focused on a product, as with ads for Masterlock, Head and Shoulders shampoo, or various aftershaves and deodorants. Some stories fall into the category of fantasy, as with cereal-box characters who come "alive" as cartoons, Ronald McDonald in the clown suit, romantic fantasies in perfume ads, or bright landscapes that erupt from boxes of bubble bath.

Other commercials attract and hold interest through *humor* (usually a subcategory of narrative in general). Some of the best comic commercials are parodies of endorsements, demonstrations, and other forms. One "scientific test," with Michael Richards (Cosmo Kramer in *Seinfeld*) as a white-coated lab scientist, manages through "Pepsi deprivation" to transform Cindy Crawford into Rodney Dangerfield; others in this series show us chimps with Pepsi-induced high levels of intelligence. A Doritos ad running in winter 1995 had the recently defeated governors of Texas and New York, Ann Richards and Mario Cuomo, talking about the difficulty of getting used to recent changes—referring not to their return to life out of office, but to the new design of the Doritos bag. Miller Brewing made use of wacky combinations of sports to give viewers full-contact golf, surfing cows, and beauty queens playing ice hockey. Energizer batteries have put their pink, drum-beating bunny into the Bermuda triangle, Roadrunner cartoons, *The Wizard of Oz,* and (courtesy of George Lucas) *The Empire Strikes Back.* This series of commercials was answered (in a way) by The Puttermans, a creepy battery-powered family showing the virtues of Duracell batteries. If we are looking to commercials to give relevant testimony about the quality of products, humor is even less likely to work logically than endorsements, because often *nothing* is being claimed in these ads.

Some ads don't bother with humor, endorsements, demonstrations, or fancy storytelling. They just shout at you. SALE! SALE! SALE! NO MONEY DOWN TILL FEBRUARY! EVERYTHING MUST GO! Furniture companies, local car dealers, and carpet stores tend to favor this hard-sell technique: It's cheap and therefore easily done at the local level; and local customers may be more motivated by price, which is difficult to give in a national campaign. These campaigns try to break through the attention barrier by shouting at the audience—by increasing the volume and/or by using a high-pitched voice and large, brightly colored letters.

Other ads establish a quick link with the audience through *allusion* to a story, program, or cultural text already well known. Some endorsements feature actors from current programs for this purpose. Dennis Hopper's character in his weird film roles (*Blue Velvet, Speed*) carried over into his shoe-sniffing

1994–1995 Nike ads. For some time after the Indiana Jones movies, commercials presented characters or situations that resembled the film character (including a campaign in late 1995 for the Marines).

A final category to mention here is that of *analogy or symbol.* Some commercials get a concept across through a link with something that can be visually represented. A 1995 ad promoted gas over electricity by showing two bathtubs full of water, one heated with electricity, one with gas—the gas one much fuller and hotter. IBM has advertised its usefulness for businesses by portraying a commuter train as a roller coaster, thus giving a visual equivalent to the ups and downs of the business cycle. Kleenex asserts that their tissues last better than other brands by having them dab at abstract faces with water balloons for noses.

Technical devices are often the basis for the style of a campaign (or an agency); these may come into and go out of favor quickly. The more common and intense the use of a technique, the faster it is likely to wear thin. Camera movements can be mentioned here: In the mid-1990s some television programs (and films) began to make use of a "rough" quality; for example, by tilting the camera a few degrees to the left, by using shoulder-mounted videos rather than wheeled carriages or booms to track through a set or along a street, and by using noticeable "jumps" rather than a smooth, seamless pan, track, or zoom. These devices (along with accompanying music) lend an aura of "realism" to programs such as *NYPD Blue, COPS,* or *ER.* They may have been popularized especially by MTV and other video channels, and they are definitely present in commercials.

Sound involves its own technical devices. Music is sometimes understated in discussions of advertising techniques; but musical styles such as rock, blues, country, gospel, jazz, and classical music are important to attract audiences of desired demographics and cultural loyalties. In addition, environmental sound is carefully recreated to reach its highest fidelity in ads; and voice-overs are often done so as to create the impression that the viewer's own inner voice is speaking about the product.

PROBLEMS

Ads As Propaganda

The discussion of news in Chapter 4 explored the concept of propaganda. In what respects does advertising differ from propaganda? Aren't they pretty much the same thing? As we saw, the origin of propaganda had to do with making converts in non-Christian lands; and it might be said that the aim of advertising, like that of proselytizing, is to make converts.

But what is there in an ad to correspond to belief? That Tide will give you brighter colors and whiter whites? That Ford has a better idea? That *Coke adds life,* or *is it,* or is *the real thing*? That, as Nike recommends, we should *just do it*? The belief component of ads is implied, not explicit: A skeptic might ask, How is it that you know you have just done it? Are they really brighter colors and whiter whites? Advertising claims are suffused with a subjectivity and vagueness that rival any religious mysticism.

Neil Postman draws an analogy between advertisements and parables in an essay called "The Parable of the Ring around the Collar": The structure of problem–resolution to be found in New Testament accounts such as the parable of the prodigal son is repeated in such contemporary (per)versions as the famous Wisk commercials. While it's difficult to be sure about matters of faith, probably the level and intensity of belief inspired by gospel parables is higher than that aroused by detergents. It's unclear whether advertisements are preaching the same or competing gospels—whether their propaganda is all on one side or a babel of competing voices. Certainly Coke and Pepsi and 7-Up, Burger King and McDonald's and Taco Bell, Levi's and Lee's and Guess Jeans are intimating in their campaigns the heresy of loyalty to competing products. But they all follow a strategy of linking the purchase of products to happiness, to a comfortable belief in materialism. They want us to buy *someone's* soft drinks and fast food and jeans, if not theirs, more or less as a disappointed distributor of religious materials might prefer that a nonconvert be of *some* belief rather than an atheist.

Commercials do not require a *deep* belief. Religious belief is traditionally granted the possibility of transformation, of renewing and recharging one's experience of the world. Ads do not claim that power, though they may hint at it through symbol and allusion. Something like the Promised Land is often visible in ads—for example, in the clear waters, white sands, uncrowded beaches, and friendly peoples of the Caribbean pictured by travel agencies, or in the romance and sensuality offered as the reward for buying the right brand of perfume or traveling on the right cruise liner or chewing the right brand of gum. But there's a different conditional in the implied grammar. Religious accounts say that if you get with the program, you will receive eternal life; ads are never so definite. The appeal is more that of daydream or fantasy than promised actuality.

Much about advertising is not understood. Advertisers often do field studies of the effects of specific ads or campaigns, in order to discover whether they will get their money's worth. But focus groups may not exactly replicate the makeup of a national or even a regional audience; and viewing a commercial in a focus-group context is necessarily artificial, and therefore different from encountering it in the context of programming. And such tests are done about specific ads rather than about advertising, in its natural state and with an eye to its accumulated effect. Some work on advertising has been done within the framework of sociology and communication, but here it's hard to devise research that isolates advertising in order to tell exactly what is being measured. Most of what is said about ads and their effects is guesswork.

While it is not possible to point with any confidence to states of belief, we can resort to expenditures as evidence. Many industries spend 5% of their budgets on ads, and some a higher percentage still: "proprietary drugs, 19%; perfumes and cosmetics, 14%; liquor, 11%; cereal, 11%; cigarettes, 8%." In 1980 this was estimated at $691 per household spent on advertising (Bagdikian pp. 115; 146). Corporations and others using advertising must believe in its effectiveness in order to participate to that extent.

But it's not just their money they are spending—it's ours, through the increased price of goods and services. It may be argued that many of these goods and services would not exist without advertising, that advertising is part of the creation of demand that keeps the economy going. Such arguments are classic propaganda: They state an article of belief in the culture's very mode of existence, its day-to-day practices. Advertising is propaganda insofar as it reinforces this kind of fundamental organizing social principle, to the exclusion of alternatives.

Ads and Effects

Much of the concern expressed about advertisements has to do with the effects they are believed to have on the audience. Children's advocates worry that those too young to understand how ads work will be vulnerable to their appeals. Public health professionals and others criticize continued advertising for tobacco (and tobacco companies' sponsorship of sporting events), because tobacco products contribute to cancer and heart disease. Ads for alcohol may help boost alcohol dependence, traffic fatalities, and lost time at work. Similar concerns are expressed about the typical diet of U.S. consumers—high in fats, sodium, and total calories—which may be influenced by commercials for fast foods and snacks. And in addition to concerns about these specific categories of ads, some see advertising as contributing to a harmful materialism in our culture.

But how much do advertisements influence these things? The relation between advertisements and increased consumption—as with pretty much any discussion of the effects of media or media texts—is very difficult to prove because of the absence of any control group. For example, there is no society identical to the United States but without advertising directed at children, to which researchers could compare what happens in the United States. Absent a strong methodology, social scientists work with statistics and with less conclusive forms of demonstration. Much of the argument about the effects of media depends on anecdotes, and these are notoriously subject to being selected and manipulated.

In the absence of rigorous and professionally defensible research, how is it possible to say anything at all about effects of advertising? Perhaps "effects" is the wrong model, tied as it is to the stimulus–response model in psychology. It might be possible to work along the lines of anthropology and sociology, instead: to gather information from those available to provide comment about what they believe is happening as they watch, read, listen to, and otherwise interact with advertisements. Discussion of what goes on at the conscious level may not be the whole story, but it's a start.

Critics of television sometimes regard it as a "mass" medium, which it is in a sense, addressing millions at the same moment. But it addresses us one by one, or in small groups, so that there's also reason to consider it an individual medium—or perhaps a mass medium disguised as an individual one. It may also be useful to think of television audiences as between masses and individuals—as medium-sized groups. We sometimes talk with friends and colleagues and family members and total strangers about television, and such conversations may serve as the basis of influencing and regulating how we interpret what we see.

A term that might be of use here is that of *interpretive communities.* This term can describe readers of texts who may be widely separated from each other in space and time, but who share fundamental assumptions about how to make sense of a text. (It's not that such "communities" construct the reading of texts—they *are constructed by* the prior assumption of how to read them.) For example, viewers of *Roseanne* and *Married With Children* might be divided according to whether they see the shows as primarily fictive, giving us made-up stories with little application to the way we live our lives, or whether they see them as fictionalized accounts of people to be seen daily around us. Further division could proceed according to whether viewers regard these programs as positive or negative, whether they identify with the lower- or lower-middle-class portrayals, and so on.

While some guesses about how to categorize an interpretive community can be made on the basis of the text, it's more useful (and convincing) to try to get at people's reactions to texts by talking with them, in order to find out what assumptions guide their readings.

ASSIGNMENT

Choose a topic or issue connected with advertising, and design ways to test your assumptions by talking with people about the topic or issue. You might, for example, be interested in how audience factors such as social class or ethnic background affect portrayals in television commercials and print ads of "the good life." Or you might collect instances of print ads in which an attractive woman looks directly at the camera, and gather reactions to these ads (individual ads or clusters of ads) from men and from women, either singly, in same-gender groups, or in mixed groups. Or you might talk with children of various ages watching television about what sorts of discriminations they can make between program and commercial.

In doing this sort of analysis, it's important not to make your generalizations go farther than they should. If I am part of an "interpretive community," I may not be consistently a member—at times I may watch advertisements or other texts critically, and at other times without paying close attention. The actor talking into the camera may at times impress me by her sincerity while at other times I may see this as only a device to create an image of sincerity. Repeated viewings change reactions, so that an ad that is surprising and funny the first couple of times can become progressively more irritating. We will do more with interpretive communities in Chapter 7, on entertainment.

Dirt

Many of our assumptions about the nature of texts come from what might be thought of as the paradigm for texts, the book. Other media texts blend into each other more easily than do books, however, and this blending, or violations of boundaries, causes problems for their analysis and their ordinary reading.

Boundaries are important to how we think about texts. Books are artifacts of several hundred pages bound in covers (paperback or hardback); their covers form literal and figurative boundaries marking those texts off from others. And in books that are compilations of essays or articles, each essay is marked off from others by separate titles, by white spaces (sometimes blank sheets), and by authors' names that mark each text as the property of its author. In *Adventures of Huckleberry Finn,* Mark Twain set explicit boundaries:

NOTICE

Persons attempting to find a motive in this narrative will be prosecuted; persons attempting to find a moral in it will be banished; persons attempting to find a plot in it will be shot.

BY ORDER OF THE AUTHOR
Per G. G., CHIEF OF ORDNANCE

Media texts rarely have such hard physical or figurative boundaries (much less explicit "hands off" warnings from the author). The nearest equivalent to a book might be a magazine—but the name *magazine* is applied to all publications that come out at intervals ranging from three months to a week, as long as they are marked as separate by volume and issue numbers, dates, and different covers. But is the relationship between one *Harper's* or *Esquire* or *National Review* and another that of identity or difference? Within a particular issue of a magazine, there are articles by different authors, under separate titles—but the boundaries between these are less pronounced, more "permeable," than with essays collected in a book. There's a kind of "author function" to the publication itself as well as to the individual author of an article or a report. Articles often coexist with advertisements or other articles on the same page. They refer to or are commented on by photographs and illustrations. (An article by Leslie Savan about tobacco companies' new marketing use of "down-home" brands such as Dave's and Moonlight Tobacco Co. appeared, quite by accident, in the *Village Voice* directly opposite a full-page ad for Moonlight Tobacco; see page 267.) A similar permeability is characteristic of newspapers, which are usually even less like books than magazines. And when we get to broadcast media, there is no physical text to hold in our hands—only words carried over the medium of radio waves. Visual media such as films may be fairly coherent, particularly if seen in a theater; but the move toward viewing films on videocassette or CD players brings them into the freer environment of the home, lessening the boundaries between medium and audience. And television is less bounded still, with its many channels, its mixture of programming and advertisement, and its frequent intertextual commentary.

The tendency for boundaries to become more permeable has been termed **dirt**. The concept of dirt has been adapted to discussions of media and other cultural phenomena from the context of anthropology, where it is used to describe the mixing of matters that are characteristically kept separate. In the context of media, certain kinds of texts are considered not only as generically separate, but as potential sources of contamination; for example, consider the professional journalist's insistence on keeping news departments separate from the money-making arms of newspapers, the advertising and circulation departments. Incursions by these into the news categories—for example, running public relations material as news, or using news coverage to promote a sports stadium, sales event, or political campaign—is a violation of ethics, a taboo. (Recall the "Dart" from the *Columbia Journalism Review* in Chapter 4.) Television news personnel have long been kept separate from advertising; for example, television anchors are among the most recognizable faces and voices on television, but they are rarely used to endorse or sell products. (Such commercial mixings are the mark of questionable news sources, as with radio figures like Paul Harvey or Rush Limbaugh, who freely endorse products and do radio commercials for their sponsors.) Similarly, boundaries between entertainment and advertisements are formally marked by transitional devices such as fade-outs, logos, or transitional statements ("And now for a word from our sponsor" or "After these messages, we'll be right back").

Dirt is the source of some of the news profession's low regard for tabloids. Tabloids provide, in something like the format of a newspaper, stories that are so obviously fantastic that they are read as entertainment—and this mixing of these purposes, spreading from print tabloids to quasijournalistic shows on television such as *A Current Affair*, is seen as supplanting public interest in responsible news reporting.

Crossing of boundaries is also a source of interest when we explore connections between the values advocated in television programming and those implied by the commercials run in a given program's time slot. Sports programming, for example, is often sponsored by beer companies, and the values tend to overlap in ways that put the sports coverage implicitly (if not explicitly) at the service of selling beer. For example, how many of these values are promoted both by sports commentators and by advertisements? (*a*) Individual effort at the service of a corporate identity (team, company, family); (*b*) wit and inventiveness in the defining of a personal style; (*c*) giving one's ultimate effort (110 percent) to achieving an artificial goal defined within the context of "the game." Similarity between the values of the programming and of the advertisements can be seen as well in the commercials and plots of soap operas. Both encourage a concern with what is right and proper behavior at the personal level: Transgressions are appropriately punished, whether a transgression is sexual misbehavior or the use of the wrong bleach. The basic act in both soaps and soap sales might be the giving of advice.

The following article by Leslie Savan traces a similar connection between readers' values and a corporate sales pitch, in this case by tobacco companies.

LESLIE SAVAN

Don't Inhale: The Tobacco Industry's Attitude-Delivery System
Cigarette companies are under fire, their very ads threatened with a partial ban, and so what do they do? They get whimsical, get hip, throw their arms around you—you readers of *Spin, Details, Interview,* the *Stranger,* the *Voice.* They design a Starbucks-like logo, offer packages with "alternative" edge, and, in general, try to blow smoke rings around your self-image.

That, of course, is the tobacco companies' good-time face. They also file hardball lawsuits, take out sanctimonious ads about the tragedy of underage smoking, twist ABC's arm for saying Philip Morris "spiked" cigarettes with extra nicotine, swear before Congress that nicotine isn't addictive, and contribute heavily to Republicans.

But almost predictably, the kings of cough suddenly switch roles to play the outsider and the upstart, as in two of their latest inventions: Dave's cigarettes, a brand ostensibly rolled by a rustic little guy who goes up against the establishment—though it's owned by establishment top-dog Philip Morris; and Moonlight Tobacco Co., a small, seemingly Young Turk company that overnight introduced seven artsy cigarette brands—like Politix and Sedona—each, in fact, a boho mask for giant R. J. Reynolds.

Marlboro-maker Philip Morris, the top seller with 45 percent of the $44.5 billion tobacco market, and Camel-trainer RJR, No. 2 with 27 percent, are only following the trend of huge corporations marketing fake-underdog brands. By muting or simply not mentioning the real corporate parent, the kid brand can come off as independent, rebellious, and somehow "Gen X." Like OK Soda for alienated youth, created (and now killed) by Coca-Cola; or kooky Zima, made by conservative Coors; or retroish Red Dog beer, owned by Miller Brewing Company—which is owned by Dave's dad himself, Philip Morris. Red Dog ads, which don't own up to their ancestry, still have some people believing that Red Dog is a microbrewery. [See Savan's interview with Daniel Zwerdling in Chapter 8.] The success of real microbreweries has encouraged counterfeit rebel sells for all sorts of enterprises. And these microscreweries, as you might call them, are always spiked with outside sources of attitude.

First, puff on Dave's, a discount smoke being test-marketed in Seattle, Portland, and Denver. The brand is based on the jokey "tale" of Dave, who "from the get-go, was determined to grow the fattest leaves in the county," as the ad copy goes. The script is shaky, implying homespun. Over a cartoon of an easy chair and a remote control (implying regular guyism) are tobacco leaves hung up by...clothespins. You can't get more Bartles & Jaymes (another big business cum mom-and-pop shop, Gallo). But Dave's does, with the fiction that "Dave works for nobody but himself."

Why the little-guy drag? Philip Morris spokeswoman Karen Daragan answers: "We're using a grassroots, unconventional approach about a fictional underdog who takes on the establishment by starting his own company." Well, yeah, but why? "We thought this was the best approach to reach consumers who want quality and character." Cigarettes are not *nicotine* delivery systems, as the FDA's David Kessler insists: They are *character* delivery systems.

As for the name *Dave*, she says, "It's common, it's mainstream, it's memorable," and that's no lie. In fact, after "Bob," whose namesake ventures are numerous, "Dave" is the marketing moniker of the moment: There's Wendy's founder Dave, Dave's Beer in Canada, the movie *Dave* about a regular shmo made U.S. president, the TV show *Dave's World*, the Kids in the Hall tune "All the Daves I Know." But mostly, Dave is the name of choice for underdogs everywhere: David against Goliath. Now Philip Morris gets to play both roles.

Although the Dave tale is intended as chuckley fiction, it may lead even savvy smokers to believe that a few facts actually grow among the weeds. "He hand cut the fattest leaves and auctioned off the rest to some other tobacco company," the ad copy reads. But when asked if the leaves are any fatter than other cigs', the spokeswoman equivocated as if I had asked if smoking is harmful, finally saying, "I don't know if the leaves are fatter, because that's a descriptive term and it's a tale." Oh.

Tall tales or not, cigarette ads provide information, helping "adults to make free choices in a free marketplace," as another Philip Morris exec (and the entire industry) insists. But other than printing mandatory tar and nicotine levels, what info in Dave's ads can help anyone make a free choice if the info's all pretend? Actually, Dave's is only a wee more make-believe than most cigarette campaigns—it's just a matter of which fiction we prefer to applique to our identity: Cowboy loner, Alive with Pleasure!, or grow-your-own authentic.

Moonlight Tobacco Co. is going for something more downtown than down-home; more David than Dave. The seven new brands sold only (so far) in New York, Chicago, and that Starbucks kind of town, Seattle, are not character-driven, like Dave's, so much as "art-driven," as RJR spokesman Frank Lester says. Clearly, the world wasn't waiting breathlessly for safer cigarettes, but for more dangerous design.

"The products are good," says Lester, "but the packages are designed to speak to the individuality of the adult smoker. This allows me to say, 'Hey, I'm not run-of-the-mill. I smoke something different.'"

"Cigarettes are something people pull out of their pocket 20 times a day," adds Dirk Herrman, Moonlight "co-founder" along with Diane Roberts (he was formerly a senior brand manager at RJR; she was in R&D). "These styles allow them to do it with a little more self-identity."

Herrman got the idea from an East German brand that rotates package designs. "One pack looked like Warhol, one like Kandinsky, one like Mondrian, and I thought, There's got to be a way to sell cigarettes through packaging alone."

Moonlight's target customer, Herrman says, is "interested in culture, in film, art, in being a part of that more than someone who sits back and reads about it in *People* magazine." And so Moonlight doesn't advertise in *People*, but in *Details, Interview, Rolling Stone*, and in alternatives like the one you're holding [i.e., the *Village Voice*, where this article appeared; an ad for Moonlight Tobacco appeared on the opposite page].

Unlike RJR's earlier, ill-fated attempts to create cigs for other "niche markets" (namely Uptown, aimed at blacks, and Dakota, aimed at "virile women"), Moonlight's efforts probably won't be accused of offending, much less of trying to kill, its target market of artistes. Dragging on death is part of the deal. The backlash against the antismoking movement has only enhanced the formula: Along with unknown quantities of additives, you inhale iconoclasm. And as the anti-p.c. backlash grows, it looks even more iconoclastic to cheer the Republican "revolution" as it defends its friends in the tobacco industry—who, in turn, fund the GOP.

Maybe that's why Moonlight dared to call one of its brands Politix. I wondered if it was so named because of the coming election year. Silly me. "It's a play on the politics of smoking," says Lester. On the package is a hand making the peace sign and the words *Lighten Up* and *Join the Party!* And speaking of society's slide from real politics to puff politix is the brand North Star; its Viet Cong–like design apparently targets communists. But no problem: Communism's just another style these days. (Filling out Moonlight's alternative carton are the elephant-emblazoned Jumbo's; the "honey-roasted" B's and Sedona (the latter is the name of a New Age mecca in Arizona); and the ur-bane City and Metro. Said an editor as he played with the colorful packs: "I'm embarrassed at how excited I am." Others' comments: "Oh, cool." "The guy who did this is a genius." "Politix tasted kind of stale."

Other than the honey-hyped brands, Moonlight cigarettes themselves are not terribly different from RJR's other smokes. But it's looks that count. City, for instance, has "granite filters," as Herrman puts it. Granite? Well, it's just the color of the paper, he says. "But there's never been a cigarette that's looked like that. It's a perceptual issue, and the individual sort of fills in on some of these things."

One thing no individual can fill in, though, is the identity of the company that actually owns Moonlight when its I. D. appears nowhere in the ads. "[RJR's name] is in every pack of cigarettes and in inserts that tell the story," answers Herrman. "But when it comes to advertising, there's only so much you can try to communicate."

Besides, who cares? "It's not a consumer issue," he says. "No consumer reads the fine print."

[From *The Village Voice,* October 24, 1995. Reprinted by permission of the author and *The Village Voice.*]

QUESTIONS
1. Can you extend Savan's examples to other products with "attitude"? In what senses can this "attitude" be said to come from the audience the ads are directed to, independently of the ads for the products?
2. What do the quotes from corporate spokespersons add to the article?
3. How would you describe the author's tone in the article? How does it connect with the "antiestablishment" position that she says these brands are tapping into?

"Dirt" is also a feature of radio and television offerings. Networks and cable channels group their offerings so as to stress connections between programming segments, then often use these groupings to sell commercial time. In winter 1996, CBS featured Elizabeth Taylor in four successful programs, all as a tie-in to a perfume marketed by her company. The device pushed CBS to the top of the ratings for that week. To find illustrations of other such groupings, look at the television guide by channel for specific nights, in order to see how each channel's identity is set forth; it's common, for example, for a network to group sitcoms so that the audience for the first tends to stay tuned for the second, and so on through the evening. A really successful show can establish an identity for the network (helped by promotion), as with *Married With Children* and *Beverly Hills 90210* for Fox; *Home Improvement* for ABC; and *The Cosby Show* and, more recently, *ER* for NBC.

Television is not a very "formalist" phenomenon: That is, analyzing one text at a time leads us to understate television's "flow." As viewers, we typically do not turn on the television for one show and then turn it off; rather, we tend to leave the set on, changing channels to find something else to watch, once our viewing momentum is up.

To certain ways of looking at the world, having firm categories is important. Information regarded as *news* carries a certain credibility that *fiction* or *entertainment* does not. Statements made by someone who is impartial or disinterested are understood differently from those made by someone with something to gain—think how it would affect your opinion of a legal decision if the judge had a financial or political interest in one of the parties involved, or your opinion of a sports contest if the referee were a known supporter of one of the teams. Firm categories can also be important to some people in connection with cultural groupings on the basis of gender: Unambiguous gender roles are preferred by some, and this is the source of objections to long hair and jewelry on men or jeans and cowboy boots on women. (Some of the mixed reaction to Michael Jackson may have come from this in-between status.)

PAUSE FOR REFLECTION

Construct a list of codes by which people in our culture are marked as clearly male or clearly female. Can you think of instances in which these markings were crossed up, subtly or seriously? What was your reaction?

Look at some print ads, or think back on television commercials, for figures that can be read as between gender categories (for example, the diver in Exhibit 5.4, or ads that present images of ethnic diversity). Are there categories in which you personally are willing to tolerate some looseness? Others in which you prefer clear separations?

Concern with dirt, or mixing of categories, is not confined to media. John Hartley suggests seven categories that are used to mark individuality: self, gender, age-group, family, class, nation, and ethnicity. Long-standing anxieties about "hyphenated" Americans (African-American, Italian-American, etc.) may have their origin in the blurriness of visibly different groups, set against the idea of the "melting pot." It may be that some anxieties about people between, say, twelve and twenty-five have their source in the blurring of categories: Teenagers are not entirely children, not entirely adults, and they participate ambiguously in love and sexuality, in the workplace, finally in identity. This uncertain status is in some situations extended to college students, some of whom are working adults, with others still financially dependent on parents or guardians.

This chapter's discussion of the concept of dirt is meant to broaden our discussion of advertisement and media out from concentration on single texts—as sometimes happens with analysis—to other areas of concern. In a sense, no texts are bounded: They have their significance in how they are received by audiences. It can be a difficult but necessary part of analysis to broaden our concerns out from specific texts to how they connect with others, because that is fundamental to understanding media and their rhetoric.

CONCLUSION

As with the ideological dimensions of other texts, the appeal of advertising isn't hidden. It can be inferred from what's there to be seen. Studying advertisements as you have done in this chapter is an exercise in a common academic activity, moving from observations about the explicit to inferences about what is implied. Ads, like other media texts, aren't hidden persuaders, but open—and fairly obvious once they are put into contexts a little different from those routinely provided to viewers. Another way to think of this point is that media (particularly television) have taught us to read ads according to one set of assumptions, which keeps texts in separate compartments. This book is devoted to developing some alternative ways of reading advertisements, and other media texts, through an interpretive framework more along lines of academic or critical inquiry.

FURTHER ASSIGNMENTS

Assignment: Ethnography

Draw on your "attentive TV viewing" practices (Chapter 2) to compile reactions to how other people react to commercials. You will need to be doing "social viewing"; that is, watching television with others present. (Be careful not to tip them off that you are assessing their responses.) For this assignment you should keep notes on scratch paper as before; but instead of trying to take notes on everything, note program, time, and other specifics, but pay particular attention to how others watching with you are responding to commercials. Do they watch commercials in much the same way as the program? Do they talk during ads? Flip the channels? Leave the room? Do the ads that catch their attention fall into any particular pattern(s)?

After observing for some time (an hour or so minimum), talk with your companions about what they recall from the commercials. Prompt them, if necessary, about specifics that you've noted. Get some sense of their general attitude toward advertising, and see to what extent this matches with their specific reactions.

Assignment

Choose a species of programming with which you are fairly familiar, and note connections between themes that express values in the programming and in some of the commercials broadcast during that time. Some possibilities: (*a*) musical programming on radio (country, rock, classic rock, easy listening); (*b*) rock videos, rap videos, and so on; (*c*) children's programming (cartoons, competitive programs); (*d*) specific genres of sports (football, tennis, golf, stock car racing, tractor pulls); (*e*) news broadcasts; (*f*) informational programming (e.g., *Meet the Press*).

Assignment

Extend some of the discussions above on classification and close reading to radio ads. How does it change your understanding of technical devices when the medium makes use of sound and language, but not visual images?

Assignment

Make use of some research materials to explore the relationship between tobacco advertising and control over what has and has not come out about the health effects of tobacco. (Books by Bagdikian and Lee and Solomon are starting points; see the Works Cited list at the end of this book.)

Assignment

Do an equivalent to your media log, but specifically about advertising. That is, choose a period of time (e.g., an hour) when you watch television or listen to the radio, make a tape during that time, and review the tape, making a list of commercials run, along with the amount of time for each. As you look back over the list, what patterns do you see? What connections might there be between the advertisements and the programming?

Assignment
Record three hours of whatever is broadcast on a commercial channel of your choice. Then, making free use of the fast-forward button on the VCR, make an inventory of commercials, connecting them to the programming being sponsored. What inferences can you draw from the association between programs and sponsors? (Compare the listing of programming for news programs in Reading the News Comparatively in Chapter 4.)

Assignment
Make your own analysis, similar to those above for Midol and the Chevrolet Camaro, of the technical devices used in a television commercial. (You will need a VCR for this assignment.) It might be advisable to record several commercials, so as to make it possible to select from these; a remote with pause button is helpful. One way to proceed is to try to get the camera movements down first, then go back through and work on description of the images, then make a third pass to capture the sound events.

Once you have prepared the description, leave it alone for a day or so; then return to it. Read it carefully to develop a sense of how the written account differs from the commercial itself. Comment briefly on how the process of doing analysis has affected your understanding of the commercial.

Assignment
Compile your own list of commercials or print ads that suggest a state of happiness associated with a product or service. Is there any consistency in the products that make such suggestions—that is, do certain categories of products and services rely more on these than do others? What sort of "promised land" is promised—love, rest, sexual satisfaction, material comforts? Have you bought products or services so advertised?

APPENDIX 5.1: PRINT ADS

Here are some print ads (Exhibits 5.7 through 5.20). As you look through them, note some of the following components of their meaning:

1. *Image:* One, or several? What does it contain? What does it resemble? Are there other images that this one refers to?
2. *Caption:* Is there anything that functions like a caption or headline? What caption would you have supplied for the image? How does the caption shape your reading of the image?
3. *Text:* Are there words in smaller print in the advertisement? If so, where are they in relation to the image?
4. *Integration of parts:* How do the image, caption, and text interact? Do you find the text or image speaking more to you? Which do you look at more, and why?
5. *Presence of logo or image of product:* How is this brought into the ad?
6. *Implied audience:* Based on your reading of the ad, what audience(s) is (are) the advertisers trying to reach? Is your sense of the implied audience a matter of the product, of technique, or of both? What details in the ad indicate it?

Exhibit 5.7 "Feel good." Used by permission of Hi Tec Sports USA, Inc.

Exhibit 5.8 "Who'd think millions of people...." Used by permission of Lands' End.

Exhibit 5.9 "You'll be done before you know it." Used by permission of Hewlett-Packard Company.

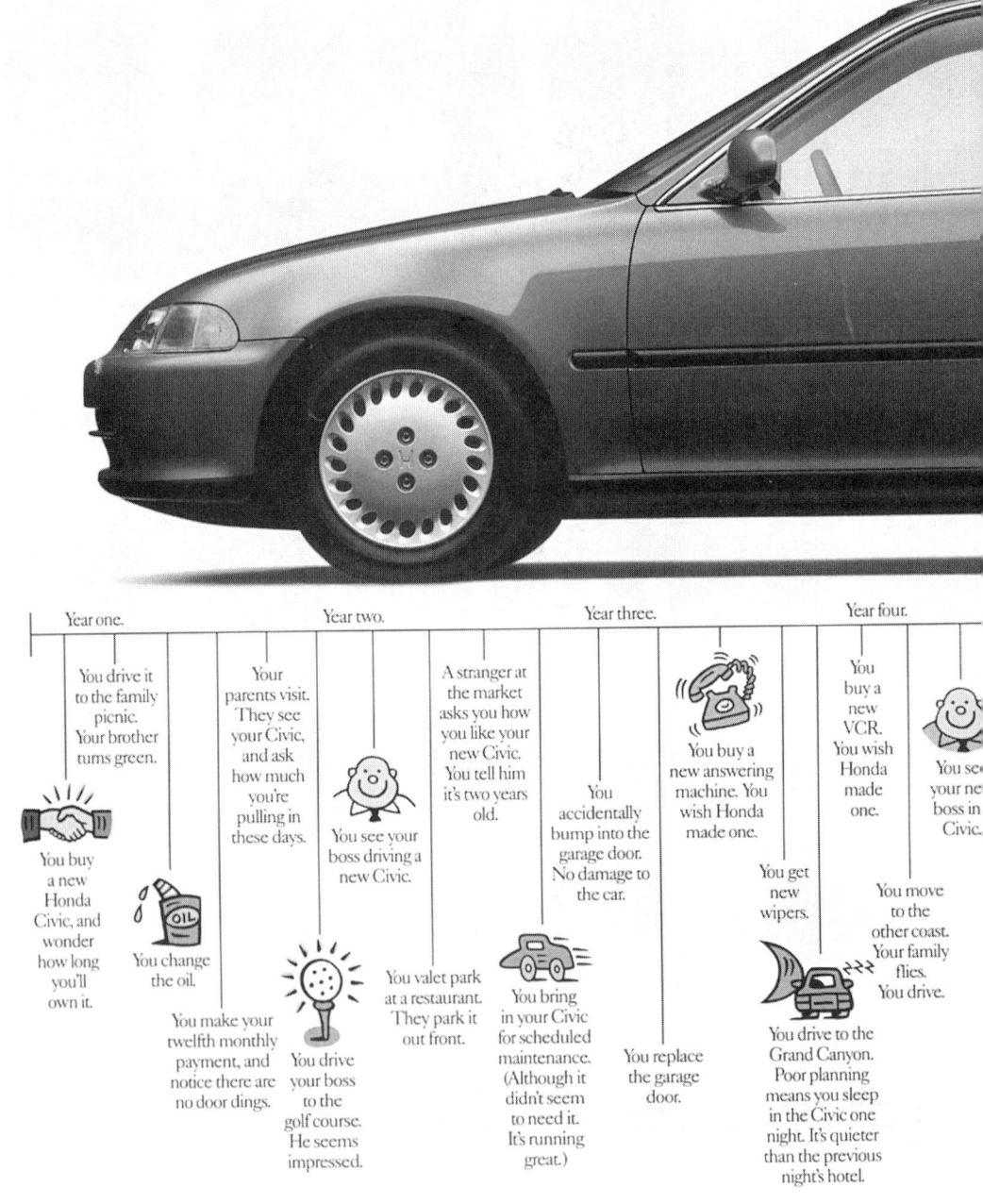

Exhibit 5.10 Honda Civic. Used by permission of Honda Corporation of America.

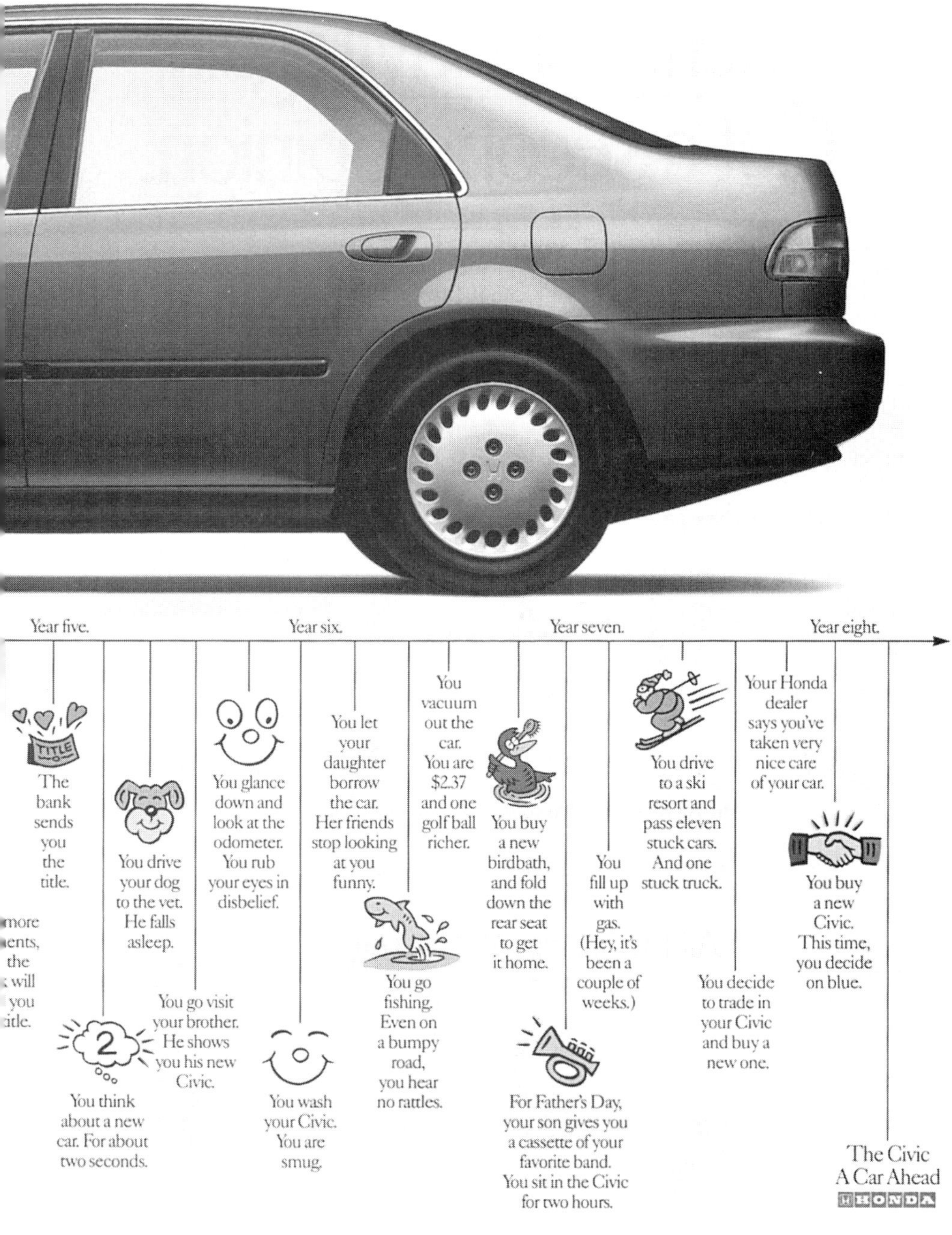

Chapter 5: Close Attention to Detail: Regarding the Commercial — 279

Year five.

The bank sends you the title.

You drive your dog to the vet. He falls asleep.

You go visit your brother. He shows you his new Civic.

You think about a new car. For about two seconds.

Year six.

You glance down and look at the odometer. You rub your eyes in disbelief.

You let your daughter borrow the car. Her friends stop looking at you funny.

You wash your Civic. You are smug.

You go fishing. Even on a bumpy road, you hear no rattles.

Year seven.

You vacuum out the car. You are $2.37 and one golf ball richer.

You buy a new birdbath, and fold down the rear seat to get it home.

You fill up with gas. (Hey, it's been a couple of weeks.)

For Father's Day, your son gives you a cassette of your favorite band. You sit in the Civic for two hours.

Year eight.

You drive to a ski resort and pass eleven stuck cars. And one stuck truck.

Your Honda dealer says you've taken very nice care of your car.

You decide to trade in your Civic and buy a new one.

You buy a new Civic. This time, you decide on blue.

The Civic
A Car Ahead
HONDA

Exhibit 5.11 "This is the blueprint...." Used by permission of Whirlpool C.A.C.

Exhibit 5.12 "The clean look." Used by permission of Grey Advertising.

Exhibit 5.13 "The warrior's most powerful weapon." Used by permission of United States Marine Corps.

Chapter 5: Close Attention to Detail: Regarding the Commercial

Exhibit 5.14 "José is a virtuoso." Used by permission of Four Seasons Hotels, Ltd.

Exhibit 5.15 "What do doctors recommend most?" Used by permission of Buick Motor

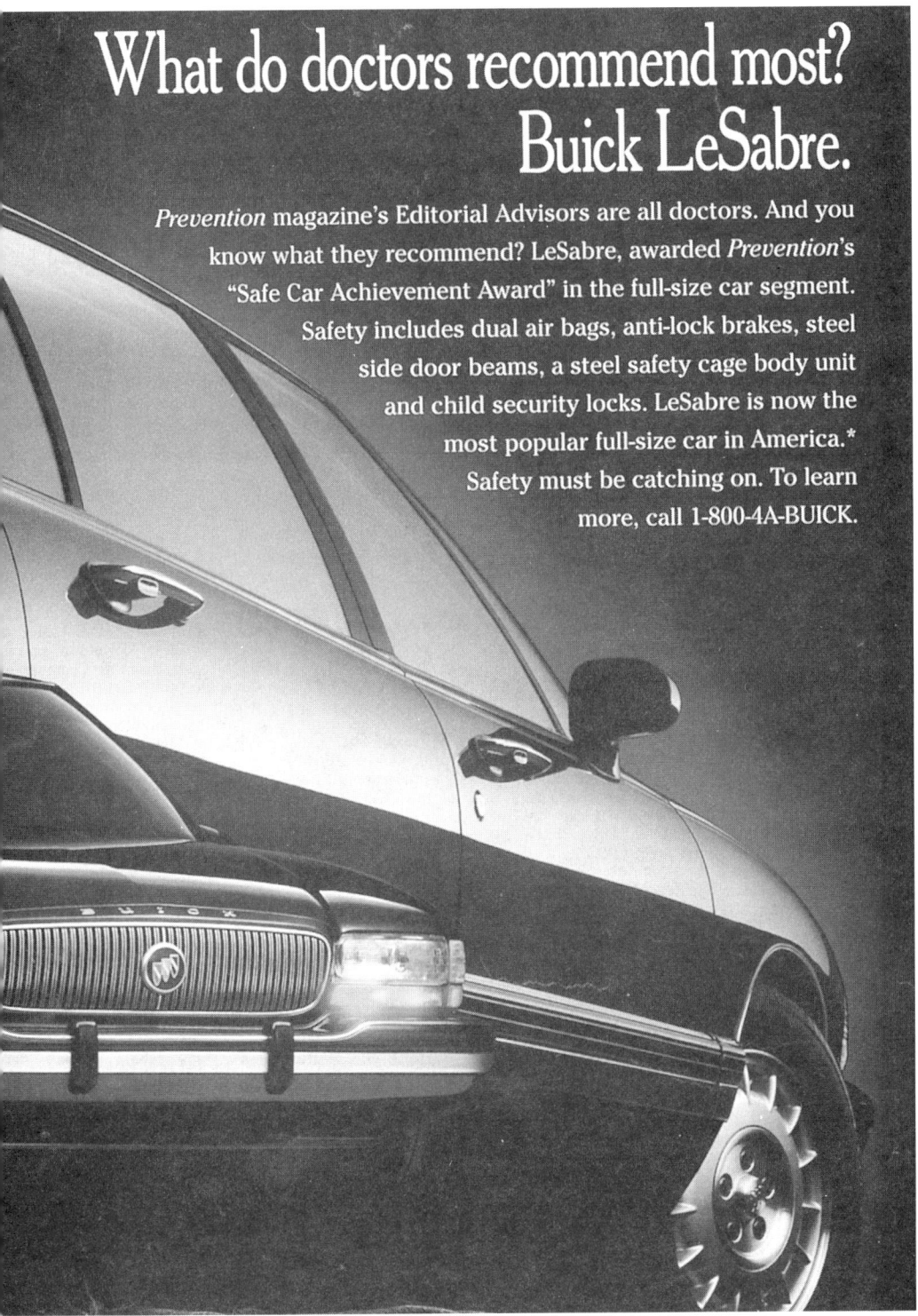

Exhibit 5.16   "The fully functional sedan." Used by permission of Mazda Motor of America, Inc.

Chapter 5: Close Attention to Detail: Regarding the Commercial

Exhibit 5.17 "The Montblanc." Used by permission of Montblanc North America.

Exhibit 5.18 "No man is an island." Used by permission of North Carolina Department of Travel and Tourism.

Chapter 5: Close Attention to Detail: Regarding the Commercial   289

Exhibit 5.19 "Listen to your head." Used by permission of Sony Electronics Inc.

Exhibit 5.20   "When exploring the remains...." Used by permission of Rolex Watch U.S.A., Inc.

6

Reading Pictures

OVERVIEW

Picture this: a studio photograph of a Welsh couple, taken about 1925. They are about the same height: The man, on the left, looks a little like Buster Keaton, in a formal suit. His tie is flowery; the collar is turned up awkwardly; there's a carnation in his lapel. His trousers are pressed with a crease sharp enough to spread butter. His hat is held stiffly in front of his waist. If he's Buster Keaton, she's Mary Pickford, dressed up under a large lacy hat. A bouquet of lilies rests in the crook of her arm. The light-colored dress is respectable but not showy, and the shoes definitely workaday. The couple stands squarely before the camera facing forward. Their names and histories are lost; but this absence gives us freedom to think about them as we like. We can make of their *images* what our *imaginations* allow. How did they get there? Who were they before they posed for the camera? And after? And where is *there?* They could be our grandparents, or the subjects of a romantic novel, or simply figures from a lost, wordless past.

The photograph described above can be found in a book about snapshots, *Say Cheese*. Its author, Graham King, labels the photograph as follows: "*The clothes are impeccable, the expressions are sanitized of all emotion, and the poses are petrified; any detail that might tell us something about this couple has been stringently excluded*" (King p. 96). This caption brings the photograph into that book's context, just as the description above brings it, in a sense, into the context of this one. Media have drawn on **the visual** for much longer than there have been photographs: Writers have needed to describe an appearance, a scene, a landscape, an event as part of narratives for a long time, because as readers we want these things to be represented to us. We want to see too.

Many kinds of writing include picturing for others—describing a scene, expressing symbolically an emotional state, or allowing a reader to see through your eyes. There are occasions when you *have* to tell others how you felt, what you saw, what the quality of your experience was. Writing may persuade by logic, but it also persuades by putting readers in touch with a way of looking at the world. The visual is an important component of writing, just as it is of media such as magazines, newspapers, books, film, and television. Long ago we began to look at the world through pictures—each of us as individuals, and cultures as well—so long ago that it's easy to forget that pictures are only a *pictured* reality, and that other pictures are possible.

"Reading pictures," as in the title of this chapter, is a shorthand way of characterizing how we interact with visual media. Here we will discuss some of the implications of visual media, and by this means we'll direct our attention to **representation.** When something is represented, in writing, in photography, or in another medium, it is in a sense both there and not: Its image is re-presented, but the image is not the thing itself. The photograph of the Welsh couple as it appears in the book contains details that are not in my word-translation—and, in turn, the photograph simplifies and leaves out elements of its subjects' appearance, by reducing them to a two-dimensional black-and-white projection. (And their appearance is a further reduction of who they are to a single, uncomfortable moment in time.) But while using the media of photography and prose, we agree to treat these representations as though they were the real thing. Representation is a crucial subject in rhetoric: How you persuade readers to adopt your representations has everything to do with your success as a writer.

Photography will serve in this chapter as a *paradigm* or model for the visual. Other media are also largely visual: Film and television draw on photography as a constituent part, just as they draw on writing and music. More and more of what we know comes to us through media that are partially or largely visual. And as audience we are well trained to read the visual, so well that we have forgotten our training. Most people in the United States now look to television as their primary source of news (or at least say they do). This is a significant change from forty years ago, when newspapers dominated as sources of information, with radio as second. This shift to visual media has undetermined consequences for our understanding of the world: What we *see* is processed differently from what we *hear* or read. It will be important, then, to consider visual media as a special case of media, in order to understand the quality of information they provide.

It may be somewhat misleading to think of our present reliance on the visual as created by film or television. The omnipresence of these forms has only intensified what was already happening through photography. Western culture has been translated more and more into pictures since the popular response to the camera in the mid-nineteenth century. And well before photography, other media drew on readers' interest in how things looked: Artists made images by drawing, painting, and sculpting, and the written equivalents of images have always been important parts of narrative poetry and prose. For reasons both biological and cultural, our understanding of the world is based largely on what we see. The vision section of the human brain is large and complex, and our capacity for sight has been made use of through the development of media. It may be that our devotion to print in recent centuries was the anomaly, rather than the recent shift to visual media.

At any rate, our increasing reliance on the visual means that, in some respects, people now *know the world* differently from two generations ago. There are ever more pictures to look at, because of the accumulation of photographic images and their circulation through advertising, forms of news and entertainment, and CD-ROM and other electronic media. Understanding what can and cannot be easily communicated visually will help us use rhetoric more successfully.

Visual phrases pepper our speech. To "see through" something is to move from what is evident on the surface to an underlying significance, to realize a deeper level. To "see *it* through" means to watch something personally from the start of a process to the finish, as a guarantee that it will get done. If we want to assure someone else that something will happen, we "show" them. These examples and others illustrate that visual metaphors are built into our language, in such a way as to suggest that sight is fundamental to how we conceive of knowledge.

As with other chapters of *Rhetoric through Media,* thinking about the rhetoric of photographs takes us to basic questions. What do we *see* when we see through visual media? Do we *see through* media when we see through media? What do media incline us to look *for,* and what to look *past*? How does consciousness of visual representation change how we understand it?

Visual texts began well before the invention of photography. When our ancestors drew on cave walls, they were telling stories of the hunt through images. Just as stories can be told through pictures, written stories can make use of words to create pictures. When we want to register something in memory, whether it's a battle, a meeting of political figures, a dance, or the expression on someone's face, we usually rely on a verbal account of its visual qualities. The presence of cameras has not made such description obsolete; on the contrary, as we have seen in studying news and advertising media, descriptive language is often used in conjunction with images to direct viewers *where* to look and *what* to look for. Captions in news photography highlight elements of a photograph and direct the reader's thinking along certain channels. So this chapter will reexamine how we think about representation, using attention to pictorial conventions as a device for making visual media less natural, so that we can better understand how they work.

PAUSE FOR REFLECTION

Have you ever noticed how many verbal expressions are based on *seeing* things? "As you can see," "focus on," and "picture this," are just a few examples. Brainstorm additions to this list—you may find it helpful to use a thesaurus. Does English make use as often of other senses as the basis of metaphors (e.g., "hear me out," "touch on this topic")? Make some lists of phrases that involve other senses, and determine which sense you can find most examples for. As you read this chapter, you may want to mark in your textbook phrases that imply the use of one or more of the senses.

Many visual metaphors derive from the root metaphor that "seeing is believing"; but, *as we have seen* in other chapters, much contemporary "seeing" takes place through the technologies of media, and this "seeing" can manipulate our understanding of reality. How does *seeing* affect you personally?

ISSUES

The Appeal of Seeing

As I write this, I'm at my desk, during my regular writing time. I have a deadline approaching, but the words just aren't falling into place. If I want to, I can wait it out, trusting that something will come; or I can reach back to some of the invention strategies I know, and brainstorm or freewrite or use another starter discussed in Chapter 3. But what I have to say is closer at hand than that, and it shouldn't require much to get the flow of words started.

What I find myself doing is *looking.* I look out the window at the house across the street, even if there's nothing happening there. I look at my desktop—cluttered, usually, but with some potential sources of interest, some things to cue my inner voice. I look at words, at objects, at pictures, at movement. I literally look for somewhere to start. Some part of me says that this looking around is a distraction, that it's just the self that wants to play trying to divert the self that is at work to meet the deadline. But another part of me says that some of my best work, and everyone's, is done through play. When I find something interesting, when I discover something about myself or a subject, it is often by letting my mind drift rather than staying on task. And some of this mental drifting occurs when I let my vision, literally and figuratively, drift.

Shift ahead to later in the evening. Like many people, I have a television in the bedroom, with a remote control device. The television is on, but I'm not very solidly hooked by the program, and during a break for ads or a slow moment in the plot, I look around for something better. In this case, I shift my vision, just as I did when looking around at the desktop. Now, however, I "look around" by moving my thumb rather than my head and eyes, and my "looking" is limited by the channel changer (which goes up or down one channel at a time) and by the television schedule. I can look only at what is being broadcast at that moment. I have the sensation of being able to choose what I see, but I can choose only from among the few options available. The contrast between looking with my eyes and looking with my thumb is this: The television seduces me into letting it provide my vision.

For reasons we don't often look into very closely, sight is very important to us, in itself and in what we do with it. We acquire an affection for those things we see daily; this may be the reason why we come to like a certain locale, car, pet, and so on, while other people find nothing especially valuable in them.

Another factor in "seeing" is that it means two different things, one literal, one figurative. The first is physical—whatever is in my field of vision, I *see*. But like everyone, I've had the experience of seeing and not seeing—that is, it's possible to see something with the eyes but not with the mind, not understanding its significance. When we say "I see," we mean more than literal sight. In this second sense, I can see only what I am *prepared* to see. Imagine someone new to some of the spectacles in the United States—for example, the Super Bowl, a political convention, the Academy Awards, the Miss America pageant. What would that person "see" in watching that event? The same things would be shown, but without guidance through the ritual, the significance would be lost. Context guides what we see, not only in rituals, but in the everyday: When I was growing up, the area's local television newscasters had no on-camera personnel who were African American—but I didn't "see" this fact because I wasn't prepared to recognize it as significant. My background pointed out certain details as important to notice, and left others aside. An important part of that pointing function is fulfilled by media. We rely on media to a great extent to see for us, in both meanings of *see*.

One way to think about rhetoric in general is to see it as a system of pointing readers toward certain things, a way of signaling what is important to notice. It has been said that "media do not tell us what to think, but they tell us what to think about." (Cohen p. 13). There's no need for a wave of paranoia about this aspect of media: All writers want to do this. In writing, we all want our readers (notice the possessive? *our* readers) to see the evidence *our* way, to understand and agree with how we reason about the world. This desire for agreement is always for the interests of some and against that of others. In other words, it's always political. Some objections to media come down to the fact that media are so very good at doing this—that media point readers' and viewers' attention so insistently in certain directions, particularly commercial ones, to such an extent that those of us without the same resources and expertise have difficulty getting others to notice our messages and our ways of thinking about the world.

One of the principal directions that contemporary media point—because it works for them to do so—is toward the visual. "The visual" can serve us as a catchphrase for making another pattern of analysis available, just as can other categories such as sound, metaphor, connections, or similar keywords that signal different patterns. There are visual elements to any written text. The meaning of a handwritten letter is not the same as that of the same letter typed on a word processor or received by e-mail. When you write a letter, it makes some difference for the meaning whether it is handwritten (in pencil, ballpoint, or fountain pen), typed on a manual typewriter, printed out in a standard computer font, or typeset in an attractive typeface. And the kind of paper also matters—letterhead, bond paper, legal pad, graph paper, or Big Chief tablet. We identify handwriting so closely with identity and personality that some people claim to be able to read *who you are* through your handwriting, as if character were told through handwriting, as in reading lines on the palm or (as was done commonly in the nineteenth century) bumps on the head. Palm reading and phrenology (head-bump reading) are generally regarded now as pseudosciences; but our selection of a style of print, as a choice of medium, can be part of the rhetoric by which we communicate. Even print is visual, in a literal way—see Exhibit 6.1.

Media, including the medium of writing, make use of what is there to use. Styles of type have come to have associations for us—not through any design of our own, and perhaps not from anyone else's design. Any publication has to take these associations into account, working within them. The same is true of other, apparently more significant elements of the visual—or, more generally, of meaning. In writing or reading, we are not free to make up whatever meanings we will; we use meanings and subjects that come to hand.

> The following fact is set in Helvetica.
>
> Helvetica, a typeface designed in Switzerland in 1957, has become very widely adopted because it suggests qualities of cleanness and purity. Walter Kacik used this type font in redesigning New York City's garbage trucks in 1968. Photos of the garbage trucks were exhibited at the Louvre and the Museum of Modern Art. Kacik chose this typeface for the trucks "because it was the best of the sans serifs and it didn't detract from the kind of purity we wanted."
>
> New York's Metropolitan Transportation Authority began to shift to Helvetica in the 1970s for its signs. Leslie Savan suggests that this was an attempt to counter people's associations with the subway. "In contrast to the subway's filth and potential for violence, the cleanly and crisply lettered signs lend a sense of authority. They assure us that the train will come and diminish the chaos created by the graffiti-scrawled walls" (Savan pp. 18–19).

Exhibit 6.1 What does this type style suggest to you?

PAUSE FOR REFLECTION

This process of using what comes to hand is like the French term *bricolage*. The French anthropologist Claude Lévi-Strauss has drawn a contrast between two personalities in working environments, the engineer and the *bricoleur*. (An approximate English translation of *bricoleur* is *junk man*.) The engineer would fit more closely the common stereotype of the scientist: Procedures need to be planned in advance. The bricoleur, by contrast, doesn't really have a system but takes things as they come, improvising by looking for whatever works without depending on an orderly arrangement.

Many writers incline to one or the other as a working principle. Think back over your own working environment: Are you a cluttered-desk sort of person, or one who needs to have order and arrangement in order to work? When you write, are you inclined to use whatever scratch paper might be available, or do you like crisp, clean sheets? Is your writing physically all over the place, or do you prefer to work with clean, typed copy?

Language is never only ours individually, and its uses almost never start from scratch. It's dynamic, changing, in a sense alive. Language and rhetoric tend toward **bricolage**—using what comes to hand—in day-to-day reality. Many things about language can be systematized, as indicated by its systematic study. But no one individual speaks exactly as do the people in language books—language lives in human beings. Each of us is continually redefining a relationship to language, and our use of media is part of that process.

> Please indicate the area(s) for which you would like your proposal to be considered. Competition for a place on the program is considerable, and many worthwhile applicants cannot be accommodated. Each proposal is given a blind reading by two reviewers, both of whom must concur; split decisions are decided by a third reviewer.
> [Helvetica]
>
> Please indicate the area(s) for which you would like your proposal to be considered. Competition for a place on the program is considerable, and many worthwhile applicants cannot be accommodated. Each proposal is given a blind reading by two reviewers, both of whom must concur; split decisions are decided by a third reviewer.
> [Times New Roman]
>
> ```
> Please indicate the area(s) for which you would like your
> proposal to be considered. Competition for a place on the
> program is considerable, and many worthwhile applicants
> cannot be accommodated. Each proposal is given a blind read-
> ing by two reviewers, both of whom must concur; split deci-
> sions are decided by a third reviewer.
> ```
> [CourierMedium]
>
> Please indicate the area(s) for which you would like your proposal to be considered. Competition for a place on the program is considerable, and many worthwhile applicants cannot be accommodated. Each proposal is given a blind reading by two reviewers, both of whom must concur; split decisions are decided by a third reviewer.
> [Tekton]

Exhibit 6.2 Contrasting type fonts.

PAUSE FOR REFLECTION

If you have a word processor with several type fonts, try out which seem most appropriate for the following genres of communication: (a) personal letter; (b) business correspondence; (c) notice informing someone of a tragic event; (d) ad text selling a snack. Exhibit 6.2 offers examples of different fonts. Which fonts seem inappropriate for which genres of communication, and why?

As with styles of text and with language, so with visual media—we never start from scratch. Rather, we recirculate bits and pieces of images that are available within our culture and accessible to us. Even if you undertake to communicate something using pictures, you will not be starting fresh. Rather, you will make use of techniques and media and conventions of seeing that have been established for you. And in looking at (and through) these media, you are working from a repertoire of visual images accumulated for you, by individual experience and by the wider culture. Learning to use rhetoric has less to do with "invention," in the sense of making something up, than it does with developing a set of skills and devices, which you use to make sense.

The idea that media recycle has been raised in previous chapters, but it may be important to return to it here; because when we take up the subject of pictures, we are a little off the usual expectations for "media." Usually that word evokes television, newspapers, and other sources of information in terms of how they select and manipulate words for verbal communication. But we may not notice that the same kind of selection and manipulation is done visually, with images. Seeing *seems* to happen automatically, even mechanically. Your eyelids open, light passes through your eye's lens and forms images on the retina, and nerve impulses convey information to the brain. The physical model is easy, just as is the technological imitation in which the camera lens replaces the eye and the film replaces the retina. But we have been *taught* to see—*what* and *how* to see—just as we have been taught to picture the world.

Part of what we have learned is the assumption that sight is easy, and that *what we see is the truth.* "Seeing is believing," goes the proverb: If we *see* something happen, we accept its reality, whether this seeing takes place in person or is done for us through some visual medium. But it's well known that photographs can be manipulated: Examples can be seen in pretty much any national tabloid, as with the "indisputable photographic evidence" that Hitler is alive in Argentina or JFK surviving secretly in a rest home. (See also Heather Bush and Burton Silver's 1994 book *Why Cats Paint,* which provides photographic "evidence" of feline artistry.)

The film *Forrest Gump* was built on such visual trickery: Its special effects were well publicized, so that viewers (presumably) didn't accept the visual evidence that Tom Hanks shook hands with LBJ, Kennedy, and Nixon. However, similar manipulations are technically possible for other kinds of narratives, such as those in political campaigns. For example, several 1994 political ads showed Democratic candidates' faces "morphing" into Bill Clinton's. Also, *Time* magazine was criticized for darkening the cover photo of O. J. Simpson to make him appear more menacing. We realize that trickery can go on with film and television—though realizing it intellectually may not prevent us from being influenced by the deception.

But a more significant point is that visual media *always* involve some manipulation of their subjects. Even when the most exacting professional canons of objectivity are observed, there is necessarily some selection going on in what is presented, and what is selected *in* means that something else is selected *out*. Also, *visual* presentation has meaning in certain culturally determined ways. It forces us to attend to certain aspects of a story, because it gives us visual "tools" to use in forming the story's meaning for ourselves. These tools predispose us to make sense of what we see through media in certain ways, and not in others.

Having news and information presented visually has become very important for many. The student journal entry below is typical in its claims for the value of television news (italics added):

> I watched NBC News with Tom Brokaw. They had great live coverages, and in-depth stories. *I learned more from the news than the papers, because I got to see with my own eyes what happened.* I also watched TV5 News. Of course, the news was localized to the area, and had some live coverages. *I liked to* see *what was going on in our area, rather than reading about it.*
>
> The news on the radio [NPR broadcast] was hard for me to understand. I couldn't get as much out of it, because I had nothing to look at. It seemed like they talked too fast. At least with the paper, I could read at my own pace.
>
> I think the papers had more detail, but *the news was more interesting because I could see what was going on.* (Marci Nowak; used by permission)

Nowak prefers television because it offers her the chance to *witness* events, which she feels involves her more directly than reading or listening would. Some of this may be a matter of individual preference: Another person might feel more at ease with a voice in her ear telling her the news, as happens on radio. But statistics support the contention that more of us rely on television than on other media to give us our basic, day-to-day information about the world. And this preference must have something to do with television's ability to show pictures, in color and with movement.

But in order to analyze rhetoric, it's important to ask questions about anything that seems *obvious* or *natural*. Our brains may predispose us to rely on sight—but outside of media, that sight is under our control, rather than selected for us by others. We can choose specifically where to look, when to blink, whether to focus on what is nearby or far away. (Ways of making sense of what we see, of course, come from our culture and experiences; these are not entirely a matter of choice.) What is there about pictorial media that convinces us that we are getting better information than we get from those media that don't rely mostly on the visual?

As we saw in Chapter 4, the format for television news permits fewer words about a smaller number of stories than newspapers or magazines. In reading the paper, you can select among many stories, but television offers no possibility for the viewer to select within one program. The amount of detail presented in any broadcast, radio or television, is a function of time, so that quantity of information can be expressed roughly in seconds. Round-the-clock coverage on news channels offers the possibility of more detailed treatment—but apart from exceptional events like the Gulf War, news is presented in cycles. Moreover, audience expectations formed by television tend to promote coverage in units ranging from a few seconds to two minutes, with few "sound bites" longer than ten seconds.

How does television overcome what might otherwise be considered a substantial disadvantage compared with print media, in terms of the information made available? Partly through its emphasis on personalities: A wise and sincere voice coupled with a respectable face and costume can convince us that what we are hearing is not only truthful but the whole story. Furthermore, broadcast media typically frame news stories in terms of their effects on individuals (as we saw in the television and radio coverage of the Japanese earthquake in Chapter 4), so that getting a suggestion of beginning–middle–end with an individual leaves us with the illusion of complete coverage. Another factor that gives the audience confidence in television coverage is skillful selection and dramatic presentation of film and video, creating the *illusion* of participation; we *feel* we are getting more than is actually there. Visual elements are crucial parts of the rhetoric of television news. And in the next chapter we will find visual elements at least equally important in entertainment media.

Seeing appeals to us, then, partly because our brains make (i.e., our evolutionary development has made) sight the most important sense—and partly because our culture has begun to stress what is seen through multiplying visual media. The ways in which we accumulate information have shifted dramatically toward the visual. Before the development of print, most information was passed along orally, through conversation, lecture, and other spoken discourse. With the invention of print, it became increasingly important to be *literate;* mass circulation of publications brought the middle classes, and eventually the working classes, into this form of information exchange. By the seventeenth century, the ability to read had developed into the paradigm of learning. There is a continuing investment, throughout our culture, in *reading* as what well-educated people *do*—and a corresponding bias against visual, mostly popular media. Beginning with film and intensifying with television, most in the United States have added the visual to oral and printed sources of information. This tendency has produced warnings from many of those committed to the written word, who fear that what is learned through pictures is biased toward surface appearances, toward the dramatic, toward the accumulation of trivial detail rather than the development of logical thought. Others may be inclined to accept visually oriented information as a reasonable equivalent of verbal—it is *different,* however, from what is expected in college writing. Whatever the justification for this concern, the emphasis on the visual is very much an accomplished fact; in the domain of news, the shift has largely taken place since the close of World War II.

Most people reading this book have grown up in the middle of this developing visual culture. Culture is always in the middle of some development; every age is an age of transition. However, the rise of television during the 1950s and 1960s was a historical process with tremendous influence on how we come to know the world. (Developments in computers and electronic communications may prove to be an even more significant change.) It may be difficult for you to conceive of U.S. culture without television. Perhaps you can get some feel by playing with the visual aspect of a television broadcast, as suggested in the Pause for Reflection below.

PAUSE FOR REFLECTION
Take a few minutes to *watch* TV—literally—without the sound. Write informally about what difference, if any, this makes. Then take the same length of time to watch the set without the picture, and write about that. (You can do this by turning the set around or by blacking out the screen.) How much difference does it make to you to have the visual image present or absent? What if the visual aspect were the only one available?

When we are accustomed to any medium, we accept its characteristics as "natural." But they are created by conventions which have developed over time, and in conjunction with institutions. It is true that "naturally" we have sound as well as vision, together, as with television; but "naturally" we do not have the *frame* provided by television. We don't have our sound and vision of the world sitting in a corner of the living room—*we* do the selecting of what is seen, by being present and by directing our gaze. But television, like film, points our heads in a certain direction—and selecting one direction means that we cannot look in others, just as a still camera must limit its picture of reality to what comes through its lens. As is the case with print media, broadcast and visual media select material to be presented to their "readers." The distinction, however, is that television, in particular, provides so convincing an imitation, with its material so carefully selected and its "flow" carrying viewers along, that it becomes easy for us to forget that any selection at all is going on. And the visuality of the medium is a large part of what encourages us to believe this.

As in other sections of *Rhetoric through Media,* then, our consideration of the visual has implications for how media present things for us to see. This reconsideration means looking at the conventions through which we participate in those media, through which as audience we complete their meaning. But because the visual is something like a primary category out of which other media build their meanings, the account of conventions here will be more basic than in other sections, involving questions about signs and how they relate to reality. Before we get to that discussion, however, three other subjects will be useful preparation: how photographs connect with stories, how photography evolved from other visually oriented media (painting and descriptive writing), and how a photograph can be read as an example of social and cultural codes that guide our interpretation.

Pictures and Narratives

It used to be said that "a picture is worth a thousand words," back when words were the currency of information. A medium that presents a pictorial image can rely on that image to *show* the reader what would take more space to *tell.* In other words, the saying illustrates that "every picture tells a story." But what stories? Whose stories? Where do they come from?

In Chapter 4's discussion of news and information, we saw that the news is incorporated by readers into stories. Stories that do not connect to ideology tend to drop from sight, while those that connect with common beliefs and worldviews are repeated and reinforced. The same principle holds for visual images: As with news accounts, our reading of visual images tells us about our customary ways of understanding the world.

In a way, the pictorial impulse is opposite to the narrative impulse. Narratives are necessarily told in some sequence: First this happened, and then as a result, that happened. Even if the narrative doesn't assert cause and effect, we supply it. Any portion of a narrative looks backward and forward—back at what has already happened, forward to what we anticipate will happen. But a picture or image appears to be a frozen moment of time. An image gives us a face, a disposition of objects, a view by the shore, as it exists when the image was made.

But as we look at these frozen images, we provide narratives. We make pictures "move," not only by imagination but by bringing them into our own stories (many of which, of course, are not exclusively or originally our own).

Yearbooks, photograph albums, picture postcards, and slides all invite us to connect with past experiences (high school, family reunions, travel, etc.). If the image isn't part of our history, it may be part of our psychology: We may fantasize along lines suggested by the image. One of the most powerful aspects of visual media is their capability of involving us by providing grounds for imagination and fantasy. As we construct our own stories out of their materials, we have an interest in maintaining those stories.

The appeal of the visible may be seen in the common advice to beginning writers to "show, don't tell." That advice reflects the idea that what we see takes precedence over what we hear. But showing and telling may not be as separable as this saying suggests. Nonpictorial media may have pictorial elements (as we will see below in the discussion of descriptive writing). Those who work with radio often contend that that medium allows listeners to picture imaginatively what is said—an idea that is confirmed by our having mental images of the voices heard on radio. Furthermore, pictorial media are shaped by the audience into narratives. Whatever is "shown" as a still photograph is immediately drawn into a story, partly constructed through the experiences of the audience and partly through categories provided for the audience. (The successions of stills that make up film and television, and the use of photos as illustrations in magazines and newspapers, are obvious examples of pictures drawn into narratives.) Sequences of photographs can be linked either with words as connective material (print, oral narrative, or voice-over) or with connections unstated but left to the viewer to provide. Such connection happens mechanically with film and television, which use sequences of photographs to simulate live movement (at thirty frames per second, the eyes cannot distinguish individual frames). Most important, however, photos work through the rhetoric of images to entice viewers to interpret them according to the stories we know and live.

ASSIGNMENT
Write informally about the narrative you find in Exhibits 6.3 and 6.4. Then compare your comments with those of others to see what sorts of different readings emerge.

This section will show some examples of ways in which photos connect with narratives. But whose narratives? U.S. culture, with its stress on the individual perspective, often prompts us to regard our narratives as uniquely ours; and, paradoxically, because our media often speak to millions at once, we usually construct these presumably unique narratives out of the same materials as everyone else. Insisting on their uniqueness, then, is ideological rather than logical.

Exhibit 6.3 Photo from *Another Way of Telling* by John Berger and Jean Mohr. Copyright © 1982 by John Berger and Jean Mohr. Reprinted by permission of Pantheon Books, a division of Random House, Inc.

Exhibit 6.4 Photo from *Another Way of Telling* by John Berger and Jean Mohr. Copyright © 1982 by John Berger and Jean Mohr. Reprinted by permission of Pantheon Books, a division of Random House, Inc.

As with other media discussed in this book, it's always relevant to ask about ownership: Who owns the images from which these narratives are constructed? Whose interests do they serve? Is it possible to use the common stock of visual images for your own purposes without being used by them?

Looking at photographs is a very familiar activity. We do it frequently, going through reminders of our most recent vacation, preparing this year's Christmas cards, leafing through a magazine, or noting the faces on the covers of *People, Us, Self,* and other publications at grocery checkout counters. As with other texts, we encounter photographs in categories, and these help to establish our modes of reading them. We rely on these categories as part of the basis by which we construct stories around photographs. Does the picture cause the story to happen? Or do we use the pictures as illustrations for our stories? Which comes first, the story or the pictures?

Most of us probably encounter photographs in a very few categories: family or tourist photos, images in print media such as newspapers or in magazines such as *Life* or *National Geographic,* or art photos. All of these, even the last, fit into storytelling in some way. You have probably seen examples of all three categories, and you could judge from stylistic cues sufficiently to tell them apart. A photograph of a green pepper, for example, might be used *(a)* to present your aunt's gardening hobby, *(b)* to accompany a recipe or news about the 4-H club, or *(c)* to create a pleasing or interesting effect through the play of light and curvature. A landscape scene might signify your great-grandparents' farm, a desirable travel site, or the tranquillity of nature. A portrait might offer an image of yourself at age twelve, a person in the news, or a representation of an inner character.

In other words, there are genres of photographs, just as there are genres of news stories, film, popular music, conversation, or television texts; and these genres function within several symbolic systems, often simultaneously. Photography as a medium cuts across several media—in this respect it is like writing or sound. Visual images are components of several media, and reflecting on their qualities may help our thinking about other media that are partially visual.

While it might be said that pictures provide us with stories "worth" a thousand words (more or less), the words might not be the same for everyone. Those with sight have all "seen" the world, but not necessarily the same portions or in the same ways. The same visual image might connect to several potential stories—but these alternatives cannot be held in mind simultaneously. It's like the black-and-white drawing of a goblet/two faces (Exhibit 6.5) in silhouette, or the rabbit/duck drawing often encountered in psychology classes: You can see the one, or the other, or both in alternation, but not both simultaneously. When there are several possible stories that a photo can connect to, how is a choice made between them? And whose choice is it?

Chapter 6: Reading Pictures 307

Exhibit 6.5

ASSIGNMENT

Look at Exhibit 6.6 and at the responses below. What is there about these comments that may be connected to the nature of the people responding? What do these people see because of who they are (i.e., how they are identified)? Does the concluding voice (labeled as "What was happening") possess an authoritative reading of the photograph? If so, why?

The comments below indicate variant readings of the photograph in Exhibit 6.6 on page 308:

Market-gardener: The eyes of these men tell you about their lives. They've never had anything, or any advantages. Today, when things are changing politically and it seems possible for man to change his fate, such people are becoming aware of the differences between different countries.

Clergyman: Who is going to reply to them? They all look at the camera, they are all waiting for something. I like this photograph. I see in it all the problems of our Christianity. Am I going to offer them the usual *spiel*, or am I going to listen to them and share their waiting?

Schoolgirl: It's a group of poor people and they are waiting to be given something.

Banker: This image immediately brings to mind the stirring of the Asian masses. As racial types, they have fine features, and their

Exhibit 6.6
Photo from *Another Way of Telling* by John Berger and Jean Mohr. Copyright © 1982 by John Berger and Jean Mohr. Reprinted by permission of Pantheon Books, a division of Random House, Inc.

expression suggests that they are questioning the why of their existence, which is probably very precarious.

Actress: My first impression: a group of men, like [in] choral music. They are waiting for an answer. Or are they just looking at the photographer? The situation is very tense.

Dance-teacher: These people believe in what? It's frightening, the way they look. One would like to offer them something. Not food—

it's not what they're asking for. They are waiting and they are worried. And what will they do to us, if we disappoint them? It's there, in that moment, an uncontrolled force, either positive or negative.

Psychiatrist: I wouldn't like to be in the photographer's shoes. Perhaps it's a political meeting. They are very serious and grave, these men. Scarcely a smile. All of them young. No old people, no children. All of the same age-group.

Hairdresser: They are holding papers in their hands. They must be waiting for a signal. It's in Asia. Men waiting to be vaccinated, or waiting to vote. Their faces are all similar. And the filth. Men waiting to be paid. They are poor.

Factory worker: What country is it? Are they Algerians, perhaps Moroccans? Are they posing for a photograph? It's hard to know what they are doing, or what they are waiting for. From their faces and their eyes, you can see that they don't eat every day.

What was happening: A tea plantation in Sri Lanka. A group of workers came to hear a talk in favour of vasectomy (male sterilisation). After the talk, thirty of them agreed to be operated on straightaway, in the mobile hospital unit outside. (Mohr and Berger pp. 52–53)

Pictures such as that above accumulate to become part of what we use to tell our stories. Collections of photographs in an exhibit, a book, or a magazine tell several stories at once: the story of the exhibit or book or magazine, the story of the photographer, and other stories relating to how the subjects in the photographs are perceived. Even a single photo may connect with several stories. In the comments above, some stories relate to political relations in the Third World (Market-gardener, Psychiatrist, Factory worker), to economic hardship (Market-gardener, Schoolgirl, Dance-teacher), and to a tense relationship inferred between the subjects and the photographer (Psychiatrist, Dance-teacher, Actress). Still photographs have long functioned as starting points for stories; this is one reason to take a camera on vacation, in order to create some props (and perhaps an excuse) for telling others about your trip.

But over time, according to Susan Sontag, a curious transformation has happened: Those under the sway of photography have begun to see the world as *already photographed.* These frozen moments we observe or consume, transferring the later looking at the photograph or slide back to the present experience, or just looking at what we see as though through the camera's lens. In other words, seeing the experience in terms of "shots" has changed how we see it in the first place. The world is there waiting to be photographed, as opposed to some other use (or nonuse).

> Our very sense of situation is now articulated by the camera's interventions. The omnipresence of cameras persuasively suggests that time consists of interesting events, events worth photographing.... After the event has ended, the picture will still exist, conferring on the event a kind of immortality (and importance) it would never otherwise have enjoyed. While real people are out there killing themselves or other real people, the photographer stays behind his or her camera, creating a time element of another world: the image-world that bids to outlast us all. (Sontag p. 11)

Being a tourist means accepting a certain relation to the immediate surroundings: You are there but exempt from really participating as do those living there. You watch what is around you, often more intensely than those who live there day after day—but it's a curious kind of watching, distanced and temporary. It may be like the kind of television watching done during chores or in the evenings: The television may be on, but those before it have no particular commitment to a program. Tourists have no special connection to a place or the people who live there: Two weeks touring through Italy allows us to see the sights and breathe in a bit of local color if we choose (or stay on the bus if we don't), but usually doesn't involve talking with any Italians beyond hotel personnel, waiters, and others who deal professionally with visitors. The knowledge gained in this way may be valuable in other contexts. Travel and adaptation to its requirements is a useful skill; those who study art or architecture or cuisine can gain a good deal from this level of contact. But the kind of knowledge available to most tourists is often similar to that provided by a good documentary. And the basic reason for this is that tourism takes all places into its own narrative, rather than discovering other narratives that may be already in progress.

PAUSE FOR REFLECTION

Does Sontag's point above describe your own experience of being a tourist? Write informally about a vacation or other travel experience that either did or did not confirm her contention.

We can get a feel for this capacity of photos to stop time by comparing stills from films with what we know of them as continuous texts.

ASSIGNMENT

Look for an image drawn from a film—a movie poster, the packaging for a videocassette version of a film, or a newspaper ad. Commonly these offer either a representation of a moment in the film or a montage of several characters or events. What are some ways in which the image so provided connects with the film?

Genres of photos and our responses to them can become material for other media, such as artistic photography. One artist working in this area, Cindy Sherman, made a series of prints in the late 1970s that presented images of the photographer *as though* they were stills from older black-and-white films (see Exhibits 6.7 and 6.8). Those looking at the photos "write" them into

Exhibit 6.7 Photo by Cindy Sherman. Courtesy of the artist and Metro Pictures.

Exhibit 6.8
Photo by Cindy Sherman. Courtesy of the artist and Metro Pictures.

narratives familiar to viewers of these films, as they might be seen from a later, ironic perspective. Sherman's photos are distinct from film stills in that these films weren't made—the viewer of the photo has to construct a plot from the photo (along with whatever movie plots, cultural stereotypes, and other materials come to hand) rather than connect it with, say, Indiana Jones in an already existing story.

ASSIGNMENT

Drawing on Exhibits 6.7 and 6.8, write a paragraph on the story each of Sherman's stills implies. Then compare with others to see what your descriptions have in common.

The paragraph below comes from an introduction to a volume of Sherman's film stills. What are some features of the writing that indicate to you that the subject is photography as art rather than other genres?

ARTHUR C. DANTO

Cindy Sherman's Stills
Of the signs and images of ordinary sub-artistic reality, few would be more commonplace than photographs—and few would carry a more powerful charge of human meaning. The baby picture, the graduation photograph, the mug shot on one's driver's license or passport, the wedding portrait, the honeymoon snapshots, the polaroids of the new house, the new baby, the new car condense the biographies of each of us (the death picture, which gave employment to so many anonymous painters of the nineteenth century, has not survived into our present system of pictorial markers of crucial moments in simple lives). The publicity glossy or the poster of the movie or rock star hangs like an icon on countless walls, bringing into homely rooms the incandescent glamor of transcendent beings, quite as vividly as the icon itself brought the truth of spiritual light into mean hovels and dark chambers. And the images which we instantly recognize constitute the common cultural consciousness of everyone who also recognizes them instantly: we form a cognitive and spiritual community with everyone who knows, without having to ask, which are the faces of Liz and Elvis, Jackie and Marilyn, Mickey and Minnie and Donald, Batman and Superman, Johnson and Nixon, John and Yoko and Ringo, Jesus and Mary. Each of these images activates whole clusters of feelings and memories and attitudes which compose a form of life—and when these images are no longer instantly recognized, then, as Hegel says, a form of life will have grown old. It is not simply that these images are ourselves, but that to participate in the life of our culture is to have internalized what we might term the language of photographic forms, to be masters of the rules that define the meaning of a photograph, whatever its content. Most of the photographs of common life had little to do with photography as an art or with the artistic ambitions of fine photography. And then, in the Sixties, along with the other signs and emblems, these humble images began to find their way into the space of art. (Danto pp. 6–7)

Let's consider one use of photography as brought into a contemporary setting. The program for the 1995 meeting of the Conference of College Composition and Communication (CCCC), held in Washington, D.C., featured the photograph of Frederick Douglass shown in Exhibit 6.9. This photographic image became part of the rhetoric of that professional meeting. Douglass, born into slavery in Maryland in 1818, was being taught to read by the wife of his owner, when her husband interrupted, declaring that literacy would ruin the boy as a slave. For the young Douglass this statement confirmed the equation

Exhibit 6.9 Photo of Frederick Douglass used for the 1995 meeting of the Conference of College Composition and Communication. UPI/Corbis-Bettmann.

between literacy and the power of self-determination and freedom. Frederick Douglass's stature as a writer (he published three versions of his autobiography, along with essays and speeches), and the close connection of his lifework with literacy, made his picture a useful icon for several thousand writing and speech teachers to carry about with them as they moved through the streets, hotels, taxis, and subways of Washington.

The picture can be identified as coming to us from the past through several textual cues: the serious expression, the style of dress, and the indistinct background, which indicates the photo's enlargement and cropping. The CCCC programs did not reproduce the photo as shown in Exhibit 6.9, but enlarged it so as to magnify its personal dimensions—Douglass was enlarged to more or less the size he would occupy on a television screen. In other words, quite apart from the historical circumstances linking Douglass to literacy and to Washington, his photograph says *history*—but the CCCC brought history to contemporary expectations of scale and sensibility. This photo, in sum, connects with stories of dignity in the face of slavery and racial prejudice, self-improvement through individual effort, use of the written word as a device for social prestige, and accommodation of past traditions to contemporary uses, among others.

Many photographs are coded in this way, as establishing an immediate connection with the past—because photography freezes the subject as it is at a moment in time. The faces in old photographs seem to look out at us from the past. Selecting Douglass's photo for the CCCC program cover meant drawing on a long tradition connecting photography (especially portrait photography) with history.

Photographs *offer* commentary, then, and they *evoke* it. Photos taken on vacation prompt stories told to others. Photographs of relatives illustrate family connections—times and places and human faces from the past. News photographs accompany print accounts of events and places that we haven't witnessed ourselves. Art photos present us with the visual as an esthetic object, inviting us to think about physical shapes and forms and their representation on paper. Important components of our world are signaled by photographs and by our practice of seeing the world as though photographed. The next section illustrates this concept by a close reading of one such photograph.

How to Read a Picture

Chapter 5 introduced the concept of *analysis*, or breaking something into its constituent parts in order to understand them and how they interact, as applied to print ads and television commercials. Other texts, such as the photographic portions of ads, can also be broken down in this fashion.

In analyzing a text, it's important to recognize that you are analyzing not only the text but your reactions to it and your application of the cultural systems that make that text meaningful. Sports broadcasts, especially those on radio, often provide expert analysts; these people not only tell listeners what is happening but set the game into other contexts—they explain this game's relations with other games, with other teams and players, and with the entire season. In doing so, they assume listeners who are at a certain level of competence: You have to *learn* to listen to a radio analysis of a baseball or football game. It doesn't come naturally. (If you want confirmation of this, try explaining a baseball game as rendered through a radio broadcast to someone from a culture that does not have these games. Or, to put the shoe on the other foot, listen to a radio broadcast of a game unfamiliar to you, such as rugby or cricket.) So a home run is significant not only for a specific game, but for the batter's season, for other batters who may be near to the top in home runs, for statistics kept for more than a century, for the pitcher's earned run average, and so forth. Baseball, more visibly than other texts, offers a web of meaning. Your response (or nonresponse) is to far more than the game in progress.

Analysis of styles of clothing can serve as a second example. How you dress makes up a text through which others read you. Elements of clothing shift in meaning continually, often rapidly. Blue jeans, for example, were identified historically with the lower or working classes. (You may remember a character from *Adventures of Huckleberry Finn,* "the King," who complains melodramatically of being kept "in blue jeans and misery.") Jeans were invented as tough and durable clothing for prospectors, and took hold as suitable attire for farmers, ranchers, and others whose work was outdoors. Professional classes dressed in "better" attire. Blue jeans became higher-status clothing through association with portrayals of romanticized life on the road, such as that seen in some 1950s films (e.g., those with James Dean) and through association with rock and roll. Internationally, jeans are the icon of westernization, prized in former Soviet bloc countries among others. Jeans became more upscale through the marketing of designer versions in the 1980s, so that now some brands are sold in the same periodicals and with the same techniques as perfume. Reading fashion can be more than an idle pastime: The wrong choices in dangerous circumstances (a certain color of kerchief, expensive sneakers) could result in physical harm.

Analysis is never isolated analysis of a text. Nothing can stay decontextualized, finally—because it will be reinserted in a context. Every text is presented and understood in context (not always the one intended). What is being analyzed, when others read your texts, is your ability to work within the codes and conventions that give that text its meaning, and to make those codes and conventions your own. This is true for your image in a photograph, your choices in clothing or cars, and your essay in a writing class.

No photographic image, then, can be entirely reduced to its literal description. It always comes in relation to something else—some other visual texts that it resembles or contrasts with, some print texts that comment on it or which it illustrates. Photographs are always to some extent intertextual. It's important to examine what the visual text calls up in its audience; but it can also be an effective rhetorical device, at times, to pretend to be encountering a visual text with innocent eyes, to see a visual text abstracted from its surroundings and framed by a blank sheet. Consider Exhibit 6.10.

Even the attempt at "innocent" description in Exhibit 6.10 crosses the borders of the photograph, however. In moving from the colors and patterns of the first paragraph to the statements of the second paragraph, the phrases bring connotations that prompt the reader to make inferences. The "deep, even suntan" and "fashionable...two-piece swimsuit" connect with *signs* which involve the photograph into a web of culturally available meanings.

> I am looking at a photograph. I am attempting to describe what is within its borders, without crossing those borders. The photograph is rectangular, wider than it is high. Three colors predominate, an aqua–blue across the top, an off-white on the lower two-thirds, and a mostly orange color across the center. The geometry of the photo runs generally diagonally from lower left to upper right.
>
> The photograph is not abstract, as these colors and geometric descriptions might suggest. Rather, it's dominated by a human figure, a slim woman who appears to be in her early twenties. The off-white color is the sand of a beach, and she's lying on it, on her back, eyes closed. Her hair, mostly pulled back under her head, is blonde; she has a deep, even suntan. She is wearing a fashionable and rather small two-piece swimsuit, and an ankle bracelet. Her arms are extended on either side, her knees slightly bent (left more than right), so that the shadow beneath them establishes a contrast with the brightly colored sand.

Exhibit 6.10 Photo used by permission of The Cancún Trust.

Reading a photograph means registering these signs and connecting them to *codes*. (We'll examine signs and codes further in the next section.)

We can say some things about the photograph in Exhibit 6.10. First, there are few details in the photograph: There's the water, the sand, and the woman pictured. She's not lying on a blanket, surrounded by the paraphernalia that people ordinarily take to the beach. She doesn't even have a bottle of suntan lotion. No beach bag, no purse, no picnic basket. There are no footprints in the sand. (Perhaps she was lowered into the scene by helicopter.) Both the sand and the water are extraordinarily pure: no seashells, seaweed, or tar spots on the shore. In other words, the picture doesn't seem to be realistic, but works as an invitation to daydream. The water is very clear; there are a few dark spots at upper left—perhaps rocks—but hardly a ripple in the surface. The sunlight throws sharp, crisp shadows, suggesting that the sky is as clear as the ocean's water. These details point beyond themselves, to a kind of abstract purity in the scene itself: There's no complication behind the picture, no history. It's as if the woman in the picture washed up on the beach. Whatever we read this photo as saying to us, it has to be linked with solitude. (The photo could also be connected with other stories of women and the sea, such as the episode of the sirens in *The Odyssey,* legends about mermaids, or Botticelli's painting of the birth of Venus.)

Some of the signs to be interpreted in this picture are appropriated for the photo from the system of fashion. First, the human figure: The woman is young, thin, and well tanned, all of which suggests a good diet and high income. (Probably she wears designer jeans.) Just as the sand and sea are not cluttered by other life forms, the woman has no jewelry beyond the elegant and minimal line on her ankle. If she were vertical rather than horizontal, the pose would suggest a crucifix; but her posture is that of repose rather than suffering—eyes closed, soaking in the sun, transfixed with pleasure rather than nails. In contrast to the subjects of many photographs, she is not looking at the camera: Eyes closed, face pointed toward the sky, her posture suggests self-absorption.

PAUSE FOR REFLECTION

Is it significant that the woman is not looking at the camera? What does that mean for you? How would the photo work differently if she were?

Some portion of the reading of such a photograph depends on what it is *not*. Signs exist within a framework of oppositions: Reading this photograph means not only observing what is represented there, but observing it in contrast to what isn't. This scene is clearly *not* an ordinary day at the beach: There's no one else pictured, and there are no seashells, footprints, or other signs of life. The scene looks as sterile as an operating room. Beaches are usually messy places. They are areas of transition between sea and land, and things are deposited there (jellyfish, pop bottles, driftwood, fishing line and nets, etc.). So clean/messy and fantasy/realism might be two sets of oppositions to apply to reading this photo. Others come to mind: rich/poor, white/black, female/male, leisure/work, rest/activity, young/old, tan/pale. What this image *presents* aligns the woman with the first term in each of these pairs. And to the extent that the image creates desire, it leads us to want to move toward these qualities.

Based on the description so far, we can infer a few things about the taking of this photo. First, it's probably not a vacation or family snap: Those involve more "natural" moments, with subjects looking at the camera or engaged in some activity rather than adopting quite so self-conscious a pose. And although the photo has some esthetic qualities, these do not pull it into the category of art image. There's a fair amount of skin showing, but the photo is not especially prurient. The most likely use, then, is advertising. See Exhibit 6.11.

The analysis above was presented in terms of the photo alone rather than of the photo in the context of the ad, in order to show how many of the image's signs come from photographic *codes* rather than from its commercial setting. In Chapter 5, we considered how text and image interact in print ads and television commercials; this example illustrates how much of the reading we bring to a photographic image is already done for us, even without the prompting of the text.

In the context of the ad, the photo is placed below another picture, which shows Mayan ruins highlighted by a prominent beam of sunlight. Between the two images is a caption: "For a thousand years there's been no better place to worship the sun." The label and the juxtaposition pull the apparent self-absorption of the photographed woman into relation with *worship.* (This association may make the crucifix-like pose significant.) The usual assumption about worship is that it involves the contemplation of a deity or a transcendent power, as part of an organized social ritual. But outside the social context, the use of the term "worship" in conjunction with an apparently rich and desirable blonde getting a suntan suggests that narcissism can be as holy as kneeling in a cathedral or bowing outside a mosque. (Is it significant that the "worship" is in the context of Mayan ruins, rather than of religions that are currently active?) In other words, the ad appropriates the tradition of religious devotion to the pursuit of solitary (sedentary? stationary?) pleasures. By presenting someone young, probably upper-class, and white as its human image, the ad manages to suggest that other sorts of tourists are not likely prospects for these leisure

For a thousand years there's been no better place to worship the sun.

Cancún. The gateway to the Mayan world. Whether you're taking in the sunset from the steps of an ancient Mayan temple, or catching the rays on our powder-soft beaches, your vacation is golden in Cancún. So come to the island that knows what sun worship is all about. Write P.O. Box 9018, East Setauket, NY 11733-3453 for a free 12-page brochure.

© 1994 The Cancún Trust

The Caribbean island of legendary pleasures

Exhibit 6.11   "Cancún." Ad used by permission of The Cancún Trust.

activities. African Americans or other ethnics, those middle-aged and up, those with young children, those who are overweight or physically unattractive, or those who prefer beaches with groups of people playing Frisbee or surfing are presumably poor candidates for this sort of "worship." The choice of photographic subject is interesting, since Cancún is just off Mexico's Yucatán peninsula—but the ad labels Cancún as a "Caribbean island." This tactic seems to be chosen so as to distance the location entirely from contemporary Mexico, as though to protect the image being sold to tourists from contamination; that may be the significance of the footprint-free beach exhibited in the photo.

ASSIGNMENT

Do your own readings of the photographs in Exhibits 6.12 through 6.14. To the extent you can do so, try to work first with what is literally present within the borders of the photograph; then work toward what elements strike you as significant and what they point toward (in other words, what they are signs of).

Exhibit 6.12
Photo used by permission of Four Seasons Hotels, Ltd.

Exhibit 6.13 © Jackson Archives/The Image Works.

The discussion above should illustrate that photographs are more than what appears on the paper: They point in other directions, toward the circumstances that produced the photographic image, toward the context within which it appears, and toward conventions that have developed over time. Looking at the system that supports such readings is our next subject.

Signs, Codes, and Conventions

Any particular element in a photograph can be regarded as a *sign*. The systems by which signs relate to each other may be called *codes*, and the rules by which we read these codes are *conventions*. The **sign** may be thought of as the unit of meaning, the basis of combinations that are linked together so as to produce texts. Much of the theory behind this discussion will be continued in Chapter 8. However, some treatment here will be useful to our reading of visual texts.

Language is made of signs. Reading the prose description of the photograph in Exhibit 6.10 requires that you decipher signs at several levels. The

Exhibit 6.14   Corbis-Bettmann.

lowest level is graphic: twenty-six letters of the English alphabet, in both upper and lower case, along with various punctuation markings, representing a larger number of potential sounds or phonemes within English. Many of the possible combinations of phonemes do not mean anything in English—that is, they are signs that do not signify. Others may mean two or three things, ambiguously, and the meaning must be distinguished according to what's nearby: If you heard this sentence read aloud, you would have to depend on syntactical cues to tell if the word *two* was the number or the adverb or the preposition. Languages themselves are systems of signs, the most highly developed and flexible sign system that we have.

An introductory textbook on writing and communication through media cannot do an exhaustive discussion of the concept of signs. A general theory of signs, or semiotics, requires time and technical expertise beyond the range of this book. What is most important is to develop a sense of how visual media work through culturally derived systems of signs, or codes. If meaning were totally present in the text and fully accessible to all readers, then there would never be any disagreement about what texts mean; but there is frequently disagreement about meaning. If meanings were entirely open to readers to do with as they liked, then there would be no basis for agreement and no possibility of deciding that there was such a thing as a wrong reading; but there are often agreements about texts, and readers will overwhelmingly reject some readings as missing the point of a text. (You may read this book differently from others in your class, but it is not open to you to make it mean *anything* you like.) So it may be said that many (possibly all) texts provide a plurality of possible readings, and they do this by giving audiences a number of signs with which to construct meaning. We construct meaning from within our comprehensions of the codes that make it possible to do so—through bricolage. This principle becomes important for our purposes; because learning these codes, and choosing how to participate in the implied systems of making meaning, is a necessary step in your use of rhetoric.

Signs, both verbal and nonverbal, are familiar to us. A surprising amount of modern communication takes place through nonverbal symbols, from the orange hand and walking figure used for Don't Walk/Walk signs to corporate logos.

PAUSE FOR REFLECTION
Collect examples of nonverbal signs, logos, and other illustrations of communication going on through symbols rather than through words.

Signs go back a long way, as shown by English pub signs, coats of arms, flags, and the cross. They are multiplied through advertising and its incorporation into portrayals of life on television and in film. And signs are continually invented, reinvented, and recycled.

One of the most familiar uses of the concept *signs* may be signaled by something like the image in Exhibit 6.15. Everyone who drives recognizes what this illustration means, because such knowledge, learned through the experience of traveling on highways and through reading a driver's manual, is required before a person can pass the driving exam. Like all signs, this one doesn't *mean in itself:* It points to something else—in this case, a curve in the road. The sign can be thought of as conveying a message, which can be paraphrased in words as *Caution: The road curves to the right ahead.* In general, then, the sign is the intersection between two conceptual parts, something that stands for something else, and the something else it stands for. In the example given, it's the road sign and the curve—or the *signifier* and the *signified.*

Immediately we get into complications. Does the representation in Exhibit 6.15 signal a curve in the *text?* Well, no—it stands for similar highway signs. (What would a curve in the text be?) But which curves, specifically, does it stand for? When pressed in this fashion, we have to admit that the sign stands for the *idea* of such curves, rather than for any particular ones. There's an ambiguity, then, in the question of which curve the highway sign in Exhibit 6.15 refers to: Does it mean the one on that road, there, 3.3 miles west

Exhibit 6.15
Curve ahead.

of Remus, Michigan? Or does it mean some ideal or fictional curve? In this case, the abstract referent takes precedence over the specific curve. This isn't a matter of different meanings: The sign's meaning would be the same even if it were misplaced. That is, if you encountered this sign before a curve to the left, you wouldn't call into question the sign's meaning—you'd say "Someone put that sign in the wrong place," and you might even call the state highway commission to complain. The complaint would be possible because of a system of meaning within which highway signs link up, one-to-one, with features of the road. A sign cannot function all on its own: It has to be perceived in relation to other signs. Such a system of meaning constitutes a **code.**

Within a code, it's possible to develop small variations. The system of highway signage is not standard across the United States: One state might put recommended speed limits for all curves that cannot be safely taken at 40 mph, while another might take this limit up to 50; or the first state might indicate one curve right after another with a squiggly arrow for the whole set, while the second state might mark each curve in sequence. But both are still using the code of signaling a curve with a yellow diamond-shaped sign featuring a black arrow. These variations in the basic code might be called *conventions.* (Conventions have been discussed in Chapters 2, 3, and 4 in the contexts of reading, writing, and news.)

The relevance of highway signs to our discussion is this: Thinking about signs is a way to refocus attention on reading visual media, reading other media, and, ultimately, reading language. You probably know how to look at highway signs and at photographs already—they are "natural" to you—because you grew up inside of those systems, just as you grew up speaking a language and living within certain value systems of your culture. All of us grow up inside a particular corner of language and culture: It may be large and generously furnished, or it may be cramped and uncomfortable, but we can't really know its dimensions until we encounter those corners inhabited or occupied by others. We can't really know how *we* read visual media until we come in contact with some alternatives to what we already know how to do. Knowing only one sort of response to a media text is a little like always living in a house on the highway beside one curve. If you could restrict knowledge to one set of codes, you would know only those codes, not the fact that there are such things as codes. For practically everyone reading this book, that issue has been settled: Media make us continually aware of others who live differently, talk differently, think differently from ourselves. The issue then becomes how to understand the alternatives and how we want to respond to them.

Codes are not individually derived. They come into being through a kind of social agreement, through which *this* stands for *that* (Mitchell p. 13). (You can of course make up your own code—a little like Star Trekkers' invention of Klingon—but it will not signify unless others agree to adopt it. See the discussion of Humpty-Dumpty under Why Ads? in Chapter 5.) Language itself is composed of signs—but there's no necessary reason or logic behind any particular sign. *Cat* has come to mean an animal with certain qualities—one that has retractable claws and soft fur, purrs when content, eats meat, runs around the house at night—distinct from the animal designated by *rat*, and yet the two words differ only by the initial consonant. These signs signify within English, but other languages point to the same animals with different words, which may be related linguistically or not. (Polish for cat is *kot* and for rat *szczur*.) Signs mean as they do, then, not out of any "natural" order, but because a definable group of people has made them mean in this direction and not that. And this is true for visual representation as it is for language.

Your discussion of the photos in Exhibits 6.12, 6.13, and 6.14 should have served as a reminder that visual codes have different meaning according to their context. For example, most of the time we associate tuxedos with men's formal dress, such as might be seen in a photo of a classical musician. However, a similar tux on a blonde woman, standing by a Shetland pony, as in Exhibit 6.14, signifies playfulness, perhaps a parody of these conventions. Another context might introduce commercial elements: An Estée Lauder ad from the 1990s featured a glamorous woman wearing a tux, above the brand name of a perfume. The photograph in this context signifies qualities such as beauty, sexual attractiveness, glamor, consciousness of being looked at, freedom, availability, unconventionality, and style—qualities transferred to the commodity being sold. Part of the codes by which we read such pictures, in other words, are elements which connect to class status, gender, and commercial use.

Not all photographs produce the same meanings, even with similar details. For example, gazing at the camera may signify something entirely different in a personal snapshot, in a photograph for advertising purposes, in a personal ad for potential dates, in a police photograph. In this case, the code is signaled by the gaze of the person photographed, while the convention varies according to context.

It may not be "natural" to you to think in these terms when you write; but as you become more analytical about your writing, you should begin to look at how your choices link up with conventions and codes. For example, something as basic as the choice of pronouns used in your text can determine much about the style and tone. This text makes frequent use of "we" and "you," in an attempt to signal something of the collective nature of classroom discussion, along with direct address to readers individually. (When looking over an early draft of this chapter, I used the search function in my word processor to count forty-seven different uses of "you," "your," or "yourself" up to this point.) Direct address functions as a code. The assumption is that a writer can say "you" and the reader will understand this as the written equivalent of one-on-one (or one-to-several) conversation. (One interesting feature of English is that the same pronoun, *you*, is used for both singular and plural. This ambiguity allows writers to address readers one by one and collectively at the same time.)

Other kinds of writings work within different codes, for which direct address would be inappropriate. Writings in the sciences, for example, usually signal that they are not dealing with fuzzy, subjective areas; and writers in the sciences tend to avoid direct address. And direct address can function differently outside of the teacherly context to be expected in a textbook: Rather than an authorial voice assuming something of the image of an instructor offering advice and direction, direct address can be a quiet and somewhat alarming private voice in your ear, speaking to desires that hardly anyone is public about.

In another convention, "you" sometimes works as a colloquial substitute for what, in the writer's opinion, people generally do; for example, in "The first thing you do when you get up in the morning is turn off the alarm clock and wish you could go back to sleep." The reader is being addressed, in a sense, but what is really happening is that the writer is expressing the judgment that this is what everyone does in the morning, but without saying so in a generalization that might be challenged. These different conventions are variations on the same code. The code is constant, but the conventions supply different uses for it.

Just as with codes, conventions usually originate in borrowing from other texts rather than being invented; however, it is sometimes possible to trace a convention to a single text, writer, or form. Conventions pass through cycles, and are sometimes taken up and widely used for a while, then dropped. (This can be seen, for example, in newspapers' adoption of color following the convention popularized by *USA Today*—which, in turn, was an adaptation from the graphic devices used on television broadcasts.) Commercials, because they are produced, shown, and dropped so quickly, may show more visibly how conventions begin and change. Consider, for example, the use of graphic text paralleling voice-over or being offered as a commentary on the filmed portion of the ad. This convention was in heavy use in ads during 1994–95; at some time in the future, the convention will become overworked, and it will be quietly dropped when it is felt to have lost effectiveness, in favor of some other devices. Another example: Television used to signal a shift to advertisements with a deep-voiced announcer's statement along the lines of "*Playhouse 90* will continue after a word from our sponsor." That convention, largely a carryover from radio drama, has largely disappeared.

Some more specific discussion of codes and conventions in photography might be helpful here. Our casual use of "pictures" to refer to photographs is a clue that the codes of visual representation were taken largely from painting into "light-writing," which is what the word *photography* literally means. Some of these codes are so ingrained that alternatives are difficult to imagine, as for example with the illusion of perspective on a two-dimensional flat surface. In the early Renaissance, painters adopted devices that created the impression of everything in a painting being seen from one point of view—that is, perspective. Paintings from other periods, cultures, or traditions that do not adopt this convention sometimes look strange to us, as though the artists hadn't figured out the trick of how to create perspective. But deciding to forgo perspective does not mark one as "primitive"—just as working in a different tradition, or set of codes. Part of what was strange in early twentieth-century artistic movements such as cubism resulted from the artists' choices not to preserve the convention of perspective—and, later, not to continue representation as it had been done. In paintings that use perspective, it is possible to trace lines that converge on one point within the picture, called the vanishing point, more or less in the manner that parallel lines seem to come together at the horizon. (Imagine that you are looking across a flat landscape at parallel railroad tracks.) The illusion of a three-dimensional organization of objects, in a painting, is created by their relative size and placement on the canvas, as well as by the play of light and shadow. Pictures are coded so that we accept this transposition without comment, as though it were a three-dimensional space that we were looking at.

Photographs continued the code of projection onto a two-dimensional surface developed by representational painting. What had been done by artists after years of study and developed craft could now be done by mechanical devices (a fact that may explain some of the early coolness between photography and painting). Other codes have developed with photography over the years: for example, the photograph as coded for *uninterpreted reality*. The camera is often presumed to be invisible, more or less as the audience for modern realistic drama is supposed to be watching through a fourth wall. In seeing a photograph, we are understood to read along the lines of *that's the way it happened.* But photographs rarely happen by accident: There's usually someone employed by an organization to hang around with a camera, and the photograph taken is developed, printed in cropped or enlarged format, and inserted into a context that shapes that supposedly uninterpreted reality, Even the "hanging around" part isn't likely to be accidental: Many public figures have become adept at staging "photo opportunities," which are thought of as events created to be photographed so as to appear in the media.

Contrary to the code identifying photographs as pure transcription of reality, then, photographs are not a moment of reality, impersonally registered and rendered to us purely, without history (and without their own histories). They are carefully selected and composed so as to give us a shaped reality—which pretends to be a moment of reality frozen on film. This code has some connections with parallel developments in other, mostly realistic texts; the next section sets out connections between pictures and their rendering in prose.

Visual Images and Descriptive Writing

Writers have long presumed on readers' familiarity with the codes of visual media. Narratives such as epic poetry, novels, histories, and biography draw on our experience of the visual to advance the storytelling and to involve us imaginatively in what is being told. Classical writers gave this rhetorical pattern names (*ut pictura poesis* or *ekphrasis*). The attempt to produce something like the characteristic of one art through another involves both the artist and audience in problems of representation. One use of descriptive writing is to pull the visual into the frame of reference of the prose.

Descriptive writing illustrates what happens when creating the equivalent of one medium in another. You may have found some difficulty in moving from studying a picture or image to describing it in words. While there may be greater or lesser success at such descriptive writing, we may as well recognize that the visual is a different medium from prose. Even if you could account for everything present in a photo, for example, phrasing it in words would not be the same.

For starters, only convention rather than any physical quality of the form compels us to look at the parts of a photo in any particular order. In looking at photographs, we commonly imitate the movement of reading (in English and most European languages) by scanning from left to right, top to bottom; but there may be an emphasis on what is at the center rather than at the periphery. But descriptions of images have to be sequential, listing the particulars one after another—and there can be only one point raised at a time, so those features that receive comment are emphasized relative to everything not receiving comment.

Before the invention of photography, if you wanted to look at pictures, you pretty much had to travel to where they were. In a cave, in a palace or someone's country manor, in a church or in a museum, the image had to be seen there. Pictures were brought out of museums and great houses into the reach of many more people in the mid-nineteenth century and after. At the same time that ordinary people appeared more and more in novels, poems, and plays, their images began to appear in photos. And more people from the middle class and lower classes began to make photographs. Technology, in addition to trying for closer and closer approximations of reality, also made these images more widely available, democratizing access to pictures—both in their viewing and in their creation.

It may be hard to imagine a world without photographs, because they are so much a part of our world. Even in the centuries before photography, it was possible to see a projected image inside a darkened box. Creating a *camera obscura* involves making a small hole in a box; light passes through that hole as it does through a camera lens, and forms an inverted image, which can be seen through a peephole in the top of the box. In the 1830s it became possible to fix such images by daguerreotyping them (a process that made a positive image), and then a little later by using the light to make a negative, which can print multiple copies. Photography uses chemicals sensitive to light to make the image in the *camera obscura* (relatively) permanent.

Taking pictures was at first a practice of specialists and hobbyists, then a means of collecting and distributing pictures from far-away events such as the Crimean War and the U.S. Civil War. More or less at the same time, photography evolved into a way for average people in Europe, Britain, and the United States to make records—their own landscapes of faraway scenes, family and other portraits, and so on, now available not only to the upper classes but to a much wider circle. Formerly, in order to have a portrait made, you had to hire a painter, which was no trivial expense. By the beginning of the twentieth century, almost anyone could make and collect black-and-white images as a way of freezing and preserving a view of the world against time and change.

Photography made instant history available more quickly to the middle-class viewer, and eventually to other classes as well. Visual images much more exact than sketches could be provided within a matter of days (faster still with the development of wire photos), and photo albums could be assembled into something like a family history. But as we have come to recognize, the fact that something is being recorded photographically changes the event being recorded. We behave differently for the camera.

The impulse to make pictures goes back well before photography. Drawing is listed in Charlotte Brontë's *Jane Eyre* as one of the attainments of an accomplished young lady. Paintings and dioramas were exhibited as a way of satisfying—or stimulating—public curiosity about remote areas (for example, renditions of views of the North American interior or the Amazon basin). A sketch with pencil or charcoal could be done fairly quickly, while a careful rendering of a portrait or landscape in oil or watercolor required much longer. Both required more time and trouble than do snapshots.

Looking at a landscape as represented visually, we are involved in constructing a story about that landscape (not our story by origin, but ours to the extent that we share it). The landscape may portray a peaceful pastoral setting, in which case the story may be one of contrast with the hubbub of contemporary city life; or it may be a wild and dramatic rendering of mountains and canyons and the play of light and darkness, in which case we may connect with stories about extreme climates and what it takes to live there.

Landscapes, though important, are not the only genre of the pictorial. Portraits are also central to both painting and photography. Looking at a portrait, we are engaged by more than a face and the fashions of the time: We are invited by the form to read *through* the surface to something like the character of the person pictured through the portrait (as with Frederick Douglass, or the woman on the Cancún beach). Just as landscapes work to encourage us to imagine ourselves in other locations, drinking in different views, so portraits put us before other persons, looking at their gaze in response to our own.

Looking at an image of another person may involve contemplation of that person, as though he or she were looking back at us; or it may involve being with or possessing that person. Or it may mean *imagining oneself* as that person, as someone who is well dressed, elegant, attractive. We are cued to receive visual representations in these two ways, in part through contemporary narrative forms such as film and television, and in part through older narratives that invite such connections. Novels—especially romantic novels, with their emphasis on the development of sensibility—have been important influences on developing this sort of identification as a way of reading.

Jane Austen's novel *Pride and Prejudice,* begun at the end of the eighteenth century and published in 1813, can give us some sense of the conventions of reading portraits before the invention of photography. A little more than halfway through the novel, the heroine, Elizabeth Bennet, vacationing with her aunt and uncle, is visiting some notable houses. They arrive at one such, Pemberley, which is owned by a Mr. Darcy, the novel's love interest (the owner is not at home). Darcy, Elizabeth's social superior, earlier proposed to her; but believing that he is proud, even arrogant, she declined his offer. Subsequently, she has discovered that her earlier estimation of him was based on prejudice and gossip, and has come to think more favorably of him—an opinion reflected in her thoughts as she examines his portrait. Her thoughts are voiced by the narrator, who is generally quite sympathetic:

> In the gallery there were many family portraits, but they could have little to fix the attention of a stranger. Elizabeth walked on in quest of the only face whose features would be known to her. At last it arrested her—and she beheld a striking resemblance of Mr. Darcy, with such a smile over the face, as she remembered to have sometimes seen, when he looked at her. She stood several minutes before the picture

in earnest contemplation, and returned to it again before they quitted the gallery. Mrs. Reynolds [a servant] informed them, that it had been taken in his father's life-time.

There was certainly at this moment, in Elizabeth's mind, a more gentle sensation towards the original, than she had ever felt in the height of their acquaintance. The commendation bestowed on him by Mrs. Reynolds was of no trifling nature. What praise is more valuable than the praise of an intelligent servant? As a brother, a landlord, a master, she considered how many people's happiness were in his guardianship!—How much of pleasure or pain it was in his power to bestow!—How much of good or evil must be done by him! Every idea that had been brought forward by the housekeeper was favorable to his character, and as she stood before the canvas, on which he was represented, and fixed his eyes upon herself, she thought of his regard with a deeper sentiment of gratitude than it had ever raised before; she remembered its warmth, and softened its impropriety of expression. (Austen pp. 271-72)

The portrait here is an index to Darcy's character, to who he really is—and his character is defined not purely as an essence, but in connection with who he is culturally (brother, landlord, master, someone who employs intelligent servants, someone who owns one of the finest houses in the country). The things he owns are an extension of who he is—and one of the things he owns, of course, is this representation of himself, read sympathetically by Elizabeth as it refers back to qualities in the original. In other words, the portrait as situated in his domain is his medium—one in which Darcy works better than in conversation, where Elizabeth is more at home.

Not everyone will perceive these qualities through Darcy's portrait. Elizabeth's aunt and uncle expect family prejudice, and so do not take at face value the housekeeper's statement that "'He is the best landlord, and the best master.... There is not one of his tenants or servants but what will give him a good name.'" They have no reason to credit this, as Elizabeth does. In other words, representations do not compel particular readings, but open up to interpretation by us as viewers according to our preparation for seeing them.

As Elizabeth's experience in the novel illustrates, we are cued by codes in portraiture to read the portrait along certain lines, and we fantasize along those lines so as to believe that we understand something about the person's essence. (Compare *Pride and Prejudice,* beginning of Chapter 43, the description of Pemberley as situated in the landscape.) Austen drew from the pictorial arts of her time to let her readers follow the forming and re-forming of Elizabeth's reading of character. Our own reading and rereading of pictures in contemporary media goes on all the time—though it's rare that we have the occasion to reconsider as carefully as Austen's character does. Most people in the novel do not do so, either: They read according to their own narratives (egotistical like the minister Collins; victimized like the rake Wickham; whining like Elizabeth's mother, Mrs. Bennet; or humbly useful like her oldest sister, Jane). Similarly, we read pictures according to how they fit into the narratives we write, or fantasize, about ourselves and our place in society.

Our usual assumptions about novels—especially those nineteenth-century novels which are still taught—are that they are "classic" texts at some distance from everyday experience. (It's also common to assume that novels, as literary works, do not persuade readers through rhetoric.) Novels, however, began as popular forms, reaching out to a wide reading public; it was only with the beginning of modern literature in the early twentieth century that some novels took on the associations of high art. Novels, in other words, are media, as surely as films or newspapers: They work with other forms to open ways for their readers to get at meaning. Austen draws on visual arts of her time such as landscape, paintings of domestic settings, and portraits, but brings these into her medium. Similarly, in your writing you will sometimes bring descriptions based on photography or film to serve your own purposes.

Visual images can idealize the subject, as in the account of Darcy's portrait. But they can also be used to mark the subject as *not like us,* perhaps as something to be hated. Among the early uses of photography was surveillance. Scientists and social scientists collected images of the criminal, the mentally impaired, and people of other races and classes, perhaps in hopes of reading through the surface to the essence of such alien behavior or being.

In *On Photography,* Susan Sontag connects photography with surveillance, with the furnishing of visual images of those to be disciplined by society.

> Photographs furnish evidence. Something we hear about, but doubt, seems proven when we're shown a photograph of it. In one version of its utility, the camera record incriminates. Starting with their use by the Paris police in the murderous roundup of Communards in June 1871, photographs became a useful tool of modern states in the surveillance and control of their increasingly mobile populations. (Sontag p. 5)

The invitation to fantasy, then, can lead in other directions besides the uplifting or optimistic. Visual images can powerfully evoke fears, stereotypes, entire categories of what cultures have stigmatized. The photos taken by Nazis of Jews, Roma (gypsies), and other nationalities, and those taken of the mentally and physically handicapped, are testimony of the potential for using photography for destructive fantasies, often in the name of science.

Descriptive writing orders the features of an image into some hierarchy of importance, and in that hierarchy is an interpretation of the scene or image. It might be thought that a photograph or other visual image does not involve such interpretation—that the image is presented to the viewer without any prodding to see this way or that. But in fact this prodding is going on in other, less explicit ways. First, any photo, even one in a family album, is selected from the stock of all those available. Even the most inclusive photo album will exclude photos that are under- or overexposed, blurry, made with the lens cap on, essentially duplicating another snap, not flattering to the subjects, and so on. Photos made for advertisements or news or magazine stories are far more carefully selected still.

Photographs accompanying a typical *National Geographic* story are drawn from 11,000 exposures (Lutz and Collins p. 368).

Also, photos are often cropped or enlarged in order to emphasize certain elements and omit others. And there are highly developed conventions by which we read photographs, conventions that help shape the viewers' interpretations.

PROBLEM

The Gaze

Who is the person in a photograph looking at? This is the question of **the gaze** in photography. There are several ways to answer this question, and all of them are important to reading a photo. A photograph might be thought of as the record of a moment, fixing the time and place as they were from a specific perspective, that of the camera lens. If we consider a photo in this way, then the person's gaze is directed at the photographer, and the question becomes one of their relationship. Is the photographer a friend? Family member? Professional photographer? Journalist, tourist, foreign visitor, employee of the intelligence service or police, or wanderer through the streets? All these imply roles that affect how the subject of the photo looks at the camera. When you are having your picture made for a driver's license or passport, your relationship to the making of the photo is different from the way you look at your kid brother popping around the corner with a pocket camera (for example). Something of the relationship between the subject and the photographer necessarily gets into the photo, in terms of facial expression, posture, setting, clothing, and so on.

Much of the pleasure of photography has always been that of *looking*. Photography developed along with tourism in the late nineteenth century: Travels to Egypt, Palestine, India, and other remote locations (many parts of the British Empire) could be registered on film and brought back for photograph albums as souvenirs (the word *souvenir* means *to remember*). The same period was also the high point of European colonialism; invariably it was the Europeans and Americans who were the tourists, taking the pictures, and the darker-skinned natives who were being photographed, with greater or lesser degrees of willingness. Very few Zulus or Hindus traveled to European capitals to tour and report back to their people.

The verb we use is to *take* pictures: At least linguistically, that suggests that the person whose image is on the print has lost something. If my image is made and reproduced, I will lose no blood, no flesh, no money—in fact, being photographed may produce tangible benefits. But that image will go places that I myself cannot; a representation of me will be out in the world. In Exhibit 6.16, photographer John Loengard comments on the experience of being photographed.

If I take a picture of my daughter, our relationship changes and she is not my daughter any more. She could just as easily be the Duchess of Malfi. If she says, "Oh, Dad, not now!" I'll treat her exactly as I would Georgia O'Keeffe if she said, "Oh, Mr. Loengard, please not now!" In my head I think, "There is a beautiful picture here and by God, short of murder, I'm going to get it. So shut up and hold still!" But what I say is: "You look wonderful. It'll just take a minute. It's marvelous. We're doing something very special."

I learned the part about a minute from a dentist. I learned the rest from Carl Mydans. For the magazine's thirtieth birthday, *Life* photographers were asked to photograph each other. Carl was assigned me. To see such an intelligent and distinguished man concentrate on the problem of taking my picture was extremely flattering. Still, I felt tense. After all, I was being scrutinized. Carl kept telling me what wonderful pictures were being made. I believed him, and soon I relaxed. I was a success at being a subject!

(You should tell these things to a person as you photograph him—even if it's a lie—which, in this case, it was. *Life* photographers, as it turned out, could photograph anything in the world except each other.) (Loengard p. 58)

Exhibit 6.16 Photo (of the author's daughter) and commentary by John Loengard, from *Pictures Under Discussion*. New York: Amphoto (Watson-Guptill), 1987. © John Loengard. Used by permission

PAUSE FOR REFLECTION

Write informally about Exhibit 6.16. What do you see as Loengard's conception of the relations between the subject (his daughter, then himself), the photographer (himself, then Carl Mydans), and the institution (*Life*, or other magazines, newspapers, or organizations that produce photographs)? What portions of this description set out these relations?

Exhibit 6.16

A photograph, then, may be more than just a single moment: Photographs are records, and therefore bear their visual messages forward through time, at least while the print is in existence. The subject in a photograph—whether conscious of this fact or not—is also looking at all those who will see that photo. A suspect having a snap taken at police headquarters is facing not only the employee who takes the picture, but also potentially hundreds of ordinary citizens in post offices, along with other police officers, should that face be put onto a wanted poster. Your face on your driver's license is also staring out at store clerks recording your identity on a check or confirming your age for purchases of alcohol, at the traffic cop who may pull you over for speeding, and so on. A model posing for Misty cigarettes is not only looking at the photographer but staring out from the pages of thousands of magazines and down from hundreds of billboards scattered around the countryside.

"Racial, age, and gender differences appear in how often and how exactly the gaze is returned and lend substance to each of these perspectives on the camera gaze. To a statistically significant degree, women look into the camera more than men, children and older people look into the camera more often than other adults, those who appear poor more than those who appear wealthy, those whose skin is very dark more than those who are bronze, those who are bronze more than those whose skin is white, those in native dress more than those in Western garb, those without any tools more than those using machinery.... The 'civilized' classes, at least since the nineteenth century, have traditionally been depicted in Western art turning away from the camera and so making themselves less available." (Lutz and Collins pp. 370–71)

The way in which the question of the gaze was phrased earlier—"Who is *the person* in a photograph looking at"—assumes a photo of one person. Often photos have two or more, and their gazes may also be significant in how we read the photo. Are they looking at each other? Looking away from each other? Both looking at something else? Is one looking at the other, while the other looks elsewhere—for instance, at the camera? The still used to advertise the film *I Love Trouble* featured an image of the two lead actors, Julia Roberts and Nick Nolte: He was looking at her, while she looked past him at the camera/ at the viewer of the photograph. Such an arrangement is fairly common in photographs of a man and a woman used in advertisements and magazine covers. One interpretation is to say that her gaze at the viewer of the photo is inviting: "I'm with him but it's really you I want," or "See what you could have if you were like me/like him?" Regardless of whether the viewer is male or female, then, the gaze at the viewer through the camera invites fantasy. (What do we make of the viewer with other sexual orientations? The disposition of this kind of photo, including casting and so on, suggests that heterosexual relations are the norm: Do gay men and women have an entry point into the photo?)

> In the normal rhetoric of the photographic portrait, facing the camera signifies solemnity, frankness, the disclosure of the subject's essence. That is why frontality seems right for ceremonial pictures (like weddings, graduations) but less apt for photographs used on billboards to advertise political candidates. (For politicians the three-quarter gaze is more common: a gaze that soars rather than confronts, suggesting instead of the relation to the viewer, to the present, the more ennobling abstract relation to the future.) (Sontag p. 38)

What does **looking** mean for our culture? Who gets to look, and how? Photographs in some ways resemble voyeurism: As someone regarding another's image in a photograph, you get to see that person, but she or he is unconscious (except possibly in a general sense) that you specifically are looking at her or him. This has some similarities to looking through a window at a person who is not conscious of being observed—except that most often the subject of a photograph is aware of being photographed.

Not everyone gets to look. In numerous social situations, it is taboo or at least unwise to look at someone else. Think about being alongside someone in your car at a stoplight—there's an unstated taboo against looking closely at the person in the car next to you. Or think about meeting people in public transportation, or on the street: Particularly in large cities or places where there are a lot of strangers and high consciousness of crime, people often avoid eye contact. Particularly women avoid eye contact, because that might invite an unwanted encounter—a gaze might be read as inviting conversation or more. So a direct gaze on a magazine or book cover, in a sense, invites you to enter that text.

Before we close, let's think for a moment about the word *subject*. If we use the phrase "the subject of a photo," it might imply something like "the story the photograph is telling, the narrative with which it connects." The subject of the blonde on the beach, in this sense, would be something like vacation as pristine solitude, or fantasy of having nothing necessary to do but lie in the sun on sand unmarked by footprints or uncluttered by seaweed, shells, and other traces of life. But another, connected meaning of "subject" would be the person photographed—connected because it is her story (as a portrayal, perhaps). (Is it her story? Or is the fantasy one established by the reader? The viewer's story is in effect written over the other.) In this meaning, "subject" brings in associations of power relations: Those living in an empire are the emperor's subjects; we are subject to laws of the state. Subject is related linguistically to *subjugate*, which means to bring someone or some area under political control.

CONCLUSION

Perspectives on visual media are a crucial part of entertainment media such as films and television. As you turn your attention to Chapter 7, you should keep this chapter in mind for continuity: What changes as the pictures begin to move?

FURTHER ASSIGNMENTS

Assignment
Write a description of a place, emphasizing the visual, but including other sensory details as needed. You might write, for example, about a favorite vacation spot, a famous scene, or a location you pass frequently. As you work on the description, isolate the specifics that seem most important in how you experience the place, and in how you think others would experience it on seeing it for the first time.

After your first draft of the description, go back and examine the order in which you present the specifics. What is the logic of the description? Do you move spatially, left to right, up to down, near to far, center to outside? Do you move temporally? What other possibilities are there for organizing such a description?

After reconsidering your draft, write a short paragraph explaining some point or purpose that your description can serve.

Assignment
Design a logo. You could make it a personal logo, a logo for your family, or a logo for any group you identify with. Think about ways to incorporate a name, title, or key word in the logo. Think about elements such as size, color, and shape. Draw on other logos or identifying signs that you see around you. What makes a logo popular, legitimate, and acceptable to others?

Assignment
Construct your own reading of the portraits in Exhibits 6.17, 6.18, and 6.19, along the lines of Jane Austen's reading on pages 332–33.

Exhibit 6.17
Photo from *Another Way of Telling* by John Berger and Jean Mohr. Copyright © 1982 by John Berger and Jean Mohr. Reprinted by permission of Pantheon Books, a division of Random House, Inc.

Assignment

Write in your journal about images—from photography, film, videos, or other sources—of public persons such as politicians, film stars, actors, and so on. In what ways have these images helped to formulate something like a "common cultural consciousness" for you personally? Fix your attention on a few (perhaps one) as illustration.

When you've written this entry, write its opposite—that is, what portion(s) of your cultural consciousness are not formulated through the accumulation of such images?

Exhibit 6.18 Georgia O'Keeffe by John Loengard, from *Pictures Under Discussion*. New York: Amphoto (Watson-Guptill), 1987. © John Loengard. Used by permission.

Assignment

Collect photos and other images that illustrate varieties of "the gaze." These may be drawn from sources such as ads, personal photos, books of esthetic photography, news photos, or campaign photos. Ascertain what each person is looking at, what the "tone" of the photo is, and so on. You may want to look at Erving Goffman's *Gender Advertisements* for a sense of what is possible.

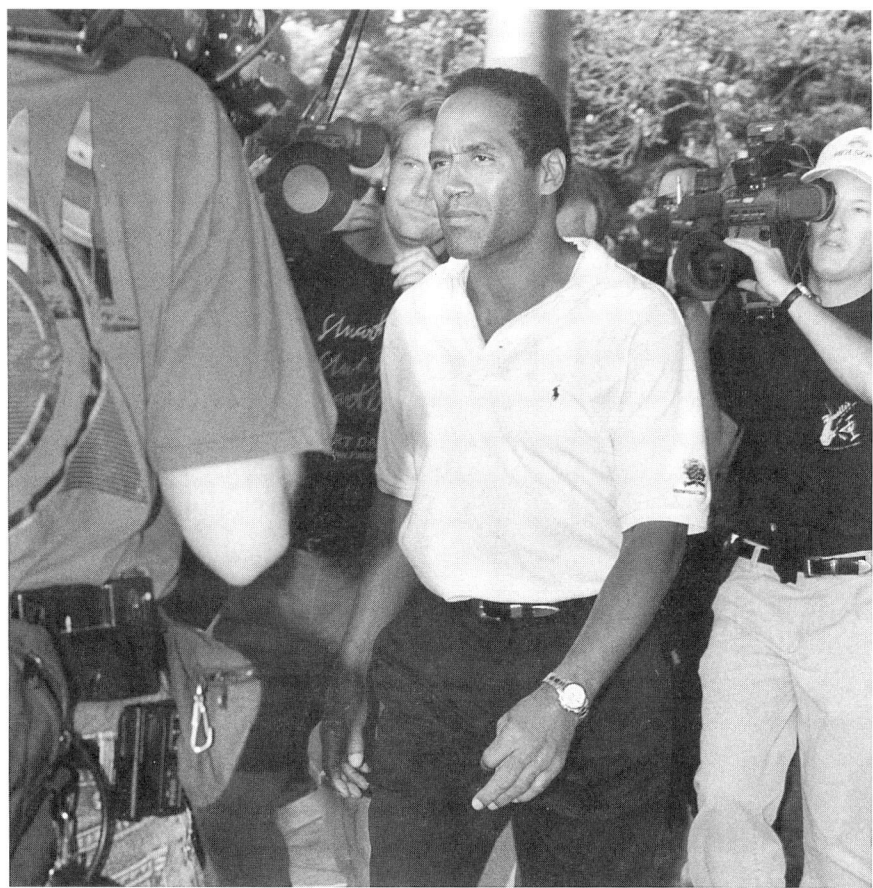

Exhibit 6.19 Reuters/Corbis-Bettmann.

Entertainment As Information

OVERVIEW

Many people new to the United States draw their first views about our customs and behavior not only from language classes and direct observation, but from our media—particularly film and television, which offer attractive windows onto our language and culture. As children, most of us looked through those same windows, supplementing what we learned at home and in school with available programming. Because we learned our lessons so well, as adults we may not even recognize how much we learned from these media—from the most common, most "natural" uses of media, those devoted to entertainment.

Entertainment texts are among the most powerful and pervasive devices for confirming the ideas and values that underlie our culture—or its fundamental ideology, known as **common sense.** One commonsense principle is that the two predominant uses of media, entertainment and information, are entirely separate. This chapter will suggest some ways in which these uses merge; I will draw on the blurring between entertainment and information as a starting point for reexamining "common sense" about media. As we saw in Chapter 4, when we read the news, we absorb not only accounts of particular events, but also stories that help make sense of them. The stories told in songs, in films, in television programs, and in other texts we use to occupy our leisure time fulfill similar functions: They pass on information as surely as does the *New York Times*. And the replication of these stories helps to define and regulate what we understand as "natural"; that is, the replication of the stories participates in cultural **hegemony,** or the institutional domination of shared cultural understandings.

Entertainment, while it may or may not be your dominant use of media, is the dominant use for the majority of the U.S. audience. But another perspective besides that of the audience must be considered: As seen by producers, *advertising* may be dominant, since entertainment texts are distributed only if the bills are paid. Entertainment media may be said to exist both to give us stories and to sell us goods and services—and it's important to reconcile these two perspectives.

Texts such as popular music, magazines, films, and sporting events have become part of the fabric of daily life. Often these are what we talk about and talk through. These and other media texts have been integrated into the rhythms of everyday activities, both in leisure time and at the workplace, so that driving or time at the desk or work site are often done with an accompanying sound track, in parallel with the routine business of our lives. After our time at work, media texts give us diversion and relaxation at day's end in forms unavailable to previous generations. Whether you believe that these forms of entertainment make our lives richer or that they intrude on private moments of thought, their presence marks a profound change from past centuries.

The first thing to say about entertainment texts, then, is that they are *always there,* offering us their mild pleasures. But at what cost? To understand entertainment and how we interact with it, we have to start with specific texts, as with the analysis of commercials in Chapter 5. But analysis of these texts is not all there is to understanding entertainment: We need to look at the systems from which these texts take their meaning, at their cultural histories or genres, and at their systems of production. We also need to examine our own readings of these texts—not only in themselves, but also for what they tell us about how we connect to the larger culture.

This chapter will serve only as a start on these questions. The topic of entertainment is perhaps the most complicated in the study of media, not least because of audience resistance: We often develop strong loyalties to our sources of entertainment and may prefer not to examine them. I may be able to tolerate analyzing advertisements or news—putting a commercial, a newspaper story, or network news coverage under the knife doesn't threaten any type of response I care very much about. But being analytical about my favorite drama or comedy, about my tastes, threatens to disrupt my fun. Why not just relax and enjoy it?

If the goal of analysis were only to interfere with other people's pleasures, it would be largely pointless. No one likes a spoilsport. But studying rhetoric means moving toward comprehending texts, both static and dynamic; and passing over entertainment texts would mean missing an important element in understanding ourselves and our uses of media. Such analysis may be more complex than analyzing commercials, just because of the texts' length. And examining their cultural functions is more difficult still. But analysis is a first step to making use of entertainment media more consciously on our terms, rather than as their producers might prefer.

What interests do these texts and systems serve? Are we as audiences free to shape meanings, or do we have to stay with those provided by others? These and other questions in this chapter of *Rhetoric through Media* will open serious discussion of mostly popular texts that usually pass unremarked. Regarding entertainment media seriously goes against the grain of how we have learned to deal with them. "Common sense" advises us that these texts are too trivial to stand up to analysis; that anything popular can't be worth spending time on; that we're better off just watching or just having fun; that if there's something we don't like, we should just switch off; that those who produce and own such texts didn't intend for them to be dissected in this way; and so on. But "common sense" is itself a text to be read for assumptions about who we are, and who others want us to be. Entertainment texts have powerful effects on audiences: Part of their means to achieve these effects is exactly this commonsense assumption that nothing of much importance is going on. As with advertising, we usually consume entertainment texts (that is, watch or read them without analysis); and we deny that what we watch or read or listen to has any effect on us, personally—though we may believe that others are probably heavily influenced.

Even though most viewers and readers don't usually analyze their own preferred texts, you have probably encountered some criticisms of entertainment texts. Most of these critiques take up one of four themes:

1. Concern with intensity and frequency of sex or violence;
2. Stereotyping of, or absence of, ethnic minorities, classes, and genders;
3. Commercialism and domination of entertainment media by a few corporations; and
4. Audience passivity or susceptibility to manipulation.

These will be addressed in our discussions of entertainment.

PAUSE FOR REFLECTION

Have you encountered one or more of the concerns listed above in articles, conversations, radio broadcasts, Internet exchanges, or other media? Do you share these in some form? Write briefly, giving an example of one concern in each category (not necessarily your concern).

You should keep in mind that, in seeking entertainment, you are not only making use of these texts; they, or their producers, are also making use of *you:* of your time, thought, and money. An attitude of critical distance is a necessary start to discovering the real cost of being entertained.

ISSUES

What's Entertainment?

Whatever we mean by using or consuming entertainment, we do it a lot. Statistics confirm that the amount of time spent with entertainment media in the United States is high, more than any other activity except for sleeping. On average we spend between twenty-five and thirty hours per week watching television (including some news and informational programming), another twenty hours listening to the radio, and lesser but still significant amounts of time with other diversions such as films, video games, and sporting events. (Some of this total includes entertainment while at work.)

In spite of the larger number of options, the amount of time spent watching television has remained pretty much constant since 1960, with time spent per set declining in proportion to the increase in the number of sets. "Television audiences remain at approximately the same size regardless of the number of channels available or what they carry, regardless of the number of viewing choices, and regardless of whether programming is planned to maximize audience size, as it is in the United States, or devised to pursue ideological goals, as it is in China and was in the Soviet Union" (Bogart p. 22).

Much of this entertainment goes on as background or low-intensity activity, which may explain why we don't notice it much.

> [In] 1981, newly elected President Ronald Reagan appointed as head of the FCC Mark Fowler, "a journeyman communications attorney... with few credentials beyond his association with the Reagan campaign team," and the whole thrust of the agency reversed itself. Under the banner of deregulation, Fowler announced that "it was time to move away from thinking about broadcasters as trustees. It was time to treat them the way almost everyone else in society does—that is, as businesses." For, as he said on a different occasion, "television is just another appliance. It's a toaster with pictures." (Engelhardt pp. 75–76)

Defining entertainment is no problem for some who, like former FCC head Fowler, are professionally responsible for regulating or producing forms of entertainment: These texts are nothing more nor less than consumer goods. Making a film or recording a song is essentially the same thing as manufacturing and marketing household appliances. The audience is offered the same range of choices and the same "buyer beware" principles as in the marketplace generally. If there are problems with your picture, just adjust your toaster.

Others see the analogy between toasters and TVs, or entertainment, as misleading. There is no *Consumer Reports* or Underwriters' Laboratory for television; and the Federal Communications Commission usually stays clear of evaluating programming. The public is offered advice from producers, sponsors, and reviewers, all of whom have financial and professional interests in any sort of guidance they may give. (We are all in some sense interested in the texts we watch and read, but most of us do not have our livelihoods invested in their interpretation.) It's not commonly argued that using a toaster changes your way of thinking in any significant way—but there are those who argue that that's precisely what goes on with entertainment media. Defining entertainment, then, will require that we look closely at how we use it.

One view of entertainment media such as television and film is as services produced for our enjoyment. This is the dominant way of thinking about these media—as commercial providers of stories. Though we often think of commercial television as a free service, its texts are paid for directly or indirectly: through cable service fees and through money from advertisers who hope to influence the public to buy their products and ideas. (We usually assume that *we* aren't the ones being influenced by advertising.) Film costs are recouped through admissions, videocassette rentals, spinoffs, and sales to broadcast media. Radio, also apparently "free," is also supported through advertising. The ads afford us the opportunity to push the seek button or channel changer and check up on what else might be available. Occasionally we stay with the commercials, which are often more entertaining than the programming.

The cost of all advertising in U.S. media in 1993 worked out to $540 per person (Bogart p. 271).

But if we think of entertainment from the point of view of a producer rather than that of a consumer, the entertainment portion of the broadcast looks a little different. For consumers, the entertainment is what the medium is *for;* but for producers, the entertainment is a device to create and hold audiences for commercials. There is some satisfaction in making good stories and enriching people's lives, but the principal measure of success is ratings, which also happens to govern how money is made in broadcasting. What broadcast media have to sell, *all* they have to sell, is their audiences. Seen from this perspective, *we* are the product. Television, radio, newspapers, and magazines all charge advertising rates based on CPM, or "cost per thousand" people watching/listening/reading. Who the "thousands" are is determined by ratings provided by companies such as A. C. Nielsen and, in the case of print media, by circulation figures. A single percentage-point change in ratings or circulation figures can mean millions of dollars' difference in ad revenues.

Each of the three major networks has about 205 affiliates, and each is permitted to own up to 12 stations outright. "In 1960 advertising revenue for the three [networks] was $820 million; in 1989 it [had] increased twelve-fold to $10 billion." Until 1991, networks couldn't develop their own shows. "The network pays a licensing fee of from $270,000 to $600,000 to the production company per half-hour episode for two showings." Then the show is eligible for syndication, which is highly profitable because further costs are negligible (Twitchell p. 213).

Thirty seconds on the 1996 Academy Awards cost advertisers $1.2 million for a worldwide audience of one billion. NBC charged $700,000 for thirty seconds of prime-time 1996 Olympic advertising.

Entertainment texts should not be thought of merely as self-contained units. To understand them, we have to look at them functionally. Entertainment media in the United States are businesses first and cultural enterprises secondarily, but it is to their advantage to disguise this fact. In order to work effectively—to continue to attract audiences and generate advertising revenue—the media usually downplay the financial motive, just as do those who work in news media. The fact that media offer their texts for money should not be surprising, since the same happens in other professions: Novelists, architects, teachers, actors, musicians, and many others combine practice of a craft with a profit motive. But it can be difficult to keep this in mind, because as audience we have an interest in playing along with the essential deception. We *want* to believe that the art is paramount; that, say, Michelle Pfeiffer is playing a character because she wants to and is good at it, not just for the millions of dollars she'll earn by doing so. But when an actor or writer admits to working for a salary, that seems to cheapen the art, to lessen its aura, to spoil the illusion. The system seduces us into believing (to some extent) that what we know to be true is at least partially false, that there's no barrier between the entertainment and the business sides of media. But in fact they interpenetrate.

It is interesting to compare first uses of media. Among the earliest print documents is the Gutenberg Bible. The first telegraph message has a biblical flavor: "What hath God wrought?" Alexander Graham Bell's first words on his telephone were a summons to an assistant: "Come here, Watson—I need you." By contrast, one of the earliest images transmitted on television—on the experimental apparatus of Philo T. Farnsworth in 1927—was a dollar sign; see Exhibit 7.1 (Barnouw p. 78; Twitchell p. 207).

However we manage to define entertainment, then, it will be necessary to keep reminding ourselves of the dual nature of these texts. If they are thought of as self-contained units, their rhetorical purpose might be said to be to divert or entertain us. As with the analysis of commercials in Chapter 5, looking at entertainment texts in this way can be a powerful critical tool. But these texts do not exist in isolation, any more than commercials do. When they are thought of in the context of the system, their effect (if not their purpose) is to influence us in some fashion. In order to figure out what that influence might

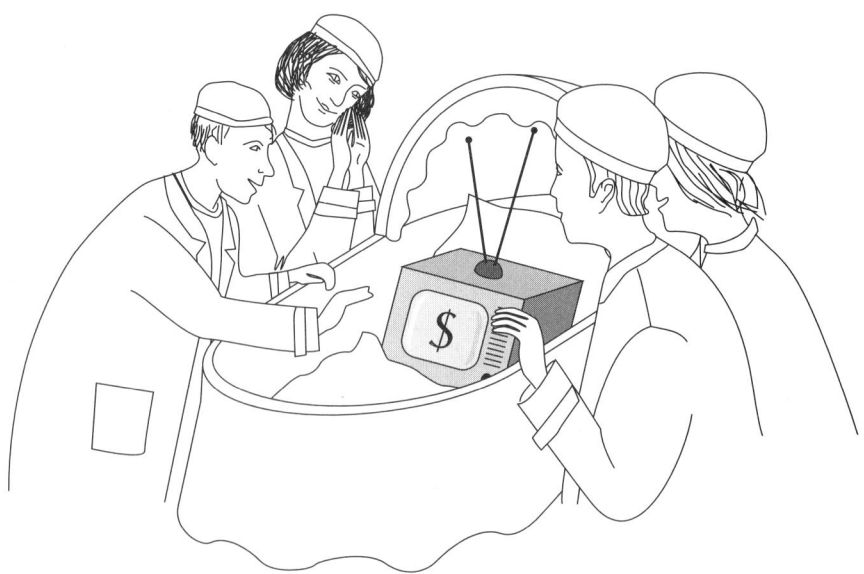

Exhibit 7.1 A new member of the family.

be, we have to develop some skepticism toward entertainment. And such skepticism is difficult because we are easily flattered into thinking that *we're* too smart, too independent, too rebellious to be taken in.

PAUSE FOR REFLECTION
Can you recall entertainment texts—rock or country songs, videos, films, television programs—that include as part of their stories characters who are rebellious or independent, and who show this by breaking away from an organization or group wanting them to conform? Focus on one such text: What is your connection with that text as you think back on it? Do you judge it critically, or do you play along, identifying with the main character(s)?

In this chapter as in others, it's important to start with your observations about entertainment media. What use do you make of entertainment media now? What have you seen about others' use of media? *What* you interact with is a first step in moving toward *why*, which is the real question about entertainment: Why do you individually, and why do we collectively, like the things we like? Why are they effective in moving us toward buying into the products and the values that come with entertainment? A plausible place to start is with observing your own uses of media for entertainment.

ASSIGNMENT
Use one of the prewriting devices discussed in Chapter 3—for example, brainstorming, freewriting, or a concept map—to come up with as extensive as possible a list of what you do for entertainment. Don't restrict your list to entertainment texts; include activities as well. You should build on your own explorations by comparing your lists with those of other students.

We may as well admit that defining entertainment rigorously is next to impossible. Definitions are supposed to refer clearly and unambiguously to what is defined; but what one person considers entertaining may not be entertaining for another, or even for the same person in different moods. Some kinds of texts and activities are widely counted as entertainment—television comedies and dramas, most films, popular music, most published best-sellers, major spectator sports, and many participant sports and activities. Other texts and activities with some similarities to these are not considered entertainment so much as something else—news in all media, documentaries, most classical music, much "serious" fiction and nonfiction, and working out or jogging.

And some activities might be thought of as entertainment by some and not by others, such as visiting a museum.

One common distinction between entertainment and art is popularity; but the number in the audience is not always a reliable guide. Several texts from the high end of the cultural spectrum draw large audiences. Film and dramatic productions of plays by Shakespeare, Shaw, Ibsen, Pinter, and others of high literary reputation attract audiences of millions annually, as shown by successful theater in Stratford (England and Ontario), New York, Ashland, and many other places. Best-seller lists of "serious" music have included Górecki's *Symphony of Sorrowful Songs* and an album of Gregorian chants by Benedictine monks. Shakespeare and Jane Austen continue to draw film audiences, as with Kenneth Branagh's versions of *Henry V* and *Much Ado about Nothing,* and the version of *Hamlet* starring Mel Gibson. Film treatments of Austen's *Emma, Persuasion,* and *Sense and Sensibility* show the viability of reasonable versions of classical novels. Respectably sized television audiences watch dramatized novels on PBS's *Masterpiece Theater.* And, conversely, many texts from the more popular end of the cultural spectrum receive critical acclaim and serious academic treatment, with the Beatles as preeminent example. Informative and high-quality magazines like *The New Yorker, Scientific American,* and *Harper's* have created and held sizable mass-market circulation figures. So the definition of a text as popular must not be linked strictly to size of audience.

Subjectivity can present problems when we are defining terms—but perhaps in this case we can use subjective responses in connection with the definition. Texts might be considered entertainment on the basis of audience response—they count if they entertain us, but not if we use them for staying informed, becoming educated, and so on. But it's questionable that audience response, on its own, can work as a principle of definition, because of aberrant or untypical readings of texts. The children's song "Puff the Magic Dragon" recorded by Peter, Paul, and Mary was seriously interpreted as really about drugs ("lived by the sea" = "lived by the C" or cocaine; "little Jackie Paper" = marijuana; etc.). At the end of the 1960s, the Charles Manson "family" read the Beatles' song "Helter-Skelter" as a call for race riots, and committed brutal murders to initiate the apocalypse.

Some readings of popular culture produce unconventional results. "Rev. Jim Brown of Ironton, Ohio, told the First Church of Nazarene congregation in 1986 that the theme song to the old TV show, *Mr. Ed,* played in reverse, contains satanic messages." According to Brown, "A horse is a horse, of course, of course," backwards, is "the source is Satan." (Shepherd, Kohut, and Sweet, p. 75).

A resident alien in the United States can learn English and many customs by watching television and listening to the radio, but does that mean we should define *Full House* as an educational program? It's likely that the *uses* for texts are just as mixed as the texts themselves—we can be both entertained and (mis-)informed by sitcoms or talk radio. If we define entertainment with audience response in mind, how do we certify which responses count?

Entertainment texts present problems in definition, then, that are similar to those we encounter in defining literature. Both entertainment texts and literary texts may be seen as having multiple purposes. Both exist in a territory between a text that is *out there* and a response that is *in here*. Both are used for a variety of purposes by readers, by producers, and by other groups within the culture.

Perhaps the best hope for a definition of entertainment texts would be through something like their cultural function. Terry Eagleton suggests in *Literary Theory* that literature is the set of texts that a culture values; perhaps entertainment texts are those that we as a culture play with.

Entertainment As Play

If entertainment consists of those things that we as a culture spend our leisure time playing with, what do we play with? What texts and activities do we look to for fun? This way of thinking about entertainment directs us to popular culture.

Reactions to popular culture generally and to specific popular culture texts are mixed. Whatever is *popular* is by definition liked by many people—which is reason for some to argue that it's good (it's liked by many, so I should like it as well), and for others that it's bad (it's liked by many of the *wrong sort* of people, so I shouldn't be seen to like it). Common sense tells us that we shouldn't take popular culture too seriously: It doesn't last long, it's not serious, there's nothing in particular to be learned from it—all considerations that may direct our attention away from the particular texts and toward the activities around them. But a case for the importance of examining popular culture may be based on its persistence: Specific popular culture texts may not last long, but popular culture *itself* is extraordinarily durable and tells us a great deal about the culture that sustains it. The texts involved in entertaining us may be ordinary, but our desire to be entertained is all the more significant for its ordinariness. We look to be entertained every day, and those daily forms of entertainment do more than is commonly recognized to shape how we think and act. This section, then, will direct attention to entertainment texts as those we play with.

Play and entertainment are terms that cover a wide range of phenomena. We play in many different ways, as children and as adults. Adult forms of play range from games of chance played with cards, dice, and slot machines (assuming that these are a matter of chance); to physical movement such as riding on amusement park rides, horses, canoes, and sailboats; to tennis, golf, softball, and other sporting contests. Both children and adults play through pretend roles—adult versions include charades and other party games, costumes, drama, and improvisation. Play would also include linguistic play—word games and acrostics, jokes and puns, proverbs, and amusing sayings. Musicians play instruments. Many arts have elements of play to them. And in addition to participant play, there's spectator play, in which we watch or listen to others display their abilities. Not all play has to involve physical action: Some can be done mentally, passively, even conceptually.

Popular culture shares some positive attributes with play. Play works as a great icebreaker: Kids make friends through play, and it's an impulse we carry over into adult life. Similarly, many areas of popular culture (sports, movies, television programs) offer areas of common ground for conversations and more significant sorts of bonding. Many adult social rituals involve play, from joke telling and amusing chitchat at parties to other matters. But play can also be threatening if it gets out of control, as may happen in frat houses or football stadiums.

Thinking about connections between entertainment and play, then, may help us to understand the rhetoric of entertainment texts. A study of rhetoric means knowing how to reach others through reading, writing, speaking, and other means. Extending this to the rhetoric of entertainment texts means knowing something about how they reach you. And it is commonly part of the rhetoric of these texts, and of play, that you don't have to study it, you *just do it*. In fact, spending too much time thinking about entertainment texts might be seen as preventing you from entering their spirit, from having fun with them.

How seriously should we take the analogy between play and entertainment? What do these activities have in common? First, both exist in opposition to a more serious category: *play* contrasts with *work; entertainment* with *information.* We have seen that distinction evoked in journal entries in Chapter 2: The writer gave information and entertainment as the two purposes for her interactions with media. Information was listed first, but the journal kept returning to entertainment, as though that were the real attraction. If we turn to media to tell us something about current events, we may do it out of something like a sense of civic responsibility. But more often than not, we turn to media to remove us from having to be responsible: Play and entertainment are temporary freedoms from responsibilities.

Concerns about play and entertainment tend to focus not on *one's own* play but on that of *others.* One concern may involve the amount or the kind of play: A child who plays too much won't give adequate attention to homework, and if you eat nothing but snacks, your nutrition will suffer. Similarly, those who spend too much time on forms of entertainment will lack information about matters of public concern (such as the environment, domestic political issues, world affairs) and will be easily influenced by propaganda, misrepresentation, and demagoguery. (Not us.) Another concern about entertainment focuses not so much on entertainment displacing informational programming, but on "too much sex and violence" or distorted or stereotypical portrayals. Such entertainment texts may be objectionable because they create and/or promote values that are undesirable. Entertainment and play, in other words, are not just activities in themselves but may be used deliberately to encourage attitudes of materialism, commercialism, selfishness, and so on rather than values we (who?) would like to see encouraged.

A study by Lichter, Rothman, and Lichter of "a month of prime-time fictional series" counted 1,005 scenes involving violence (some with multiple violent acts). "One out of five violent scenes...involved gunplay, and nearly half...included some kind of serious personal assault beyond mere slaps, punches, destruction of property, and the like." Also, during the month studied there were more violent scenes in promos for television programs and films—1,313—than featured in the programs themselves (Lichter, Rothman, and Lichter, *Prime Time*, pp. 31–32, 37).

One cable film service, such as HBO or Cinemax, averages as many violent acts in primetime as ABC, NBC, and CBS combined (Lichter, Rothman, and Lichter, *Prime Time*, p. 31).

Planned Parenthood estimated 1987 annual sexual references on afternoon and evening shows at 67,000 (10 per hour) (Lichter, Rothman, and Lichter, *Prime Time*, p. 80).

Those who express concern about the quality of media often gesture in the direction of "junk" of one sort or another; defending media usually takes the form of pointing out some excellent material that is available as entertainment. Both of these responses miss the point: Film and television and radio and print media all offer *both* some excellent materials *and* some that are sensational, prejudiced, empty, unbalanced, or twisted. The quality of entertainment, like the quality of information, depends to a great extent on the selections made by the audience, on how all of us choose to play.

Just as some entertainment texts provide information, some play is in a sense work. The same activities might be considered as work or as play, depending on the circumstances. When I go to the tennis courts, that's play; when Andre Agassi goes, that's (usually) work. For most of the audience at a drama, it's play; but when a magazine reviewer goes to a drama, it's work. Much of the publicly expressed resentment about labor troubles in baseball (and other sports) begins in the idea that young men (and a few women) are paid millions per year for playing a game—playing it very well and justifying hundreds of millions of dollars in television time, advertising contracts, and revenues from attendance, but still playing a game. Writing, which you may be accustomed to thinking of as work, is a form of play for many, particularly in fiction or poetry. Anyone who has served on the editorial staff of one of the hundreds of small literary magazines knows that there are thousands of aspiring poets anxious for their writings to see print.

One distinction that might be drawn between work and play is that advocated by Mark Twain: If they pay you to do it, it's work; if you pay them to do it, it's play. Work is what you *have* to do, play is what you *want* to do. How the activity is categorized greatly affects the attitudes and perceptions of those taking part.

We can conclude from the examples above that play and entertainment are both characterized by a kind of purposelessness, or rather purpose defined from within the frame of the activity. They are done for the activity *in itself*, not for something that it is a means to (such as a paycheck). But play and entertainment *signify*. Play signifies as something you do not have to do, but choose to do—and that is the basis of its symbolic value. There are associations between the ability to play *when* and *how* you want, and socioeconomic class: Only those with the economic resources can engage in more expensive sorts of play, such as golf (country club memberships) and yachting. These sorts of play become partly forms of display, a way to show off class status (connected to money, but not directly equated to it). Lower-class sorts of play have their own display as well, such as bowling jackets and noisy identification with sports teams. Class associations guarantee that informal business negotiations take place on the fairway or in the locker room, not at the bowling alley or video arcade.

We can get at some of the concerns about entertainment texts, then, by characterizing these as forms of play. (Of course, not everyone finds these matters objectionable.) First, there's the concern that *too much* play is going on. Media sources of entertainment have multiplied since the invention of the printing press, and this growth has accelerated since the development of electronics—and there's a worry that if we spend so much of our time at play, the culture generally will go downhill. Cable TV has brought more channels, which has meant not more television watching, but more *fragmented* television watching.

Second is the worry that there's the *wrong kind* of play going on—harmful play. Entertainment texts, it is said, encourage extra- or premarital sex, violence, stereotyping, or other harmful activities by showing these as "natural."

As with its portrayal of other serious social issues, television presents a highly selective view of sex.

"In general, television focuses on the joys of sex, not its problems. A typical network hour in 1988 had one or two mentions of sexual intercourse and nine or ten other sexual innuendos, but no mentions of birth control. References to sexually transmitted illness occurred only once in ten program hours. While adultery was depicted much more commonly than in the past, no moral judgment was passed two-thirds of the time. Prostitutes were portrayed sympathetically, as victims of an unjust social order. In the 1990s unorthodox sexual practices and (with the growth of the AIDS epidemic) sexually transmitted diseases have become everyday subjects of media content, accepted as part of the normal business of life" (Bogart p. 158).

As with objections to the amount of time spent on entertainment, this complaint has a familiar ring to it: Similar concerns about media and sexual behavior were expressed about silent films in the 1920s, culminating in 1930 in the Hays film code, which required, among other things, that a man and a woman in a bedroom keep at least one foot apiece on the floor. The influence of media on morals was worrisome long before this century—in the publication of newspapers and popular magazines (for the lower classes) in the nineteenth century, and in the effects of novels in the eighteenth. (The charge's persistence doesn't mean that it has no merit: Public morals may indeed have been corrupted by all these things.)

According to a study in the *Journal of Broadcasting and Electronic Media* in fall 1991, there was one sexual act or reference every four minutes during prime time (Lichter, Rothman, and Lichter, *Prime Time*, p. 38).

Sexual activity between unmarried couples is so naturalized on prime-time television that, in 220 scenes, only 9 percent "concluded that having sex would be wrong or inappropriate for any reason," while 22 percent offered no judgment, and 69 percent were positive (Lichter, Rothman, and Lichter, *Prime Time*, p. 39).

Concern about sex and violence stem from a conflict with what is seen as the *right* way to behave; in other words, the media texts violate someone's sense of good and appropriate behavior. (We are playing in the approved ways, but those approved ways teach us behavior which may not be best.) Other objections to the values of entertainment texts come not because they conflict with, but because they *confirm* dominant systems of belief. This objection to entertainment media is based not only on their encouragement of commercialism, but on their tendency to reinforce existing power relations between women and men, and between groups in the United States that have power and those who are relatively powerless, thereby helping to recreate and cement these relations. In other words, entertainment media are used (whether deliberately or accidentally) to keep the audience thinking the "right" sorts of thoughts.

One of the principal conflicts in how we think about media, then, is the conflict between ourselves as free agents in our use of media for entertainment and the belief that media powerfully influence audience behavior. One or the other has to go—either we are not so free, or others are less prone to influence than we think. To get a start on resolving this conflict, it will be useful to explore it from your perspective in writing. However, it's characteristically difficult to observe your own feelings and thoughts, and more difficult to communicate these to others in ways that you want to be even moderately public.

PAUSE FOR REFLECTION

If creative writing is sometimes thought of as play, to what extent can other writing be so considered? What kinds of writing that you have done in the past have encouraged or allowed an element of creativity? What sorts of creativity? Do you feel freer to create in some media (e.g., through electronic media or longhand) than in others?

Most of the contexts in which you do writing probably make writing seem like work, not play; writing for school or work assignments usually means trying to meet others' expectations. But many genres of writing leave at least some room for invention, for discovering satisfactions in the way language lets you express things. The greatest latitude for play in language is often in poems, many of which give the poet the latitude to invent both subject and format. Other genres such as reporting, conventional short stories, song lyrics, and letters may allow or encourage certain kinds of playfulness. Probably the degree of fun you can have depends more on audience than on genre.

There can be a surprising degree of crossover from kinds of entertainment to writing. One area is in play with language: Even business occasions permit or even encourage opening and closing anecdotes or jokes, whose relevance to the subject may be rather distant. These function as icebreakers for establishing some contact between speaker or writer and audience; and they can also serve as a small bit of pleasure to go along with what might be considered dry "content." Another sort of play, less conventional than the opening anecdote, might be the subversive joke or anecdote, one that apparently fits audience expectations yet begins in some way to undermine them, bringing the more careful reader to reexamine the assumptions brought to the text.

As we have seen, many forms of entertainment involve the telling of stories. Readers may find discussions of abstract or distant concepts difficult to "relate to"—wars in other parts of the world, the escalating national debt, threats to the health care system, control over systems of media. All such abstractions can be understood more directly when conveyed in terms of stories about individuals who are affected by them. News coverage has increasingly borrowed this technique—essentially an entertainment device—from fiction. You need to be wary of such a mixture, however, both as writer and as reader. As writer, you have a responsibility to select stories that are fair and representative; as reader, you should be aware that stories are often chosen in ways that essentially distort what is being communicated.

A woman in New Mexico, Stella Liebeck, bought coffee from a McDonald's drive-thru. Attempting to put cream and sugar in while the car was stationary, she spilled the coffee, causing third-degree burns to her groin, inner thighs and buttocks, which required skin grafts and seven days of hospitalization. Initially, she asked McDonald's to pay her medical expenses; after their refusal, it came out that "in the past decade McDonald's had received at least 700 reports of coffee burns ranging from mild to third-degree" caused by their policy of keeping coffee at 180–190 degrees Fahrenheit.

"After hearing such testimony, the jurors found McDonald's liable and awarded $200,000 in compensatory damages," deducting $40,000 for Liebeck's contributory negligence. They further assessed $2.7 million in punitive damages, which was reduced by the judge to $480,000 (Ruiz, pp. 10–11).

What is interesting about the McDonald's story in the Fact above is that it helped generate calls for limitation on lawsuits. Compare these reports to the Fact account:

- George Will, *Newsweek:* "A jury awarded $2.9 million to a woman who burned herself when, in a moving car, leaving a McDonald's with a cup of coffee between her legs, she spilled it. She said the coffee was hot."

- *New York Times:* "Life used to be blissfully simple: the coffee hot, the drinker sitting and sipping. But now everyone's hither and yon, perching take-out coffee in mid-dash. And spilling it. And suing someone."
- Jeff Pelline, *San Francisco Chronicle:* "America has a victim complex" because of "such surreal cases as the woman who recently won a $2.7 million verdict after spilling coffee on her leg in a McDonald's restaurant."
- Paul Huard, National Association of Manufacturers, on *CNN:* "What we have here is a system which has just gotten completely out of control. When a plaintiff can pick up a million or two for spilling hot coffee in her lap, you have to know there's something wrong."

Paul Ruiz's article in *Extra!*, compiling these reactions, notes that "Media pundits are promoting far-reaching changes in the U.S. legal system on the basis of half-truths and fables" (pp. 10–11).

What gives the McDonald's coffee story its currency is its usefulness as an anecdote. Stories are used rhetorically to score points. Ms. Liebeck's burns get rewritten into both a sick joke and an illustration that things have "just gotten completely out of control." Note that the story is *not* rewritten as a criticism of a business's callous disregard of its customers' safety; we may infer that that was not the interest of those writing about the incident. The writer's points are rendered more effective because of the story's entertainment value, and repeated in part out of a kind of playfulness. "Did you hear about the woman who got $3 million from McDonald's because she spilled coffee on herself..."—the anecdote was circulated far more widely than its combined news sources, and circulated in distorted fashion. The story was still being repeated in summer 1996, on the Comedy Central program *Politically Incorrect.*

The circulation of this and other stories should serve as a reminder that entertainment media, like other media, do rhetorical work. In this case, the story served to soften up public opinion for federal legislation limiting damage suits, a law that would have been considerably to the advantage of large businesses dealing with substances more dangerous than hot coffee. For example, such a law might allow those responsible for toxic waste spills to avoid responsibility for millions in damage. You might consider such a law good or bad—but it goes considerably beyond the effects of spilling hot coffee.

In earlier discussions of news media, we observed pressures on the news to be more entertaining in order to attract larger audiences. Such movements across categories of texts—whether the point is to use an entertaining tidbit to jazz up the news, or to use an entertainment medium to argue for political or social action—provide an ambiguous, mixed text. This mixing is the subject of the next section.

More Dirt

Dirt was defined in Chapter 5 in the sense of transgressions of categories—but the information that entertainment texts provide has to be "dirty," because providing information is not usually considered to be part of the definition of entertainment.

Why does it matter if categories are transgressed? First, category violations make it more likely that the sender of any message will be misunderstood ("You thought I was serious, but I was joking," or vice versa). It's precisely to prevent this sort of miscommunication that airports post signs warning passengers not to joke about carrying weapons when going through security. Both as audience and as writers, we need to be conscious of the hazards of not keeping sources of information straight. Second, there are many kinds of media, including some entertainment texts, that incorporate ambiguity and misunderstanding into their rhetoric. To understand how entertainment texts are received, therefore, you should consider some instances of dirt.

In order to frame this chapter's discussion of dirt, I am going to take you on an imaginary tour of my house on an average weekend morning. Imagine whatever sort of house comes to mind for you—but imagine it a mess. Breakfast dishes, along with a few from the previous night, are not exactly stacked in the cabinet. Clothes are still where they were let fall. Books, magazines, newspapers, and other printed material are scattered on coffee and lamp tables. You don't have to look too far to find wrappers, bits of paper, dustballs, and other odds and ends. It's all good stuff (at least, I think so—except for the dustballs), but the problem is that so much is out of place. The logical place for dishes is clean and in the cabinet (or at least in the dishwasher). Clothes belong in the laundry basket, washer and dryer, or closet and drawer. Books and magazines go on shelves or magazine racks; newspapers should be read and either clipped or recycled. Garbage goes in the garbage can, dustballs belong outside. The place is a pit—it's *dirty*.

Dirt can refer literally to soil, accumulated over millennia from rock and decaying organic material and highly valuable for raising crops. But dirt that is out of its place is ready to be swept or vacuumed up and put back in that place. In other words, "dirt" takes on a metaphorical as well as a literal meaning—whatever is out of place, in the wrong category, or between categories takes on some of the taboo qualities of dirt in the household.

We use *dirty* in this metaphorical sense to indicate that something is wrong and needs cleaning up. Sexual activity outside approved categories is sometimes called dirty (as in the phrases *dirty movies* or *dirty books*). "Dirty," then, means something is out of place or taboo. Any member of a culture comes to have a sense of that culture's understanding of what is appropriate behavior, what organizing principles should hold. Whatever threatens those principles, whatever might violate the categories on which the cultural system of order is based, may be regarded as "dirty," like disorganized household objects.

We have different responses to "dirt," depending on what the context is, and who we are in the culture. These responses range from feeling a very strong impulse to keep experience separated into well-marked and orderly categories, to finding this sort of order predictable and dull. Life in large cities can be exciting, with something new going on all the time—but those new events may be personally threatening; and over the last several decades many people have moved to suburbs, which lack such an immediate vitality, in exchange for lawns and trees and what might be considered a safer, "cleaner" way of living.

Something out of place transgresses a custom or unwritten law in our culture. These transgressions might be as trivial as talking loudly in a library or driving ten miles per hour below the speed limit; or they might be more serious, such as insults or damage to property (e.g., driving a car on a golf green, spitting in public, or egging a car). In fact, the word *transgress* means literally to go across a border. But what sorts of borders are we talking about?

The crucial borders for this culture and some others pertain to what defines the individual. Categories such as those cited in Chapter 5—*self, gender, age-group, family, class, nation,* and *ethnicity*—are important to this definition: They provide potential for ambiguous, "dirty" examples. For those within our culture, these categories seem to be natural and permanent; however, other cultures may deemphasize one or more, or disregard them entirely. For example, U.S. popular culture has stressed concerns and anxieties of one age-group in particular, teenagers, since the 1950s, by presenting their stories in films, popular music, and advertising. But being teenaged is a relatively recent concept that didn't especially concern our nineteenth-century ancestors. (The arbitrary nature of the grouping *teenager* is illustrated by its English origins. Grouping people between thirteen and nineteen doesn't make sense in languages other than English: Nothing special happens to those numbers in French or Spanish, for example, and in Slavic languages the relevant suffix runs from eleven to nineteen.)

Teenagers constitute a useful marketing category: Defining them as a category allows consumer goods to be packaged to sell to and through peer groups. Being between children and adults, teens are often regarded suspiciously. Sometimes this is rationalized in some fashion: Teenagers may be watched closely in stores because they allegedly shoplift more than people of other ages. Traffic cops may watch for teenaged drivers on the theory that they are more likely to cause accidents. Parents may watch teenaged children more closely for signs of sexual activity because of their "hormones."

PAUSE FOR REFLECTION

In preparing collections of print ads for Chapter 5, you may have selected some that target teens as the audience. Add to these any others you encounter, as well as relevant television commercials. How do you know the age and presumed concerns of the audience? Which of your ads suggest some sort of transgression as part of the appeal?

Being between ethnic identities can also bring suspicion. An extreme instance would be the comment of a high school principal in Alabama who went so far as to cancel the school prom in order to prevent interracial dating: He told a student in his school, the daughter of a black and a white parent, that she was "a mistake." Eventually he lost his job over this violation of a taboo against racism.

Entertainment texts have the potential to present controversial issues in such a way as to help us think through, and feel through, their implications. One of the conventions about dramatic narratives is that they involve a conflict of some kind—no conflict, no story; and often the conflict involves a clash in views provoked by a dirty category. This can be as trivial as the cat versus prey plots of the *Tom and Jerry* or *Sylvester and Tweety-Bird* cartoons: Tweety-Bird's owner regards him and Sylvester as pets, but Sylvester is inclined to consider the bird as a snack. Or the conflict can be the sort of struggles between self-definition and meeting parental and social obligations to be seen in the plots of John Hughes films (*The Breakfast Club, Ferris Bueller's Day Off*) or in the short-lived TV drama *My So-Called Life*. Any sort of drama has to condense into the framework of the text a transition of some sort, a set of events that have some effect on the participants (and, presumably, the audience). Sometimes the conflict is re-created in reactions to an entertainment text—for example, in the clash between the view that children's entertainment should be (relatively) free of disturbing incidents and the view that children should be permitted entertainment by more adult subject matter.

The list of formulaic comedy plots in Exhibit 7.2 is adapted from Eisner and Krimby, *Television Comedy Series*. Note how many of these plots involve ambiguities between categories. The list refers to "classic" comedy—many themes could be updated. For example, "moonshine" could be replaced with marijuana (as in an episode of *Roseanne* in which the parents find one of their kids' joints and smoke it).

> Lookalikes of one or more characters [ambiguity between self and other].
>
> Spies and espionage [ambiguity between nationalities].
>
> Redecorating the house with disastrous results [for example, any episode of *Home Improvement* is likely to feature the comic contrast between Tim Taylor's supposed competence as a handyman and what he actually manages to do].
>
> Someone's new girl/boyfriend is using them for some reason.
>
> Jealousy—characters are envious of each other or someone else.
>
> Grandparents (usually same cast in elderly makeup).
>
> Someone's mother is coming for a visit.
>
> A new haircut or dye leads to complications (baldness, strange color, etc.).
>
> The anniversary (or some big event that someone usually forgets).
>
> Moonshine, which usually has the characters drunk at the end.
>
> The makeover of an "ugly duckling."
>
> A wild adventure in a department store.
>
> A character mistakenly believes he is dying.
>
> A trip to the amusement park should be fun but isn't.

Exhibit 7.2 Formulaic comedy plots. From Joel Eisner and David Krinsky, *Television Comedy Series: An Episode Guide to 153 TV Sitcoms in Syndication.* Jefferson, N.C.: McFarland, 1984, pp. 2–3.

Events associated with the Vietnam War continue to be "dirty" as well. The majority view in the United States, in this as in other matters, connects our country with "the right side"; but many events in the war (such as the My Lai massacre) called that self-categorization into question. The issues remained unresolved even twenty years later, when one of the chief architects of U.S. involvement in the war, Robert McNamara, admitted in his memoirs his long but heretofore unstated belief that the United States could not have won. (His making money from sales of his memoirs has been criticized as a "dirty" combination of confession and profit.) In contrast with the Vietnam war, U.S. participation in World War II was much less ambiguous, but still has the potential for sharp reactions. This can be seen in the controversy over the Smithsonian's plans for an exhibit of the *Enola Gay,* the airplane that dropped the atomic bomb on Hiroshima. The exhibit called into question whether it was necessary to use the bomb and kill close to 100,000 people, when Japan was apparently close to surrender; veterans' groups protested vigorously what they saw as a rewriting of history to make the United States morally culpable.

As a result the exhibit was canceled and the museum director pressured into resigning.

There is, then, an inherent "dirtiness" when entertainment texts shape "real-world" attitudes. Events portrayed in "stories" are to some extent reflections of reality, and to some extent selected for dramatic purposes. There's a "dirtiness" between the claim to represent truth and the need to tell a convenient story. Sometimes the shaping of attitudes happens implicitly, sometimes by design.

The military establishment has helped to shape more positive portrayals of U.S. actions in wars, by allowing use of military bases and equipment for some films and denying it to others. Some films receiving such cooperation included *The Green Berets*, a 1968 film starring John Wayne as a member of the Special Forces in Vietnam; *Rambo III*; *Red Dawn*; *Invasion USA*; *Top Gun*; and *The Hunt for Red October*. Films with an antiwar or ambiguous message, on the other hand, received no such cooperation. These included *Attack* (1956); *On the Beach*, a 1959 film about the world after a nuclear attack; and *Steel Helmet*, whose script involved the killing of a North Korean prisoner of war. When Francis Ford Coppola filmed *Apocalypse Now*, he had to rent military equipment from the Philippines (Parenti pp. 26–27).

From the standpoint of reaching audiences, ambiguity can be of considerable advantage to producers of entertainment texts. Violence in films such as *Pulp Fiction* or *Boyz N the Hood*, or in comparable television programs, can be justified by appeals to realism in some cases, or can be enjoyed for a vicarious thrill in others—but both those who deplore real-life violence and those who enjoy its fictional portrayal watch.

Those who defend violence in entertainment texts may comment that it only reflects reality; but it's a curious sort of reflection. Television violence is carefully tailored to the requirements of telling stories. The world of TV fiction "is an unusually violent place, but the violence is blissfully unattended by pain and suffering." Murders in prime-time television occur at a rate 1,000 times higher than in real life. "TV murders do not result from quarrels—as they overwhelmingly do in the real world—but in the course of another crime" (Bogart p. 160).

While in real life we don't usually see violent events, they are naturalized in our television viewing experience. By age eighteen, according to Newton Minow, a child has seen on average 25,000 televised murders (Bogart p. 347).

One result of the heavy yet sanitized portrayal of violence on television and in films is that viewers come to believe that their world is a far more violent place than it is in fact—and to act on that belief. This belief comes from "dirt" between entertainment texts, which show events which are invented, and real experience. Polls in 1994 cited increasing crime as the public's number one concern, when crime rates had in fact been decreasing for several years. A principal source of dirt, then, is difficulty in distinguishing between fictional portrayals and reality.

Yet another instance of blurred categories can be seen in the edging of news and information toward entertainment. Televised talk shows transgress this distinction, with their often sensationalized presentations of serious topics. A similar mixture of motives can be found in other sorts of popular culture, from traditional carnival midways, to their modern descendants such as World Wrestling Federation events and tractor pulls, to the *National Enquirer* and other supermarket tabloids. There may be members of the public who believe that "Five US Senators Are Space Aliens," that celebrities are regularly taken on interplanetary trips by UFOs, that Elvis lives, and so on; there certainly are people who read such stories out of a combination of amused fantasy and ironic superiority to anyone who might buy into these "news" stories. But both sorts buy and read the tabloids. And tabloids fall into the "dirty" category of being not really news, not really entertainment.

Entertainment texts also approach history from their direction—in genres such as the "nonfiction novel" of the 1960s, the pseudodocumentary (*Zelig, Roger and Me, Forrest Gump*), and ambiguous texts such as Oliver Stone films (*JFK, Nixon*). Computer techniques and other film devices have made it possible to insert Tom Hanks as Gump into televised scenes with Presidents Kennedy, Johnson, and Nixon, and Anthony Hopkins as Nixon into the 1968 Republican Convention.

Ambiguous texts and genres may be variously interpreted, then—but not in entirely open ways. Rather, as we interact with these texts, we do so along lines established for us by culturally established systems of understanding. We have only a few ways to "read," and they are not *our* inventions. I have established this point with respect to news, by outlining some of the "stories" that we read news into. Something like this can be shown with entertainment texts as well.

"Dirty" categories, as subject of some anxiety, are often treated in sitcoms, as we saw in Exhibit 7.2 above. An episode of *Seinfeld* broadcast in fall 1994 can illustrate how these ambiguities connect with audiences' circumstances. *Seinfeld* has a more wide-open situation than most sitcoms, and thus has a wider latitude than a typical sitcom built around a family. It features four regular characters, as well as a few who reappear occasionally. Jerry Seinfeld, as actor and character, blurs to some extent the distinction between fiction and reality. As with some other sitcoms, the program carries the lead actor's real name; his character in the comedy is a comedian, and frequently the episodes either open or close with a monologue that is thematically related to the events of that week's program. Typically, *Seinfeld* episodes interweave vignettes involving the four main characters. Elaine (Julia Louis-Dreyfus), Jerry's former girl friend, keeps up friendly relations with Jerry and others. George (Jason Alexander) is a rather neurotic figure; Jerry's across-the-hall neighbor, Kramer (Michael Richards), is an exuberant oddball likely to come crashing into the apartment at any moment. In several episodes, Jerry and George are trying to sell NBC on the idea of giving them a sitcom which will be "about nothing"—a self-referential concept that seems to violate the program's "self." *Seinfeld* plots (such as they are) are built out of vignettes running along two or three parallel plot lines that intertwine and offer comment on each other. Structurally, this allows a "dirty" flow between characters' stories. One consistent theme in the program is a prevailing concern with manners and sexual anxiety: The characters' preoccupations are likely to be their latest love interests (particularly those of George and Elaine). The characters' anxiety results from their histories of less-than-successful love affairs, and in turn may contribute to the latest failures.

In one episode, Jerry and Elaine have finished dinner at a restaurant. His car has been parked by a valet (shown only at a distance), who leaves a very strong odor in the car—which Jerry says is "BO." But the plot's complication comes from the fact that, as Jerry notes, "the O" has not managed to stay with "the B." Most of the comic developments in the episode come from Jerry's attempts to get the odor out of his car, and his and Elaine's attempts to get the odor off his jacket and other clothes, and out of her hair. Jerry returns to the restaurant and insists that the manager pay half of the cost of getting the car cleaned, gaining his agreement by the device of locking him in the car. As the episode progresses, the odor's persistence is more and more solidly established, until Jerry begins to speak of it in terms drawn from horror movies: "It's the Beast!" "You need a priest to get rid of this thing!"

Viewers who might wonder about the source of such a potent odor will have to be content with two glimpses of the valet. One, early and indistinct, occurs before there's any reason to pay attention to him. The second, when Jerry and George return to the restaurant, takes a bit longer. The actor playing the part isn't visually identifiable as "ethnic" (i.e., is "white"), unless having a mustache counts; but the fact that Jerry has to communicate with him in gestures might suggest that he's not an English speaker.

The other half of the same episode's plot concerns Susan, a former girlfriend of George's whom he meets in a video store. George notices her from the back, holding hands with another woman, and comments to himself, condescendingly, "a lesbian sighting!" In talking with her, he discovers that she became lesbian after breaking up with *him,* and the anxiety aroused by this revelation preoccupies him throughout the episode. As it happens, Kramer later becomes involved with Susan's girlfriend, Mona; this provokes George to bitterly exclaim, "I drive them to lesbianism, he brings them back!" Homosexuality has long been taboo in mass entertainment—though it has been somewhat more freely treated in films than on television because of films' greater audience selectivity. Treating lesbianism in prime-time TV is relatively novel; in the same TV season, a briefly notorious episode of *Roseanne* involved her kissing a woman friend. These are episodes rather than regular characters; television, in this instance, is not exactly breaking new ground. (Female homosexuals appear to be more palatable than male, at least in comedies.) Treatment of homosexuality on television is done very gingerly, restricted to a kiss or hand-holding, without much reflection on more concrete instances of sexuality. (George's question for Susan has to do with who leads whom when they dance.) Becoming gay, in its television treatment, appears to be about as consequential as becoming Republican: When Mona defects, George counsels Susan not to worry—"You're beautiful, you're intelligent—you'll meet other girls." Sexuality, as a component of self, is unstable on television: In a later season, Susan becomes hetero again and gets engaged to George.

One interesting feature of this episode is what it does with juxtapositions. There are two instances of parallels that function to draw attention to similarities. The more minor of these occurs late, when Seinfeld is trying to get the smell removed from his car while Elaine is working on making her hair smell sweet again. The smell expert is telling Jerry about how they will use "de-ionizer" to get rid of the stench; in the parallel segment the hair expert is talking about using dilute vinegar and other solutions to remove the smell from Elaine's hair, with the last resort being tomato sauce. Jerry eventually gets into his car, after spending $250 to have it deodorized, and begins to pound the steering-wheel in frustration, shouting "It still smells!" Elaine leans back over the hairdresser's sink, with the curt request, "Sauce me." The other parallel, extended throughout the episode, is implied in the alternation between BO and lesbianism. Both are sources of social discomfort and embarrassment for at least one of the *Seinfeld* characters. Both BO and lesbianism put the desirable other out of reach (at least for George). During a conversation over lunch, Susan encounters *another* of George's alumnae, who says to her, "That's a lovely vest," and another acquaintance begins, much to his dismay. Tomato sauce and vests, consumer goods, are integrated into the plot as ways to deal with serious concerns such as lesbian relationships and displaced body odor.

What categories are crossed in this episode of *Seinfeld*? First, gender and personal identity: There's a transgression in even acknowledging the existence of categories other than heterosexual on prime-time television. Susan, formerly heterosexual, is lesbian, while Mona, formerly lesbian, becomes heterosexual (at least briefly). George, who would like to be a real *mensch*, feels himself responsible for Susan's "metamorphosis," while Kramer, whom George sees as a comic figure, brings about a conversion back to hetero. Second, personal matters become public—the valet's odor is transferred to Jerry's car, and from there to various other locations (his jacket, Elaine's hair). The valet's ethnic background is unclear, but there's at least a suggestion that he's foreign. In most respects, however, the show's meaning is *underdetermined*—that is, one could agree with the surface meaning of George's comment that "lesbians are hip," or with the desire he expresses for Susan, which goes somewhat against this sentiment. One could read the comedy as normalizing being gay, or as giving it a minor stigma—on the level of body odor, perhaps, but not to the level of religious condemnation. It's possible to read Jerry's (or *Seinfeld*'s) problem with odor as saying, in effect, "foreigners stink," or to read his preoccupation as exaggerated and comic. In other words, the program works in some respects to promote examining stereotypes (Susan responds to George's question about leading while dancing by telling him, "You really are an idiot"), and in some respects to sustain and reinforce stereotypes. *Seinfeld* uses "dirty" categories, as we have seen, to have it both ways.

A shorter illustration of how "dirt" can mix the entertaining with the commercial can be seen in advertisements. One entertaining commercial for Doritos, shown in March–May 1995, was set in what are supposed to be two hospital newborn rooms. The first, captioned "Life Without Doritos," is filled with crying babies and despairing attendants. The second, captioned "Life With Doritos," has female attendants with bags of chips happily moving among babies who are singing a jazzed-up version of the Young Rascals' 1960s hit "Good Lovin'." (The babies are obviously not newborn, but somewhere around six months.) Special effects are used to make the babies' lips move along with the lyrics. At the end, two (male) doctors walk by, amazed at what they are seeing.

The Doritos ad has some things in common with more usual entertainment texts (that is, with those that are not directly commercials). It's cute—no one ever went broke relying on U.S. consumers' appetites for cute children. It's funny—matching the bass and tenor voices and the women's backup with the babies provides a mild chuckle, as well as creating curiosity about how they got the babies to do that. It's simple—the "Life Without/With Doritos" labels avoid anything too complicated for the form, just as do most television comedies and dramas, most popular songs, and most films. And it's fast-paced—the music is up-tempo, and the camera cuts reinforce the quick movement.

The ad corresponds to entertainment texts in other respects, too: It's a match with what we may take to be the dominant ideology. Gender roles, for example, are reinforced in the ad, just as were dominant sex roles in the *Seinfeld* episode described above. Male doctors are outside the glass, observing and maintaining authority over this experiment (life without/with Doritos), while the particular actions needed for infant care are assigned to female nurses. And the "Good Lovin'" song gives the lead part to the male tenor, with prominent bass carried by a (light-skinned black) male baby; the girls sing backup, and three of them are on screen together, instead of getting their own solos. (All the infants are white except for the bass-singing child, who also appears to be spun around and around at one point.)

Another form of "dirt" should be mentioned here—the crossing of the boundary between entertainment and commercial enterprises as businesses. Entertainment texts—television programs, films, songs, and other sorts—are money-making enterprises, as much as are commercials. But they generally downplay or discount the extent to which they are formed as commercial enterprises. The largest U.S. manufacturer of household cleansers, Procter and Gamble, also produces six daytime dramas (a.k.a. soap operas)—illustrating the blurred nature of these programs. These dramas originated with the need to attract a sympathetic, mostly female audience for ads, going all the way back to *Oxydol's Ma Perkins* in the 1930s.

"Dirt" in the sense of creating an association across the boundary between program and advertisement has been a factor since the heyday of radio. Advertisers sponsored programs in their entirety, building associations between Hellmann's mayonnaise and the *Happiness Boys*, between Pepsodent toothpaste and *Amos 'n' Andy*, and so on. Pillsbury's *Today's Children* was described by *Broadcasting* magazine in 1935 as "homey drama that appeals to 'just folks,' the mothers, the homemakers, the flour users of America." Stars of these programs stepped out of character to endorse the product in personal appearances as well as during radio ads; perhaps the best known of these was Jack Benny's famous opening line, "Jell-O again" (Bogart pp. 104–05).

Entertainment texts present themselves as how it "naturally" is, whether in commercials, daytime dramas, or sitcoms. In the Doritos commercial described above, nurses are female, doctors are male, as often happens in reality;

the "Good Lovin'" song was by a male group, and songs from that period often had "girls" singing backup. And, anyway, it's all in fun—it shouldn't be treated as something that's so serious. The same comments are generally made about more substantial entertainment texts—that they simply reflect the culture, and that being entertainment, they shouldn't be subject to serious analysis.

But that's exactly the point: The connection with and reinforcement of *how it "naturally" is* gives entertainment texts (and advertisements) their hold on the audience. They invite us to see a mainstream view of our culture as a matter of natural order. Hospital infant care rooms are not natural locations (much less such rooms that serve Doritos or feature pop music prodigies); they are culturally created sites. But we are invited to *think* of them as natural, even while recognizing the manipulation going on with computers and camera tricks. The selection of the song for the ad reinforces the notion that males (even babies) "naturally" sing lead, females sing backup, and doctors are the authorities in the hospital hierarchy.

What happens to us as audience in watching this commercial? Mostly, I think, we are charmed and amused. The babies are cute, the music is catchy, and the matching of visual and auditory lets viewers see the ad several times without getting sick of it. On repeated viewings, we may be interested in specific details—how the digitizers got the babies' lips to move in sequence with the lyrics, how the three girl babies' arms are coordinated to move in phase, and so on. Also, a good retreatment of a familiar tune can keep us listening several times (on radio as well as on television)—"Good Lovin'" is familiar from top-forty play in the 1960s and from frequent play on "oldies" programs since. In the song lyrics, medical advice is summoned as proof that what is needed is to have one's desires gratified, whether for good lovin' or good snackin'. All the fantastic movement in the Doritos commercial naturalizes the other fantasy of the commercial, that the specific product will make us feel as lighthearted and happy as the babies and nurses appear to be. It may also suggest that hospitals are places where no procedures take place that are more invasive than rediapering—an illustration that commercial messages are never simply confined to the product.

There are several responses available to any entertainment text, as there are to this Doritos ad—but none of them is an individual creation. Rather, as viewers we select—or are selected by—one of several alternatives. We might do the television-watching equivalent of snapping our fingers and tapping our toes—that is, relax and enjoy the music and visual images, without being particularly attentive to the ad; and in this case "Doritos" would get insinuated into the backs of our minds. We might take a more attentive stance toward the ad, in which case the computer-generated special effects and other details might draw our attention. We might read the ad as satirizing rather than confirming male authority (the bewildered doctors and with-it nurses give some support to this reading). Or we might take a more specifically critical stance, along the lines suggested above concerning gender and race.

Entertainment texts frequently offer several varieties of fantasy that encourage audiences to connect with versions of *how things are.* How things are, in most cases, prove to be how they are in *this* culture, and in a particular version of this culture, offered as though it's part of the natural order. To the extent that we are seduced by cuteness, good music, and lights and movement into agreeing with the characterization of the cultural as the natural, we buy into the cultural hegemony of "common sense."

Why Do They Want You to Play?

As we reflect on the extended comparison above between forms of entertainment and play, our attention should be directed toward both audiences and producers—that is, why do *we want* to play, and why do *they want us* to play?

Play can be considered a vehicle for learning. On the playground, children learn to associate with other children: They learn to negotiate differences, to engage in common activities; they learn (and develop) their physical capabilities. They learn what is expected of them within specific roles related to gender, race, class, and other markers of identity within a culture. They learn about language use, in ways perhaps more influential than what goes on in the classroom. They learn, in short, who they are in relation to others. Similar points may apply with entertainment texts, for adults as well as for children. Just as with the playground example, forms of entertainment are powerful devices for socializing us as members of a culture with specific roles related to our genders, races, classes, and so on.

Adults sometimes have motives for getting children to go play, beyond just "do what you want." Sending the kids out to play can be a way of getting them out of your hair; some forms of play teach values that adults want children to have; and, if the adult is not a parent but, say, a dealer in toys or sports equipment, there's a commercial motive as well. In other words, there's "dirt" between the supposedly pure reasons for play and the uses to which it's put. These uses are connected with *hegemony,* or the devices that institutions use to maintain and re-create the culture's dominant sense of the "natural" order. *Hegemony* in general terms means "the ways in which a governing power wins consent to its rule from those it subjugates" (Eagleton, *Ideology* p. 112); and entertainment texts, along with other media, can be considered as part of this process.

The concept of hegemony was developed by Antonio Gramsci within the framework of twentieth-century Marxism, but has grown somewhat beyond its original context. To simplify somewhat, any industrialized society can be considered as organized into several classes—classically, three (the ruling class, the middle class, and the working class), though those may be further subdivided. The ruling class has at its disposal mechanisms of force to put down revolts (the police, criminal justice systems, and so on) but is better served if violence can be avoided through hegemony—getting those not in power to want what the rulers want them to want.

Entertainment texts fit into the model of hegemony in several ways. First, if the workers can be entertained (by circuses, movies, sports, and other forms of popular culture), then they are less likely to cause political trouble. (This has been called the "safety valve" theory of entertainment.) Second, entertainment texts can be useful in getting across a version of reality that encourages those not in power to remain content with their station. Entertainment might, for example, be helpful in directing attention to heavenly rather than earthly rewards; in persuading workers that if they work well and consistently, they can get a shot at some form of power; or (a tactic very much in evidence in the 1980s and early 1990s) in spreading the cynical belief that what average people do won't matter anyway, because the system is too large and complex to be affected by their efforts.

One example: An argument made against *The Cosby Show*—by Sut Jhally and Justin Lewis, as well as by Mark Crispin Miller—was in part directed at its participation in hegemony. The premise that the Huxtables achieved their high economic and social status through individual effort communicates to viewers (of all races) the belief that we too can succeed, and that if we don't, it's our own fault. The ideology that this view ties into is sometimes called "the American dream": It is highly individualistic and well adapted to a free market economy.

While some part of the content of entertainment texts may be disinterested, most entertainment activity in the contemporary United States exists within the context of a set of commercial values: The most widely recognized reason for entertainment is to make money. Initially in this section, then, we should take note of the commercial motivation behind entertainment. The other, less generally acknowledged set of reasons why "they want you to play" has to do with persuading audiences to certain sets of values.

We as audiences are so generally familiar with entertainment as a form of making money that we often forget *how much* money-making has come to be accepted as part of entertainment. Sales and accompanying profits have come to be accepted as measures of a text's quality, as with "gold" and "platinum" records, best-selling books, high-rated television programs, video rentals, attendance at sporting events, and so on.

When you read newspaper accounts of television ratings for the week, you may not automatically equate these to dollars—but television executives do. "A rating point is worth $140 million to a network" over a year. "Each rating point on a network show brings in over $8,000 for a 30-second spot, and there are seven such spots in a half-hour show.... A hit like *The Cosby Show* at its peak was worth over $100 million a year" (Bogart p. 138).

Commercial motives have become so intertwined with entertainment that we do not always observe a distinction any more. Many films gather money from sources other than audience attendance.

"The film *Batman* earned half a billion dollars from product licensing arrangements, more than twice its box-office revenues" (Bogart p. 39).

"Product placement" is of considerable interest in film and television. "Film studios routinely receive up to $250,000 for introducing branded products into films. Philip Morris reportedly paid $350,000 to get Lark cigarettes displayed in *License to Kill*, a James Bond thriller." [Philip Morris had a relative bargain in the film *Superman II*, getting 22 placements of the Marlboro logo for $42,000 (Manning p. 34).] A Coke machine was brought into a school cafeteria in *TV 101*. "Dell has published romantic novels that insert the brand name Bel Air before every reference to a cigarette.... An average of 11 plugs per hour for specific products and brands appeared in 1993 on each of the three major network owned and operated stations in Chicago, over half of them on news shows" (Bogart pp. 72–73).

The producers of *ET* didn't get a satisfactory offer for "product placement" from the Mars candy company, the manufacturers of M&Ms, so they changed the screenplay to have the alien enticed by Reese's Pieces. Sales of Reese's Pieces increased by 66 percent immediately (Jacobson and Mazur pp. 67–68). Makers of *Demolition Man* worked out a promotional scheme with Taco Bell: In the script, the future involved fast-food wars, resulting in Taco Bell's being the only restaurant left. With routine film budgets frequently exceeding $30 million, product placements can be important sources of income—so it's probably safe to assume that any product package, neon sign, billboard, or logo seen in a film was inserted not as the result of the creator's vision so much as to fulfill contracts with corporations.

In addition to stories provided through film and TV, hegemony works through the stories present in sporting events. The prevailing myth about sports is that it's a physical contest matching strength and skill in a pure competition. While it's possible for us as watchers to hold to this myth by directing our concentration appropriately, sports has been largely contaminated by its development as a business, through tie-ins with media and corporate sponsors. Old film footage of tennis players, Olympic stars, and others from decades ago is striking for the absence of something we now take very much for granted—sports product logos. If you watch a contemporary tennis match, practically any ranked competitor will be wearing a hat, shirt, or shoes bearing logos by Nike, Reebok, or other recognizable brands of sports apparel. These are the result of payments from corporate sponsors that may considerably outpace players' earnings from the sport itself. Baseball fans long ago lost their innocence about its being just a game, with sports contracts escalating dramatically as owners competed for expensive free agents. And the Dallas Cowboys' owner, Jerry Jones, incurred the wrath of the National Football League by striking his own deals with Nike and Pepsi-Cola. Within a commercially dominated society, it's hard to blame players for getting what they can—their salaries serve as indicators of their value, which is increasingly defined in terms of entertainment and audience draw rather than performance on the field. The protests of sports fans are a lament for the passing of a myth.

Commercial sponsorships have become a considerable part of the sports environment as well, with rotating billboards next to the scoring table, home plate, or end zone, where TV cameras will pan past them. Corporate symbols are thus part of the "natural" environment for sports. About a decade ago, traditional bowl games added commercial labels to their titles, so that we now have the Thrifty Car Rental Holiday Bowl, the F S & G Sugar Bowl, and the Poulan Weed Eater Independence Bowl. Tobacco companies have become a substantial part of minor sports, with Marlboro's logo (and associated "gear") highly visible in auto racing, the Winston Cup as the pre-eminent award, and Virginia Slims for years heavily involved in sponsoring women's tennis tournaments. Because tobacco advertising has been forbidden on television since 1971, identifiable logos are an important back-door way to plug the product on screen. (The city of New York is requiring Madison Square Garden to remove cigarette signs from every point at which they could be picked up on camera for televised sporting events.) Sports events can be powerful texts for affecting audience attitudes, which is the source of their attraction for commercial enterprises.

Until 1955, Marlboro was a "women's" cigarette with so-so market share. That year the Philip Morris company began its "Marlboro Man" campaign, which promoted an identification with independent, Western men, and sales rose to their present volume (Atwan, McQuade, and Wright, *Edsels, Luckies, and Frigidaires*, p. 69).

It may be necessary to suggest some reasons for objecting to endemic commercialism, because it's become so naturalized. If you see nothing but commercial television, you may not recognize that there's an alternative. By contrast, however, European television is underwritten by fees paid to the government; there are a few ads, but these are grouped together at the end of the program, rather than being dispersed throughout. Europeans seeing American television for the first time are shocked at the level of interruption we accept. (There's some similarity between the European "public service" tradition and U.S. public television, which has program announcements about corporate underwriters such as Mobil, Archer-Daniels-Midland, and General Electric, but no ads per se.) Under the European system, there's less possibility for advertisers to bring pressure on programming in order to make it suit commercial ends.

In 1965, congressional hearings on the influence of advertisers over noncommercial television and radio produced this memo from the advertising manager of Procter and Gamble to their advertising agency:

> There will be no material on any of our programs which could in any way further the concept of business as cold, ruthless, and lacking all sentiment or spiritual motivation.
>
> If a businessman is cast in the role of villain, it must be made clear that he is not typical but is as much despised by his fellow businessmen as he is by other members of society.
>
> Special attention shall be given to *any* mention, however innocuous, of the grocery and drug business as well as any other group of customers of the company. This includes industrial users of the company's products, such as bakeries, restaurants, and laundries. (Bagdikian pp. 156–57)

Times have changed, as a study based on content analysis of evening programs shows. In 1992, "business characters were twice as likely to be bad guys and three times as likely to commit crimes as were characters in other occupations.... Over three out of four shows that contained discussions of business dealings treated corporate or entrepreneurial activity as corrupt or unethical." This change can be explained in part by shifts in program genres: Early cop shows such as *The Untouchables* showed organized crime as the bad guys (Lichter, Rothman, and Lichter, *Prime Time* pp. 65–67).

Corporate sponsors have a great deal to do with the content of entertainment programs. After all, they are the ones paying the bills, and their interest in bringing the public enjoyable and worthwhile programming is subordinate to the interest in providing an effective context for their advertising.

"We're looking for opportunities for vignettes, where we can surround our commercial with interesting programming to sustain the viewer's interest and then mug him with a commercial." (George Mahrlig, quoted in Bogart p. 109)

This involvement with content may reach the level of suggesting or requiring revision of the script.

Much of the work of commercial television goes on outside the viewer's frame of reference.

The Advertising Information Service, which is owned by twenty-one large advertising agencies, employs twenty people to screen shows for problems. Examples of what they do: A scene in which wild dogs chase a girl on an episode of *Little House on the Prairie* was cut because one of the sponsors was Puppy Chow. No cat food commercials appeared on *Alf* because the alien threatens to eat the family cat. General Motors wants to be sure that none of its commercials are in the neighborhood when Michael Moore is touting his anti-GM movie *Roger and Me*. The Advertising Information Service is not in the least concerned about the steady infiltration of product placement into prime-time television. Quite the contrary. They check to be sure that Coca-Cola has a red coke machine in the series *TV 101*, that Alf is eating only Hershey bars, that Oneida silverware is identifiable on the tables of *Dynasty* and *Dallas,* and that Budweiser beer is drunk at Roseanne's house while Stroh's is served over at Cheers. (Twitchell p. 219)

The innocent might think along lines such as these: Entertainment texts are produced (by individuals or groups) in such a way as to reflect artistic purposes. Some of these may be high-cultural, artistic works—novels by contemporary equivalents of William Faulkner, for example, or serious poems and plays. Others may not try for that level of achievement or complexity, but produce what would still be respectable work in a more popular genre; for example, films such as those of George Cukor, Alfred Hitchcock, Orson Welles, or the Ealing Studios in postwar England. Decisions of all sorts, from plot and characterization to film editing and musical scores, are based on artistic integrity; actors are chosen on the basis of their abilities, their capacities to play the roles assigned, their working together with the director and in ensemble, and so on.

What is the audience's motivation for accepting this myth? It has the simplicity of familiarity: We understand intention in everyday activities such as food preparation, so it's possible to conceive of producers of media texts as "preparing" their texts according to a pure ideal, as we might have a Platonic steak dinner in mind when cooking up the Thursday night feed. The myth explains events in terms of origins—we feel we know something about the nature of a text or event if we know who did it. And it ties into a metanarrative of our culture, that the deserving have every chance to rise to recognition (that's how we know they are deserving). A consequence of this metanarrative is the belief that those in prominence are there because they deserve to be by merit. Rather than one monarch ruling by the grace of God, this myth provides us several hundred stars who shine because of their own light. And we can hope or fantasize to be among them in our own areas some day.

Increasing commercialization eroded this myth, however—and well before television. After writing a dozen or so novels, several of which are now recognized as among the best this country has produced, William Faulkner found it necessary to go to Hollywood and write screenplays. Writers of previous generations such as Herman Melville and Mark Twain had to work out their own compromises with the market (in Melville's case, without much success). The analogy with literary texts breaks down with film: Who is the author? The writer of the screenplay, the director, or the producer? From its outset, film has been a commercial medium: Actors have always been cast on the basis of their ability to draw audiences, as well as their acting talents. Films do not have their existence as independent texts so much as they do as vehicles for actors and directors—it makes sense to speak of a typical Brian De Palma or George Lucas film, or to speak of a John Wayne or Meryl Streep or Arnold Schwarzenegger film. Films have always been produced with an eye to their prospects for commercial success, and this has had its effects from the earliest decision to write a particular sort of proposal for a screenplay up to the choice of which scripts to produce, when and how to release films, and so on.

But there are levels of intensity to commercialism. Producing entertainment texts has always been a question of balancing the producer's artistic vision and sense of "what the public wants" with what it is possible to finance and distribute (in other words, sell). A story that is felt to be *only* about making money is likely to be unsuccessful. And certain kinds of stories are more likely to be made available to us as audiences than are others—anything too intense, too complex, or too discouraging may not find commercial sponsorship. (This may account for the relative dominance of comedy over tragedy in film and television recently.)

So one answer to the question at the opening of the section is this: They "want you to play" so they can make money. Some of that money is funneled back into production of entertainment texts, so that *their* sorts of play can continue. But much of it goes to pay for investors and production companies through the framework of commercial enterprises. It is in this sense that Mark Fowler's description of television as "a toaster with pictures" can be seen as appropriate—reduced to its commercial dimensions, TV is a product, a household appliance.

The "authors" of entertainment texts, then—those with professional commitment to or commercial ownership of entertainment texts—are in a "dirty" position between aesthetic play and commercial gain. The fact that most entertainment texts lose money may be accounted for by the problems of the marketplace: Determining what will sell is an inexact science. Todd Gitlin's conversations with television producers and executives showed that they had no way to judge consistently about whether a new show would succeed:

> Often I began an interview by saying that I was trying to understand how decisions got made about what to put on the air. There was one initial response that I heard so frequently it amused me at first, and later I came to expect it. It was usually said with a smile. "If you figure it out, please let me know"; or "I've been in this business X years, and *I* don't understand it." (*Inside Prime Time* p. 21)

In other words, making a television program, like making a film or record album, like writing a book or producing a play, is a risk, more or less like starting a business. You assess your chances, based on what consultants tell you or on what your hunch is about the public mood, and give it a shot. On average, *something* is going to click, even if it's nearly impossible to judge what.

Television programmers try to minimize the chances of failure by testing out their productions.

Because programmers abhor risk, almost every new show is screened by a "live" audience. This occurs in a nondescript building on Sunset Boulevard known as Preview House. Promised free entertainment and door prizes, viewers line up in

> the afternoon and fill out information forms. About four hundred people will finally be chosen. They take assigned seats. The operators of the Stanton–Lazarsfeld Program Analyzer know that, for instance, the occupant of seat 12A is in the eighteen to twenty-five-year-old group, has two children, and makes between $11,000 and $14,000 a year. If the production is a sitcom, the audience is first shown a *Mr. Magoo* cartoon (called "the magoo" in the trade), which has a pretested level of "laughs." There is a point in the cartoon when Mr. Magoo falls off a mountain which has "tested funny," and reaction to this moment has more to do with what America watches on television than anything else. If the preview audience does not meet the laugh levels of "the magoo," then the evening is scrapped, and the data discarded. Once accepted as a test audience, the viewer twists a dial that measures likes and dislikes, and he or she is asked to respond to each joke on a 1 to 100 scale. Questionnaires follow as well as discussion groups. This information is coded and computerized. (Twitchell p. 224n)

Even when audience response has been checked by test showings and pilots, the decision to schedule a television program or film depends to a large extent on intuition. But this intuition, based on an assessment of what can be done within the borders of the medium, is what we need to form a better idea about. What will people respond to? What will we like, what will speak to us? More than one producer has been driven out of the business by trying to guess: The question pertains to something that functions for the culture (or a part of the culture) more or less as the unconscious functions in Freudian psychology.

The term for what we are talking about is *ideology,* the set of beliefs and values that are largely taken for granted within a culture, which largely define what that culture is and maintain its particular forms of expression. (The custom is to speak in the singular, ideology, though there are numerous competing ideologies in circulation at any given time.) Ideology will be a central term in the next chapter, so I will not discuss it extensively here. However, a working hypothesis might be that we tend to like entertainment texts that fit comfortably within our own ideologies, and to resist those that conflict with them.

One theory that may be useful in suggesting connections between entertainment texts and cultural values of the audience is set out below. Arthur Asa Berger makes use of work by Aaron Wildavsky, a political scientist, to explain "genre migration," or the tendency for audiences of entertainment texts to shift their preferences with age.

ARTHUR ASA BERGER

Genre Migration

Number and Variety of Prescriptions	Strength of Group Boundaries	
	weak	*strong*
many	fatalists	elitists
few	individualists	egalitarians

Hierarchical elitists justify inequality, show deference to superiors, value order, sacrifice parts for the whole.

Competitive individualists believe freedom of contract is basic, that humans are self-seeking, that government should protect property, and defend the country.

Egalitarians stress equality of needs, criticize hierarchy and individualism, which form the "establishment."

Fatalists see life as based on chance, luck.

[Aaron] Wildavsky argues that two dominant questions arise in any cultural theory—"who am I?" (that is, what group do I belong to?) and "how should I behave?" (that is, what rules should I obey?). By setting up a four-celled figure that considers group boundaries and the number and variety of prescriptions in a culture, he arrives at these political cultures.

The question of interest is: Can Wildavsky's schema be used to understand the appeal of certain genres? And more precisely, would certain political cultures, by view of their values and beliefs, tend to be more interested in some genres than others? I assume that people watch television programs, go to films, and read books that support and reinforce their values and beliefs and avoid texts that challenge these beliefs. Let us assume, for argument's sake, that we have readers and viewers of texts who like the genres they should like. What might we find? This exercise is highly speculative, of course, but it does yield some interesting results.

Hierarchical Elitists	**Competitive Individualists**
News (international)	Sports
Classical mysteries	Westerns
Spy stories	Mysteries (private eyes)
Egalitarians	**Fatalists**
Stand-up comedies	Soaps
Zany comedies (Monty Python)	Country/Western music

I assigned international news to the hierarchical elitists because these programs tend to be about the comings and goings of the various elites who run countries and make decisions of national and international importance. Elitists would also like the classical mysteries because they tend to be about elites—the classical English ones often involve aristocratic types who live in large mansions with servants, family members who lust after inheritances, and so forth. Elitists would also be drawn to spy stories because they frequently involve the adventures of elite figures (or pseudo-elite figures, like James Bond, who likes his drinks shaken but not stirred and has other seemingly aristocratic tastes).

Competitive individualists, I would argue, should be drawn to sports contests—especially ones like tennis and golf that involve individuals competing with other individuals. Were westerns still popular, individualists would be drawn to them, in that many feature the lone cowboy who single-handedly cleans up a corrupt town and vanquishes evil. And, of course, competitive individualists would follow the adventures of "private eyes," detectives who solve crimes and find murderers, generally competing with and outwitting the police (who are often shown as inept and frequently hinder the private eye).

For the egalitarians, the most significant genre would be comedies—especially the kind like *Monty Python* that ridicule society and its institutions (and various elements in society, as well, such as the hierarchical elitists found in government, the church, etc.). Humor can be a means of resistance to the powerful elements in society who control the media and run the government. Humor is generally a liberating force, an antiestablishment force (though it can also be used by the elites for their purposes).

...What Bakhtin points out is that humor is, by its very nature, a subversive force and one that destroys the sense of solemnity and distance that those we have called hierarchical elitists use to justify inequality. Humor enables people to see things realistically, by bringing things "close" and enabling people to inspect them.

The kind of comedy that egalitarians would logically like would be that found in the better stand-up comedians, which often deal with the fiascos and absurdity of political life, and comedy shows that have a satirical or absurdist aspect to them.

Finally, for the fatalists, if we follow the logic of their beliefs and values, we end up with country and western songs, which often deal with the trials and tribulations of common people who find themselves fired from their jobs, deserted by their loved ones, and so on. These motifs are also found in soap operas, which deal with the same kinds of things, though generally they involve middle- and upper-class characters who tend to be professional, or businessmen and women. Soap operas are complex texts that offer gratifications to all of the political cultures, though logically they should be of most interest to the fatalists, who can identify with the problems the characters in soaps face and perhaps aspire to the kinds of lifestyles they lead.

Logically, fatalists should not watch films or television programs that show that one can succeed on the basis of individual initiative, that show that society functions because of the doings of elitists (who have a sense of obligation to those beneath them, unlike the competitive individualists), or that stress the things that everyone has in common rather than the things on which they differ. Whether fatalists or any of the political cultures consume the genres they *should* is a difficult question. Because texts are so complex, they often offer gratifications that make them of interest to members of political cultures that on the basis of pure logic should not be attracted to them....

It is difficult to determine with any precision the way people migrate from genre to genre as they get older. As far as radio is concerned, if our informant is to be believed, it is quite reasonable to assume that as we get older, our tastes may change somewhat, and we migrate from the rock music of our teens to soft and easy music in our thirties and forties, as well as news and talk shows. Research indicates that the audiences of talk shows tend to be made up of people over fifty.

Let me offer a highly speculative table on genres and the life cycle, based on discussions with child librarians, radio broadcasters, and others in the media.

There is a logic to our interest in specific genres.... As we get older and move through the life cycle, we face certain psychological challenges that we need to deal with and, presumably, different genres help us deal with specific problems. We are not conscious, I would add, of the problems we face or of the forces leading us to the different genres, but just as children need fairy tales when they are around five years old, and for a few years or so after that, so do adolescents need the kinds of music they listen to and the kinds of stories they are drawn to in books (for those who read books), on television and in the movies.

Stage in Life Cycle	Genre of Interest
Babies	Lullabies
Children (5 to 7)	Fairy tales
Early teens	Love, adventure, mystery
Teenagers	Science fiction, sports
Young adults, adults	News, sports, soaps, cops, etc.
Middle aged	News, soaps, etc.
Senior citizens	News, talk shows, obituaries

[From Arthur Asa Berger, *Popular Cultural Genre: Theories and Texts* (Foundations of Popular Culture, vol. 2), pp. 60–63, 66–67. Copyright © 1992 by Arthur Asa Berger. Reprinted by permission of Sage Publications, Inc.]

QUESTIONS

1. How well does Wildavsky's categorization (381) fit actual people? Think of examples from your own experience of a "hierarchical elitist," a "competitive individualist," an "egalitarian," and a "fatalist." Do you consider yourself to fit into one of these categories? Why or why not?
2. How would you extend Berger's list of genre preferences (381–83) to fit some other types of programs not covered here? Consider the following, among others: music videos; medical dramas (*ER, Chicago Hope*); situation comedies (*Roseanne, Friends,*

Murphy Brown, Cybill); evening dramas (*Beverly Hills 90210, thirtysomething, Baywatch*); police dramas (*Law & Order, Murder One*).
3. Berger assumes "that people watch television programs, go to films, and read books that support and reinforce their values and beliefs and avoid texts that challenge these beliefs." Does this describe your own choices in entertainment texts?
4. To what extent does the choice of programs reflect who people already are, and to what extent does it make them into that kind of person (at least provisionally)?
5. What do you think of the idea that audiences migrate through genres of popular culture as we age? Has this been true for you? Do you think these "genres of interest" should be modified or enlarged?
6. Does the idea of a cycle through age-groups conflict with the idea of categorizing by "political cultures"? That is, do we move from being "egalitarian" to "elitist," for example, as we age? Or do we stay consistently within one pattern, but select different texts to reflect that consistency?

Both the "political cultures" and the "seven ages of man" systems in Berger's essay can be connected with entertainment texts in such a way as to show that these texts reinforce ideologies. For example, in the mid-1960s, those who supported the U.S. involvement in Vietnam—out of patriotism, trust in national leaders, commitment to traditional ideals of masculinity, opposition to Communism, or other associated values—valued entertainment texts that harmonized with their beliefs, such as John Wayne movies, the 1965 song "The Ballad of the Green Berets," and USO shows conducted for the troops by Bob Hope and others. Those opposing U.S. involvement in Vietnam favored peace over national loyalty, or argued for reexamination of conventional male/female roles, or found the rhetoric of the Cold War inappropriate to describe what they saw as a contemporary version of colonialism—and their preferred entertainment texts included *M*A*S*H* (the film), *Easy Rider, Eve of Destruction*, folk music by Bob Dylan and others, and hard rock that put to electric accompaniment its attitude of general rebelliousness to authority.

You should not assume from this description that ideology comes in either/or separations. There are subtle gradations of ideology, and bits and pieces that circulate fairly freely; we tend to combine these in ways not entirely consistent with each other. As Berger and others point out, entertainment texts are complex: This means that they may appeal simultaneously to different age groups and personalities, who literally see different portions of the texts or interpret ambiguous characters or events in such a way as to confirm their presuppositions. So long as this keeps everyone happy, it allows producers of entertainment to stay successful and permits the regulation of potentially conflicting beliefs. But an important point to raise is that not only are *texts* often complex and contradictory—so are *selves*. We may *become* the person addressed by a text, at least for the time of our interaction with it.

PAUSE FOR REFLECTION
Sometime when watching a film or television program you take seriously, or when paying full attention to popular music, put some questions to yourself about the kind of person these texts invite you to be or pretend to be. What do you (pretend to) want to do at that time? Is this wish lasting or temporary? How does it fit with your more usual persona in dealing with others?

Playing a role, whether patriotic support of or principled opposition to overseas military engagement, has a way of enlisting our sympathy, our energy, and our thinking into causes recommended by others. We become what we play. That's the thinking behind another theory of the production of entertainment texts: that they are made in order to consolidate the position of those in positions of relative power in society. We should now consider entertainment texts such as those mentioned above in connection with hegemony.

Objections to the hegemony model take several forms. The first might be to deny the relevance of a class system to U.S. culture. (We're all equal, we're all middle-class.) Another is to deny the existence of a ruling class capable of orchestrating hegemony. But orchestrating—or even awareness—isn't necessary, if both this "ruling class" and those who are its subjects are working within an ideology that denies its relevance to what they "choose" to do. In other words, if you were to talk with the ad agency that produced the Doritos spot discussed under More Dirt above, or with the office in the corporation that worked with the agency to produce it, you would probably find little explicit discussion about hegemony. Certainly the TV producers who talked with Todd Gitlin (page 379) didn't see themselves as orchestrating hegemony. Within the subculture of those producing ads, what producers want is consciousness of (and positive associations toward) a brand name, and the camera movements, music, and narratives of the ads are just rhetorical means to get that. In other words, the producers of texts are at work within a set of assumptions so seamless that alternatives do not suggest themselves. This is not peculiar to those who produce ads or entertainment texts: As audiences, we typically read within these assumptions in the same fashion. Entertainment texts offer us a set of potential connections, and we fill these in, connecting what is left to us in a way analogous to completing a crossword puzzle or tracing between the dots. And it's important to their hegemonic function that these texts solicit our participation, because that gives us an investment in connecting the dots in that specific way. As John Hartley puts it, hegemony is an attribute of "us," not just "them" (137).

We saw how this drawing of connections works in Chapter 6, in the Cancún ad with the mountaintop temple and the woman on the beach "worshipping the sun." These two potent visual images are connected (along with the text) by readers of the ad, and we make a greater investment in connecting them that way because we seem to have done it ourselves. If hegemony is effective in its workings, it's because we have decided to play along. But have we?

The Audience's View

As Chapter 2 explained, in order to understand media, it's not enough just to look at texts. It's important to get some sense of how those texts are received by audiences. Some critical views of media are based entirely on analyses of texts, as though once a text's parts were enumerated, that was the end of the matter. It would simplify things greatly if all we needed to do was to analyze a text—but there's the issue of its reception. What are we seeing, hearing, reading, understanding, as we encounter that text? Answering that question means trying in some way to take on the audience's perspective—not only your own and projections from that, but others' perspectives as well.

What is an audience, anyway? How does one get to be part of an audience? Imagine a few hundred people in an auditorium, arranged in rows of comfortable theater-style seats. They come from a wide assortment of places: large, prosperous houses on the golf course, ordinary tract houses in the suburbs, condominiums, apartments, mobile homes, motels. They come from large cities, small towns, and farms; from in-state and out of state and even a few from other countries. They range in age from, say, nearly ninety to a few months. What makes them into this singular collective noun, an *audience*?

Each person in that grouping is grouped by coming there, and takes on an identity by that fact. All members of the audience have multiple identities—locality, type of residence, nationality, political allegiance, and many other factors help us to name these. But at the moment, their identity is *as* an audience, which is paradoxically both multiple and singular—like the *you* in this book. They are named as audience by the text they have come to hear (the word *audience* is built on hearing). This text invites them to play a role, or rather, one of several roles.

But they—*we*—don't all agree to play audience roles in the prescribed ways. For convenience we can divide audience responses into three, though there are many shadings between these. An audience member can go along with the text's proddings and prescriptions, laughing at the jokes, weeping at the sentimental parts, cheering the heroes, and hissing the villains. This could be called the **dominant response,** since that's presumably what most are doing, playing the role to which they are called. An alternative might be chosen by someone who doesn't really want to be there, who is intent on **resisting,** or playing an oppositional role. Resistant responses include that of the person who laughs at tear jerkers, or who becomes indignant at jokes felt to be in bad taste. The comic commentary carried on by the characters in *Mystery Science Theater 3000* is a good example of an oppositional role. A third position is loosely between these, **negotiating** between the role that the text invites the audience to play and an unwillingness to be so compliant.

PAUSE FOR REFLECTION
Think back on texts (entertainment or information) for which you have played each of these three roles.

How much choice does an audience have, as an audience? In our fictional example, there was no compulsion to come to that event: Many thousands of other potential audience members stayed away. But in staying away they are not part of the audience—they are not named to that role. Once we are within the framework of continuing to be an audience—because otherwise we can have nothing to say about a text—how much freedom do we have then? Are we limited to interpreting a text, or reacting to a text, exactly as its author (or corporate body functioning as an author, what Foucault calls an *author-function*) intends for us to do? How much freedom can we assert in these matters? The question has importance far beyond entertainment texts. For example, in matters of law, how limited are we to the text of the Constitution? There's a recurrent debate about whether the Second Amendment pertains to individual ownership of guns, or the maintaining of state militias such as the National Guard. Historians and scholars are pretty much agreed that the original context was keeping an organized army for public order; but a substantial portion of the public (along with the NRA and those who manufacture firearms) holds to an oppositional view, in effect rewriting the amendment so as to apply to personal firearms.

The gap between the mass addressing of audiences and the individual choice of preferred texts is spanned by hegemony. We play along with producers' roles, encoded in media, because we want to—we are led to want to, because the roles are familiar or flattering. Understanding this concept leads to thinking of media (not just entertainment media) as "Consciousness Industries," a term coined by Hans Magnus Enzensberger. Dallas Smythe wrote in *Dependency Road:*

> Today, the mass media (press, television, radio, magazines, books, cinema) are the central means of forming attitudes, values, and buying behavior—consciousness in action, to put it succinctly. They are the "shock troops" of Consciousness Industry. It is obvious to all—and is the main concern of liberal and radical critics—that the way the mass media select and present news, portray ethnic groups in the "entertainment," and handle public controversial issues powerfully affects people's behavior. (p. 4)

Smythe's discussion is echoed by others, such as Len Masterman: "[T]heir main product is *people* who are ready to buy consumer goods and to pay taxes and to work in their alienating jobs in order to continue buying tomorrow" (p. 225). In other words, in our culture media are a crucial factor in producing audiences who are good consumers, keeping the economy moving by buying products, and who play the part of good citizens by collaborating in the political system (vote, pay taxes, don't engage in terrorism, keep protests under strict limits, etc.). So, for example, the corporate interest in maximizing the sale of consumer goods leads to encouraging the ideology of individualism, with such offshoots as the prevailing view in the United States that it's up to us as individuals to protect ourselves by owning handguns, installing security devices in our cars and homes, and so on. The logical consequence of this ideology is an image of crime as caused by essentially bad individuals (rather than, say, by poverty, poor education, and absence of jobs), with the solution being to figure out who the bad guys are and lock them up. But the interaction between audience choice and ideology is a tangled problem.

Ways of thinking about the audience range through a number of possible positions. One emphasizes audience passivity: Thinking of viewers of "mass media" suggests a television audience of "couch potatoes" and other vegetable imagery. This picture coexists uncomfortably with the image of audience as consumers in a free media marketplace, choosing the programs and forms of entertainment they prefer. To put it bluntly, the audience can't be both simultaneously: Either we are dupes drifting at the will of programmers, or we are rational and informed individuals selecting among available choices. (Or, more likely, both in alternation.) Those inclined to see the audience as passive may see various dangers—the danger of commercial interests virtually compelling the public to spend money unnecessarily or unwisely, or of supposedly liberal media conspiring to corrupt public morals. Others, inclined to credit the audience with more ability to choose, may downplay talk about media texts' effect, stressing instead what are called *uses and gratifications.* In this model, the audience is not the tail but the dog, wagging various forms of media by its preferences. The concern is focused then not so much on the producers of entertainment texts as on the audience: *Why don't you like better things?*

The degree of control audiences have over texts is a matter of dispute. For some, audiences are relatively passive—citizens of television's "vast wasteland," in Newton Minow's notorious phrase. But audience passivity can be overestimated: Audiences aren't simple pawns of media programmers, or else every song, every program, every work of popular fiction would be a hit.

Ways of accounting for what will draw an audience and what won't have not been very successful. The various ways of rating media don't make good predictors: The Nielsen and other ratings simply indicate that a set is on; journals and other devices have been developed to keep track of individual responses, but these have not helped a great deal. Even "the magoo" has not been infallible.

Some media critics have made use of case-study approaches in an effort to get better information from members of the audience. Case studies can help a great deal in bridging the gap between the "mass" scale of television, film, and other forms of entertainment that address hundreds of thousands at once, and the individual perspective most people bring to entertainment. Case studies allow us to conceive of audiences as (temporary) communities, who use entertainment texts as material for exchange, as things to talk about. Some very interesting studies have been done using soap operas as texts that initiate social interchanges.

PAUSE FOR REFLECTION

To what extent do you think of the audience for an entertainment text as a community? Do you yourself affiliate with others in the act of watching a film? A television program? Attending a concert or listening to a musical group? Talking with others about a sporting event or team? Is it enough just to think about a text to qualify as a member of that community? What are some areas of similarity and difference between these sorts of communities and more literal ones?

> Television audiencehood is a pervasive social and cultural reality in the late twentieth century. In a multitude of ways, sometimes routine, sometimes exceptional, television plays an intimate role in shaping our day-to-day practices and experiences—at home but also outside

it; at work; at school; in our conversations with friends, family, and colleagues; in our engagements with society, politics, and culture (Ang, in Newcomb p. 367).

Getting some sense of the audience through case studies or ethnography can be an important corrective to projections from the text or from our fears about the text. The strength of these research tools is that they fill in a lot of the silences left by ratings and other measures. The weakness is that generalizing from a small number of people can be risky.

PAUSE FOR REFLECTION
How is your class representative of the U.S. population as a whole, and how does it differ? Does your class qualify as a "community"? You should touch on at least the following: age, region, income level, class (i.e., working class, middle class, etc.—make sure that "middle" is split and defined), kind of neighborhood (inner city, suburban, rural), racial composition, gender, ethnic backgrounds, religious backgrounds, political preferences, level of education. Is your class relatively homogeneous? Relatively heterogeneous? How do you see media (especially entertainment media) as representing or speaking to the concerns of others like you in these respects?

In making use of case studies and ethnography, keep in mind the limitations on extending your conclusions. Your class is small in relation to the audience for any medium; as college students, your classmates are probably younger and better educated than the U.S. population on average; and there may be other factors that skew the reactions relative to the population at large. But it is necessary to start somewhere. All of us ground our observations about media and rhetoric in our own personal understandings of these things—that is, on a sample of one.

Media texts do have implied audiences. One purpose of the analyzing of such texts that we've done in previous chapters has been to work from texts such as news reports and commercials toward a sense of whom the text is aimed at, whom it names as its audience (not necessarily its real audience). Elements such as the choice of spokesperson or protagonist and visual and verbal styles are codes by which we can infer an implied audience. (For a discussion of codes, see Signs, Codes, and Conventions in Chapter 6.) But the audience as *implied* by the text is not the only consideration—it might be possible in that model for the text to select among available readers or viewers, attracting the notice of some and sending others reaching for the channel changer or turning the page to another article. Rather, the more interesting consideration is that some texts *name* us as their audience and entice us to play along—in some sense to *become* their audience.

The way in which texts name us to become their audiences—in a sense, their subjects—is called *appellation* (see Appellation and Ideology in Chapter 8). Audience cooperation and interest are assumed—and by that assumption, created. (The advertising campaign for the film *Sliver* made use of the line "You like to watch, don't you," both to suggest something about the film's plot and to cast the viewer explicitly into a role as voyeur or voyeuse; promotions for *Strange Days* adopted a similar strategy.)

In the discussions of specific problems below, this should be one of the standard questions: How does the image of the audience created entice you as reader or viewer to play along? Regardless of whether the text is a daytime drama or sports broadcast, documentary or fantasy film, *Masterpiece Theater* or tabloid talk show, country or alternative song, it invites you to play a role, to become (at least provisionally) the kind of self willing to interact with it. Those who are concerned about what they see as bad taste in media are objecting only in part to the media texts themselves—the real objection is to their fellow citizens who are attracted to texts they themselves despise, think pernicious, or find in bad taste. So we should have a look at the concept of taste before getting to specific programs.

PROBLEMS

Taste

In order to consider audience preferences in entertainment, we have to look at the troublesome but necessary topic of taste. Creating and manipulating preferences is the principal means of building markets in modern economies. As we observed in Chapter 5, this manipulation is done readily and openly in advertising—and as with advertisements, many viewers of entertainment texts admit that *others* are influenced, but not they themselves.

What we like is usually regarded as the product of our own essential and unchanging nature—which conflicts both with the evidence that our tastes change over time, and with the assumption widespread in the culture that we act according to a rational calculation of self-interest. (If rational considerations were all that mattered, there would be less consumption of tobacco, alcohol, sugar, high-cholesterol foods, expensive and overpowered cars, and so on.) Whatever we think accounts for taste, it's not all out on the surface. If asked "Why do you like that?" our first response is likely to be "I don't know.

Because. You like it too." Coming to awareness of our reasons may require us to examine esthetics and other issues that we may not want to look into, or believe to be all that important, in the first place.

Another source of difficulty in talking about taste is resistance to being told by others what we *should* like. This "being told" goes back in some cases to adults' tendency to insist on children's finishing the green stuff on the plate if they want any dessert. It finds a parallel in suggestions that readers should show maturity through preferring some things to others. And a third source of difficulty in dealing with taste is the analogy sometimes drawn between cultural and political elitism, as though there were a necessary connection between liking what millions of others like and being in sympathy with them about other matters.

Perhaps we can use the literal sense of taste as a starting point for considering these matters. Before I sit down to my desk in the morning, I brew up some coffee. I could get started without black coffee, but something would be missing (besides, of course, the caffeine). My wife likes the smell of my coffee but won't drink it herself. A friend says that coffee is good but that *my* coffee will float a spoon—he dilutes it with water or milk. When my father visits, he may drink some coffee, but he prefers decaf (and, in fact, instant).

These variations on tastes in coffee are a way of presenting the subject of taste as it is usually thought of: something trivial and relatively inconsequential. In the ultimate scheme of things, it doesn't matter very much whether I drink coffee or not, or what the style of that coffee is. But apparently trivial distinctions of this sort can mask very significant differences: Taste is sometimes an indicator of sharp divisions in daily practice, which in turn are markers for differences in matters such as class or belief. A Mormon friend may not drink coffee because of a belief that it's forbidden by God, or at least by church dogma. My preference for strong coffee may come from traveling abroad. Choosing weaker coffee may derive from health concerns—cut the caffeine and you may save your heart. Coffee may be associated with pretty much the only permitted excuse to break from routine and talk with coworkers—a permissible form of resistance that serves as a safety valve. Many differences in taste that escape notice—about our preferences in entertainment as well as preferences in hot beverages—may prove to be valuable clues to what our likes and dislikes are based on, and what our choices in these matters signify.

PAUSE FOR REFLECTION
Can you think of other seemingly trivial preferences and the ways these connect to deeper issues?

In Chapter 6 we looked at signs, codes, and conventions as they apply both to everyday objects, such as highway signs, and to the complicated but largely unconscious practice of reading visual media. These signs, codes, and conventions are just as basic to entertainment texts or others as they are to traffic flow. Thinking about traffic flow as a text may serve as a useful exercise (it may at least keep you diverted the next time you are stuck in rush hour). Part of that text would be the official rules of the road (speed limits, no passing and school zones) and what we might think of as traffic manners (when to let another car into the line, how much room to allow behind the preceding car, when to dim lights, which lane to cruise in on the freeway). Anyone who has been on a U.S. road knows that there are several approaches to driving—which we might think of as several "tastes" in "reading" the text of traffic. The various road systems make these texts possible, but such texts are completed by all the drivers—who "write" these texts while driving, and who are in turn part of the texts that other drivers write. For example, if you see a driver lane-jumping in heavy freeway traffic, you may close the distance between you and the car ahead in order to prevent a jump into your lane—writing your text, for the moment, as competitive rush-hour driving. Or you may respond by easing back, either out of a generous spirit or out of concern for avoiding a possible accident, thus writing your text as (a) "We're All In This Together" or (b) "My Goal Is To Get Home Safely; I Don't Know About Yours."

Entertainment texts are not complete in themselves; in other words, they need our participation, our "writing," in order to attain full meaning. *Home Improvement* has been one of the most popular comedies on television since its introduction, and part of its popularity has been its playful adaptation of issues very much in circulation within the culture generally—particularly differences between men and women, at home and in the workplace. The first episode illustrates *Home Improvement* as a text for viewers to "write": Tim Taylor (Tim Allen) strongly associates his role as handyman and his use of power tools with traditional masculinity. (One of the shticks in the early months of the show, downplayed in later episodes, is a tendency to grunt on camera, leading the fictive *Tool Time* audience in a deep-voiced chorus.) At one point in the show, Tim's assistant Al Bourland (Richard Karn) hands him a drill; Tim says that that sort of drill would be OK for a girl, and then gets from Lisa (a very attractive woman) a much larger tool with more power.

The desire for more power (symbolically and literally) gets Tim in trouble at home. His wife, Jill (Patricia Richardson), who is the mother of three boys and anxious about her adequacy as a housewife, is preparing for a job interview. Tim, over Jill's protests, wants to demonstrate the usefulness of more power in their dishwasher by hooking up a stronger air compressor to blast dried egg yolk off a dirty dish. He installs the compressor despite her objections, and the demonstration blows the dish out the back of the dishwasher.

Audience responses to this episode can take several forms. There are several texts open to us to write, according to our tastes or, at a deeper level, according to our ideologies or who we are in our culture. There is material present for seeing Tim Taylor as a well-intentioned fool, along lines suggested by Mark Crispin Miller, as the latest "Dad-centered" joke. In terms of classical drama criticism, Tim is an *alazon* or braggart figure riding for a fall; and Jill, the boys, Al, and occasional visitors are *eirons* or ironic voices (the contemporary equivalents of the tricky servant or court fool), able to cut through Tim's pretensions with actions or observations closer to what most of the audience presumably believes or thinks. But not all the jokes go one way: In some instances the joke is on Jill or the boys, and Tim comes out ahead. These open the way for a "writing" of the text that is aligned with what might be called "Men in Power." The preferred reading in this case would be to see Tim as an imperfect example of right relationships between men and women, rather than as a demonstration of the inadequacy of his perspective.

There are, of course, more possibilities. It's possible to see *Home Improvement* as another instance of television's talking to a select but substantial fraction of its audience but "writing out" others: those who have no hope of owning a home, those who prefer love relations with people of their own sex, those who find changes in how men and women relate to each other to be so threatening that you shouldn't joke about it, and so on. Presumably most such people would choose not to watch or talk about *Home Improvement,* and if asked about it would say that *it's just a matter of taste.* Appeals to taste are often polite but insistent ways of changing the subject.

Taste, then, is anything but trivial. *What we like* is an index to *who we are* in relation to the larger culture. There are two prevailing positions on issues of taste, and both are in some respects evasions of difficult and possibly threatening issues. First, what might be called the *de gustibus* position. The Latin *de gustibus non est disputandum* expresses the idea that there is no point in arguing about tastes. In this view, we like what we like naturally. Accepting *de gustibus* might suggest that human beings are as they are and don't change tastes—but it's fairly easy to see that's not true. Many tastes are acquired.

Second is the position that taste corresponds roughly but reliably with class. What you like, according to this explanation, is not a matter of nature but of social origins. A preference for espresso or cappuccino might be a marker for more expensive (read higher-class) tastes, whereas flavored coffees might be suburban and middle-class, and plain ordinary coffee solidly middle-class or lower. Class preferences become obvious when those writing about taste are denouncing the vulgarity of much popular culture, as for example in the list from James Twitchell:

> I tell [my kids] that Madonna videos are vulgar, as are Stephen King novels, *Screw* magazine, Van Halen, John McEnroe, Las Vegas, the Trump Tower, dances like the Lambada, Mr. T., professional wrestling, Batman, Opal Gardner, "graphic novels," Velcro, Cher, costume jewelry, almost anything reported on in *People*, Joan Rivers, clothing with someone's name on it, Geraldo Rivera, anything that the adjective "loud" can be used in front of, Rupert Murdoch, Richard Simmons, Houston, Texas, Joan and Jackie Collins, Benny Hill, the late Billy Martin, *USA Today*, confrontainment television with Mort Downey, Jr., paintings on velvet, electrified musical instruments, monstrous bodybuilding, Barry Manilow concerts, Ed Koch's campaigns (when he was running for mayor of New York City), political advertising in general, the second edition of the *Random House Dictionary*, Brian Bosworth, Mick Jagger, Donald Trump, any Aaron Spelling production, men's suits that shine, the Philip Morris Company trucking around the Bill of Rights, Countess Mara ties, Rodeo Drive boutiques, almost all top-forty music and rap music, diamond jewelry for men, any movie with a sequel, music by Michel Legrand, Forest Lawn, paintings by Leroy Neiman, full-length leather coats, George Steinbrenner, Larry Flynt, Jerry Falwell, Hawaiian shirts, Tammy Bakker, Disneyland and World, Chuck Barris, anything on prime-time television with a market share of more than 10, any large building by John Portman, belt buckles that look like silver dollars, roller derbies, anything that shines.... "Everything fun is vulgar to you, Dad," they say, as I continue listing away. (Twitchell p. 14)

PAUSE FOR REFLECTION

What do you make of Twitchell's list of what's "vulgar"? Could you compile either your own extension of this list, or a counterlist—say, a list of what's snooty? What defines "vulgar"? (Look up the word's root.) How does it compare to the near-synonyms "tacky" and "kitschy"? (You may notice that, at least in this passage, Twitchell permits the same ironic undercutting of his role as Dad and authority figure that most sitcoms encourage in their conceptions.)

Neither *de gustibus* nor popular culture as vulgar carry us very far, however, toward understanding how entertainment looks from the audience's perspective. Both are judgments about the audience taken from the outside. Both regard taste as static: According to the first account, someone who appeals to you about your likes and dislikes is suggesting that you change your essential nature; according to the second, such a suggestion is a criticism of your social status, of who you are. Using the singular word *audience* masks the fact that what we have are audience*s* that are divided from each other precisely by likes and dislikes, by taste.

Radio stations select their formats in such a way as to *drive off* listeners not in their preferred demographic category:

> The "top-forty" hit tune format, with its mixture of genres, gave way to stations whose selections were locked into a particular musical type. Recordings were selected for broadcast through a practice known as "negative programming" to produce minimum aversion among the targeted group of listeners and meet advertisers' requirements. A broadcasting executive: "We did shrink our teens by intent and we have improved the 25- to 49-year-old figures by eliminating hard rock." (Bogart p. 114)

If we take seriously the idea implied in the Fact above, that entertainment media exist for the purpose of grouping people into audiences in order to sell advertisements, then our individual likes and dislikes aren't particularly of interest to those who produce media texts—only how those preferences can be used to shape demographics. You can test this out by observing which products are advertised at specified hours of the day and in association with certain program categories, on radio or television. Products sponsoring Paul Harvey or pre-rock and roll popular music suggest that most listeners are in an upper age bracket, divided by gender; those for sports talk radio would be across a wider spectrum of ages, but more male than female; "classic rock" reaches baby boomers of both genders; "soft rock" would be similar by age, but shifted more to women; "progressive rock" younger on average, with top-forty rock younger still, and so on.

Dividing programming by demographics, again, tends to stress biological or other factors beyond our control. But most of our market preferences are taught and maintained by media and other devices. Women do not automatically gravitate toward soap operas any more than men do to sports programs (and, in fact, men who have time available in that part of the day sometimes get "hooked" on soaps). What is of interest is deciding what factors in programs work to create and maintain audiences.

As we have seen, *entertainment* is a term that covers a highly diverse set of texts and activities. The following sections are meant to demonstrate some ways of reading entertainment, and to suggest some areas of further work. This chapter (and this book) will reach its full potential only when readers extend the discussion to the ever-evolving media materials around them.

The cliché is that there's nothing new under the sun; the reality is that new entertainment texts are appearing all the time, and even some new forms of entertainment—but they fall into consistent and rather conservative cultural relations. As audiences, we may not always be looking in the same places, but we *are* generally looking for the same sorts of diversions.

Popular Music

Entertainment texts come in many forms. One of the most pervasive in twentieth-century U.S. culture, and one that this culture excels in, is popular music.

To gain a sense of how popular music connects with some of the themes discussed in this chapter, it may be useful to work initially with music at some distance from our own time and place. You may want to use "Swinging on a Star," discussed below; this song was featured in the 1944 film *Going My Way*, starring Bing Crosby; it has been recorded by Crosby, Frank Sinatra, and Liza Minnelli, among others.

The music is catchy and interesting, and keeps you wanting to sing along. The pattern set out in the lyrics is an alternation between the low and down-to-earth (animals) and high aspirations—both figuratively and literally (swing on a star, carry moonbeams home in a jar). These hopes are equated with being "better off than you are"; *better* is an ideal not linked to anything material, so that the ambiguity serves to inspire both moral uplift and getting ahead in the world. Such a double reference to spiritual and physical resembles what happened to the New England Puritan ethic. Some of the more prominent Puritans held the conviction that God would give a sign of his favor to the elect; over time, with the prosperity of that section of the colonies, this religious certitude evolved to an acceptance of material prosperity as evidence of moral rectitude (an attitude very much with us today). That acceptance can be traced in attitudes found in the United States after World War II—self-satisfaction with our prosperity and assertions of the moral rightness of our way of life, in contrast to communism, which is defined as the negation of these virtues. This may seem to be a lot of freight for such a light song; but entertainment texts work by signaling ideologies already present in listeners.

The opposite pole to "swinging on a star" is to be an animal of some sort—and not just any sort, but an animal with traits disagreeable to the society listeners are invited to join. The mule, the first mentioned, is definitely working class. "His back is brawny and his brain is weak, / He's just plain stupid with a stubborn streak." The "animal" lines are spoken/sung by the boys in the film—the contrast between their amateurish performances and Crosby's smoothness may indicate the distance between being (not just swinging on) a star, and playing an urchin or being a child extra in a film. The pig, the lyrics' second animal, introduces personal hygiene and manners to the discussion (dirty face, disgraceful shoes, sloppy eating habits). The fish is like the mule in wanting to avoid education, but his form of resistance is deception rather than stubbornness or just being gross. "To fool the people is his only thought, / Although he's slippery, he still gets caught." The last of the animals, the monkeys, aren't described in similar images; presumably it's enough just to mention monkeys. (It may be significant that the monkeys are the only animal referred to in the plural.) Monkeys are notorious for wanting to play rather than study and work seriously. What's at work in this song? What traits do the animals have in common? They all like to have their own way—expressed here as individual willfulness—rather than cooperating with others in school, war, and other valuable social enterprises.

Crosby performed this song in the character of a young priest in *Going My Way*. In the film, before taking religious orders, he had had a career as a swing pianist and songwriter; and he draws on these talents to try to earn some money for St. Brigid's Church. (The contrast with the older priest is one way the film presents its ideology: The way to revitalize the church is to be cool and hip, not to hold to traditional, stiff ways.) In the course of the film, Crosby cajoles some of the neighborhood boys into serving as a choir (which they do very capably), and a woman friend (obviously disappointed to see him in his clerical collar) who is a renowned opera star agrees to perform the song "Going My Way" for potential publishers. They don't like that song, but they hear "Swinging on a Star" as they are walking out and seize on it as hit material. In other words, the song's placement in the plot of the film enacts the kind of vague and improbable success that the lyrics encourage the audience to long for.

How does one get from good table manners, willingness to go to school, and the other traits opposite to those of the animals, to "swinging on a star"? The songs don't offer a program for this transformation, other than going to school and working hard. It might be objected that not everyone who goes to school and works hard manages to perform fantastic astronomical feats, or even to become the sort of Hollywood star represented by Bing Crosby. But the aspiration to "be better than you are" may promote a positive attitude, which helps to keep the whole socioeconomic machine going.

ASSIGNMENT

Look for other songs from this period (i.e., popular film music and songs from between the world wars) that encourage thinking about advancing oneself in a distant and vague way. Examples: "When You Wish upon a Star" from *Pinocchio*, or "Over the Rainbow" from *The Wizard of Oz*. Later musicals would be good points of comparison, such as *My Fair Lady*, *West Side Story*, or *The Sound of Music*.

Songs today are likely to be less direct than "Swinging on a Star" in encouraging audiences to pull together for the common good. That sort of message was more common earlier in U.S. history, and especially during World War II. Particularly after the period of prosperity following the war, attitudes encouraged by popular music became more likely to connect with individual consumption than with pulling together to get a good education and reach for the stars.

Of course, many songs take an oblique, even satirical, stance. "New Age Girl," for example, directs attention to ways of living presumably not shared (sincerely) by the speaker of the song. The girl "don't eat meat, but she sure likes the bone." The lyrics below, to "Mr. Sellack," mix satire and pathos.

THE ROCHES

"Mr. Sellack"

Oh, Mr. Sellack,
Can I have my job back?
I've run out of money again.
Last time I saw ya,
I was singing "Hallelujah,
I'm so glad to be leaving this restaurant."

Now the only thing I want
Is to have my old job back again.
I'll clean the table,
I'll do the greens,
I'll get down on my knees and scrub behind the steam table.

Oh, Mr. Sellack,
I didn't think I'd be back.
I worked here last year, remember?

I came when Annie was going on vacation
And I stayed on almost 'til December.

Now the only thing I want
Is to have my old job back again.
I won't be nasty to customers no more;
When they send their burger back, I'll tell them
"Thanks, I'm sorry."

Waiting tables ain't that bad.
Since I've seen you last,
I've waited for some things that you would not believe
To come true.

Give me a broom and I'll sweep my way to heaven,
Give me a job, you name it.
Let the other forty million, three hundred and seven
People who want to, get famous.

Now the only thing I want
Is to have that old job back again.
I'll clean the table,
I'll do the greens,
I'll get down on my knees and scrub behind the steam table.

[Song by The Roches, used by permission of DeShufflin Inc.]

"Mr. Sellack" isn't as straightforward in its treatment as some other songs (Joni Mitchell's "Big Yellow Taxi," Pete Seeger's "Little Boxes," or Simon and Garfunkel's "Big Bright Green Pleasure Machine," to pick three from the 1960s and 1970s)—it mixes in some sympathy for the speaker's disillusionment at chasing after fantasies of fame. Still, popular songs should illustrate that the point of reading entertainment texts this way is not to look for Deep Meaning. Connections with ideology are not hidden, but obvious. Finding connections to ideology in entertainment texts doesn't require you to play the tape backwards or interpret the album cover for Satanic symbols: The direct sorts of connections are effective enough.

Rock is a popular form, and it's not easy to decide how much connection to draw with histories of the artistic genres from which it draws. Like many popular arts, rock tends to convey the message that the past doesn't matter, that it's irrelevant (or, worse, boring), that individual actions and attitudes do and should outweigh thinking about culture. It's more than just convenient that this message connects with consumerism: Messages to live spontaneously in the moment can easily translate into encouragement for following impulses to buy things or for living in such a way as to require spending a lot.

Violence

One of the hot-button issues in discussions of entertainment in recent years has been the representation of violence, particularly in films and on television. The following three essays set out useful perspectives on this issue.

CARL M. CANNON

Honey, I Warped the Kids: The Argument for Eliminating Movie and TV Violence
Tim Robbins and Susan Sarandon implore the nation to treat Haitians with AIDS more humanely. Robert Redford works for the environment. Harry Belafonte marches against the death penalty. Actors and producers seem to be constantly speaking out for noble causes far removed from their lives. But in the one area over which they have control—the excessive violence in the entertainment industry—Hollywood activists remain silent.

The first congressional hearings on the effects of TV violence took place in 1954. Although television was still relatively new, its extraordinary marketing power was already evident. The tube was teaching Americans what to buy and how to act, not only in advertisements, but in dramatic shows, too.

Everybody from Hollywood producers to Madison Avenue ad men would boast about this power—and seek to use it on dual tracks: to make money and to remake society along better lines.

Because it seemed ludicrous to assert that there was only one area—the depiction of violence—where television did not influence behavior, the TV industry came up with this theory: Watching violence is cathartic. A violent person might be sated by watching a murder.

The notion intrigued social scientists, and by 1956 they were studying it in earnest. Unfortunately, watching violence turned out to be anything but cathartic.

In the 1956 study, one dozen 4-year-olds watched a "Woody Woodpecker" cartoon that was full of violent images. Twelve other preschoolers watched "Little Red Hen," a peaceful cartoon. Afterward, the children who watched "Woody Woodpecker" were more likely to hit other children, verbally accost their classmates, break toys, be disruptive, and engage in destructive behavior during free play.

For the next 30 years, researchers in all walks of the social sciences studied the question of whether television causes violence. The results have been stunningly conclusive.

"There is more published research on this topic than on almost any other social issue of our time," University of Kansas Professor Aletha C. Huston, chair of the American

Psychological Association's Task Force on Television and Society, told Congress in 1988. "Virtually all independent scholars agree that there is evidence that television can cause aggressive behavior."

There have been some 3,000 studies of this issue—85 of them major research efforts—and they all say the same thing. Of the 85 major studies, the only one that failed to find a causal relationship between TV violence and actual violence was paid for by NBC. When the study was subsequently reviewed by three independent social scientists, all three concluded that it actually did demonstrate a causal relationship.

Some highlights from the history of TV violence research:

- In 1973, when a town in mountainous western Canada was wired for TV signals, University of British Columbia researchers observed first- and second-graders. Within two years, the incidence of hitting, biting, and shoving increased 160 percent.
- Two Chicago doctors, Leonard Eron and Rowell Heusmann, followed the viewing habits of a group of children for 22 years. They found that watching violence on television is the single best predictor of violent or aggressive behavior later in life, ahead of such commonly accepted factors as parents' behavior, poverty, and race.

    "Television violence affects youngsters of all ages, of both genders, at all socio-economic levels and all levels of intelligence," they told Congress in 1992. "The effect is not limited to children who are already disposed to being aggressive and is not restricted to this country."
- In 1988, researchers Daniel G. Linz and Edward Donnerstein of the University of California, Santa Barbara, and Steven Penrod of the University of Wisconsin studied the effects on young men of horror movies and "slasher" films.

    They found that depictions of violence, not sex, are what desensitizes people. They divided male students into four groups. One group watched no movies, a second watched nonviolent X-rated movies, a third watched teenage sexual-innuendo movies, and a fourth watched the slasher films *Texas Chainsaw Massacre, Friday the 13th, Part 2, Maniac,* and *Toolbox Murders*.

    All the young men were placed on a mock jury panel and asked a series of questions designed to measure their empathy for an alleged female rape victim. Those in the fourth group measured lowest in empathy for the specific victim in the experiment—and for rape victims in general.

The anecdotal evidence is often more compelling than the scientific studies. Ask any homicide cop from London to Los Angeles to Bangkok if TV violence induces real-life violence and listen carefully to the cynical, knowing laugh.

Ask David McCarthy, police chief in Greenfield, Massachusetts, why 19-year-old Mark Branch killed himself after stabbing an 18-year-old female college student to death.

When cops searched his room they found 90 horror movies, as well as a machete and a goalie mask like those used by Jason, the grisly star of *Friday the 13th*.

Or ask Sergeant John O'Malley of the New York Police Department about a 9-year-old boy who sprayed a Bronx office building with gunfire. The boy explained to the astonished sergeant how he learned to load his Uzi-like firearm: "I watch a lot of TV."

Numerous groups have called, over the years, for curbing TV violence: the National Commission on the Causes and Prevention of Violence (1969), the U.S. Surgeon General (1972), the National Institute of Mental Health (1982), and the American Psychological Association (1992) among them.

During that time, cable television and movie rentals have made violence more readily available while at the same time pushing the envelope for network television. But even leaving aside cable and movie rentals, a study of TV programming from 1967 to 1989 showed only small ups and downs in violence, with the violent acts moving from one time slot to another but the overall violence rate remaining pretty steady—and pretty similar from network to network.

"The percent of prime-time programs using violence remains more than seven out of ten, as it has been for the entire 22-year period," researchers George Gerbner of the University of Pennsylvania Annenberg School of Communication and Nancy Signorielli of the University of Delaware wrote in 1990. For the past 22 years, they found, adults and children have been entertained by about 16 violent acts, including two murders, in each evening's prime-time programming.

They also discovered that the rate of violence in children's programs is three times the rate in prime-time shows. By the age of 18, the average American child has witnessed at least 18,000 simulated murders on television.

But all of the scientific studies and reports, all of the wisdom of cops and grief of parents have run up against Congress' quite proper fear of censorship. For years, Democratic Congressman Peter Rodino of New Jersey chaired the House Judiciary Committee and looked at calls for some form of censorship with a jaundiced eye. At a hearing [in 1988], Rodino told witnesses that Congress must be a "protector of commerce."

"Well, we have children that we need to protect," replied Frank M. Palumbo, a pediatrician at Georgetown University Hospital and a consultant to the American Academy of Pediatrics. "What we have here is a toxic substance in the environment that is harmful to children."

Arnold Fege of the national PTA added, "Clearly, this committee would not protect teachers who taught violence to children. Yet why would we condone children being exposed to a steady diet of TV violence year after year?"

[Reprinted with permission from *Mother Jones* magazine, June–August 1993. Copyright © 1993, Foundation for National Progress.]

JOHN LEONARD

TV and the Decline of Civilization
Like a warrior-king of Sumer, daubed with sesame oil, gorged on goat, hefting up his sword and drum, Senator Ernest Hollings looked down November 23 from a ziggurat to intone, all over the op-ed page of the *New York Times*: "If the TV and cable industries have no sense of shame, we must take it upon ourselves to stop licensing their violence-saturated programming."

Hollings, of course, is co-sponsor in the Senate, with Daniel Inouye, of a ban on any act of violence on television before, say, midnight. Never mind whether this is constitutional, or what it would do to the local news. Never mind, either, that in Los Angeles last August, in the International Ballroom of the Beverly Hilton, in front of 600 industry executives, the talking heads—a professor here, a producer there, a child psychologist and a network veep for program standards—couldn't even agree on a definition of violence. (Is it only violent if it hurts or kills?) And they disagreed on which was worse, a "happy" violence that sugarcoats aggressive behavior or a "graphic" violence that at least suggests consequences. (How, anyway, does television manage somehow simultaneously to *desensitize* and to *incite*?) Nor were they really sure what goes on in the dreamy heads of our children as they crouch in the dark to commune with the tube while their parents, if they have any, aren't around. (*Road Runner*? Beep-beep.) Nor does the infamous scarlet V "parent advisory" warning even apply to cartoons, afternoon soaps, or Somalias.

Never mind, because everybody agrees that watching television causes antisocial behavior, especially among the children of the poor; that there seems to be more violent programming on the air now than there ever was before; that *Beavis and Butthead* inspired an Ohio 5-year-old to burn down the family trailer; that in the blue druidic light of television we will have spawned generations of toadstools and triffids.

In fact, there is less violence on network television than there used to be; because of ratings, it's mostly sitcoms. The worst stuff is the Hollywood splatterflicks; they're found on premium cable, which means the poor are less likely to be watching. Everywhere else on cable, not counting the court channel or home shopping and not even to think about blood sports and Pat Buchanan, the fare is innocent to the point of stupefaction (Disney, Discovery, Family, Nickelodeon). That Ohio trailer wasn't even wired for cable, so the littlest firebird must have got his MTV elsewhere in the dangerous neighborhood. (And kids have been playing with matches since, at least, Prometheus. I recall burning down my very own bedroom when I was 5 years old. The fire department had to tell my mother that the evidence pointed to me.) Since the '60s, according to statistics cited by Douglas Davis in *The Five Myths of Television Power*, more Americans than ever before are going out to eat in restaurants, see films, plays, and baseball games, visit museums, travel abroad, jog, even *read*. Watching television, everybody does *something else* at the same time. While our children are playing with their Adobe Illustrators and Domark Virtual Reality Toolkits, the rest of us eat, knit, smoke, dream, read magazines, sign checks, feel sorry for ourselves, think about Hillary, and plot shrewd career moves or revenge.

Actually watching television, unless it's C-Span, is usually more interesting than the proceedings of Congress. Or what we read in hysterical books like Jerry Mander's *Four Arguments for the Elimination of Television*, or George Gilder's *Life After Television*, or Marie Winn's *The Plug-In Drug*, or Neil Postman's *Amusing Ourselves to Death*, or Bill McKibben's *The Age of Missing Information*. Or what we'll hear at panel discussions on censorship, where right-wingers worry about sex and left-wingers worry about violence. Or just lolling around an academic deepthink-tank, trading mantras like "violence profiles" (George Gerbner), "processed culture" (Richard Hoggart), "narcoleptic joys" (Michael Sorkin), and "glass teat" (Harlan Ellison).

Of *course* something happens to us when we watch television; networks couldn't sell their millions of pairs of eyes to advertising agencies, nor would ad agencies buy more than $21 billion worth of commercial time each year, if speech (and sound, and motion) didn't somehow modify action. But what happens is far from clear and won't be much clarified by lab studies, however longitudinal, of habits and behaviors isolated from the larger feedback loop of a culture full of gaudy contradictions. The only country in the world that watches more television than we do is Japan, and you should see its snuff movies and pornographic comic books; but the Japanese are pikers compared with us when we compute per capita rates of rape and murder. Some critics in India tried to blame the recent rise in communal violence there on a state-run television series dramatizing the *Mahabharata*, but not long ago they were blaming Salman Rushdie, as in Bangladesh they have decided to blame the writer Taslima Nasrin. No Turk I know attributes skinhead violence to German TV. It's foolish to pretend that all behavior is mimetic, and that our only model is Spock or Brokaw. Or Mork and Mindy. Why, after so many years of M*A*S*H, weekly in prime time and nightly in reruns, aren't all of us out there hugging trees and morphing dolphins? Why, with so many sitcoms, aren't all of us comedians?

But nobody watches television the way congressmen, academics, symposiasts, and Bill McKibbens do. We are less thrilling. For instance:

On March 3, 1993, a Wednesday, midway through the nine-week run of *Homicide* on NBC, in an episode written by Tom Fontana and directed by Martin Campbell, Baltimore detectives Bayliss (Kyle Secor) and Pembleton (Andre Braugher) had 12 hours to wring a confession out of "Arab" Tucker (Moses Gunn) for the strangulation and disemboweling of an 11-year-old girl. In the dirty light and appalling intimacy of a single claustrophobic room, with a whoosh of wind sound like some dread blowing in from empty Gobi spaces, among maps, library books, diaries, junk food, pornographic crime-scene photographs, and a single black overflowing ashtray, these three men seemed as nervous as the hand-held cameras—as if their black coffee were full of jumping beans, amphetamines, and spiders; as if God himself were jerking them around.

Well, you may think the culture doesn't really need another cop show. And, personally, I'd prefer a weekly series in which social problems are solved through creative nonviolence, after a Quaker meeting, by a collective of vegetarian carpenters. But in a single hour, for which Tom Fontana eventually won an Emmy, I learned more about the behavior of fearful men in small rooms than from any number of better-known movies, plays, and novels on the topic by the likes of Don DeLillo, Mary McCarthy, Alberto Moravia, Heinrich Böll, and Doris Lessing....

[T]elevision is always there for us, a 24-hour user-friendly magic box grinding out narrative, novelty, and distraction, news and laughs, snippets of high culture, remedial seriousness and vulgar celebrity, an incitement and a sedative, a place to celebrate and a place to mourn, a circus and a wishing well.

And suddenly Napoleon shows up, like a popsicle, on *Northern Exposure*, while Chris on the radio is reading Proust. Or Roseanne is about lesbianism instead of bowling. Or *Picket Fences* has moved on, from serial bathers and elephant abuse to euthanasia and gay-bashing.

Kurt Vonnegut on Showtime! David ("Masturbation") Mamet on TNT! Norman Mailer wrote the TV screenplay for *The Executioner's Song*, and Gore Vidal gave us *Lincoln* with Mary Tyler Moore as Mary Todd. In just the past five years, if I hadn't been watching television, I'd have missed *Tanner '88*, when Robert Altman and Garry Trudeau ran Michael Murphy for president of the United States; *My Name is Bill W.*, with James Woods as the founding father of Alcoholics Anonymous; *The Final Days*, with Theodore Bikel as Henry Kissinger; *No Place Like Home*, where there wasn't one for Christine Lahti and Jeff Daniels, as there hadn't been one for Jane Fonda in *The Dollmaker* and Mare Winningham in *God Bless the Child*; *Eyes on the Prize*, a home movie in two parts about America's second civil war; *The Last Best Year*, with Mary Tyler Moore and Bernadette Peters learning to live with their gay sons and HIV; *Separate but Equal*, with Sidney Poitier as Thurgood Marshall; and *High Crimes and Misdemeanors*, the Bill Moyers special on Irangate and the scandal of our intelligence agencies; Graham Greene, John Updike, Philip Roth, Gloria Naylor, Arthur Miller, and George Eliot, plus Paul Simon and Stephen Sondheim. Not to mention—guiltiest of all our secrets—those hoots without which any popular culture would be as tedious as a John Cage or an Anaïs Nin, like Elizabeth Taylor in *Sweet Bird of Youth* and the Redgrave sisters in a remake of *Whatever Happened to Baby Jane?*

What all this television has in common is narrative. Even network news—which used to be better than most newspapers before the bean counters started closing down overseas bureaus and the red camera lights went out all over Europe and Asia and Africa—is in the storytelling business. And so far no one in Congress has suggested banning narrative.

Because I watch all those despised network TV movies, I know more about racism, ecology, homelessness, gun control, child abuse, gender confusion, date rape, and AIDS than is dreamt of by, say, Katie Roiphe, the Joyce Maynard of Generation X, or than Hollywood has ever bothered to tell me, especially about AIDS. Imagine, Jonathan Demme's

Philadelphia opened in theaters around the country well after at least a dozen TV movies on AIDS that I can remember without troubling my hard disk. And I've learned something else, too.

We were a violent culture before television, from Wounded Knee to the lynching bee, and we'll be one after all our children have disappeared by video game into the pixels of cyberspace. Before television, we blamed public schools for what went wrong with the Little People back when classrooms weren't overcrowded in buildings that weren't falling down in neighborhoods that didn't resemble Beirut, and whose fault is that? *The A-Team?* We can't control guns, or drugs, and each year two million American women are assaulted by their male partners, who are usually in an alcoholic rage, and whose fault is that? *Miami Vice?* The gangs that menace our streets aren't home watching Cinemax, and neither are the sociopaths who make bonfires, in our parks, from our homeless, of whom there are at least a million, a supply-side migratory tide of the deindustrialized and dispossessed, of angry beggars, refugee children, and catatonic nomads, none of them traumatized by *Twin Peaks.* So cut Medicare, kick around the Brady Bill, and animadvert Amy Fisher movies. But children who are loved and protected long enough to grow up to have homes and respect and lucky enough to have jobs don't riot in the streets. Ours is a tantrum culture that measures everyone by his or her ability to produce wealth, and morally condemns anybody who fails to prosper, and now blames Burbank for its angry incoherence. Why not recessive genes, angry gods, lousy weather? The mafia, the zodiac, the *Protocols of the Elders of Zion?* Probability theory, demonic possession, Original Sin? George Steinbrenner? Sunspots?

[Reprinted with permission from *The Nation* magazine, December 27, 1993. Copyright © The Nation Company, L.P.]

TODD GITLIN

Imagebusters: The Hollow Crusade against TV Violence
I have denounced movie violence for more than two decades, all the way back to *The Wild Bunch* and *The Godfather.* I consider Hollywood's slashes, splatters, chain saws, and car crashes a disgrace, a degradation of culture, and a wound to the souls of producers and consumers alike.

But I also think liberals are making a serious mistake by pursuing their vigorous campaign against violence in the media. However morally and aesthetically reprehensible today's screen violence, the crusades of Senator Paul Simon and Attorney General Janet Reno against television violence are cheap shots. There are indeed reasons to attribute violence to the media, but the links are weaker than recent headlines would have one believe. The attempt to demonize the media distracts attention from the real causes of—and the serious remedies for—the epidemic of violence.

The sheer volume of alarm can't be explained by the actual violence generated by the media's awful images. Rather, Simon and Reno—not to mention Dan Quayle and the Reverend Donald Wildmon—have signed up for a traditional American pastime. The campaign against the devil's images threads through the history of middle-class reform movements. For a nation that styles itself practical, at least in technical pursuits, the United States has always been remarkably quick to become a playground of moral prohibitions and symbolic crusades.

If today's censorious forces smell smoke, it is not in the absence of fire. In recent years, market forces have driven screen violence to an amazing pitch. But the question the liberal crusaders fail to address is not whether these violent screen images are wholesome but just how much real-world violence can be blamed on the media. Assume, for the sake of argument, that *every* copycat crime reported in the media can be plausibly traced to television and movies. Let us make an exceedingly high estimate that the resulting carnage results in 100 deaths per year that would not otherwise have taken place. These would amount to 0.28 percent of the total of 36,000 murders, accidents, and suicides committed by gunshot in the United States in 1992.

That media violence contributes to a climate in which violence is legitimate—and there can be no doubt of this—does not make it an urgent social problem. Violence on the screens, however loathsome, does not make a significant contribution to violence on the streets. Images don't spill blood. Rage, equipped with guns, does. Desperation does. Revenge does. As liberals say, the drug trade does; poverty does; unemployment does. It seems likely that a given percent increase in decently paying jobs will save thousands of times more lives than the same percent decrease in media bang-bang.

Now, I also give conservative arguments about the sources of violence their due. A culture that despises and disrespects authority is disposed to aggression, so people look to violence to resolve conflict. The absence of legitimate parental authority also feeds a culture of aggression. But aggression per se, however unpleasant, is not the decisive murderous element. A child who shoves another child after watching a fistfight on television is not committing a drive-by shooting. Violence plays on big screens around the world without generating epidemics of carnage. The necessary condition permitting a culture of aggression to flare into a culture of violence is access to lethal weapons.

It's dark out there in the world of real violence, hopelessness, drugs, and guns. There is little political will for a war on poverty, guns, or family breakdown. Here, under the light, we are offered instead a crusade against media violence. This is largely a feel-good exercise, a moral panic substituting for practicality. It appeals to an American propensity that sociologist Philip Slater called the Toilet Assumption: Once the appearance of a social problem is swept out of sight, so is the problem. And the crusade costs nothing.

There is, for some liberals, an additional attraction. By campaigning against media violence, they hope to seize "family values" from conservatives. But the mantle of antiviolence they wrap themselves in is threadbare, and they are showing off new clothes that will not stop bullets.

The symbolic crusade against media violence is a confession of despair. Those who embrace it are saying, in effect, that they either do not know how, or do not dare, to do anything serious about American violence. They are tilting at images. If Janet Reno cites the American Psychological Association's recently published report, *Violence and Youth*, to indict television, she also should take note of the following statements within it: "Many social science disciplines, in addition to psychology, have firmly established that poverty and its contextual life circumstances are major determinants of violence.... It is very likely that socioeconomic inequality—not race—facilitates higher rates of violence among ethnic minority groups.... There is considerable evidence that the alarming rise in youth homicides is related to the availability of firearms." The phrase "major determinant" does not appear whenever the report turns to the subject of media violence.

The question for reformers, then, is one of proportion and focus. If there were nothing else to do about deadly violence in America, then the passionate crusade against TV violence might be more justifiable, even though First Amendment absolutists would still have strong counterarguments. But the imagebusting campaign permits politicians to fulminate photogenically without having to take on the National Rifle Association or, for that matter, the drug epidemic, the crisis of the family, or the shortage of serious jobs.

So let a thousand criticisms bloom. Let reformers flood the networks and cable companies and, yes, advertisers, with protests against the gross overabundance of the stupid, the tawdry, and the ugly.

But not least, let the reformers not only turn off the set, but also criticize the form of life that has led so many to turn, and keep, it on.

[Reprinted with permission from *The American Prospect*, winter 1994. Copyright © 1994 New Prospect, Inc.]

QUESTIONS
1. Write a sentence or two for each of the three essays above, condensing each writer's argument concerning television violence. (For each reading, be sure to check your sentences carefully to make sure they match up with the main point of the entire essay, not just with an illustration or an early point.) How do the writers' perspectives differ?
2. What do you see as the importance of naming specific people and giving illustrations in each essay?
3. Besides specific illustrations connected to their arguments, what else do these writers refer to? What is the reason for these references?
4. What kind of evidence and argument could potentially convince you to change your perspective on the subject of TV violence?

Children's Entertainment

As you read the two movie reviews below, look for labels or short descriptions of the positions taken by reviewers and by those represented in the review. (Is it possible to hold two or more such positions?)

DAVID FOSTER

Sexist? Racist? Violent?

Sexist. Racist. Homophobic. Violent. Even, perhaps, a threat to democratic ideals. What kind of depraved entertainment could generate such bitter epithets? A Snoop Doggy Dogg video? An Andrew Dice Clay concert?

Would you believe *The Lion King*, Disney's G-rated, coming-of-age saga that's well on its way toward becoming the highest-grossing animated film in history? Believe it.

Some parents, psychologists and pundits read between the lions and see not family fun but shocking violence and offensive stereotypes: subservient lionesses, jive-talking hyenas, a swishy Uncle Scar, a father's murder.

"The movie is full of stereotypes," Harvard psychologist Carolyn Newberger complained in an op-ed piece for *The Boston Globe*.

"The good-for-nothing hyenas are urban blacks; the arch-villain's gestures are effeminate, and he speaks in supposed gay clichés."

The movie's plot is a sort of Hamlet-meets-Abbott-and-Costello-in-the-jungle: The lion king Mufasa is murdered by his evil brother Scar, who then lays the blame on Mufasa's son and heir, Simba.

Riddled with guilt, Simba runs away and is befriended by a warthog named Pumbaa and a meerkat named Timon who teach him to forget his troubles. Scar takes over and the kingdom plunges into chaos.

Eventually, Simba returns to overthrow Scar and reclaim his rightful crown. In between, there's lots of singing and dancing and a few bad vaudevillian jokes.

Criticism isn't new for Disney. Parents still fret about the death of Bambi's mother.

Some feminists are uncomfortable with the prince-as-savior themes in *Sleeping Beauty*, *Snow White and the Seven Dwarfs*, and *Cinderella*. More recently, some Arab-Americans denounced *Aladdin* as racist.

Ann Adams of Cotuit, Mass., said she hadn't planned to take her 3 ½-year-old daughter to *The Lion King*, but gave in after listening to Allison count the days to the movie's premiere.

Now she wishes she hadn't. She feels deceived by the movie's G rating.

"It's supposed to be a family show, a movie that you can take any child to," Adams said. "We ended up sitting in the lobby for half the movie. Bambi was a piece of cake next to this."

Adams cited the scene most often criticized: the murder of Mufasa, in which the lion falls to his death as Simba watches. That scene, along with the climactic battle between a grown Simba and Scar, has prompted some psychiatrists to recommend that preschoolers and sensitive older children not see the film.

"It's well beyond what I'd want to take a 2- or 3-year-old to see—just the wickedness of it," said Dr. Laurie Humphries, who heads a committee on television and the media for the American Academy of Child and Adolescent Psychiatry. "These are pretty bad guys."

But that's just the start of a spirited Disney dissection.

The Lion King is "a fundamentally sexist film," wrote *Detroit Free Press* columnist Neil Chethik.

Simba's young sweetie, Nala, may beat him at wrestling early on, but when things go bad under Scar's rule, she and the other lionesses become "impotent victims whose only hope is to find a male lion who can save them," Chethik wrote.

Then there are Scar's henchmen, those slobbering hyenas.

Jane R. Eisner of *The Philadelphia Inquirer* found a harmful message in the helplessness of Scar's subjects, who wait for the royal Simba to save them.

"Anybody at Disney heard of 'empowerment?'" she asked.

"If we are ever going to move into the next century with political and organizational structures that truly reflect the wants and needs of the populace, we must teach our children to see beyond the dependency of early childhood, beyond the sense of entitlement and victimization so many embrace and into a world where they believe they can and should and will be responsible for themselves."

Wow. Is this a deep cartoon, or what?

"These people need to get a life," said Disney spokeswoman Terry Press. "It's a story. It's fiction."

Press offered a point-by-point defense.

Mufasa's death? "It's made very clear in the movie that Simba is not responsible for the death of his father."

Sexism? Without his girlfriend Nala's prodding, Simba would not return from exile. But that's beside the point, Press said: "It's not her story. It's his story, about his coming to terms with who he is."

Racism? "The hyenas are voiced by Whoopi Goldberg and Cheech Marin," Press said. "Do you think Whoopi Goldberg would lend her voice to a character that is racist? I don't think so."

Press said the movie's popularity speaks for itself. It grossed $199.7 million in ticket sales in six weeks.

"People are going back again and again, so it must have some resonance," Press said.

Consider another expert opinion from Olympia, Wash., where Reed Nightingale, age 5, lives.

"It was good," he said. "Simba won the fight."

[From *Saginaw News*, July 26, 1994. Reprinted by permission of Associated Press.]

QUESTIONS

1. What can you tell about the basis of the objections to *The Lion King* voiced through David Foster's account? What position(s) on entertainment texts do the objections share?
2. What do you take Foster's reaction to be toward these objections? How do you know from the article?
3. List the responses offered by the Disney spokesperson toward the criticisms of *The Lion King*. How valid are these responses in addressing the issues raised?

TERRENCE RAFFERTY

No Pussycat

Disney's new animated feature, *The Lion King*, is a coming-of-age story about animal royalty. It's *Bambi*, but with carnivores. Like Bambi, the fawn who was known as the Prince of the Forest, this picture's hero, Simba, is born to the purple: his father, the mighty lion Mufasa, rules a vast stretch of the African plains, and Simba, the first-born son, is the heir apparent. Before he can ascend to the throne—that is, the large rock, jutting phallically over the plains, from which the monarch surveys his kingdom—he has to make cute friends, court a soft-eyed female of the species, learn a lesson or two, and see a parent die.

The key event in *The Lion King* is Mufasa's death, in a scene that may actually jerk kids' tears more shamelessly than its ignominious counterpart in *Bambi*. For more than fifty years, the death of Bambi's mother has reigned as the undisputed champion of childhood-trauma inducement, but, in the way of the world, nothing can last forever. Bambi, fleeing hunters, turns around, sees that his mother is not behind him, and cries out for her in the silence of the snowy forest. The directors of *The Lion King*, Roger Allers and Rob Minkoff, milk the pathos of their child hero's loss in a way that makes the earlier film seem tasteful, almost austere. Simba nudges Mufasa's corpse like a kid trying to wake his father on a Saturday morning, and keeps up, for a while, a steady stream of poignantly hopeful chatter: "Dad? Dad, come on, you gotta get up." Finally, the cub gives up, closes his eyes, and snuggles under his father's lifeless paw. As if that weren't enough, the movie then burdens its lovable hero with a crushing sense of guilt: Simba's evil uncle, Scar (who wants to be king), persuades him that he was responsible for his father's death. It's clear that this isn't so—Scar, we know, was the killer—but that may not matter to impressionable kids, who aren't strong on critical distance: they're meant to identify with Simba completely, to feel whatever he feels.

When *The Lion King* isn't busy dredging up deep-seated insecurities and terrors, it serves up soothingly banal musical numbers (composed by Elton John and Tim Rice) and silly, rambunctious comedy. You're grateful for the comic relief, and even, in a way, for the insipid songs: the musical sequences provide ideal opportunities to take the kids to the bathroom, the candy counter, or the shrink. The berserk alternation of moods has always been a hallmark of the "classic" Disney style, but the tone of *The Lion King* is unusually volatile: the movie is such an extreme example of the you'll-laugh-you'll-cry aesthetic that we begin to suspect that the filmmakers are just flaunting their power, showing us that they can manipulate our responses at will.

Watching a movie that is as haughtily sure of itself as *The Lion King*, you become docile and passive: you learn to accept the scraps that the filmmakers throw your way. The picture is a heedless jumble of incompatible elements: aside from *Bambi*, its primary influence seems to be, of all things, the Disney version of *The Jungle Book*, which is one of the studio's liveliest, least pretentious full-length cartoons—a movie whose loose, anything-for-a-gag spirit is closer to the Warner Bros. style than to the traditional Disney grand manner. It makes no sense to combine family tragedy and goofball farce (in a cartoon, no less), but if you're just trying to survive the experience, taking what meagre nourishment you can find, then you pounce on the comedy routines: although they're all leftovers, a few are sort of tasty. Jeremy Irons' vocal performance as Scar is an elegant ripoff of George Sanders' readings as the sly tiger in *The Jungle Book*. Like Sanders, Irons gets laughs by evoking a hilariously exaggerated air of aristocratic languor. His voice drops wearily at the end of every line: it's as if Scar were so comfortable with his evil nature that he had become bored with it. The most memorable character in the picture—a peppy, skeptical, New York-accented meerkat named Timon—might have stepped directly out of *The Jungle Book*. At his best, Timon (animated by Mike Surrey and read, with showstopper timing, by Nathan Lane) is funny enough to be a Warners character: he's like Bugs Bunny, whose brash personality is an obvious model for Timon's. The meerkat wisecracks constantly, stretches himself into shapes that do not exist in nature, and tends to get carried away when he sings and dances; his lunatic rendition of "The Lion Sleeps Tonight" is, by a long shot, the movie's comic highlight—an unexpected morsel of pure joy.

It's slim pickings, though. The animation, computer-assisted in some of the more elaborate sequences, is sometimes impressive, but rarely impressive enough to overcome a certain impersonality—a stubborn mechanical coldness. And the animators, annoyingly, persist in trying to mimic live-action photographic effects. Time and again, they shift focus from a figure in the background to one in the foreground, or vice versa. The eye rejects the technique. No matter how thoroughly we may have surrendered to the "magic" of animation, we're still aware that we're looking at *drawings:* we expect perspective, but we know that in this two-dimensional world there's no reason for anything ever to be out of focus. The sight of a hard-edged figure moving against a fuzzy background doesn't make the action seem more real; it just makes the image look a little cheesy.

But animation technique is the least of this movie's problems. What really ruins *The Lion King* is its deeply peculiar concept of nature: the movie celebrates the exercise of brutal physical power without ever quite acknowledging it. Mufasa's kingdom—later Simba's—is presented as a paradise, a harmonious ecosystem stretching as far as the lion's eye can see. In the picture's opening sequence, animals of all species gather on the plain, loyal subjects, for the king's presentation of the newborn heir. The music (a dreary tune called "Circle of Life") swells; the assembled multitudes look awestruck. The scene is a louder, more grandiose version of the beginning of *Bambi,* in which the fawn prince makes his debut to the acclaim of the forest animals—the bunnies, the birdies, the chipmunks. Sickening, sure, but the audience can believe, on some level, in the cheerful coexistence of these gentle little critters. In *The Lion King,* though, you look at the obediently lined-up animals and you can't help wondering, What the hell are they so happy about? Most of the creatures gazing reverently up at their present and future rulers are, in fact, the lions' *food.* Are they all hypnotized? It looks like Jonestown out there.

The movie tries to account for the impossible blissfulness of the Pride Lands (as the lions' kingdom is called) by having Mufasa—boomingly vocalized by James Earl Jones—deliver homilies to his son on the delicate balance of nature. Lions, he explains, do eat antelopes, but when lions die their bodies eventually become grass, which is eaten by the antelopes. "We're all connected," he pontificates. Easy for *him* to say; it seems unlikely that the antelopes share this philosophical serenity. But, despite the unequal power distribution in the Pride Lands, the only unhappy campers appear to be the weak, envious Scar and a bunch of hyenas, who help him usurp his brother's throne. The picture becomes even nuttier when Simba, after a long exile from the Pride Lands, returns to the kingdom and witnesses the devastation that Scar's reign has produced. The lush plain has become a wasteland, because all the animals, except for the few remaining lions and Scar's hyena courtiers, have left. Again, questions arise. Are we supposed to believe that the animals are picky about who's having them for dinner? The implication is that they're honored to be preyed upon by Mufasa but that, ever since Scar and the hyenas took over, getting eaten just isn't what it used to be. (Mufasa's ecology lectures did lend a touch of class to the proceedings.)

At the end, Simba, now fully grown, stands on that thrusting rock with his friends and his family and holds up his own new cub. (Reprise of "Circle of Life.") The Pride Lands are green again, his subjects have returned, and they are, if anything, more worshipful than before. The lesson that *The Lion King* imparts to its audience—which the filmmakers must hope is as rapt and as cowed as the congregation of animals on the plain—is: It's O.K. to be prey.

[Reprinted by permission; © 1994 Terrence Rafferty. Originally in *The New Yorker,* June 20, 1994. All rights reserved.]

QUESTIONS

1. Do you see Terrence Rafferty's objections to *The Lion King* represented in Foster's article? If so, where, and in what form?
2. How would you imagine the Disney spokesperson responding to Rafferty's criticisms?
3. If you have seen *The Lion King,* try to recall your responses to the film, particularly to the scenes described in Rafferty's review. Does reading the descriptions in the review change your response to the scenes? Why or why not?

Science Fiction

*If you wonder how he gets his food
And other science facts
Remember that it's just a show
You should probably just relax*

—Theme song to *Mystery Science Theater 3000*

Star Trek and other science fiction television programs and films are not just good stories: They have taught us many things. For one thing, they teach us that there are technological solutions to many problems, including getting around the laws of physics. Is the speed of light an absolute limit to traveling between stars? Distances through space would require generations (not just "the next generation")? No problem—just invent a "warp drive" or a "worm hole," and that small inconvenience is disposed of. Long-term health problems from living outside gravity (and, incidentally, high expenses involved in shooting actors in free fall)? Just assume artificial gravity. Supplies of food and drink between stars a little sparse? Invent (in the script) a computer that can brew a cup of Earl Grey out of thin air, and quietly assume that human wastes and by-products aren't an issue on board. Vacuum of space doesn't carry sound for dramatic "fighter" dogfights? OK, just ignore it. Psychological problems from boredom? Computer-generated holographics can put your whole crew on a simulacrum of an eighteenth-century sailing ship, and even convincingly douse crew members forced to walk the plank.

The problem with our learning from science fiction texts such as *Star Trek* lies in our incapacity to keep what we learn in separate categories—dirt again. Viewers of science fiction films are presumed to understand that the "long time ago, in a galaxy far away" relieves the storytellers of the responsibility to present "realistic" stories—everyone knows that we can't move so readily across thousands of light years, that if we do encounter other cultures in space there's no necessary reason (besides casting) why they should take such humanlike forms. But the "let's pretend" aspect of science fiction, particularly as augumented by special effects, conflicts with the realistic codes that have developed with film and television.

These pretend solutions make good viewing, but they have the side effect of persuading audiences that anything that looks inconvenient about technological development can be assumed to be solvable in the future. That assumption contributed to billions spent on a "Star Wars" defense during Ronald Reagan's presidency (later revived in congressional proposals): The public was invited to imagine satellites in space that would zap nuclear missiles from the Soviet Union (we would, of course, freely share this technology with them). Such technology, if it could be developed, would give us a first-strike capability; it would violate treaties against antimissile systems; and the supposed "nuclear shield" would have to be 100 percent perfect, because one little malfunction could mean millions of deaths. No matter: Persuasive fictions had prepared us to ignore what we knew about science and technology (not to mention politics) in favor of fantasy, and as a result money continued to flow into defense-related industries rather than in competing directions (e.g., education, ecology-based research, public assistance, or retiring the national debt).

The desire to imagine a Star Wars defense has a certain resonance with the song "Swinging on a Star," which is also quite specific about the bad effects of not going to school, not working to be "better than you are"—but quite vague about how one gets to "carry moonbeams home in a jar."

Race and Entertainment Media

A good test issue for links between entertainment texts and ideology is race. Films have a checkered history, from our present perspective, of dealing with race, as shown in films of past generations, such as *The Birth of a Nation* or 1930s films such as *Imitation of Life* and Hal Roach comedies (The Little Rascals, some Laurel and Hardy films) and the Three Stooges. Radio and early television were consistent in reflecting the same sort of period racism.

Shifts in treatment of race can be documented beginning in the 1960s. One of the best-known television shows of the period from the mid-1980s through the early 1990s was *The Cosby Show. Cosby* was received gratefully as a corrective to television portrayals of African Americans. In the 1950s black Americans were depicted primarily through programs such as *Amos 'n' Andy,* adapted from the radio show that now stands as shorthand for racial stereotypes. Prime-time America encountered African Americans in the 1960s through the occasional series such as *Julia* (Diahann Carroll) and *I Spy,* which featured Bill Cosby as the hip sidekick to Robert Culp. While these shows did not offer negative stereotypes, they weren't particularly grounded in realism; they could be seen as an attempt to counter the racial tensions of the mid-1960s. Compare also "relevance" programs of this time, including *East Side, West Side; The Defenders;* and, more trivially, *The Mod Squad* ("one white, one black, one blonde"). A few more shows featuring blacks appeared in the 1970s, such as *The Jeffersons* and *Sanford and Son;* these have been criticized as reinforcing racist portrayals. By contrast, *Cosby* portrayed "comedic black characters with dignity and humanity" (Jhally and Lewis p. 2). The (relative) warmth and depth of characterization of the show was a relief for most viewers after the shallow and flat versions of *anyone* in television, not just blacks; and the show stayed at or near the top of the ratings throughout its existence.

In large part owing to Bill Cosby's success, blacks are present in prime-time television in greater numbers than their percentage of the population—18 percent in 1992–93, with 77 percent white. However, this greater representation has not carried over to other ethnic groups, none of which were represented in numbers greater than 1 percent (Lichter, Rothman, and Lichter, *Prime Time* p. 53).

"Unhappily, blacks account for over one-third of all Americans arrested for serious crimes, nearly half of those arrested for violent crimes, and a majority of those arrested for murder. On prime time, by contrast, ... only 8 percent of criminals were black" (Lichter, Rothman, and Lichter, *Prime Time* pp. 61–62).

Critical reaction to *Cosby* has been mixed, however: In the effort to distance itself from negative portrayals and comic stereotypes, the program was criticized as too distant from the day-to-day concerns of most blacks. The Huxtables, both New York City professionals (obstetrician and lawyer), seemed always to be able to find time for relaxed social activities and conversations with their children. As is often the case in television comedy, problems seemed to be easily resolvable, if not in one half-hour episode then in two. Henry Louis Gates, Jr., has criticized the Huxtables' portrayal as being "in most respects, just like white people," with the result that the show reinforced the myth that economic and social problems are the responsibility of individuals rather than systemic problems.

Since *The Cosby Show* went off the air, no program has succeeded in bridging the differences in viewing preferences between white and black audiences.

Viewing preferences for blacks and whites differ markedly: "[E]leven of the twelve top-rated series in black households revolved around black lifestyles and culture," with the single exception, at number 10, being *Married with Children*. As for white viewers' preferences, "only *Hangin' with Mr. Cooper* made the top twenty list," at number 20 (tie), while "[t]hree of the black top ten—*Roc, Out All Night,* and *In Living Color*—finished one-hundredth or lower among whites." U.S. viewers are strikingly segregated: Overall top-ten choices are not widely watched by African Americans, who rank *Roseanne* at number 15, *Home Improvement* number 47, *Murphy Brown* number 64, and *Love and War* number 76

(Lichter, Rothman, and Lichter, *Prime Time* p. 55). Subsequent polls published in newspapers show the pattern continuing, with only two shows common to the top twenty in both overall and African-American lists—*Monday Night Football* and *Seinfeld* (number 20 for African Americans).

Stereotypes

The topic of stereotypes is as relevant to entertainment as to news. Complaints about stereotypes may be somewhat unfair: So long as we don't hold especially firmly to them, stereotypes can serve as rough approximations to guide us in encounters with the unfamiliar. But stereotypes in media may be a different matter, if they contribute to bias and constitute the basis of tangible harm.

Stereotypes have been part of comedy since there has been comedy; tragedy, by contrast, is more likely to present characters who are sharply different from others. Roman and Greek drama offers prototypes of the young airheaded lovers, the braggart, the tricky slave, the miser, the complainer. These characters seem to be constants of human societies, if their presence in plays from Euripides and Aristophanes through Shakespeare and Molière to Neil Simon is any indication. Like fiction and other narratives, comedy makes use of familiar characterizations for convenience and ease of communication with the audience. Tragedy, in contrast, seems to emphasize those factors that individuate characters rather than stress their essential sameness. Another way to put it is that comedy tends to give us ensembles in which the relations between the various characters are what's important, while tragedy deals in fundamental isolation. Comedies often end in a marriage, tragedies in a funeral; marriages introduce the participants to the web of human relationships, while funerals bring reflection on how death occurs to each alone (even if it occurs simultaneously with other deaths).

Sitcoms, like comedy generally, deal freely with stereotypes. The distinguishing feature of sitcoms is the continuing relationship of the participants within a "situation." Stage comedies portray an action within a few hours of fictional time in which things happen that fundamentally change the characters involved. In marked contrast to this, sitcom segments on radio and television seem to exist outside any relationship to other episodes. With rare exceptions, one sitcom episode does not follow another. The events in the characters' lives do not accumulate, week by week or year by year—though there may be some suggestion of this if the sitcom includes children, who inevitably age over the life of the program.

What makes up a "situation"? Any premise that serves to relate characters, such as the upstairs/downstairs working-class lives of the Kramdens and

Nortons in *The Honeymooners*, the family reactions to Archie Bunker's prejudices in *All in the Family*, the man-and-two-women-as-roommates premise of *Three's Company*, the employees and regulars in the *Cheers* pub, and so on. Sitcoms went through a gimmicky phase in the 1960s, with magical females in *I Dream of Jeannie* and *Bewitched*, a talking horse in *Mr. Ed*, Halloween caricature families in *The Addams Family* and *The Munsters*, the shipwrecked crew on *Gilligan's Island*, and an automotive reincarnation in *My Mother, the Car*. Even successful sitcoms tend to have a run of only a few years at best, as the premise goes through several phases—novelty, popular success, familiarity, staleness, cancellation, and (sometimes) syndication. Perhaps more than television dramas, the most successful sitcoms (at least since the 1960s) tend to pick up on current issues and trends—that may be why they seem to be so much of the moment, and why they come to have a dated feel a decade later.

Sitcoms very rarely are explicitly didactic: The nearest they come to trying to instruct the audience would be through the negative example of a character who overreaches or behaves foolishly and receives an appropriate penalty. However, the extent to which sitcoms try to stay current means that they often position their stories in relation to the presumed ideology of the audience, which means an implicit advocacy of values. For examples of how this happens, see the discussion on pages 393–94 about *Home Improvement*, or the discussion of *Seinfeld* on pages 366–69.

FURTHER READING

Concerns about the cultural effects of entertainment media are summarized by Todd Gitlin's conclusion to his book on prime-time programming.

TODD GITLIN

Conclusion—Inside Prime Time

[Cable TV] is likely to create only minor, marginal chances for a diversity of substance—and fewer and fewer as time goes on. The workings of the market give Americans every incentive to remain conventionally entertainment-happy. Conglomeration proceeds apace. Homogeneity at the cultural center is complemented by consumer fragmentation on the margins. Technology opens doors, and oligopoly marches in just behind, slamming them. There can be no technological fix for what is, after all, a social problem.

The problem is the texture of American life. Americans rely on television's conventions because television suits the partitioned nature of everyday existence.... Most of us believe that real life is private life, real ambition private ambition. The public world is a corrupt necessity, a jungle to be dropped into only when we have a direct—that is, private—interest at stake.... As long as we understand the private and isolated to be the central sphere in which we define ourselves and live our real lives, we are primed for television, which is modern domesticity's eery umbilical connection with a larger world. Having dropped out of the public realm, because there are few institutions that might provide the arena for rich and informed public speech, we rely on television to stay "in touch." Instead of having the means for direct communication of what we might have in common—media in the literal sense—we get "the media."

That is why television has become a cultural force of such enormous proportions.... [W]hen a television set is switched on for almost seven hours a day in the average American household, the curious power of this electronic machinery begins with the fact that it requires so little of us. Turning a single set off seems almost beside the point. While we nod off, or get up to go to the refrigerator or the bathroom, the images go on living their strangely insubstantial yet ubiquitous lives. We hear about them at work, or from our children, or parents, or friends, or encounter them transfigured into the styles of people in the street....

[J]ournalistic and academic critics of particular shows and genres, or of specific features of television, like violence, miss the essential point about TV's force. The images register with us as symbols, as diversion and ideology at the same time, by virtue of the fact that our guard is down when we watch. It is certainly true, as many researchers remind us, that we screen these symbols differently according to who we are and how we already see the world. We notice and soak up and ignore selectively, although not always consciously. The presence of the medium is such that we don't so much reflect on the meanings or (most of the time) study them; we swim in them.... "Ideology" to Americans usually smacks of a foreign disease: something that afflicts other people. But ideology means nothing more or less than a set of assumptions that becomes second nature; even rebels have to deal with it.

[From *Inside Prime Time* by Todd Gitlin, pp. 332–35. Copyright © 1983 by Todd Gitlin. Reprinted by permission of Pantheon Books, a division of Random House, Inc.]

FURTHER ASSIGNMENTS

Assignment

Individually, you should choose one of the factors mentioned in the Pause for Reflection on pp. 390 and explore ways in which that has influenced or determined your preferences in media. For example, how has your social class or region affected your reaction to a film? Be careful not to oversimplify.

Assignment

Write informally (a journal entry or short essay) about a text or category of texts that might be considered as entertainment *and* information. Suggestions: radio or television talk shows, films set in other historical periods, "educational" video games ("Where in the

World Is Carmen Sandiego?"), a popular novel, children's books. Account for what you consider to be the entertaining elements and the informative elements. What do you see as the effect of their combination in your chosen text? Is this combination controversial?

Assignment: Inferring Audience from Text

The purpose of this assignment is to see what you can tell about the implied audience for an entertainment text by that text itself. (Most of the comments below are directed toward television; but they are likely to be readily adaptable to film, and they might work, with some careful rethinking, for music, print texts, video games, and so on.) This assignment will work better if you choose something new to you: If you watch primarily sports programs and comedies, watch a soap opera; if your viewing tastes run to dramas, turn on a hockey match. If you never watch MTV, this is your chance. If you range throughout commercial television, watch a televised church service. If you don't listen much to radio, do that. The amount of time and attention will depend on the text.

Many entertainment texts offer a center of attention—a main character or protagonist, someone for the audience to identify with. That person may do unwise things, particularly in comedies, but is basically likable. Some texts may offer a range of possible centers of attention, in essence dividing the audience. Identify this center of attention and give some thought to how and why the person works in this fashion for the text.

In addition to the center of attention, there are often combinations of single characters who contrast with the central character(s) in some way, usually in connection with what happens (i.e., dramatic contrast). Does this dramatic contrast also work thematically? That is, can the events of the plot also function symbolically, with the contrast extended beyond individual characters to types that they stand for? If so, is this a necessary inference, or only a possible one?

Here are some suggestions for issues you might want to consider in your account of the audience as inferred from the text. You should probably choose one or at most two issues to develop in your essay, though you might want to make notes on most or all to think it through.

1. *Gender.* Is the text pitched toward men primarily? Toward women primarily? Toward both? What are the features of the text that support your conclusion? (E.g., announcers; character(s) that the audience is invited to identify with; themes in the text.)

2. *Class.* What is the economic and social status of the audience? How do you know? (Be careful not to put down "middle" and stop there—what defines "middle class"?)

3. *Race or ethnicity.* What markers are there for race? For ethnic background? How are these presented? What seems to count as "normal" in the text? How do you know? What kinds of race/ethnicity are not present?

4. *Age.* Here, as in race and ethnicity, you should work from presence/absence and from inferences about those who are presented.

5. *Occupation.* What do the characters do in their work? Is this represented? If so, how? If not, why not—and what is the effect of its absence?

6. *Region.* Is the text situated anywhere? How is this established, and how important is it to how the audience might regard the text? Are there characters from other defined regions? If so, how are they represented?

7. *Sexuality.* Does the text deal exclusively with heterosexual characters? Does their sexual orientation become an issue in the text? If so, how? If not, what are the effects of its being quietly assumed?

8. *Social organization.* Are the characters part of a family? If so, what is the implied norm for the family unit? If what is portrayed is not a family, what is it? Associates at work? Single people? What other possibilities are there? What alternative sorts of organizations are shown in the text, and what inferences might be drawn from them?

If you find yourself stereotyping the audience (particularly if you assume that they are people not like yourself), ask yourself about your basis for knowledge. In other words, is it a development from the entertainment text itself? From direct personal experience? From what friends and family have told you?

Assignment

Compile a list of your likes and dislikes in entertainment texts and consumer preferences, but make choices you believe would appeal to someone you regard as a figure of authority (instructor, boss, parent). Compile a second list that would appeal to peers, friends, or others on a social basis of equality. Compile a third list for those who regard you as a figure of authority (younger brother or sister, children, employees). (Invent people if no one comes to mind.) In addition to entertainment texts (films, television programs, radio stations, styles of music or musical performers, leisure reading), you might include other leisure activities, forms of transportation, clothing, foods, and other matters of taste that can function as codes for who you are. (Category headings may be a help in this.)

After making extensive lists, look through them carefully. If there are differences between the three lists, why? If there are overlaps, why? Are there kinds of texts or activities that can comfortably fit on all (i.e., that might be said to have appeal across a wide spectrum)? Are there texts or activities with narrow appeal?

These lists are differentiated according to social status. What other systems might be used to draw up different lists? (Possibilities: church membership or political convictions.)

Assignment

Test the radio categories listed on page 396, and add your best guesses about the demographics of other sorts of radio programming such as R&B or country. What can you tell about the demographics for television programs such as the following: *CNN Crossfire; Headline News;* network evening news; morning news programs; morning or after-school cartoons; *Melrose Place* or other Fox network dramas; MTV; stand-up broadcasts on the Comedy Channel and other cable networks; daytime soap operas; ESPN; *American Gladiators;* the Nashville Network; and so on.

Assignment
Do some informal writing about songs you are familiar with, in whatever style. Think not only about lyrics, but about music as well, and about how a song connects with others within its stylistic framework. What attitudes and values do songs connect with (positively or negatively)? Are there elements of the larger culture that benefit from those attitudes and values? If so, how and why?

III

Reconsiderations

8

Discovering Contexts and Deeper Purposes

OVERVIEW

When you are engaged in critical reading and writing, it is sometimes important to step back from immediate questions and activities in order to ask what it's all for. In critical reading this "stepping back" can take the form of observing your own habits of interpretation as compared with those of others. In writing, it can mean turning away from drafting and developing ideas in order to look at larger contexts (metacommentary). These are questions directed *to* rather than *through* the practices of reading and using rhetoric.

Perhaps the most important element of writing is not writing itself, but thinking. Some kinds of writing tasks occur in contexts that allow you to work easily within conventional expectations—routine business letters, summarizing and reporting on research articles, who-what-where-when in news reporting, or accounts of hypothesis–experiment–conclusion sequences in lab reports. Once you learn the form, the rest is straightforward. But other writing tasks require critical thinking—that is, examining the origins and purposes of conventional expectations themselves. It is challenging but valuable to develop a habitual critical stance, both toward the systems within which your rhetoric functions and toward your own participation in those systems.

Developing this capability for critical thinking means looking at contexts and deeper purposes for rhetoric. We have already made a start on this, focusing on specific media such as news, advertisements, and photography. This chapter will provide a more systematic introduction to critical thinking through exploration of the concept of *ideology.*

By now you've had some practice at recognizing rhetorical forms and purposes in media texts and finding their relevance to your own purposes for writing. You've worked with conventions of particular forms of media, drawn some connections between those forms, and considered some issues that cut across genres. And you've found some rhetorical forms in some media that can be applied to the problem of reaching audiences in writing. But beyond these initial connections, what do different forms of media have to do with each other? Can *media* be treated as one subject, or should they be seen as phenomena only distantly related to each other?

These questions are crucial to how we see rhetoric through media, and ultimately to the use we make of rhetoric. If the very different sorts of media we are considering are intrinsically separate from each other—newspaper journalism, rock music, billboards, electronic bulletin boards, pamphlets, shopping channels on cable TV—then any connections we find are likely to be either borrowings or coincidences. If that's the case, we'd better change the title—it's not rhetoric, but *rhetorics,* with different rules applying in each case. And the rhetoric involved in writing essays would be different from all these as well.

If it were true that the various forms of media we've been working with were distinct and disconnected from each other, then they would work as an accumulation of bits and pieces. In that case they would be like marbles in a circle or pool balls on a table, and the relations between them would depend only on what happened to collide with what, and when. The only sort of order to describe media, in that case, would be roughly that of the dictionary or encyclopedia, with alphabetical sequence or chance the best we could do.

But there *is* an order that can describe the movements of marbles or pool balls and can account for their position and movement: the laws of physics, which scientists have formulated through the long process of observing events, forming hypotheses, and testing these through experiment. Might there be some such laws that apply to media and our uses of media? If so, what can we determine about their nature?

If there's an underlying unity to the rhetoric of different forms of media, then we can hope to bring these different forms into some relation with each other, and apply what we learn about their rhetoric to the writing that we do. This book argues that there is a common ground to these various media, although one not so widely acknowledged or firmly established as that of physics. If we draw back a bit from specific media and media texts, it may be possible to look at deeper meanings of media and their relations with culture more generally. Such relations are established by the structure of ideas and values within a culture—its ideology.

Chapter 8: Discovering Contexts and Deeper Purposes

This chapter will begin with a summary of such principles of connection, and will ask you to test these theories against your own experience of media texts and the effects of their rhetoric. The goal is to extend our sense not only of *how* such rhetoric works, but of *why* it works.

Ideology isn't always addressed in treatments of rhetoric. You may have encountered the phrase *critical thinking* before now in classes that directed attention to the importance of problem solving: Critical thinking has become an important goal in mathematics, the sciences, sociology, political science, and other disciplines. Previous chapters of this text have anticipated the topic by looking at the nature and effects of media such as news and information programming and advertising, and by thinking through relations between those and writing. However, critical thinking often stays within one discipline, and it doesn't usually get to the sorts of questions that ideology makes available: What work does this text, this position, this way of looking at the world, do? Whose interests does it serve?

This chapter will ask you to consider not only the meaning but the implications of ideology. What does it mean to participate in a world in which every text is seen as coming from an ideological position? How can you develop the ability to read that ideological position from the text and context? How do text and context relate to your own interests, to what you want to accomplish?

Discussing ideology will require us to venture onto grounds of critical theory, which means introducing some terms and concepts that are more abstract than may be customary. Another potential difficulty with this material is that these questions require a discussion of politics, in a class and subject that some prefer to see as apolitical. But even supposedly apolitical matters have political effects. Politics is inescapable: If you avoid political questions, you simply leave it to others to make decisions for you. The question is not whether you are to be involved in politics, but what sort of politics you will engage in—that involving considered action in what you understand to be your own and others' best interests, or that involving withdrawal in favor of someone else's interests. Such thinking about politics, however, doesn't require affiliation with a specific position or political party. The point is to become informed about the consequences of several possible positions in order to be able to make an informed choice. Choosing not to know means leaving yourself subject to easy manipulation by others.

Before introducing the concept of ideology directly, we will be approaching it through some matters related to media that are connected to it: specifically, the questions of how media represent reality, how labels work to present ideological positions, and how ideology may be inferred from conventions of behavior.

ISSUES

Representation and the Natural

A central theme of this chapter will be an examination of some general principles behind the impulse to claim that positions set forth in media are "natural." In order to understand ideology, we need to consider what is assumed to be "natural" in media texts and our readings of them.

This morning as I write, I have on the desktop a glass of After the Fall brand Georgia Peach juice, available (it says) from "natural foods stores." The label is fairly representative of how code words are used in marketing; it tells me that my glass "contains 100% fruit juice" sweetened with "ALL NATURAL INGREDIENTS." To the right of this on the label is a short essay for compulsive label-readers, which uses the word *natural* three times. Label readers will note that most of the juice in Georgia Peach is not peach juice. "Ingredients: water, white grape, pear, and apple juice concentrates, peach and apple purees, lemon juice concentrate, *natural* flavor. Our juices contain the *natural* pulp that *nature* intended, so please shake well." I count six appearances of the word *natural* on the small label, more than any other substantial word except "juice." We might ask whether it's right to call this Georgia Peach juice "natural" if it's mostly white grape, pear, and apple with a little peach pulp added. We certainly could puzzle a good deal over what is meant by the word *natural* as it appears on the label. And we could ask how After the Fall determined what "nature intended." But the more interesting question is why the manufacturers felt compelled to insist so much on the word *natural.* Why is it so important to them, and presumably to us as consumers?

You can confirm the importance of naturalness as a marketing device by making a trip to the supermarket. A few minutes in a grocery store produced the examples listed in Exhibit 8.1.

One explanation for all this *natural*ness might be that those who market these products are aware of a widespread concern that much of what we eat and drink is not "natural" but artificial; companies use the rhetoric of labels and advertising to try to distinguish their products from those of their competitors.

But what does "natural" mean if it can be so easily claimed for so many manufactured products? The term is so widely applied as to be practically meaningless—except in its emotional effects, which are evidently still quite powerful. The category of "natural," in other words, is a cultural construction: We decide (*we* collectively—not the body of people reading this book, sitting in an actual classroom, or otherwise brought together, but we as a culture)

> 1. West Virginia brand ham, "with natural juices," (i.e., not with water added—but isn't water natural?)
> 2. Dannon Coffee Natural Flavored Lowfat Yogurt (is coffee flavor natural to yogurt?)
> 3. America's Choice brand Mozzarella Natural Cheese ("excuse me, sir; where do you keep the unnatural cheese?")
> 4. Minute Maid All Natural Fruit Punch
> 5. Florida's Natural brand grapefruit juice
> 6. Chiquita brand juice with natural flavoring
> 7. Sunkist old-fashioned 100 percent natural frozen concentrate for lemonade, as well as "all natural" pink lemonade (is lemonade naturally pink?)
> 8. Eggo strawberry and blueberry "naturally and artificially flavored waffles" (here we get the best of both worlds)
> 9. Natural Light beer, "with nothing artificial added"
> 10. Busch beer, brewed with natural ingredients
> 11. Ben and Jerry's ice cream, "Vermont's finest all-natural ice cream" (presumably there might be a finer artificial ice cream, or part natural ice cream, in Vermont)
> 12. Brownberry Natural Wheat Bread
> 13. Kellogg's Complete Bran Flakes, with "natural whole grain goodness"
> 14. Quaker 100% Natural Crispy Whole Grain Cereal
> 15. Del Monte Fruit Naturals in its own juices [sic]

Exhibit 8.1 Selling the natural.

what to consider natural and what artificial. That construction takes place through the workings of "common sense" the categories are "natural" to us because we take them for granted. This whole notion of *taking for granted* is integral to the concept of ideology.

PAUSE FOR REFLECTION

Do a freewriting on the question of what is *natural*. After the freewriting, look back over your text for examples of the natural as represented.

Visit a grocery in order to look for other words that function as "natural" does here—vague words that have the effect of making you feel positive about the product or its use, while not committing the manufacturer to anything in particular. Write about these in your journal.

A character in a play by the seventeenth-century French dramatist Molière suddenly realizes, in the middle of a conversation, that he is speaking prose.

This realization occurs when something the character has been doing without thinking about it—something that comes naturally to him—suddenly becomes artificial, and he begins to think about its meaning. In beginning to think critically about media, you may have seen their texts as "natural" as well, by taking them pretty much for granted as you have found them. Asking analytical questions about what is offered as entertainment or information tends to denature such texts. By now you should have seen ways in which *the real* is constructed and represented (or re-presented) to us. This constructed naturalness is most convincing to us when we neglect to look critically at the conventions of a medium.

Elements of what you have observed for many years on television and in film, radio, newspapers and magazines, and other media texts, should be considered as representations rather than transcriptions of "reality." In order to get at the nature and workings of ideology, then, it will be useful to think about representation, because making the processes of representation visible will highlight what is usually taken for granted.

Our thinking about visual media in Chapter 6 dealt with some of the symbolic systems those media use for representation. Something can be represented to us only as we understand it through the conventions of that medium (or some other conventions). René Magritte's print (Exhibit 8.2) plays with the assumptions of representation in art.

Classroom discussions of this print may begin in some confusion as the class tries to adjust the assumptions about reading a visual image to this image plus caption. "Why does it say 'This is not a pipe'? It *looks* like a pipe." "I don't get it." "OK, if it's not a pipe, what is it?" Eventually someone comes up with the key observation: "It's a *drawing* of a pipe." Then there's a general groan, of the sort that you might hear after a bad pun. Of course, we knew it was a drawing of a pipe... the illustration, however, serves to underscore the invisibility of conventions. It's natural to see the visual portion of the print as a pipe, and unnatural to inquire into the basis of its representation. Magritte's work here is not (only) a bad joke, but an illustration of how "naturally" we accept representation in artworks and, by extension, in other media. We agree to call a two-dimensional black-and-white drawing a pipe, in much the way that we agree to consider some print marks on a page or a pattern of black, gray, and white dots a human being. From "inside" the convention of representation, the thing represented is accepted as "real," even if we maintain a consciousness of its fictionality.

Just as it's "natural" to assume an equation between a drawing of a pipe and a pipe, so in discussing a televisual text it's "natural" to equate an image of a person with a person. But do we forget, when we are watching television, that that's what we are doing? In one sense, obviously not. But if you ask

Exhibit 8.2 René Magritte, *"Ceci n'est pas une pipe"* ("This is not a pipe"). © 1997 Herscovici, Brussels / Artists Rights Society (ARS), New York. Used by permission. From the Los Angeles County Museum of Art, purchased with funds provided by the Mr. and Mrs. William Preston Harrison Collection.

what's happening, you'll get an account of events as described within the TV show so far—"the professor's wife has been killed by a letterbomb, and they're trying to trace the murderer by use of chemical residues"—as if it were a news report. Entertainment media sometimes attract audiences with a wish to escape: The use of the entertainment invites a pretended shift in reality for the period of the program. But it's a matter of some concern whether some of the effects of that pretense cross over into the way that we think about reality altogether.

In Exhibit 8.3, of course, it's not a person, but an *image* of a person on television (more precisely, a drawing of the image of a person on television). TV's images are created for us thirty times a second, as an electronic beam moves very rapidly across 525 lines on the television tube. The electronic beam imitates a person sufficiently closely that we see, or agree to see, no difference. But it's habitual to pass over the awareness of the transmission of that image through media and to say that that's a person, just as it's habitual to

This Is Not A Person

Exhibit 8.3
Tom Tomorrow (Dan Perkins). Used with permission.

say of a landscape shown on television or film that that's Bosnia or the Lake District or Prince William Sound or France during the time of Louis XIV. In similar fashion, readers of newspapers may regard photographs, which are cropped and positioned so as to illustrate a point being made by the newspaper, as though they are reality. It's important to the success of these media that we participate in the pretense that the media make no difference, that they transmit a version of the way things are as clearly as a window allows us to see through it.

Representation is made possible by an implicit agreement within a culture, with its specific forms determined by the technology and social practices available (Mitchell p. 13). But in our time, the rapid changes in these mean that we have multiple systems of representation available to us. The extent of agreement about representation is breaking down—a threat or an opportunity, depending on how you look at it. It is now not only possible but likely that a media text is the product of many "senders" with conflicting sets of values that contend within the text, carried over a medium with multivalent possibilities, and received by audiences who read the same text within conflicting and contradictory sets of worldviews.

To sort all this out, we need to look at the question of ideology, of what is "beneath the surface" of texts. Part of the contention of this text is that, if ideology is beneath the surface, it's not very deep. A little practice will enable you to sort out significant ideological markers as these serve to guide or manipulate your interpretation of texts.

PAUSE FOR REFLECTION
Did you catch yourself, in looking at Exhibit 8.3, thinking "Of course it's a person"? To what extent do you see other cartoon characters—*The Simpsons*, the *Peanuts* kids, the figures in *Calvin and Hobbes*—as people?

Characteristically, media invite readers to read texts according to the model of the window. When you look through a window (provided the glass is not too dirty), you see what is outside, not the window. But what is seen through the window depends on where you stand: The perspective changes slightly according to the angle of view. And the "glass" on which televisual images are projected is not *clear,* any more than is the screen on which film is projected or the paper on which photographs and newspapers are printed. Rather, these are two-dimensional surfaces on which we have learned, through conventional systems that have grown up in the culture inside of which we exist, to interpret versions of "reality."

Claims to faithful representation of "reality" through a medium are sometimes called **realism,** and news sources make such claims, explicitly or implicitly. Consider the slogan of the *New York Times,* "All the news that's fit to print"; the names of newspapers like the Cleveland *Plain Dealer,* the *Christian Science Monitor* (something that keeps watch), the *Times,* the *News,* the *Record*—all these titles are claims to record history impartially. (They are not called "*a* record" or "a *version* of the news.") On television, *Headline News* has used the phrase "Give us thirty minutes, and we'll give you the world." Television reports from the scene of a disaster are often accepted as *what happened,* despite their being framed as "reality" by conventions that have grown up around disaster reporting. But much about the representation of, say, an earthquake is shaped by media conventions, and is to that extent fictional. They are, after all, called news *stories.*

To start with the obvious: If you watch earthquake footage, your own walls and floors do not move. Television shows you *reality elsewhere.* Perhaps this is what seems so bizarre about the appliance-shop video camera hooked into a monitor. It's not just that we see ourselves on TV, which is disorienting enough, with no left–right reversal as we see in the mirror. It's seeing real-time TV, right there where it's happening. The mirror is a representation which we have come to accept as "reality"; the televisual representation is therefore strange. If, instead of having mirrors in our bathrooms we all had television cameras and monitors, it would be the mirror image that would look strange to us.

As I discussed in Chapter 6, television combines sound with a two-dimensional image governed by the conventions of framing and perspective that have developed as part of Western pictorial art since the Renaissance. The camera typically brings us only a few degrees of the landscape, considerably narrower than the view of human eyesight. (Anyone who has tried to photograph the Grand Canyon can testify to the discrepancy between what's there to be seen all around you and the image brought home to be put into the photo album.)

In addition to the problem of the frame in visual media, we must consider selection: Anything presented on television or other media has been selected for us. As we saw in Chapter 4, producers, editors, and writers select from a fairly large quantity of footage a few minutes, sometimes only seconds, to put into the larger context of the news broadcast (whether a special report or the evening news). One element of this selection is locality. A major earthquake in California rates important placement on the national news, whereas the same earthquake in Armenia would probably get only a few seconds' air time. This may be explained by the assumption that in the United States we care primarily about ourselves (not unique to us, of course); most news broadcast here concerns events that affect people here. For example, coverage of Iraq's 1990 invasion of Kuwait was heavy because of concern over oil prices and the possibility of U.S. military intervention in the crisis.

The framing and selecting of television news that we considered in Chapter 4 takes place with an eye to the essential message of the televisual medium: what might be called its *as-if reality*. Television sets things up for you *as if* you were present on the scene, usually without acknowledging the presence of camera or other technical devices. Such televisual representation requires film or videotape footage: If it's expensive or inconvenient to send reporters to the site of a story, then that story will receive less prominent treatment than another that is easier to cover. A "talking head" reading a report on camera does not represent what happens as if "you are there" (the title of a 1950s CBS series of fictionalized historical accounts, done as if in a news report). But if the representation of being there is done seamlessly enough, it will be accepted (in some sense, at least) as *what really happened*.

The *as if* convention can be found in the stylistic conventions of newswriting, which require reporters to write as if they were eyewitnesses, but to efface themselves from being participants in the events described. An "invisible eyewitness" can be very convincing as to the truth of what is represented—but there is little opportunity *within that medium* to question the representation. Furthermore, the presence of the press may change what is observed into a "media event." Those who deal with the press, such as corporate executives, politicians, or public relations officers of organizations, know that reporters' presence changes what is happening.

There is nothing intrinsically sinister or deceptive about this pretense at invisibility in representation. And if we are deceived, it is at least partially *self*-deception. We are expected to know, as readers, that newspaper and other texts are shaped to suit our presumed values and desires. We have been taught this game, and for the most part we play along. There are, of course, examples of deliberately fraudulent representation in all genres of media, particularly advertising. But most editors, reporters, producers, and others are fair and professional, within their understandings of professional behavior. However, their media have grown out of practices that bring their own (often invisible) sets of values.

The paradigm of a medium that must address an at least partly cynical audience is advertising. Commercials often inspire skepticism in television viewers. But as we saw in Chapter 5, some features of commercials are likely to be accepted as representative of "reality," just as with other televisual texts. Viewers *know* that the commercial is pretended reality, presented from the seller's point of view. In watching ads, we are expected to make adjustments in the ad's "reading"—but this adjustment must take place on the conscious level, and commercials often work at other than conscious levels.

To take one example: Actors in commercials often speak directly to the camera, as though they were conversing with *you*, individually and directly, as a friend would. The conventions of face-to-face conversation promote a certain vestigial trust in commercials that mimic this form of communication, leading us to accept the commercial message as coming from sincere and truthful people. Commercials frequently use actors who are not well known, cast so as to represent particular demographic groups, as if to say that the words and images of the ads come from those in the desired group. The representational message, in this case, is that the product or service is endorsed by "one of us." (Another genre, of course, is the endorsement by a celebrity, who brings an aura of public recognition to the product.)

There are also iconic forms of representation—those that draw meaning from symbols such as a scientist's lab coat, which signifies that what is presented in the ad has been technologically or scientifically tested. (This if *stated* would be fraudulent; but it can be *suggested* by way of symbols and other elements of meaning offered through the visual rhetoric of the commercial.) These and other facets of representation are so familiar that they are generally not consciously recognized by viewers: They are at once obvious and hidden, like Edgar Allan Poe's purloined letter.

PAUSE FOR REFLECTION
While engaged in attentive viewing, watch television commercials with an eye to *symbols*. What are ways in which ads make use of symbols as part of their rhetoric? What are some ways in which writers make use of symbols?

One of the most important principles to remember, then, is that while media provide us with *representations* of reality, it is conventional for viewers to look past the representations to "reality." (The proverb that "pictures never lie" is one that any practiced photographer knows to be hollow.) The equation of representation with reality is fundamental to the workings of ideology, which always is offered as "truth" about reality. One area in which this equation can be seen is that of captioning, or the labeling of photographs to influence how they are read.

Labeling

Visual media are never purely visual: They come with labels. Newspaper photographs do not run just as photographs—they have cutlines (captions) and small headlines below or above, and frequently photographs are run as illustrations for accompanying stories. Something like labeling happens in television coverage as well, with either voice-over or text juxtaposed with the image. (This may not be so obvious as the captions in the newspaper, because on television photography moves, and it is not preserved in so convenient a form as print.) Labeling is a central device for instructing us in how to understand media representations; see Exhibit 8.4.

We might expect labels on photographs of human beings—seeing a face makes us curious about who it is. But in media even photos of "nature" are labeled in such a way as to instruct us how to understand them ideologically. A photograph of a lightning bolt as in Exhibit 8.5 on page 440, for example, could be captioned in connection with multiple themes:

- The power of electricity, with lightning as a familiar illustration
- Static electricity
- The discovery of electricity (Ben Franklin, etc.)
- Noise on AM radio, much of which is caused by lightning
- Deaths of two golfers by lightning
- Destructive power of nature
- The power of God to strike down human beings at any time

Chapter 8: Discovering Contexts and Deeper Purposes **439**

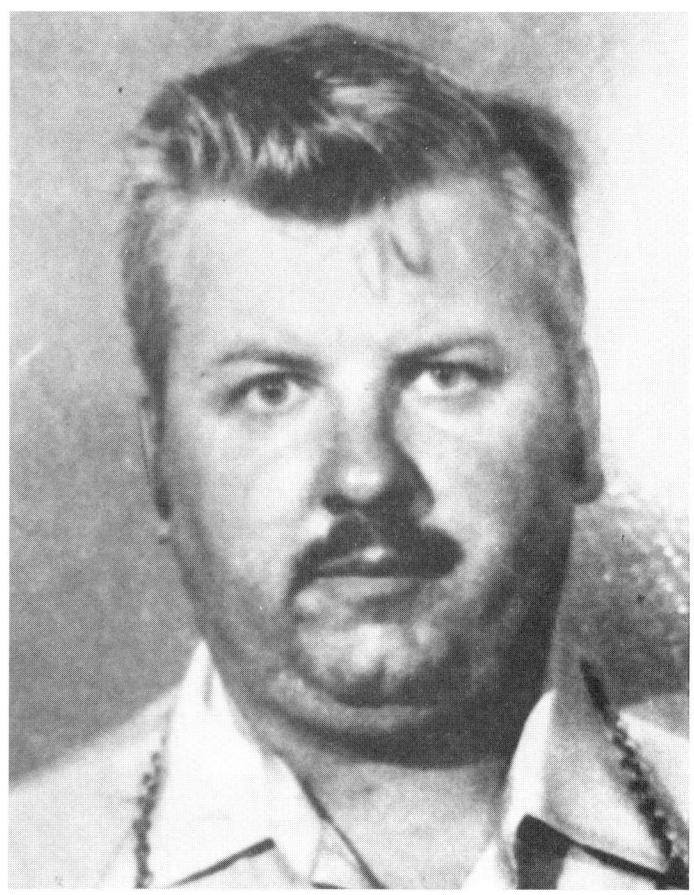

Exhibit 8.4
The man in this photo is *(a)* a kindly uncle; *(b)* a small-town banker; *(c)* a convicted mass murderer; *(d)* a transvestite. UPI/Bettmann.

- Photographic technique (how do you manage to photograph a lightning bolt, anyway?)
- The necessity to plan ahead when backpacking, in case you're caught in a thunderstorm

A photograph similar to Exhibit 8.5 appeared in a *National Geographic* special issue on water—with the following caption:

The Cycle of Water

With the flash and boom of an Arizona storm, nature goes about its eternal recycling program. Rainwater eventually evaporates and rises to form clouds that release new rain. Humankind has yet to perfect its own management of this essential liquid asset.

Exhibit 8.5 How might this image be labeled? © Daniel Wray/The Image Works.

Notice how many elements of the *National Geographic* caption are *extrinsic* to the photograph: emphasis on the water cycle; the locale in Arizona; mention of "nature"; the presence of "humankind," implied by the camera but normally left tacit; and the idea that water is an asset to be managed. Terms used in the caption imply an ideological position—cyclical nature is something that "humankind" has the right and the capacity to control for its own purposes. To some extent, photography has developed its own ideology-linked conventions; but particularly within other media texts such as newspapers and magazines, the combination of photograph with caption allows a photograph to be given a particular spin. In other words, it's common for a photograph to come with instructions as to how to read it (some verbal, some supplied by the context). And just as the photograph is conventionally value-neutral, its own ideology invisible within the system of reading photography, so the combination of photo-plus-caption is conventionally value-neutral.

Let's consider an example: the front page of the *Saginaw News* for January 8, 1995. A boxed area occupies the left-hand three-quarters of the page. Within the boxed area are two large photographs and two smaller ones. The top photo shows a man leaning over slightly, holding his arms close to his chest; the photo just beneath (Exhibit 8.6) is of about six people sitting around

Exhibit 8.6 Photo from the *Saginaw News,* January 8, 1995. Used by permission.

a table in a restaurant. The labels in and around the boxed area tell us what to make of these photographs—and together with them constitute a narrative, which in turn is part of a larger narrative. The headline over the whole box is "Murder moves north": Several anecdotes provided by people featured in the photos (and others) have to do with events in which non–Gladwin County residents were responsible for crimes there.

Some of the statements that function as "captions":

Above, Timothy S. Yarbrough, 32, shows how he wrestled with Robert A. Morgan, 38, on June 13, 1994, when Morgan tried to kidnap his own infant daughter. Yarbrough shot Morgan to death in what was ruled a justifiable homicide. William E. Nash, 46, and his wife, Mari, 43, discuss the rash of homicides at Robin's Restaurant in Gladwin. . . .

"It's city folks doing (the crimes). Some of the older folks are really upset. They say the flatlanders are movin' in and taking over." Cheryl M. Eagleson, 37, a cashier at Ace Hardware in Gladwin. . . .

"I'm definitely more careful now. Every week there's a break-in. It used to be if we had one a year, we'd think that was quite bad." Arthur D. Anderson, 74, a lifelong Gladwin County resident.

[Above the headline, a statement from the county sheriff:] "We are a violent society. Just because someone has to drive 200 miles north of Detroit doesn't change that. If he's a criminal, then he's a criminal 200 miles north of Detroit."

The photos and captions are mutually supporting. If we were to consider Exhibit 8.6 without story or labels, there's nothing by which we could conclude that these people are talking about an upsurge in crime. At the same time, the headline and accompanying stories can describe events but wouldn't have the same impact without pictures of people's faces.

While the newspaper accounts don't offer an explanation of the "eight murders in two years" in the rural Michigan county, they offer labels that encourage the reader to plug the story's details into a narrative: It's people from "the city," from farther south, from Detroit, who are coming in. The label "criminal," however, seems at odds with the man trying to kidnap his own daughter. Whatever we make of that story, it's more complicated than bad people coming up from the big city. What there is of the dead man's story remains defined from the viewpoint of the man who killed him (boyfriend of the baby's mother) and from the mother's account of his "stalking" her in order to gain custody of their child.

Another narrative that the story may be made to fit is that told by the National Rifle Association. According to the article, the NRA wants to use the story in ads "to support its stand that citizens should have the right to own guns and keep them in their homes."

In other words, the newspaper account and photographs provide material that is pressed by the captions into one narrative (criminals moving from the corrupt and violent city to the formerly peaceful countryside), even when some details of the account point to a different story (conflict between parents over child; attempt to seize the child, ending in shooting). The newspaper reporters and editors do the labeling, through summarizing and simplifying the comments of those interviewed, in order to speak to readers in nearby Saginaw and other cities about crime in Gladwin.

One of the best ways to see how ideology connects with the reading of a photograph is to try your own labels and see how they compare with those of others.

ASSIGNMENT

Examine the photographs in Exhibits 8.7 through 8.11. One or two come with captions, so that you can see how these guide interpretations of the photo. Others are without captions. Working in small groups in class, discuss some possibilities for how the photos might be labeled. (The print ads grouped at the end of Chapter 5 can also be used for this purpose.) You also should consider some alternatives for the ways in which Exhibits 8.7 and 8.8 are labeled.

Outside of class, look for five to ten other examples of captioning and write on its effects in your journal or in an informal writing.

Exhibit 8.7 "Another day." Used by permission of Evian Natural Spring Water, Great Brands of Europe, Inc.

Exhibit 8.8 "Time is to be treasured." Used by permission of Citizen Watch Company and Meyer Jewelers.

Exhibit 8.9 Photo used by permission of Statue of Liberty National Monument.

PAUSE FOR REFLECTION

Also consider Exhibits 8.12 through 8.14, reproductions of artwork by Barbara Kruger. Kruger characteristically brings together a photo and a text, and her art depends on a dissonance between these that defamiliarizes both photo and text as well as the customary relationship between them. Often Kruger's photos include black-and-white illustrations drawn from older work, framed in a striking red border, with white-on-red lettering for the caption. You might consider, in your discussion of captioning, how her work offers a commentary. It's a commentary at odds with the more common conventional ways of captioning photographs, which make the act of captioning invisible and "natural."

446 RECONSIDERATIONS

Exhibit 8.10 Photo by Lewis Hine. Used by permission of George Eastman House International Museum of Photography and Film.

Appellation and Ideology

Another term for labeling, one that connects more directly to its theoretical aspects, is *appellation* (also *interpellation*). A French Marxist theorist, Louis Althusser, developed the term in the 1960s to apply to the sort of labeling done in captions and elsewhere. In French the standard form of introducing yourself by name is *je m'appelle* so-and-so; literally, "I call myself" so-and-so. We fre-

Exhibit 8.11   Photo used by permission of the Museum of the City of New York.

quently call ourselves by one of various possible labels (first name, last name, occupation, practitioner of a hobby, etc.). Depending on the context, I could call myself a man, a father, a professor, an author, a tennis player, a *Doctor Who* fan, a dog owner, a careful driver, and so on. Each of these terms implies a relationship to other aspects of contemporary culture, sometimes by affiliation (other tennis players, athletics, those governed by cultural codes more upper- or middle-class than, say, bowling), sometimes by opposition (man and father are male; dog owner might be read as anticat—which I am not, being a cat owner as well). My choosing a label for myself *projects* an identity; it tells others how I want to be known. Notice that I have several choices, several components of who I am, and that it is through selection that I present myself. Even your appellation, then, is rhetorically significant.

You may have noticed the appellation used at the beginning of the preceding paragraph, in which Louis Althusser becomes "a French Marxist theorist." It's a rare privilege to be able to do what the French idiom literally says—to *call yourself*. Often, you receive your appellations, as in this case, from others.

Exhibit 8.12
Photomontage by Barbara Kruger.
Courtesy Mary Boone Gallery, New York.

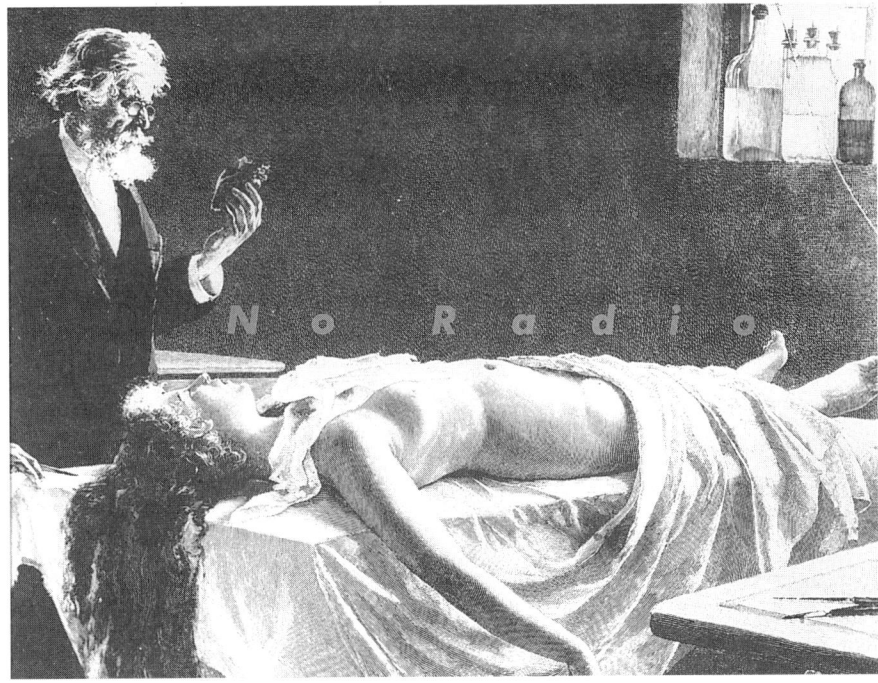

Exhibit 8.13 Photomontage by Barbara Kruger. Courtesy Mary Boone Gallery, New York.

In your classes, you may be identified by first name; by last name; by Mr./Ms./Miss/Mrs. + last name; by "You in the back row"; and so on. And within these settings, you name others, thus (prospectively) bringing them into a defined relationship with you. For example, how do you address your instructor? As "Doctor"? "Professor"? "Professor" or "Doctor" + last name"? By first name? You may find it customary to use one mode of address, and very difficult to shift to another—you may be accustomed to speaking to your teachers in the more formal register marked by "Ms./Mr." or "Dr." + surname, and may have an almost physical resistance to using the first name, even when specifically requested to do so. (Languages other than English sometimes have even more strict prohibitions against such informality than is the case in U.S. usage. Several European languages have different verb forms for formal address and for speaking with close friends, family, and pets: If, in French, you use the familiar *tu* form with a stranger, you may provoke a violent response because of the insult.)

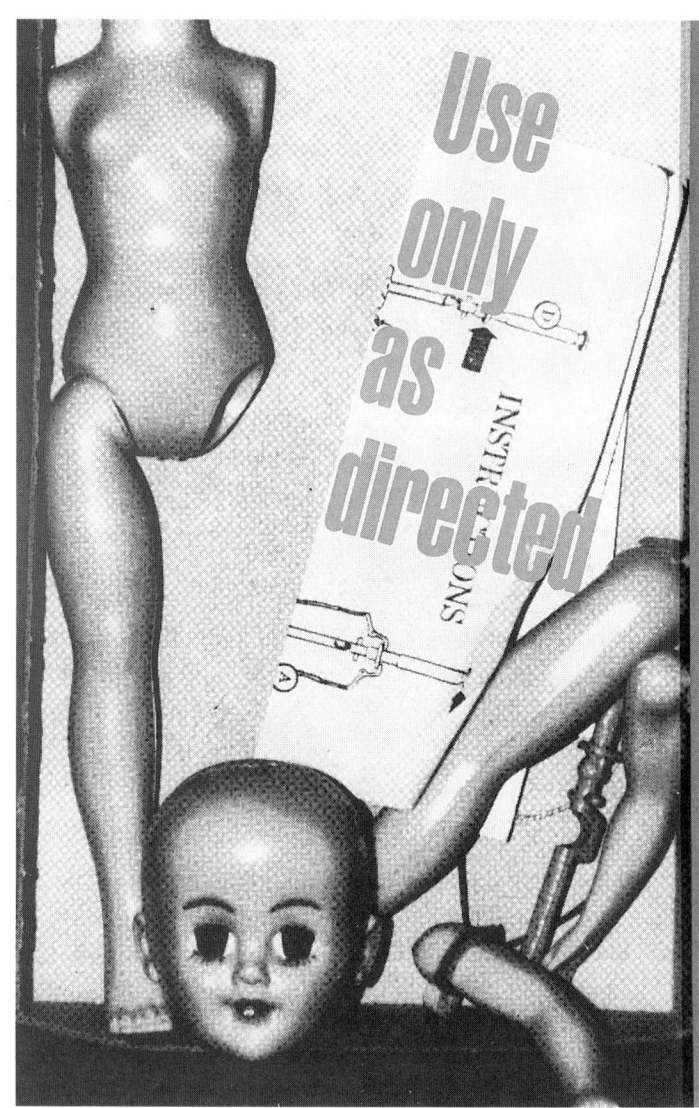

Exhibit 8.14
Photomontage by Barbara Kruger.
Courtesy Mary Boone Gallery,
New York.

PAUSE FOR REFLECTION

Draw up a list of people that you are most comfortable with when you use their first names or nicknames. Then provide a second list of people to be addressed by "Mr./Ms./Miss/Mrs." + last name. What sort of logic do you see in your lists? Do you have a nickname? Whom do you encourage or permit to use it?

Interestingly enough, when writing papers on poetry or novels, students often find it easier to talk about female writers by first name than they would male writers: If the subject is the novel *Pride and Prejudice* or the poem "I heard a fly buzz—when I died," essays may refer to the writers as "Jane" or "Emily," whereas it would be highly unusual to find, in papers on *Hard Times* or "The Love Song of J. Alfred Prufrock," references to "Charles" or "T. S."/"Tom."

PAUSE FOR REFLECTION
Try this out with media celebrities: Compile a list of ten male and ten female, and see which you would be inclined to address or speak of by first name, which by last.

Louis Althusser uses the phrase "Hey, you there!" as the prototype of appellation. Being addressed in this fashion, as might happen on the street, automatically interpellates us as **subjects.** To be a subject is to be under someone's authority, whether that of a policeman, a king, the law of the land, administrative control, or whatever. ("Under the power or authority of another; owing obedience or allegiance to another," as the *American Heritage Dictionary* phrases it.)

We generally prefer having the freedom to call ourselves our choice of names, rather than being called something by someone else. But despite our preferences, we *are* "called" by others, repeatedly or even incessantly, because we necessarily have some relation to them that is not of our own creation. For example, you are interpellated as *student* because you have enrolled in a course and met the requirements for continuing in that role. (The particulars of what it means to be a student vary, of course, depending on the institution.) And while in class you may be called on to answer a question or offer a comment. Many, perhaps most, appellations are not up to individual choice: When you cease to be a student, you will be a former student, perhaps a graduate or alumna/-us; had you never enrolled, you would have been appellated as a nonstudent (perhaps high school graduate, member of the public, or some other term). Everyone fits into the larger cultural system in multiple ways; and the labels or appellations by which we know each other have a great deal to do with how we interact, because they connect with how we treat each other, which in turn connects with ideology.

The larger cultural system and ideology can be inferred from what does and does not feel "natural," or what is and isn't "common sense." Another way to bring to consciousness what is natural is through looking at what is prohibited and why. Every culture has a set of taboos—actions or words that are prohibited. Taboos are easier to see in other cultures, because our own taboos have, for us, the force of "natural" law. Some taboos are very culture-specific, while others are widespread. Virtually every culture has a taboo against incest, though what counts for incest differs widely. (For example, marriage between first cousins is taboo in many parts of the United States but is permissible in others.)

Taboos can be flash points for conflict because of the mixture of differing ideologies in contemporary society. For example, premarital sex is taboo within certain subcultures in the United States, engaged in but not approved in some, and generally acceptable in others. Taboos on homosexuality or oral and anal sex (legally defined or appellated in some states as "sodomy") vary considerably according to region and social group. For some groups words such as *God* or *fuck*, in spoken language or in print, are taboo in all uses; in others, permitted in certain contexts (such as in a joke book, in a textbook if italicized, or in a college course if cited as a linguistic example); and for still others (including some college classes), permitted to be spoken or written freely. For some groups one or more of the following are taboo:

- Dating, intimate contact, or marriage between people of different races
- Dating, intimate contact, or marriage between people of widely different class or economic status
- Dating or intimate contact between teacher and student
- Dating or intimate contact between a man and a woman of widely disparate ages
- Dating or intimate contact between man and man or woman and woman

The Alabama principal who canceled the senior prom to prevent interracial dating was trying to prevent violation of one taboo felt with particular force in his area of the South; his actions, in turn, violated a professional taboo against open expressions of racism by educators and those in positions of authority.

Taboos are generally conceived—within the cultures in which they operate—to be a matter of nature or of religion. *It just isn't done* is offered as a characteristic explanation, and the question "Why?" may be not only unexpected but subversive or irreligious. And yet the differences between cultures as to what is or is not taboo would indicate that taboos are cultural, not biological, in origin.

PAUSE FOR REFLECTION

What instances of taboos can you name? Generate a list, based on (a) your understanding of the community in which you live; (b) matters specific to your family or relatives; (c) matters specific to your circle of friends. Are there words or phrases or actions that are permissible in some localities but not in others? (E.g., at a baseball game but not in a classroom or church or library? One can start a "wave" in a stadium, whereas in a library or church service, perhaps not.) What are penalties for some of these taboo actions? How do others show that taboos are important to observe?

Taboos extend from matters considered to be of major importance, like the prohibitions against racism or incest, to those that seem to be of less importance, such as being rowdy in museums, addressing "social superiors" by their first names, or walking into the wrong bathroom (even if you know it's empty). The Pause for Reflection above should illustrate that not all of what we undertake to do has carefully thought-out and consciously held reasons behind it. Rather, it's only with some reluctance that we can bring ourselves to transgress practices we have absorbed along with the rest of what we term culture. The set of customs, beliefs, ideas, myths, and so forth that gives rise to taboos and to other examples of what "goes without saying" is ideology. This discussion allows us to sense something of its force.

Ideology: Definitions and Illustrations

Taboos are touchy matters because they connect to the values and fundamental assumptions of what it is to be a member of your culture. In that sense, they are closely connected to the most general meaning of the term *ideology*. Used in this general sense, ideology is one of those abstractions that, like radiation, cannot be experienced or sensed directly, but whose existence must be inferred from other phenomena. Two of these phenomena include labeling—who is labeled, by whom, and for what purposes—and taboos on certain acts or expressions. So long as everyone is working within the same set of values or ideology, there is agreement on what is "natural" or good. But when there are conflicts in values or ideologies (as is more and more frequently the case in contemporary culture), differences become visible—differences along lines of gender, race, class, and other fault lines. It has been said that we read not *into* a text but *out of* one.

PAUSE FOR REFLECTION
Consider the following hypothetical situations. What sorts of "texts" are they "read out of"? For each, what would you probably do in terms of gestures, spoken words, or other sorts of interchange?

First, think what you would do individually in the circumstances described. Then talk through these responses with others in the class, explaining your rationale for differences (if any). Last, and most important, what does this activity tell you about the assumptions or values to be seen in these and similar encounters? How are these behaviors coded in the labels you would use in each case?

1. You reach a large, cumbersome door just ahead of a sexually attractive person, close to your own age.
2. Same situation as #1, except the person is someone you don't consider to be attractive.
3. Same situation as #1, except the person appears to be having a little difficulty walking, perhaps because of age or disability.
4. Same situation as #1, except the person is in her or his early teens.
5. Same situation as #1, except the person is someone who would be commonly regarded as your social superior (minister, community figure, professor, etc.).
6. Same situation as #1, except the person is your supervisor or professional superior.

Write informally about what you expected other students to say, what they in fact said, and any differences you found between your responses and theirs.

By now you may have recognized differences among individuals in your class, as well as more generally in the culture, regarding what is seen as the "natural" order of interactions between people. Matters such as age, race, gender, level of education, and income level are used as bases for establishing and maintaining relationships with others—singly or in groups, in person or through media. Conventions for these ways of interacting are grounded in ideologies, whether shared or conflicting. In order to develop an account of how such differences develop and why they are significant for a study of media, we will have to examine something of the background of the term *ideology*.

One problem evident in discussing ideology is the problem of trying to be objective about subjective beliefs. If it's someone else's beliefs under scrutiny, you may be seen as the bloodless scientist dissecting the butterfly in order to understand the nature of beauty (to borrow one classic formulation); if it's your own belief under examination, then you may be prone to the same special pleading as anyone else. What's needed is a **double consciousness,** a consciousness that is at once analytical toward the phenomena under discussion and capable of acknowledging participation in them. (The perspective taken toward media and their texts throughout this book may be seen as an attempt at encouraging a double consciousness.) But the attempt to maintain such a double perspective can be fatiguing.

The meaning of the word *ideology* slips, depending on the context. There are three principal, contrasting senses of the word; and it is important to keep these straight, so that your own thought and communication with others are as clear as possible. In the case of ideology, the slippage is not only a result of our imprecision about words: It is a crucial part of how the concept has developed in Western culture. (The discussion of ideology in this chapter and elsewhere is indebted to the entry for "ideology" in *Keywords,* by Raymond Williams, and to *Literary Theory* and the first chapter of *Ideology* by Terry Eagleton.)

FALSE CONSCIOUSNESS

The term *ideology* was first used in the context of the French Revolution to refer to the science or study of ideas, in a formulation parallel to bio*logy* (the study of life), psycho*logy* (the study of the mind), and other -logy words. The word *ideology* was coined by Antoine Destutt de Tracy, an aristocrat who became a spokesperson for the French Revolution. His hope, and that of others who picked up the term, was that *reason* would free the student of ideas from the influence of ideas. (In studying the rhetoric of media, we may be motivated by similar hopes.) However, the attempt to free reason from "the prejudice, superstition and obscurantism of the ancien régime" was itself an ideological attempt, as part of a power struggle that put appeals to "disinterested nature, science, and reason" to political uses. Ironically, Tracy and other "ideologues" became scapegoats after France's defeat in its war against Russia, for pursuing theories instead of "a knowledge of the human heart and of the lessons of history." At the outset, then, discussions of ideology got mixed up with the term's use in struggles to gain and hold onto political power.

The fundamental problem with the topic of ideology, then, is subjectivity—the would-be analyst of ideology necessarily has ideological interests, as do those who are not involved in such analysis. In practice, what usually happens is that people engaged in discussions of ideology make an implicit or explicit claim to be independent of ideology; that is, not to have any interests at stake in the analysis. (Such a position is usually an honest belief, but at times it may be disingenuous.) Most commonly, you will find uses of the term *ideology* to be pejorative: "ideology" describes someone else's warped or narrow ideas. The term is used to criticize another's position in an argument as being dominated by a "contrived" set of ideas or dogmas. Those "theoretical" ideas are opposed to those of the speaker, which are presumably natural and commonsensical—perhaps based on "a knowledge of the human heart and of the lessons of history." (For illustration, consider denunciations of the U.S. president as dominated by a "liberal ideology," or of the Congress as having undergone an "ideological takeover." Both charges are accompanied by a tacit claim to be free of ideology.) The early and still dominant sense of the word *ideology* involves an accusation that someone else is being "political" while the speaker is free of such motives. Ideology is conceived to be conscious distortion of a position the speaker knows to be the truth. The further someone's position is from the "common sense" of the dominant or majority ideology, the more likely that position is to be attacked as ideological.

Ideology is frequently conceived in terms of "left" and "right," or "leftist" and "conservative." (The popular opposition of "liberal" and "conservative" is a misnomer: "Liberal" describes a position in which individuals have the capacity and right to decide for themselves, and is in fact a centrist position attacked by both left and right.) The political extremes are sometimes fairly close to mirror images of each other, as you can see if you compare the tactics and pronouncements of the student left of the 1960s and early '70s with those of current white separatist and vigilante groups and antiabortion activists. (However, this symmetry does not mean equal influence or access to media: In U.S. political discourse since the 1980s, the right has attained a wider measure of power by affiliating with corporate organizations such as the Olin Foundation.)

The opposite of *ideological* would be not ideological in the opposite direction, but *pragmatic* or *practical.* The implication is that those who are practical are not ideological but are able to shift viewpoints and adapt to circumstances—to cut deals and work out compromises. However, this ideal of pragmatism is *itself* an idea or theory or ideology, even if not consciously or consistently held. The governing principle of pragmatism—not getting carried away with theories—is itself a theory which has carried many away.

While the term *ideology* arose in the aftermath of the French Revolution, it was developed and used most effectively by Karl Marx and others who formed a theory of society based on conflicts between classes. Marx outlined what he saw as the competing interests in society through his theory of the class system: The economic interests of three classes, according to this theory, dominate all interactions. Marx explained the workings of society by a theory of continual antipathy between interests of the ruling class or capitalists, the working class or proletariat, and the middle class or bourgeoisie (a tripartite structure that remains largely intact though more complex in later versions). Analysis, in this system, is used to rationalize the continued dominance of the ruling groups. Marx thus established the primary sense of ideology as fantasy or illusion, "false consciousness": not only false because it doesn't fit with (nonideological) reality, but also false ethically, because it distracts those in the dominated classes from understanding how the world really works, keeping them (us) out of any real power.

"False consciousness" continues to be the most common meaning given to the term *ideology,* with particular emphasis on the rigidity of one's opponents' ideas. Those who endorse this model of ideology, whether fundamentalist conservatives or Marxists, tend to think of issues in terms of two sides, "us" and "them," "good guys" and "bad guys." The narrative that supports this view of ideology is most often a conspiracy: God's legions against Satan, greedy capitalists keeping the oppressed workers ignorant and underfed, communists or the Elders of Zion conspiring to subvert and destroy the moral fiber, and so on. The assumption here is that the truth is evident to all, even the opponents, but that they are denying common sense by twisting facts to suit their interests. Those who accuse others of being dominated by ideologies claim to possess a correct and accurate version of things, a transcendent understanding of truth.

The concept of false consciousness can also apply to interested groups of people who are assumed to be willing to distort what they know to be the truth in order to gain sympathy or adherents (a behavior popularly taken to be "political"). Statements made by advertisers marketing their products, by union leadership during contract negotiations, by campaign spokespersons during an election year, by editorial cartoonists, by "political" talk show hosts are assumed to be drawn from available "facts" in order to influence what listeners and readers believe. The "rhetoric" of such statements is characterized by slanted evidence and special pleading. (See Bad Rhetoric section in Chapter 10.) In this model, it is assumed that ideological statements are made consciously; it may also be assumed, or at least claimed, that the audience understands the conditions of "reading" these statements and that, as with advertisements, it's up to us to watch out for our own interests. The difficulty of reading such interested rhetoric is that we are invited to become the text's ideal audience, and thereby appellated as something we want to be: that is, as cleverer than the next person, or on the winning side, or part of a larger, more attractive group. And this encourages us not to examine the ideas offered.

Thinking about ideology in these terms presumes that there is a grounding in truth, in reality, in God's word, or in the way things are—in some transcendent viewpoint outside of ideology—which is available to and understandable by "the common man," either naturally or after guidance by the enlightened. (The pose of enlightenment may come from a credentialed expert, from an "Aw, shucks" sort of ordinary fellow, or from a variety of other types of sources.) But increasingly in the twentieth century, it has become more difficult to sustain such a transcendent viewpoint, whether derived from Judeo-Christianity, from dogmatic strains of Marxism, or from some other perspective. Charges that "the other side" is dominated by ideology frequently mask hypocrisy and cynicism, from the United States and its geopolitical allies just as surely as from those labeled Communists. "To seek some humble, pragmatic political goal, such as bringing down the democratically elected government of Chile, is a question of adapting oneself realistically to the facts; to send one's tanks into Czechoslovakia is an instance of ideological fanaticism" (Eagleton, *Ideology* p. 4).

Claims that Marxist, Christian, or other theories give access to objective truth about human affairs—whether based on revelation or on scientific knowledge of political economy—are increasingly regarded with suspicion. For one thing, these claims tend to denature each other. It was easier, in Europe before the Reformation, to honor claims by "the Church" to a licensed interpretation of the meaning of the Scriptures, because there was little competition. After Luther, however, there were many voices claiming a right interpretation of God's word, and the rigorous licensing of interpretation by the Catholic Church was met with the Protestant notion that individual believers had to do their own interpretation, guided by study of the Bible and the Holy Spirit. (Regulation of individual believers presents its own problems, as shown by Protestantism's later fragmentation.)

Similarly, it was possible in the early twentieth century to believe in a communist utopia in which the state would wither away, and to give credence to a "dictatorship of the proletariat" in the Soviet Union. Knowledge of purges and genocide under Lenin and Stalin percolated through the Soviet bloc even during Stalin's lifetime, however, and became public knowledge after Khrushchev's denunciation of Stalin in 1956. The dissolution of the Soviet Union was a political recognition of what had been generally recognized if not acknowledged by those living in its political sphere, that the claims to scientific knowledge of political economy served principally as cover for cynical dominance by the managerial class or *apparatchiki*. There are still "true believers" in the communist idea (mostly in retirement homes), but such belief requires a great force of will in the face of what may be the predominant attitude in the United States and Europe now, a generalized cynicism.

Relativism

A second, contrasting sense of ideology, then, has arisen along with the inclination to doubt the existence or possibility of a transcendent position from which to discover or pronounce upon truth. Increasingly, *ideology* is being used to refer generally to any set of beliefs or assumptions by which one's world is ordered; the term is applied not only to conscious decisions but to unconscious matters taken for granted. This second sense is not reserved for those with whom we do not agree but applies as well to practices of our own culture. This position is sometimes labeled (by those assuming a true belief)

Chapter 8: Discovering Contexts and Deeper Purposes 459

as "relativism," and it tends to sit more comfortably with current, more democratic sensibilities than do claims of transcendence.

According to this definition of ideology, it's not a matter of consciousness, but of material practices. "The set of ideas which arise from a given set of material interests, or more broadly, from a definite class or group" (Williams p. 156) does not equate to the "false consciousness" perspective on ideology, because these ideas derive from the system rather than from anyone's consciousness as shaped by that system. Regarding ideology as a set of beliefs or assumptions or practices, basic, usually not articulated, and frequently even unconsciously held, means extending some legitimacy to ways in which others think, even if those ways are different from your own views. For example, in discussions about the custom of opening (or not) a door for another person, some differences may emerge along lines of gender or region. These may have next to nothing to do with the "false consciousness" way of regarding ideology, and yet there are differences between your expectations of how you treat other people casually, and how others in your class may. Conspiracy theories don't usually extend to the level of common interactions between people, and yet these, too, seem to be subject to ideology: Rules of precedence through doors may be trivial in themselves, but the understandings they indicate about how women and men deal with each other are anything but trivial. Do women get to speak in church? Do they get to be preachers or priests or bishops? Who speaks up in public meetings? Who gets called on in class, and who volunteers answers? Are these trivial matters?

One controversy about ideology, which has consequences for thinking about rhetoric, may arise from a confusion between these two meanings of the term. If one speaker regards ideology as deliberate distortion, while another extends the term to any set of beliefs or values, it's hard to see how any real conversation can take place. Such is the situation, for example, in disputes about abortion, in which one group defines *baby* as a fetus at any developmental stage back to the fertilized egg, while another considers *baby* to mean an independent living human being, quite different from a fetus in its early stages of development. As a consequence, what is for one ideology a minor surgical procedure is for another a second Holocaust. This is clearly not only a verbal dispute. But the terms of discourse (it can hardly be called a debate) rigidly circumscribe the possibility for any exchange of ideas or successful rhetorical appeal to sides other than one's own.

Producing good rhetoric under these conditions is difficult. Is the goal to speak to the like-minded, motivating them to action against evil opponents? Or is it to understand and perhaps persuade those of differing viewpoints? As a writer, you have to determine how to respond, according to your own values—

but tolerance for others' views is a norm in academic discussions, and it is an attitude usually found more persuasive than "preaching to the converted."

PAUSE FOR REFLECTION

Have you been in a situation where you had an extended conversation or exchange of views with someone on a matter that was the source of strong disagreement between you? What was the subject? What were the positions taken? And how did you manage to carry on your discussion?

What are some subjects besides abortion that tend to bring about strong disagreements in the contemporary United States? How do you write so as to motivate those who agree with you on such topics? How do you write so as to reach those who don't? At what stage do you reevaluate your own beliefs?

All of us derive from others in our culture (family, friends, cultural institutions such as schools) our fundamental sense of how our lives should be ordered. These ideas of proper order are present throughout what we do, ranging from relationships between women and men to how we treat our children to what household or workplace duties are appropriate. Calling these "ideological matters," without further clarification, however, brings connotations of ideology as mistaken thought—and no one is likely to tolerate frontal challenges to her or his customary worldview.

A CONCEALED STRUCTURE OF VALUES

A third sense of ideology, that adopted in this book, retains some aspects of the other two meanings. The term *ideology* is applied to underlying values and assumptions, not reserved for conscious distortions; but these values and assumptions are given a specifically political spin. Ideology by this definition would be "the largely concealed structure of values which informs and underlies our factual statements," as this is connected with the "power-structure and power-relations of the society we live in" (Eagleton, *Literary Theory* p. 14.).

Note that under this definition, as under the second above, there is no getting "outside of ideology"; and as with that definition, it's not necessary to have a position of untranscendable authority from which to pronounce on others' ideologies. But this definition reflects ideology's political function of maintaining power relationships. Ideology works to reproduce the existing social orders within society; its conscious and careful examination can be the basis of questioning these orders.

To see ideology in terms of power relations means to contemplate, from the essentially democratic assumption of social relations that holds in the

United States, the fact that some people have more and some less power. It should not be surprising that many within the same system look at it differently, depending on whether or not that system keeps them warm and well fed. As we saw in Chapter 7, the ideological devices by which those in power maintain their advantage are collectively called hegemony.

Antonio Gramsci (and some others) developed the concept of hegemony in order to explain why working classes and others who are disadvantaged in the social order not only do not rise up in revolt, but actually buy into the social hierarchy that defines them as less deserving. The short answer is that they (we) are taught to accept our position as the natural order of things. In an earlier century this natural order would have been phrased as the divine right of kings, the expectation that God will take care of us or will sort out the just and unjust when the last trumpet sounds, the wrongness of identifying happiness with material wealth rather than moral values, and so on. With the lessening influence of religion in Western cultures in this century, some of that teaching has been taken on by forms of entertainment, principally media: first cinema and then television (as well as popular books, magazines, and newspapers) have kept us diverted and to some degree isolated from each other, so that we don't get together into troublesome groups and demand higher wages or adequate health care. Another hegemonic device is the invention and encouragement of divisions among the lower (and increasingly among the middle) classes, through such matters as sports rivalries. Sports gives a safety valve, an outlet for competition in a form that never seriously threatens the interests of those in positions of power.

Hegemony provides a useful interpretive lens for looking at some of the more popular elements of media and culture—but it has only one story to tell, and that one gets old after a while. It's always media as the middlemen, taking orders from the powerful in order to get us masses to stay in line. But hegemony runs into a good deal of resistance from "common sense": The idea of U.S. culture as dominated by a ruling class may be hard to sustain, because contemporary culture is so diversified. And it might be argued that some popular media offer the potential for resistance, not simply delivering hegemonic propaganda.

One ideological position that does hegemonic work is the assumption that each of us is a self-creating individual. This is so much an article of faith that even suggesting that there are limits to individualism may bring sharp denials. There's a moment in *Monty Python's The Life of Brian* in which Brian, the other guy from Nazareth, is talking to a crowd in the street below, trying to persuade them that he is not the Messiah and that they should leave him alone. They shout things back at him such as "Only the true Messiah denies his divinity," which leaves him no possible response. He tells them "You don't need to follow anybody." They respond, in unison, "We don't need to follow anybody." He shouts, "You're all individuals"; they respond, again in unison, "We're all individuals." The claim to uniqueness may come from reasoned observation; but more often, it's a statement of faith or dogma. It's ideology speaking through us.

If we want to develop a capacity to act independently rather than be falsely persuaded that we do so, we should learn to distrust or at least look skeptically at what appears to be "natural." The established order in our culture is obvious to us because it's familiar. But if because of ideology we see "constructed" ideas as "natural," are there such things as "natural" ideas at all? Something that was truly "natural" would be universal, existing in all cultures, and with the later twentieth-century developments in transportation and communication we should be able to find these.

Seen from that perspective, very few matters are candidates for "human nature." The need for food and drink, for sleep, the sexual drive: These are all biological matters—and beyond these, problems arise with the concept of "the natural." Even with matters such as sexuality or religion, concrete practices and the accounting of these within any culture's system are so distinct that it becomes difficult to find a relationship. In other words, we should scrutinize any claim that an activity or practice or belief is natural for the possibility that we are being urged to accept something without examining it.

Perhaps whatever is repeated comes to feel natural to us. Not many things are repeated more often to us than our names, and it is in part how we are named that defines us in relation to others. Mrs. Smith is named in relation to Mr. Smith; Dr. Jones is named as a *doctor,* usually more prestigious than plain *mister;* Elizabeth has a different, more grandiose connotation than Liz, Lizzie, Eliza, Betty, or Beth; and traditional English (or French) names such as Richard, Michael, George, Anne, or Catherine have a different "feel" to them (and therefore fit their subjects differently) than clearly Continental names such as Justine, Katrina, Marlene, Gunter, Boris, or Horst. These are different, in turn, from Irish/Scottish names (Ryan, Ian), which in turn are different from names deriving from other cultures or which are made up. Names connect you to a tradition, well before you have any say in the matter.

PAUSE FOR REFLECTION

Studies suggest that women with names such as Elizabeth, Catherine, or Anne are more likely to rise in social and professional ranks than those with names such as Brandi, Susie, or Rose. How would you go about confirming or contradicting this?

We are named in ways besides our names, as noted above. We're named as informed readers, as good citizens, as constituents, as customers, as consumers, as Ford owners, as neighbors, as parents of schoolchildren, as taxpayers, as good credit risks... and all these are part of invisible webs that link us to other portions of our culture. Cultures develop numerous ways, having more to do with flattery than compulsion, by which they interpellate each of their members as *subjects.* If you happen to share in the ideology that makes these connections, the result is that you feel at home in the larger culture (or at least your corner of it). If, on the other hand, you identify with those who do not feel so addressed— too old, too dark, too female, too foreign, too gay, too poor, too uneducated—this centering can come to feel like a pull away from who you are (more precisely, an appellation of you in terms you do not accept). This sensation has been described as undergoing "innumerable small murders of the mind and spirit" (Gornick p. ix).

PAUSE FOR REFLECTION
Brainstorm a list of appellations for yourself. Include those that are flattering, those not very positive, and those neutral. When your list gets to about twenty terms, look at each one and try to determine (1) who it is that applies that term to you, and (2) what uses there might be in doing so.

Althusser devised a concept to account for how ideology as "'lived' relation to the real" is put into effect—Ideological State Apparatuses (ISAs). The notion of ISAs is offered to account for the continuance of the views of "the ruling class" even without frequent intervention of police, the army, or the criminal justice system. The frequency and intensity of strikes and work stoppages has diminished since the Depression, so that violence in labor negotiations is much rarer than formerly. A partial explanation is that "workers" have been "better educated" so as to be more sympathetic to management. The means of such "education" are the various organizations Althusser calls ISAs.

The concept of Ideological State Apparatuses was developed in order to fill in a "hole" in classical Marxist theory—in which the ruling class, the working class, and the middle class all exist statically, without attention to how they can be reproduced over time. Althusser (p. 143) suggests that there are a number of overlapping and somewhat competing ISAs that fulfill this reproductive function:

- The religious ISA (the system of the different churches)
- The educational ISA (the system of the different public and private schools)

- The family ISA
- The legal ISA
- The political ISA (the political system, including the different parties)
- The trade-union ISA
- The communications ISA (press, radio, and television, etc.)
- The cultural ISA (literature, the arts, sports, etc.)

Althusser sees these as working closely with the ruling ideology. In pre-revolutionary France, the aristocracy worked most closely with the religious ISA to instill values that kept it in power; after the revolution, the new ruling class, rising from the newly powerful bourgeoisie, devalued the religious ISA, giving more emphasis to the educational ISA, which Althusser sees as dominant in contemporary society.

This principle is something to be kept in mind when we hear complaints that schools aren't teaching "values" any more. Which values? Whose values? In whose interests? Everyone benefits—from the viewpoint of Althusser's "ruling class"—if ISAs can do their work. Calling out the army or police to maintain order, as happened during the Democratic Convention of 1968 or two years later with the Ohio National Guard at Kent State, is not only expensive and destructive but even counterproductive. It's far better to develop what Richard Nixon appellated as "the silent majority," because then the government's policies on behalf of "the ruling class" can continue even over (token) opposition.

Writing in the 1960s, Althusser contended that the educational ISA was then dominant. Such an argument may be harder to sustain now: While it is true that educational institutions have considerable control over the time and materials of U.S. children from age five to seventeen in the great majority of cases, and for at least another four years in a slight majority (those who pursue college degrees), education's dominance in this country has been contested for some time by a conglomerate of communications and cultural ISAs generally labeled "the media." As is frequently pointed out, U.S. high school graduates have on average spent as much time watching television as they have in school, and when other media such as radio and popular music are figured into the total (sometimes in the form of secondary or tertiary consumption; i.e., listening to the stereo and reading a magazine while the TV is on), clearly it can no longer be said that the educational ISA, in conjunction with the family, is exclusively in control of forming cultural values. Moreover, the media ISA is finding its way into the educational one; for example, in the promotion of Channel One, a combination of news, public affairs, and commercials pitched to teenagers and shown in thousands of classrooms daily.

From another perspective, elements of the political ISA, speaking on behalf of the business establishment, are contesting the educational ISA (though not in these terms) as too expensive, too professionalized, and too driven by ideas about education that differ from "common sense" (i.e., their own education from a generation ago). And the educational apparatus is also criticized by an alliance of family and church ISAs for its positions on "sex education" and on scientific matters such as evolution that impinge on their ideology. But the primary challenge to the power of the educational ISA comes from media.

The relevance of ideology to discussions of media should now be clear: Media, as the preeminent "consciousness industries," have become contemporary culture's most efficient devices for shaping and sustaining the dominant ideology by marginalizing those of the "outs." This is the basis of many attacks on media, as expressed by those who (like myself) are part of the educational ISA, those in religious or family ISAs, or even (and ironically) those in the media themselves. In U.S. society the dominant or "common" ideology has evolved to become largely empty of what is often thought of as political content. It is most often phrased as affirmation of what is sometimes called "the free market." This ideology isn't particularly concerned about "liberal" or "conservative" views (none are really leftist), so long as consumers continue to consume, laborers to labor, and corporations to manufacture. Perspectives on this system are held to be the spontaneous creation of free-thinking, self-creating individuals. No attention is typically given to how this "individualism" is itself created and replicated—but you will find many media texts that contribute to it.

As Althusser describes the mechanism, ISAs, while they may compete to some extent with each other for prominence, all are subsumed under the "ruling ideology" established by the "ruling class." It might be possible to reverse the sequence and say that the ruling class is established by the ruling ideology. This is a chicken–egg problem: Both arise out of the same action. The means by which those in control maintain that control, without resorting (more often than they do) to bloodshed, is to create a mechanism of desire by which most of those in subordinate positions *want* to fit into the system, and the others cause as little trouble as can be arranged. This management of desire is hegemony. One place where we can see hegemony most clearly at work is in ways in which media texts reinforce definitions of appropriate roles within society: These texts do not create such definitions out of thin air, but build from material already extant. A brief illustration might be found in the 1988 film *Die Hard*.

Reading *Die Hard*

Die Hard starred Bruce Willis as a somewhat rebellious and obnoxious but thoroughly professional New York cop, John McLain. It's Christmas, and

McLain has gone to visit his wife Holly (Bonnie Bedalia) and children in Los Angeles, where Holly has taken an important position with a large Japanese firm, the Nakasone Corporation. McLain has worked up some gestures of reconciliation, hiring a limo for their use after the firm's Christmas party. He is more than a little ill at ease in the firm's luxurious headquarters and in California generally, but is relaxing in Holly's office, feeling the thick carpet on his bare feet, when shots ring out. A group of international thieves pretending to be terrorists have occupied the building and taken control; the leader is a German, Hans Gruber (Alan Rickman). McLain manages to evade their roundup of the employees and for most of the film plays a role as "the fly in the ointment," subverting the thieves' attempts to fortify their position and break open the corporate safe. Reluctant (for obvious reasons) to use his real name on the walkie-talkie he captures from one of the thieves, McLain identifies himself (after a contemptuous comment by Gruber) as Roy Rogers. He manages eventually to kill Gruber and another accomplice with his last two bullets.

Through several devices the film encourages viewers to identify with McLain. He takes heroic, independent action against opposing forces—not only the superior forces of the international "terrorists," but also the official procedures of the LAPD, who first consider his calls for help to be crank calls and warn him to get off reserved radio channels; then send out a lone patrol car ("*Ein mann*," the Germans sneer) to investigate; then attempt to counter the thieves' defenses "by the book." The LAPD are replaced in turn by the FBI, whose greater firepower is matched only by their arrogance, as from their helicopter they try to gun down McLain (who has just saved fifty or so hostages from being blown up by explosives set on the roof). Another, less evident set of oppositions is that represented by Holly Gennaro's (or Mrs. McLain's) professional aspirations. Her career, and some implied marital tensions, have led her to move to the West Coast and to adopt her maiden name, a move that a sleazy coworker takes as license to hit on her. (He has bought her a Rolex, which features in the death of the leading villain.) The film works by developing and then resolving these tensions, more or less along the same rhythms as the succession of fights with the villains (all won, at the cost of greater and greater exhaustion, by McLain—except that the last "terrorist" is dispatched by the black patrolman who has been the one outside voice of common sense that McLain has had for support).

The police and FBI forces rely on institutional procedures. These are ineffective because the Germans have better procedures (and more firepower). On the other hand, the individualist and improviser McLain manages to come out ahead by remaining flexible. The thieves use a rocket to blow up the Humvee that the police attempt to use to enter the building; in response, McLain wires some explosives to a computer monitor on top of a chair, drops the apparatus down the elevator shaft, and takes out two combatants along with most of the ground floors, and nearly himself as well. He anticipates, as if by "natural" common sense, what the Germans' next move will be. The media comes in for some criticism too in *Die Hard* (and in the sequel *Die Harder*): An enterprising television reporter manages to scoop his colleagues by being on the spot for the large explosion. His staff figures out who John McLain is, and gets an interview with his children by threatening their housekeeper with deportation. The TV interview allows Gruber to make the connection between McLain and his wife Holly, greatly increasing her danger. At the conclusion of the film she has the satisfaction of responding to a question by punching the reporter in the face on camera.

The film, in other words, works as a parable of the superiority of American individualism and improvisation over both U.S. bureaucracy and foreign procedures, in the course of which the hero wins back his wife from the blandishments of the (Japanese) multinational corporation. All these social messages are encoded in the plot and other aspects of the film—although films are highly complex texts, and there are enough elements provided in this one for viewers to hold alternative interpretations. A strong element in almost any reading of the film, however, would have to be a ringing endorsement of individual action as opposed to the procedures of large organizations: A viewer of this film might take away an image of John McLain, bloody but unbowed, challenging kidnappers, assistant chief of police, sleazeball corporation executives, and others burdened with behaving as others require of them rather than taking independent initiative to do what's right. The message is essentially the same as that of many advertising campaigns, from Virginia Slims' "You've come a long way, baby," to Nike's long-lived "Just Do It": Pay no attention to others' warnings or considerations or analyses; act on what you feel and believe to be right or desirable. Transported out of the fictional world of *Die Hard* to the economic world of the marketplace, this message keeps us buying, on credit if necessary.

In addition to the functions we have seen in media texts—telling us stories, providing information about world events, giving us a sense of fashion, and other "pragmatic" functions—media disseminate and reinforce cultural values in ways that (as we have seen) connect to power relationships between individuals and other segments of society. It is in this regulation of power relationships that ideology moves to the third definition presented above: that of a concealed structure of values underlying what we say and do. Ideology in this sense blurs with the notion of hegemony as not only the set of ideas or values that support a text, but the ideas or values it is desirable for those reading that text to have. If we ask the question "Desirable for whom?" we raise the question of whether there is such a thing as a "ruling class" in the contemporary United States. It is part of the prevailing view that we make decisions as individuals, not as "classes"—beyond the blunt factor of income, in the United States we tend not to think of ourselves as members of classes. And yet there are undeniably affiliations in U.S. society that have a great deal to do with competing claims for power.

These competing claims can be seen in present complaints about "media." Some of these attacks on media come from the political left: To a large extent, media tie into consumer culture, creating unsustainable appetites for fossil fuels, wood, and other resources that incline developed nations to continue exploitation of others. Some come from political conservatives: Media present an image of the United States that attacks our nation unfairly, calling our good intentions into question; in covering domestic issues, media put forth "political" ideas about gender and racial roles. ("Mainstream" views are considered to be "natural," and therefore are supposedly not political or ideological.) Some attacks come from religious conservatives who see sexual attractiveness used in commercials and narrative lines as corrosive to their own beliefs about appropriate moral behavior. "Media" are quickly becoming scapegoats, which is an indication of the rapidly growing recognition of their pervasive influence in contemporary culture, and a response to some of the media's more evident transgressions of the assumption of neutrality.

Louis Althusser saw competing and collaborating ISAs at work in the overall interest of the ruling ideology. How do we apply this competitive model to the contemporary United States? Instead of a ruling class, the contemporary United States has several competing groups—the very rich, corporate executives, the political establishment, prominent cultural figures, those in control of media—whose interests sometimes overlap and sometimes compete. It is far from clear that their ideologies coincide. And how is it possible to determine and pronounce on someone's ideology while working within a theory that denies the possibility of nonideological vision? Althusser's model seems to reintroduce the need for a transcendent viewpoint, a position above theory, by which the whole system can be considered—which takes us back to ideology as false consciousness.

Perhaps a metaphor could be of use here, that of ideology as a lens. In this metaphor, no one sees 20–20: There is no clear and undistorted view of "reality," but there are views through lenses of various prescriptions. By this metaphor, there is no getting outside of your own subjectivity to assess ideology from an unbiased viewpoint; but you may get some sense of your own biases and try conceptually to compensate for them. And in rhetoric it is equally important to anticipate the ideologies of your audience, in order to determine how many and what sort of illustrations and supporting examples to use. In other words, there are ideologies, and ideologies: To say that a position is ideological is ultimately to say that it's human.

The interesting question then becomes not "What is it?" but *"What work does that position do?"* What are the effects of the ideological position taken? If the purpose of a statement is to get more Democrats or Republicans elected, that might be seen as good or bad in itself; but as the one peak of the hierarchy around which to organize an entire moral system, it's implausible. Is the goal to make the system work? To address injustice and inequity? To make as much money as you can? Many ideologies oversimplify what's at stake, saying, in effect, "Trust me—I have the answer." The answer offered may be *Get 3,000 card-carrying Communists out of the State Department,* as with McCarthy in the 1950s; or it may be *Stand back, deregulate, and let the market do its magic;* or it may be *Trust the experts, because they have degrees and should know better than you do.* Ideologies provide the hope of simple answers, as though there's one guiding principle by which to reorganize culture. Examples: God will straighten everything out in the end; when the dictatorship of the proletariat is at hand, the work will be completed, and eventually the state will wither away; fire wasteful government employees, cut fraud and abuse, and distribute the savings through tax cuts; figure out which are the good people and which are the bad, and promote the good and build enough new prisons to lock away the bad. These have all the appeal and all the shortcomings of oversimple answers.

The problem, finally, with some Marxist analyses of ideology, like the other positions alluded to above, is that they feed on the naive hope of a simple answer. In this case the "simple answer" is that the "ruling class" uses media to disseminate manipulative messages to keep people consuming, cynical towards any significant political action, and still working away rather than thinking clearly. But rather than a conspiracy among some mutually recognizing "ruling class," another possibility might be a kind of ideological atheism—what if the entire system runs without any control? The Ruling Class doesn't get together for lunch at the club; the Freemasons' secret handshakes and passwords don't amount to much. The place is full of customers, and no one's behind the counter.

Rather than one dominant ideology, twentieth-century communication and the shift in culture have produced several contenders for dominance.

1. We have the economic version in *the belief in the free market,* which allows a lot of people and interests to be stepped on in its name. The market ideology reached its recent high-water mark during the deregulation of industries and undermining of the Environmental Protection Agency and other

agencies under Reagan and, to some extent, under Bush—and made a return to some extent with the 104th Congress during the Clinton presidency.

2. We have conservative fundamentalism, going back to the Goldwater campaign of 1964, at its peak during the Reagan administration, and still influential in the Republican Party and to some extent among Perot supporters. This viewpoint might best be described as a *populist cynicism*.

3. We have a somewhat liberal democratic stance, a kind of *moral free market*—which does not elevate the Market to the leading principle, but doesn't look ahead to the Last Judgment or want to incarcerate all the Bad Guys as the answer. The key term here is "tolerance": You do what makes you happy and allow me to do the same, and don't make judgments or smoke in my nonsmoking section or break apart oil tankers or kill civilians. (Oddly, this ideology describes some NRA members not usually labeled as liberal.) This sort of liberalism has at its core the self-determining individual (John McLain would probably be an NRA member). This is probably the dominant U.S. ideology, going back to the Constitution with its checks and balances and careful restrictions on state power.

4. And we have those devoted to *collective organization through Worthy Causes*—people who understand that working one by one, individually, won't be able to counter the economic weight under item 1 above, and who want to get like-minded people into lobbying groups to make some social/cultural changes. (For example, the Sierra Club and public interest lobbying groups.)

These four ideological positions offer contrasting explanations of what needs to be fixed in present U.S. society. It's interfering groups or the government, who won't let business do its thing. It's Satan influencing the misguided to pursue their own desires rather than do what they know is right. It's greedy business interests or misguided Christian fundamentalists who want to limit personal freedoms. It's selfish pursuit of what you want to do (own assault weapons or abort fetuses) rather than consideration of what the consequences of that might be for others.

All these positions have spokespersons who make use of media to some extent, but in far from equal numbers. Discussions about welfare reform and health care begun by the Clinton administration attempted to look to a wide range of interests dealing with both issues—except that those who receive public assistance and those who are currently uninsured had far less presence in the discussion than those with enough money and prestige to see that their interests were considered. (See Keeping Informed in Chapter 4.) It is evident, as A. J. Liebling said, that freedom of the press is restricted to those who own one; and that a higher socioeconomic or cultural position increases one's access through media. But the familiarity of descriptions 1 through 4 above should demonstrate that all four positions (along with some others) are finding their way into public consciousness. Media are mostly allied with the moral free market, because that's the approach closest to a "ruling ideology" in the United States now. It grows out of our Enlightenment principles of the "pursuit of happiness": The individual is assumed as a starting point, and the society is built up from that ideology. But a careful consideration of media may create doubt about this position, because media participate in *building* the individual—that is, to the extent they work in symbols and language and ideology, media are "consciousness industries." Starting as the moral free market does with the Imperial Self, then, is not in itself sufficient.

Working in groups to improve matters (collective action) may be more promising, but other ideological positions keep it from attaining dominance. Who calls the shots for the group? Why can't I get my say there? Who's really in control here? These are "special interest groups," as opposed to presumably unaffiliated individuals or to the business interests already organized along the "natural" principles of the free market. Unions don't have your interests at heart—they're just out for profit. The bleeding-heart liberals just want a greater share of your profits. You can't trust so-called professionals to know what they are doing. And so the capability of groups for making change gets undercut, and the uneasy alliance/competition between these continues.

What this model comes to is this: *Ideologies are fictions, some of which come to be accepted as myths.* They are made-up accounts of how the world works; and they draw, as convincing fictions do, on versions of experience that can be recognized by readers. (If I'm fortunate, this book will prove to be a convincing fiction, and what I say here will be recognized by you as an adequate account.) These accounts are necessarily selective and partial, because no fiction can embrace the world. People make up ideologies, collectively, and then forget that they are fictions, at which time their status passes over into myth. Others ideologies look back to originary figures who are more familiar (Marx, Christ, Joseph Smith, Newton). The trick when you are reading a fiction is to offer conditional belief while being aware that it is conditional; and while this has worked for some persons in the past, it remains to be seen whether such can be an organizational principle for a culture. But awareness of how ideology supports the various phenomena of culture is a starting point.

Reading Media Texts for Ideology

To get some sense of how a "'lived' relation to the real" (Althusser) might connect to a media text, it may be of some use to look at a student essay written by way of illustration, about the most openly ideological genre of contemporary media texts, advertisements. (You may wish to look as well at the essay on page 252 in Chapter 5.)

LISA STRANEY

Analysis: Nike Ad

1. Birds chirping. Footsteps.
2. Tracking head and shoulder shot of woman walking quickly R. to L., arms in full swing, past leafy green trees. Wearing royal blue sweatshirt and also passing small, dark background figures (park).
3. Fem. voice-over: *"I walk because when I was a child, I walked like a child, and…"*
4. Motion slows, sound of wind, large brown leaves blowing (woman smiles, inhales): *"when I grew up, they started to drive."*
5. Cut and pan up to black birds flying in treetops—startled noise vaguely like turkeys gobbling, which echoes.
6. New fem. voice-over: *"I walk because…"*
7. Quick cut to close-up of man in dk. gray dress suit crossing in front of blue luxury car. (Sound: barking): *"…if I didn't, my dog would disown me."* Power window lowers, Great Dane pokes snout through and barks at camera (viewer).
8. Cut to close-up of old man in black overcoat and hat, at L. with back to camera. He's overlooking a white beach (arm resting across fence) which has a small silhouette of a couple holding hands in U. R. corner.
9. Man raps fingers. Church chimes.
10. (Same) fem. V-O: *"He's already quite bitter."*
11. Cut to pan of bike rack (blurred, foreground) with same walker coming from R. past a tree and another couple (background) walking in opposite direction.
12. Louder chimes. New fem. V-O: *"I walk because I was beginning to look like my couch."*
13. (Organ music joins chimes as) New woman enters. Close-up, crossing in front of woman above. Royal blue sweatshirt, black biking shorts; arms swinging w/ fists. Each step accented w/ a background "clunk."
14. New fem. V-O: *"I walk because there is life here."*
15. Pan from legs to face—mouth open, deep breaths, focused.
16. Cut to close-up of pair of white Nikes walking toward camera against wet, bluish grey concrete.
17. (Same) fem. V-O: *"No desks…"*
18. Gradual slow-mo: laces rising and falling as shoe hits the ground.
19. (New) fem. V-O: *"…no answering machines…"*
20. Cut to close-up of woman's perspiring face, looking down and off to side—mouth open, against deep blue background and clothes.

21. Slow-mo. as she blinks, accented by a chime and an echoed clang.
22. New fem. V-O: "...*no telephones that scream for me.*"
23. Cut to new woman walking in slow-mo in dark blue/black, swinging arms, bike shorts/sweatshirt tied around waist.
24. New fem. V-O: *"And, if they scream..."*
25. Pan up from legs to head toward bright blue sky with huge fluffy clouds.
26. Wind and chimes heard, getting louder.
27. Cut to yet another woman (in black) w/ pulled-back blond hair walking in slow-mo (head and shoulder shot), across bright green grass.
28. New fem. V-O: *"...I don't have to answer."* (Above head turns to side while crossing screen.)
29. Assorted noise: muffled shouts of men and women groaning, calling "here, here," etc....volume increasing with more organ music and chimes added, ending with a short, loud low pitch ("Um"?)–sounding like monks. Then quickly silence.
30. **Just Do It** appears in center of screen in white against black. Faint bird chirps.
31. **Just Do It** fades to [Nike logo] on the same black screen. Sound of birds now more defined.

Comments: This particular ad for Nike walking shoes is aimed at women who are (given its style and quick pace) approximately 30-something or younger. It is also crammed full of technical events, too many to reasonably include, but there were some recurring images I found stronger and more interesting than others.

Perhaps the most obvious effect was the overlapping, fast-cutting camera work following several different women, voices, and locations; almost a collage of young women patched together, as if to say all kinds of women walk, for all kinds of reasons—these are the "all kinds of" women. Nike was trying to push this broad, "universal" image of active young women, or at least the popularity of walking and attention to health. All of the women in this ad were thin, however; and one woman's comment about looking like her couch was inappropriate and potentially offensive. Certainly this is not a composite image of women (not even healthy ones). Health, weight-consciousness, and stress reduction were used heavily as selling points.

Their use of color grabbed my attention, mainly because of its prevalence of rich, deep dark blues, grays, and blacks. The remaining colors therefore contrasted and were made significant (lime green grass/trees, sky blue, white clouds and sand). Why did they choose this to stand apart? They all represent nature as fresh, appealing and colorful. Nike means getting you out there in the rainbow of "natural" color; it means to tempt you to get in touch with your "outdoorsy" side.

Another effect I tend to remember was the use of slow motion. At the end of most cuts, the walking slowed, enabling us to see the walker more closely. This technique was also paired with sound, another prevailing characteristic I was drawn to. For example, echoes and clanging usually occurred during close-ups, when the motion in turn would slow down. Perhaps the clanging, clunking thuds of close-up shoes and close-up eyelids slamming was meant to give the impression of work, toil... while the birds, whose sounds framed the ad, symbolized peace/reward for using this product and working hard (Neil Postman's "glimpse of Heaven/Hawaii" conclusion).

The sound of howling wind (at various intensities) was also accompanied by slow motion. Going against the wind, the logic used here is easy enough to understand. There were other sounds not quite so straightforward, making them I think very important. The chimes & church organ began subtly and grew to a crescendo, ending with a monkish note. Walking now not only means getting in touch with the beautiful physical world, but apparently it's good for your soul too.... Maybe wearing Nikes can evoke a religious experience? Although at first nonspecific and easily filterable background fodder, the sounds of birds and religion became clearly as hand-picked as the striking contrast in coloring and the skinny women. Nature and religion, then, got added to the list of selling points, as did inner *and* outer beauty.

[Used by permission. Quotes from Nike commercial reprinted with permission of NIKE, Inc.]

Lisa Straney's analysis of this Nike ad draws attention to the ways in which some of the technical events in the commercial draw on and reinforce certain cultural values—concern for health and exercise, love of nature, nonsectarian religious associations, and so on. These are used artfully to build a connection between ideological commitments viewers may already have, and the ideas of buying a specific product. You have already written similar analyses of commercials in Chapter 5, but Straney's essay makes a point that is important in this context: Reading any media text means working from "surface" details to some sense of the ideological subtext.

ASSIGNMENT

Working with the definition of ideology as an underlying set of values or assumptions about how things ought to be, find a media text for analysis. For this assignment, generally, simpler is better: An advertisement from a magazine or Sunday supplement would probably be a good choice, though films, cartoons, or television programs are possibilities if you are ambitious. First write informally, registering details of your chosen text and your reaction to these; then look back over your work and organize your comments so that what you have to say comes across to another reader who might not share your assessment.

Ideology and Metaphor

It should be clear by now that discussions about ideology are grounded in an ongoing dialogue about the nature and values of culture. Ideological positions are encoded in words or phrases: *family values; quotas; fair and free elections.* Many of those writing in and about media see media texts as part of what has been called "culture wars"—for example, in Pat Buchanan's speech before the Republican Convention of 1992. Much of the rhetoric of these debates is drawn from a particular ideology that views life as a contest between the forces of Good and Evil, in which there can be no compromise—no extension, finally, of any legitimacy to another viewpoint except insofar as that viewpoint agrees with or furthers one's own. Others involved in these supposed "wars" may be similarly absolute about single issues—such as abortion, women's rights, or gun ownership—while keeping open about others, such as economic policy, foreign policy, or political party affiliation, except as they affect these specific questions.

The use of metaphor can often influence how ideas are examined. For example, the metaphor *culture war* inclines us to see two sides in absolute combat, as does to some degree the notion of "debate"; but complex issues often have several positions possible, and it does not help in articulating one's thinking on a complex matter to be pushed into one of two absolute positions. The war image can be effective short-term rhetoric, however. For example, in discussions of U.S. policy in Nicaragua during the mid-1980s, Washington's rhetorical stance posed the matter as a struggle between "freedom fighters" and "Communists" allied with Cuba and the Soviet Union. When involved in a war, one must often choose sides out of patriotism or loyalty rather than using close and careful consideration. For that reason, the metaphor of war is useful for motivating those who already agree with you, but not for examining the content of your and others' thought.

An excellent illustration of the ideological power of metaphor is the work of George Lakoff (with Mark Johnson, in *Metaphors We Live By*, and with Mark Turner, in *More Than Cool Reason*). Lakoff categorizes several instances of metaphors used to characterize (falsely) events in the Gulf War. "The state-as-person system" characterizes a country as an individual, war as "a fight between two people, a form of hand-to-hand combat." "The fairy tale of the just war" imposes on international events a plot in which people are cast as villains, victims, and heroes (Lakoff, "Metaphor and War" p. 232). Or war is considered to be "a competitive game," in which victory is characterized as kicking Iraqi butt—not as the actual deaths of tens of thousands of mostly noncombatants. To illustrate one deceptive result, seeing Iraq as a person "highlights the ways in which states act as units, and hides the internal structure of the state. Class structure is hidden by this metaphor, as are ethnic composition, religious rivalry, political parties, the ecology, the influence of the military and of corporations (especially multinational corporations)" (p. 236). At the conclusion of the war, and periodically since, the United States has been reminded of the diversity of what we had been calling "Iraq" by the attacks on the Shiite minority in the south (their marsh homelands, an ecosystem that had existed for thousands of years, was being drained by the government as "improvement") and the Kurds in the north. Military defeat of "Saddam" solved none of the "hidden" issues listed by Lakoff, and the continuing problems in the Middle East illustrate the insufficiency of the metaphors through which the situation has been conceptualized.

Metaphors, then, are necessarily accompanied by value judgments. Not only do they allow us to express opinions inventively and colorfully, but they frame how we understand issues—and in that framing, they connect with ideology. When we decide what to say or write, our language shows traces of our thought; and the language that most naturally comes to hand is full of implied or explicit metaphors that give useful indications of assumptions.

I used the phrase "comes to hand," thus metaphorically indicating that language is a tool employed for something, perhaps bricolage (see page 297 in Chapter 6). *Bricolage* means taking what's "at hand" to construct something that will get by. And this is a pretty good image for writing, at least in my experience—writing means making use of the tools you have (that metaphor again) to get something down, then coming back to tinker with it. Such tinkering, as we have seen, can best be done in different stages.

PROBLEMS

The Example of "PC"

Another metaphor that does ideological work—and we will want to consider for what—is "political correctness." This phrase has wormed its way into public discourse with the help of media. It started as an ironic in-joke on the "left"—a way to be slightly self-mocking about one's real opinions so as not to appear doctrinaire. Then the phrase was picked up by conservatives and used as a club against any reining in of one's impulses whatsoever. Do you now use "African American" or "black" when you used to say "Negro," or perhaps even "nigger"? That's PC. Do you say "disabled" (or, more clumsily, "differently abled") when your original impulse is to say "crippled"? That's PC. Do you say "women" when your unrestricted impulse is to say "girls" or "broads" or "bitches"? That's PC.

These offensive examples are cited to make a point: Usually when the subject of political correctness is trotted out, it's linked to some particularly extreme example, a spurious charge of sexual harassment or an awkward circumlocution designed to fudge unpleasant realities. However, there are some taboos that no one in public life will violate, some words or phrases that are considered too offensive—and why isn't the avoidance of these labeled as "politically correct"? These phrases and others are still privately used, but quietly, so as to avoid exposure and public embarrassment.

In virtually all cases, a complaint about "political correctness" comes from someone in a position of power or identified with a relatively powerful group, who would "naturally" speak jokingly or offensively about someone in a position of lesser power—middle-aged white man about younger woman; white about black; "American" of West European ancestry about "American" of Central European, Asian, Latin American, or Native American ancestry; and so on. The speaker (usually male) is restrained by fear of embarrassment, but he gets a little of his own back by muttering sarcastically, "PC." Seen in this context, cries of "political correctness" are yelps of protest against having one's (verbal) power brought under any limitations. The Pause for Reflection below and the two newspaper reports that follow explore aspects of the PC phenomenon.

PAUSE FOR REFLECTION

In the 1970s the student body of the University of Texas voted to change the team name from Longhorns to Armadillos, a plan that was vetoed by the State Board of Regents. In the last few years there have been more team names along other principles: natural phenomena (Avalanche, Heat, and Fire now go with the Miami and Tulsa Hurricanes) or local totems (the Saginaw Gears and newly christened Lansing Lugnuts). Some of these poke fun at the more serious, aggressive style of naming.

BRIAN E. ALBRECHT

Team Names Still Stir Controversy

More than a baseball battle will be waged when the Indians face the Braves in the World Series.

To some, the Series represents an opportunity for pressing demands that sports teams drop names and logos they describe as racial insults to American Indians–the

Indians, with Chief Wahoo, and the Braves, with their fans' "tomahawk chop," being glaring cases in point.

Opponents of racially oriented team names and logos have met with limited success in terms of focusing public attention on the issue. And some newspapers have discontinued using those terms and images in recent years.

The Portland, Ore., *Oregonian* has said it will continue using only "Cleveland" and "Atlanta" to identify the teams in the World Series. The Minneapolis Star Tribune dropped the team nicknames two years ago. That's a start, say critics.

Vernon Bellecourt, national representative of the American Indian Movement and president of the National Coalition on Racism in Sports, told *USA Today:* "We're not going away until we can get rid of the Big Four: the Kansas City Chiefs, the Washington Redskins, the Indians and the Braves.

"We're not going to accept racism in our national pastime."

Critics also note that behavior prompted by these team nicknames can be even worse: fans in Atlanta doing the "tomahawk chop," or dressing in feathers and "warpaint" in both cities, imitating Indian chants and whoops....

Chief Wahoo was created by Walter Goldbach in 1947. He has said then-owner Bill Veeck was looking for a "fun, happy-go-lucky cartoon thing" to symbolize the Tribe. Goldbach's design was later updated to the current version by the late *Plain Dealer* cartoonist Fred Reinert....

At one point, Atlanta had its own version of Chief Wahoo in Chief Noc-A-Homa—a guy in a feathered headdress who would emerge from a teepee beyond the outfield fence in Fulton County Stadium to do a war dance upon each Atlanta home run.

Indians spokesman Bob DiBiasio said yesterday that the team name is a way of honoring the legacy of Sockalexis, first American Indian to play in the major leagues. As for the Chief Wahoo logo, DiBiasio said, "I think overwhelming fan support is pretty much the reason why we are continuing with it. Let's just play baseball."

Braves President Stan Kasten would not comment on the issue.

Local opposition to the "tribalization" of baseball includes Juan Reyna, chairman of the local Committee of 500 Years of Dignity and Respect. Reyna said one problem lies in getting people to admit there is a problem.

"People are in a state of denial—talking about political correctness, or however they want to brush it off," he said. "They need to recognize it's an abuse. We've been taking pictures of these people going crazy at the stadium, so maybe they should reconsider who's the savage here.

"These people keep acting out this fantasy of what they think Indians are like. Then, when they meet a real Indian, they start dancing around, doing the chop, and they think it's funny, they think it's a joke. But when you encounter it every day of your life, it gets boring real quick."...

One need not have a World Series to experience the controversy. At the Western Reserve Historical Society on University Circle, the issue has become part of a display featuring the old 37-foot-tall Chief Wahoo sign that topped the Stadium from 1962 to 1993.

This display includes statements from representatives of both the "Save Our Chief" fans group and the Committee of 500 Years of Dignity and Resistance.

Writing on behalf of Save Our Chief, Sarah Goss Norman said: "Win or lose, Chief Wahoo has been smiling down on Cleveland baseball fans for almost 50 years.... Today's meaning behind the Chief—eternal happy hope that good things will happen—has proven popular."

The exhibit also invites and displays written comments from visitors. These include:

"...this false face / Red Sambo / With its Uncle Tomahawk grin / And Pinocchio lie of a nose...."

And, "Chief Wahoo is a *proud* symbol of a great team. The team was named to *honor* an American Indian player—the logo was meant then and now as a symbol of fun and good times...."

With such opinions seemingly entrenched in opposing dugouts, perhaps the only surety is that this particular battle won't be decided in a ballpark.

[From the Cleveland *Plain Dealer*, October 20, 1995. Used by permission.]

CANDY HAMILTON

Where a Tomahawk Chop Feels Like a Slur

For many, the protests by native Americans over nicknames and tomahawk chops by fans of the Cleveland Indians and Atlanta Braves are little more than a World Series footnote. A politically correct sideshow.

But here in South Dakota, high school athletes from the Lakota Indian reservations face derisive caricatures and gestures at nearly every competition. Taunts of "dog eaters," "squaw," "dirty old Indians," as well as war whoops and tomahawk chops greet the Lakota teams when they compete off the reservation.

"When one of our people was lying on the floor hurt, I could hear people yelling, 'shoot her, shoot her,'" recalls former Red Cloud basketball player Michelle Carlow.

Racism is nothing new for Pine Ridge Reservation athletes. "This is South Dakota, and we've been living with it," says Brian Brewer, Pine Ridge athletic director.

Conflict between local tribes and whites here goes back to even before General Custer's last battle at Little Bighorn in the late 1800s and the standoff at Wounded Knee in 1973. Lakota tribes are still trying to win back the Black Hills near Rapid City, S. D.

The issue flared again here even before the World Series match-up put a spotlight on Indian mascots. Jason Brave Heart, student council president at Little Wound High School, called a joint meeting of reservation student councils to discuss the Bennett County High School (BCHS) homecoming activities, centered around the team name, Warriors.

"It's not the issue of the mascot itself," Brave Heart says. "It's the mockery. They do things [dressed as Indians] that Indians don't do. A warrior is a common Indian man who protects his family and nation," he explains.

Members of the BCHS homecoming royalty, who are non-Indians, use the names big and little "chief," wear buckskin and feathers, and this year tried to adapt a Lakota prayer ceremony into the pre-game festivities.

"[The taunts] have to stop somewhere," says Red Cloud High School Coach Dusty LeBeau. "We have to stop it in our own homeland. At Bennett County, they were acting like they were praying to the four directions. Indians don't make a game of the way we pray, but it's nothing to them," says Mr. LeBeau, coach of the 1995 boys state basketball champions. His team will not play BCHS until their homecoming celebration changes.

The Bennett County school superintendent and principal agree some changes are needed, but the school board has to make them. Superintendent Chris Anderson says any change would likely mean a recall of the board. One member, in fact, won election campaigning on "no change."

Moreover, after Sara Trimble, a Lakota and BCHS cheerleader, protested the homecoming activities in 1994, her classmates ostracized her for the rest of her senior year. Some students threatened to throw eggs at her if she cheered at the homecoming game.

Of the four reservation high schools, only the Crazy Horse Chiefs use an Indian logo, a feather bonnet, though no one wears them at games.

A Lakota chief earns the right to wear a headdress, one feather at a time, through bravery, fortitude, and generosity. "Our kids know real chiefs," says school board president Francine Red Willow. "They know what it takes to become one. For us we really are honoring Crazy Horse, our ancestor."

Although he calls the Indian logos demeaning, Pine Ridge School Superintendent John Haas puts mascots well below budget cuts on his problem list. "We are barely holding this school together," he ways. "If this will help us get money for Indian education, it'd be worth it."

Still, some progress has been made in raising awareness about racial sensitivities. The South Dakota High School Activities Association adopted policies on racial taunting in 1994, when slurs directed at a black player caused a melee at a Black Hills football game. "All these years at state tournaments, we've put up with it," Brewer notes.

[From the *Christian Science Monitor*, October 25, 1995. Used by permission of the author.]

What is there that places the center of gravity, in this discussion, toward the use of such sports nicknames? Why is it that the burden of proof is on those associated with Native Americans to argue that, say, the presence of Chief Noc-A-Homa or 45,000 Florida State fans doing the tomahawk chop is offensive, rather than on those who would like to keep such names to argue that they should be permitted? One explanation, a partial one, is ideology's ability to naturalize: Having grown up with Washington Redskins, we easily accept that appellation as part of the natural order. Another, not incidental answer is that making any change would cost money (team uniforms, logos, and the intangible but very real fan loyalty and investment). Another possibility is that resistance to change is diversionary: If groups on the margins can be kept worrying about (relative) trivialities like sports logos, they may not be able to lobby effectively for better social programs, health care, or control over natural resources.

In the following reading, John K. Wilson expresses deep concern over some groups' uses of the "politically correct" label.

JOHN K. WILSON

The Myth of Political Correctness
"Are you politically correct?" asked the cover of *New York* magazine. Readers were told to test themselves. "Do I say 'Indian' instead of 'Native American'? 'Pet' instead of 'Animal Companion'?" I had to confess that sometimes I said "Native American," mostly to avoid confusion with the Indians in south Asia. I didn't know that saying a word could make me a fellow traveler with the thought police. But the "Animal Companion" part puzzled me. By this definition, I wasn't politically correct; in fact, by this definition I'd never met anyone who was politically correct. Do people really say "animal companion" instead of "pet"? Does anyone accuse those who use the word pet of being a "speciesist"? Would anyone take them seriously if they did? I began to suspect that the "political correctness" movement was no more than the product of someone's paranoid imagination. Being asked "Are you politically correct?" is like being asked "Are you in favor of the international conspiracy of Jewish bankers who control the world?" Of course I'm opposed to an international conspiracy of Jewish bankers controlling the world, but I also know that no such conspiracy exists....

As I began to examine the stories about political correctness, I noticed a curious double standard. Whenever conservatives were criticized or a leftist expressed some extreme idea, the story quickly became another anecdote of political correctness. But when someone on the Left was censored—often with the approval of the same conservatives who complained about the PC police—nobody called it political correctness, and stories of this right-wing intolerance were never mentioned in articles and books on PC totalitarianism. My own experience made me question the existence of the "PC fascism" I had read about. And as I began to study the terrifying tales of leftist McCarthyism, I found that the truth was often the reverse of what the media reported. While some stories about PC are true and deplorable, the scale of censorship is nowhere near what most people think....

Conservatives manufactured the political correctness crisis and skillfully pushed it into the national spotlight. This does not mean that all examples of political correctness are pure invention; leftists do sometimes show intolerance toward those who fail to toe the party line. But leftist intimidation in universities has always paled in comparison with the far more common repression by the conservative forces who control the budgets and run colleges and universities.

My claim is not that American universities are perfect defenders of free expression or that political correctness is pure invention with no basis in reality.... [But the] myth of political correctness has created the illusion of a conspiracy of leftists who have taken over higher education and twisted it to serve their political purposes. Attacks on political correctness have misled the public and unfairly maligned a large number of faculty and students. Worse yet, the crusade against PC has silenced the deeper questions about quality and equality that our colleges and universities must face, and a greatly needed debate has been shut down by the false reports and misleading attacks on higher education....

The conservative backlash against universities has been funded by right-wing foundations and supported by liberals and journalists who dislike the academic Left. Using a long list of inaccurate anecdotes, endlessly recycled in conservative and mainstream publications, the right-wingers have distorted and manipulated the debates about higher education. Presenting conservative white males as the true victims of oppression on campus, they have convinced the public that radicals are now the ones who threaten civil liberties. This is the myth of political correctness that conservatives have created and successfully marketed to the media and the general public....

The liberals' original "I'm not politically correct" was an ironic defense against those who took extremism to new extremes, who demanded absolute consistency to radical principles. The conservatives warped this meaning to convey the image of a vast conspiracy controlling American colleges and universities....For conservatives, "I'm not politically correct" became a badge of honor, a defense against a feared attack—even though no one had been seriously accused of being politically incorrect....

While claiming to be silenced, conservatives now use PC to silence their opponents. In August 1993, Joe Rabinowitz, news director of WTTG-TV, the Fox station in Washington, D.C., wrote a memo to the chair of Fox Television, urging the firing of "politically correct" employees. To hunt down these employees he consulted with conservative media critics like L. Brent Bozell III, chair of the Media Research Center, and Reed Irvine, head of Accuracy in Media. As the American Association of University Professors observed, "Charges of 'political correctness'... have a way of taking on their own coercive tone." If an opponent could be dismissed as politically correct, there was no need to reply to any substantive arguments....

By expanding the meaning of *political correctness* to include *any* expression of radical ideas, conservatives distorted its original meaning and turned it into a mechanism for doing exactly what they charge is being done to them—silencing dissenters. Michael

Bérubé points out that "the term 'PC' is doing the work that the term 'liberal' did for Bush in 1988: it's trying to dismiss large potential constituencies for cultural activism, and to narrow the bounds of permissible political debate."... The genius of using a term like *political correctness* was that people would never declare themselves politically correct, so it was virtually impossible to counter the conservative attacks when a culture of soundbites defied the kind of analysis needed to refute the presumption that political correctness existed.

[From John K. Wilson, *The Myth of Political Correctness: The Conservative Attack on Higher Education.* Durham, N.C.: Duke University Press, 1995. Used by permission.]

Political correctness may be defined as a poor fit between what someone is for rhetorical reasons compelled or inclined to say/write, and what the person actually would say or write if free to seek expression without worrying about others' opinions. It's a way of signaling resistance, of claiming an ironic stance. Irony is usually considered to be more subtle than this: The claim of political correctness is *announced* irony—a protest against having to respect other people's positions at all, a move against diversity, as though, when the hundred-thousandth gripe about "political correctness" is made, then we will agree that we don't have to worry about diversity any more. So then complaints about PC are laments for the good old days, when we could just ignore blacks, women, and others with their noisy and expensive demands.

And "diversity"? Perhaps it could be defined as acknowledgement of a principle that the "mass" audience isn't homogeneous, that there are reasons for those of different races and genders to differ on issues. Given the tone of media discussions of politics in the 1990s so far, those expressing positions that are of use to others holding or seeking political power will continue to call names and intimidate opponents, particularly those disadvantaged by the system who lack access to respond meaningfully.

Media are made use of by those in politics, "think tanks," corporations, public relations officers, and others; and because of economic or political or ideological affiliations, or because of their conventions of reading, media present the viewpoints of these various interests as "natural." The result is to multiply the power of the viewpoints of already powerful people, to the exclusion of others who do not have such easy access. The highly partisan nature of such discussions as it has evolved since Richard Nixon's presidency has made reasoned discussion of public issues even more difficult, raising the level of cynicism in the public generally and giving ideology a bad name.

There are "political"—more precisely, ideological—implications in everything that you write and say. There can be no getting away from these. In some circles, it may be rhetorically useful to trot out the cliché one more time and complain about having to be "politically correct"—but in any writing in which you have to be responsible for defining terms and using words according to academic standards of fair and precise argument, you should expect to be challenged on this term. And you should recognize that complaining about having to be "politically correct" is a coded way of saying that you'd really prefer to align yourself ideologically with political positions sympathetic to racism, sexism, and other forms of prejudice against the relatively powerless in society.

Nostalgia

"Nostalgia isn't what it used to be." —Anonymous

Etymologically, *nostalgia* is return-home pain, or a longing to return home; and homesickness is a tone frequently struck in nostalgic media texts such as popular music and films. Generally *nostalgia* has come to be extended beyond a literal longing for one's home to a longing for the idea of home, or perhaps for an idealized version of the past. This sentimental version may be either of one's own or of a cultural or historical past, and usually strikes a note of contrast with an unhappy or complicated present. Its affiliation with ideology deserves a closer look.

The nostalgic message is basically *pastoral*—away from complications, from complexity and entanglement and responsibilities, back to a childhood or a simpler time. This return to an evocation of the past has obvious appeals. For those in middle age or older, it's a way of harkening back to when we were young and vigorous; for the young, nostalgia may serve as a way of evading the complications of relationships or trying in some way to understand an earlier period. Part of its appeal for the young may be that of the exotic or strange. Another part of the appeal may arise from a longing for a break from routine.

Nostalgia is a mode frequently used by media. The top-forty radio stations of the 1960s have now been resurrected in "classic rock" formats. These serve several purposes: They expand a thin contemporary playlist, afford DJs occasions to reminisce and recall for readers some valued texts, and promote tours by some of these groups. Rock history runs much deeper now; chronologically anything from Bill Haley and the Comets on is available.

But it should be noted that nostalgia is selective, reconstructing the past as do all histories. Much of this popularized history understates the roots of rock in blues, gospel, swing, country, jazz, and other sources that rock plundered and popularized. Furthermore, it focuses attention largely on "stars" rather than, say, one-hit groups—the equivalent of literature's focus on "major authors" rather than on minor authors or movements. This version of "classic rock" is somewhat gender-biased, perpetuating into the present the past dominance of male singers, as well as the values that those singers' songs promulgated. And in the emphasis on performance, "classic rock" seriously understates the importance of merchandising of the music industry and the creation of taste, suggesting that the major rock successes got there because they deserved it or were lucky, rather than by the energetic marketing of their records.

ASSIGNMENT

Listen to some classic rock for ways in which these texts recirculate past ideologies. For example, the Beach Boys' "I Get Around": "None of the guys go steady, 'cause it wouldn't be right / To leave your best girl home on a Saturday night," or Dion's "The Wanderer": "Well, I'm the kind of guy who'll never settle down."

Nostalgia is present in film releases and television programs as well as in popular music. The film *American Graffiti* spawned a series of TV stories grounded in pre-Vietnam youth, with *Happy Days,* any number of classroom programs (*Welcome Back, Kotter*), and the sustenance of TV syndication drawing on the proven market here; it also spawned films, *National Lampoon's Animal House* and *Peggy Sue Got Married.* (And there's the postmodern appropriation of nostalgia in the 1995 Weezer video of "Buddy Holly," which inserts the group into a compilation of *Happy Days* vignettes.) Outside the 1950s and 1960s matrix, there's the pastiche George Lucas developed in the *Star Wars* films (drawing on echoes of the Buck Rogers/Flash Gordon sort of serials), and the Steven Spielberg development of the serial hero in *Raiders of the Lost Ark* and its sequels. As with rock music, the *Raiders* pastiche allows the continuation of certain gender-based attitudes—the spunky, somewhat feminist character of Marion (Karen Allen) is overwhelmed by the more knowledgeable and heroic Indiana Jones (Harrison Ford) figure.

The *Back to the Future* trilogy is another illustration of nostalgia in film, but in this case striking a pose of simultaneous hip superiority to the past. Marty McFly lands back in 1955 and more or less controls the situation—not only by what he knows about his parents and other events in their future, by his recognition of a *Honeymooners* episode, and by his general hipness, but also by his own pastiche before the fact, in playing a 1980s version of "Johnny Be Good" at a dance, where it is heard by one Marvin Berry, supposedly Chuck's cousin.

Since the mid-'70s, several film versions of comics and comic books have arisen—*Superman, Batman* (drawing as well on the campy 1960s version that resurfaced on the FX cable network), *Teenage Mutant Ninja Turtles,* and *The Flintstones.* In the Richard Lester portion of the first Christopher Reeve *Superman* film, there are some physical comedy jokes brought in as part of the way to establish that this nostalgia is all joking, all for play, as happens in *Back to the Future.* When Clark Kent is searching for a place to change clothes, he takes a longing look at a pay phone—no longer in a booth—before going through a revolving door to change into his tights.

There are now entire cable networks (Nickelodeon, FX, much of the Family Channel) largely given over to television programs of the 1960s and 1970s, effectively perpetuating for today's children the ideologies inscribed in these texts, while allowing parents to visit their own (selected) televisual past. Nostalgia may be seen not only in the presence of *Lassie* and *Mork and Mindy* and *The Muppet Show* but (in the case of the Family Channel) in religious programming. Harkening back to a stable world has something of the nostalgia-for-the-end that can be found in some fundamentalist religious beliefs: Rather than expecting happiness here, we should look to Heaven, where all mysteries will be made clear and all wrongs will be righted. The ideological message sent in this case is "deferred gratification": Don't expect to be rewarded now, but wait patiently and your needs will be met.

PAUSE FOR REFLECTION

Is there anything like nostalgia in news? Consider the effects of historical background stories, "Whatever happened to X?" features, and accounts in December of the year's major events.

Several explanations might be offered for the frequency and intensity of nostalgia in media. First is the market: Audiences prefer things that are familiar. We can relax and not worry so much about paying attention if we already know the outlines of the story. Second is the economics of production: It's easier for filmmakers to sell producers and financiers on the idea of a story with its roots in the popular culture than on something novel (such as a Dublin band doing the Motown sound, as in *The Commitments*). Third, there's ideological work being done when media show (even if in jest) a stable and familiar world in which familiar patterns are observed (clean lawns, hard-working white people, deferent blacks, token villains, no real threats). One message here is that the (constructed) nostalgic view is the past—there's no changing the past (absent a time machine). Part of the message, too, might be that one need not aspire to change anything in the present, either—there's destiny at work. It may be significant that in the more positive future that closes the first

Back to the Future film, Marty's father turns out to be a science fiction writer: Science fiction, surprisingly, is a powerful vehicle for nostalgia, as is suggested by the early dismissive phrase, "Space Westerns." Nostalgia is integral to the continuing appeal of *Star Trek* (see page 122 in Chapter 3).

Nostalgia can be found in many aspects of U.S. culture. Take sports and sports coverage—baseball as "the American game," for starters, or the insistence on keeping records and making comparisons with past figures. Once one's sporting career is over, one can look forward to appearing as a commentator, spicing the broadcast with a rich supply of lore. Resistance to changes in the game is often based on appeals to the past.

Observations of past historic events often adopt nostalgic tones, as in some of the coverage in June 1994 of the D-Day Normandy invasion. The celebration did ideological work in highlighting the heroic advance on the Nazi occupation in northern France—and in understating what the Russians had been doing in the war for more than a year before. Almanacs provide observations of days as they pass; "The Writer's Almanac," a regular feature broadcast daily on public radio by Garrison Keillor, is one example of such. Keillor's radio fiction around "Lake Wobegon" is a powerful and witty evocation of nostalgia as well as a commentary on present society. Frequent comparisons between Keillor and Mark Twain also function nostalgically. Twain is a one-man trope for nostalgia—his image is selectively based on *Tom Sawyer* and *Huckleberry Finn* (as opposed to the acerbic pieces of his last twenty years), and the ideological work done by Tom Sawyer in keeping Nigger Jim under control and grateful should be noted in this context.

The tone of nostalgia reaches outside both literary and standard media texts to other cultural phenomena: classic car shows, habits of collecting things (pop bottles, beer cans, memorabilia of the sort to be found in various restaurants), reproduction of posters, "sock hops," and so on.

ASSIGNMENT: NOSTALGIA

Extend the discussion of nostalgia by looking for further examples beyond those offered. Is the primary tone in each case sentimental recollection? Is there some judgment of the past mixed in with the favorable recall? Can you determine what sort of selection went into the presentation of what was valued in the past? What facets might have been left out? What seem to be the guiding principles behind such selection as goes on?

Are there moments of nostalgic recollection in your family (such as your parents reminding you of things you did when you were a toddler)? What kind of effect do these have on you and on them? Are there favorite films, television programs, or songs for you for which the appeal involves nostalgia? What are the effects of holding to this tone?

FURTHER READING

BOB GARFIELD

Pizza Hut Has the Crust to Roll Out "Incorrect" Celebs
So Donald Trump, Dennis Rodman and Rush Limbaugh are on the Pizza Hut payroll, starring in the three latest celebrity spots from BBDO Worldwide, New York.

Well, isn't that great. You make a name for yourself being an erratic, arrogant, egocentric, rude, blustering boor, and then you get your commercial deal. The bigger the jerk, the better the deal. We can hardly wait to see who's in the next pool of spots.

Louis Farrakhan? Charlie Manson? Pol Pot?

(Note from the Ad Review Legal Dept.: In no way does this feature intend to demean, defame or disparage anyone, or to any way equate Donald Trump with Pol Pot, who murdered an estimated 5 million to 10 million of his own people. We apologize to Mr. Pot for any misunderstanding.)

It's dispiriting to see another example in our celebrity-obsessed culture of fame and notoriety being confused with substance and character. We're almost to the point where, who knows, some half-wit parasite of a witness in a murder investigation could wind up getting movie deals or something. But we grudgingly have to concede this is a pretty good campaign.

The spots introduce stuffed crust pizza, and with the help of these leading public nuisances, the point of difference is well communicated.

Unlike most celebrity-spokesman users, who resort to Q-rated personalities in place of an advertising idea, BBDO and PepsiCo know how to employ celebs in *support* of an advertising idea. The selling contrivance here is the notion of eating pizza "incorrectly"—i.e., crust first—and thus the agency recruited the most incorrect characters it could find.

Some of them work better than others. Dennis Rodman, the San Antonio Spur forward who makes Charles Barkley look like a goodwill ambassador, turns out to have lots of charm and acting skills in addition to his major personality disorder. When his famously clean-cut teammate David Robinson counsels him to loosen up and eat his pizza backwards, and Rodman replies, "Whoa, Dave, you crazy, man. You crazy," it's a sweet and funny moment.

But Limbaugh, as per his persona as bilious reactionary demagogue/demigod, is merely pompous and obnoxious. He isn't being the good sport poking fun at himself; he's just in character as self-proclaimed infallible broker of truth. Those who buy into his act will enjoy seeing good ol' Rush being Rush. But many pizza eaters will despise Pizza Hut for further enriching a mean-spirited and disreputable broker of hate.

Then there's The Donald, who shows up in what looks like his (former) Plaza Suite with his former Plaza sweetheart. Yes, it's he and Ivana, dressed to the nines, seemingly in the midst of a naughty tete-a-tete.

Donald: "Do you really think this is the right thing for us to be doing, Ivana?"

Ivana: "What will people think?"

Donald: "Let 'em talk... It's wrong, isn't it?"

Ivana: "But it feels *so* right."

And so, ha ha ha, instead of running around with the married man who ran around on her, she shares a crust-first pizza pie with her exhibitionist ex. It is only the latest in the 15-year series of Donald Trump indignities, which he, for his own part, confuses with achievement.

But don't blame Pizza Hut or BBDO. Sirhan Sirhan wasn't available.

[Reprinted with permission from the May 1, 1995, issue of *Advertising Age*. Copyright, Crain Communications Inc., 1995.]

BOB GARFIELD

Pizza Hut Mail Bag

In nearly 10 years of doing this column, in spite of sometimes saying rather caustic things about clients, agencies and their advertising, the AdReview staff had until recently received a grand total of three nasty letters (our favorite opining, simply and elegantly, "Bob Garfield is a nitwit.")

But then we wrote about the Pizza Hut commercial featuring Rush Limbaugh, in which we questioned the wisdom of BBDO casting somebody who many pizza eaters—our staff included—regard as a blight on the airwaves.

Many, many readers took this opportunity to criticize us for sneaking our personal opinions into our personal-opinion column, and for reflexively spouting left-wing dogma.

Well, *mea culpa*. As regular readers know, we at AdReview are in lockstep with the liberal media elite, and don't write a word without clearing it with Teddy Kennedy. We have never expressed anything remotely like conservative thought; we believe death-row inmates should get work-release to ref midnight basketball and we were personally involved in the Vince Foster murder plot.

Thus were we chastened by the barrage of mail, the latest and most eloquent piece of which arrived on our desk only today. [One reader] wrote that the column exemplifies "the kind of mean-spirited knee-jerk leftism which makes it increasingly impossible for this country to address its problems in an intelligent, civil, reasoned manner."

"In short, Mr. Garfield, get [expletive deleted]."

[Reprinted with permission from the June 19, 1995, issue of *Advertising Age*. Copyright, Crain Communications, Inc., 1995.]

CONCLUSION

The topic of ideology remains unfinished: Related considerations are present in all the chapters of this text, and there is obviously much more that could be said. The subject is large, complex, and rather more philosophical than a writing text can afford to be. If this chapter has been successful, the "false consciousness" model of ideology has been countered by more accurate, useful, and generous versions of the term. One of the ideals frequently evoked as part of U.S. culture is the extending of legitimacy to others' views, and a broader concept of ideology should contribute to this.

Resistance to reading texts with a consciousness of ideology often takes the form of appeals to "common sense." This chapter has argued that appeals to common sense are powerful ideological persuaders. There isn't any avoiding theory, because to do so is to do theory without knowing what you do.

Media are powerful influences partly because of the widely held illusion that they are innocent and objective transmitters of reality. Part of this myth of objectivity is based on the assumption that audiences are neutral consumers of media. But in fact, audiences are active participants in receiving messages; and we transmit other messages in turn. Knowledge of how media work their magic is indispensable to developing greater independence from others' manipulation. Making ideological factors and ideological markers more visible to audiences is an important part of attaining greater independence. Students of media should recognize that neither they nor their instructor nor the educational system are free of ideologies. Attempting to analyze contemporary culture is necessary even if impossibly complex.

FURTHER ASSIGNMENTS

Assignment

Choose a representative body of material and look for numbers of citations, and substantial treatment, of local, state, national, and international news. Your body of material might be a week of your local newspaper, a national newspaper such as *USA Today* or the *Christian Science Monitor*, a major daily paper such as the *Washington Post,* or references you have kept on radio news such as *All Things Considered* or on television news such as that shown on CNN or one of the broadcast networks. What can you tell about your medium's expectations of its audience, based on such selection?

Assignment

Drawing on a newspaper or magazine, look for instances of labeling, either through captions beneath photographs or through headlines from associated stories.

Assignment

Can you think of other films which connect to an ideology similar to that described in the discussion of *Die Hard* (in Reading *Die Hard*, above)? Choose one and develop a description of its plot and characters with attention to ideology.

Assignment

Break a taboo. Choose one item from the list you made—one that will not bring legal, ethical, or psychological consequences—and break it. Report back to the class on what the taboo was, how difficult you found it to break, and so on.

Assignment

List as many sports nicknames as you can, and classify them. What conclusions can you draw about ideology and the conventions of naming in a sports context?

Assignment: Ideology and Jokes

Over the course of a week or so, collect jokes that make mention of ethnic, religious, or otherwise marked groups in society. Compile several examples in your journal. If you can, ask others for their recollections of jokes that may not be current—your parents, other family members, and so on. (Instances: Polish jokes; Jewish jokes; jokes told on blacks or Indians, women drivers, blondes, Chinese, etc.) You may want to watch some routines by stand-up comics, or parody programs such as *Saturday Night Live* or *In Living Color*, for comparison.

As a class or in small groups, discuss which groups were featured in the jokes you found. Did you find analogous jokes told about different groups? Did jokes isolate and build on stereotypes about these groups? How many jokes took as their targets people in positions of relative power? How many, the relatively powerless?

What is the role of humor in these matters? Where do jokes originate? What keeps them circulating? Can you determine something about ideologies that support humor?

Assignment

Collect phrases containing names of ethnic or national groups, such as French leave, French kissing, Dutch treat, Indian giver. Leaving aside those which are simply descriptive (e.g., Italian olive oil or French bread), what can you infer about how the named ethnic or national groups are regarded? If someone in the class has lived outside the United States for some time (or if you know someone who has), see if that person knows any comparable phrases using "American."

Collect examples of uses of the phrase "political correctness" in order to see who is complaining and about what.

Revision: Bringing Drafts to Completion

OVERVIEW

Previous chapters have connected purposes for writing with news, advertising, visual media, and entertainment. In working with texts from these media, you have been writing observations and drafts as ways of working through texts' implications for you as a user of media, including writing.

In this chapter you should turn your attention again to your own drafts, and how to make them more rhetorically effective through revision. Revision is usually invisible. Books and printed articles do not routinely show any stage but the final, finished work. The same can be said of films: Screenwriters revise a lot of material out of finished scripts, which are further cut by directors in shooting—and most of the film shot is left on the cutting-room floor. Television drama and comedy are assembled in much the same way as movies; and reports for radio and television news may require several takes. Live drama is developed to performance standards through rehearsals. Seen from one perspective, whatever is not used in these media is wasted—but it might also be said that the additional material was necessary in order for the perfected version to exist. Revision is a crucial part of the professional writer's craft—but it's also part of that craft to keep the fact of revision out of the audience's sight and attention.

This chapter is not the first in *Rhetoric through Media* to direct attention to what is usually kept out of sight and mind. Also largely invisible are the extent to which news is constructed in stories, to fit reporters' and editors' and publishers' judgments of what their readers need and expect to hear; the ways in which entertainment texts draw from and reinforce ideologies of their culture; and the technical devices through which television commercials reach (i.e., manipulate) viewers. But revision's invisibility has a direct impact on your work as a writer. If you don't *see* revision happening in other people's texts, you may come to believe that you are the only one who has to revise anything, because (you think) you are just not very good. But revision goes on in all aspects of text production—offstage. Professional writers do not do their writing in one pass. They know that they have to continue to work at making drafts better, and they have a repertoire of devices to help with this process. This chapter should help you add to your own repertoire, by offering some devices through which you can do better revision and thus produce better texts.

This chapter, then, is about bringing your work to completion. There are two principal subjects here: finding **strategies** for finishing a text, and developing **tactics** for carrying through on revisions. (Strategies are overall perspectives; tactics are point-by-point decisions. Generals and national leaders decide strategies, while tactics are carried out in the trenches. Both are necessary for a campaign.) Much of this is not work for a textbook: What you need to do to revise your text has to come largely from your own analysis of that text. Ultimately, a lot of the decisions governing revision are specific to a given essay—your subject, audience, and persona, and what you know about them. But specific procedures may serve as starting points. Finally, some examples of writers carrying out their revisions will help show how revision proceeds in helping a text to find its eventual form. Also, part of this chapter will be concerned with incentive for revisions. A major part of the work of revision is realizing what is expected. Portfolios and class publications can be beneficial for getting clear on expectations.

Of course, not everything relevant to revision is confined to this chapter. Some of the devices for moving from initial observations to draft form discussed in Chapter 3 can be applied to the problems of later drafts. Decisions about audience, style, and logic are relevant to revision, and these will be taken up in Chapter 10. And skill in working with conventions (Chapters 3 and 6), analysis (Chapter 5), and ideology (Chapter 8) is also important for revision. Examining your strategy as a writer facing revision, and developing some tactics for carrying a draft further than may be customary, are what the chapter is all about.

ISSUES

It may be useful to start with an obvious question...

Why Revise?

Suppose that on your desk is a piece of your writing that has gotten to a certain stage. You've done enough prewriting to think through its issues in order to get started. And the first draft on your desk is suitable to be read by others, so long as they understand that it is work under construction. Now what?

Some of us, whether students or writers in other contexts, are content to leave most of the writing we do at that level. Like the grocery in Garrison Keillor's fictional hometown of Lake Wobegon, Ralph's Pretty Good Grocery, we may be happy just to have a pretty good draft. Not every piece of writing has to be a masterpiece, and in some cases you've done enough if you can show that you've done some thinking on a project, even without the extra effort.

But on occasion the stakes are higher. Sometimes, as a writer, you need to show that you can finish a piece well, that you are capable of raising your game a notch. In these circumstances, pretty good isn't good enough. If you are writing for a new situation, such as your first year in college, or an application for graduate school or a corporate position, you may not *know* yet what is expected in these contexts. You need the experience of taking your material through progressive revisions in order to realize how much is possible.

What you want to be able to produce, then, is writing that you won't have to apologize for. You want the reader not to think, "This is OK, under the circumstances," but to forget the "circumstances" part. There are times when you don't want to be just the fastest runner in the slow group. You want to be able to bring your writing to completion.

The word *completion* has several synonyms and close relatives. Its etymological sense is to fill something up. One standard dictionary, the American Heritage, offers the following discussion of *completion* and its near relatives:

> *Complete, close, end, finish, conclude, terminate.* These verbs mean to bring something to, or to arrive at, a stopping point or limit. *Complete* suggests the final stage in assembling parts into a whole: *complete a building*, or bringing a project to fruition: *complete a novel. Close* applies to stopping an action, either when it is completed: *The church service closes with a benediction,* or when it cannot be continued: *Lack of support caused the play to close. End* emphasizes finality: *end*

a career. Finish, often interchangeable with *complete,* is especially applicable to what one has set himself to do. *Conclude* adds to *complete* and *close* a sense of formality: *They concluded tariff negotiations. Terminate* more specifically suggests reaching an established limit in time or space.

So rather than suggest that your work *terminates* when you run out of time or *ends* when there is nothing more to be said on a subject, it's more suitable to try to bring it to *completion, fruition, fulfillment.*

In order for this completion to happen, you will have to do some further work with your writing. (This is probably not a surprise to you.) *What* and *how much* further work will depend on the context in which your writing will be read—on the audience and its expectations, on the subject matter, and on what kind of stance you claim for your knowledge. As readers, we expect more and better from certain texts than others. We don't look for the depth of thought and research in a short paper assigned in the first year that we expect in a major paper or thesis. First-year students are generally less practiced writers than seniors, and both are less practiced than professional writers. But first-year students often want to *become* seniors and professional writers, and their practice in writing will make this possible.

Part of the expectation for completed writing is that you bring your energy not only to having good ideas, but to giving them the best setting you can. Students routinely produce insights as good as those of publishing critics and writers—in some cases, better. But the difference is that the professionals know that more has to be done and are equipped to stay with the topic to *ensure* that more is done. Insights can be found in journal writing: The difference is that, in a draft, you lead the reader up to your insights through framing your discussion so that the importance is clear and the opportunity not wasted. Essays lead up to a climax, just as do short stories, novels, films, television dramas, and other narratives. Practice in getting best value for your insights is what revision is all about.

On occasion students talk about revision as though they had had a few years added to their sentences. *I'm going to revise my essay—the teacher's not happy with it yet.* This conception suggests a model of revision as *time served* (the sentence as sentence): Take some additional days, poke around at the margins a bit, and perhaps rewrite a bit on the basis of a literal reading of any comments provided by the instructor. No one is likely to be happy with the result, because in such cases there's *no revision taking place.* Revision is *re-vision,* seeing again, and in this scenario it isn't happening, because the writer really isn't convinced that any changes needed to be made. The motivation comes from outside.

Good writing has to belong to its writer first of all—but not exclusively. It has to belong to its readers as well. A better model for this process of interchange is conversation, in which what you say belongs both to you and to those you are communicating with. Thinking of writing as conversation may help us past the "stuck" point of a dispute over writing as property. Writers have always had cause to complain that *it's my essay, but I have to write it their way.* As I have often mentioned in previous chapters, writing as communication is not complete until it has been read and understood. You need the audience for your writing to have meaning. Writing involves "saying" something, to someone, in a form more lasting than speech. But writing is never a one-time utterance or a pronouncement. Rather, it's part of an extended interchange, and revision is your opportunity to *say it better,* to *complete* what you started to say initially.

Much of what separates successful writers from the rest is their persistence. They are able to stay with a piece longer, to recognize its potential and bring that out through patient reworking. Writing is recursive. You should not expect to write one thing, once, and be done with it. Performing artists don't record songs or perform scenes in one take; rather, they rehearse to get it right before letting the tape roll or going onstage. You have to return to the same issues and concerns, patiently, at times when you can bring them your *best* attention. (How much of your writing is done with the television or stereo on? Editing can be done in some hurly-burly, but re-vision requires quiet.) Some professional writers are the sort to have brilliant flashes and insights and get these down as rapidly as possible. Others are more like patient researchers. First-draft work by some successful writers of both sorts is really awful—many first-year college students do better first drafts. But the difference is that the professionals have learned to *stay with it,* to carry some internal sense of what a finished version looks like, and have developed strategies and tactics to get from the rough first draft to the finished version.

One tactic already mentioned in Chapter 3 is to divide the work of writing into stages. Because writing is recursive, there is something like revision going on at several stages, from the first notes jotted down for a topic to the time you hand your essay to a reader in completed form. But conventionally, **revision** is used to refer to those phases of writing that occur after the initial draft. Several separable activities go on from that point, and recognizing what these are should give a sense of their importance to your work. One such phase, *global revision,* involves activities such as development and reorganization, in which you are frequently working in units of a paragraph or larger. Another, later phase, *editing,* takes place at the sentence level or below. (In shorter pieces of work, it may not be necessary to separate revision from editing; when the writing gets to be more than a page, however, it probably needs a second pass.) Studies have shown that relatively inexperienced writers make virtually all their changes as editing, with very little if any global revision going on.

Not every writer excels at all phases of writing. You write from who you are. Some people are best at the imaginative phase, and will spin out wonderful concepts; some are best at taking ideas and developing their connection to concrete applications; and some are best at revising so as to round materials out. These last have a considerable advantage at getting the most out of their material, so revision is a skill well worth your time to develop. You cannot expect to become a complete writer until you can revise well.

Writing As Conversation

Let's return for a moment to the analogy developed above, *writing as conversation*. Writing may not appear to be a conversation, because the other voices don't "speak" in the same time and place. Some "other voices" are heard earlier—in texts that have been spoken, written, and broadcast by others. These voices may be experienced directly, or gotten at secondhand (or at greater remove). These participants in the conversation usually offer us received ideas, and we shouldn't sell such ideas short. *"Be careful when you go on the streets at night."* You probably heard something like this from your parents or others before anything bad happened to you, and perhaps before anything bad had happened to them either. We get secondhand not only advice but our culture's opinions and judgments about what are the right choices to make, the right values to have, the right thoughts to think. Very little of what we think started with us. (This is not an original idea. . . .) So only a few of these received ideas are the sort to be traced to specific texts. (Exhibit 9.1 takes off from this idea.) When you find a text that serves as the source of an idea, it's a rare object. Hold on to it and look at it very closely.

Other participants in the conversation speak later. If our writing is *to* someone—as opposed to talking to ourselves, which is not automatically a bad thing or a sign of insanity—and if it is in a medium that allows response, that person may talk back. Writing done for a class usually has responses from the instructor, and often from other students as well. Newspaper articles inspire letters from readers, comments from other writers and editors, and other forms of response—such as regular paychecks or notices of dismissal. Electronic exchanges draw reactions in similar kind. Books are reviewed, cited, praised or damned or ignored by other writers as well as readers, and adopted or passed over for classes. Not all of the conversation is in a form to be heard by the writer; but it's out there.

> Imagine that you enter a parlor. You come late. When you arrive, others have long preceded you, and they are engaged in a heated discussion, a discussion too heated for them to pause and tell you exactly what it is about. In fact, the discussion had already begun long before any of them got there, so that no one present is qualified to retrace for you all the steps that had gone before. You listen for a while, until you decide that you have caught the tenor of the argument; then you put in your oar. Someone answers; you answer him; another comes to your defense; another aligns himself against you, to either the embarrassment or the gratification of your opponent, depending upon the quality of your ally's assistance. However, the discussion is interminable. The hour grows late, you must depart. And you do depart, with the discussion still vigorously in progress.
>
> **Questions**
>
> 1. In Kenneth Burke's parable above, what are the areas of similarity between this conversation (?) and writing?
> 2. What is similar to exchanges in and through media?

Exhibit 9.1 Writing as conversation. Quoted passage from Kenneth Burke, *The Philosophy of Literary Form: Studies in Symbolic Action* (Berkeley: University of California Press, 1973), pp. 110–11.

Conversation is not always or entirely a matter of what goes on between us and others. Writing is also the visible and public part of a conversation that we have with ourselves. *Do I want to say that in that way? Do I want to be the person this sounds like? What about this objection?* We may not consider it conversation so much as reflection or meditation, but it's important for good revision.

What is odd is that it should be necessary to *say* "think about your writing as part of a conversation." What else would writing *be* except "talking" to someone else? How is it that our culture has created the sense that writing is a matter of the writer and the blank paper, in an upstairs room somewhere, with imagination and nothing else? Such a myth may heroize the writer, by stressing the individual elements of creation; but it's crippling to more collaborative aspects of writing.

If you think of your writing as part of a conversation, then, one of your strategies for revision should be to notice the other voices. As in any conversation, you have to listen carefully. Whom or what are you writing in response to? Who are you, to be able to write to them? Who else has an opinion on these matters? What values and thoughts and ideas do they have already, which your writing tries to interact with? How can your writing make a difference in this collection of voices? Specific questions should follow from these, depending on the subject—and you should draw up your own checklist of standard questions that you hope will make more evident the other participants in the conversation and their positions. (Sometimes you will have to prepare for your voice in the conversation by doing more and more selective reading. Improving a draft often means finding out who else has written on your subject, encountering their ideas, and incorporating them or responding to them.) Whether the conversation is with others or with yourself, a key principle is to pay attention to all parties in the conversation.

ASSIGNMENT

Choose a public issue now under discussion and trace some of the currents in your and others' thinking about it. For example, a discussion of *affirmative action* might involve several parts: the ideal of equal opportunity as presented in documents such as the Declaration of Independence; the concept that, in America, we all are able to attain the status we deserve through hard work (sometimes called *the Protestant ethic* or *the work ethic*); prejudice because of race, age, gender, or other factors; public attitudes toward government and toward corporations; the tension between defining people as individuals and defining them as members of groups; terms and metaphors in circulation, such as *quotas* and *the glass ceiling*; and so on. You may be strongly committed to one perspective on this issue—but set out all the constituent parts as fairly as you can, without allowing terminology to predispose value.

ILLUSTRATION: VECTORS ON O. J. SIMPSON'S ARREST AND TRIAL

By the time the first draft of this chapter was written, the first anniversary of O. J. Simpson's arrest for murder had passed, along with the first surge of interest in what would come out at trial, and most people had become mightily bored with the proceedings. Now, long after the verdict and several hundred news and tabloid stories, the subject may be old enough to use as an example of how currents or vectors are always at work in our "conversations."

Here are the products of my own brainstorming on the topic of O. J. (others would produce a different list):

- Sports hero and public figure from films and TV commentary
- Visible and successful black man
- Agreeable personality
- Notoriety of car chase—bizarre events
- Revelations of past domestic abuse; man-on-woman violence

- Overexposure of trial news
- Expectations from court stories (film and television) of speedy and dramatic wrap-up
- Reaction to disappointing "fall" of positive figure: cynicism, *schadenfreude*
- Regard for court system

One way to represent the several currents at work in your and others' thinking on an issue is by diagramming **vectors** (quantities with both magnitude and direction). The length of the arrows showing the vectors is meant to suggest the magnitude of force with which the considerations are felt. You can set up the terms representing the directions of feelings in whatever way seems important to you: The graph in Exhibit 9.2 uses the y-axis for positive and negative associations, the x-axis for private/public or individual/collective. Such a representation is offered as an illustration of how an issue is seen, in subjective terms.

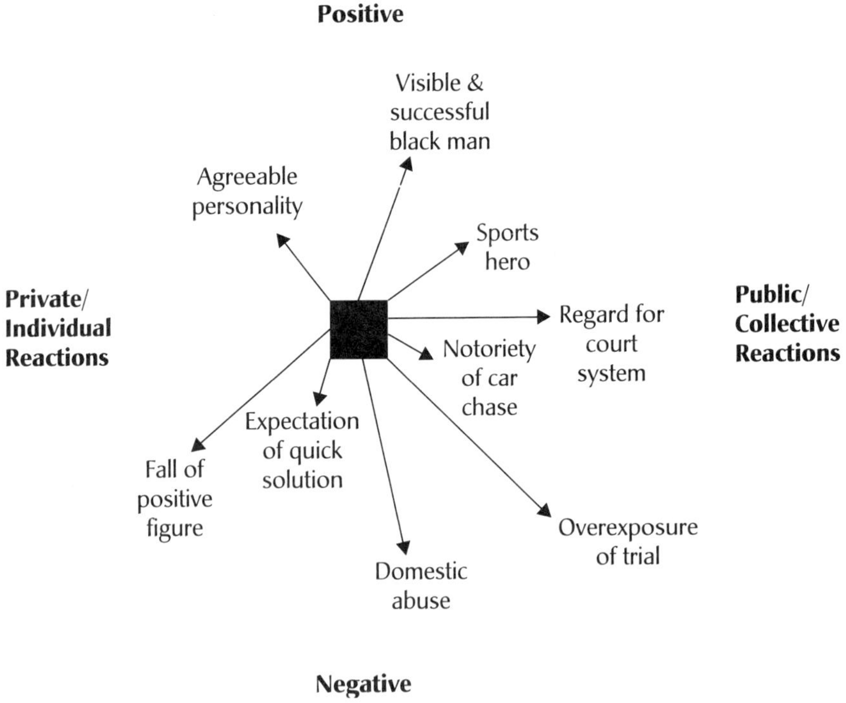

Exhibit 9.2 Vectors on O. J. Simpson's arrest and trial.

As can be seen from this illustration, my own set of vectors on O. J. Simpson shows that I am pulled in several directions, both positively and negatively, and in considering both personal responses and my thinking about public issues. Positive factors: O. J. Simpson as a visible and successful black man, an agreeable personality, and (less important for me personally) a sports hero. Negative: the notoriety of the car chase (bizarre, but not all that significant in itself), the overexposure of the trial and my own wish for a quick resolution, my reaction to domestic abuse, and the fall of a positive figure. All these factors pull in opposite directions, so that careful preparation could predispose me to think more about some than others: For example, a writer who stressed the public aspects might succeed in leading me to deemphasize my personal reactions; or a writer could emphasize the superficial similarities between this narrative and the archetypal fall of a tragic hero, thus strengthening my own cynical response.

Thinking in terms shown by Exhibit 9.2 may help you remind yourself that, on practically all issues worth writing about for a college class, your reader is likely to have a complex set of reactions. Analyzing these can help you direct your discussion, at the revision stage as well as at the first draft stage.

Examining my responses to the O. J. matter has led me to adopt certain partial reactions—in effect, to put on certain masks. There's a mask of sorrow at discovering the apparent wrong committed by a public figure, the mask of sober trust in the public system of arrest and trial, the mask of outrage at domestic abuse and alleged murder, and the mask of sour satisfaction (the German word *schadenfreude* means "shameful joy") at yet another "hero" unmasked. (All these are modified in response to the verdict.) Which is my "real" reaction? I'm not sure. I have a different response depending on the context called forth, which means that I am prepared to use the O. J. matter rhetorically in a variety of ways.

It can be very interesting to objectify your self in this way—to put on opposing masks, in a sense, or to respond to a different appellation—so as to stage a conversation. And such a conversation is not always so intentional as this one; for example, many writers keep a log of dreams. Dreams can be part of this conversation as well, both literal dreams we experience while sleeping, which may be thought of as conversations between unconscious and conscious, and daydreams or fantasies we indulge in while awake. Writers sometimes keep dream journals, because material for poems and stories may come up in its sharpest and most vivid form when we are asleep or just waking. You should not expect to make public use of all your dreams and fantasies— normally we have private thoughts that we keep private, because they violate taboos on appropriate behavior—but it can be useful to reflect on them yourself and see what they tell you about the other, less public portions of who you are.

Strategies and Tactics for Revising

You probably have gotten the message by now that you need to do more revision, and that you should begin by assessing what you already do for revision. So where do you start?

METACOMMENTARY

You can extend observation of yourself into a tactic. Write to yourself; that is, make use of **metacommentary,** or commentary on your commentary. *What I was trying to say in this passage was... what I want to do next is to... what I should be doing here, which isn't coming out so well, is....* You can go back and revise these and similar statements later, along with the *I think that*s and *I suppose that*s and other expressions indicating that what is said is only your opinion. (Of course it is; whose else would it be?) These phrases and other bits of metacommentary may be false starts, which can be edited out later—but they can help get you to clearer recognition of what you are trying for in a piece of writing.

Metacommentary is important in the intermediate stages of revision, then, as a way of breaking the ice in the conversation. The conversation with yourself, or perhaps with your self as you were a few days earlier in groping through the draft, may be engaged more easily if you use the margins and white spaces between the lines to reopen and reengage the earlier vision of your work.

PAUSE FOR REFLECTION
Write about how you revise your work. Think about essays written for the class in which you are using this text or, if it's early in the semester, for a preceding class for which you wrote significantly.

- Approximately what percentage of the total time in writing (including prewriting) was spent after the first completed draft?
- Considering the paragraph as a unit, how much of your revision involved units larger than a paragraph? (For example, transposing paragraphs or developing a point into a new paragraph or several.)
- How much of the revision was on units less than a paragraph? On units less than a sentence (for instance, substituting or inserting a word or phrase, changing punctuation marks)?

- What motivated your changes? Were you making adjustments in syntax and punctuation in order to make your writing grammatically correct? Or were you making changes in order to improve your style? In order to develop your topic? To explore another direction that occurred to you after the first draft? To reflect what you learned through further reading on your subject?

As you respond to the questions above, reply according to what you actually do, not according to what you think your instructor or others would like to believe you do.

A student wrote the following cover essay reflecting on her use of metacommentary in revision.

Many of the points brought up by classmates in...discussions helped me to submit a better final essay. I can honestly say that I considered the majority of the points raised during these critiques when revising my final essay.

The first thing I did to revise my essay was to use the nutshelling technique [see page 506] to rewrite my opening paragraph. I then made a list of the specific suggestions and objections raised by my classmates and instructor. Using this list, I then examined each of the paragraphs which I had written. I eliminated some of the paragraphs which got off the point of the essay. Since I was using the O. J. Simpson trial as an example of the negative effect media is having on our judicial system, I eliminated references to other high-profile court cases.

I also found the suggestion of looking at the essay from a stranger's point of view quite beneficial. By looking at it through someone else's eyes I could see some specific questions which might be raised. I tried to use this technique of using the literal point of view to eliminate some of the ambiguity in my writing.

The revision suggestion which was made in class of actually reading the finished work aloud also worked well for me. I have the habit of reading back things the way I think I wrote them, instead of reading the actual words printed on the page. This device helped me to find many mistakes which I had made. [Used by permission.]

The first strategy to think about, in revision, is to go from large to small. When rethinking your first draft, you will probably want to explore further dimensions of the topic, to deal with new ideas or give more space to the implications of those already outlined. These changes are part of thinking through the subject in order to do global revision. If changes are being made to clean up your prose, improve style, or make your writing grammatically correct, there's probably little or no development going on. In this case, **editing** better describes what you are doing. Revision is done in order to treat the subject adequately, to deepen what you are prepared to say; editing is done with no intention of expanding the subject, but in order to improve the small considerations that might affect how your writing is received. (Small is still important.) When you are seriously developing a topic, it's more efficient not to let yourself be distracted by considerations of whether or not to transpose a phrase, or by turning to a dictionary or thesaurus for advice. Just from practical considerations, if you edit prematurely, you may spend time correcting sentences that will be cut later.

Ideas need time to show themselves. They don't leap onto the paper or into RAM. (At least mine don't.) There needs to be a dialogue between the writer and the piece of paper (or electronic equivalent), in which the writer puts something down and reflects on it. One important purpose for doing revision at all is to get your best thinking down on paper; first ideas may not be the best, or may be good but underdeveloped.

COMPUTERS AND REVISION

Computers make possible a new set of tactics for revision. Many involved in the teaching of writing believed a decade ago that computers would change how writing was done. The widespread use of computers in writing still has that potential. Think back on what it meant to write in the 1970s and before, when there were three media, the last inaccessible until publication: handwriting, typing, and printing. Until the later nineteenth century, all writing was done by hand (or occasionally, as in Henry James's case, late in his career, by dictation). Mark Twain was the first to submit a manuscript to the printer in typescript. By the early twentieth century, it was possible for writers to work at the typewriter—but the ease and rapidity of writing there made it a temptation to write too quickly. Ezra Pound made a point of hitting the space bar three times between words, as a device to remind himself to give every word more weight. See the interview with Ernest Hemingway under How Writers Write in Chapter 3 for an account of how Hemingway used longhand and typing.

In both handwritten and typed drafts, the word remained the unit. If a writer wanted to move larger pieces of text around, the best device available was to cut and paste. But the adoption of word processors in the 1980s has made some material changes in revision: It is now no more work to transpose paragraphs than it was formerly to change the spelling of a word.

But the widespread adoption of computers in writing labs, with their style checkers, thesauruses, and other applications, is not an unmixed benefit. The computer makes it possible to write drivel and make it look professional. Printed in an attractive font on a laser printer, poorly written prose can appear as finished as the printer's end product did back in the 1970s. In doing revisions on a computer, therefore, you have to become used to the idea that your drafts will *look* more complete than they are.

The medium of the computer also holds other traps for writers. First, the mechanism offers less resistance than did either pencil and paper or a manual typewriter. Because there are no key jams, your speed of composition is limited only by small motor skills. You never have to stop to change a sheet of paper, and you never need to white out or erase mistakes. (Spell-checkers, however, do not deal well with homonyms: *To/too/two* and *there/their/they're* are still yours to catch. And there are always words such as formal names that are not in the computer's dictionary, which you have to pay attention to.) A second issue is that, because of the size of the screen, you can see only twenty lines or so at a time. This means that, if you want to see what you wrote a few paragraphs before, you have to jump about with the cursor or a search function, and it's usually inconvenient to shift about in this fashion.

Advice for writing on computers, then: Print frequently and work with hard copy. Don't become accustomed to doing all your work on screen, no matter how much you want to conserve paper. You need hard copy of the first draft in order to see and evaluate your organization, and you need hard copies of subsequent drafts in order to do proper editing. Some programs allow a split screen, so that you can work with eight to twelve lines in two drafts simultaneously: You can use this tactic not only for revising close passages, but also for keeping a short outline or list of points in view while composing a first draft. Finally, most important: Save early and often. If you are not sure that you want to lose an earlier version, save it under a different title. But make backup copies on floppy as well as hard disk. I would estimate that up to 10 percent of students have told me at some time in the semester that they had to retype drafts or rewrite a paper entirely because of some computer problem. Power outages or mechanical problems can happen at any time: Unfortunately, using a computer makes it possible for you to lose an entire document, rather than just a page or two.

A Few Tactics for Revision

With these strategic principles established, what are some tactics which might work to extend and improve your revision?

Leaving It Alone This may sound like curious advice after so much emphasis on the fact that most writers do not revise enough. But one reason that few changes are made in drafts is that the material is *too* familiar: Your voice (in print) is still too much in your ears. It often helps to leave it alone for a while:

to let a span of time pass—twenty-four hours, perhaps more—so that you can approach the language of the first draft as though it were that of a stranger. Ask yourself, sentence by sentence and paragraph by paragraph, what would your reaction to this text be if it were someone else's?

Sometimes revision doesn't go well because you are too close to the subject. Or you've worked with it so much that you are bored with it and don't see what else you can do. In that case, *stop.* Nothing good can come of writing that is forced, and this is as true for revision as for drafting. (Sometimes you have no choice—and then the best you can do is get through however you can, and try not to get yourself in that position again.)

Leaving the text alone can be effective advice for both global revision and editing. When you revise, considerations such as overall development and soundness of ideas are important; when editing, you will be reconsidering matters such as organization within the paragraph, transitions, style, and word choice. Both activities are made more difficult if the text is too recent.

You should not let the text sit *too* long, however. It is possible to leave your work in the drawer so long that you don't recall what it was you were trying to accomplish. If that happens, your revision may turn into a salvage operation or a fresh start.

Nutshelling   A cliché for reconsideration: "What were you trying to accomplish, in a nutshell?" To "put it in a nutshell" in this context means phrasing in a sentence or two what the main point of the draft is. What, above all else, are you trying to accomplish? You may feel that you've done this adequately with a well-formed thesis sentence—in which case your "nutshell" would be a paraphrase. But even paraphrasing the thesis sentence you have already written means some reconsideration of what that is in light of its potential. Spend some time with your nutshelling, and try to get a concise and elegant statement that conveys the essence of your text as you want it to be.

The nutshell then can serve as a means of returning freshly to parts of your text to test how sound they are. As you read deliberately through your draft, ask about each of the major parts of the essay, "How does this connect with that?" Does the rephrasing of the main point suggest an organization? If so, you may use that as a means to reconsider the sequence of paragraphs.

Often, a nutshell can help you refocus your attention on persona and audience: What will my audience be most curious about in my draft? Who do I seem to be in this text in order to give that to them?

Bombing the Draft   I've watched children play with a computer program called MacPaint: In addition to a variety of devices that make variously colored and textured traces on the screen, there's a logo of a bomb (the familiar cartoon icon—round, with a burning fuse at the top). When you click this icon and move it to the screen, a bomb goes off, with appropriate sound effects, clearing the screen for more MacPainting.

Unless you write with a program more sophisticated—or less—than mine, you probably don't have the literal capability to "bomb" anything in your text. However, you might use the concept to examine how important any portion of it is. What would happen if *this* paragraph or *this* section were bombed? Would anyone notice? Your essay may have started out covering two or three main points or questions, but perhaps in the writing you find that one of them has become far longer than the others—it seems to be more important, the questions are more complex, you yourself are more interested in that aspect of the issue, or you believe your audience will be. What would happen if you shifted your topic to be about the questions you want to give rein to, rather than those you were committed to in the beginning? The more you look at your essay, the more it seems to wobble; it's top-heavy on the point you really want to write about, but you feel some commitment to develop the other points you started out with.

Nuke 'em. That is, produce a version of your essay without those points altogether. This can be done more readily with a computer: You simply highlight the sections you think you might do without, and delete them, printing up a draft in the new form. (You can do the same thing by cutting and pasting hard copy.) Be careful, however, *not* to erase the old draft until you are *sure* that you want the bombed parts to stay gone.

Intentions change, even after the first draft. This may occur because you have written to the end of a topic and found that, for some reason, it doesn't interest you. Or you may have set out with three or four areas to explore, and found that when developed, one of these is a good deal more complex than you'd first imagined. Most first-year college writers consistently underestimate the development of topics expected by their readers—perhaps because of the superficial treatment available in most media texts' dealings with serious issues. Whatever the reason, your draft allows you to see what you have to say, and you should claim the freedom on subsequent drafts to modify that in order to make it better.

Impersonation   When using the impersonation technique, you take on a persona distinct from your own to read your work. You pretend to be a reader with interests other than finishing this draft and turning it in for evaluation. This exercise asks you to become something of an actor and invent a mask or persona for practical use.

One such persona, valuable for these purposes, is that of an imagined opponent. It's easy to write for ourselves and our friends: We already agree, and we need little convincing. Some peer critiques—readings from other students—have a similar fault: When reading the essay of someone who sits next to you in class, you may be reluctant to point out everything you think may be wrong about an approach. To do so might make an enemy, or might define for yourself an identity in the class that you'd prefer not to have. It's not normally your function to be an editor and critic in a classroom setting. But if you can imagine a reader of your text who takes a sharply contrasting view, and address your arguments to that person, it may help improve your work.

Impersonation can help bring up for conscious inspection some of what is assumed in a draft. All of us take some matters for granted in writing—we have to, or communication would be impossible. But some of what we assume needs to be scrutinized: Points of ideology, for example, are exactly the matters that need to be explored in a piece of writing, rather than assumed to be held in common. It can be a useful tactic in revision to take a key idea in the draft and say to yourself, "What if my reader thinks differently about this?"

Two passages from student essays may help illustrate how impersonation can help bring about reconsideration of an essay. As you read, pay attention to the writer's persona: What words and phrases in the essay go to construct that persona? Impersonate a critical reader as you work through the essays below.

SHANNON PEACOCK

From "Dais-ed and Confused"

It all started when I registered to vote last year. A local election was in three more weeks. Every day I received pamphlets and letters in the mail, which stated what candidates were the right choice and tried to persuade me one way. The candidates had signs in different families' yards all around the township. By the time election day arrived, I was too confused to vote because it seemed whoever I chose would mess up our system, whether it was raising taxes or cutting school supplies....

Why does this frighten and anger me? Maybe because I am new to the voting world or maybe because I am young and do not understand the politicians today. Both are true, but overall I think it frightens me because it is very overwhelming. What I mean by this is that we are bombarded with all the candidates. There are just so many people running for so many positions. Yet these people anger me as well. I do not like to hear about the candidates' affairs that have nothing to do with the election. [Used by permission.]

QUESTIONS

1. How would you describe the writer's persona here? What would be some possibilities for contrasting roles, either for her or for a reader of this text?

2. What might be the basis for seeing candidates' personal lives as relevant to their fitness for holding office (as in the case of Bill Clinton in 1992)? How much of President Clinton's success or failure in office do you attribute to allegations of adultery?
3. Can you offer another perspective on raising points in a campaign that people may judge (as this writer does) to be irrelevant? (For example, political operatives sometimes take the position *any means to an end*—if an issue, even a nonissue, is effective, use it.)
4. Are there circumstances in which confusing potential voters can be considered to be good? (What if it helps your side to win?)
5. How would this writer's discussion be strengthened if she were to take account of some of the motivations behind negative campaigning?

ERIC NELSON

From "Words Mean Things and Integrity Matters"

The national media have a role to play as the devil's advocate, and as such they report negatively on many issues. Part of their job is to stir controversy. But be aware that some of the word and presentation choices are a decision of a reporter's personal preference and style, while others are designed for effect.

For example, Connie Chung, co-anchor of the CBS Evening News, recently conducted an interview with the mother of the Speaker of the House, Newt Gingrich. She was on assignment for the CBS broadcast *Eye to Eye*. During this interview Mrs. Chung asked Mrs. Gingrich to whisper the answer to the question, "What does your son think of the First Lady?" Mrs. Gingrich had declined to answer on camera but agreed to whisper it privately; [in] confidence. The violation of that trust and the decision to report the confidence conveyed a disregard of journalistic integrity for the sake of a sound bite. The paramount issue is the meaning of the word *confidence*, not what was said. CBS's defense is that *Eye to Eye* is an entertainment show, not news broadcast. Shaky ground for their national anchor to stand upon, and a thin veil to hide their true editorial agenda. Our only retribution is by sending letters in response, or to vote by action. I have made a choice not to watch CBS news programs....

There are many forms of accessible information from pure fact to pure fiction. We see shows like *Hard Copy* and *A Current Affair* broadcasting a new form of entertainment that is presented with the look and feel of traditional news. Traditional news broadcasts have also borrowed from the entertainment world. I watch, listen to, and read many personalities who espouse a particular view or ideology.

Talk show hosts from Jim Hightower to Rush Limbaugh have interesting topics and discussions. They tell you where they come from, what they believe, and that they are an entertainment program based on current events. In many cases, broadcasters or publishers change the definitions and standards they are bound by to suit their momentary need, and in doing so, shirk their editorial and journalistic integrity. Every time this happens our right as Americans to have a "free press," without bias, is diminished. Men like Edward R. Murrow or David Brinkley have been eclipsed by the business of news. [Used by permission.]

QUESTIONS
1. As with the preceding essay, how would you describe the writer's persona? What are some possible contrasting roles?
2. What is it about the news texts mentioned that the writer objects to?
3. Consider the use of "entertainment" in the section above: CBS defends Chung by arguing that *Eye to Eye* is an entertainment program, and the author here argues that Rush Limbaugh's programs are to be understood as entertainment. Choose the role first of a defender, then of a critic of hybrid "news/entertainment" programs.
4. Does the writer contend that reporters on newslike entertainment programs, or their employing institutions, should or should not advocate particular views or ideologies?
5. Assuming the writer wants to continue to criticize Connie Chung while supporting talk shows and "tabloid" television programs, what would your advice be on ways to do this effectively?

Academic argument is best done with points that are open to dispute. If you believe (for example) that all right-thinking people *have* to agree with your position on a topic, if you imagine that all disagreement on a point is evil, then you are probably not working on material that is a good topic for college writing. (You have only one "mask" or persona available to you, and you believe that others must have the same mask as well. One size does not fit all.) Topics for discussion in a university setting have to be "in play"—that is, you have to be able to envision alternatives. Otherwise you are taking on either easy targets or impossible ones. (This is why some instructors forbid certain topics, such as abortion: Past experience shows that reasoned argument usually goes out the window because of emotional commitment to a position.) Some people take on intense levels of commitment on political issues, particularly as the election nears: "Don't try to unsettle me with the facts, I've already made up my mind. . . ." What can be troubling to us as writers is that these are often exactly the topics we feel are most important—but they have to be addressed at a time and in a manner that the audience can profit from, rather than according to our schedule.

Sample Revision: "Media in the Courts"

The following is an extended account of one student's revision, from earliest draft, submitted for reading by instructor and class, through intermediate version, to the completed version.

Media in the Courts (uncorrected 5/23 draft)
I think that broadcasting criminal trials on television is having a negative effect on our judicial system. I believe that televising trials effects the jury, witnesses, judges, attorneys and most importantly the outcome of the trial. This in turn is causing a negative effect on society as a whole.

How does television effect the jury? The juries are subject to media scrutiny. After the trial it is almost as if the media puts the jury members on trial. Although the jury members are not seen on television during the trials, the jurors who have been excused in the O. J. Simpson trial have had their names and faces plastered all over the media. While certain jurors seem to thrive on the attention, others have tried to be left alone and have been pestered by the press. Furthermore, jurors are not excused without the press revealing their names, occupations and the reason for their dismissal from the jury. There was a woman who was recently excused from the Simpson trial who reportedly was on the verge of a nervous breakdown. I am sure that the intense media scrutiny added to the poor woman's distress. The woman had done nothing wrong, she was just doing her civic duty.

I feel that this will severely limit the quality of the jury pool. We are apt to get a jury consisting of opportunists and publicity hounds. These type of jurors view the trial as their moment in the spotlight. A jury is supposed to be a fair and impartial body of your peers. One of the Simpson jurors was released fairly early on in the proceedings when it was revealed that he was keeping notes in order to write a book about the trial. I wouldn't say that he was fair or impartial.

The jury system is already severely limited by constraints of time and availability. Unfortunately most citizens can ill afford to take much more than a few weeks off from their job to serve on a jury. The fear of harassment following a verdict, the certainty that the press will not only reveal your name but most likely air pictures of you could send many potentially good jurors scurrying to avoid this service.

Broadcasting trials can also have a negative effect on witnesses. Some witnesses are really not witnesses at all, such as Rosa Lopez in the O. J. Simpson trial. It appears that her story may be a total fabrication. Sensation seekers become witnesses and may embellish their story for profit.

Legitimate witnesses may be afraid of the attention and media frenzy. Personally, if I were a potential witness I would not want my face broadcast all over the world. The witness is not the criminal. It is one thing to have your name in print, but when every crazy in the world can turn on their TV and see your face it invites problems.

The media, especially tabloid journalists, go overboard, they interfere with investigations and trials. The police are competing for information with the media. Sometimes if a witness is paid to talk on television or to give a story to a magazine before they give a statement to the police or grand jury it can cause this testimony to be thrown out, without any regard to the importance of the testimony. There was some controversy over some men who allegedly sold O. J. Simpson a knife, and who sold their story to the National Enquirer between the time of their grand jury testimony and the pre-trial hearings.

Some of the trials which were broadcast either on CNN or Court TV are the trials of William Kennedy Smith, the Menendez brothers, the trials involving the Rodney King police beating, the Reginald Denny beating trial and currently the O. J. Simpson trial. I believe the verdicts in these past trials and most likely in the Simpson trial have all been influenced by television.

The acquittals for the policemen who beat Rodney King and the hung jury in the Menendez case are prime examples. Is it fear that motivates the jury?

I think that the real problem with televising these trials so extensively is that the criminals become celebrities, and the celebrities who are trial are not judged to be criminals. I think that it also desensitizes viewers to the reality of the crime. Viewers become so caught up in the legal semantics of the trial that the real issue as in the Simpson case, did he or did he not murder two innocent people, is lost.

If the verdict which is arrived at is not a just verdict because it was adversely affected by being broadcast on television then than this affects all of us. Society as a whole will suffer if criminals are allowed to go free and if all citizens do not receive a fair trial. [Used by permission.]

This version was presented in class and was well received. But the class procedure was to rethink the essay and make revisions, so the student collected comments in writing from other students and instructor and made herself the following set of notes to guide further work:

Notes from Instructor & Classmates

- The press followed Rosa Lopez to El Salvador.
- How would I change it?
- Compile examples from one trial and link them chronologically.
- How would you balance the problem you describe here with society's interest in a free press, informed public, etc.?
- Media going overboard with coverage.
- Second paragraph re: jurors good; Ending paragraph effective.
- Less "I feel" or "I think."
- Positives.
- Not admitting evidence is only fair to the defendant but—if the evidence hadn't been.
- Court TV—better than CNN.
- Media is trying to let us know the reality in our society—what is really going on in courts.

Exhibit 9.3 shows the revisions made in this first draft of "Media in the Courts." Reading a revised draft can be frustrating and difficult; because if the

Uncorrected 5/23 draft

I think that broadcasting criminal trials on television is having a negative effect on our judicial system. I believe that televising trials effects the jury, witnesses, judges, attorneys and most importantly the outcome of the trial. This in turn is causing a negative effect on society as a whole.

How does television effect the jury? The juries are subject to media scrutiny. After the trial it is almost as if the media puts the jury members on trial. Although the jury members are not seen on television during the trials, the jurors who have been excused in the O. J. Simpson trial have had their names and faces plastered all over the media. While certain jurors seem to thrive on the attention, others have tried to be left alone and have been pestered by the press. Furthermore, jurors are not excused without the press revealing their names, occupations and the reason for their dismissal from the jury. There was a woman who was recently excused from the Simpson trial who reportedly was on the verge of a nervous breakdown. I am sure that the intense media scrutiny added to the poor woman's distress. The woman had done nothing wrong, she was just doing her civic duty.

Revision of 5/23 draft (changes in italics; cancellations in brackets; metacommentary in boldface)

[I think that broadcasting] *The intense coverage of certain* criminal trials on television is having a negative effect on our judicial system. [I believe that televising] *Extensive coverage and broadcasting of trials* [e]affects the jury, *the* witnesses, *the* judges, *and the* attorneys. *But the* [and] most important[ly the] *effect may ultimately be on the outcome* of the trial *itself*. [This in turn is causing a negative effect on society as a whole.] *It appears that the O. J. Simpson trial is fast becoming an example of this breakdown in the judicial process.*

How does television [e]affect the jury? The juries are subject to media scrutiny. After [the] *a major* trial it is almost as if the media puts the [jury members] *juries* on trial. [Although] *The judge does not allow* the jury members [are not] *to be* seen on television during the *Simpson* trial[s][,]. *However,* the jurors who have been excused in the [O. J.] Simpson trial have had their names and faces plastered all over the media. While certain jurors seem to thrive on the attention, others have tried to be left alone and have been [pestered] *hounded* by the press. Furthermore, jurors are not excused without the press revealing their names, occupations and the reason for their dismissal from the jury. *Several jurors has been dismissed when it was revealed that there was some kind of domestic abuse or violence in their past. True, they probably shouldn't have been sitting on this particular trial. But they are not public figures and do not need to have their names and past debated by the media.* There was [a woman who was recently excused from the Simpson trial] *also another dismissed Simpson juror* who reportedly was on the verge of a nervous breakdown. [I am sure] *There is no doubt* that the intense media scrutiny added to the poor woman's distress. [The] *This* woman had

Exhibit 9.3 Revision of first draft of "Media in the Courts." Used by permission.   *continues*

I feel that this will severely limit the quality of the jury pool. We are apt to get a jury consisting of opportunists and publicity hounds. These type of jurors view the trial as their moment in the spotlight. A jury is supposed to be a fair and impartial body of your peers. One of the Simpson jurors was released fairly early on in the proceedings when it was revealed that he was keeping notes in order to write a book about the trial. I wouldn't say that he was fair or impartial.	done nothing wrong, she was just doing her civic duty. *She also did not deserve to have her name and emotional problems dissected on T.V.* [I feel that this] *All this media scrutiny* will severely limit the quality of the jury pool. We are apt to get a jury consisting of opportunists and publicity hounds. These type of jurors view the trial as their moment in the spotlight. A jury is supposed to be a fair and impartial body of your peers. One of the Simpson jurors was released fairly early on in the proceedings when it was revealed that he was keeping notes in order to write a book about the trial. [I wouldn't say that he] *No one can argue that this juror* was either fair or impartial. *He was seizing the opportunity to make a fast buck off of other people's troubles. If this juror had not been removed—would his verdict have been influenced by his goal to write a book? definitely. Maybe he would feel a hung jury would make better material than a guilty verdict, or vice-versa. It is fortunate that this juror was removed, but how many potential novelists still lurk within the jury?*
The jury system is already severely limited by constraints of time and availability. Unfortunately most citizens can ill afford to take much more than a few weeks off from their job to serve on a jury. The fear of harassment following a verdict, the certainty that the press will not only reveal your name but most likely air pictures of you could send many potentially good jurors scurrying to avoid this service.	The jury system is already severely limited by constraints of time and availability. Unfortunately most citizens can ill afford to take much more than a few weeks off from their job to serve on a jury. The fear of harassment following a verdict[,] *and* the certainty that the press will not only reveal your name but most likely [air] *broadcast* pictures of you could send many potentially good jurors scurrying to avoid this service.
Broadcasting trials can also have a negative effect on witnesses. Some witnesses are really not witnesses at all, such as Rosa Lopez in the O. J. Simpson trial. It appears that her story may be a total fabrication. Sensation seekers become witnesses and may embellish their story for profit.	Broadcasting trials can also have a negative effect on witnesses. Some witnesses are really not witnesses at all, such as Rosa Lopez in the O. J. Simpson trial. It appears that her story may be a total fabrication. Sensation seekers become witnesses and may embellish their story for profit. *Rosa Lopez may have gotten more than she bargained for, when she left the US to return to her native country. She was pursued and followed there.*

Exhibit 9.3 *Continued*

Legitimate witnesses may be afraid of the attention and media frenzy. Personally, if I were a potential witness I would not want my face broadcast all over the world. The witness is not the criminal. It is one thing to have your name in print, but when every crazy in the world can turn on their T.V. and see your face it invites problems.

The media, especially tabloid journalists, go overboard, they interfere with investigations and trials. The police are competing for information with the media. Sometimes if a witness is paid to talk on television or to give a story to a magazine before they give a statement to the police or grand jury it can cause this testimony to be thrown out, without any regard to the importance of the testimony. There was some controversy over some men who allegedly sold O. J. Simpson a knife, and who sold their story to the National Enquirer between the time of their grand jury testimony and the pre-trial hearings.

Some of the trials which were broadcast either on C.N.N. or Court T.V. are the trials of William Kennedy Smith, the Menendez brothers, the trials involving the Rodney King police beating, the Reginald Denny beating trial and currently the O. J. Simpson trial. I believe the verdicts in these past trials and most likely in the Simpson trial have all been influenced by television.

The acquittals for the policemen who beat Rodney King and the hung jury in the Menendez case are prime examples. Is it fear that motivates the jury?

Legitimate witnesses may be afraid of the attention and media frenzy. [Personally,] *From a personal standpoint*, if I were a [potential] witness *in a major trial* I would not want my face broadcast all over the world. *After all* The witness is not the criminal. It is one thing to have your name *appear* in print, but when [every] *any* crazy in the world can turn on [their] *his* T.V. and see your face *and the house where you live, well* it invites problems. *Who is to say an avid trial watcher may not [make] hold the juror responsible for a verdict which is not to his liking.*

The media, especially tabloid journalists, go overboard, they interfere with investigations and trials. The police are competing for information with the media. Sometimes if a witness is paid to talk on television or to give a story to a magazine before they give a statement to the police or grand jury it can cause this testimony to be thrown out, without any regard to the importance of the testimony. *Although throwing this testimony out is only fair to the defendant, it is interference by the media which can cause a crucial bit of evidence to be disallowed.* There was some controversy over some men who allegedly sold O. J. Simpson a knife, and who sold their story to the National Enquirer between the time of their grand jury testimony and the pre-trial hearings.

Omit mention of other trials.

[Some of the trials which were broadcast either on C.N.N. or Court T.V. are the trials of William Kennedy Smith, the Menendez brothers, the trials involving the Rodney King police beating, the Reginald Denny beating trial and currently the O. J. Simpson trial. I believe the verdicts in these past trials and most likely in the Simpson trial have all been influenced by television.

The acquittals for the policemen who beat Rodney King and the hung jury in the Menendez case are prime examples. Is it fear that motivates the jury?]

Exhibit 9.3 Continued

I think that the real problem with televising these trials so extensively is that the criminals become celebrities, and the celebrities who are trial are not judged to be criminals. I think that it also desensitizes viewers to the reality of the crime. Viewers become so caught up in the legal semantics of the trial that the real issue as in the Simpson case, did he or did he not murder two innocent people, is lost.

If the verdict which is arrived at is not a just verdict because it was adversely affected by being broadcast on television then than this affects all of us. Society as a whole will suffer if criminals are allowed to go free and if all citizens do not receive a fair trial.

Insert e.g. 1) judge influence
2) attorneys—defense
—persecution
3) Benefits

The judge in the Simpson trial has undoubtedly been influenced by the exhaustive media coverage. The constant criticism in the press over the length of the trial plus jurors complaints have caused Judge Ito to speed up the trial. This can actually be viewed as a positive effect. [because]

The attorneys in the case are also affected by the media coverage. Prosecutor Darden has stated publicly that all the sensationalism sur-round[ed]ing the trial has disillusioned him. He intends to give up [the] his job as a public prosecutor when the trial is concluded. Of course, if the trial results in a mistrial or a guilty verdict which is appealed he may well get in another ten years on this case alone.

Marcia Clark, another prosecutor, has had her life, including a child custody battle, laid open to public scrutiny. Although Ms. Clark is a civil servant she is not a celebrity and also does not warrant this invasion of her privacy.

[I think that t] The real problem with televising these trials so extensively is that the criminals become celebrities, and the celebrities who are on trial are not judged to be criminals. [I think that it also] *The viewer becomes* desensitize[s]d [viewers] to the reality of the crime. **Rearrange** [Viewers become so caught up in the legal semantics of the trial that the real issue *is lost.* [as i]*In* the Simpson case, [did he or did he not] *the* murder two innocent people [, is lost] *sometimes becomes secondary to the bickering of the legal counsels and the media discussion of Marcia Clark's hairstyle.*

New close
If the verdict which is arrived at is not a just verdict because it was adversely affected by being broadcast on television than this affects all of us. Society as a whole will suffer if criminals are allowed to go free and if all citizens do not receive a fair trial.

Exhibit 9.3 *Continued*

Chapter 9: Revision: Bringing Drafts to Completion 517

The defense attorneys have not been adversely affected by the media coverage. On the contrary, Johnny Cochrane, one of OJ's lawyers, has just opened a new office in Los Angeles which is focused on entertainment law. The publicity surrounding the trial has also brought Mr. Cochrane new clients. He is representing victims of the Oklahoma bombing in a class action suit against the [fertilizer] company whose fertilizer was allegedly used in creating the bomb.

All the affects of the intensive media coverage have not been [positive] negative. Some benefits from the OJ Simpson trial specifically could be the focus on domestic abuse and violence. It has made people aware of domestic violence in a way they never were before. [The] A wife beater is not necessarily someone poor or uneducated. Spousal abuse can occur in any home[s of celebrities] the rich, the famous or the [home] house next door.

Another positive [a]effect [of] which comes from televising trials is that viewers become aware of the complexities of the judicial system. The fascinating field of DNA research has come to the forefront. [Viewers] Viewers have also gotten to know the origin of the phrase, "the wheels of justice turn slowly." Real criminal trials are not resolved as quickly as in a Perry Mason made-for-TV movie.

Use?

It remains to be seen whether or not O. J. Simpson will be judged guilty or innocent. That is not the question I raised here. The [question] issue [of] was whether or not he [received] will receive a fair trial and if [that was] the verdict was affected negatively by the intense media coverage. Regardless of the outcome, innocent, guilty or a mistrial I feel that the jury system is not fail-proof but it is [one] the best method available in our [American way of judgment] democratic society. Each accused criminal has the right to be treated fairly by the system. The freedom of the press should not infringe on the defendant's right to a fair trial.

Exhibit 9.3 Continued

5/23/95 DRAFT

MEDIA IN THE COURTS

The intense coverage of certain criminal trials on television is having a negative effect on our judicial system. Extensive coverage and broadcasting of trials affects the jury, witnesses, the judges and the attorneys. But the effect may be on the and most importantly outcome of the trial itself. It appears that the OJ Simpson trial is fast becoming an example of this breakdown in the judicial process.

How does television affect the jury? The juries are subject to media scrutiny. After a major trial it is almost as if the media puts the jurors on trial. The judge does not allow the jury members to be seen on television during the Simpson trial. However, the jurors who have been excused in the Simpson trial have had their names and faces plastered all over the media. While certain jurors seem to thrive on the attention, others have tried to be left alone and have been hounded by the press. Furthermore, jurors are not excused without the press revealing their names, occupations and the reason for their dismissal from the jury. Also another dismissed Simpson juror who reportedly was on the verge of a nervous breakdown. There is no doubt that the intense media scrutiny added to the poor woman's distress. This woman had done nothing wrong, she was just doing her civic duty. She also did not deserve to have her name and emotional problems dissected on T.V. All this media scrutiny will severely limit the quality of the jury pool. We are apt to get a jury consisting of opportunists and publicity hounds. These type of jurors view the trial as their

[Margin note: What it was revealed that there was some kind of domestic violence in their past, true, they probably shouldn't been sitting on this particular trial — but they are not public figures and do not need to have their names past debated by the media.]

Exhibit 9.4 Excerpts from marked-up first draft of "Media in the Courts." Used by permission.

Chapter 9: Revision: Bringing Drafts to Completion 519

moment in the spotlight. A jury is supposed to be a fair and impartial body of your peers. One of the Simpson jurors was released fairly early on in the proceedings when it was revealed that he was keeping notes in order to write a book about the trial. No one ~~could argue that~~ this juror ~~I notices say that he~~ was fair or impartial. He was seizing the opportunity to make a fast buck ~~either~~ off of other people's troubles. If this juror →

The jury system is already severely limited by constraints of time and availability. Unfortunately most citizens can ill afford to take much more than a few weeks off from their job to serve on a jury. The fear of harassment following a verdict ˄and the certainty that the press will not only reveal your name but most likely ~~use~~ broadcast pictures of you could send many potentially good jurors scurrying to avoid this service.

Broadcasting trials can also have a negative effect on witnesses. Some witnesses are really not witnesses at all, such as Rosa Lopez in the O.J. Simpson trial. It appears that her story may be a total fabrication. Sensation seekers become witnesses and may embellish their story for profit. Rosa Lopez may have gotten more than she bargained for, when she left the US to return to her native country. She was persueded to followe there.

Legitimate witnesses may be afraid of the attention and media frenzy. ~~Personally~~ From a personal standpoint, if I were a ~~potential~~ witness in a major trial I would not want my face broadcast all over the world. After all ˄The witness is not the criminal. It is one thing to have your name appear in print, but when ~~every~~ Any crazy in the world can turn on ~~their~~ his T.V. and see your face and the house where you live, well it invites problems. Who is to say an avid trial watcher may not make the juror responsilbe for a verdict which is not to his liek.

The media, especially tabloid journalists, go overboard, they interfere with investigations and trials. The police are competing for information with the media. Sometimes if a witness is paid to talk on television or to give a story to a magazine before they

Exhibit 9.4 *Continued*   *continues*

The defense attorneys have not been adversely affected by the media coverage. On the contrary, Johnny Cochrane, one of OJ's lawyers has just opened a new office in Los Angeles which is focused on entertainment law. The publicity surrounding the trial has also brought Mr. Cochrane new clients. He is representing victims of the Oklahoma bombing in a class action suit against the fertilizer company whose fertilizer was allegedly used in creating the bomb.

All the affects of the intensive media coverage have not been negative. Some benefits from the OJ Simpson trial specifically could be the focus on domestic abuse and violence. It has made people aware of domestic violence in a way they never were before. A wife beater is not necessarily someone poor or uneducated. Spousal abuse can occur in any homes, the rich, the famous or the house next door.

Another positive effect which comes from televising trials is that viewers become aware of the complexities of the judicial system. The fascinating field of DNA research has come to the forefront. Viewers have also gotten to know the origin of the phrase, "the wheels of justice turn slowly." Real criminal

Exhibit 9.4 Continued

writer has seriously engaged with the topic, there are cancellations and revisions all over the place—writing on the backs of pages, inserts, cut-and-pastes, writing sideways in the margins, Post-its, and other physical violence done to the text. Exhibit 9.4 shows examples. Computers have made some of this work invisible, because much of the surgery is done on successive versions printed up, or left in memory. (Surgery as a metaphor is too kind. The process may be more like amputating a limb and then seeing if the patient can walk straight, a dozen or more times successively.) Exhibit 9.4 is readable only because the student is a fairly neat writer.

If you look back at the "Notes from Instructor & Classmates" and at Exhibit 9.3, you'll see that the writer has engaged seriously with the other voices represented by her notes. (Much other advice was offered during the class presentation; the discussion went so far as to turn into a debate with another student on the appropriateness of televising trials, and he wrote his own essay on the subject, presented the following week.) None of this student's writing space or metacommentary is spent on lamenting how other students didn't get what she was trying to say, or feeling wounded; such criticism as there was became a prompt for further work, a stimulus for re-vision.

Below is the final version of "Media in the Courts." Changes after the revised draft are in italics. Note that these changes are clearly editing, while changes from first to second draft combined some editing with revision. Not all the cancellations are shown on this version.

Media in the Courts (Final Version)
The intense coverage of certain criminal trials on television is having a negative effect on our judicial system. Extensive coverage and *the live broadcast* of trials affects the jury, the witnesses, the judges, and the attorneys. But the most important effect may ultimately be on the outcome of the trial itself. It appears that the O. J. Simpson trial is fast becoming an example of this breakdown in the judicial process.

How does television affect the jury? The juries are subject to media scrutiny. After a major trial it is almost as if the media puts the ju*rors* on trial. The judge does not allow the jury members to be seen on television during the Simpson trial, however the jurors who have been excused in the Simpson trial have had their names and faces plastered all over the media. While certain jurors seem to thrive on the attention, others have tried to be left alone and have been hounded by the press. Furthermore, jurors are not excused without the press revealing their names, occupations and the reason for their dismissal from the jury.

[New paragraph] Several jurors ha*ve* been dismissed when it was revealed that there was some kind of domestic abuse or violence in their past. True, they probably *should not be* sitting on this particular *jury, but* they are not public figures and do not need to have their names *revealed* and past debated by the media.

[New paragraph] There was also another dismissed Simpson juror who reportedly was on the verge of a nervous breakdown. There is no doubt that the intense media *pressure* added to the poor woman's distress. This woman had done nothing wrong, she was just doing her civic duty. She also did not deserve to have her name and emotional problems dissected on *television.*

All this media *attention* will severely limit the quality of the jury pool. We are apt to get a jury consisting of opportunists and publicity hounds. These type of jurors view the trial as their moment in the spotlight. A jury is supposed to be a fair and impartial body of your peers. One of the Simpson jurors was released fairly early on in the proceedings when it was *discovered* that he was keeping notes in order to write a book about the trial. No one can argue that this juror was either fair or impartial. He was seizing the opportunity to make a fast buck off of other people's troubles. If this juror had not been removed would his verdict have been influenced by his goal to write a book? Definitely. *Perhaps* he would feel *that* a hung jury would make better material than a guilty verdict, or vice-versa *and cast his vote accordingly.*

The jury system is already severely limited by constraints of time and availability. Unfortunately most citizens can *not* afford to take much more than a few weeks off from their job to serve on a jury. The fear of harassment following *the trial* and the certainty *that your name and picture will most likely be broadcast nationwide* could send many potentially good jurors scurrying to avoid this service.

Broadcasting trials can also have a negative effect on witnesses. Some witnesses are really not witnesses at all, such as Rosa Lopez in the O. J. Simpson trial. It appears that her story may be a total fabrication. Sensation seekers become witnesses and may embellish their story for profit. Rosa Lopez may have gotten more than she bargained for, *the press followed her when she left the United States to return to her native country.*

Legitimate witnesses may be afraid of the attention and media frenzy. From a personal standpoint, if I were a witness *in a major trial,* I would not want my face broadcast all over the world. After all, the witness is not the criminal. It is one thing to have your name *appear* in print, but when any crazy in the world can turn on his TV and see your face and the house where you live, *this* invites problems. Who is to say an avid *fan* may not *blame you, the witness, for the a guilty verdict and come after you.*

The media, especially tabloid journalists, go overboard, they interfere with *trial* investigations. The police are competing for information with the media. Sometimes if a witness is paid to talk on television or to give a story to a magazine before they give a statement to the police or grand jury it can cause this testimony to be thrown out.

Although *disallowing* this testimony is only fair to the defendant, it is interference by the media which *may eliminate* a crucial bit of evidence.

[New paragraph] There was some controversy over *two* men who allegedly sold O. J. Simpson a knife. [New sentence] *These men* sold their story to the National Enquirer between the time of their grand jury testimony and the pre-trial hearing.

The judge in the Simpson trial has *obviously* been influenced by the media. The constant criticism in the press over the length of the trial plus jurors complaints have caused Judge Ito to speed up the trial. This can actually be viewed as a positive effect.

The attorneys in the case are also affected by the media coverage. Prosecuter Darden has stated publicly that all the sensationalism surrounding the trial has disillusioned him. He intends to give up his job as a public prosecutor when the trial is concluded. Of course, if the trial results in a mistrial or an *appealed* guilty verdict he may well get in another ten years *of public service*.

Marcia Clark, another prosecutor, has had her life, including a child custody battle, laid open to public *discussion*. Although Ms. Clark is a civil servant, she is not a celebrity and *this trial* does not warrant an invasion of her privacy.

The defense attorneys have not been adversely affected by the media coverage. On the contrary, Johnny Cochrane, one of O. J.'s lawyers has just opened a new office in Los Angeles *specializing in* entertainment law. The publicity surrounding the trial has also brought Mr. Cochrane new clients. He is representing victims of the Oklahoma bombing in a class action suit against the company whose fertilizer was used *to make* the bomb.

All the *effects* of the *intense* media coverage have not been negative. Some benefits from the Simpson trial could be the focus on domestic abuse and violence. *This trial* has made people aware of domestic violence in a way they never were before. A wife beater is not necessarily *some poor, uneducated person.* Spouse abuse can occur in any*one's* home, the rich, the famous or the house next door.

Another positive effect which comes from televising trials is that viewers become aware of the complexities of the judicial system. The fascinating field of DNA research has come to the forefront. Viewers have gotten to know the origin of the phrase, "the wheels of justice turn slowly." Real criminal trials are not resolved as quickly as in a Perry Mason movie.

The real problem with *publicizing* these trials is that the criminals become celebrities, and the celebrities who are on trial are not judged to be criminals. The viewer becomes desensitized to the reality of the crime *and the victim is forgotten. Trial watchers* become so caught up in the *media hype surrounding* the trial that the real issue is lost: *two people were brutally murdered.*

The jury system is not fail-proof, but it is the best method available in our democratic society. Each accused criminal has the right to be treated fairly by the system. The freedom of the press, *and the public's right to know,* should not infringe on the defendant's right to a fair trial. *If the defendant does not receive a fair trial because of the negative effects of media coverage then our judicial system has failed. This debate regarding the O. J. Simpson case will go on long after the trial has concluded regardless of the final verdict.* [Used by permission.]

QUESTIONS

1. What are some of the strategies and tactics for revision that are left implicit? That is, what are some patterns of change followed by the writer that were not written out under "Notes from Instructor & Classmates"?
2. If you believe the final version is an improvement on the earlier versions, why? What particulars in the text make it better?
3. Even the version above may have room for further work. What are some additional changes you would make in this text? Can you see a pattern to your recommendations?

One of the hardest questions about revision is this: To what extent is revision text-specific? That is, how much revision has to be keyed to the topic and writing situation for a given piece of writing, and how much can be made part of a writer's own general system for revision? If all revision were connected to the subject and mode of treatment of a given text, then there would be little point in writing a chapter about revision, because it all would have to be done in individual consultations. Experience suggests, however, that successful procedures for revision can be freely adapted to serve in many different situations. Most checklists for revision should include considerations such as those shown in Exhibit 9.5.

Revision always involves rethinking, and further suggestions about rethinking appear in Chapter 10 in the context of the discussion of "bad rhetoric"—poor or misleading logic that is sometimes present in media texts. That chapter also offers additional suggestions for editing.

Editing, even more than revision, is centered on specific texts and writers. The principal consideration for editing is to develop your own checklist of things you know from past experience to watch out for. If you confuse homonyms such as *its* and *it's, there* and *their,* you probably know it by now. Put those on your list, and look up the distinction. If you have the habit (as I do) of using "this" to refer to a possibly vague preceding idea, check that usage—you can use a computer to highlight that word or others as a way of checking your work. If you tend to comma splices or other misuses of commas, you can highlight all your commas and look closely at them. But editing is your responsibility. Mistakes at this level function like radio static: An occasional pop or two can be overlooked by most listeners, but at some level almost everyone will stop listening.

- Make sure that paragraphs are adequately developed both for the subject matter under discussion and for the audience and context.
- If you feel you don't know enough about a point, find out—use search procedures to find relevant material from indexes, databases, and other resources. (On many subjects, your audience will expect you to have taken some trouble to find out; and in other cases, doing the research will improve your authority.)
- Expand your work—don't just tack more material on at the end. As shown by the "Media in the Courts" example, effective revision often means reconsideration throughout. The effect can be like watching the printing on the side of a balloon expand as it is blown up.
- Be more generous with the introduction and conclusion. Less-experienced writers are often impatient to get to the main subject and may give too little consideration to what is needed to frame the subject and establish its importance, both generally and for the specific audience. Similarly, essays by beginners often conclude by leaving the impression that the writer has run out of things to say; but you should use the conclusion effectively to stress the importance of the subject. (Avoid conclusions that simply repeat the essay's main points: These may leave the impression that you believe your reader is so bored or stupid that you have to say what you have to say repeatedly.)
- Make sure that you have reasons to support your assertions. There's always something taken for granted in an essay—but it's usually better to argue a point that doesn't need much treatment than to assume agreement where you shouldn't.

Exhibit 9.5 A checklist for effective revision.

Collections of Writing

One activity recommended in Chapter 5 involved making collections of advertisements. Here we will discuss what is involved in making collections of your own work, either individually in the form of a portfolio, or collaboratively in a class publication. (See Chapter 11 as well.) Much of our effort in writing goes into topics for single essays, and often we concentrate so hard on those single tasks that we may miss connections with other texts. But connections with our other texts can help us prepare our work for audiences beyond the instructor.

PORTFOLIOS

Most of what is suggested in *Rhetoric through Media* about writing can be done by readers on their own initiative, and there's nothing to prevent you from gathering your work into a folder and calling it a portfolio. Portfolios, however, usually are assembled and read for institutional purposes: Their form and purpose, the genres of works collected, and the uses for portfolios all involve more than just a matter of individual choice. Specifics about portfolios will have to be provided by an instructor, counselor, or other official representative of your college. If you are reading this book for a class that is not using portfolios—doing all your writing in discrete assignments that are separately graded—most of this section may not apply to you.

There are two general uses of portfolios in college classes. One, the more common outside of writing classes, is what might be called the **exhibition portfolio.** The exhibition portfolio serves as a way for students to select what they consider their best work to show others, as with art prints or photography. And increasingly, portfolios are being used as devices for students to demonstrate competence in writing for institutions, through a collection of essays done for several classes. (These are usually the student's own choice, made according to assigned genres.)

Others will probably have something to say about how you assemble an exhibition portfolio. Is the purpose of the portfolio to show a prospective employer some of your professional capabilities? To show an admissions committee for graduate school some of your best undergraduate work? To demonstrate writing proficiency in several classes for a university committee? These are related but separate purposes, and your choices and portfolio organization will differ accordingly. Find out what is needed, by seeking written information or by talking with faculty or staff responsible for criteria by which portfolios are read or prepared. For example, some uses of exhibition portfolios will require pieces as originally submitted, including instructors' comments; for others, you will be expected to provide clean copy that looks as professional as possible—that is, without instructors' comments.

Probably both written handouts and advice on portfolio criteria will be rather sketchy. Official guidance about exhibition portfolios is likely to be sparse because no general statement can fit precisely the individual characteristics of writing. A good way to proceed would be to add to whatever rubric is provided through your own metacommentary. Begin by exploring what writing you have to work with and how that fits the required or recommended categories; part of the expectation for portfolios is that you use them to show your ability to work within the guidelines to your own purposes. What do you see in your writing that makes it of interest for the portfolio? What will others want to see, and how does this writing fulfill that need?

The principal task for you, in assembling an exhibition portfolio, is to convert it from a collection of disconnected pieces into a unity. This may take more than a table of contents, and you should find out if further revision of the pieces in the portfolio is expected or permitted. Usually you are dealing with work done over several months, perhaps several years, much of which was written with no thought about what would eventually be next to it in the portfolio. What can you discover in associating these disconnected works as though they were connected? You should write (informally) exploring this question—perhaps incorporating some of your thoughts into a cover essay or introduction—because those connections are principally what your reader will be trying to discover, and you may be able to frame the response to the question in beneficial ways.

For the purposes of this class, your instructor may want you to collect several pieces of finished work about media. If that is the case, you probably have a rubric for your portfolio already, in the form of a course syllabus or other handouts. For instance, in one semester's class I asked for the following types of essays:

- Observation of a media consumer;
- Close technical analysis of a commercial;
- Definition of a genre of media text;
- Discussion of the ideology implied by a media text; and
- Self-evaluation as a media critic.

Again, metacommentary is crucial: It's not enough just to collect your writing according to your own estimation, and it's not enough just to follow others' requirements. The implicit requirement in such a portfolio is to make a bridge between these, to show that your own accomplishments in writing can fit others' requirements. In other words, you need to demonstrate that the product of your own thinking can be made to serve social and cultural needs. (Is this hegemonic? Yes. Welcome to college. But as I've said before, the most successful writers will manage to maintain their own independence at the same time that they satisfy institutional requirements; that is what marks them as successful.)

While some English classes use exhibition portfolios, most adapt portfolios to a different purpose, following the development of writing over a wider span of the writing process. Portfolio selections in this mode, or **draft portfolios,** include a substantial portion of writing done for the class—informal as well as formal, with prewriting devices, journal entries, research notes, and successive drafts of the same paper all included. Draft portfolios emphasize writing as a process, as this and other chapters of this book have done.

Draft portfolios have been around for some time now. Their purpose is to improve work at several phases of the writing process. There have been conferences on the subject, and articles and books on their practicability and use. If your instructor has designed your class around portfolios, that choice has certain consequences for you: It means that you have the opportunity, and the expectation, of staying with a piece for longer.

In contrast with the more usual pattern of writing assignments (assignment–paper–grade, assignment–paper–grade), a draft portfolio fosters a different approach. Consider, to begin with, what you typically do with the instructor's comments on papers. If the paper is graded, there's a strong temptation to regard the essay as over and done with. What you look for, mostly—what I looked for—is the bottom line, the grade. If it suited my expectations, then I would read anxiously over the comments in the margins, hoping to find "good," "fine," "excellent" in the instructor's handwriting, and fearing the "but" and "you haven't shown" and, worse, the grammatical codes to be found there. But all this reading was done in regard to work that was *in the past;* it had no particular relevance to the next assignment. This was especially true of end-of-semester papers, which often were the last I expected to write for that instructor.

Especially diligent students will read end-of-paper comments as suggestions and hints for the next time, whether in that class or the next one, perhaps even going so far as to keep a log of comments. However, most will not do so. Portfolios can work effectively to modify these practices by separating *evaluation* from *suggestions for improvement.* Suggestions from the instructor and other readers are all relevant to the eventual grade, so there is incentive to give them special attention.

Portfolios are congenial to thinking about writing as a process—and this has both advantages and disadvantages for you as a writer and for the quality of your writing. If your writing is characterized by surface-level problems—sentence-boundary errors such as fragments and comma splices, vague reference, mispunctuation, and so on—one-shot assignments may encourage you to concentrate too soon on editing rather than giving time and energy to development, organization, and the difficult job of thinking well about your topic. Some portfolio systems encourage approaching writing in a sequence, getting the overall approach first before fine-tuning terms and phrases. Such "fine-tuning" is not to be underestimated—but it is better done at a later stage of composition.

One considerable advantage of the draft portfolio system is that it encourages trying things out, because you know that you can always reconsider them later. If every draft is graded, then you may be encouraged to take "safe" positions. With some subjects, it may be better to write from within your first set of conceptions, then modify or reconsider with the help of readers' responses.

The advantages of draft portfolios can prove to be disadvantages as well. First, you don't usually have unambiguous feedback on your work in terms of grades. While you can get some feedback by conferring with the instructor, it's possible to become either unnecessarily anxious or overconfident. Also, too much concentration on writing as process can make it possible to defer thinking of your work as a product altogether (at least during that semester). Writing for others means meeting their expectations as well as your own; this usually requires that sooner or later you come to a conclusion. Having the leisure to treat subjects more carefully may create a dependence on having all the time you think you need, on having others offer constructive criticism, and so on; but most real-life writing situations do not allow unending deferral or helpful criticism.

But if it's kept in mind that most writing involves deadlines, draft portfolios offer distinct advantages for student and instructor. The principal of these is greater student control over, and responsibility for, writing. You have to learn how to make your writing as good as it can be, depending on your own resources rather than those of instructors, writing centers, and others in your situation. Almost no one is privileged to have an editor employed to offer advice about what is good and should be kept, what is weak and should be improved or cut out. While it is possible to enlist friends or family as editors, too much use of this tactic may cause you to lose friends and alienate family. You need to internalize your "editor" as another of your characters for impersonation. Developing an editor on call will give you more confidence in judging how your writing works for the various situations in which it may be required.

Whether it's draft portfolios or collections of finished writings, portfolios encourage a wider view of the writing task, which may enable you to see patterns in your work. If criticism of one paper is focused on the short introduction or lack of a conclusion, reviewing that criticism may get you thinking about your introductions and conclusions on other assignments. In other words, portfolios may encourage you to think about your own work rhetorically, rather than focusing exclusively on the content of an assignment.

PAUSE FOR REFLECTION

As a guide to a persona to be adopted during revision, write out some characteristics of the "editor" you need. What are some other masks that would be helpful for you to put on?

CLASS PUBLICATIONS

Writing for a class publication is in some respects like writing for an exhibition portfolio—except that the collection involves other students' work rather than just your own. Writing by students is necessarily seen as *student writing*. One device that may remove your class's work from that category, to some extent, is the use of a class (or university) publication.

Creating a class publication obviously is not an individual effort: It requires some planning and legwork, interaction in some cases with university staff and administration, at least minimal funding or use of a copy machine, and time and effort not given directly to the preparation of individual student essays. (Another alternative would be an electronic class publication.) These are more than incidental costs.

Roles in preparing the publication need to be divided up. Most instructors will not want to serve as editors—the point of the publication is to turn responsibility over to students. Preparing a class publication means discussing several parts of the enterprise: deciding what the title and purpose of the publication is, determining which essays will be published, organizing these into sections and some sequence, providing illustrations (if any) and transitional material, and so on. Then there are the activities that correspond to what we have been calling "editing": getting acceptable copy from writers, establishing and policing a consistent format for the publication, and so on. (If writers are to prepare camera-ready text, then just getting the same type font and size, preparing page numbers, and enforcing margins can be a major headache.)

There can be substantial benefits, however. Writing for a class publication creates an audience beyond the instructor and, in some cases, beyond the classroom setting. In writing for a publication, you will develop some sense of the wider context that the publication provides, and of how your own essays interact with others included. Seeing your work as part of a larger project, published and bound, can make your writing more than just another semester's assignment, recorded only as a letter on your transcript. And there are advantages for the instructor as well. Many collaborative assignments are just that—assignments. Students are paired off to read each other's work, lacking much of a context for peer critiques beyond what they can provide from previous writing classes. But publications may give wider notice for good-quality work.

Class publications can provide local visibility for the class's work. Classroom versions of "real writing" often do not escape the classroom context—they remain practice assignments. A class publication may fall into this category as well, so it is desirable to try to get legitimacy for it by continuing publication semester after semester, by going to a professional-looking format rather than Xeroxed pages, by involving writers from other classes and other departments, and so on.

CONCLUSION

The principal message of this chapter is as follows: Don't close prematurely. This is good advice in writing first drafts as well as revisions. Sometimes, because of pressure to meet a deadline, boredom with a subject, or just impatience, we want to get finished with a piece of writing. This desire can be understandable, but the result may be to give too little concentrated attention to an issue or a perspective on an issue. Part of the message in this chapter is to *slow down*. If you can't give your writing the concentration it deserves, you need to take a break, get away from it for a while, and then come back when your mind is fresh and your attention level renewed.

Much of this chapter involves advice. As with other sorts of advice, it's largely up to you to decide whether to take the advice and how to apply it. It is possible to take a good piece of advice and convert it into a disaster through misapplying it. That is the importance of seeing your writing as conversation, not only with some distant writers and readers, but with the local ones as well. You have others in your class, an instructor, and probably other resources as well. Don't be shy about asking for their opinions. They are who you are writing for.

FURTHER ASSIGNMENTS

Assignment
After having read through the chapter's discussion about revision as conversation, the specific strategies and tactics suggested for revision, and the extended examples of revision and editing above, return to your own list of procedures for revision. Which of them seem most likely to produce fruitful re-vision? What are some additional procedures that you might consider for extending and deepening your work? As you respond to these questions, do so in two personae—first as someone not interested in doing any more writing than necessary, and second as someone without regard to time and energy needed for later drafts.

Assignment

Take three pieces of incomplete writing (anywhere from freewriting to first draft) and write metacommentary about each. What would it take for you to bring these to completion? Consider how you would apply the tactics discussed in this chapter; then choose one piece of writing for further revision.

After that revision is completed, write a reflective piece on the changes you made and the extent to which your metacommentary was helpful.

10

Developing Style and Audience Awareness

OVERVIEW

Much advice about style in writing is contradictory. Some takes the form of simple advice that works well for some circumstances but should not be applied in all. ("Avoid passive voice.") Some extends one set of preferences about style to all circumstances. ("Simple sentences have more punch.") And some disconnects style from content, suggesting that you can change style as easily as you might change your clothes.

But style is less the clothes than the body, or perhaps the flesh over the bones. It grows out of interaction between the writing persona, the subject or field that provides context, and the implied audience for the writing. Initially the subject area establishes a field for possible treatment; within this area, the text creates roles, not only for the writer, but for readers as well. Style is effective when there's a fit between these roles and actual readers; problems arise when readers do not want to play the roles inscribed for them through the text.

We can improve how style works for us by renewing our sense of audience in writing—in particular, by observing how audience is inscribed in media texts and by examining our own reactions to these scripts. Audience roles and writers' personae are created by an accumulation of small decisions. Your choices in words, sentence length and structure, and appropriate figures of speech are drawn from the uses of language already available to you. As with other aspects of rhetoric, many of these uses of language are supplied by popular commercial media.

Thinking more consistently about writing as rhetorical, then, can offer specific guidance for stylistic choices. One style does not fit all; as writers, we need several models. These can best be gotten by reading widely and reading critically. Prose is itself a medium in wide use; and you can analyze it, much as you analyzed films or television programs or popular music in previous chapters, to see how it works rhetorically.

Some concerns related to style have already been discussed. Chapter 2 discusses the audience's uses of media. Chapters 4, 6, and 7 all consider audience in the contexts of news, visual media, and entertainment. Analysis, taken up in Chapter 5, directs attention to how the overall nature of a text is constructed from a series of smaller choices. Metaphor, and audience as called into being, are topics in Chapter 8. And the cross-connections between media texts and those you have been writing are stressed in every chapter. So a concern with style pervades *Rhetoric through Media*. However, the relation between style and audience is important to consider separately. Like rhetoric, style as a concept has had some bad press. Rhetoric's reputation has suffered from the excesses of texts that use verbal devices to cover for emptiness or weak logic. Style is not subject to the same negative associations as rhetoric; but it is similarly thought of as dispensable, as though style were somehow extraneous to the real substance of an argument. The concept of style as external is reinforced by the use of the term to describe clothes, jewelry, and other devices used (at least theoretically) to make ordinary people look glamorous.

But style is not simply decorative. It's common, for example, to speak of musical style, which is based on instrumentation, phrasing, melody, harmonic structure, repetition and development of motifs—in short, those elements that *make* the music. In cinema, we can speak of a director's style as the result of preferred camera angles and movements and the way the cuts are put together—and again, these are not ornaments, but the decisions that make the film. And in writing, style is a matter of word choice, syntax, organization at the paragraph level, rhythm, presence and selection of figures of speech, and so on—those essential matters that make up the writing. Style is not something added at the last minute, like a sprig of parsley or a carrot curlicue alongside the main course. Style *is* the main course.

Usually when you ask for a description of writing style, you get an adjective: peppy, clear, turgid, abstract, chatty, and so on. These labels are only marginally helpful, because they express a mood or reaction in the reader rather than how these are created. What you decide in your writing, there, right *there*, and in the next line—those bit-by-bit decisions are what make up style. We can adapt Tip O'Neill's statement about politics: All style is local. The principles that produce style relate to persona, subject, and audience—and, further back than these, to ideology. But these overall terms are built, as it were, brick by brick. In thinking about style and audience, then, it will be more useful to see what some of these choices have been for other writers, to develop a grammar of terms for discussing writing style, and to consider how style is constructed by writers and readers within ideological parameters. Along with the positive, we'll look at some negatives—that is, at styles that exhibit poor use of language or logic.

ISSUES

Some Bad Advice about Style

Before you can make use of a length of knotted rope, first you have to undo the knots. Some of the knotty problems we encounter with style come from our attempts to apply well-meant advice in too general or contradictory ways. These may be represented as a succession of voices in a chorus:

Voice #1: Make your writing flow. It should come out gracefully, naturally, like the current of a river.

Voice #2: Don't just pour out any old words that come to mind. Give your paragraphs and sentences transitions that link the parts of your subject to an overall structure.

Voice #3: Use style that is appropriate to the subject; don't talk down or up.

Voice #4: Make your style fit your audience's abilities and interests.

Voice #5: Write the way you talk.

Voice #6: Don't use long, involved sentences. Develop a declarative, hard-hitting style.

Voice #7: Avoid choppy, short sentences that make your prose rushed or breathless.

Voice #8: Form your style on others' models—let your writing follow rhythms established by others.

Voice #9: Let your style find its own cadence; don't imitate.

Voice #10: Don't worry about style until late in the writing process—first explore your subject and your position towards it.

Voice #11: Style is the first thing you establish, because that makes your sentences.

You get the idea. The "chorus" is not singing from the same page in the songbook. As with other writing advice, much of what is said about style is (or appears) contradictory. What might be appropriate for one circumstance should not be extended to all circumstances. Because we are encouraged to look for easy solutions, we usually look for a knife to cut away tangles rather than trying to straighten them out. This section will concentrate on untangling some common advice about style, and offering alternative ways to think about the relation between *what* you write and *how*.

Probably you have heard a writing teacher advise you to "write the way you talk." As advice, this may be useful as a coded statement along the lines of "Keep it simple, stupid"; but its usefulness may not go much beyond that level. To start with, we don't keep very good accounts of how we talk. Writing as a technology is defined by its being more permanent than speech. In other words, it's possible to keep examples around of how you write; but unless you are Richard Nixon, tape-recording your conversations for posterity, you probably don't have anything comparable for your spoken words. "Write the way you talk" is code for something else—perhaps "Stay with language you know well." But there are occasions when you should not do this.

Second, as any literal transcript of dialogue will show, our recollection of our speech edits out a lot—the characteristic "you knows" and "uhs," the repetitions, the false starts all disappear in transcription.

 Hugh Grant's explanation to Jay Leno of his arrest with a prostitute offers a model illustration of incoherent speech rendered in print: "It's not easy, um...that, um, people give me tons of ideas on this one. I keep reading new psychological theories.... I think it would be bollocks, really, to hide behind that. I think you know in life what's a good thing to do and what's a bad thing. I did a bad thing, and there you have it" (*Esquire* p. 50).

In this sense, we *don't* write the way we talk—we shape our writing to suit an imagined audience. Any reporter taking down a quote knows to edit it, selecting from the literal statements the portion desired, so that what might be a conversation of several minutes becomes a sentence or two in print—but that sentence or two eliminates a lot of verbal static that neither the newspaper nor the source wants to see reproduced, and it is selected to represent what the reporter understands to be the quoter's main purpose.

Probably, "Write the way you talk" can be decoded to something like "let your writing flow the way your conversation does," or "Let your writing express a persona as you do 'naturally' in speech," or "Don't try to complicate what you write in order to impress the reader." These may be helpful as general suggestions, but they may not fit some of your writing situations. If I were a nurse making notes on a patient's condition, for example, I would not want my writing to "flow." Graceful expression is not particularly valued in medical documents, and brevity is very much preferred to a chatty account. If I were giving an eyewitness account in court, I might not want a "natural" persona—I'd have to suppress my normal ebullience and imaginativeness (if these are "normal" qualities I think I have) in order to communicate through style that I am rational, subdued, and trustworthy. If I'm doing a report on a subject in a lab science I don't understand very well, I'm likely to stretch my vocabulary in order to impress a very specific reader, a science teacher or lab assistant, by my ability to handle complex topics, such as the connection between the material from the lab and the concepts discussed in the chemistry or biology textbook.

Better advice than "write the way you talk," then, would be to tailor your style to whatever writing situation you find yourself in. So how do you do that? A starting point would be to look at how we think about style in our culture already. As Exhibits 10.1 and 10.2 suggest, there are two dominant models for thinking about style: *style as ornament,* and *style as clarity.* Both have some usefulness as concepts, and both involve traps.

STYLE AS ORNAMENT

If you think about improving style as a process of going back through a draft and adding more impressive words and colorful metaphors, you are assuming that style is ornamental. There's a long tradition behind this position: Style is treated as ornament in the five parts of rhetoric as codified in classical Greece and Rome:

1. *Invention,* the search for persuasive ways to present information and formulate arguments
2. *Arrangement,* the organization of the parts of a speech to ensure that all the means of persuasion are present and properly disposed
3. *Style,* the use of correct, appropriate, and striking language throughout the speech
4. *Memory,* the use of mnemonics and practice
5. *Delivery,* presenting the speech with effective gestures and vocal modulations (Bizzell and Herzberg pp. 3–4)

In this classical division of rhetoric, style is thought of as largely a matter of figures of speech and other supposedly superficial matters, detachable from "invention" or "arrangement." The five-part division above is still with us to

Exhibit 10.1 Style as ornament. Bob Daemmrich/ The Image Works.

some extent: Invention, arrangement, and style are still concerns in modern rhetoric. Memory and delivery have had to be modified somewhat as "rhetoric" has come to mean not only speaking but writing for highly diverse audiences and purposes, through media of many sorts. Even in speaking, use of a script or written text has made memory far less important than formerly:

Exhibit 10.2 Style as clarity. © Eastcott/Momatiuk Photography/The Image Works.

Many public occasions permit the use of TelePrompTers, so that there is no need for public speakers to memorize or improvise on selected themes. (Many do, of course.)

In the classical system of rhetoric, there is a clear separation between finding the truth, which is the purpose of *dialectic,* and stating it persuasively for an audience, which is the concern of *rhetoric.* But what if these two categories prove less clear-cut than their labels suggest? Determining what public policies are appropriate and wise, deciding what is necessary for a good life, evaluating our information about civic affairs—these concerns all must be addressed from *within* discourse. Some contemporary theories of language argue that there can be no separation of dialectic and rhetoric: Thinking takes place *through* language, not outside of it. Finding the truth and persuading others about it are collapsed into a single action, understanding the world in human terms as *constructed* through language.

Media texts sometimes encourage us to see style as ornament. Outside of the context of writing, style most often connotes something superficial, as in the case of style in clothing. Style in performance arts may also be considered a matter of ornament. We may speak of actors or singers as giving a part their own style, by nuances of phrasing or delivery that are part of their approach as performers. But, again, there's the contrast between the substance of the performance (the song or script) and these little extra touches.

This conception of rhetorical style as ornament runs deep in our culture, as may be seen by the figures of speech that draw a contrast between words and actuality. We are sometimes ready to dismiss *words* as insubstantial next to *things* or *actions*. Many of our proverbs are based on this belief: *Sticks and stones may break my bones, but words will never hurt me. Money talks and bullshit walks. A man of words and not of deeds is like a garden full of weeds. Do as I say, not as I do. Practice what you preach.* Aspects of contemporary society are often described in terms of a contrast between *what's on the surface* and *reality*, and we may be accustomed to thinking of words as superficial.

But what generally happens in such a model is hasty or haphazard or hypocritical use of language; and the damage is multiplied by the use of such language in advertising, political campaigns, and other circumstances in which we have come to expect lies or at least superficialities. When we are accustomed to hearing that "Coke adds life," what should we expect of language? What sort of truth is expressed by the claim that Chevrolet is "like a rock" or "the heartbeat of America"? Such figurative statements do not persuade through an impartial determination of truth, followed by the use of persuasive devices to move audiences to act on that truth. The Platonic–Aristotelian model doesn't apply well to advertising, modern culture's predominant form of persuasion. Rather than the sequence above—first dialectic to find the truth, then rhetoric to persuade others of our conclusions—we may be more accustomed to a model in which *all we have* is persuasive language, disconnected from truth. As the audience for advertising, political persuasion, and some other forms of media, we come to expect to be lied to. In these circumstances, style seems to be neither constitutive nor superficial, because it's detached from all connection to reality.

But if we think about musical style from the perspective not of performance but of composition, style is *all there is* to music. That is, musical styles are what *make* the music. If you change the notes of a Chopin mazurka to make "the same music" in a different style, you *change the music*. Transpose the piece from piano to accordion, synthesizer, or orchestra, and that's a change in the music as well (though in this case you might still be entitled to call it "Chopin").

In similar fashion, style in writing or speech isn't a costume, but is made of language, the very material of consciousness. Language is what makes writing, speech, discourse—the field of rhetoric. Language is basic to media. If the language is changed, the message is changed (perhaps not very much, as you might judge it, but changed).

PAUSE FOR REFLECTION

In "Politics and the English Language," George Orwell cites a translation of a passage from the King James Version of the Bible (from Ecclesiastes) into twentieth-century bureaucratic language:

> I returned and saw under the sun, that the race is not to the swift, nor the battle to the strong, neither yet bread to the wise, nor yet riches to men of understanding, nor yet favour to men of skill; but time and chance happeneth to them all.

Here it is in modern [i.e., bureaucratic] English:

> Objective considerations of contemporary phenomena compels [sic] the conclusion that success or failure in competitive activities exhibits no tendency to be commensurate with innate capacity, but that a considerable element of the unpredictable must invariably be taken into account.
> (p. 360)

A third version might be worth setting alongside these. Orwell's target in this essay is bureaucratic language, but *any* restatement changes the nature of the statement. Here is the same passage in the 1970 New English Bible:

> One more thing I have observed here under the sun: speed does not win the race nor strength the battle. Bread does not belong to the wise, nor wealth to the intelligent, nor success to the skilful; time and chance govern all.
> (Ecclesiastes 9:11)

Why does style matter so in a translation of the Bible?

Many of our proverbs were put into their present form by Benjamin Franklin. Some of Franklin's public-spirited activities were meant to encourage the general public to improve its lot by acting more wisely; so, to encourage saving, he invented sayings like "A penny saved is a penny earned" and "A groat a day's a penny a year," and popularized them through *Poor Richard's Almanac* and other writings. These proverbs are a little different from what we usually think of as inventions—usually technological gizmos such as improved stoves or bifocals (two of Franklin's creations) rather than machines made of words. But they are nonetheless inventions. Try to come up with an alternate way of saying "A penny saved is a penny earned," and you see its ingenuity. Other versions don't work particularly well, and not just because of their lack of familiarity.

PAUSE FOR REFLECTION

In informal writing, come up with an attitude or behavior that you believe would benefit others to practice or avoid. Invent several short phrases that might work as proverbs do, to encourage or discourage that behavior.

Another way to think of Franklin's proverbs is through the concept of hegemony. These little sayings may be effective in getting the general populace (i.e., people normally less industrious and less well read than Ben Franklin) to act in ways that are to the advantage of those who are (economically, socially, politically) over them. That is, people who save money (the two quoted above), get out of bed early ("Early to bed, early to rise, makes a man healthy, wealthy, and wise"), tell the truth ("Honesty is the best policy"), and are thrifty with food and other materials ("Waste not, want not") benefit others besides themselves. Can you think of other, more recently invented proverbs or slogans meant to have similar effect? For example, "Friends don't let friends drive drunk" from public service announcements, or Anheuser-Busch's version, "Know when to say when."

The style of these proverbs and sayings can't be separated from their meaning. The verbal form of proverbs, then, is not ornamental. And the same point applies to the longer forms of language that are more customary for college and other writing.

STYLE AS CLARITY

If language is a medium for conveying thought, then the more direct and simple and clear we can make our language, the more accessible our thought will be to readers. You get better views through clean glass than through dirty. This principle is the basis of another approach to style, one devoted to the ideal of clarity. You have probably received advice, from teachers or textbooks, to *make your writing clear*. The purpose of writing, in this view, is to communicate—and if your writing adopts features of style that present obstacles to readers, then your communication will be limited or prevented entirely.

The advice to cultivate a clear style may appear at first to be the opposite of that based on style as ornament. Ornament suggests that first you get a sense of what you have to write, and then you look for some nice metaphors and analogies to pretty it up, or perhaps you take some of your ordinary word choices and substitute something more impressive. Clarity as a model directs you to simplify, to shift away from Latinate word choices and supposedly inessential figures of speech to the basic matter of the thought. Though these pieces of advice point in opposite directions, they are based on the same concept—style as separable from thought.

Clarity as an ideal goes back at least to Puritanism. The general Protestant suspicion of ritual and ornamentation was carried over not only into houses of worship, but into aspects of daily life such as furnishings, china, eating utensils, and written texts such as sermons and poems. The esthetics of plain style is evident in nineteenth-century U.S. folk art and architecture, and in many of the fine arts as well—but its lasting influence may be due more to the early twentieth-century esthetic of industrial efficiency promoted by Frederick Taylor. In association with this devotion to efficiency, we have many expressions related to business: Get down to business; get down to brass tacks. A businesslike style is lean and mean, perhaps Spartan—it doesn't tolerate much ornament or prettying up.

The pursuit of clarity has become a cause for some writers and teachers of writing, as though clumsy or imprecise writing were a moral fault. For example, Joseph Epstein, introducing *The Complete Plain Words* (1988):

> As a university teacher, I find myself, among my students, from time to time wielding a small Augean broom. Why do I bother? It won't do to say, *à la* John Wayne in the role of federal marshal, "Cause it's my job, ma'am." It is closer to the truth to say that woolly circumlocutions, psychobabblous phrasing and sentiments, and language used as if it were a game of horseshoes (in which one expects points for being close) offends me. What it offends is my sense of decorum. (p. vi)

Holding forth clarity as an ideal can be useful as a device to persuade us to look closely at the language through which our thought exists—so the concept may be practical, even if flawed. But why is there an interest in developing and practicing a "clear" style? In the analogy between clear prose and a clean window, we don't spend a great deal of time noticing the window. It might seem that clear writing places the writer in the background, perhaps even absent altogether. This "placing in the background" can be seen in *The Elements of Style,* a text influential in how style has been discussed in college writing courses. A small book, it consists of bits of advice compiled by Will Strunk, a professor of English in the 1920s, edited and with an introduction and an additional chapter by E. B. White. White's number-one rule about style is this: "Place yourself in the background." That advice not only fits with the "window" metaphor but provides a feel for how White humanistically values the moral dimension of writing:

> Write in a way that draws the reader's attention to the sense and substance of the writing, rather than to the mood and temper of the author. If the writing is solid and good, the mood and temper of the writer will eventually be revealed, and not at the expense of the work. Therefore, the first piece of advice is this: to achieve style, begin by affecting none—that is, place yourself in the background. A careful and honest writer does not need to worry about style. As he becomes proficient in the use of the language, his style will emerge, because he himself will emerge, and when this happens he will find it increasingly easy to break through the barriers that separate him from other minds, other hearts—which is, of course, the purpose of writing, as well as its principal reward. Fortunately, the act of composition, or creation, disciplines the mind; writing is one way to go about thinking, and the practice and habit of writing not only drain the mind but supply it, too. (p. 70)

Notice the adjectives, or adjectives derivable from other words, describing the writer as White wants the writer to be: unaffected, careful, honest, proficient, disciplined. The goal is to "break through the barriers that separate [the writer] from other minds, other hearts." Composition is equated with creation, and facility in writing comes from "practice and habit."

White's narrative in this section of *The Elements of Style* is a softer but equally directive version of the ideas of his mentor, Professor Strunk. Strunk is affectionately mocked in the introduction as a drill sergeant issuing commands: "Omit needless words"; "Choose a suitable design and hold to it"; "Place the emphatic words of a sentence at the end." *Follow authority* is the message from Strunk; White's take on this is that readers follow better if you let them believe it's their own idea. The narrative behind White's account downplays rhetoric: Writers who are "honest" will submerge themselves in the subject, letting style emerge from an open account of who they are. The role offered the writer is a curious sort of seduction by hard work. Most of the text is a succession of "elements" or prescriptions, which if followed will produce not only clarity but forcefulness:

> The active voice is usually more direct and vigorous than the passive.... The habitual use of the active voice... makes for forcible writing. This is true not only in narrative concerned principally with

action but in writing of any kind. Many a tame sentence of description or exposition can be made lively and emphatic by substituting a transitive in the active voice for some such perfunctory expression as *there is* or *could be heard*. (p. 18)

The models White held forth as exemplars (selected for the 1956 edition) are mostly those considered greats—Hemingway, Faulkner, Whitman, Frost, Dickens, along with a writer less read, Jean Stafford. We are advised to aspire to their level of achievements by disciplined attention. White follows the literary practice of the time by citing mostly male authors, a practice which may be grating now.

Reading White's chapter, we receive not only these "elements" but advice on why we should follow them. "[D]o not forget that what may seem like pioneering may be merely evasion, or laziness—the disinclination to submit to discipline. Writing good standard English is no cinch" (p. 84). In spite of all the proscriptions of the first portion of the book, style is characterized not as a matter of following rules *externally*, but of *living* them—and there's no better short definition than this of hegemony: "[A]s an elderly practitioner once remarked, 'Writing is an act of faith, not a trick of grammar.' This moral observation would have no place in a rule book were it not that style *is* the writer, and therefore what a man is, rather than what he knows, will at last determine his style" (p. 84). The pursuit of clarity in writing, then, can translate into advocacy of a certain style of living and thinking. It may be argued that if an idea cannot be expressed so that the reader can get it at first glance, there's something wrong with the writing. The writer of a lengthy or complicated account in prose may be judged a pretentious snob, or may be thought to be trying to confuse the audience or withhold information. But some subjects require us to be immersed in the way of seeing the world that comes with specific disciplines: These cannot always be translated into words of one syllable. Attacks on jargon sometimes turn into antiintellectualism.

Richard Lanham has called for style to be taught as *visible*, stressing the enjoyment of language: Rather than expecting language to disappear, allowing readers to transcend language in order to get to the reality represented, his book *Style: An Anti-Textbook* advocates attention to the material of words. Attention to language in style is comparable to noting the technical and generic features of television, film, print news, and other media. You will become a better practitioner of the medium of writing to the extent you can pay attention to the details through which these media work.

If we determine to work for a clear style, this leaves another question: How do we know when a style is "clear"? Usually this adjective translates into the question "Did you find it hard to read?" That places the definition onto subjective grounds, so that clarity becomes a property not of a text but of its suitability for a specific audience. What might be clear in *Harper's* could be obscure in *People*.

For this reason, awareness of the audience is a necessary part of the subject of style. The audience's understanding is based in part on matters such as word choice and syntax, but in part on ideology. Stephen Jay Gould's essay on the evolution of Mickey Mouse might be perfectly "clear" to the audience for *Natural History* or *The Panda's Thumb,* because those readers would be familiar both with the general concept of evolution and with the possibility that popular culture, including Disney figures, carefully crafts its texts to the audience's psychological needs and desires. But for readers who are affiliated with a fundamentalist reading of the Old Testament's account of creation in six days, or who have not encountered the idea that popular culture is closely fitted to (mass) psychology, the essay might not be clear at all.

There are a few fairly easy stylistic principles, discussed in the next section, that can make your writing more direct, if that is what you judge will be most effective for your audience. But you should keep in mind that clarity is one rhetorical tool among many; it's a choice among options, not a matter of virtue.

Reducing Unnecessary Difficulty

In the section above, we considered clarity as a metaphor for writing style. It has to be a metaphor: Words cannot literally be *clear,* any more than glass can transmit an equivalent of what's on the other side in words. Clarity as a goal comes from what might be called the rhetorical device of the *disappearing author:* In this model, as White suggests in the passage cited earlier, the good writer will withdraw as much as possible from participation in the writing, letting the audience *see through* the prose to the subject. But this is a strategic withdrawal, not one done out of shyness.

There are reasons to question the "disappearing author" model of good writing. For one thing, it's misleading, possibly dishonest. Every writer is an active participant in the text, selecting from a very large number of possible choices, in words and phrases, sentence structure and length, figures of speech, and other components of writing style. Such selection may not always be conscious—in fact, it's most efficient when it takes place unconsciously. It takes place according to an ideology (sometimes working back and forth between several); and insofar as the author is invisible, the invisibility makes that ideology seem to be a product of nature or common sense.

Despite these reservations about "clarity," there are good reasons not to choose sentence structures or other formulations that make the reader struggle more than necessary with your prose. We sometimes write prose harder than it has to be, because other writers who are our models have done so as well. This section of the chapter will offer some programmatic choices that can promote a more direct style, without elevating it into an ethical principle.

Most veterans of English classes have in their past a dark figure hovering over the page—the Grammarian. English teachers are unfortunately legendary for mysterious scribblings in the margins. Some of these are Sibylline pronouncements about style; others are offered as correction for such violations of syntax as sentence fragments, comma splices, and errors in agreement between subject and verb. One of the great puzzles about U.S. education is the intensity with which these humble sins are attacked—not just by English teachers, but by newspaper columnists and others with a professional claim to competence in advising others about what is good English. The persistence of "bad grammar" is offered as evidence that the schools aren't doing their job.

PAUSE FOR REFLECTION

Look for some newspaper or magazine commentary on language use—for example, columns by William Safire, James J. Kilpatrick, George Will, or John Simon. What accounts for the presence of their work on op-ed pages?

Some of this intensity is connected with an ideology that associates style of speech and writing with class and moral worth. For well over a century, children have had *ain'ts* and double negatives beaten out of them, third-person singular verbs and correct use of the apostrophe beaten in; and this practice of regulating public speech and writing has been professionalized and given over to the schoolteacher.

Concern with *correctness* and the common misconception about English as a matter of prissiness are rooted in the idea that style is ornament, something exterior to thought—and that if you can only avoid making mistakes, then you will have produced good writing. Style in this case would be a matter of what you avoid doing. Don't use "ain't." Don't dangle modifiers. Use "hopefully" only to express the state in which one is full of hope. Lapses from these standards are seen as symbols of ignorance, weak will, or even moral decay: If we ease off on the split infinitive, who knows what moral turpitude will be next? Laxity in policing dialect is linked with laxity in policing drug use. The result of this approach to style may be like that expected of an athlete who concentrates on not making errors or turnovers: You don't try to *do anything*. Error-free writing may not be good thinking. It may be *safe* thinking, or thinking that shies away from any transgression of the status quo. That may be the connection between this conception of style or good writing and the ideology that accompanies it: Get the person worried about correctness, and you don't have to be concerned with really fundamental questions such as power and economic resources. Or, in slightly different terms, within the workings of institutions, if you can focus attention on *how* a decision was made, you can divert attention from whether it was right.

Fixation on style as micromanaging has grown out of the concept that thought is expressed in language, and that we do have some choice in the matter of style. The possibility of choice is an axiom of George Orwell's essay, "Politics and the English Language." Orwell has been enrolled, after his death and somewhat against his political inclinations, into what has been in recent years mostly a conservative fixation on the connection between "sloppy" language use and moral rot. But Orwell's essay is an attack on dishonesty in language, as expressed through style and other features of language use.

Style is a consideration not only in single sentences but in individual words chosen. English carries its history in its formation of words: for example, the abundant lists of words with *-man* as suffix, held over from the social organization in which those who performed such actions were generally men. Since the 1970s, publishers and professional organizations like the National Council of Teachers of English have produced guidelines to nonsexist language to encourage the notion that agents such as authors or decision makers can be of either gender. Sometimes it requires a bit of agility to avoid automatically writing *businessman* or *congressman,* but generally you can manage it without doing much violence to the prose or to your ability to write what you want. In this case and in some (now conservative) concerns about "decline in language use," style is read in a culturally political context: Automatically using "he" to refer to an action that could be performed by either gender—or, for that matter, using "she," or "he or she," or "s/he"—is a choice rooted in ideology. As a writer, your style aligns you with one of a number of ideologies, no matter what your intentions to avoid affiliation may be.

It may be debated whether language teachers should serve as grammar police. But we should recognize that much talk about style includes what people in general call "grammar." "Bad grammar" identifies a person as lower class rather than middle class, and this class affiliation has a lot to do with the intensity of grammatical pronouncements. "Good grammar" might be better thought of as a matter of suitability for an audience: If your audience is one that will rise in indignation because you have offered a plural pronoun in reference to a singular indefinite antecedent ("Everyone will have their favorite term"), then you have to anticipate how you want to meet those expectations.

Concern about sloppy writing has a point: If language is the medium of thought, then public discourse that is poorly thought out and hastily assembled should be improved. But often the denunciations stay at the sentence or word level, without connection to ideology. They sometimes take as targets phrases that are in colloquial use—and that's what troubles the critics, that they are in use. Much of what is objected to by grammar columnists is written and spoken, not only among ordinary people, but by respected writers. (The response might be "They should know better"—but it should be assumed that they *do* know better, and prefer their own language to that advocated by the columnists.) The grammar columnists' attempt to "purify the dialect of the tribe" may translate into offering their own language (and ideology) as normative or desirable, in ways others would consider to be elitist. Besides, raising the intensity of attacks on minor problems makes it likely that little if anything will be said about the major whoppers.

Probably the biggest of these whoppers is the fit, or lack of fit, between dialectic and rhetoric—the disconnection between finding the truth as the writer perceives it and presenting that truth to the reader by means of the resources of writing, including style. Much rhetoric used by contemporary media is not based on even a subjective model of truth—it deliberately deceives or misinforms. Some of these deceptions are much more heinous than the ordinary "whiter than white" lines of advertising, as they signal a way of thinking or ideology with consequences far wider than the selection of a brand of detergent. For example, the widely circulated statement by a U.S. officer during the Vietnam war that "We had to destroy the village in order to save it"; or the use of the phrase "ethnic cleansing" by Bosnian Serbs to cover widespread deportation, beatings, rapes, and killings of their Muslim fellow citizens. Next to these, ordinary bureaucratic gobbledygook is fairly venial, as sins go. That aspect of rhetoric will be taken up under the section below on bad rhetoric. Here we are looking at the middle range—neither the weeding out of colloquial usages nor Orwellian "doublespeak," but ways to improve on the habitual clumsiness of first-draft writing. (Note: "Doublespeak" is in use, as from Orwell, to refer to writing that uses words to deny reality; it's not to be equated with bureaucratic style in itself, though there may be a good deal of overlap.)

In order to improve writing at this middle level, it may be useful to categorize some of the sources of problems. The advice about style in this chapter is largely drawn from *Style,* by Joseph M. Williams, a book intended especially for writers who want to improve on institutional prose.

1. **Selection of words with Latin rather than Anglo-Saxon origins.** English society changed after the Norman conquest in the eleventh century: For some centuries after, the nobility spoke Norman French (derived from Latin) while the common people used Old English, so that English vocabulary is enriched by two sets of parallel terms with slightly different meanings. Ordinary farm animals, while alive, are named by words descended from those used by the farm workers of the time who cared for them: *cow, pig, sheep*. But their meat, processed for the nobles' table, is named by words which come from the French: *beef, pork, mutton*. Military terms on land are those used by the nobility: *campaign, advance, retreat, bivouac*. But the terms used by common soldiery are not: *gun, sword, tent*. The Normans weren't generally sailors, so our names for things on a boat come from Anglo-Saxon. Using the generally longer words derived from Latin, then, has a long association with the upper class, and we still try to impress others with these words. For example, it's acceptable in polite society to use Latinate words such as *copulate, fornicate, excrement,* or *urination,* while there's something crude about their Anglo-Saxon equivalents. The issue may be whether your audience would consider you as really learned, or just trying to show off. Advice: Consult a thesaurus and consider using, when possible, the plainer English word.

2. **Overuse of passive rather than active voice.** Active voice means that the *agent* in a sentence is also the subject: *The car rolled down the driveway.* Here the sentence's action is performed by the car, which is the subject. Passive voice hides the agent, sometimes in a prepositional phrase or absent from the sentence altogether: *It was decided to delay action on the proposal.* In that sentence you can't tell who did the deciding—the agent is missing altogether. Perhaps there's a chair for a meeting, or perhaps some body came to that conclusion by consensus. Passive voice is a common feature of organizational prose: It allows decisions to be treated as though they were natural facts, as automatic as the rising of the sun, rather than choices made by human beings. *Your proposal, although meritorious, was rejected.* Notice that nowhere in the sentence can you find the agent(s) judging the proposal to be meritorious but rejecting it. (The agent might appear in a prepositional phrase such as *by the steering committee.*)

Passive constructions generally add a few words—always a helping verb such as "was," often an extra syllable *-ed* to the participle, and often a prepositional phrase if the agent is explicit.

Passive voice is most appropriate in contexts in which the agent doesn't matter: *Mail is delivered at ten o'clock.* The important elements of the sentence are *mail* and the time of its arrival. The question of who delivers the mail might be judged unimportant to the context, and so left out.

3. **Where possible, convert nominalizations to corresponding verbs or adjectives.** *Nominal* refers to how something is named—the part of speech that names something is a noun—and a *nominalization* is a noun formed from another part of speech, usually a verb or adjective. For example, *fortification* comes from *fortify, decision* from *decide, ugliness* from *ugly,* and so on. Nominalizations frequently end with a *-shun* suffix (*-tion* or *-sion*), but not all such words are nominalizations (for example, *tradition*).

You should reduce use of nominalizations, for the same reasons you should limit use of passive voice: They can make your prose vague and abstract, even opaque. Frequently, nominalizations are coupled with verbs of being, giving the impression that they describe qualities that simply are. But nominalization—in fact, style—is a verbal representation made by human beings and institutions with political purposes. Nominalizations can obscure these purposes. In many cases, you can make a sentence more vivid and concrete by reworking the nominalization so as to use a verb (or adjective) and finding or inventing an agent to serve as subject. Instead of *The realization of powerlessness to bring about change is terrible,* try *Realizing that you are powerless to bring about change is terrible.*

4. **Reduce or avoid altogether strings of nouns.** In the effort to economize on the number of words used, some writers put three or four nouns together in sequence: *college textbook distribution control center; Odessa weight reduction clinic operation hours.* (English, unlike some languages, allows nouns to function in this way as adjectives.) Some such phrases become familiar in local contexts, so that we don't recognize them as problematic; but if we are addressing an audience outside that context, they stick out.

One device for controlling the noun–noun problem is to break the strings up, using prepositional phrases or relative clauses. The examples above might occur in sentences such as:

> *The college textbook distribution control center supplies desk copies for 100 instructors per week.*
> *The Odessa weight reduction clinic operation hours are 8–4:30 weekdays.*

But the strings of nouns can be clipped:

> *The center for distributing college textbooks supplies desk copies for 100 instructors per week.* (or) *The center distributes college textbooks to 100 instructors per week.*
> *The clinic for weight reduction in Odessa is in operation from 8:00 to 4:30 weekdays.* (or) *The Odessa weight reduction clinic is open 8–4:30 weekdays.*

Revisions along these editorial guidelines can be done easily, almost automatically, once you get the hang of it. The next pattern of stylistic changes requires a little analysis. You have to look closely at sentences to determine which portions are most familiar to your audience and which provide new information—that is, which portions you want to emphasize and which to bury.

The **topic** of a sentence is everything in the sentence that precedes the verb. Sometimes this will be short—

<u>Cars</u> *are necessities nowadays.*

sometimes slightly longer because of the presence of a phrase or clause—

<u>People who live in glass houses</u> *should wear bathrobes.*

and sometimes quite long indeed.

<blockquote><u>When in the Course of human events, it becomes necessary for one people to dissolve the political bands which have connected them with another, and to assume among the Powers of the earth, the separate and equal station to which the Laws of Nature and of Nature's God entitle them, a decent respect to the opinions of mankind</u> requires that they should declare the causes which impel them to the separation.</blockquote>

Usually in English subjects precede verbs. There are syntactical constructions that throw the subject and verb into reverse order (as this sentence, which begins with *there are*). But mostly we encounter *first* subjects (agents), *then* verbs (actions). As we read or listen to sentences, we are linguistically oriented toward verbs: Until the verb arrives, we don't know what sort of action is being performed within the small drama of the sentence. A stylistic habit of folding into the topic all the modifiers—particularly prepositional phrases and subordinate clauses—can tax the patience and short-term memory of readers.

Notice that I've avoided calling this a good or bad stylistic choice. Such decisions depend on the audience; and as the example above from Thomas Jefferson shows, there is some highly accomplished prose that does not follow modern prescriptions for simplicity and directness. Part of the reason is that contemporary readers are likely to have less patience than their eighteenth-century counterparts. But writers not only find audiences as we are—they *invite* us to become a certain sort of reader, and in many cases we cooperate. If writers did not in part create their readers, then no one would ever have read any novels by William Faulkner.

PAUSE FOR REFLECTION
Faulkner's most highly regarded novels invite readers into acts of stylistic daring, so that part of the drama of the novel is trying to anticipate just how much the author can get away with. Consider sentences like the following, from *Absalom, Absalom!*:

> Yet on the day when I went out there to stay that summer, it was as though that casual pause at my door had left some seed, some minute virulence in this cellar earth of mine quick not for love perhaps (I did not love him; how could I? I had never even heard his voice, had only Ellen's word for it that there was such a person) and quick not for the spying which you will doubtless call it, which during the past six months between that New Year's and that June gave substance to that shadow with a name emerging from Ellen's vain and garrulous folly, that shape without even a face yet because I had not even seen the photograph then, reflected in the secret and bemused gaze of a young girl because I who had learned nothing of love, not even parents' love—that fond dear constant violation of privacy, that stultification of the burgeoning and incorrigible I which is the meed and due of all mammalian meat, became not mistress, not beloved, but more than even love; I became all polymath love's androgynous advocate. (pp. 181–82)

We won't analyze this sentence—but you might notice how much of it comes in the middle of something else. It's as though there's an interruption between "perhaps" and "and," another between "because I" and "became not mistress," and other attempts to clarify and explain, ironic because the narrator's clarifications all add up to one huge, confusing mass of a sentence.

Faulkner's readers do not stumble on this sentence, or on many others that approach its level of intensity, in the first few paragraphs of the novel. We work up to it, through the author's high variations in length of sentence and phrase, word choice, and presentation of character, so that we "know" Miss Rosa Coldfield (the narrator of this passage) and understand the style of writing through that knowledge. Judging "good writing," then, requires putting it into context, and considering its use within that context.

So one piece of advice if you are in pursuit of clarity—and it's your choice, based on how you assess the complexity of the subject and what your readers will tolerate—is to shorten the topic, so as to lessen the distance between subject and verb. Examine the preceding sentence: It has an unusually long topic, thirty-three words. It could be rewritten so as to follow its own recommendation. *So you should shorten the topic in order to lessen the distance between subject and verb, based on how you assess the complexity of the subject and how much your reader will tolerate.* Is this version better? There are trade-offs in any stylistic choice: The loss in the second version has to do with what happens at the end of the sentence, called the **stress.** The most dramatic point in a sentence is the end: It functions like the last phrase in a musical composition, echoing in the mind long after the notes have died out. When we read a sentence, silently or aloud, we pause for punctuation, with longer pauses for periods, exclamation points, and question marks, and shorter pauses for colons, semicolons, dashes, and commas. (These are rests, not grand pauses, cadences, or conclusions.) The final pause leaves the last phrase or term with greater emphasis, which is why "stress" is a useful concept: It links sentence position with rhetorical function.

The first sentence in the preceding paragraph is organized so as to build a kind of suspense (Where is the author going with this? What's the advice being built up to here?), not only through the dependent clause beginning with *if,* but through the use of an appositive phrase beginning with *and it's your choice,* so that the sentence resounds with dramatic emphasis on *lessen the distance between subject and verb.* That's what I wanted you to come away with in that sentence, what I wanted to stress. The second version is also a useful sentence, but it stresses something different, *how much your reader will tolerate.* As a writer, you have to decide which element in any sentence you want to emphasize, and place that last.

Notice that neither sentence concludes with a relational word or phrase such as *however* or *on the other hand.* These are generally less important than other parts of the sentence, as they do not present content. They are related to how the portions of the subject under discussion fit together, rather than what they are in themselves. It's often better to place these connecting terms in the middle of the sentence, which is the least emphatic part.

In general, you should begin the sentence with topics using terms and phrases that are carried over from the preceding sentences, or which are familiar to the audience from common experience. What we want to stress is the information that is new to the discussion or most unfamiliar to the audience. In this way, we can adapt the presentation of our information to readers' conventional expectations for prose.

Thinking in these terms about sentences means shifting away from the description of style as single adjectives to a somewhat more technical knowledge of how sentences work—and of how *your* sentences work. This knowledge gives you some tools to shape your style. It also draws your attention away from the subject of the writing and toward what you are doing, step by step; and for that reason it might best be considered in revision rather than in early stages of the writing. But reexamining your style can and should take place at all points in the writing process. Some stylistic revision should go on early, during or even before your first draft. Thinking of sentences in these terms can become habitual, so that you make choices that lead toward ease for the reader—or not—automatically.

Style As Constitutive: Or Would You Rather Be a Dog?

In Chapter 7 under Popular Music there was a short discussion of the 1940s popular song "Swinging on a Star," with its transitional pattern in the lyrics, *"or would you rather be a ———."* The song's first three verses invite the listener to imagine being a mule, a pig, or a fish, and describe those animals (along with monkeys, in the fourth verse) as self-limiting because they are selfish and stubborn, dirty, tricky, or interested only in playing rather than going to school and working with others to achieve idealistic goals.

Other texts may invite us to play roles such as these, not negatively but positively. Style is one of the rhetorical features that leads us to want to play along with a text, the better to absorb its content. This invitation to play along is the subject of this section. The reading audience has its own interests to consider, so a crucial function of style is to tempt the audience to identify their interests with the writer's.

Our thinking about style in language connects with ideology. The style of any text grows from interactions among the writer and her or his experiences and culture, the subject and the world of discourse that defines it, and the audience and its collective experiences and culture. From your perspective as writer, these three interconnected factors may be characterized as follows: what you are projecting as your *persona*, or your self as represented in the writing; the *subject* or topic as it can be set forth in the form of writing, the genre in which you are working, and the system of conventions that are part of these; and the *audience* or readership you anticipate for your work. These terms have been important to the discussion of rhetoric throughout this book. But their relationship is crucial for a discussion of style, because how they interact is what makes style. Your writing in effect creates your own role in the prose and offers roles for the audience to play in relation to the subject, and your success as a persuasive or argumentative writer will depend to a great extent on how well you do in casting the drama of your work. Rhetorically successful writing will lead your audience to want to play the role(s) assigned to them.

For example, in the proverbs quoted on pages 541–42 above, the texts invite speaker and listener(s) to acknowledge and repeat common wisdom. When we quote a proverb, it is understood not to be our own idea—rather, we are citing what is known to everyone, though perhaps forgotten in the particular instance. Quoting the proverb may serve as an indirect reminder about what is judged to be appropriate action, but judged with the force of collective opinion (expressed generally) rather than just the speaker's own thought (expressed specifically about this case). The proverb provides two possible roles for the listener: being corrected—that is, agreeing to the general wisdom of the proverb and its application; or not being corrected, rejecting the proverb or its application. For example, "I know 'A penny saved is a penny earned,' but I really *need* a Discman." Hearing the one about "early to bed, early to rise" may place the listener in the healthy, wealthy, and wise category—or among the unhealthy, the not so well off, and/or the foolish. (Powerful incentives on the morning after the night before.)

Most roles created by style involve choices more complex than these. Proverbs may seem old-fashioned not only because of their eighteenth-century style of expression, but because of the assumption of wisdom based on what everyone knows: Our own ideologies tend to assume (and encourage) individual differences, as in "It's a free country" or "Everyone's entitled to their own opinion."

PAUSE FOR REFLECTION
This last statement may not be a proverb. What if my own opinion is the opposite of this—that everyone has to earn the right to their own opinion? Would I be entitled to that opinion?

As a writer, you will want to practice anticipating what readers will do in response to your text—to understand and make use of the roles you provide for them.

As you think back on texts in your experience, it may seem that a near infinity of styles are possible, in writing, in speaking, in reading, in producing other sorts of media texts. But these styles are far more constrained than might at first appear, because of a number of factors. Generally, these can be categorized by the three interconnected factors noted above—persona, subject, and audience. As diagrammed in Exhibit 10.3, these factors can be conceived not only by single words, but by questions: Who are we? What is the nature of the medium through which this style exists? Who is our audience?

Who we are translates into a limit on what we can do. As a writer, I cannot use words that I don't know. I can learn new words through consulting a dictionary or thesaurus, reading texts that use unfamiliar terms, or talking with others—but such learning is slow and prone to mistakes, and it may affect my ability to reach others if I slip up. But beyond what might be thought of as physical limitation on what can be written, there's who we are *in this text*. The

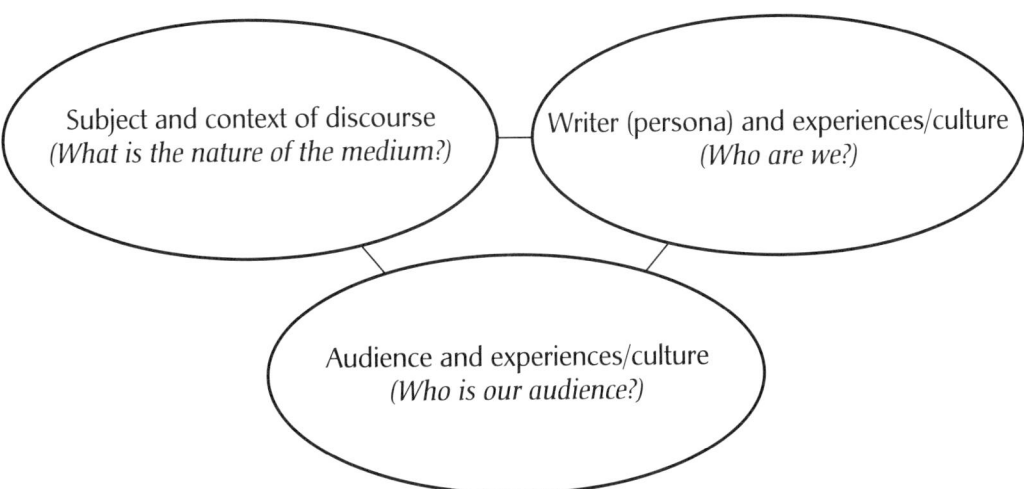

Exhibit 10.3. Three factors that govern style.

persona we adopt puts forth a certain side of our more complex selves, selects a set of our traits for display, and pushes other potential selves out of sight. No matter how exemplary a person you are, there's a side of yourself that you would rather not show to your classmates, your professor, or others in public generally.

Additional limits come from who our audience is. I may have words and other choices available for use but decide not to use them—because of a suspicion that my readers or listeners would find these out of keeping with who I'm supposed to be in this text or, more important, inappropriate to the uses they want to make of that text. We don't usually do a survey of the audience we are writing for, as happens with some media texts, but we do have an internalized sense of what will and will not be possible.

That internalized sense generally comes from what we understand to be conventions within the genre in which we are working—in other words, from the subject, which is always more than just the narrowly conceived topic. Stylistic choices grow out of what can be done within a medium and genre: Limiting factors may include budget, judgments of decision makers (producers, directors, editors, overseeing governmental agencies, advertisers), technical limitations, and so on. You probably don't consider providing illustrations for most of your college papers, for example, because finding and producing illustrations can be time-consuming and would require different resources than you might have available. As we have seen in previous chapters, various media encourage certain stylistic choices and discourage others.

These factors, persona, audience, and subject, are impossible to separate, and the discussion here doesn't really attempt to do so: The medium and genre are in some ways prior decisions, which strongly influence if not determine who the audience is, or who we are in that context. Our understanding of what is possible in a medium directs us to make certain stylistic choices to show forth certain aspects of our selves for the audience, which is also selecting a side of itself in order to read that medium and that text. Whereas it initially seemed that style presented the writer with many thousands of possible options, what we have found is that other factors screen those choices quickly and effectively. When you are accustomed to working in a medium, many of the options do not even present themselves to you.

In other words, stylistic options grow out of other decisions, some of which you control and others of which you inherit. You can't make choices that are not available to you by reason of either your previous experience or what can be done in your medium. The persona or writing "self" is a role that a writer plays, just as actors play roles. It should not be confused with the biographical/historical self (though most writers stay reasonably close to the self they represent in day-to-day interactions). The persona necessarily changes somewhat with context and audience. (And sometimes within a text—the "self" constructed can be dynamic.) It's important to stress self as *role* here, in order to prevent the common assumption that *who you are* doesn't change. That common misconception leads to "I write the way I write because that's who I am, and I can't change that." The writing persona can't be equated with "who I am," because the persona is a construction, a mask made from words. (*Persona* means "mask.") Your words have the capacity to last long after you, and you have some choice in what self you create for this purpose.

Style, again, really isn't a separate topic. We sometimes assume that we can make "the same thing" in a different style; but if you change your words, your sentence length, or other aspects of what you write, you change what you write. In other words, it's not true that style is a simple expression of "natural" personality or essential character: Style is created. You can be a different (writing) self through the choice of words and other devices. And you can be it not only in writing: The self you project may change the self you presently are.

PAUSE FOR REFLECTION

Take a draft as you have already conceived of it. Freewrite about some other personae you could adopt with that subject. What would be the effects of such a change? Write two or three paragraphs (especially the introduction) in order to test this out.

This model, style as the product of the interaction between subject/medium, persona, and audience, accounts for how style evolves and how changes in style *can* take place. But it doesn't address why those participating would *want* changes to take place. What is there to lead us to want to adopt new features in our vocabulary, syntax, and other features of style, beyond the generalized desire to succeed in communicating and in understanding a subject? That question is usually answered by the context that gives rise to writing. It's left to institutions in society (college, workplace, the family, etc.) to give us motivation, and these institutions work by deep-seated connections with ideology.

Hegemony and Style

An example, simpler than most texts, may help to illustrate the dynamic linking style to hegemony. As noted above, style is often described as the outgrowth of an essential self—in other words, in terms of individualism. Your style is what differentiates your work from that of others. But our eagerness to claim "an individual style" doesn't just appear out of thin air. It's linked to the familiar ideological message of many texts within our culture: You are yourself, unique; no one else is like you, no one else is so valuable for those unnamed qualities you possess. (Usually the next line in these and other claims, ironically, links this uniqueness to the purchase of a product manufactured in millions of identical units.)

An illustration of how this shift between individual uniqueness and mass merchandising occurs can be found in an advertising campaign begun in late 1994. (As in other sections of *Rhetoric through Media,* advertising is used here to provide a convenient illustration of modes of communication also found in news and entertainment media.) One of the most heavily advertised categories of products is beer, as brewers (like manufacturers of soft drinks, cigarettes, detergents, and snack foods) strive mightily to differentiate substantially identical products and build consumer loyalties. The two largest breweries in the United States, Anheuser-Busch and Miller, found their marketing position eroded at least marginally by the development of microbreweries—local companies producing beer in smaller batches, judged by some consumers to be of higher quality than the major advertised brands. The threat was not so much to sales as to image: Budweiser ("the king of beers") and Miller maintained their shelf space and market presence, but their image was threatened by the possibility that consumers might see their products as little better than generic beers, with discriminating consumers paying more for the likes of Samuel Adams, Old Detroit Ale, Third Coast, Columbia, and many other brands.

Two corporate strategies in this situation are to claim high quality for your own product or to create your own "microbrewery" with the marketing clout of the large corporation. Budweiser followed the first strategy, running ads which said they started out as a microbrewery in 1856, but got bigger and better. Miller took the second, instituting the "Plank Road Brewery" (Miller's plant in Milwaukee is on Plank Road) to manufacture and market Red Dog beer.

Not much happens in contemporary marketing if you just put your product up for sale and let it spread by word of mouth. You want to define for potential customers what it means to buy *that* brand rather than their customary choices. Buying beer has become an act of affiliation: As consumers we communicate to others through our marketing choices, which constitute a matter of personal style. We talk back by buying. In keeping with the target audience (beer drinkers who want to move away from being identified as mass consumers), the Red Dog ads stressed individualism, bucking a trend, charting your own course, and so forth—all familiar ideological features.

You are your own dog: This deep thought appeared in television and radio commercials, in print ads, and on billboards, in a mock-up of an old manual typewriter's font, as though consumption of this mass-produced beer were the end result of exploring individual taste without the encouragement and assistance of contemporary advertising devices. In this campaign the co-opting of individualism into compliance with commercials and the desire for mass-marketed products is reinforced repeatedly. The tactic can be seen in sentimental as well as assertive versions; for example, Carly Simon's refrain line "Nobody does it better. . . . Baby, you're the best," as used for a Special Olympics public service announcement. We believe these claims—we want to believe them—because they are flattering, and in important ways true. Genetically, each of us is unique. We *are* our own dog. (Genetically, every fly is unique.) But it's the practice of advertising to reduce this presumably individual self to several traits and emphasize those so as to simplify the rhetorical task—and as we cooperate, we agree to become that simplified self. We play the role of consumer-as-dog, and come when we are called. Exhibit 10.4 looks more closely at the slogan "You are your own dog."

If the Red Dog ad copy said "You are a dog," the corporation couldn't expect to sell much beer. It's not very flattering to be called a dog. The ad speaks to persons, not to canines. Or if it said "You are your dog," that line might work for some products, perhaps as an incitement to buy good-quality dog food. But "You are your own dog" works as we have seen appellation work in Chapter 8: It invites the (human) reader to imagine him-/herself as a dog, to be doglike in some respects. And such appellation is basic to hegemony.

> ## You are your own dog.
>
> 1. Someone is speaking/writing to the reader singly, individually—*you*.
> 2. The *you* is equated to something else: *are* works as an equal sign here.
> 3. *Your* indicates possession, in this case *self*-possession, in contrast to being a dog possessed by others (my, her, his, their, our) or labeled by adjectives (American, junkyard, handsome, big, plug-ugly). You belong to yourself, in contrast to belonging to something else, someone else, some group.
> 4. **Own.** Owning connects to property. Jim in *Huckleberry Finn* tells Huck that he owns himself, and he's worth $800, and that's a lot. He's going to work to free his own wife and children next, so that he can own them or they can own themselves. The statement says, you own yourself.
> 5. **Dog.** Here the dissonance comes in—a comic dissonance, to be sure, but dissonance. We expect some other word. **Dog** is a minor insult; sometimes affectionate ("You sly dog!") and sometimes not ("Son of a bitch!").

Exhibit 10.4 The Red Dog slogan: a closer look.

The dog pictured in the commercial and advertisements is a bulldog. Bulldogs are not pretty; they are reputed to be tenacious and assertive; they don't take any guff from anyone. (The name comes from the practice of breeding dogs for sport to attack and hang onto bulls. Supposedly, people competed to see who had the best litter of pups; the ultimate test was to attach a dog to a bull and see if it would hang on even when the dog's head was cut off.) So, by implication, if the ad campaign calls us to be a dog, it has to be one that has qualities we admire, at least in some imagined context. Haven't we all played at being a dog at some time—in childhood, while entertaining others' children or our own, and so on? So the ad invites us to play this role again, but in association with a product.

We are invited to imagine being a certain kind of dog, then, but a dog with only certain qualities—those outlined in the commercial or extensions of it. The bulldog on the TV isn't shown doing a pile in the park or hiking his leg on a tree, for instance, though those are familiar and "natural" acts for dogs. He's not sleeping long hours of the day, though this is part of the daily regimen for all the dogs I know. He's not shown being friendly to an owner (licking hand or foot, coming when called, etc.), though he is clearly a domestic dog rather than a wild animal—bulldogs do not flourish in the wild. In other words, the aspects of dogginess shown in the commercial contradict what we know to be the truth about dogs. They are not their own dog; they are kept animals. And rationally, we know that dogs and other animals in commercials are *trained* to perform; the dog in the picture certainly was *not* his own dog, any more than was another brewer's symbol, Spuds MacKenzie (who, incidentally, was female).

In the two readings that follow, a radio interview and a print commentary reflect further on the Red Dog ad campaign.

DANIEL ZWERDLING

Interview with Leslie Savan

Daniel Zwerdling, Host: Leslie Savan has the kind of job that would drive a lot of Americans absolutely stark-raving crazy. Leslie, you watch TV ads for a living.

Leslie Savan, Columnist, *Village Voice*:   Yes, I do.

Daniel Zwerdling: And your brain is still functioning to tell us about it?

Leslie Savan: *[laughs]*   Right. It's functioning mostly because I have to distance myself from them in order to watch them and take something from them, you know, find patterns. What's really going on out there in ad land. What are they trying to tell us, and what's working and what's not and why.

Daniel Zwerdling: And you write about all of that in a regular column for the New York newspaper the *Village Voice*, and I understand you have been itching to tell us—to warn us maybe is a better word—about some ads you've been seeing lately that are brainwashing us Americans.

Leslie Savan: Right.

Daniel Zwerdling: Leslie Savan, take it away.

Leslie Savan: OK. Well, there's two campaigns right now that I think are really pristine examples of a trend in advertising that we're seeing more and more—ads that tell us, essentially, join us and become unique.

Daniel Zwerdling: Join us and become unique.

Leslie Savan: Right. Exactly. These ads tell us that we're unique, independent, nonconforming, secretly rebellious individuals, you know, and we just can't wait to express that by buying the product that they're selling us. In other words, they sell us—they sell millions of us the same exact product so that we can find our individuality.

Daniel Zwerdling: And ad number one is?

Leslie Savan: Well, I think that we should start with Red Dog. Red Dog is a new beer which came out in October. It features a very gruff looking bulldog. He's really a sort of a contrarian and he wears a spike collar around his neck. He's always grousing about other dogs, usually smaller dogs—poodles, chihuahuas, or otherwise lap dogs—who are just sort [of?] slaves to their owners and to people. They can't think for themselves. They can't be individuals.

[excerpt from Red Dog commercial]

Bulldog: Look at 'em makin' fools of themselves. And for what? A pat on the head and a dog biscuit?

Woman: What do you think of that Red Dog?

Daniel Zwerdling: We're at some sort of weird circus or something. There are all these frou-frou dogs around who are being put through their paces and literally being ordered to jump through hoops.

Leslie Savan: Exactly. They're at a dog show and they're jumping through hoops and Red Dog has somehow meandered in through there and he's just grousing about it. He thinks this is so humiliating to them. And so Red Dog sort of makes this personal campaign to tell these dogs they don't have to be treated like that.

Daniel Zwerdling: There's a part of it that's almost scary. I mean, at one point the Red Dog, the bulldog, jumps onto the guy who's holding the hoops and knocks him down.

Leslie Savan: I mean—

Daniel Zwerdling: Sort of like, it's almost like a barroom brawl, you know, let's punch that guy out.

Leslie Savan: Red Dog is the force for nonconformity and for doing your own thing and being a rebel. So he's trying to appeal to each of us individuals and tell us we don't have to be like the rest of the crowd and we're different from them and better. And the way we can feel that way the most quickly and in the most guaranteed method is to buy the product, to buy Red Dog.

Daniel Zwerdling: And product number two is?

Leslie Savan: Product number two is for Saab. Saab is a Swedish car, and they have a campaign and a slogan that seem almost identical to Red Dog's, although they're very different. On one hand, Red Dog is geared toward a 25- to 29-year-old male drinker mostly; Saab is much more upscale and is aimed at older people because they can afford the Saab to begin with. And yet they both have almost an identical slogan. Red Dog's slogan is, you are your own dog. Saab's slogan is, find your own road.

[excerpt from Saab commercial]

Announcer: You could never wear a suit again. You could not laugh when it's not funny. You could go off and write that novel, climb that mountain, buy those shoes.

Leslie Savan: The Saab campaign is done in a very nice animation. Sort of looks like *New Yorker* cartoons animation. And one of them features a woman who is told that, you know, she never has to wear a suit again. She can climb her own mountain. She can do her own thing. She can fly in the face of convention.

[excerpt from Saab commercial]

Announcer: —Or drive there. Find your own road. Saab.

Daniel Zwerdling: Isn't this really a very old advertising message? I mean, what about the Marlboro man? He's been around for years and years and years and years and years, and he was saying, "Be an individual, just smoke our cigarette."

Leslie Savan: Well, one interesting thing about this is that when Red Dog first came out it wasn't identified as to who owned it. It just said Plank Road Brewery. And a lot of people thought it was a microbrewery, somehow an alternative, something sort of funky and new and different. It turns out, of course, that Red Dog is owned by Miller Brewery, the number two brewery in the United States. And Miller, of course, is owned by Philip Morris, which brings us back to Marlboro.

Daniel Zwerdling: Oh.

Leslie Savan: And I spoke to the spokesman for Miller and she said what I found was a fascinating contradiction. She said Red Dog is very much a premium, mainstream beer. It's an alternative to the mainstream but it's in the mainstream. So they want to have it both ways.

Daniel Zwerdling: Well, Leslie Savan, of the *Village Voice*, I am very different. I'm going to chuck this darn job, so I don't think I'm going to talk to you probably again. I'm going to go mountain climbing or something. Nah, maybe I'll just buy a Saab. Listen, thanks for talking with us today.

Leslie Savan: OK. Thank you.

[© Copyright National Public Radio® 1995. This news report by NPR's Daniel Zwerdling was originally broadcast on National Public Radio's *All Things Considered* on June 4, 1995, and is used with the permission of National Public Radio. Any unauthorized duplication is strictly prohibited.]

IRA TEINOWITZ

Rich Lalley, Red Dog

In May 1994, Rich Lalley got a call from his boss, Miller Brewing Co. VP-International Dick Strup. He had spotted an interesting campaign for a Canadian beer from Miller's partner Molson Breweries.

"He asked me if it made sense to the U.S., and if so, how to do it," says Mr. Lalley, 39, Miller's director of new-business development at the time.

The ads that so captivated the Miller executives were created by BBDO Worldwide, Toronto, and featured Oscar-winning actor Tommy Lee Jones as the voice of a wayward dog.

"I thought the advertising campaign was as good as I had ever seen, and I've worked on beer advertising for years," says Mr. Lalley, who spent 10 years working for D'Arcy, Masius, Benton & Bowles on Anheuser-Busch advertising.

The product itself, however, was less captivating. Molson's Red Dog was a specialty, heavier-style malt brew but its silver packaging translated in the U.S. to expectations of a lighter beer.

While Miller felt the advertising had broad appeal, it quickly determined the actual beer wouldn't work well here.

The decision was made to use the advertising for a mainstream, slightly heavier brew under the Plank Road Brewery label. Product packaging was redesigned by Design Partners, but the advertising that started it all moved to the U.S., executed again by BBDO's Toronto office.

Miller introduced Red Dog in the Southeast last October. It was hoping to achieve the equivalent of a 0.8% national share and to begin expanding distribution nationally in early 1995. Two months later, with share figures averaging nearly double the target—and Anheuser-Busch nipping at its heels with a rival named Red Wolf—Miller sped up the timetable.

By January, Red Dog was in most markets and the bulldog was on its way to being a popular figure in the U.S.

Miller claims Red Dog has a 0.8% volume share of the national beer category in the market that most dogs them and a 3.5% share in Chicago, its most howling success.

"This thing is a real phenomenon," says Mr. Lalley, who has since been named group director–Miller trademark brands, charged with marketing responsibility for all brands carrying the Miller name.

Miller also has seen some unexpected benefits—several million dollars in apparel licensing fees.

[Reprinted with permission from "The Marketing 100" in the June 26, 1995, issue of *Advertising Age*. Copyright, Crain Communications Inc. 1995.]

The Red Dog ad campaign is a useful illustration, then, of a crucial feature of media: They work most successfully when they invite or call the audience to play a role that is in some sense flattering or entertaining. By choosing a role, as readers we assert our own sense of style. When we bring such ads our participation—whether the mode is sentiment, humor, patriotism, cynicism, anger, or other attitudes—we become invested in that identity. And we care more about that text and medium because of that investment, which is emotional as well as rational. But identity is always limited: In the case of media texts, it is limited to a relatively few traits or qualities, which are open enough to invite participation by a fairly large number of people. (Being a dog requires different aspects of dogginess, depending on whether the dog is relating to a potential mate, a rival, a small animal to chase, a meter reader, a vet, and so on.) Whether it's because we are pretending, we're having fun, or we're forgetful, we select certain qualities in our fictive identity and repress others, and in some instances this repression has significant consequences.

Communication for most academic purposes is not the same as the advertisement described above. The consumer-as-dog concept involves a complex irony/fantasy that is unlikely to work well in academic genres. The role that your prose creates for your audience will probably not be too far from the position the audience already holds in the social hierarchy—that is, if your primary audience is the instructor in a course, often the instructor's expertise in the subject you are writing about is greater than yours, and your relationship means you'd better not be too flip about it. But it may be of some help to think of your writing as creating a role for the reader to play—the role of recognizing you as promising student, someone whose sincerity and strong interest may supplement inexperience or narrowness of research.

Readers, then, show a sense of style in responding to the roles available in a text. We "dogs" come perkily and eagerly, dog-with-a-ball ready to play. We come for some food, when it's time to eat. We come sulkily: After a nap or when you're an old dog, it's hard to be bouncing around like a pup. We come expecting to be punished, when we've misbehaved. We come ready to take a nip. We come to challenge a rival dog on our territory. We come to chase a squirrel or other prey. These canine responses, drawn from a repertoire according to the situation at hand, are generally triggered by something else (the tone of the owner's voice or something in the environment). In other words, style is **display**. We use it to communicate to others what we are thinking and feeling, thereby establishing our relationship with them.

Most discussions of audience don't really give attention to the role the audience is asked to play. The audience for writing is imagined to be passive, reading and deciphering along lines that the writer has set out. But our discussions of media have shown us audiences that are anything but passive. Texts draw us in to *participate*. When we listen to popular music, we follow cues in that text to conceive of the general situation suggested by the lyrics and music along lines in our own experience. In other words, we rewrite the song into our own lives to some extent, and if it doesn't fit we dislike that song (or genre) and edit it out of our consciousness (or avoid it in the first place). If we attend a film or read a story, we commonly look for someone to "identify" with—usually a protagonist who is portrayed as having certain qualities of character that we like to believe we have, or a protagonist who is placed in a situation that in some respects resembles ours. Our response to the film or story involves a complex matching between the fictive situation portrayed (or the part written into that text for us) and our own, and the less we like what we see, the more distant and critical our likely stance. But as audience, we are invited to take part.

Much of our popular and critically acclaimed fiction, many films, much popular music, and practically all television starts from the ideological presumption that you as an audience member do not want to be lumped together with anyone else—a contradiction, in the context of mass media. So even if the manufacturers of Miller Beer want consumers to march in lockstep to their retail stores to buy six-packs of their product, they won't (usually) find it effective to write us roles in which we do so. Rather, we will be given humorous and somewhat offbeat commercials like those combining an agricultural show with a surfing competition, producing surfing cows ("Cowabunga!"), which flatter us as viewers into thinking we thought of these clever combinations. And material from these and other commercials finds its way into conversations and jokes, as with the crowds at sporting events in the 1980s shouting "Less filling!" "Tastes great!" in imitation of the Lite Beer campaign of the time.

The role of self as independent individual has been used to sell concepts less innocuous than the consumption of beer. Generalized suspicion and distrust of news media, for example, is a standard component of many attacks on government; in some versions these are assembled into conspiracy theories, as discussed in Chapter 8. Set against these media bad guys is a network of heroic and vigilant individuals grouped into resistance and opposition—gun owners as "patriots," militia members, subscribers to "true" media that express the way things really are, Sagebrush Rebels, or opponents of American intervention on the side of oppressive governments in the Third World. (This last account is a holdover from the 1960s and 1970s: Though the rhetoric is familiar, these particular heroic opponents are numerically a much smaller presence in the 1990s. See the discussion of Bad Rhetoric later in this chapter.)

The role of audience as cynic (distinct from rebel) has been prepared for us by many precedents. An easy place to start would be the Cold War: During this period official rhetoric and many stories (both fiction and news) offered the division of the world into two sides, that headed by the Soviet Union and that headed by the United States. *We* were for truth and freedom; *they* were for suppression of freedoms and world domination. Against this very appealing and dramatic story came the Vietnam War, with hundreds of thousands of soldiers placed into the middle of a conflict for which that black-and-white scenario gave them no satisfactory role. Whatever was going on, it didn't much resemble the "fighting for freedom" rhetoric being officially provided; and many actions that were at best morally ambiguous were denied, distorted, or otherwise twisted. The government became the catch-all agent of these perversions, and much of the present antigovernment rhetoric has its root in that great national loss of innocence.

Another complex of events that helped to create the present cynicism was Richard Nixon's presidency, with its series of presidential decisions and the cover-up labeled as Watergate. Many of Nixon's actions had some related precedents in the behavior of other politicians. But political misbehavior was first taken to new and higher levels, then publicly exposed during the Watergate hearings and the series of revelations over a three-year period. Cynicism toward political figures was extended by the treatment given to Watergate in the films *All the President's Men* and *Nixon,* in other texts, and by repeated reference in political statements comparing Watergate with other governmental actions and attempts at secrecy.

These actions, with quite specific historical and political contexts, have for many in the United States become generalized to an equation of politicians with crooks. Anyone who wants to be elected to high office is "naturally" suspect for wanting power. (The longer they serve, the more corrupt they may be presumed to be.) All of the traditional and established "rhetoric" of idealism and moral behavior is assumed to be insincere, a mere cover for what the political figure really wants. And the media figure in the role of either dupe or accomplice—unlike the voice of truth, which uncovers all this, flattering the audience for its insightful cynicism.

Conspiracy theories are more readily accepted because of their wide distribution in fiction and film. They make good stories. Films such as Oliver Stone's film *JFK* (itself legitimated by books such as *Rush to Judgment*) predispose readers to disregard official explanations and believe conspiracy theorists' charges. Those who buy into conspiracy theories such as those of "Mark from Michigan" (prominently mentioned in April–May 1995 in connection with the Oklahoma City bombing), followers of L. Ron Hubbard or Lyndon LaRouche, or more mainstream conspiracy buffs, are encouraged to think highly of themselves for knowing how things *really* are—for being their "own dog"—as opposed to being taken in by news with widespread credibility, such as CBS or the *New York Times*. At some level, as pointed out by many following the Oklahoma City bombing, angry antigovernment rhetoric contributed to that act. Individualism, cynicism, paranoia, and conspiracy theories are not just verbal selling points, like all ideological hooks—they have "real world" effects. Rhetoric works in a continuum. In ancient Greece it might have been possible to imagine that you were talking only to those present, along with a few others who might give accounts to others, in rare cases in writing. But with print the range of reportage increased, and by now words can be multiplied without the usual sorts of filters: A speaker can invent and disseminate by radio a story such as the one about two CIA agents who "confessed" that the bombing was a governmental plot, and can have the story copied electronically via the Internet through fax machines, bulletin boards, and distribution lists to journalists, historians, and others who are interested.

In this section, we've seen how style in media texts can be hegemonic, helping institutions persuade us to want to play roles that benefit them. Although the examples cited above may be seen as negative, writers always want to persuade readers: The important thing is determining whether the goal is in our interest. Buying a certain brand of beer is rather trivial; buying generalized cynicism about government is not.

Style and Audience

Audience is one of the great mysteries in rhetoric. Simply put, how do we know when our writing is working well? How can we tell about others' responses to a text (assuming we know what our own are)? Is it enough just to infer audience from the text?

Generalizations about audience are not easy to back up. Broadcast media and some print media use surveys and rating systems for information about how their texts are received—techniques that are necessary because these media deal in very large numbers. When questioned about the small size of the Nielsen sample, a representative of the agency that conducts the survey compared it to taking a blood sample: You don't have to test *all* of the patient's blood to make some statements about its composition. But the analogy is faulty—human beings are not blood cells, and it has yet to be shown that human behavior is as homogeneous as that of a quantity of blood. Our reception of texts may be skewed unpredictably by factors difficult to account for in a survey.

One consideration in thinking about audience is that audiences and texts interact. Neither is stable, because the text is received by an audience whose members bring different expectations to their reading, and whose reactions to the text may differ widely from each other, as well as changing during the time of the reading. As we saw in the previous section, audiences agree (or not) to fit themselves to the appellations provided by the text. In some media, there's a channel of feedback so that the author or producer can adjust while the text is being produced. For example, an actress on stage can tell something about the audience's reaction and adjust, sometimes unconsciously, during the performance. Newspaper columnists may not get helpful responses to one column, but over a series of columns a pattern of feedback accumulates. And as you write essays for the same instructor, you come to know a reasonable amount about the probable reaction to an essay.

In a different sense, audiences speak back within the context of the market. Ratings for broadcast media, and circulation figures for print media, are the basis of advertising revenues: They make possible our culture's most effective form of "speaking back," through money. Mostly mass audiences fragment. There are a very few media texts that reach large portions of the potential audience—the Super Bowl, last telecasts of *The Cosby Show* or *Cheers,* or news coverage during a national emergency or catastrophic event. Generally, however, the huge potential market is divided in many directions, according to the use for media (entertainment or information), the time of day, demographics, and other factors.

Another way to look at this fragmentation would be to say that the text calls its audience into existence. Any text speaks to its potential audience in a certain fashion, through specific features that differentiate those of us who are willing to respond to its modes of address from the many others who aren't. For example, a radio broadcast of a baseball game creates its listeners *as* radio listeners of a baseball game: of a familiar voice as announcer, almost always male, often a former player, someone who is knowledgeable about baseball in general and the home team in particular, someone who is supportive of the home team but not too openly partisan, and so on. We are created as listeners in response to these attributes, as loyal rooters but not crazed fanatics. We participate in a long ritual of listening to and decoding words and phrases, and to some extent visualizing action on the field. We may integrate the radio broadcast with some other activity, such as an outdoor chore or a day at the beach. Other people may happen by and ask what the score is, thereby identifying themselves as fans and potential listeners, and joining in talk about the sport. In this way, the text of the radio broadcast, and more generally the text of baseball, creates its audience.

A second example might be daytime dramas ("soap operas"). The potential audience has to be available at home during the hours of broadcast (at least, it did before the availability of video recorders); beyond that point, the text creates an audience that is interested in fiction recreating close, personal interaction and centering on love, family relations, and gossip. These programs very rarely reach a sense of closure but continue on indefinitely into the future. As with the example of baseball and other sports for (mostly) men, soaps provide material for further conversation among their fans (mostly women); digests and fan magazines are published for both groups, extending the created audience into print media and multiplying conversation. Both baseball and soaps provide the means for some kind of fan input, through sports talk programs, mail to networks, and magazines like *The Sporting News* and *Soap Opera Digest*.

In both radio broadcasts of baseball games and television broadcasts of daytime dramas, audiences tune in—or not—knowing pretty clearly the general kind of program to expect. As with most media texts, we know when we choose to interact with it the general nature of the text, and part of the gratification it provides is that it completes this anticipated sense, though usually not in exactly the way we may have anticipated. The bloop single with two out that opens up to a big inning, the plot twist that brings Renee and Ralph into a torrid relationship, are matters that the audience may not specifically predict will happen—but the events themselves are of common types (whether matters of chance or carefully guarded secrets of writers and producers). But what creates *us* as the audiences for these texts, what brings us to the awareness of the kinds of texts we will encounter, is (among other things) their style: the series of small, often nearly invisible decisions that name us as their audiences. We are named as audiences of these texts in part by genre and medium. But style is the discrete acting out of the general decisions that are forced by the one large decision of genre and by the need to work within the genre's guidelines in a particular text.

Thinking of your writing as creating its audience can give you a great deal of power as a writer. Previously we've thought of writing as taking place inside of systems of conventions and culturally developed codes that seem to imprison the writer in a network of predetermined meanings. And behind the scenes we have ideology, inclining both writer and reader in ways we may not fully understand, ways not entirely in our interest. But if you can conceive of ways to create an audience for your writing, by making stylistic choices *within* the frameworks of ideology and technological/rhetorical possibilities, then you will have found the way to make writing as a medium work for you.

ASSIGNMENT
View or listen to two specific texts. One can be a portion of a baseball game, on television or radio or at a baseball stadium (substitute another sport if it's football or basketball season); the other should be an episode of a soap opera. These can be done outside or during class, at the instructor's discretion; but do your viewing attentively. That is, keep some scratch paper at hand to write down points of style: words or phrases that are characteristic to that text, that connect to your previous understanding of what you will find, or that are surprising departures from what you expect to find. Then, together with others in the class, pool your observations to build a sense of what makes the style of that kind of text. What are some of the small decisions that create style?

Second, where are the possibilities for divergence in the audience? That is, where do you as audience have a choice about what to make of that text? What kinds of opportunities are there for differing fans or nonfans to express their views? What various uses can be made of the same texts?

Words, Words, Words

As we have seen, style is constructed from many possible choices and guided by factors such as audience, purpose for writing, genre, and other contextual matters. It's important to look at the smallest units of construction, the words chosen.

If we are accustomed to thinking of style as ornament, then the particular words used are beside the point. Other words could be chosen just as well: There are always more words available. Getting proper word choice is as trivial a matter as flipping through a thesaurus to look up some alternatives (or calling on a computer program to do that for you). But if style is thought of as constituting our writing, as well as other media, then choice of words is crucial.

In order to have a choice, you have to have things to choose from. What you can write will depend on the words you have available; so you should begin to extend your vocabulary. This can be done programmatically, by a course of study. A more usual way is to develop some procedures for learning words as you encounter them. You should read texts that stretch your vocabulary—not too much at first, because your comprehension of a text falls off if you have to look up five to ten words per page. Read a short passage of text, marking unfamiliar words in pencil or highlighter (if it's *your* text—not the library's); then come back and look those words up, *writing out* the definitions in a log for future reference. As you look the words up, work them into sentences so that their use begins to feel more natural.

A college-level thesaurus and dictionary are important tools for any writer. Thesauruses give synonyms, so that if you are close to the word you want but can't quite think of it, you may jog your memory by seeing it there. (It's not a good idea, however, to try to use the thesaurus to avoid repetition by simply plugging in a synonym for a word that you feel is used too much.) The thesaurus is a good tool for poking around in, to expand your sense of what language is capable of.

The dictionary is more precise than the thesaurus: Rather than giving several hundred possibilities, many of which won't fit your context, it provides principal definitions for one word at a time. (Often there are some synonyms given, but that's not a dictionary's main purpose.) The dictionary is also the best source for a short etymology, indicating something about the word's history.

Most of your reading will probably be from texts written to explain a concept or idea; many media texts, however, exist for other purposes, such as entertainment. It might be of interest to do a glossary for an entertainment text—for a broadcast text you would need to have a transcript or other permanent version—to see what its key words might be.

Some writing uses words not so much for communication as for atmosphere. Beverly Gross's essay below illustrates how working with a specific word can open up an entire range of meanings.

BEVERLY GROSS

What a Bitch!
What one learns from the dictionaries: There is no [such] classifiable thing as a bitch, only a label produced by the act of name-calling. The person named is almost always a female. The name-calling refers to alleged faults of ill temper, selfishness, malice, cruelty, spite, all of them faults in the realm of interpersonal relating—women's faults. It is hard to think of a put-down word encompassing these faults in a man. *Bastard* and even *son of a bitch* have bigger fish to fry. And an asshole is an asshole in and of himself. A bitch is a woman who makes the name-caller feel uncomfortable. Presumably that name-caller is a man whose ideas about how a woman should behave toward him are being violated.

"Women," wrote Virginia Woolf, "have served all these centuries as looking-glasses possessing the magic and delicious power of reflecting the figure of man at twice its natural size." The woman who withholds that mirror is a bitch. Bitchiness is the perversion of womanly sweetness, compliance, pleasantness, ego building. If a woman is not building ego she is busting balls.

Ball-buster? The word is a nice synecdoche (like *asshole*) with great powers of revelation. A ball-buster, one gathers, is a demanding bitch who insists on overexertion from a man to satisfy her sexual or material voraciousness. The bitch is probably his wife. But balls also bust when a disagreeable woman undermines a guy's ego. The bitch could be his wife, but also his boss, Gloria Steinem, the woman at the post office, the woman who spurns his advances.

Bitch, the curse and concept, exists to ensure male potency and female submissiveness. Men have deployed it to defend their power by attacking and neutralizing the upstart. *Bitch* is admonitory, like *whore*, like *dyke*. Borrowing something from both words, *bitch* is one of those verbal missiles with the power of shackling women's actions and impulses.

The metamorphosis of *bitch* from the context of sexuality (a carnal woman, a promiscuous woman) to temperament (an angry woman, a malicious woman) to power (a domineering woman, a competitive woman) is a touchstone to the changing position of women through this century. As women have become more liberated, individually and collectively, the word has taken on connotations of aggressive, hostile, selfish. In the old days a bitch was a harlot; nowadays she is likely to be a woman who *won't* put out. Female sensuality, even carnality, even infidelity have been supplanted as what men primarily fear and despise in women. Judging by the contemporary colorations of the word *bitch*, what men primarily fear and despise in women is power.

[Reprinted from *Salmagundi*, a publication of Skidmore College, by permission of *Salmagundi* and the author.]

QUESTIONS

1. Do words like *bitch* retain a certain shock value for you as a reader? What are some other words which have the same effect? Why?
2. Is there a distinction between the use of *bitch* and other italicized words in the essay and their use in other contexts, such as casual conversation or a family argument? If so, why is there a difference? Do you ever hear this word used in its original context, to speak (without emotional overtones) about a female dog?
3. Over some period of time (a week or so), keep notes on when you hear words such as *bitch*—spoken by whom, to whom, with what apparent intention. Does your sampling of uses confirm Gross's assertions in the essay?
4. Check the entry for *bitch* in the thesaurus, then any corresponding terms you can think of for a man. Does the thesaurus give support for Gross's points?
5. Gross cannot come up with a corresponding "power" word used by women toward men, parallel to *bitch*. Can you? How would you frame a response to her article?

We commonly expect advertisements to mislead us, at least a little. Because of this, we may have grown accustomed to that particular sort of misuse of language. But the use of misleading words seems a little different in personal ads, because it's one's own qualities being spoken of. Look through personal ads from local newspapers or weeklies for key words that work as a kind of code; try to figure out what the writers are actually saying about themselves.

ASSIGNMENT

How would you write in "personal ad" terms the following information?

Don't be turned off, but I'm twenty pounds over my desired weight.
I'm divorced.
Don't have kids, don't want kids.
I'm looking for a man/woman with plenty of money.
Money isn't nearly so important as having fun.
I'm willing to consider only a certain age range.
I'm single, and don't want calls from people who are divorced or married.
Send me your picture.
Don't reject me, but I'm bald as an egg.
I want to reach someone who's gay, but most people who read this publication are not.
My education level is pretty advanced, and I want to make sure that anyone responding to the ad is someone I can talk to and respect.
I don't have a high education, and I don't want the pressure and anxiety of someone who does.
I really like outdoors activities in an ecological mode.
I like some outdoors things, but with machines (ORVs, snowmobiles, Winnebagoes, etc.).
I'm a couch potato.
I like to socialize with other people
I've been burned before....
I'm not looking for a serious commitment, just someone to have fun with.
I'm ready to settle down and get married, if I find the right person.
Sex is a high priority.
Companionship is a high priority.

Bad Rhetoric

Previously in this chapter, style has been a matter of words and phrases as they connect with roles that are written into texts for both writer and audience. The basis for communication according to these roles is good faith between writer and reader. However, much contemporary communication is *not* a matter of good faith—or even of the predictable differences in viewpoints that derive from contrasting ideologies—but of deception. Rhetoric, like technology, is amoral. Medical devices can cure or kill; artillery can defend or attack; explosives can be used to build tunnels or bomb buildings. The same rhetorical stratagems that can be used to persuade audiences of the writer's understanding of the truth and move them to action can also be used to belittle, attack, even destroy others. What this section calls *bad rhetoric* is not strictly speaking a matter of style; but it has a great deal to do with audience.

Discussions about media in other chapters have often emphasized ways in which media texts' rhetoric parallels writing. Unfortunately, there are parallels as well between some of the negative aspects of rhetoric present in media texts and written rhetoric. It should be recognized that much of this is bad rhetoric—bad in the sense of being poorly constructed, in some cases, as well as bad ethically.

Responsible instruction in rhetoric has as its purpose the fair use of rhetorical skill—that is, of rhetoric in the service of what the writer understands to be the truth or the good. But as audience, we have to be on guard against manipulation, even while granting a wide range to differing understandings of truth. Rhetoric can be used to mislead or disinform, as in propaganda (see Chapter 4 and 5), as well as to motivate readers to buy a product irrespective of its benefits. There are several characteristic devices, some associated with style, used for deception; and I'll discuss these below, in hopes that awareness about them can help us counter their effects.

Note, however, that simply listing some of the rhetorical devices used to mislead will not provide immunity from them. Bad rhetoric is effective because many listeners *want* to be persuaded by it. It speaks to our preconceptions, to our comfortable ideologies; it invites us to believe in a simpler or more interesting account of events. Before we turn to categories and devices of bad rhetoric, let's briefly review the ethical dimensions of rhetoric in general.

Part of the problem with sifting bad from good rhetoric is volume. As media have multiplied beyond printed books and newspapers to magazines, photography, films, radio, television, and newer electronic media, there's an understandable tendency to read more rather than reading better or more critically. Faced with an overload of texts, we usually tend to select those texts that fit most comfortably with our ideology—exactly the sort of situation best suited for the use of propaganda to reach selected segments of the audience.

Not all bad rhetoric is propaganda—that is, not all is the result of intentional distortion. Some occurs when people repeat others' distortions without examining them; and some is erroneous logic. Examples of bad rhetoric can be found irrespective of political colorations and social and economic status.

But at present, more examples can be found in politically conservative writings. Media play to their audience, and the conventional wisdom as of 1996 is that political sentiments are tending to the right. Some significant factors may be cited here: the growth of conservative foundations and think tanks such as the Heritage Foundation, the Cato Institute, and the Olin Foundation; the increased influence of religious groups such as the Christian Coalition in political affairs; the development of talk radio as a means of shaping and amplifying conservative public opinion; the disarray of organizations more to the political left, such as the AFL-CIO and NAACP; and as antecedent cause, the willingness of some business groups to spend money in promoting not only specific candidates but a specific variant of a free-market ideology.

The Olin Foundation supports conservative magazines to the extent of $15 million annually, underwriting conservative student newspapers such as the *Dartmouth Review*, which has produced conservative figures such as Dinesh D'Sousa, author of *Illiberal Education*, an attack on alleged "political correctness" in universities, and William Cattan, a speechwriter for President Bush. As John K. Wilson notes, there are no comparable systems of grants to promote leftist ideas (Wilson pp. 27-29).

In sum, examples of bad rhetoric can be found on left and right—but at present the right is in the ascendancy, and money and political influence give prominence to examples of right-wing bad rhetoric.

In the discussion of gathering and evaluating news and information (Chapter 4), we considered the concept of objectivity. There is no meter to test fairness: Rhetoric always does its work in an ideological context, and we always read out of our own texts. But there's a fundamental distinction between a text that summarizes opposing views and attempts to show why they are mistaken, and a text that suggests to its audience that they need not consider opposing views at all. The first is an interested argument, and may well be fair; the second is propaganda.

Propaganda in English usage has strongly negative connotations, owing to its association with totalitarian states' attempts to control thought through the agencies of communication and education. Leading up to World War II and after, those outside Nazi Germany tried to come up with an explanation of how Hitler could come to power and maintain political control over what the West wished to see as a modern and enlightened country. One explanation was effective propaganda—dominance of discussion through newspapers, radio, films, and other forms of communication. The same means of control were examined during the Cold War, when they were at work in the Soviet

Union and other Communist countries. The usual assumption is that propaganda in this sense is possible only under strict state control: Multiple sources of media and the absence of censorship mean that we in the present-day United States are not subject to anything like propaganda.

From outside the ideological framework of free-market individualism, however, it's difficult to be so complacent. During the Cold War, the United States spent substantial sums of money on the Voice of America, Radio Free Europe, Radio Marti, and other broadcasting organizations dedicated to telling our side of the story. These organizations have avoided the "big lie" sort of deception—but their subjects and mode of presentation still enable them to function as propaganda for our system. We prefer it because it is ours.

There are degrees of distortion, then. No text is entirely free of bias, because no text is without a perspective on the events it describes—but there are degrees of fairness. Labeling something as propaganda, or pointing out that those who produce the text have something to gain by influencing us, ought not automatically to prevent our considering that text. Even habitual liars occasionally tell the truth.

The more interesting question is to and about the audience: Why are we taken in by manipulative and deceptive statements? As we saw in connection with the Red Dog advertisements, the audience is attracted by being invited to play a certain role. Propaganda is most effective in working through seduction—that is, effective propaganda starts from beliefs and values already in circulation and flatters us into agreeing with them. Being told that "America is number one," for example, builds our confidence and self-esteem. We *want* to think so; and if news is carefully selected for us so as to build that impression, we will be pleased, and we'll continue to be an enthusiastic audience for that news. (Bad news can also be flattering, by confirming a negative viewpoint: As I've pointed out before, few sour pleasures are more gratifying than the opportunity to say "I told you so.") Effective propaganda works by telling us what we want to hear, quietly connecting that with what others want us to hear, and downplaying conflicting messages.

Being able to dismiss something as propaganda is a shortcut, so that you can avoid the necessity to consider its claims in order to be fair or well-informed. (Calling someone else's argument "propaganda" is in fact one of the most common forms of propaganda, *name-calling:* It invites us to ignore someone else's stated reasons in advance of seeing what they are, because they are already labeled as "propaganda.") But there are no shortcuts—only practice at being able to distinguish between fact, opinion, and inference, and at being able to work out what ideological work arguments are being used to advance. A good test question for propaganda would be this: Is the effect of the argument to open up discussion, or to close it down?

Perhaps we should consider all attempts at persuasion as propaganda—especially those we already agree with—and judge each (1) by how well it considers and represents opposing views, and (2) by what its aims seem to be. If propaganda represents opposing arguments fairly and can tolerate dissent, that's different from propaganda that caricatures or silences opposing views in order to prevent its audience from thinking differently.

Here are some brief descriptions of categories of bad rhetoric. Some are most likely to involve deliberate deception; some are most probably incautious logic; others might be either.

- **Inconsistency between standards.** In this form of bad rhetoric, what is expected of one person (opponent) is more rigorous than what is expected of someone else (friend, self). Use of this kind of rhetoric may involve **stacking the deck** or **slanting evidence** so that it makes your case look stronger relative to someone else's. **Double standard** or **special pleading** means choosing wording or inventive phrasing so as to favor your friends. Compare Bertrand Russell's "conjugations": "She is fat; you are overweight; I am pleasingly plump, full-figured, etc." *The best response:* Insist on equal treatment for friends and enemies of the writer.
- **Selective sample.** A familiar device, especially in political rhetoric, is to present a small number of cases, perhaps a single case, in such a way as to suggest (or let the reader infer) that this sample is fairly representative, when in fact it's carefully chosen against the preponderance of cases. This is also known as **hasty generalization,** basing the formation of a general law on too small or specialized a set of cases. *The best response:* Note limitations on the sample size, and look for plausible alternatives.
- **Limited alternatives.** Often a fairly chaotic and complex state of affairs will be presented as though it were reduced to a very small number of options, perhaps only two—when in fact there may be several possible points along a spectrum. A variant of this **false dilemma** is the **slippery slope,** which suggests that event A should be avoided because it leads to B, which leads to C, which leads to D, which would be catastrophic. A slippery slope argument can be sustained only if it is in fact proven that all those steps necessarily would follow the first. *The best response:* Look carefully to see if all alternatives are given and are carefully argued; if they're not, provide others.
- **Repetition.** Surprisingly, much of what is presented as argumentative rhetoric in popular usage is nothing of the kind, because no proof is ever offered. Rather, all that listeners get is restatement, sometimes using synonyms; and restatement often proves to be quite persuasive, particularly if the same charges are carried by different media texts. These media may be drawing from the same report, but the fact that all of them carry the news leads to

the audience's increased belief in the truth of what is reported. *The best response:* Note that repetition is going on, and discount for volume.

• **Labeling.** Various forms of labeling go on: **name-calling; stereotyping,** focusing on just one aspect of a more complex human being; **scapegoating,** or letting one person bear responsibility for many or for an institution; **demonizing the opponent;** mud-slinging; imputing guilt by association. Labeling is most often negative, but it exists in a positive direction as well. *The best response:* Search out a more neutral label or estimation, one that doesn't depend on lumping the subject of the term in with disagreeable or agreeable others.

• **Straw man.** A common device in good rhetoric is to summarize opponents' positions before showing what is in your view wrong with them—but this turns to bad rhetoric when someone sets up a "straw man," portraying opponents' positions as more extreme or weaker than those actually held. *The best response:* Correct the statement of your position; edit or revise the attributed position in order to get it right.

• **Complex question.** This device builds part of what is under debate into the question, as an assumption. *The best response:* Divide the question into its component parts and deal with them separately.

• **Language play.** Some people use tricks with words to do rhetorical work, either by joking, ridiculing opponents, using wordplay to distract attention from serious points, or taking a word in two (or more) different senses. *The best response:* Insist on taking words and ideas seriously; make sure that definitions remain the same in all parts of an argument.

• **Irrelevant argument.** Sometimes an unscrupulous user of rhetoric will restate a question in such a way as to make it easier to reply to, thus **changing the subject.** Another device is to charge the opponent with something like the very same fault, the **tu quoque** or "you do it too" reply. Another sort of irrelevancy is to raise an unrelated issue or **red herring.** The **false analogy** is a special sort of red herring, involving an extended comparison between two matters that actually differ in significant ways. An appeal to a **bandwagon** is an invocation of the irrelevant fact of an idea's popularity. *The best response:* Insist on staying with the point.

• **Authority.** Comments by an authority are relevant if the authority is in an appropriate field or is in a position to know. Actors in doctor suits are no more expert in cold remedies than anyone on the street. Often this sort of authority is acquired by **association.** Appeals to authority may be based not on expertise but on celebrity, or on averageness or plain-folks identity. *The best response:* Ask what the relevance of the "authority" is to the idea or concept being advocated.

In academic writing, you can be most persuasive by establishing and maintaining your credibility. Bad rhetoric can be damaging to your relations with your readers.

RUSH LIMBAUGH AND RHETORIC

The talk radio figure Rush Limbaugh has much to teach us about the contemporary use of bad rhetoric. Limbaugh's political position, while not so explicitly stated, consistently adheres to the populist conservative strand of Republican thought identified with Ronald Reagan and with some associated business interests. Limbaugh has built a national following on radio (and to a lesser extent on television) through a rhetorically skillful combination of humor and attacks on others.

Talk radio hosts have attacked others by directly racist remarks: Bob Grant (WABC, New York) has referred to blacks as "screaming savages" and prayed for Magic Johnson to die of AIDS; Limbaugh once told a black caller to "Take that bone out of your nose and call me back."

Readers of this text are probably not hearing of Limbaugh for the first time. His programs were widely syndicated before the 1992 election, and talk radio programs are credited with helping to increase the level of dissatisfaction that led to the Republican victories in the 1994 congressional elections. From that standpoint, the rhetoric of Limbaugh and his ilk has been tremendously effective.

There is now no "liberal" equivalent to conservative talk shows, for several reasons: The main one is that such shows depend on a strong reciprocal connection with a substantial, politically active ideological position. To the extent that a liberal position can be found, it's present within some management and governmental positions and characteristically seeks the "balance" of *on the one hand this, on the other hand that* to be found in mainstream news texts. That is, liberalism is by definition **centrist**, taking cover in balance and rationality, at least putatively. Conservative talk shows, as they have evolved, offer a mixture of rationally defended positions and fallacies of the sort described above as "bad rhetoric," so that one can either attack or defend the programs.

Limbaugh's program has built a cadre of highly loyal followers, who take pride in calling themselves "dittoheads." William Lantry offered the following analysis via e-mail:

< I don't think he believes half of what he says—he says it for effect, for a laugh, to tell a good story. >

I'm afraid I must strongly disagree. [Limbaugh's] job is to sell advertising. He does this by appealing to those people who have the money to buy products. By using a strange mixture of Campbell and Burke, he succeeds. He identifies the preexisting emotions of his listeners, attempts to reinforce them, and then offers a catharsis of those emotions through action. This catharsis can come from voting a certain way, from engaging in intimidation or even political violence, or even from buying products.

And this, I believe, is the function of the callers: he can constantly test his identification of the emotions of his audience through on-air conversation, modifying his identifications as he goes. This is what separates him from previous commentators of similar political leanings (I'm thinking especially of Paul Harvey, and others of that tradition).

His use of the rhetoric of identification is actually stunning. I have an aunt who was a university professor for three decades, who made a career teaching a form of applied rhetoric. She was thus well versed in the fallacies. When I listed a few he engaged in, she agreed that he was less than honorable in his practices. Then she said a striking thing: "He speaks my mind. When you attack him, you are attacking me." Not even his claim to be the voice of truth really disturbed her. [posted on H-Rhetor list, May 21, 1995; used by permission.]

Columbia Journalism Review reported a collateral effect of Limbaugh's popularity—the requirement to adjust the weather.

When weatherman Sean Boyd [of KMJ, Fresno, California] began predicting rain for the day of the second annual KMJ-sponsored barbecue and picnic in honor of the conservative commentator, his bosses high-pressured him to put more sunshine in the forecast lest supporters stay away from the profitable event; when he refused,...they threw him out in the cold.... They couldn't, however, deny that their ousted weatherman had been at least meteorologically correct: during the Al Gore Tree-Hugging Contest, it started to drizzle, and by the time the Miss Dittohead Swimsuit competition got under way it was raining quite liberally indeed. (*CJR* p. 17)

The media-watch group FAIR (Fairness and Accuracy in Reporting) has done a useful report on Rush Limbaugh. FAIR's stated goal is to focus "public awareness on the narrow corporate ownership of the press, the media's allegiance to official agendas and their insensitivity to women, labor, minorities, and other public interest constituencies." In the July/August 1994 issue of *EXTRA!*, FAIR set claims made on Limbaugh's program alongside other sources. It's possible for audiences to spend more than twenty hours weekly watching or listening to Rush, so there's a lot of air time to fill; FAIR's contention, however, is that much of the program is deliberate misrepresentation—propaganda—that has not been scrutinized by mainstream media. According to a standard definition, "As generally understood, propaganda is opinion expressed for the purpose of influencing actions of individuals or groups... with reference to predetermined ends" (Lee and Lee p. 15). In other words, propaganda differs from scientific inquiry, because with science you don't make your mind up first what you want to come up with, then go look for it; with propaganda, however, that's exactly what happens. As FAIR reported, Limbaugh's statement on the thinning of the ozone layer fits this definition.

> [According to Limbaugh,] Mount Pinatubo in the Philippines spewed forth more than a thousand times the amount of ozone-depleting chemicals in one eruption than all the fluorocarbons manufactured by wicked, diabolical, and insensitive corporations in history.... Mankind can't possibly equal the output of even one eruption from Pinatubo, much less 4 billion years' worth of them, so how can we destroy ozone? (Limbaugh pp. 155–57; cited in FAIR report p. 1)

Those who worry about such matters as the thinning of the ozone layer, Limbaugh goes on, are "environmental wackos," "dunderheaded alarmists and prophets of doom." The problem with the Mount Pinatubo claim is that it slants evidence, misreading a specific fact with a predetermined end in view—a classic definition of propaganda.

The assertion that depletion of the ozone layer is due to natural causes rather than chlorofluorocarbons (CFCs) is misrepresentation of fact. CFCs are chemicals found in refrigerants (and before 1978 in aerosol cans); they are not water soluble and therefore rise to the stratosphere, where they are broken down by ultraviolet light (UV). The free chlorine from CFCs interacts chemically with the stratospheric ozone, reducing its thickness and its effectiveness as a filter against UV. But chlorine from natural sources such as volcanoes is dissolved by rain and water vapor before it can reach the stratosphere and be broken down by UV radiation.

The potential beneficiaries of this particular piece of propaganda are business interests: Because of the threat of environmental damage and harm to human health, corporations have been pressured to stop manufacturing

CFCs and switch to other materials for refrigeration. Most have done so willingly, but misrepresentation like Limbaugh's is useful in fostering a belief that government should lessen its regulation of the chemical industry. This misrepresentation is possible because mass media audiences typically are not well informed about science and do not recognize the sleight of hand being performed.

One of the characteristic devices in contemporary propaganda is to find a conflicting source, then claim that matters are still under dispute, so it would be premature to force anyone to change their practices until all the facts are in. Informed scientific opinion is pretty well agreed on what is happening to the ozone layer—an agreement documented in *Science* magazine and supported by statements from atmospheric chemists such as Dr. Sherwood Rowland: "Ozone depletion is real, as certain as Neil Armstrong's landing on the moon. Natural causes of ozone depletion are not significant" (FAIR report, p. 2). Limbaugh draws on sources as well, but on none with scientific credibility: His principal source is *Trashing the Planet,* a book by Dixy Lee Ray, formerly governor of Washington and chair of the Atomic Energy Commission under Ronald Reagan. Ray's main source, in turn, is the editor of a magazine published by a group associated not with scientific research, but with Lyndon LaRouche. It's an old but effective trick to cite sources in conflict with the mainstream of informed opinion, so as to give the impression that "the jury's still out." Tobacco companies have distributed generous grants, through the Tobacco Institute, to researchers willing to "cook" their research enough to give the companies some cover and help avert legislation that might hurt tobacco sales. But Limbaugh's device above adds name-calling to the misrepresentation: Those who follow the preponderance of scientific opinion are labeled as "the agenda-oriented scientific community"; in this way their expertise is dismissed before the listener can ever encounter it. This rhetorical device is called **poisoning the well,** and it's a familiar trick in political campaigns—however, it introduces a level of distortion highly unusual in the context of a program received by its audience as "news."

Limbaugh receives generous treatment from mainstream news organizations, which some audiences rely on to check things out. The reason for the generosity is probably that negative reports through television or newspaper on someone with twenty million loyal listeners can be counted on to produce hostile attacks, which in turn might hurt the TV or newspaper audiences. When in 1954 Edward R. Murrow of CBS News attacked Senator Joseph McCarthy, CBS felt the economic and political effects for some years afterwards (along with reaping praise for their courage). But at least McCarthy could be censured by the Senate for his misdoings, and could lose an election.

Radio hosts are not elected; and so long as audiences are there, advertisers are happy.

Some other examples of Rush Limbaugh's uses of bad rhetoric, organized by device:

Name-calling: "Don't let the liberals deceive you..."; a critic of feeding grains to cattle, rather than eating more grains and vegetables ourselves, is called an "ecopest"; name-calling of President Clinton is frequent, as in "draft dodger"; the National Organization of Women is labeled "feminazis," Madonna is called a "Smut Queen," antiwar activists are "long-haired maggot-infested FM radio types," Greenpeace "environmental wackos," Senator Carol Moseley Braun a "blithering jewel of colossal ignorance," and so on (Keliher p. 44).

Personal attack, abuse, ridicule: "Those of you who want to take off the Clinton/Gore bumper stickers, just go get a handicapped parking sticker instead, and people will know why you voted that way" (Keliher p. 29). Limbaugh told a joke on television about "the White House dog"—holding up a picture of Chelsea Clinton. "One of the things I want to do before I die is conduct the homeless Olympics.... [Events would include] the 10-meter Shopping Cart Relay, the Dumpster Dig, and the Hop, Skip and Trip" (*Los Angeles Times,* 1/20/91). A Mexican national won the New York Marathon, according to Limbaugh, because "An immigration agent chased him for the last 10 miles" (*USA Weekend,* 1/26/92). "Kurt Cobain was, ladies and gentlemen, I just—he was a worthless shred of human debris" (TV show, 4/11/94). "Environmentalists want forests to stay so they can grow pot without detection" (Keliher p. 40). "To whatever extent this nation is racist, that racism is fueled primarily by the rantings and ravings and inconsistencies, the absolute idiocies of people like Jesse Jackson and Benjamin Chavis"; compare also "The NAACP should have riot rehearsal. They should get a liquor store and practice robberies." "There is racism in this country, but it is not as bad as people think" (Keliher pp. 52, 54).

Irrelevance: Distracting audiences by bringing up unrelated matters is an effective way of avoiding an issue. Limbaugh brings up the Genesis story about Joseph's public role in Egypt as a justification for tax cuts, when what Joseph did was to impose a tax on grain so that, in a lean year, there would be enough for people to eat (radio show, 6/28/93); he defends U.S. health care as the world's best, on the basis of how well it serves those who are covered by insurance or can afford to pay for treatments—but ignores general measures of U.S. health care such as life expectancy or infant mortality. Justifying the claim that the U.S. poor are better off than the mainstream in Europe, he mentions matters such as car ownership and apartment size rather than income level or public amenities.

Double standard: Part A. Comment on Janet Reno's statement that "as Attorney General her priority would be to protect the rights of the accused": "What about the victims? What about the rights of the law-abiding? Who cares about the criminals?" Part B. Several months later, on "the four police officers being retried for beating Rodney King": "What about double jeopardy? Self-incrimination? What about the officers' fifth-amendment rights?" According to the *Minneapolis Star,* Limbaugh used a minor physical impairment to avoid service in Vietnam, which has not prevented his criticizing President Clinton for not going.

Questionable authorities: Many of the citations Limbaugh provides in his lengthy response to the FAIR criticisms draw on work only slightly better than the LaRouche journal mentioned previously. The response about health care draws on someone from the Manhattan Institute with a Ph.D. in constitutional law, not a medical degree. Defending the statement that "there are more American Indians alive today than there were when Columbus arrived," Limbaugh turns to an article in the Heritage Foundation magazine that states that "some Indian groups are more populous today than in 1492." But in fact, that population is estimated to have stood at 5 to 15 million then; to have been reduced to 250,000 in the late nineteenth century; and to be back up to 2 million today.

As the paragraph above indicates, some of the background for Limbaugh's material comes from research groups with specifically conservative agendas—the Heritage Foundation and the Cato Institute, to name two. These groups fulfill a worthwhile function in adding to the amount and quality of available information—but using their work selectively to discount much greater samples of studies, developed through the effective fact-checking mechanisms of professional work in science, is slanting evidence.

Recognizing and Correcting Bad Rhetoric

Pointing out bad rhetoric is, unfortunately, a weak device for correcting it. Those who identify logical fallacies, propaganda, and other contributions to muddying up the already complex task of understanding our world are not automatically able to do better. Rush Limbaugh is a rich source of misstatement and factual misrepresentation—but pointing this out does not negate the effects of Limbaugh's rhetoric, even for those reading *EXTRA!* or other refutations. Besides, devoted Rush listeners will have made up their minds without looking into logic, because what they hear fits their ideological predisposition.

What might be called "mainstream media" do little better in this respect. Many stories repeat charges cited somewhere else, so that it's often difficult to find, much less evaluate, the original basis for a story.

One anecdote about "political correctness" was recycled in at least thirty-five articles and books (Wilson pp. 21, 169).

As noted in Chapter 4, news media cannot give sufficient context in themselves for readers to be able to judge most information, and the media clutter that surrounds us means that we increasingly lack the basis to provide our own refutation of fallacies and false charges. Many news stories begin as public relations devices initiated by research groups, the staffs of public officials, or corporations with an interest in having a particular story appear in a certain way—and most newspapers and magazines do not do well at placing these in context for their readers, because reporters are usually not expert in the relevant fields. This leaves us as the audience in the position of needing very much to evaluate the adequacy of the information provided, while lacking the tools to do so. We can't all become experts ourselves.

Lacking an effective agency of fact-checking, there are a few strategies we ourselves can try, in a quick-and-dirty fashion. First, we can develop a list of publications that have a reputation for accuracy. It's more likely that publications such as *Harper's* or *The New Yorker* among magazines, or the *New York Times* or *Washington Post* among newspapers, will go to greater lengths to confirm and contextualize material, because they have larger staffs and professional reputations to lose. (The track record for *Time* magazine is more checkered: See the discussion of Cyberporn in Chapter 11.) Magazines that deal more in entertainment or rumors than in "hard news" should be read with even more skepticism than these.

Second, we should develop a capacity for screening for sources. What voices are speaking through this material? If a report is based on one or a very few sources, its plausibility may be reduced. What is their interest in speaking to us through this medium? If there's money to be made or influence to be gained, that might throw doubt on the motives of the report.

Third, we should develop the capacity to watch our own reactions to what we read and hear. Alfred Lee and Elizabeth Lee offer some advice about analyzing propaganda that can be usefully applied in this case:

> ASCERTAIN the conflict element in the propaganda element you are analyzing. All propaganda contains a conflict element in some form or other—either as cause, or as effect, or as both cause and effect.

BEHOLD your own reaction to this conflict element....

CONCERN yourself with *today's* propagandas associated with *today's* conflicts.... It is all too easy to analyze some old example of propaganda, now having little relation to vital issues.

DOUBT that your opinions are "your very own." They usually aren't....

EVALUATE, therefore, with the greatest care, *your own propagandas*. We must learn clearly *why* we act and believe as we do with respect to various conflicts and issues—political, economic, social, and religious....

FIND THE FACTS before you come to any conclusion.... We must ask: Who is this propagandist? (etc.)

GUARD always, finally, against omnibus words [words that carry all sorts of meanings]. (Lee and Lee pp. 16–18)

FURTHER READINGS

This chapter has alluded to "doublespeak," the term developed by George Orwell in *Nineteen Eighty-Four* and adapted since then to numerous real-world examples. William Lutz has spent much of his career collecting, analyzing, and denouncing examples of doublespeak, many of which are published by NCTE in the *Quarterly Review of Doublespeak*, which Lutz edited until 1994. Below is an excerpt from the first chapter of *Doublespeak*, Lutz's 1989 book drawing on his work.

DOUBLESPEAK

William Lutz

There are no potholes in the streets of Tucson, Arizona, just "pavement deficiencies." The Reagan Administration didn't propose any new taxes, just "revenue enhancement" through new "user's fees." Those aren't bums on the street, just "non–goal oriented members of society." There are no more poor people, just "fiscal underachievers." There was no robbery of an automatic teller machine, just an "unauthorized withdrawal." The patient didn't die because of medical malpractice, it was just a "diagnostic misadventure of a high magnitude." The U.S. Army doesn't kill the enemy anymore, it just "services the target." And the doublespeak goes on.

Doublespeak is language that pretends to communicate but really doesn't.... Doublespeak is not a matter of subjects and verbs agreeing; it is a matter of words and facts agreeing. Basic to doublespeak is incongruity, the incongruity between what is said or left unsaid, and what really is... between the word and the referent, between seem and be, between the essential function of language–communication–and what doublespeak does—mislead, distort, deceive, inflate, circumvent, obfuscate....

There are at least four kinds of doublespeak: [euphemism, jargon, gobbledygook, and inflated language.] Identifying doublespeak can at times be difficult. For example, on July 27, 1981, President Ronald Reagan said in a speech televised to the American public that "I will not stand by and see those of you who are dependent on Social Security deprived of the benefits you've worked so hard to earn. You will continue to receive your checks in the full amount due you." This speech had been billed as President Reagan's position on Social Security, a subject of much debate at the time. After the speech, public opinion polls revealed that the great majority of the public believed that the president had affirmed his support for Social Security and that he would not support cuts in benefits. However, only days after the speech, on July 31, 1981, an article in the *Philadelphia Inquirer* quoted White House spokesperson David Gergen as saying that President Reagan's words had been "carefully chosen." What President Reagan had meant, according to Gergen, was that he was reserving the right to decide who was "dependent" on those benefits, who had "earned" them, and who, therefore, was "due" them. . . .

Doublespeak . . . is language designed to alter our perception of reality and corrupt our thinking. Such language does not provide us with the tools we need to develop, advance, and preserve our culture and our civilization. Such language breeds suspicion, cynicism, distrust, and, ultimately, hostility.

Doublespeak is insidious because it can infect and eventually destroy the function of language, which is communication between people and social groups. This corruption of the function of language can have serious and far-reaching consequences. We live in a country that depends on an informed electorate to make decisions in selecting candidates for office and deciding issues of public policy. The use of doublespeak can become so pervasive that it becomes the coin of the political realm, with speakers and listeners convinced that they really understand such language.

[From *Doublespeak* by William Lutz, pages 1–2, 15–16, 20. Copyright © 1989 by Blonde Bear, Inc. Reprinted by permission of HarperCollins Publishers, Inc.]

QUESTIONS

1. Lutz's examples are drawn primarily from Republican administrations, as the book was published in 1989. Search for more recent instances of doublespeak from Democratic sources as well as Republican.
2. How would you compare the tone of Lutz's essay above to that of the shorter excerpt from E. B. White (page 544 above)?

FURTHER ASSIGNMENTS

Assignment
You may have read a novel and then seen a film adapted from that novel (or vice versa). For example, *Jurassic Park, Schindler's List, The Russia House, The Hunt for Red October,* and many other films began as novels (in some cases, with the simultaneous intention of

being made into films). Many "classic" novels have been made into films as well (*Jane Eyre, Wuthering Heights, Nineteen Eighty-Four, Lord of the Flies, Bleak House, The Age of Innocence.*)

In order to make a film from a novel, some complicated adaptation is required, so as to render description in visual form, to represent what might be the novel's internal representation of character through the camera, and so on. The same problems of adaptation apply to converting a novel into a television program. (The point could also be extended to converting a stage play into a film, or comic book characters, as with *Casper, Batman, Superman,* etc.)

Choose one example of a film and novel, both of which you know. What did you find to be significant differences between the novel and film? Did you see the film first and then read the novel, or vice versa? Which form seems to take priority for you, and why? What features of the novel did the film treat in a fairly straightforward way, and what were shortened or cut entirely? Are there elements of one medium that are not easily or well done in another (for example, a character's internal reflections in prose; or visual atmosphere in film)?

Assignment
Working in groups, brainstorm about proverbs until you come up with a fairly substantial list—twenty or thirty ought to be no problem. Then work through the list to see if you can come up with common stylistic qualities for proverbs as a form. What makes proverbs memorable? How is it that they stay around, in oral form, for as long as a dozen lifetimes? How did you come to learn these proverbs? Did people in the group know the same proverbs, or did you recall some which no one else had known? Are proverbs media?

Assignment
Pick up a real estate brochure and prepare a glossary. What do words and phrases such as *handyman's delight* and *bungalow* mean in that context?

Assignment
Do some browsing in the periodicals section of your college library, picking out ten or so publications (newspapers, popular magazines, academic journals, etc.). For each, look at a representative article: What indication does it give of the basis for its information? Does it present the author's original research? A digest of someone else's research? The author's beliefs and opinions, without their being framed as something to be confirmed? Others' beliefs and opinions? "Common sense"? Gossip?

Assignment
Take some recent writing of yours—a draft in progress or a recent essay—and pull from ten separate paragraphs what you think of as ten important sentences. If possible, draw these from a mixture of early, middle, and late positions in the paragraphs. Note what the topics are, by underlining them, and what the stresses are, by double underlines. Then

revise the sentences so as to reduce the length of topics and to increase the importance of stresses. Put these back into their paragraphs and revise the rest of the paragraphs. What difference do these changes make?

Assignment

Make a glossary. In the past, you may have been assigned readings that presented a short text with certain words in boldface—those that the editor thought might be new or difficult for readers. The boldface print alerted you to look in the text or at the bottom of the page or end of the piece for explanations.

Choose a short piece of writing that presents moderate difficulty for you, and prepare a glossary for that text. Mark all unfamiliar words, to make sure you get those; then make another pass through the text and mark words that seem to you important to understanding the text, whether or not they are unfamiliar. Look up all these marked words, and write a short definition for each. Make use of a thesaurus to find some synonyms and opposites.

Finally, write briefly how it was you came to choose those words as important, rather than some others that might have been chosen. If you looked just at the list of words in your glossary, would you have something of an idea of what the text was about?

11

Expanding Media Resources

OVERVIEW

In previous chapters we have reflected on several forms of contemporary media—print media (newspapers and magazines), broadcast media (radio and television), advertising, film, and others such as popular music. But if we regard media as devices for communication, many other forms exist, from the logos and symbols of sports organizations on caps to home pages on the World Wide Web. Our discussions have not touched on all available forms of media. To do so would not be practical or possible, because new forms evolve out of older forms. In a book on understanding rhetoric through media, the very fact of change is an important element of media's rhetoric.

Media are *dynamic:* This crucial element is the starting point for this concluding chapter of *Rhetoric through Media.* Dynamic is the precise word: It means *continuously changing,* and it relates to *power.* One of the principal sources of the power of media is their capacity for change. Not only do particular texts offered through media change, daily or moment by moment (in contrast with books, which are relatively enduring), but over time media themselves incorporate new content, themes, and even technologies from other sources.

The process of change is familiar by now: New technology allows a modification in what media can provide; market forces scout out funding and deliver promotion; and audiences gravitate toward novelty and convenience, as their leisure time, level of income, and other factors allow. These changes may come as gradual developments rather than sharp breaks; the forms of media, the nature of those forms, and the particular conventions of texts evolve from what is already in existence.

One contention of this book has been that, whatever the superficial diversity and plenitude of media texts, there is an underlying *unity*. Media texts, whether supplying information or entertainment, tell us stories we want to hear, consistent with the stories their producers and other persons of influence want us to hear. (Their wants most commonly have to do with maintaining a political and cultural presence and with making a profit.) In many respects we still want the same things as earlier generations: novelty, diversion and confirmation of our beliefs and values about the world. Where previous generations anticipated new books, films, and songs, we add to these new television programs, computer games, and technological methods of communication. In one sense, these are recurrently new; but in another, they are variations on the same process.

For a symbol of this variety-in-sameness, consider the daily newspaper. How much does its attraction really depend on changing news stories? For all the shifts in content, the newspaper looks very much the same, month after month, year after year, maintaining the same masthead and style of type and general feel. This sameness and regularity are at least as much the message of the newspaper as any stories printed there. There are faster ways to get the news—but newspapers afford us ways of thinking about aspects of our lives in terms of both superficial change and underlying continuity. Newspapers and other media flourish only if they make a connection to ideologies in the culture, both drawing from their themes and topics to communicate to an audience, and reinforcing them through repetition.

Our analysis in previous chapters has been devoted not only to reading media and their texts, but to *writing*. Writing as a medium supports other media, and it allows us to apply in our own texts some of the rhetorical features of media. In this final chapter, by looking at some current developments, we will consider as well how we may be able to make media work for us—how we may be able to get media to provide better versions of what we want and need rather than what producers of our culture's principal media texts find it convenient and desirable for us to have. What we need to do, in order to escape the limitations of playing roles of consumers, is to use media more interactively. If most of the audience is effectively closed out of interacting with television (see Exhibit 11.1) and film and print media, we can make use of other media, whether it's by Xeroxing a flier or posting a message to others via the Internet.

Exhibit 11.1 Drawing by R. Chast; © 1993. from *The New Yorker,* April 5, 1993. Used by permission.

What other forms of interactive media, besides those discussed so far, are of importance to you, either now or potentially? You share with millions of others in the United States the ability to express your views through media as diverse as graffiti, bumper stickers, or billboards (at the low-tech end), or e-mail, faxes, and computer bulletin boards (at the high-tech end). Not much can be said on bumper stickers—they don't get much deeper than "Choose Life" or "Question Authority." (Exhibit 11.2 gives other examples.) But the Internet as a medium holds some promise for more significant interaction.

The title of this chapter, then, is deliberately ambiguous and deliberately points in two directions at once. The first sense (*expanding media resources,* with *expanding* as an adjective) connotes that media resources are increasing, and that fact is something that we need to notice and reflect on. The second

> **WE VOTE PRO-LIFE**
>
> **MY KID BEAT UP YOUR HONOR STUDENT**

Exhibit 11.2 Seen on the back of a Chevrolet Suburban.

sense (*how to expand* media resources) suggests that it may be possible for *you* to expand your use of media, to take matters more under your own control through new forms. *Resources* strikes a parallel with natural resources: These forms of information are out there, and as you are already connected to them, you may as well reflect on how these connections work and turn them to your advantage. Unlike coal and oil reserves, however, media resources seem to be multiplying, not diminishing. "Expanding" may also echo the phrase *expanding universe,* which is an appropriate image for rapidly growing communications. The problem at present is not scarcity but clutter. So this chapter should offer some sense of the problems implied by that clutter, and some procedures for testing the adequacy of your information and for adding to it in directions that you find useful and interesting.

Literacy in the most narrow terms is the ability to read and write. But as media expand from print to broadcast to electronic formats, literacy may come to refer less to puzzling out words and sentences, and more to puzzling out how to use computers and other electronic devices to get the information you need. It doesn't matter what marvels are available potentially through your telephone line if you don't know how to find them. This chapter, then, offers a few early reflections on the implications of electronic media, particularly the Internet—some of its potential as a medium for our use, and some inherent and potential dangers in reading it incautiously.

ISSUES

Collections As a Basis for Your Own System

A theme for much of what has gone before: To the degree possible, you need to claim a degree of independence from media. That is, rather than playing the role of a relatively passive receiver of others' ideas and values as transmitted through media, you need to read these transmissions critically and consider the extent to which it is in your interest to act according to them. (Note the difference between "the extent to which you *want* to act..." and "the extent to which *it is in your interest to act.*") This book is written according to the assumption, or faith, that action based on such analysis is possible. You necessarily *start* with the categories and modes of thinking provided by your relationship with the general culture, but you don't have to finish there. Defining and in some cases changing that relation is one of the things that education is for. Understanding these things on a theoretical level is important, but a study of rhetoric should also have practical effects.

You have been asked at various times to write your way toward clarification. Writing as a medium brings the writer into the picture. It does no good to understand the rhetoric of media if we make no attempt to apply that knowledge, in our reading of media texts or in our own uses of rhetoric.

One such application, at the outset of this chapter, is to reflect on your uses of other media besides the principal ones touched on in the preceding chapters. To get some feel for this use, you should form your own **collections** of texts. Collections are a way of associating texts into genres or forms of media with their conventional categories or labels torn off, so to speak. Taking texts such as photographs out of their previous contexts and finding or inventing other contexts is a way to reconceive of the texts in what may be closer to your own terms. The project of tracing their relations and properties can offer you a basis for authority over these texts—authority based not on institutional presence but on the knowledge gained from analysis.

When you were younger, you may have had collections of comic books, sports cards, or memorabilia of some sort. These literal collections allowed you to take physical possession of materials, in order to establish a kind of conceptual control over them. What you are to collect now is not so much physical objects as rhetorical texts. These could be print ads (as in Chapter 5), representations of faces in cartoons, styles of printing, or travel brochures; or (less physically) examples of themes from popular music, descriptions of "coming attractions," television theme songs, or road-racing video games. These and other texts work within their own systems of rhetoric, and when you observe them and articulate that rhetoric, you are doing meaningful critical work. Part of becoming more independent of others' rhetoric, then, is to look for ways to form your own concepts, rather than recycling what is provided you. In the assignment below, prompts are offered as suggestions—but you should look for your own concepts as reflected through collected texts, rather than simply choosing one of those suggested.

ASSIGNMENT

Within the forms of media previously discussed, we have considered genres of texts with their own conventions (front-page stories, features, advice columns, sports reporting; talk radio, Top 40, "classic" rock, country; sitcoms, soap operas, documentaries). This assignment will ask you to perform as a media critic by categorizing some texts in unconventional ways. Your categories should serve as the basis of your own collection of media texts. (Some texts may not be convenient for physical collection—in that case, you may use photographs or sketches, or simply describe them sufficiently so that your readers recognize what you are talking about.)

You might want to use this assignment to do one of two things: (1) to call attention to an underrecognized genre of texts; or (2) to reconfigure texts so they reflect an issue that you feel to be of significance.

Some illustrations—though it is important to the assignment that you come up with your own ideas rather than simply developing others' suggestions:

1. *Genres:* "Legible clothing," including T-shirts, sweatshirts, and caps; "coming attractions" for films; music used in sound tracks; political advertising; text displayed on the outside of feature film cassettes; industry publications (e.g., those for auto dealers, medical personnel, or funeral homes).

2. *Issues: (a)* How do print advertisements make use of color? Of printed text? How do they reflect assumptions about gender, race, class, age? How are markers such as glasses and hair color used? *(b)* What are some ways in which assumptions about technology are reflected in texts? (Sources might include owners' manuals, print and broadcast ads for products such as computers, ways in which technology is reflected in narratives such as films and television, and offhand comments in newspaper or magazine articles.) *(c)* How do some categories of texts represent foreigners, "the Other," people not like "ourselves"? How do these texts lead "us" to define "ourselves" as being unlike "them"? Sources might include travel brochures and ads, political ads, or the sort of identification promoted by talk radio programs. *(d)* How do photographs and drawings reflect assumptions about gender?

Collections provide a basis for classifying texts. And how we classify texts may have important financial and cultural consequences. A lawsuit brought before the Supreme Court in 1996 concerned a spreadsheet program called Lotus 1-2-3. Borland International, Inc., wrote completely independent software, but used the same system of commands as are used in Lotus 1-2-3 to execute it; Lotus Development Corp. sued for copyright violation. If these commands are classified as being like a publication, as that company argued, then the appropriation of the commands is theft of intellectual property. But

Borland argued that these commands are like the system of buttons and switches in an airplane's cockpit, necessary to make the machinery run. It's the machinery that is legally protected, not the buttons and switches and overall cockpit design. The relatively new medium of computer software has brought about this legal dispute: It's more likely that users of media will be able to participate in establishing conventions when those media are new than when the ways of thinking about them are already set up. (Because the Supreme Court was split 4-4, the lower court's decision in favor of Borland stood.)

Change based on technology will be a principal theme in the rest of this chapter—but observing the categories of these new media texts does not depend on their electronic nature. Rather, we observe and associate categories of texts according to patterns already established in the culture.

What to Expect

Writings about the future of media express, by turns, optimism, pessimism, and bewilderment. Optimism may be based on just the fact of technological development and its potential for increased personal expression and communication. One of the earliest writing in this visionary mode was Marshall McLuhan, who beginning in the 1960s pointed to the implications of new media for local and global communication. Others have argued that improvements in computers and communications extend decentralization and democratization. No longer do Saginaw and Topeka have to wait for news to emanate from centers of power such as New York, Washington, and Los Angeles; now smaller locales get news electronically from all over the world. No longer does information have to be sanctioned by professionally trained journalists working through established institutions; now anyone with a few hundred dollars for a computer, modem, and telephone line can collect information and disseminate it to all who want it. More than a few people now are following the countercultural dictum: "If you don't like the news, make your own."

But these changes offer reason for concern as well as for hope. Institutions provide important checks on information, screening what is distributed, confirming the facts published (with greater or lesser success and reliability), and providing a consistent range of interpretations to be considered. Institutions reflect and re-create existing ideologies—but in some instances that may not be a bad thing. Relying on one source of information, no matter how prestigious, is risky; but an assortment of major news media provides some cross-checking as well as echoing, so that readers can be reasonably confident that aberrant interpretations will be weeded out or at least highlighted for consideration. But whatever safeguards there are with mainstream media do not apply at all to much electronic media. If I download a text from an Internet source, there is no practical way of determining much about who it comes from or what the writer's expertise and interests might be.

The growth of electronic media, then, can provide a basis for pessimism as well as optimism. In addition to questions about their reliability, there is the fact that electronic media are not equally available for all. (See Exhibit 11.3.) While e-mail makes nearly instant communication possible, you have to have a computer and a connection—which means it's a benefit chiefly for people in the middle class and up, especially those further along in educational status. (As with all new media, it helps to have money.) E-mail exchanges, as we shall see, fall somewhere between the genres of letter and conversation, with much of the informality of talk, but also its sloppiness. The existence of thousands of talk groups allows users to pursue individual interests, no matter how esoteric—but those groups set up are sometimes very far removed from the civic and public concerns of our culture's principal providers of information. (Some titles: alt. devilbunnies, alt.fan.howard-stern, alt.tarot, alt.tv.tiny-toon, alt.angst, alt.aol-sucks, alt.backrubs, alt.binaries.pictures.erotica, alt.binaries.pictures.erotica.blondes, . . . female, . . . male, . . . orientals.) Many of these provide diversion, and are likely to be at least as positive and healthy as much of what is available through established media, but which texts do they replace, and which supplement?

Exhibit 11.3 Doonesbury © 1994 G. B. Trudeau. Reprinted with permission of Universal Press Syndicate. All rights reserved.

PAUSE FOR REFLECTION

If you use a computer to participate in a chat group or to browse the Web, how much time goes into that activity? Keep a record over some period of time, as you have done with the media log: How well do the on-line texts you read and write fit with the common division between information and entertainment?

If you do not use a computer for this purpose, find someone who does and talk with her or him about that use. How much time is spent? Did that time subtract from what was previously spent with other media such as television and newspapers? From some other activity (work, sleep, family interaction)?

There is ample material to support both optimistic and pessimistic views about the growth of electronic media. What is clear is that the established forms of media now have a powerful potential source of competition, one heavily decentralized and dependent on phone lines rather than broadcast or print systems of distribution. (Keep this economic competition in mind as you read accounts of public debates over regulating the Internet.) Whether these changes are on the whole good or bad—and for whom—is still to be determined, and the changes are occurring well in advance of deciding.

As with other considerations, you must work out for yourself the extent and nature of your participation in electronic media. Some may never take much interest in the latest brave new world, while others already live there. But the existence of electronic media cannot help but change the communications system, and rhetoric, for everyone, regardless of our level of participation in it.

PAUSE FOR REFLECTION

Your response to electronic media is probably related to your fundamental view of technological change. What are some of the personal factors that have influenced how you think about technology? Write informally accounting for some of these. (Some starters: the space program; fictions associated with technology, such as science fiction novels, stories, and films; income level; parents' occupations and educational status; geographical region [i.e., urban, suburban, rural]; individual factors such as visits to the National Air and Space Museum.)

Electronic Media

Electronic media is not a very precise term, but it's probably the best available. Considered literally, the phrase would include just about everything, because pretty much all forms of media now are at least partially electronic. While the term *electronic* could apply to everything since alternating current, it would probably be more appropriate to connect the term in its contemporary sense to the invention of the transistor and its consequences for technological development. Transistors brought miniaturization, and along with that, a steady availability of consumer goods reduced in size and price, and increased in speed and capacity. We now think nothing unusual about having music personally available while walking or running, or about being able to telephone from a car or a boat. These media, and the belief in continuing technological improvement, have become routine.

It would take a tremendous effort to produce media texts now without electronics—the communications equivalent of sailing a clipper ship or doing farming without heavy machinery or chemicals. Even a medium as apparently simple as photography is not free from electronics: Modern cameras use electronic devices for setting apertures and exposures, and even an old camera would have its film developed using electronics. (One manufacturer has developed a camera which stores images *digitally,* using no film at all.) And if photography has become electronic, other media are now even more so. Contemporary newsrooms use computers rather than typewriters and typesetting equipment, and some newspapers and magazines now have on-line editions. Computer technology is taken for granted in radio, television, film, and the music industry. Obviously electronics plays a central role in video, CD-ROM and computer games, and in how we now retrieve information through libraries. So marking one branch as "electronic media" is almost meaningless.

But we need a term to include, but go beyond, the medium loosely referred to as the Internet. Electronic media, for our purposes, will include all sources of information accessed through a computer, as opposed to simpler electronic devices such as a television set, stereo receiver, or CD player. Our emphasis will be on the mode of *consumption* rather than production. Much of our attention will be directed to the Internet, a loosely defined medium accessed by any computer connected to other computers, and the World Wide Web, which adds visual images and sound to graphic text. Other electronic media include computer games and devices such as CD-ROM systems. These media have some essential differences from those customary and commonly available in the 1980s—and not only because of the technology of their manufacture. The computer makes possible an essential difference in media texts, a high degree of *interactivity.* This section will offer some perspectives on this branch of media in the context of their rhetoric.

A description of the Internet is unnecessary for many readers of this book. The Internet grew out of a network of computers set up as ARPANET in 1969 by the U.S. Department of Defense. Others from universities and research groups were quick to recognize the advantages of networking, and in the

1970s the Internet was used primarily for scientific applications. Commercial and other groups logged on in the mid-1980s (LaQuey pp. 25–26). Growth since then has been exponential, proceeding from larger universities and other computing centers to other sites and from the United States, Western Europe, Australia, and Japan to most other countries.

The Internet's origins in the scientific and academic communities have meant that the recent shift to commercial providers is encountering some resentment. Some of the enthusiasm for the Internet comes from its relative freedom from structure and hierarchy. E-mail texts have the same appearance whether they're sent by Bill Gates or by Forrest Gump. It's a technology ideally suited to the myth of independent, individual action—*myth* in this case meaning a narrative that is illusory, because those "anarchic" individualists are making use of a system initiated and heavily supported by the federal government and quasi-governmental research agencies (not to mention those aspects of government-funded research that underwrite the existence and development of computer technology).

 The term *cyberspace* was coined by William Gibson in his 1984 novel *Neuromancer* and was called in that context a "consensual hallucination." Its popularization illustrates the flow between fiction, media, and common usage.

There are occasional attempts to encourage collective action within the individualist ideology of the Net. The excerpt in Exhibit 11.4 is from an Internet document proposing a blacklist of Internet advertisers who violate certain

> The Greencard Lawyers are right when they say in their book that Internet advertising is legal, incredibly cheap and can reach a huge audience. In order to prevent a death of the Internet comparable to that of TV, we need to make inappropriate electronic advertising more expensive.
>
> To do this without violating the general anarchistic and grass roots spirit of the net, I propose a blacklist scheme. Offenders and their offensive actions are described in a document which is distributed widely over the net. The expectation is that individuals will decide on their own what would constitute an appropriate punishment and will then go ahead and carry it out.
>
> 30,000,000 potential customers sounds attractive, doesn't it? How about 30,000,000 people pissed off and telling all their friends to boycott your business?

Exhibit 11.4 Excerpt from "The Philosophy behind the Blacklist of Internet Advertisers." Internet posting by Axel Boldt. Used by permission.

taboos. Many with e-mail accounts resent unsolicited electronic advertising, for reasons similar to those of fax machine owners who resent others' use of their own machine and materials to produce advertisements.

Social and cultural connections (or their equivalents) have developed with the technology of the Internet. There are now "virtual communities" that provide professional and personal satisfaction that supplements if not replaces the more familiar sort available face-to-face, by conventional mail ("snail mail"), and by telephone. Most of these electronic "communities" will never literally commune. An interesting feature of these communities is that *all* that defines them is the labeled interest, as expressed purely through the medium of the talk group. They are appellated by what makes them possible. Am I the same person when I interact with other "community" members on comp.os.msdos.programmer, misc.fitness.aerobic, rec.arts.books.marketplace, soc.culture.bosna-herzgvna, alt.coffee, alt.cristnet.second-coming.real-soon-now, alt.fan.tolkien, and alt.buddha.short.fat.guy? This might be seen as community purified to its ultimate end, or just as community simplified by leaving out complexities. (See readings in this chapter by Gans and Kadi, pages 655 and 658.)

The Internet's size and complexity are invisible to those not hooked in in some fashion. What is being called cyberspace exists, if it exists, outside of ordinary activities altogether, so that you need never notice it. Even so, it is having an effect on media, in ways yet to be determined.

A large number of us in the United States are or shortly will become connected through the Internet—but most of us will use only a tiny portion of its potential. It might be possible to characterize four levels of involvement, from most intense to most casual:

- **Internet wizard:** Local expert or above; the person you go to see to find out what you need to know. Often but not always paid to help people; knowledgeable about UNIX, can use file transfer protocols (FTP) to download programs, capable of setting up server organizations. Most users don't have and don't need that level of expertise.
- **Internet dancer:** Something of an enthusiast, the dancer knows about ways to find things on the Internet—but they are the things he or she is interested in; frequent user for specific purposes, but may not know how to meet others' interests; has equivalent of an academic's knowledge of the library, compared to that of a librarian. Some readers of this book have already reached this level of competence, and others will do so after a few dozen hours logged in.
- **Internet talker:** Uses the Internet as the connection to a bulletin board or Usenet group, and spends majority of net time writing and reading within the framework of that group. Knows that there's all sorts of sup-

posedly wonderful information out there, but that isn't what draws this user to the keyboard.
- **Internet message-poster:** Predominant use is to send and receive short messages by e-mail. (The technology makes it just as easy and fast to do this to Sweden or New Zealand as to the office next door.)

During the attempted coup in Russia in 1991, some of those besieged in the Russian Parliament were communicating with the rest of the world—and with each other, in offices three blocks from each other—by way of an e-mail list in San Francisco.

If the medium of the Internet were more familiar, we would see parallels between these and different modes of reading the newspaper or watching television. We may skim the paper at times and read closely at others. There are TV channel surfers and those deeply involved in a few specific programs, those who watch indiscriminately and those who are professionally knowledgeable about television, and so on. These categories are of interest because the Internet is new as a medium, and extremely flexible. It combines elements of phone messages, memos, library resources (for short texts), graffiti, talk radio, swap shop, gossip post, personal ad column, professional work session, magazine, professional journal, fantasy outlet ... whatever its users want it to become. One use is not necessarily better than another: It depends on your purpose in using (and being used by) the medium. In this the Internet is like other media devices that use rhetoric. In the case of electronic media, not only are the technologies still being invented and marketed, but their uses are still being discovered.

PAUSE FOR REFLECTION

One of the fascinating aspects of the Internet at this historical moment is that no one can say what it will ultimately become. Its potential is still being worked out. The analogy might be drawn between the invention of the computer, which makes all this possible, and a car "plunked down in the jungle"—it can do all sorts of things, like "supply lights, bedding, radio communications, tape players, heat, air conditioning, a shield against arrows and bullets, and a loud horn to frighten away fierce animals." But you would never know what the car's manufactured purpose or potential was unless you had it on a highway. "For the first 10 years of the personal computer era..., we have used our computers like cars in the jungle. We have plumbed their powers for processing words and numbers. All too often, home computers have ended up in the closet unused. We have often failed to recognize that most of the magic of computing stems from the exponential benefits of interconnection" (LaQuey p. 33, quoting George Gilder).

One common use is news groups—forums for interchange, in which people associate according to a topic (or topics) of interest and write to each other. (For example, "alt." groups, such as alt.barney.dinosaur.die.die.die.) Many who do not write for these enjoy "lurking," or reading through others' submissions. Or you can subscribe to lists, so that others send you smaller or larger e-mailings on given topics.

Along with virtual communities may come virtual conferences, such as the National Electronic Open Meeting on "People and Their Governments in the Information Age" held May 1–14, 1995. The means of participation were through WWW browser, e-mail, Internet providers such as America OnLine and Prodigy, or 800 number to find a Public Access Site nearby. David Gardner of the National Telecommunications and Information Administration posted this announcement of the virtual conference:

INTRODUCTION

The Information Age offers the opportunity to make government more responsive to the needs of the American people. The Clinton Administration wants to hear from Americans about the type of services and benefits they would like to receive electronically from all levels of government. As a result, the Administration is sponsoring a national electronic open meeting from May 1–14, 1995. . . .

HOW THE MEETING WILL BE CONDUCTED

The meeting will consist of five e-mail discussion groups. . . . Each discussion group will be devoted to a specific topic relating to "People and Their Governments in the Information Age." Each topic will be hosted by one or more experts, who will provide an introductory statement to initiate the discussion and who will also take part in the discussion.

Attendees will participate in the conference by replying to the hosts' introductory statements, posting statements or comments, and by replying to the statements and comments of other attendees. We are seeking the broadest possible level of participation emphasizing input from a wide spectrum of Americans. The open meeting will focus on five topics:

    Services—from emergency help and health care to business licenses.

    Benefits—from Social Security and food stamps to small business grants.

    Information—from declassified secrets and economic statistics to satellite maps.

    Participatory Democracy—ensuring everyone's chance to be heard in a democracy.

    Technology—how the technical portion of electronic government will work.

[Used by permission.]

One of the functions that the Internet and World Wide Web provide is information—and for information a crucial skill is how to find what you need.

Search Procedures

The Internet is essentially a huge volume of documents accessible to users. The problem is therefore not quantity of information, but access. How do you find what you want or need? One common analogy for the Internet compares it to a huge warehouse with no filing system, or at least with one that is unknown to new or casual users. If you want to know what is on shelf 8 in row 32, file 114, there's no convenient way to know except to go and look. As you might imagine, there could easily be valuable material in the warehouse, but you can't find it.

This section will briefly discuss some search procedures for finding material on the Internet. Much of this is essentially the same as searching on-line library catalogs. Don't let the whimsical names of search programs put you off: Gophers and Webcrawlers are highpowered search routines that can be a great help. What is available to you locally will be different from what I have; so the best bet is to check one of the many Internet guides, or talk with your local Internet guru.

One key to the Internet's appeal is its interactive nature. This is in contrast to most media, which are largely one-way, conceived of as "mass media." The net enables contact between millions worldwide, but one at a time. Its interactivity connects it with other computer applications, which are familiar thanks to twenty years of video games (starting with Pong, tank games, Space Invaders, Pac-Man, etc.). The difference, though, is that rather than responding according to the lines determined by a program, you can now get responses from other people who are, like yourself, at a keyboard. No matter how obscure your interest or enthusiasm, it's possible to turn up someone who shares it, or who will adopt interest in order to continue the (virtual) contact. This may serve as an electronic version of the Star Trek fan groups discussed under Readers' Roles in Chapter 3.

Another familiarizing feature is the monitor's resemblance to a television screen. As faster computers find their way into home use, it becomes practical to have images transmitted via World Wide Web, similar to CD-ROM images, so that you can have (for example) a color picture of how the earth looks from the space shuttle, or the face of someone you are talking to over the phone, which changes every quarter second or so, depending on the quality of your modem. You may also find symbols offering identification—the logo of a Usenet group, or a small, discreet advertisement inserted into a text. (Unlike television, the user can choose to click the ad or not, and get a longer pitch: The system's interactivity means that users can, in effect, skim past a thirty-second TV ad or, if desired, turn it into a thirty-minute infomercial.)

Usenet groups fall into several categories. One list, developed by Gene Spafford and edited by David C. Lawrence, provides the following hierarchies (used by permission):

> **comp** Topics of interest to both computer professionals and hobbyists, including topics in computer science, software source, and information on hardware and software systems.
> **humanities** Professional and amateur topics in the arts and humanities.
> **misc** Groups addressing themes not easily classified under any of the other headings or which incorporate themes from multiple categories.
> **news** Groups concerned with the news network and software themselves.
> **rec** Groups oriented toward the arts, hobbies, and recreational activities.
> **sci** Discussions marked by special and usually practical knowledge, relating to research in or application of the established sciences.
> **soc** Groups primarily addressing social issues and socializing.
> **talk** Groups largely debate-oriented and tending to feature long discussions without resolution and without appreciable amounts of generally useful information.

Some names of these groups, particularly under the *alt.* heading, make for entertaining reading in themselves:

alt.adjective.noun.verb.verb.verb	alt.bonehead.joel-furr
alt.aol-sucks	alt.cows.moo.moo.moo
alt.bigfoot	alt.consciousness

alt.fan.furry.muck
alt.fan.ren-and-stimpy
alt.galactic-guide
alt.happy.birthday.to.me
alt.legend.the-bob
alt.lifestyle.barefoot
alt.music.smash-pumpkins
alt.out-of-body
alt.paranet.paranormal
alt.polyamory
alt.religion.islam
alt.religion.scientology

alt.religion.wicca
alt.sex
alt.sex.bondage
alt.sex.fetish.fashion
alt.sex.fetish.the-bob
alt.silly-group.spiffo
alt.sport.foosball
alt.sports.football.pro.jville-
   jaguars
alt.support.asthma
alt.support.attn-deficit
alt.support.big-folks

Like any form of communication, the Internet has its jargon. Those new to the Net (like myself, "newbies") will encounter alien-looking addresses; acronyms (FAQ—frequently asked questions—are one device intended to keep down the number of postings of familiar questions; RTFM is code, with the first two words being "read the" and the last "manual"); adapted smiley faces; and other textual features (use of > for quotations, use of asterisks and caps for *EMPHASIS*, etc.). This jargon is best acquired through use in that format rather than here.

There are search programs accessible to help you find information on the Internet and World Wide Web (WWW). These work more or less as do on-line catalogs in libraries, so you will need to develop your search procedures using these regardless of whether you go on-line yourself or not. However, because the computer brings everything together at one physical location, the search procedures, once you learn to work with them, are potentially simpler than looking for material in the library with print indexes.

The basic principle behind both on-line catalogs in libraries and search protocols such as Gopher and WWW search programs like Lycos and Yahoo is that of hypertext (discussed further below). The old system of card catalogs can be thought of as a very shallow hypertext. Consider the organization diagrammed in Exhibit 11.5. The first division, between "Author–Title" and "Subject," indicates where you should walk: If you are looking for information about the Spanish Civil War, you will want the subject catalog, so you know to look in the fourth card cabinet. Left or right? Here you get to the second level of divisions, among letters of the alphabet—and "S" sends you to the nearest section between the fourth and fifth cabinets. The third level of division is indicated by the labels on each drawer, so you would look well along in the Ss, farther toward the Ts than toward the beginning of the S section—and if you are experienced in these matters, you would read the top row to find the last heading that precedes "Spanish." Then the fourth level would be

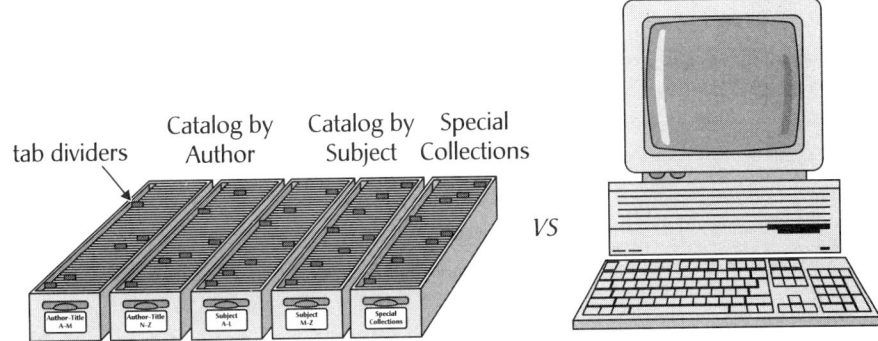

Exhibit 11.5 Organization of a library card catalog.

to scan down the row until you got to the very drawer; the fifth would be to look inside the drawer for the appropriate divider before the words *Spanish Civil War*, and then from that point you would look one by one at each card long enough to tell whether it was relevant.

Within the card drawer you would want to pay attention to "see also" suggestions that are part of the subject headings, and you might want to consider related books that treated your subject as part of a more general consideration (fascism, international relations leading up to World War II, and so on).

This search procedure works reasonably well, and so it is in some ways replicated in on-line catalogs. Rather than a hierarchy based on physical location of cards, however, hierarchies are set up by other principles: Subject or type is one of the most common (are you looking for information of any kind on a subject, or are you interested in browsing by type of files?). Frequently, if you click *subject*, the next level asks for keywords to govern the search. Here, the more specific you can be, the better: If you enter something very general such as *environment* or *media*, the computer will labor long and hard to count all the relevant titles, and then report back to you with an impossibly long list to scan. (Recently I ran a keyword search in Michigan State University's on-line catalog for anything with the word *media*, and it came back with more than 1500 entries—and the program does not allow scanning more than the first 100.)

PAUSE FOR REFLECTION

If you have Internet access, you probably can use a gopher that will give you access from your computer to an on-line catalog for a library at another university. (Try http://moondog.usask.ca/hytelnet.) Check out holdings in two or three such libraries, using a keyword search and checking to see if they have a particular book in their collection.

Search programs are generally self-explanatory, and they vary according to Internet providers. However, there are some pieces of advice that may be useful.

Keep track of how you got where you are. It's not unusual to branch "down" ten or fifteen times in order to get to a useful file or document, and no matter how easy or obvious it seems, you can easily forget how you got there. Write the path down (the cyberspace equivalent of dropping bright pebbles or unwinding string through a maze).

Learn how to save material and download it for printing (particular instructions vary according to the search and transfer programs). Initially, your tendency will be to print everything, but this runs up time and costs for paper and cassettes. Be selective in what you decide to save, what to print, and what to read and make notes about.

Allow time for screw-ups. Electronic media are subject to frequent interruptions. Universities and other providers often close down for a day or two to upgrade material; during peak periods, getting on may be difficult or impossible (often because your fellow students are carrying on in chat groups); or a bad connection, a bug in the software, or a thunderstorm can disrupt your work.

Hypertext

Like some computer games, CD-ROM materials, and databases, much of the Internet is set up as **hypertext.** When using one of the several WWW or Internet aids available, you will notice that several words per screen ("page") are bold or differently colored: point the mouse and click, and these open up. They may offer something as minor as a two-sentence gloss of a term, or as major as a whole branch of inquiry. If you were reading a book, you would have to flip pages to find any explanation longer than a few sentences; but the hypertext equivalent is potentially almost infinite in length.

The crucial change in media that rely on hypertext is this: Hypertext departs from the mostly linear structure of a book. You are expected to read a book from left to right (or, in some other cultures, from right to left or top to bottom) and from front to back, occasionally dipping into other sections if you are browsing or if you find something to scrutinize closely. But any keyed point in a hypertext document can open up for further side trips, while those who believe they know this information need not bother to click those points. Two readers, based on their choices to click or not, will read different hypertext documents.

As a form, hypertext has evolved from print media and computer programs (among other ancestors). It provides a radical departure from the technology of the book, which has been dominant for 500 years at least, because of its shift away from a linear model. We've seen in previous chapters that two readers already do not encounter the same text, because of individual vocabularies, experiences, understandings, and ideologies. They may encounter the same words, phrases, and images, but these are constructed into different unities. Hypertext, however, incorporates these differences into its physical structure, building this branching effect of reading explicitly into its nature. Hypertext acknowledges what published writers have long known, and what newspapers have evolved so as to permit: People do not necessarily (or even usually) read in a straight line. We jump around according to our interests and attention span, and hypertext permits such jumping—although with a more limited field of vision. Often you may know only in the most general terms what you will find when clicking a designated spot, and the experience has more to do with exploring unknown territory (with no physical risk) than with usual models of reading.

Despite its media ancestors, hypertext is still new, and it may be decades before writers and readers think in terms that make full use of the technology. It may be that, in the future, texts like this book will be written originally in hypertext format, so that instead of propping a 600-page book on your lap or tabletop, you will be reading from a CD-ROM disk on a computer screen. Somewhere between three and ten words per "page" will be boldfaced or differently colored, and the reader will click these for definition, further explanation, illustrations, accounts, and so on. The esthetics of "reading" in this fashion—scrolling down a document rather than turning pages—and other matters will take a while to sort out.

PAUSE FOR REFLECTION
Write informally a short "thought experiment": What would your response be to "reading" in a society in which there were no books—in which *all* sources of information came in hypertext format rather than in book form?

Hypertext has the potential to make the reader less the *subject* of the writer, or at least to modify the terms of that subjecthood. (See page 451 in Chapter 8.) That is, when reading according to conventions of print technology you have to stay fairly close to the line of the text. It is possible to skip around a bit, but in many cases that skipping is fairly random: You can pass over a chapter here or there, drawing on chapter titles and headings as rough guides, but you won't know much about what you have missed. Most readers will be assumed to be reading sequentially through the text. But readers of hypertext will follow roughly the pattern of visitors to a theme park. When you go to, say, Disney World, you must pass through the admission gate, but then there are many attractions—rides, gift shops, restaurants, shows, exhibits, and so on. Crowd control—making the visitor a subject—is established at each attraction as a unit, but overall visitors retain the capacity to choose as much or as little as desired. As the example suggests, when you read a book, readerly freedom may be an illusion, not really consumer choice. Hypertext is a closer approximation to "consumer choice"—among carefully circumscribed options—and, for better and for worse, allows a wider diversity of reader paths through a text.

Internet As Source of Information: A Test Case

We have seen some of the potential of the Internet to transform how information is gathered and processed. Also we have seen that the nature of the medium changes what can be said or what is likely to be said. This section will provide illustrations of both positive and negative aspects of electronic media.

Electronic media can offer rapid, almost immediate reactions to current events. Newspapers require physical distribution, but with electronic media speed of distribution is hardly a factor—the time involved is a matter more of readers' time noticing, reflecting, and writing than of anything inherent to the medium. For illustration, we will use electronic accounts of an event in the news in April–May 1995 (close to the time this chapter was first drafted) as a test case for what electronic media can and cannot do well.

Internet enthusiasts point out the medium's democratic tendencies: The words come across the screen in the same way no matter who sends them, with minimal letterhead or signature or other marks of corporate or social status. Those writing in talk groups can and often do adopt alternate personae rather than writing as themselves. As pointed out in the FAQ section of alt.sex, you know *nothing* about the person across the terminal: Factors such as age, appearance, body size, even gender are masked by the form. Some people find this status liberating, others unnerving.

What is seen as democratic about the medium, in the context of e-mail and talk groups, may be a source of difficulties when we are in search of information. In order to believe what we read, we look to the quality of the source—the **ethos,** or character and beliefs, of the source. An illustration: Someone tells me the Charisma is a good car. Whether I trust that information depends on who it is that tells me. Is it someone knowledgeable about cars?

Someone who knows my needs and opinions? A Charisma salesperson? As we have seen, news accounts and other forms of information do not come to us innocently—they come intimately connected with interests (and ultimately ideology), and knowing the source of a piece of information is a vital shortcut to judging how it is going to be accepted.

Some of the information available on the Internet comes with a label. Many mainstream publications now have on-line versions (the *Wall Street Journal, Time, Christian Science Monitor,* and so on), and others will have joined in by the time this sentence sees print. These borrow their status from the print versions. Governmental agencies are major providers of information: casual Internet surfing will show participation by NASA, NOAA, Congress, the White House, CIESIN, and many other agencies. Lobbyists and interest groups make very skilled and precise use of Internet *lists* to call attention to current issues, in order to motivate public response and influence congressional and presidential decisions.

Other information is provided by groups whose names may mask their ideological positioning and agenda. In these cases, the information may be accurate—or it may be manufactured out of thin air. Because readers have even less knowledge about the source of information on the Internet than with other media, we are thrown even more on our own devices to evaluate it.

An illustration may show the capacity for sending both information and reactions through the Internet. One of the major events in the news for the first half of 1995 was the bombing of the Alfred P. Murrah Federal Building in Oklahoma City, by means of a fertilizer bomb set off in a rented truck parked outside. The primary Internet sources for material about the bombing considered here are two subscription lists (two out of potentially hundreds). The first, H-Rhetor, is read largely by professionals whose concern is "rhetorical analysis in the study of history"—academics in history, rhetoric, and sociology, among other fields. The other list is Okla-Net: Its audience was journalists, researchers, and others with a specific interest in the bombing and (potentially) related phenomena such as militia groups and conspiracy theories. Much of the material read for this section was collected and distributed through this list, often with explicit disclaimers about its reliability—in the spirit of "here's some of what's being sent around the Internet on this topic."

This material is of interest for this chapter for two main reasons: It illustrates some ways in which rhetoric is used in electronic media, and it demonstrates some of the potential dangers of incautious acceptance of such materials. The H-Rhetor postings through early May largely dealt with the rhetoric about the bombing: Was the president's public reaction to the tragedy a justified argument that some right-wing rhetoric had gone too far, or was it political opportunism? How broadly should his comments about "hate speech" be construed? Was the effect to restrict free speech or expand it? What are the historical contexts for the existence and visibility of self-described "citizen militias"? Did the bombing constitute "demonstrative rhetoric," to be seen as a kind of rhetoric in itself? How did news and other media construct those who set off the bomb (initially presumed to be from the Middle East) as "the other" in order to identify the crime with flakes and weirdos and people "not like us"? Some of what President Clinton said follows.

Excerpt from President Clinton's speech (as posted on CRTNET)
In this country we cherish and guard the right of free speech. We know we love it when we put up with people saying things we absolutely deplore. And we must always be willing to defend their right to say things we deplore to the ultimate degree. But we hear so many loud and angry voices in America today whose sole goal seems to be to try to keep some people as paranoid as possible and the rest of us all torn up and upset with each other. They spread hate. They leave the impression that, by their very words, that violence is acceptable. You ought to see—I'm sure you are now seeing the reports of some things that are regularly said over the airwaves in America today.

Well, people like that who want to share our freedoms must know that their bitter words can have consequences, and that freedom has endured in this country for more than two centuries because it was coupled with an enormous sense of responsibility on the part of the American people.

If we are to have freedom to speak, freedom to assemble, and, yes, the freedom to bear arms, we must have responsibility as well. And to those of us who do not agree with the purveyors of hatred and division, with the promoters of paranoia, I remind you that we have freedom of speech, too. And we have responsibilities, too. And some of us have not discharged our responsibilities. It is time we all stood up and spoke against that kind of reckless speech and behavior. (Applause.)

If they insist on being irresponsible with our common liberties, then we must be all the more responsible with our liberties. When they talk of hatred, we must stand against them. When they talk of violence, we must stand against them. When they say things that are irresponsible, that may have egregious consequences, we must call them on it. The exercise of their freedom of speech makes our silence all the more unforgivable. So exercise yours, my fellow Americans. Our country, our future, our way of life is at stake. I never want to look into the faces of another set of family members like I saw yesterday—and you can help to stop it. (Applause.)

This citation can serve as an illustration of one of the strengths of the Internet: Those who heard the discussion about the president's remarks, by means of a television sound bite or other news reference, could (given some familiarity with electronic searching) chase down a longer excerpt or even the entire speech and have a better basis for forming a judgment.

Several challenging exchanges took place on H-Rhetor following the bombing on April 19. (As this list offers exchanges between professionals in their field, postings are generally signed with addresses that mark the writer's professional status.) The first comment draws on the bombing as an extension of what has been called "hate speech":

[Regarding] the arrest of one of the apparent bombers in the Oklahoma City tragedy, and interviews on ABC Nightline with their neighbors[:]

I wanted to articulate this: I believe we have descended into a pornography of self-indulgence in the use of hateful terms. It is no longer enough to say, I sure hope Clinton has only one term. Now it must be said that Clinton does not deserve to live—that his wife does not deserve to live. It is not enough to say that you hope your basketball team finds a way to beat the star of the other—you say, I hope that s.o.b. breaks his leg. Or worse, I have heard "hit him hard; make him pay; injure him."

Oh, we don't really mean that. Like we don't really mean those epithets.

But I believe it is self-indulgence; I believe that we use those phrases because there is a thrill there, a thrill of being willing to be dangerous, to be serious.

That is why I call it a form of pornography. Getting a thrill out of sounding tough, dangerous, hardened, baaaad.

It puts together what was bothering me—I know that when "you", the speaker, use an epithet, you really probably don't mean it the way it was meant in, say, Selma Alabama in 1954. Yet you and I both know of its heritage. So—you are able to stay "pure", and yet indulge in impurity. You haven't DONE the deed. Just played with it a little. The rhetoric that they had come to indulge themselves in, in the Michigan Militia, was the rhetoric of war. It is a war. If innocents are slaughtered, so be it.

And the rhetoric, it would appear, finally did come to action. After indulging vicariously in the deed, in speech, someone finally committed it, for the ultimate adrenalin high.

What do others think? (Mary Schweitzer; used by permission)

Several exchanges followed, both positive and negative, on the issue of intensified "rhetoric."

> Thank you...for your insightful analysis of the Oklahoma City events. Adding to the pornographic thrill you talk about is, I think, the relief I sense among many talk show callers and hosts that since they're talking only or mostly to people of their own political persuasion, they're freed from having to make a case for their views. They can just spout (unsupported) claims. Most public conversation on politics, at least as I read or hear it in the media or listen to it in my classrooms, strikes me as an exchange of claims. There's hardly any talk about evidence (too boring, not entertaining enough). This is why I think talk show hosts and politicians who talk in incendiary terms about the evils of the federal govt. (without much evidence beyond a few juicy anecdotes) must share some responsibility for last week's bombing (if in fact the bombers were members of one of these militia groups). (Rick Penticoff; used by permission)

Another response follows a common talk group practice, citing a bit of a previous posting before commenting. (Quotation is made easy by the medium.)

> > about evidence (too boring, not entertaining enough). This is why I think talk show hosts and politicians who talk in incendiary terms about the evils of the federal govt. (without much evidence beyond a few juicy anecdotes) must share some responsibility for last week's bombing (if in fact the bombers were members of one of these militia groups). <
>
> Oh?—that's terribly interesting. In what sense must our "talk-show hosts" and politicos "share some responsibility for last week's bombing?" Are you suggesting that we legislate against such "incendiary" speech? or in any way hold our talk-show hosts and politicos liable?—in what sense are they culpable? Or, are you using the term "responsibility" in some more, vague, abstracted, and therefore meaningless sense—are you merely posturing? Are you suggesting that we criminalize dissent against our Federal government?—whether that dissent be spoken by a terror-bomber or a member of our Congress? (I suppose that the threshold of criminality lies in the term "incendiary"—by what criteria do we judge a given discourse to be "incendiary?") Or: are you merely suggesting that those who engage in such irresponsible speech are, in some vague sense, "evil?"—and therefore worthy of censure upon moral, though not legal grounds? In which case, of course, you haven't criminalized dissent, you've merely ren-

dered those who disagree with you as unworthy of inheriting the Kingdom—you've merely polluted the debate.

Both you and our beloved President, I believe, made a grave error in judgment when you decided to politicize the murderous Oklahoma City terror-bombing: attempting to suggest a link—by means of an elision—between the bombing and expressions of legitimate political opinion, particularly political opinion that is (almost) invariably opposed to our current administration (e.g. ranting right-wing shock-jocks), does not merely smack of the grossest sort of political opportunism—it smacks of something far worse.

Must those who oppose our benevolent Federal Government or its policies only speak to us in gentle words and whispered tones?—must they bow and scrape the dust before they speak? And mustn't those who opposed the Vietnam War, the Gulf War, the war in El Salvador, or who continue to oppose the War on Drugs, and other policies of our Federal Government, also "share some responsibility?"—they too, spoke to us and continue to speak to us in "incendiary terms" against our Federal Government.

Comments follow other comments, in reaction that goes on for some time.

I think [the previous posting's] assessment of Clinton's rhetoric and its effects is just plain wrong. I sat in a very crowded auditorium at Iowa State University a week ago and listened to Clinton address the issue of hate speech and its relationship to the bombing. The crowd responded in an enthusiastic manner (wild applause and whistles) to what Clinton had to say. In addition, public polls that I saw reported on television last week seemed to indicate that the public is giving Clinton a favorable rating for his handling of the Oklahoma situation....

After listening to Clinton speak at ISU, I was extremely surprised to hear news reports in which radio talk show hosts complained about Clinton's attacks on them. The news reports played back Clinton's comments about hate speech in that context. The only hate speech I thought of during Clinton's speech, however, was the material I had heard from members of the Michigan Militia and the white supremacist groups that had been aired on network news programs. I didn't think of Rush, Ollie, or any of the rest (perhaps because I choose not to listen to them, so their words aren't really on my mind). Certainly, Clinton must take responsibility for his words, and their potential effects, just as he is claiming others must. Perhaps the phrase "hate speech" paints with a too-broad brush. But somehow, to me, it seems appropriate; those people who see themselves included in that brush stroke might do well to contemplate the words that they use....

Whatever Clinton says or does will be interpreted politically, if for no other reason than in our democratic system, our president is always a political animal, that is the only way a person becomes and remains president. Clinton (as has every president) has been accused of being "political" even in dealing with natural disasters, so what are the odds that his response to a terrorist attack might somehow be seen as "above" or "beyond" politics? The attack's nature as a political statement is bound to foreground the politics of the country's #1 politician. (Michael Hassett; used by permission)

These exchanges show some of the range of the medium. The professional approach is evident in all the postings: The writer of the first excerpt is interested in *articulating* her concern about kinds of discourse she has observed; the second draws the inference that many of these discussions involve "an exchange of claims" with no reasons or support given; the third challenges the limits to which the first two would go in order to circumvent such speech; and the fourth raises questions about the third posting's interpretation of presidential rhetoric. But the format is much more informal than customary professional exchanges. The first writer frames her account in a first-person narrative (not reproduced here) and uses allusion rather than quotation to illustrate "the use of hateful terms." The second excerpt opens with direct address to the writer of the first, calling her by name (not reproduced here), and frames conclusions in the tentative "I think" form. The third is also informal, but in an angrier key, making some fairly sharp use of sarcasm as well as direct address. (This could be considered a mild instance of "flaming.")

As often happens in disputes about rhetoric, the grounds of discussion have shifted. Specifically in discussions about "hate speech," frequently one set of participants argues on behalf of near-absolute rights of free speech, pointing out that any limitation can ultimately threaten dissent and the expression of ideas, and for that reason our society has to tolerate even (especially) those statements we find abhorrent (such as racism). Another set of participants focuses not so much on what forms of expression are permitted as on what forms are desirable or good—calling not for censorship or suppression but for counterspeech, for the voicing of arguments in opposition. The first two excerpts above raise questions about what is wise or good or proper, while the third returns to the criterion of what is permitted.

ASSIGNMENT

Write informally about problems you see that follow from the conflict discussed above. Rather than staying with the particular examples alluded to by these writers—"hate speech," statements by talk radio hosts, the Ku Klux Klan, or others often mentioned in this regard—work with examples from your own experience, if possible.

Under what circumstances, if any, do you feel it is appropriate to denounce others? (Rapists, child murderers, sports opponents, the opposition party?) What, if anything, do you feel should be done about attacks?

Another contributor to H-Rhetor invites discussion about the effects of labeling in reports about the bombing.

Dear All,

Not that this is actually part of the Clinton rhetoric about the bombing, as far as I am aware (I've gotten more about recent news on his rhetoric from this list than from reading/seeing/hearing on my own)—but I am still intrigued, if that's the word, about the initial act of assigning the blame to "terrorists". My local paper, the San Francisco Chronicle, had a huge headline that read "Terrorist Bomb Stuns Nation." Now, of course, in its way, it was certainly a terrorist bomb.

But it's the context-laden meaning of "terrorist" I am interested in (which my first-year writing class has just been studying). When we Americans read "terrorist", the word has Middle Eastern connotations, and sure enough, people jumped quickly to scapegoat Muslims. A sad, sad commentary on our nation.

My intrigue: if people jumped to scapegoat "foreigners" for this evil action, what happens to these people and their ideas of "evil" when it turns out that it was White Midwestern Americans all along? How do we deal with the goat we're scaping when it's one of us? To a certain extent, remarks on this thread have dealt with some of that (Limbaugh, et alia). I am just curious—do other people have ideas on this, or has anything come out yet to indicate a national attitude (I know, there is no such thing, but I'm speaking very generally)?

Sincerely,

Kirsten Anderson (Used by permission)

The subscription list also serves as a location for reaction to other forms of rhetoric, such as news reports (above) and talk radio. In the following excerpt, note that because e-mail does not permit underlining, the convention for emphasizing a word or phrase is to put a line before and after.

> I've listened to Rush Limbaugh's radio show pretty regularly since 1989, and I've noticed something interesting since the OK City bombing. After the bombing, but before McVeigh was arrested, there was some widespread speculation that some brand of 'Middle-Eastern' terrorism was responsible. During that period, Limbaugh suggested that the appropriate (meaning correct & right) response, should that be the case, would be for the U.S. to go to war over it; he also said that he wasn't sure if the country had the political will to do it (war with whom wasn't specified).
>
> After McVeigh was arrested and Clinton spoke in OK City, Limbaugh has worked very hard to sell the idea that looking into motives for the bombing is beside the point, and that we ought to concentrate on catching the individuals responsible for the act (yes, I think the concurrent discussion on the list re individuals is pertinent). Limbaugh has worked hard to characterize the perpetrators as anarchists and nuts, and has complained about them being characterized as "right-wing extremists," arguing that the same term has been used to characterize the Republican program in Congress—and unfairly conflates the two. Motive, he argues, has nothing to do with the situation; only individual responsibility is involved.
>
> What I find particularly interesting is that this is the reverse of Limbaugh's usual rhetorical method. His usual practice (which he is, I think, very good at), is to find as extreme an example of someone he opposes as possible, and then use that person or group to characterize the entire position. He does this with feminism, the ecology movement, and liberalism in general. When he gives his general critique of liberalism, one of the things he emphasizes is its place on the continuum: liberal–socialist–communist as all being merely not-all-that-different aspects of the same thing. Now he is suddenly at the other end of that kind of thinking. To try to escape from the kind of all-consuming identification that he normally practices, he (and others) are spending time making _distinctions_ (e.g., he's not an anarchist [like the bombers]; he doesn't want _no_ government, he wants _less_ government, etc.). From a rhetorical point of view, the change in the style of his show when he does this is noticeable: his strength is as a

polemicist, and the energy of the show suffers when he has to shift gears to an explanatory mode. (Paul Turpin <turpin@scf.usc.edu> Graduate student Annenberg School for Communication University of Southern California, Posting 28 April 1995; used by permission)

Most discussion via electronic media has much less reflection about rhetoric than do these postings. With the other list, Okla-Net, those subscribing are principally journalists; some other researchers and interested parties also took part. A secondary part of this list was material found in electronic circulation and passed on, with or without comment (usually with an exaggerated distance, more or less as with stories found in tabloids). Journalists' professional skepticism is raised by some of the claims in the report that follows and some of those cited below. Some of the exchanges have the tone of coffee-room chat, as with the parenthetical opening of this report:

{Purloined from the "American Patriot Fax Network." I would have thought that an underground fax network would carry stuff from the Internet (of which there *is* some), but for some reason, it's got it's own whole world of wild stuff. I'll repost tonight when I have more time. Stay tuned—got the GAO Budget Report on the Treasury Dept from Aug. 1993, some wild accusations from a retired L.A. law officer regarding the weapons at Waco, but this was the best, so I had to post it *now*:} {Oh, yeah, all signatures on my copy have been whited-out and are represented here with 'XXXXXX'}

Affidavit of XXXXXXXXXXXX

I hereby certify that I make the following statement of my own free will and do so under the penalty of perjury.

I am an attorney employed by the UNITED STATES JUSTICE DEPARTMENT, my place of employment is, Constitution Avenue & 20th, Washington, D.C. I am a seven (7) year employee of the United States Government.

On February 20, 1995, I was asked to be part of a team that was to prosecute a group of terrorists who had blown-up a government facility. This group was represented as being a training exercise that would develop into an autonomous branch of the Justice Department....

The material goes on to describe in some detail an exercise by the federal government involving the bombing of a federal building that the anonymous deponent says was identical to one he'd seen a photograph of earlier that month.

> I have requested that I be given safe haven as a result of this disclosure, and it has been granted. I am and have terminated [sic] my employment with the Justice Department....
> DATED THIS 21ST DAY OF APRIL, 1995
>
> XXXXXXXXXXXXXXXXXXX
>
> WITNESSES:
>
> XXXXXXXXXXXXXXXXXXXXXXXXXX
> Attorney at Law
>
> XXXXXXXXXXXXXXXXXXXXXXXXXX
> Member U.S. House of Representatives
>
> XXXXXXXXXXXXXXXXXXXXXXXXXX
> Attorney at Law
>
> XXXXXXXXXXXXXXXXXXXXXXXXXX
> Lt. Col. U.S. Army Retired
>
> XXXXXXXXXXXXXXXXXXXXXXXXXX
> Private Business Owner and Citizen

PAUSE FOR REFLECTION
What are the effects of having a communication in the *form* of a legal document, but with no possibility of confirming its truth because of the means of distribution?

Most postings on this Okla-Net over May and June 1995 were given to items similar to the two categories above: either news dispatches or "you're not going to believe this" excerpts from conspiracy groups. Other examples, too lengthy to use in this chapter, included transcripts of a radio show by "Mark from Michigan," a figure who surfaced in connection with the Nichols brothers who figured in the bombing investigation, and of an interview with a woman who took the various threads of the conspiracy in the direction of direct presidential involvement. Besides the bombing per se, postings also discussed the Aum Shinrikyo group in Japan, also in the news at the time; made comparisons with other "cults"; and of course talked about militia groups.

These items read more like news reports and less like analysis of their rhetoric or historical background, as with H-Rhetor's postings.

Cyberporn

Another illustration of interaction between electronic media and more established forms can be seen in the flurry over what was highlighted in a cover story by *Time* magazine as **cyberporn.** Pornography is notoriously hard to define; the concept is subjective and subject to variations in local standards, and it does not become easier through association with computers. What is of interest for understanding media is how "research" of at best questionable validity was inflated into a matter for national attention, and how this attention continues to color public thinking about the Internet.

Time's initial article (July 3, 1995) was based on a study conducted by an undergraduate engineering major, Martin Rimm. Rimm used computer software developed by Brian Reid, director of the Network Systems Laboratory, to count the number of times certain Usenet groups were accessed—his choice of seventeen adult Bulletin Board Systems (BBSs) that he considered "pornographic"—by students at Carnegie-Mellon University during one week in January 1995. Rimm got his study accepted for publication in the *Georgetown Law Review*—under the title "Marketing Pornography on the Information Superhighway: A Survey of 917,410 Images, Descriptions, Short Stories, and Animations Downloaded 8.5 Million Times by Consumers in Over 2000 Cities in Forty Countries, Provinces, and Territories." As has been pointed out by critics of the study, a law journal is not a usual medium for publication in the social sciences; and in this case the author chose a journal with no rigorous review process (Godwin). Rimm then used that agreement for publication as a means of interesting a reporter at *Time* in the story, on the unusual condition that the study not be shown to external reviewers.

The resultant *Time* article touched off a storm of protest, not only by defenders of freedom of the press or speech (or whatever term applies to the Internet), but by those doing any sort of research with statistics. A very few examples are cited below; as of early 1996, many more could be traced through a keyword search on "cyberporn."

- Brian Reid, who invented the software used in the study, has been working on ways to measure Usenet readership for nearly a decade. He believes it is impossible "to get measurements whose accuracy is within a factor of 10 of the truth." Reid notes that such studies are meaningful only for tracing change over time, not on the basis of one survey (Reid).

- Carnegie-Mellon students do not constitute a representative sample of the population at large, being 75 percent men and more highly skilled with computers than average university students.
- Rimm's study counts *all* access the same—a quick peek, a comment aroused or outraged, a downloading of an allegedly pornographic image, all get counted.
- "[I]f you happened to peek at alt.binaries.pictures.erotica.gerbils and either punted the group in disgust (marked all messages read) or just read one misposted message about anti-porn legislation, his snooper-software will count you as having viewed all the nasty pictures on a.b.p.e.g. You deviant, you. —Declan [McCullagh]."
- The study grossly inflates what it purports to count. Donna L. Hoffmann and Thomas P. Novak note that the figure of "917,410 sexually explicit pictures, descriptions, short stories and film clips" quoted in *Time* turns out to be "a total of 2830 images for analysis" on the Usenet; "out of 11,576 World Wide Web sites in December 1994, Rimm found only nine web sites, which is only eight one-hundredths of one percent, contained R or X-rated Adult Visual Material" (Hoffman and Novak). Any survey done of such a small group cannot be legitimately extended to "Over 2000 Cities in Forty Countries, Provinces, and Territories."
- *Time*'s figure of "83.5% of images" as pornographic is based on a small proportion of Usenet groups, primarily those with "sex" in the titles in commercial BBS services—compared to thousands of such groups having little or nothing to do with such content. This is comparable to assuming that the photographs to be found in *Playboy* and *Penthouse* are representative of those in all U.S. magazines. Or, as Mike Godwin (Electronic Freedom Foundation) puts it, "Even from the abstract, it was apparent that the bulk of Rimm's data came from 68 'adult' BBSes—to generalize from commercial porn BBSes to 'the Information Superhighway' would be like generalizing from Times Square adult bookstores to 'the print medium'" (Godwin).
- There are ethical expectations for researchers in the social sciences involving (among other things) getting the informed consent of those studied, and not carrying on studies that will harm the subject. In this case, no one's consent was gained beforehand for investigation of what the CMU students reasonably believed was a private matter (their computer records), and the university began steps to censor access to the Internet as a result of the study (Jim Thomas).
- Not relevant to the logic of the study, but connected with ethos: At the same time he was gathering data and alerting CMU officials to the fact that their students were downloading "pornography," Rimm was marketing a man-

ual called *The Pornographer's Handbook: How to Exploit Women, Dupe Men and Make Lots of Money* (Brock Meeks).

PAUSE FOR REFLECTION

Think back on news coverage and other material on "cyberporn": How much have you heard about "pornography" on the Internet? How much of that can be traced back to the study discussed above, hopelessly flawed and published without peer review?

The *Time* version of the article was amplified by accompanying artwork. In addition to the cover illustration—a wide-eyed, open-mouthed child staring across a computer keyboard—the magazine featured drawings of a child staring into a dark alley at a computer with a lollipop, and of a man having sexual relations with a computer.

Conveniently timed publication of this story found its way into discussions in Congress, where Senator James Exon was holding hearings on a Communications Decency Act designed to outlaw not only "pornography" but "obscenity" on the net; the *Time* article was read into the *Congressional Record* by Senator Grassley.

> MR. GRASSLEY. Mr. President, there is an article from *Time* magazine and an article from the *Spectator* magazine that I ask unanimous consent to have printed in the record at the end of my remarks.
>
> THE PRESIDING OFFICER. Without objection, it is so ordered....
>
> MR. GRASSLEY. Mr. President, this morning I want to speak on a topic that has received a lot of attention around here lately. My topic is cyberporn, and that is, computerized pornography. I have introduced S. 892, entitled the Protection of Children from Computer Pornography Act of 1995.
>
> This legislation is narrowly drawn. It is meant to help protect children from sexual predators and exposure to graphic pornography.
>
> Mr. President, Georgetown University Law School has released a remarkable study conducted by researchers at Carnegie Mellon University. This study raises important questions about the availability and the nature of cyberporn. It is this article I ask to have printed in the record.
>
> Later on, on this subject, some time during the middle of July, I will be conducting hearings before the full Judiciary Committee to fully and completely explore these issues. In the meantime, I want to refer to the Carnegie Mellon study, and I want to emphasize that this

is Carnegie Mellon University. This is not a study done by some religious organization analyzing pornography that might be on computer networks.

The university surveyed 900,000 computer images. Of these 900,000 images, 83.5 percent of all computerized photographs available on the Internet are pornographic. Mr. President, I want to repeat that: 83.5 percent of the 900,000 images reviewed—these are all on the Internet—are pornographic, according to the Carnegie Mellon study.

PAUSE FOR REFLECTION
Note the slippage between the information provided in *Time* magazine's article and how it was discussed in Congress ("the Carnegie Mellon study," "83.5 percent of all computerized photographs available on the Internet are pornographic").

Of interest on this issue was the reaction on the Internet: Not only were there angry postings denouncing Rimm's study, *Time* magazine, and others such as the Christian Coalition who used the misleading accounts in mailings; but documents relating to the entire affair were immediately made available via the web. (All the texts cited above were downloaded from a posting at Carnegie-Mellon in October 1995.) Just as the Net makes it easy to multiply and disseminate rumors about the government or other objects of conspiracy theories, it also makes it easy for responsible critiques of media treatments to be answered.

ASSIGNMENT
If you have access to World Wide Web, use a search procedure to look up documents on the cyberporn controversy. Keep track of your search paths and compare sources with others.

Does your college involve itself in any sort of censorship of, or restriction of access to, electronic media? If so, who is responsible for making such decisions, on what grounds, and with what procedures?

How does this issue of restricted access compare to the treatment of printed materials in the bookstore or college library? To what students living on campus may buy or subscribe to privately? To what is legally accessible for those living off campus?

With electronic media, you have to take even more responsibility than with mainstream media for what you accept. No reader of contemporary U.S.

media—including television talk shows, tabloids, radio talk shows, and the customary sorts of deceptive rhetoric practiced by many advertisers—should need to be reminded that the audience must be on guard against any and all media texts.

But in addition to the usual difficulties of calculating for self-interest (yours and theirs) and watching for logic traps, reading texts on the Internet presents additional problems. First, it's relatively easy to set up as an Internet provider. In addition to organizations that are relatively known quantities—on-line news services by established news organizations, information services offered by governmental agencies, and the like—others provide material without the sorts of oversight and screening given by professional organizations. Indeed, the absence of such regulation is part of the Internet's attraction.

PAUSE FOR REFLECTION
The Internet doesn't push any texts at users—users have to look for material. Donna Hoffmann, an associate professor of marketing at Vanderbilt and an expert in Internet marketing, points out that "When you watch TV it comes right to you, but on the Internet, you're in an environment with 30 million channels. It's up to you to decide where to go. You don't have to download the images on alt.sex.binaries."

The material cited above should serve as a sample of texts available in "cyberspace." Some are seriously meant and can be dangerous; some are outlets for collaborative fiction and verbal play, which is positive. And there are good and interesting materials produced by individuals from the margins of institutions. So, on the whole, discourse is richer for the existence of the Net. But the benefits of access and having one's say must be weighed against the absence of interpretive criteria for believability.

Note that familiar rhetorical devices are in use in public discussions about the Internet. For example, in news accounts and in speeches in Congress, speakers present a few selected examples and silently allow the inference that these are typical. (See page 579, under Bad Rhetoric.) Yes, sexually explicit material is available on the Net, along with bomb recipes, "flaming," and many other questionable sorts of texts. But these are a small proportion of the totality, whose alleged harm should be weighed against the usefulness of the valuable materials.

It's an old debate, one going back to television, films, and print: Each new medium makes available texts which *some* of us believe *others* of us should not have. (Do you ever hear anyone argue that *they themselves* should not have access to anything?) The deciding group (that with power to control access) may include parents, educators, cultural leaders, religious groups, and governmental officials; the group decided *for* may involve children, teenagers, lower classes, deviants, or "the masses." Those pronouncing on the dangers of "cyberporn" are the equivalents of those who denounced *Lady Chatterley's Lover* or *Lolita* in the 1950s. Every supposedly new threat to public morals can be seen as the continuation of the age-old tension—between individual freedom of access and collective responsibility to restrict texts so as to ensure that they fit current ideology. In societies more hierarchical than the United States, the task is simpler: Established cultural organizations, social groups, the church, and so on hold much less questioned positions of authority. But the fact that the United States is designed on the liberal ethos of individual choice puts advocates of social control in a far more delicate position—particularly as they often speak strongly for individual choice in other frameworks, such as the "free market."

As you think about these issues, remember that many participants in the debate have vested interests. Print and broadcast media—which publicize the debates, keeping them on the agenda—stand to lose some customers. Hours spent surfing the Internet are hours not spent reading magazines or newspapers or watching television, and the medium therefore represents a potential drop in revenue. Perhaps more crucial than numbers is the threat to prestige: Material delivered by computer does not now depend on a news organization to filter it in accordance with professional journalistic canons, or to arrange it in keeping with the sense of importance implied by the hierarchy behind front-page and lead stories.

Part of the agenda behind media coverage of the Internet might be to encourage potential Net users to gravitate toward "safe" systems such as America OnLine and CompuServe, rather than the unpoliced use available publicly through some universities and libraries. A parallel exists here with radio: Initially radio was free and public, but shortly the first free stations were shifted over to commercial licensees. Something of the sort may happen with the Net as well—this would be another instance of control through economics rather than through censorship.

Another consideration: If attention is directed to texts potentially available to minors or terrorists (foreign ones, that is—not the homegrown variety), then the public will be diverted from the prospect of quasi-military groups already active and stockpiling firearms. Calls for investigation of government agencies can be useful in such a diversion. Rhetorical devices used to direct public opinion to other times and places is evident in several of the excerpts printed in this section.

Electronic communications are being used by other activist groups besides conspiracy theorists. One "Online Activism Resource List" gives sixty lists ranging from the American Library Association to the United Church of Christ to discussions of cable and computer regulations to the Sierra Club to discussions of new gophers to help for "internauts." The list is available through the Electronic Frontier Foundation (info@eff.org), courtesy of "CRAM: The Cyberspatial Reality Advancement Movement."

The Internet, then, is like other technologies: Whether these facilitate communication, like electronic media or, before that, television, radio, cinema, photography, or print itself, or whether they are involved with other matters, technologies can be used with thoughtfulness in regard to their effects on others, or can be exploited in spite of their effects on others. They can be used to maintain or to counter dominance. They can entertain or call out the troops. Now that we have examined some of the more extreme electronic texts above, it might be appropriate to shift attention to some more academically routine information gathering.

Library Material

Any treatment of ways for you to expand your media resources should mention, at least briefly, the one place in any educational institution that is specifically devoted to that task: the library. You are probably familiar with using the library, to some extent; this section of the chapter will concentrate largely on ways that technological developments such as electronic media have affected how you find information.

Searching for additional information, or for others' perspectives on a subject, can be beneficial at all stages of a project. You might want to browse for material early on, just after the brainstorming or clustering phases of prewriting, so that you can improve your sense of what others might expect on a topic. Or you might be gathering material during drafting or early in the revision portion, so as to provide additional support and authority for your contentions. Or you might undertake library work late in the revision phase. Material gathered from other sources can be useful both in extending your own knowledge of a subject and in helping you frame that knowledge rhetorically so as to make it effective for your audience.

First, a basic problem: *We don't know what we don't know.* This is not a truism or a redundancy, but a problem basic to knowledge. You have to know a little bit about a subject to realize what there is still to learn about it. If you are completely in the dark, it makes it impossible to search for information, in the library or elsewhere. I have a pretty good idea that I don't know much about nuclear physics, at least beyond the *Our Friend the Atom* level—but the reason I possess this knowledge is that I had physics in high school and college, subscribe to *Scientific American,* and thus have some inkling of the fact that there's much terrain in that field that I haven't explored (and won't). Realizing the extent of my ignorance, then, is the first stage in my finding something out.

Knowing that you need to know more is part of getting a "feel" for your audience. In addition to needing to find information because of the nature of a subject, you need to think about its rhetorical uses. Most often, your writing self will be one that knows at least something on the topic at hand; and a fundamental way of taking a convincing position with an audience is to have a persona that brings relevant material in with ease and assurance.

One way to conceive of the problem is to think of a set of concentric circles (though a network or spider web might be a more precise analogy). The innermost circle represents your own observation based on experience. You know about matters directly pertaining to you—the specific cars you have owned, your dog's behavior on walks, the way your own body feels and reacts to sunshine and atmospheric pollen, words and ideas you have encountered. These and other experiences make up a wide pool of data—but a small pool compared to the total potential. The next largest circle would represent what others (parents, friends, teachers, ministers, people on the street) have told you personally from their experience. (Although this circle is larger based on number of sources, it is smaller in relation to the total data that each of us depends on.) The third circle is that normally considered to be the province of media: observations made by others and available to you. Everything now known is contained in this circle—though there are many potentially knowable facts which are not yet there, such as the number of stars in our galaxy, whether there are other intelligent forms of life, the origin of the universe, or how to track atmospheric data sufficient to predict specific weather conditions a month in advance.

(To simplify the analogy, I've been assuming that what is in question is a matter of information—for example, average July temperatures in Anchorage—rather than a matter of interpretation—for example, whether your [grand]parents would enjoy a summer tour of Alaska. What you do with information you obtain, after all, is not something to be looked up in the library.)

Looking up reports of others' experiences is itself an experience, one which is finite. You can look up anything, but you can't look up everything. The problem is access: What you might wish to know is probably out there, but you need some search procedures likely to help you find it.

With some subjects, you can go only so far with your personal experience. You may have heard something from an acquaintance or read a story in the newspaper that piqued your interest—how do you go about finding out more? How can you use what you can find to build your authority and plausibility on a subject? And how can you improve your perspectives on a topic? You can do all these things better by improving your ability to work with resources, such as those commonly available in college or public libraries.

A common feature of first-year writing courses is the "research paper," in which students are expected to show competence at summarizing, paraphrasing, and effectively quoting material in their essays. This is a crucial ability to develop for college success, and it should not be passed over. But frequently students (mis)conceive of the "research paper" as gathering information and then designing the paper around what they have managed to find. A more appropriate sequence would be to write what can be done on a topic—write what interests you or what you believe to be important—from within that first circle; and then look for related material from the other two. **Research,** then, should be a function of the need to use media to improve your knowledge on a subject.

When doing research, be careful that you don't take sources for granted. Just because a statement is in print doesn't mean it's unexceptionable truth. Many major publishers have careful editorial procedures, but some mistakes slip through—and other publishers pretty much print what they are hired to print. Part of the skill of reading books is reading the publishers' reputations and knowing which are seen as most careful, which less professional. Increasingly, some published material tends to slant evidence in order to make it fit a predisposed conclusion.

(You should probably suppress the impulse to look in the encyclopedia. Material in print encyclopedias suffers from a long time lapse between writing and publication; additionally, encyclopedias are necessarily very general and sparse with bibliographies.)

A significant change in research methods began in the 1960s with easy availability of copy machines in libraries. Previously, students had to copy out or paraphrase relevant passages from books and journals on note cards or in other formats. After copy machines became widespread, it became relatively cheap and easy to Xerox whole chapters or articles and highlight or underline relevant passages. Both note cards and copies have pitfalls, however: On cards, you must be careful to distinguish passages taken from other texts from your own thinking on the subject. This is one reason keeping a journal for metacommentary on research is important: Metacommentary, or your own comments on the search process, can help you keep straight what are your own ideas and what are insights gathered from others. As for copying materials, you have to strike a balance between expense and convenience. The easiest procedure may be to photocopy everything in sight—but then you have the task later of sorting through a lot of paper, most of which will go straight to the recycling bin. Or you can think carefully as you work, transcribing materials into your own handwriting (or onto a laptop)—but that makes for the maximum of time in the library. The best plan is to expect everything to take longer than you think it should, and budget time for drifting about.

Even apart from the easy availability of copiers, libraries have changed dramatically even since the mid-1980s, and they will continue to change as more standard resources become available in database or CD-ROM format. (Eventually, many resources may generally be available *only* in electronic formats.) What is available in your library will probably differ from what could be found in others. This section of the chapter will provide a sample search so as to indicate the kinds of search procedures you might want to develop on a topic, rather than taking up specific indexes to be found in some libraries but not others.

At one time it might have been thought that electronic media would eventually substitute for print media, allowing for savings in space, costs, and personnel. It appears now that the last two (at least) are unlikely. While keeping back issues of journals on microfilm or microfiche does save space, it may or may not be cheaper to bind back volumes than to buy reduced versions from University Microforms. Indexes, for the present, are commonly produced in both print and CD formats, and during some transitional period, most libraries will have to buy *both*. If you have the electronic version, then you have to buy the hardware to read it as well as CDs with the information. (Will CDs be around as long as books have been?) While both forms are being maintained, there's little space being saved, and no cost saving.

Some of what was said in the Search Procedures section about finding things on the Internet also applies to on-line catalogs. Libraries now have generally gone to on-line catalogs, though some have kept card catalogs for materials acquired before a cutoff date. On-line cataloging makes it possible to check catalog holdings whether an item is in a distant library or on the shelf where you are. This can be a great help when you are doing a bibliography and have forgotten to write certain information down.

Electronic formats may help a little or a lot with searches. As with the discussion of searching on-line sources for information, you have the use of a powerful computer to find material stored electronically. If you know the author or title, these can be entered, and immediately you have the call number, a brief description, and (a great time-saver) information as to whether what you are looking for is checked out or not. With most on-line catalogs, if you have the author's last name only, you will get a list of others nearby alphabetically, and you can scan these in hopes of jogging your memory.

But the most powerful advantage to on-line catalogs is with the subject search. The library's mainframe computer will scan all the holdings and give you a list of what's there on a subject. But you have to use such a search carefully: If the search term is too general (too inclusive), you will get far more titles than you can narrow down conveniently. One way of limiting such a search is to add a term—say, media + U.S.; media + violence; media + advertising (specific means of doing this vary with the system).

Before you begin fiddling with the on-line catalog, it may be worth the time to look up your subject in the Library of Congress Subject List (usually available near the catalog terminals). What seems to you like an easy and obvious keyword may not be the way the subject is filed in the LC system; also as with a thesaurus, you may turn up some related terms that will be more useful to you.

Particularly with media-related topics, your most current sources may not be in book form. It often takes two years or more for material to find its way into publication in book form, then to be distributed, cataloged, and made available in the library. And while the principles in media-related topics often remain the same, particular instances shift about. For example, Ben Bagdikian's book *The Media Monopoly* pointed out in the early 1980s that media organizations in the United States tended to consolidate and become concentrated, thus limiting the diversity of sources available to the public. Bagdikian and his publishers have brought out three revised editions (at least) since then, in order to bring the particular illustrations up to date. The phenomenon being described remains the same; but if you wanted to locate up-to-date information on matters such as corporate mergers, or find out whether it is permissible for newspaper publishers to own television stations, other sources might be important, because Congress might have changed the law since publication of the latest edition (or the edition available to you) of the book. Therefore, working with media often requires consulting periodicals.

Access to information in periodicals can sometimes be gotten through indexes, although sometimes it's a matter of blind luck. A good place to start would be the *Reader's Guide to Periodical Literature.* Print versions of the *Reader's Guide* are usually bound by year; more recent listings are available in quarterly and monthly versions. This means that a topic needs to be two months old, at least, in order for it to appear. You may need to consult several volumes to find what you want. The *Reader's Guide* is organized alphabetically by subject, but with an index for authors as well. (Some of this may be simplified with a CD version.)

The *Reader's Guide* is of use primarily for popular journals. If your topic takes you toward more scholarly material, you should look to other sources. For language and literature, the *MLA International Bibliography* is the standard. *The Education Index, Social Sciences Index, The Humanities Index, The Business Index,* and others apply to those fields.

If you need to consult newspapers in addition to magazines for your topic, then several indexes may be of use. Check first to see what newspapers are kept on file in your library. Most common would be the *New York Times* and *Washington Post,* together with whatever state and local newspapers apply. These should be supplemented with databases such as *Newsbank.* As a test case, I did a search on this index for *militias* and found 159 citations through June 3, 1995. It is possible to read the articles on screen, then print them on paper (with local limits on materials permitted) or copy them to disk for later use—all this takes time, and one problem with library searches on databases may be waiting in line to use them. Materials on this subject that I printed up included the following: a speech on the subject from the *Congressional Record* by Representative Schroeder of Colorado; articles on militia groups in the *Philadelphia Inquirer,* the *Washington Post,* the *Arizona Republic,* the *Indianapolis News,* the *Los Angeles Times,* the *Chicago Tribune;* and reports from two wire services, the AP News Service and Reuters. In addition, I was able to scan references in other newspapers such as the *St. Petersburg Times,* the *Vancouver Sun,* the Memphis *Commercial Appeal,* the *Dallas Morning News,* and so on. Most of these are not available in my local library, and local coverage does still have a very different flavor from national.

You should note, however, that what you get in a database is just the text of the article; the medium is somewhat different from the form in which most readers find it, in the middle of advertisements and photographs and other articles, with continuations inside somewhere. Often the electronic version is the full text as written, whereas the printed version may have been cut to fit space available. What you have, then, is the article as it might have been read in its most complete form; but many readers would have skimmed part of it, perhaps not paying full attention, as is often the way with newspaper materials.

Newsbank is an electronic database, relying on transmission as needed. Other indexes make use of CDs: for example, *ProQuest.* (Keep in mind that, as with electronic databases, you are getting just the article, without its context in the magazine or journal proper. CD-ROM formats are of little use, for example, when you are working with print advertisements.)

The hope that electronic media would save in library personnel was probably misguided, at least in the short run. Any savings on these media are likely to be counterbalanced by the need for library personnel to work as information brokers, helping users learn to adopt to ever-changing forms.

You should probably work with a hierarchy of questions, something like those below, in order to shorten your search:

- What indexes, data bases, and so on apply to your subject?
- What forms of media are most likely to be relevant to your topic?

- How can dates, times, and so forth be used to narrow search fields?
- How much is "enough" on this topic? What will the audience expect, what will the length of the writing task allow, and what are you ready to provide?

Unless you are very fortunate, you will have to contend not only with the unfamiliar nature of the search for material, but also with others using these resources. This may mean signing up in advance to use a database or CD index, or waiting for a catalog terminal to open up. Be prepared to work efficiently when you do get a crack at these resources.

Most libraries are set up for printing citations, at least at some terminals. As with the use of microfilmed materials or the question of what and how much to photocopy, you have to determine the importance of this service. Printing everything up costs time and materials; but the printer can usually get call number and title on the page faster than you can.

Some Reservations about the Internet

The readings below, by Herbert J. Gans and M. Kadi, offer some further food for thought on interactive electronic media.

HERBERT J. GANS

The Electronic Shut-Ins: Some Social Flaws of the Information Superhighway
The American business community believes firmly that technological progress cannot and should not be halted, and its promoters paint glorious utopias for every new technological breakthrough. The promoters of the latest breakthrough, the information superhighway, come with their own utopia, which portrays an ever more comfortable, convenient and enjoyable culture of consumption.

Being promoters, however, they forget that many past breakthroughs and utopias failed to satisfy the demands (old or new) of actual consumers and are now ignored even by technological museums. The notion of technological determinists—that if you build new technology people will come—is assured only in the movies, where such people can be ordered from Central Casting.

Unfortunately, media professionals and researchers are sometimes also overly infatuated with new technologies and their associated utopias, and a considerable amount of media theorizing is a spin-off from technological determinism. Nonetheless, whether the superhighway's promised innovations in activities such as home employment, shopping, banking, interactive television (including television socializing) and the 500-channel television menu, will actually be salable to real people remains to be seen.

Obviously, the promoters of the superhighway seek to make their customers more dependent on their phones, computers and television sets than ever before. The desired dependence makes good business sense, for presumably many of the new phone calls, computer input and TV button pushes required by the highway have a price that will appear on the next monthly bill.

However, that dependence also has what sociologists call a latent function, an unintended and apparently unrecognized effect: It could turn the highway travelers into virtual electronic shut-ins. If customers use the highway as envisioned by its promoters, they would be more tied to their homes than the fabled "couch potatoes" (whose frequency, incidentally, has never been empirically demonstrated).

I use the term shut-ins purposely, for in the past sick and old people imprisoned in their own homes have always been pitied. Pity for shut-ins reflects the fact that we are social animals, requiring a good deal of regular social contact, of various degrees of intensity and closeness, in order to function properly. In fact, other people are good medicine, for we know from health research that adequate "social support" is an important factor in recovering from serious illness, and the lack of such support is correlated with higher rates of mortality.

Some of that regular social contact comes from the activities that the superhighway promoters now want to move into the living room. Shopping, albeit a chore for some, is an opportunity or an excuse to meet friends, neighbors and even just familiar-looking strangers. That opportunity, immortalized by the mythic country general store, is still available even in the giant shopping malls, but it would shrink severely if people do as much of their shopping at home as the highway promoters hope. In addition, electronic home shopping would require an increased trust in the merchants who sell basic necessities and in their merchandise, at least until programmers find a way to computerize squeezing the tomatoes.

Even fully interactive television is not the same as face-to-face social contact. The belief that, in the future, people would hold many of their gatherings on interactive television seems dubious, except during snowstorms and floods. For one thing, the social equivalents of squeezing the tomato, such as face-to-face interaction, gestures and other body languages, do not come across so well on television. For another, today a lot of people still associate social gatherings with the sharing of food and drink, an ancient way of expressing closeness that would be fatally diminished by transit through optic fiber.

Admittedly, the superhighway could make life more pleasant for those already shut in, as well as for the socially isolated and people with distinctive interests who already crowd today's computer highways. However, traditional social gatherings continue to be immensely important. For example, virtually all the studies indicate that the frequency of family visiting today has not decreased, despite all the changes in the modern family and the punditry about its decline. Television viewing may take up more hours in people's leisure time, but it is a routine activity, while visiting remains a more special one.

Even the 500-channel TV set has some unrecognized social flaws. As a routine activity, television viewing is also a low-intensity one, for people often watch while they are talking and conducting other family or household business. (This may help to explain why interactive television schemes have taken off so slowly.) But choosing one of 500 channels is not a low-intensity activity, and I wonder how many people are willing to expend the time and energy to make such a choice. The breakfast food industry today supplies lots of alternatives for the morning meal, but it has not yet required customers to choose from among 500 alternative cereals, granola bars and egg dishes.

Ultimately, even in its most prosaic forms, social life is not only a basic necessity but a basic pleasure. Perhaps the new technology, or other as yet unpredictable future events, will end people's dependence on today's social life and social support systems, but I am skeptical. Actually, the highway promoters' utopia is currently a staple of dystopian fiction. Novels set in futuristic cities or among survivors of a nuclear war are often populated by characters who are shut in their dwellings to protect themselves against inhospitable climates or rampaging mobs of one kind or another.

Last but not least, the promoters of technological utopias, and even the theorists of technological determinism, rarely mention the price tag attached to many innovations. But if the highway is to be successful, it has to make a profit. In the economy toward which we seem to be moving, however, in which the reasonably secure and decently paying job is on the decline, disposable income and impulse spending, on which the living room sectors of the highway depend, will become scarcer for many. At that point, the financially strapped may rediscover a truth from an earlier era: that the cheapest leisure-time activity, other than "free" television, is visiting with the neighbors.

[Reprinted from *Media Studies Journal* 8:1 (winter 1994), by permission of The Freedom Forum Media Studies Center, Columbia University.]

QUESTIONS

1. Gans uses the framework *utopia/dystopia* to describe descriptions of the life made possible by the "information superhighway." A utopia is an ideal society (first called by that name in Sir Thomas More's book from the 17th-century). What other contexts do you have for descriptions of utopias? For their opposite, dystopias? Have you encountered the kind of optimistic descriptions of postmodern electronic society that Gans refers to?
2. Implicit in the sales pitches that Gans alludes to is the idea that consumer choice is made individually, without reference to effects on social factors such as how people interact with each other. What are some other features of contemporary life in the United States in which ignoring these social factors becomes an issue?

3. Inventing for yourself a persona aligned with those Gans calls "promoters," write back to his article, setting forth some positive sides of what his essay regards negatively. (Possible stances might include those of a technological visionary, an economic booster, a provider of needed services, an advocate of expanded consumer choice, or someone emphasizing positive human and social aspects of interactive technology.)

M. KADI

Q: How Tall Is the Internet? A: Four Inches Tall

> *Computer networking offers the soundest basis for world peace that has yet been presented. Peace must be created on the bulwark of understanding. International computer networks will knit together the peoples of the world in bonds of mutual respect; its possibilities are vast, indeed.*
>
> —Scientific American, *June 1994*

Computer bulletin board services offer up the glories of e-mail, the thought provocation of news-groups, the sharing of ideas implicit in public posting, and the interaction of real-time chats. The fabulous, wonderful, limitless world of communication is just waiting for you to log on. Sure. Yeah. Right. What this whole delirious, interconnected, global community of a world needs is a little reality check.

Let's face facts. The U.S. government by and large foots the bill for the Internet, through maintaining the structural (hardware) backbone, including, among other things, funding to major universities. As surely as the Department of Defense started this whole thing, AT&T or Ted Turner is going to end up running it, so I don't think it's too unrealistic to take a look at the Net as it exists in its commercial form in order to expose some of the realities lurking behind the regurgitated media rhetoric and the religious fanaticism of net junkies.

The average person, J. Individual, has an income. How much of J. Individual's income is going to be spent on computer connectivity? Does $120 a month sound reasonable? Well, you may find that a bit too steep for your pocketbook, but the brutal fact is that $120 is a "reasonable" monthly amount. The major on-line services have a monthly service charge of approximately $15. Fifteen dollars to join the global community, communicate with a diverse group of people, and access the world's largest repository of knowledge since the Alexandrian library doesn't seem unreasonable, does it? But don't overlook the average per-hour connection rate of $3 (which can skyrocket upwards of $10, depending on your modem speed and service). You might think that you are a crack whiz with your communications software—that you are rigorous and stringent and never, ever respond to e-mail or a forum while you're on-line—but let me tell you that no one is capable of logging on efficiently every time. Thirty hours per month is a realistic estimate for on-line time spent by a single user engaging in activities beyond primitive e-mail. Now consider that the average, one-step-above-complete-neophyte user has at least two distinct BBS (bulletin board system) accounts, and do the math. Total monthly cost: $120. Most likely, that's already more than the combined cost of our utility bills. How many people are prepared to double their monthly bills for the sole purpose of connectivity?

In case you think 30 hours a month is an outrageous estimate, think of it in terms of television. Thirty hours a month in front of a television is simply the evening news plus a weekly *Seinfeld/Frasier* hour. Thirty hours a month is less time than the average car-phone owner spends on the phone while commuting. Even a conscientious geek, logging on for e-mail and the up-to-the-minute news that only the net services can provide, is probably going to spend 30 hours a month on-line. And, let's be truthful here, 30 hours a month ignores shareware downloads, computer illiteracy, real-time chatting, interactive game playing, and any serious forum following, which by nature entail a significant amount of scrolling and/or downloading time.

If you are really and truly going to use the net services to connect with the global community, the hourly charges are going to add up pretty quickly. Take out a piece of paper, pretend you're writing a check, and print out "One hundred and twenty dollars—" and tell me again, how diverse is the on-line community?

That scenario aside, let's pretend that you have as much time and as much money to spend on-line as you damn well want. What do you actually do on-line?

Well, you download some cool shareware, you post technical questions in the computer user group forums, you check your stocks, you read the news and maybe some reviews—hey, you've already passed that 30-hour limit! But, of course, since computer networks are supposed to make it easy to reach out and touch strangers who share a particular obsession or concern, you are participating in the on-line forums, discussion groups, and conferences.

Let's review the structure of forums. For the purposes of this essay, we will examine the smallest of the major user-friendly commercial services—America OnLine (AOL). There is no precise statistic available (at least none that the company will reveal—you have to do the research by HAND!!!) on exactly how many subject-specific discussion areas (folders) exist on America OnLine. Any on-line service is going to have zillions of posts—contributions from users—pertaining to computer usage (the computer games area of America OnLine, for example, breaks into 500 separate topics with over 100,000 individual posts), so let's look at a less popular area: the "Lifestyles and Interests" department.

For starters, as I write this, there are 57 initial categories within the Lifestyles and Interests area. One of these categories is Ham Radio. Ham Radio? How can there possibly by 5,909 separate, individual posts about Ham Radio? There are 5,865 postings in the Biking (and that's just bicycles, not motorcycles) category. Genealogy—22,525 posts. The Gay and Lesbian category is slightly more substantial—36,333 posts. There are five separate categories for political and issue discussion. The big catchall topic area, the

Exchange, has over 100,000 posts. Servicewide (for the smallest service, remember) there are over a million posts.

You may want to join the on-line revolution, but obviously you can't wade through everything that's being discussed—you need to decide which topics interest you, which folders to browse.

Within the Exchange alone (one of 57 subdivisions within one of another 50 higher divisions) there are 1,492 separate topic-specific folders—each containing a rough average of 50 posts, but many containing closer to 400. (Note: America OnLine automatically empties folders when their post totals reach 400, so total post numbers do not reflect the overall historical totals for a given topic. Sometimes the posting is so frequent that the "shelf life" of a given post is no more than four weeks.)

So, there you are, J. Individual, ready to start interacting with folks, sharing stories and communicating. You have narrowed yourself into a single folder, three tiers down in the America OnLine hierarchy, and now you must choose between nearly 1,500 folders. Of course, once you choose a few of these folders, you will then have to read all the posts in order to catch up, be current, and not merely repeat a previous post.

A polite post is no more than two paragraphs long (a screenful of text, which obviously has a number of intellectually negative implications). Let's say you choose 10 folders (out of 1,500). Each folder contains an average of 50 posts. Five hundred posts, at, say, one paragraph each, and you're now looking at the equivalent of a 200-page book.

Enough with the stats. Let me back up a minute and present you with some very disturbing, but rational, assumptions. J. Individual wants to join the on-line revolution, to connect and communicate. But J. is not going to read all one million posts on AOL. (After all, J. has a second on-line service.) Exercising choice is J. Individual's God-given right as an American, and, by gosh, J. Individual is going to make some decisions. So J. is going to ignore all the support groups—after all, J. is a normal, well-adjusted person, and all of J.'s friends are normal, well-adjusted people; what does J. need to know about alcoholism or incest victims? J. Individual is white. So J. Individual is going to ignore all the multicultural folders. J. couldn't give a hoot about gender issues and does not want to discuss religion or philosophy. Ultimately, J. Individual does not engage in topics that do not interest J. Individual. So who is J. meeting? Why, people who are *just like J.*

J. Individual has now joined the electronic community. Surfed the Net. Found some friends. *Tuned in, turned on, and geeked out.* Traveled the Information Highway and, just a few miles down that great democratic expressway, J. Individual has settled into an electronic suburb.

Are any of us so very different? It's my time and my money and I am not going to waste any of it reading posts by disgruntled Robert-Bly drum-beating men's-movement boys who think that they should have some say over, for instance, whether or not I choose to carry a child to term simply because a condom broke. I know where I stand. I'm an adult. I know what's up and I am not going to waste my money arguing with a bunch of neanderthals.

Oh yeah; I am so connected, so enlightened, so open to the opposing viewpoint. I'm out there, meeting all kinds of people from different economic backgrounds (who have $120 a month to burn), from all religions (yeah, right, like anyone actually discusses religion anymore from a user standpoint), from all kinds of different ethnic backgrounds and with all kinds of sexual orientations (as if any of this ever comes up outside of the appropriate topic folder).

People are drawn to topics and folders that interest them and therefore people will only meet people who are interested in the same topics in the same folders. Rarely does anyone venture into a random folder just to see what others (the Other?) are talking about.

Basically, between the monetary constraints and the sheer number of topics and individual posts, the great Information Highway is not a place where you will enter an "amazing web of new people, places, and ideas." One does not encounter people from "all walks of life" because there are too many people and too many folders. Diversity might be out there (and personally I don't think it is), but the simple fact is that the average person will not encounter it because with one brain, one job, one partner, one family, and one life, no one has the time!

Just in case these arguments based on time and money aren't completely convincing, let me bring up a historical reference. Please take another look at the opening quote of this essay, from *Scientific American*. It was featured in their 50 Years Ago Today column. Where you read "computer networking," the quote originally contained the word *television*. Amusing, isn't it?

[Reprinted by permission from *h2so4* no. 3 (winter 1994–spring 1995).]

QUESTIONS

1. Before you read this chapter were you aware that the basic hardware for the Internet is largely supported by the federal government (through the Department of Defense and other agencies and grants to universities)? How would you go about finding out how much the total cost of the support is? Who benefits, directly or indirectly, and who does not?
2. Does Kadi's charge that "connectivity" is an option only for people in the middle class and up ring true in your experience? What are the implications for who gets connected?
3. How would you describe Kadi's persona in the article? What features of style go into making up that persona? How does it fit the essay's argument?
4. Both Kadi and Gans offer reasons for skepticism about the benefits of individual consumer choice as it affects the existence and nature of the Internet. What are the reasons, and how do they differ?
5. Explore potential responses to the writer's viewpoint. (For example, you might argue the benefits of affiliation with people "just like yourself.")

CONCLUSION

This chapter has not attempted to go beyond a rudimentary discussion of a few electronic media as these have developed so far. For additional practical advice on use of electronic media, one of the many guides on using the Internet, or better yet, a more experienced friend or professional should be your next step. For particulars on your own library resources, reference librarians should be the resource of choice.

But what this chapter has undertaken is to reflect on the rhetoric of electronic media in a way parallel to the explorations of media in other chapters. Electronic media are not windows on the world any more than is television or film; their statements have to be considered and applied by readers, just as are those of news media or entertainment texts, or the statements of political figures and others in positions of authority. You should develop the habit of looking carefully at those you rely on for guidance.

FURTHER ASSIGNMENTS

Assignment

Find a videotape or broadcast of a television show dating before 1960—if possible, one with original advertisements and promos. What elements in that program strike you as different because of the technology? (Consider not only the absence of color but the number and mobility of cameras, the use of taped or live audiences, exterior/interior shots, and so on.) What elements have to do with different conventions for television programming apart from technology?

Works Cited

Albrecht, Brian. "Team Names Still Stir Controversy." *Cleveland Plain Dealer,* Fri., Oct. 20, 1995, 1–A, 14–A.
Althusser, Louis. *Lenin and Philosophy and Other Essays,* trans. Ben Brewster. New York: Monthly Review Press, 1971.
The American Heritage Dictionary of the English Language, ed. William Morris. Boston: Houghton Mifflin, 1981.
Amesley, Cassandra. "How To Watch *Star Trek*." *Cultural Studies* 6:2 (1992), 323–37.
Ang, Ien. "Understanding Television Audiencehood." In Newcomb 367–86.
Atwan, Robert, Donald McQuade, and John W. Wright. *Edsels, Luckies, & Frigidaires: Advertising the American Way.* New York: Delta, 1979.
Austen, Jane. *Pride and Prejudice.* New York: Penguin Books, 1972.
Bagdikian, Ben H. *The Media Monopoly,* 4th ed. Boston: Beacon Press, 1992.
"Barcia Joins Conservatives." *Midland County Review,* January 23, 1995, A1.
Barnouw, Erik. *Tube of Plenty: The Evolution of American Television,* 2nd rev. ed. New York: Oxford University Press, 1990.
Berger, Arthur Asa, *Popular Culture Genres: Theories and Texts* (Foundations of Popular Culture, vol. 2) Newbury Park, Calif.: Sage Publications, 1992.
Berger, John, and Jean Mohr. *Another Way of Telling.* New York: Vintage, 1982.
Bizzell, Patricia and Bruce Herzberg. *The Rhetorical Tradition: Readings from Classical Times to the Present.* Boston: St. Martin's, 1990.
Bogart, Leo. *Commercial Culture: The Media System and the Public Interest.* New York: Oxford, 1995.
Boldt, Axel. "Excerpt from 'The Philosophy Behind the Blacklist of Internet Advertisers." <http://math-www.uni.paderborn.de>

Brooks, Brian S., et al. *News Reporting and Writing,* 3rd ed. New York: St. Martin's, 1988.

Burke, Kenneth. *The Philosophy of Literary Form: Studies in Symbolic Action.* Berkeley: University of California Press, 1973.

Bush, Chilton R. *Newswriting and Reporting Public Affairs.* Philadelphia: Chilton Book Co., 1970.

Bush, Heather, and Burton Silver. *Why Cats Paint.* Berkeley: Ten-Speed Press, 1994.

Calabrese, Tracy. "Murder Moves North." *Saginaw News,* Sunday, Jan. 8, 1995, A1, A4.

Cannon, Carl M. "Honey, I Warped the Kids: The Argument for Eliminating Movie and TV Violence." *Mother Jones,* Jul./Aug. 1993. Reprinted, *Utne Reader,* May/June 1994, 95–96.

Carroll, Lewis. *Alice's Adventures in Wonderland and Through the Looking-Glass.* New York: Macmillan, 1963.

———. *The Annotated Alice,* Martin Gardner, ed. New York: Clarkson N. Potter, Inc., 1960.

Cohen, Bernard C. *The Press, the Public, and Foreign Policy.* Princeton, N.J.: Princeton University Press, 1963.

Cohen, Jeff and Norman Solomon. *Adventures in Medialand.* Monroe, Maine: Common Courage Press, 1993.

Danto, Arthur C. "Photography and Performance: Cindy Sherman's Stills," Sherman 5–12.

"Darts & Laurels," *Columbia Journalism Review,* July/August 1995, 17–18.

"Dubious Achievement Awards of 1995." *Esquire,* January 1996, 46–67.

Eagleton, Terry. *Ideology: An Introduction.* New York: Verso, 1991.

———. *Literary Theory: An Introduction.* Minneapolis: University of Minnesota, 1983.

Eisner, Joel, and David Krinsky. *Television Comedy Series: An Episode Guide to 153 TV Sitcoms in Syndication.* Jefferson, N.C.: McFarland & Co., 1984.

Elbow, Peter. *Writing Without Teachers.* New York: Oxford University Press, 1973.

Engelhardt, Tom. "The Shortcake Strategy." In Gitlin, *Watching Television,* 68–110.

Epstein, Joseph. "Introduction," Sir Ernest Gowers. *The Complete Plain Words,* rev. by Sidney Greenbaum and Janet Whitcut. Boston: David R. Godine, 1988.

Fairness and Accuracy In Reporting (FAIR). "The Way Things Aren't: Rush Limbaugh Debates Reality." *Extra!,* Jul./Aug. 1994 <www.peacenet.apc.org/fair/limbaugh-debates-reality.html.>

Fallows, James. *Breaking the News: How the Media Undermine American Democracy.* New York: Pantheon Books, 1996.

Faulkner, William. *Absalom, Absalom!.* New York: Random House, 1936; reprinted. New York: Vintage, 1986.

Fish, Stanley. "Literature in the Reader: Affective Stylistics." *Is There a Text in This Class? The Authority of Interpretive Communities.* Cambridge, Mass.: Harvard University Press, 1980, 21–67.

Foster, David. "Sexist? Racist? Violent?" *The Saginaw News,* July 26, 1994, C4.

Gans, Herbert J. "The Electronic Shut-Ins: Some Social Flaws of the Information Superhighway," *Media Studies Journal* 8:1 (Winter 1994), 123–28.

Gardner, David. "Announcement of National Electronic Open Meeting." [HATCHG@jkhbhrc.byu.edu].

Gitlin, Todd. "Imagebusters: The Hollow Crusade Against TV Violence." *The American Prospect* Winter, 1994.

———. *Inside Prime Time.* New York: Pantheon Books, 1983.

———, ed. *Watching Television: A Pantheon Guide to Popular Culture.* New York: Pantheon, 1986.

Godwin, Mike. "Time Waited For No One (Or At Least Not For Me): Why I Picked a Fight With The Newsmagazine That Fed The Great Internet Sex Panic." *Hotwired* [www.hotwired.com/special/pornscare/godwin.html]

Goffman, Erving. *Gender Advertisements.* Cambridge, Mass.: Harvard University Press, 1979.

Gold, Jeffrey. "Talk-show Host Accused of Fraud," Associated Press text from *San Diego Union,* 30 Dec. 1994, A1.

Gornick, Vivian. "Introduction." In Goffman, vii–ix.

Gould, Stephen Jay. "A Biological Homage to Mickey Mouse." *The Panda's Thumb: More Reflections on Natural History* (New York: W.W. Norton, 1980), 95–107.

Gramsci, Antonio. *Selections from Cultural Writings,* ed. David Forgacs and Geoffrey Nowell-Smith; trans. by William Boelhower. Cambridge, Mass.: Harvard University Press, 1985.

Gross, Beverly. "What a Bitch!" *Salmagundi,* Summer 1994; reprinted, *Utne Reader,* May–June 1995, 45–46.

Hamilton, Candy. "Where a Tomahawk Chop Feels Like a Slur." *Christian Science Monitor,* Wed., Oct. 25, 1995, 3.

Hartley, John. "Encouraging Signs: Television and the Power of Dirt, Speech, and Scandalous Categories." In Rowland and Watkins, 119–41.

Hassett, Michael. "Posting on Oklahoma City Bombing Rhetoric." [HATCHG@jkhbhrc.byu.edu.] (May 2, 1995).

"Hightower Gets the Mickey Mouse Treatment," *EXTRA! Update,* December 1995, 4.

Hoffman, Donna L., and Thomas R. Novak. "A Detailed Critique of the Time Article: 'On a Screen Near You: Cyberporn'" [http://www2OOO.ogsm.vanderbilt.edu/dewitt.cgi] (July 3, 1995).

Jacobson, Michael F., and Laurie Ann Mazur. *Marketing Madness: A Survival Guide for a Consumer Society.* Washington, D.C.: Center for the Study of Commercialism, 1995.

Jeffords, Susan, and Lauren Rabinovitz, eds. *Seeing Through the Media: The Persian Gulf War.* New Brunswick, N.J.: Rutgers University Press, 1994.

Jenkins, Henry. *Television Poachers: Television Fans and Participatory Culture.* New York: Routledge, 1992.

Jhally, Sut, and Justin Lewis. *Enlightened Racism.* Boulder, Colo.: Westview Press, 1992.

Kadi, M. "Q. How Tall Is the Internet? A. Four Inches Tall." *h2so4,* Winter 1994/Spring 1995. Excerpted as "Welcome to Cyberbia," *Utne Reader,* March-April 1995, 57–59.

Kehher, Brian. *Flush Rush.* Berkeley, Ca: Ten Speed Press, 1994.

King, Graham. *Say "Cheese": Looking at Snapshots in a New Way.* New York: Dodd, Mead, 1984.

Kinsley, Michael. "The Intellectual Free Lunch," *The New Yorker,* Feb. 6, 1995, 4–5.

Lakoff, George. "Metaphor and War." *East Bay Express,* Feb. 22, 1991; reprinted in McQuade and Atwan, 231–37.

―― and Mark Johnson. *Metaphors We Live By.* Chicago: University of Chicago Press, 1980.

―― and Mark Turner. *More Than Cool Reason: A Field Guide to Poetic Metaphor.* Chicago: University of Chicago Press, 1989.

Lanham, Richard A. *Style: An Anti-Textbook.* New Haven, Conn.: Yale University Press, 1974.

Lantry, William. "Posting About Rush Limbaugh." [HATCHG@jkhbhrc.byu.edu] (May 21, 1995).

LaQuey, Tracy. *The Internet Companion: A Beginner's Guide to Global Networking,* 2nd ed. Reading, Mass.: Addison-Wesley, 1994.

Lawrence, David C., ed. "Hierarchy of Newsgroups."

Lee, Alfred McClung, and Elizabeth Briant Lee. *The Fine Art of Propaganda.* New York: Octagon Books, 1972.

Lee, Martin A., and Norman Solomon. *Unreliable Sources: A Guide to Detecting Bias in News Media.* New York: Carol Publishing Group, 1990.

Lentricchia, Frank, and Thomas McLaughlin, eds. *Critical Terms for Literary Study.* Chicago: University of Chicago Press, 1990.

Leonard, John. "TV and the Decline of Civilization." *The Nation,* Dec.27,1993. Reprinted as "Why Blame TV?," *Utne Reader,* May-June 1994, 90–94.

Lichter, S. Robert, Stanley Rothman, and Linda S. Lichter. *The Media Elite.* Bethesda, Md.: Adler & Adler, 1986.

——. *Prime Time: How TV Portrays American Culture.* Washington, D.C.: Regnery Publishing, 1994.

Loengard, John. *Pictures Under Discussion.* New York: Amphoto, 1987.

Lutz, Catherine, and Jane Collins. "The Photograph as an Intersection of Gazes: The Example of *National Geographic.*" In Lucien Taylor, ed., *Visualizing Theory: Selected Essays From V. A. R. 1990–94* (New York: Routledge, 1994) 363–84.

Lutz, William. *Doublespeak.* New York: Harper, 1989.

MacDougall, Curtis. *Interpretative Reporting.* New York: Macmillan, 1968.

McKibben, Bill. *The Age of Missing Information.* New York: Random House, 1992.

McQuade, Donald, and Robert Atwan, eds. *Popular Writing in America: The Interaction of Style and Audience,* 5th ed. New York: Oxford University Press, 1993.

Mander, Jerry. *Four Arguments for the Elimination of Television.* New York: Quill, 1978.

Manning, Michael. "How To Win the Tobacco War." *New York Review of Books* July 13, 1996,31–35.

Masterman, Len. *Teaching the Media.* New York: Routledge, 1985.

Mayle, Peter. *Up the Agency: The Funny Business of Advertising.* New York: St. Martin's, 1990.

Meeks, Brock. "Jacking in from the 'Point-Five Percent Solution' Port: Washington, DC—Time Magazine's Credibility Is Hemorrhaging." *Hotwired* [http://www2OOO.ogsm.vanderbilt.edu/novak/brock.rimm.review.html.] (July 4, 1995).

Miller, Mark Crispin. "Deride and Conquer." In Gitlin, *Watching Television,* 183–228.

Mitchell, W. J. T. "Representation." In Lentricchia and McLaughlin, 11–22.

New English Bible. Oxford and Cambridge University Presses, 1970.

Newcomb, Horace, ed. *Television: The Critical View,* 5th ed. New York: Oxford University Press, 1994.

Orwell, George. "Politics and the English Language." *The Orwell Reader* (New York: Harcourt, Brace, and Co., 1956), 355–66.

Parenti, Michael. *Make-Believe Media: The Politics of Entertainment.* New York: St. Martin's, 1992.

Penticoff, Rick. "Posting on Oklahoma City Bombing." [HATCHG@jkhb-hrc.byu.edu] (April 24, 1995).

Plimpton, George. "Ernest Hemingway." In *Writers at Work: The Paris Review Interviews,* Second Series, ed. George Plimpton (New York: Viking, 1963), 215–39.

Postman, Neil. "The Parable of the Ring Around the Collar." In McQuade and Atwan, 96–99.

——— and Steve Powers. *How to Watch TV News.* New York: Penguin, 1992.

Pynchon, Thomas. *V.* Philadelphia: Lippincott, 1963; reprinted, New York: Bantam, 1964.

Rafferty, Terrence. "No Pussycat." *The New Yorker,* June 20, 1994, 87–88.

Reid, Brian. "Critique of the Rimm Study," (July 5, 1995).

Rivers, William L., and Alison R. Work. *Writing for the Media.* Mountain View, Calif.: Mayfield Publishing Co., 1988.

Rowland, Willard D., Jr., and Bruce Watkins, ed. *Interpreting Television: Current Research Perspectives.* Beverly Hills, Calif.: Sage Publications, 1984.

Ruiz, Paul. "Media Deform the 'Legal Reform' Debate." *EXTRA!,* May-June 1995, 10–11.

Sale, Kirkpatrick. "Fighting the Darkness." *Utne Reader,* July-August 1995, 37.

Savan, Leslie. "Don't Inhale." *The Village Voice,* October 24, 1995, 20, 22.

———. *The Sponsored Life: Ads, TV, and American Culture.* Philadelphia: Temple University Press, 1994.

Schrag, Robert L. "Sugar and Spice and Everything Nice Versus Snakes and Snails and Puppy Dogs' Tails: Selling Social Stereotypes on Saturday Morning Television." In Vande Berg and Wenner, 220–32.

Schweitzer, Mary. "Posting on Oklahoma City Bombing Rhetoric." [HATCHG @jkhbhrc.byu.edu] (April 22, 1995).

Schwoch, James Mimi White, and Susan Reilly. *Media Knowledge: Readings in Popular Culture, Pedagogy, and Critical Citizenship.* Albany: SUNY Press, 1992.

Shepherd, Chuck, John J. Kohut, and Roland Sweet, eds. *News of the Weird.* New York: Plume, 1989.

Sherman, Cindy. *Untitled Film Stills.* New York: Rizzoli, 1990.

Smythe, Dallas. *Dependency Road Communications, Capitalism, Consciousness, and Canada.* Norwood, N.J.: Ablex, 1981.

Sontag, Susan. *On Photography.* New York: Farrar Straus & Giroux, 1977.

Stafford, William. "A Way of Writing." *From Writing the Australian Crawl: Views on the Writer's Vocation.* Ann Arbor: University of Michigan Press, 1978, 17–20.

Strunk, Will, and E. B. White. *The Elements of Style.* New York: Macmillan, 1979.

Teal, Karen Kurt. "The Loop Writing Process," Wallace 31.

Teinowitz, Ira. "Rich Lalley, Red Dog." *Advertising Age,* June 26, 1995.

Thomas, Jim. "Some Thoughts on Carnegie Mellon's Committee of Investigation." [http://sun.soci.niu.edu/~cudigest/rimm/rimm2/] (Sept. 15, 1995).

Tichi, Cecelia. *Electronic Hearth: Creating an American Television Culture.* New York: Oxford, 1990.

Turpin, Paul. "Posting on Oklahoma City Bombing Rhetoric." [HATCHG@jkh-bhrc.byu.edu] (May 1, 1995).

Twitchell, James B. *Carnival Culture: The Trashing of Taste in America.* New York: Columbia, 1992.

Vande Berg, Leah R., and Lawrence A. Wenner, eds. *Television Criticism: Approaches and Applications.* White Plains, N.Y.: Longman, 1991.

Wallace [Sargent], Elizabeth, ed. *What's Happening with Writing at Western Oregon State College?* Monmouth, Ore.: [Western Oregon State College], 1991.

Weltner, Linda. "The Joys of Mediocrity." *New Age Journal,* Sept./Oct. 1993; reprinted, in *Utne Reader* January-February 1994, 99–100.

Williams, Joseph M. Style: *Ten Lessons in Clarity and Grace.,* 3rd ed. Glenview, Ill.: Scott, Foresman, 1989.

Williams, Raymond. *Keywords: A Vocabulary of Culture and Society.* New York: Oxford University Press, 1976.

Wilson, John K. *The Myth of Political Correctness: The Conservative Attack on Higher Education.* Durham, N.C.: Duke University Press, 1995.

Zwerdling, Daniel. Interview with Leslie Savan. *All Things Considered,* June 4, 1995.

Index

advertisements
   recalling ads (pause), 231
   Chevrolet Camaro ad, 252
   collecting ads, 235, 238
   Saturday morning ads and gender stereotypes, 237–38
Albrecht, Brian, 487
All Things Considered, transcript of earthquake report, 308
Althusser, Louis, 446, 451, 463–65
Amend, James, 173
American Sign Language, conventions (assignment), 60–61
Amesley, Cassandra, 121–29
Anderson, Kirsten, 619
analysis, 227
   Chevrolet Camaro ad, 252–54
   technical events, 246, 248–49
   photograph, 315–21
   photograph (assignment), 321
   clothing, 316
appellation
   audience named as audience, 386, 391
   definition, 446
   how you appellate others (pause), 450
   media call us to play role, 566
   text calls audience into existence, 570
attentive TV viewing (assignment), 36
audience
   fictive and real, 69
   shift from early-stage writing to draft, 85
   testing entertainment programs, 380
   audience's view of texts, 386–91
   models for audience, 388–89
   audience divided by preferences, 396
   inferring audience from text (assignment), 421, 572
   audience and style, 569
   audiences interact with text, 570
Austen, Jane, 332–34
author
   "author-function" in media texts, 265
   corporate "author" of media texts, 378
   disappearing author and invisibility, 546

bad rhetoric, 575–81
   effective because audience wants to believe it, 576, 578
   categories, 579
Bagdikian, Ben H., 633
Banks, Gary, 230
Barcia, Jim, 146
Berger, Arthur Asa, 380–83
Berger, John and Jean Mohr, 305, 307–309
Bloch, Sonny, 203
Boldt, Axel, 602
bombing
   tactic for revision, 506
   Oklahoma City, 613–23
boundaries transgressed by dirty texts, 362
brainstorming—prewriting technique, 112
bricolage, 297
   working environment (pause), 297
   writing as bricolage, 476
Broadcast News, 90–92
Burke, Kenneth, 498

Calvin and Hobbes, 43
camera positioning, 248
Cancun Trust ad, 320
Cannon, Carl M., 401
Cantu, Sabrina, 148
captioning, 240, 243–45, 440–42
Carroll, Lewis, 233
CBS Evening News
    sequence of news stories and ads, 1/19/95, 179
    transcript of earthquake report, 1/19/95, 213–17
CCCC meeting, 313–15
censorship on the Internet, 627–28
Chast, Roz, 594
checklist for editing and revision, 524–25
class
    class and forms of play, 356
    population of class as representative (pause), 390
    class and taste, 394
    ruling class in U.S., 468
    class publications, 530
Clinton, Bill, speech after Oklahoma City bombing, 614
close reading of photograph, 315
clutter, 34, 50–52
CNN
    sequence of stories and ads, 1/19/95, 180
    transcript of earthquake report, 1/19/95, 208–12
code
    definition, 326
    signs, codes, and conventions, 322–30
Cohen, Bernard, 398
Cohen, Jeff and Norman Solomon, 56–58
Cole, Stacey, 153
collection
    of ads (assignment), 238
    of writing, 525
    as basis for own system, 595–98
    assignment, 597
Columbia Journalism Review, 582
comedy plot formulas, 363–64
commercial
    system threatens journalistic canons, 165
    news as business, 170–73
    carefully tested, 232–33
    analyzing TV commercials, 246
    categorizing commercials, 254
    commercials and shallow belief, 261
    product placement, 374–75, 377
    commercials and sports, 375
common sense
    as story, 191
    as fundamental ideology, 344
communication
    never innocent, 32–33
    face-to-face vs. mass, 33
    TV news communicates through visual imagery, 185–86
community
    interpretive community of *Star Trek* watchers, 125
    interpretive communities, 263
concept map, 115–17
consciousness industry, 388
constellation, 236
construction
    writing as constructing a representation of self, 121
    essays construct roles for readers, 129
    constructing other contexts for ads, 236
consumer
    model of reading, 29
    keyword, 40
    poor model for media use, 41
context
    Japan as context for news stories (pause), 187
    other contexts for ads, 236
    context determines "right" and "wrong" in writing, 295
    nothing can be decontextualized permanently, 316
conventions, 58–67
    skillful writers use rhetorical conventions, 30
    etymology, 59
    as rules of play, 65–66
    in writing and writing classes (pause), 67
    and speech genres, 84
    breaking conventions is conventional, 89
    different conventions for prewriting and drafts, 117–19
    in print and broadcast news, 157–64
    signs, codes, and conventions, 322–30
conversation
    and speech genres, 84
    give and take required, 84
    different from news, which is one-way, 142
    research as conversation between sources, 152
    as model for writing, 496, 497–99
critical thinking, 427, 429
culture, 183
    keyword, 32
    determines visual codes, 302
    difference as theme in U.S./Japan stories, 181–87
cyberporn, 623–29
cynicism
    and media, 204
    and cynical audience for advertising, 437
    as a role, 568

development and freewriting, 109
Die Hard, 465–67

difference
    cultural difference as "story" in Japan
        coverage, 187
    race, class, and gender difference in the gaze, 335
dirt, 194
    news as "dirty" category, 175
    and ads, 264-71
    and entertainment texts, 361
Disney
    The Lion King, 410-19
    acquisition of ABC, 163
Ditri, Jennifer, 23-24, 46
Doonesbury, 599
Doritos, 369-72
double consciousness, 454
double vision, 82
doublespeak, 549, 588-89
Douglass, Frederick, 313-15
drafting, 117-21
    stage of writing process, 80
    etymology, 118

editing, 503
Empower America—transcript of health care ad, 193-94
endorsement—as ad technique, 256-57
Enola Gay, exhibit in Smithsonian, 183, 364
entertainment
    and news, 174
    themes in critiques, 346
    texts we play with, 353
    concern about texts, 356
    media do rhetorical work, 360
    and violence, 401-409
    and children, 410-14
    science-fiction, 415-16
    race, 416
    and stereotypes, 418
Epstein, Joseph, 543
essay, 67
    defined by conventions, 93-94
    between public and private, 118
ethos, 612

FAIR, 582
fairness and objectivity, 201
Faulkner, William, 353
flow
    and advertisements, 270
    discourages analysis, 302-303
Floppy-Eared Friends, 15
fonts and genres of communication (pause), 298
Foster, David, 410

Franklin, Benjamin and proverbs, 541
freewriting, 112-15

Gans, Herbert J., 635-38
Garfield, Bob, 488-89
gaze
    directed by TV 302
    at/from photos, 335
    collect photos to illustrate (assignment), 341
gender
    and children's TV ads, 237
    part of codes for reading photos, 338
genre, 8
    speech genres, 84-85
    borrowings between, 92-93
    of photos, 306
Gitlin, Todd, 407, 419
global revision, 503
Goffman, Erving, 542
Gold, Jeffrey, 203
Gramsci, Antonio, 461
Grant, Hugh, 536
Gross, Beverly, 573
Gulf War and propaganda, 165, 200

Halstead, Michael, 49, 116
health care discussion as test case for adequacy of media, 192-96
Health Care Reform Project ad, 195
hegemony, 315
    and entertainment texts, 372-74
    objections to model, 385
    and ideology, 461
    and style, 559
Helvetica type, 297
Hemingway, Ernest, 102-108
heuristics as prewriting device, 113
Hightower, Jim, 163
Home Improvement, 393-94
Humpty-Dumpty and verbal reality, 233-34
Hurst, Teri, 95-99
hypertext, 610-12

ideology, 20
    maintained by stories, 199
    and entertainment texts, 380
    subtle gradations, 384
    as basis for underlying unity to media, 428
    three contrasting definitions, 454-61
        false consciousness, 455-58
        relativism, 458-60
        concealed structure of values, 460-62
    history of term, 456

ideology *(continued)*
  claims to transcendental viewpoint, 457–48
  as lens, 468
  test principle: what work does position do?, 469
  appeal of simple answers, 469
  four competing ideologies, 469–71
  as fictions moving to myths, 471
impersonation, 501, 507
  as editor (pause), 529
individual
  ideology of independence and stories, 147–48
  uniqueness as ideology, 304
  individualism and ideology, 567
induction and deduction, 239
information as map, 158
interests
  in media texts, 54
  of news producers, 166
  must be acknowledged for fairness, 202
Internet, 600–606
  search procedures, 606
  Usenet categories, 607
  as source of information, 612
  need to confirm information, 627
interpretation
  ability needed for media literacy, 30
  "facts" come already interpreted, 199
  differing interpretations of photos, 307–309
  interpretive communities, 263
intertextuality, 73–74
  and ads, 236
  and photos, 298–99
invisibility
  conventions are normally invisible, 59
  in news texts, 436–37
  author, 546
Ideological State Apparatuses, 463–65

Jamieson, Kathleen Hall, 194
Japan
  discussion of, 1995 Kobe quake, 181–84
  cultural differences with U.S. as theme in news reports, 183–87
Jeep ad, 241
journal
  keeping a journal, 21
  movement from journal to draft, 95
  metacommentary in journals, 109

Kadi, M., 638–41
King, Graham, 291
Kruger, Barbara, 445, 448–50
Kukla, Aaron, 252

Kurt, Karen, 114–15
Kuwait—propaganda treated as news, 200

labeling, 438
Lakoff, George, 475
Lanham, Richard, 545
Lantry, William, 581
Laser sailboat ad, 242–43
Law and Order, 20
leaving a draft alone—tactic, 505
Lee, Alfred and Elizabeth, 587–88
Leonard, John, 404
Lichter, S. Robert, Stanley Rothman, and Linda S. Lichter, 55
Limbaugh, Rush, 488–89, 581–86
  e-mail analysis of rhetoric, 620
Lion King, The, 410–19
Loop Writing Process (cartoon), 114
Lutz, Catherine and Jane Collins, 338
Lutz, William, 588–89

McAfee, Stacey, 48
McDonald's coffee lawsuit, 359
McKibben, Bill, 71–73
magazines' readership and ads (pause), 236
Magoo—test for entertainment audiences, 379–80
Mander, Jerry, 246
Masterman, Len, 388
Maxson, Mark, 47
media, 5
  as addressed, 6
  genres, 7
  writing as medium, 7
  reading media as activity, 29
  media literacy, 30
  communicate through symbol systems, 32; 35–36
  doing without media, 43–45
  strategies for reading media, 52–54
  writing as a medium, 82–83
  genres of media texts (pause), 85
  media logs and news (pause), 143
  narratives and news media, 143–46
  stories in media circulation give news currency, 145–46
  concentration of media ownership, 158
  importance of reading news media comparatively, 179–81
  media's capacities differ (TV, print, radio), 185–87
  health care discussion as represented in media, 192
  and propaganda, 197
  duplication of Gulf War propaganda, 200
  media serve and make use of those in power, 200
  media see for us, 295–96

media recycle, 298-99
one subject, or many?, 428, 593
model for reading—window, 435
reinforce ideologies, 467
reading media texts for ideology (assignment), 474
metaphor, 475
appellate audiences to flatter, 566
dynamic, 592
electronic media—positive and negative qualities, 600
electronic media—exchanges on Oklahoma City bombing, 615
anonymous "fax"—Oklahoma City bombing, 621
media deprivation (assignment), 45
media elites, 55-58
"Media in the Courts", 510-23
media literacy, 30
media log (assignment), 9-14
medium—contexts, 30-34
metacommentary, 109, 502
  important to use in research, 631
metaphor and ideology, 475
Midland County Review, 146
Midol—advertisement transcript, 249-52
"Mr. Sellack", 399-400
Monty Python's The Life of Brian, 461
Morning Edition—transcript of earthquake report, 1/20/95, 220-24
myth, 21-22
  of the born writer, 82, 100
  stories and myths, 144

names and social class (pause), 462
narratives
  that make sense of news, 143-45
  master narratives about news, 143
  meta-narratives or master narratives, 151
  narratives and ads, 245
  pictures and narratives, 303
National Geographic, 439
natural
  conventions appear as natural, 59
  conventions make media seem natural, 302
  representation and the natural, 430
Nelson, Eric, 509
news, 25
  and information as cultural systems for providing information, 142
  early use of *newspaper,* 142
  news and stories, 142
  stories about news, 143-45
  and stereotypes, 150
New York Times Index, 155

What counts as news?, 157-62
concentration of news outlets, 162-63
and interests, 153
as rhetorical, 165
newspapers read comparatively (assignment), 167
news article as genre, 167
conventions of news (print and broadcast), 167
contrast news and essay conventions, 168
news does better at informing about events than processes, 168
and commercial interests, 170-73
news is profitable, 171
and entertainment, 174
comparative reading of news, 177
audiences are trained to read news, 178
news always an interpretation, 189
keeping informed: health care discussions, 192
news and propaganda, 197
ideal of objectivity, 201
news approaches tabloids, 366
Nike ad, 472-74
nostalgia, 484-87
  assignment, 487
Nowak, Marci, 46, 300
nutshelling—tactic for revision, 506

objectivity, 201
Ohio Northern University, 17
Oklahoma City bombing—electronic exchanges, 613-23
Okla-Net, 622
Olin Foundation, 577
Orwell, George, 541
outline as prewriting device, 113-15

Peacock, Shannon, 508
Penticoff, Rick, 616
persona, 5
  from *mask* in Greek drama, 169-70
personal ad (assignment), 575
Phillips Petroleum ad, 243-45
photography, 31
  as paradigm for visual, 292
  world already photographed, 309-10
  and tourism, 335
  and labeling, 438
  captions for photos (assignment), 442
play
  texts give readers roles to play, 16
  choice of how to play along with texts, 121-22
  symbolic value, 356
  and hegemony, 372
Plimpton, George, 102

political correctness, 476-84
    political dimension to charges, 477
    recycled stories, 487
politics, 429
popular
    not strictly size, 352
    popular music, 397-401
portfolio
    exhibition, 526
    draft, 527
Postman, Neil and Steve Powers, 173
pragmatism, 456
Prainito, Tara, 240
Pretty Woman, 18
prewriting—stages, 80
    as its own genre, 86
    further division—looking for subject
        vs. further development, 109
    kinds of prewriting, 112-17
    goal to subdivide tasks of writing, 117
process, 399
propaganda, 197
    viewing propaganda films (assignment), 197
    judge by its effect, 199
    not "brainwashing", 200
    advertisement as propaganda, 260-62
    and bad rhetoric, 577
    and Rush Limbaugh, 583-86
    checklist, 587-88
proverbs (pause), 542, 555-56
public
    usage vs. trademarks, 234-35
    currents in public discussion (assignment), 499
purposes, 81
Pynchon, Thomas, 184-85

Rafferty, Terrence, 412
readers
    roles, 121
    Star Trek readers, 122-29
    readers' roles in viewing *Star Trek* (pause), 121
reading
    reading media as activity, 29
    reading requires writing and vice versa, 30
    reading traffic, 393
realism, 435
Red Dog beer ads, 559-62
reducing unnecessary difficulty (style), 549-55
representation
    and reality, 119
    persona as representation of self in writing, 119
    media representations as selected versions
        of reality, 119
    both "there" and "not there", 292
    conventions—natural seeming, 432
    multiple systems, 434
research—need to know, 631
    checklist, 634
resistance to ads, 230-32
revision—stage of writing, 80
    usually out of sight, 492-93
    as re-vision, 495
    phases after first draft—global revision
        and editing, 496
    process as subject for writing (pause),
        502-503
    and computers, 504-505
    tactics, 505-508
rhetoric, 4
    pragmatic way of thinking about language,
        135-36
    of news texts, 165
    ads as good texts for examining, 225-29
    and dialectic, 539
Rimm, Martin, 623-28
Roches, The, 399-400
Roedel, Meredith, 50
rules and conventions, 6

Saab commercial, 563
Saginaw News article, "Murder Moves North", 440
Sale, Kirkpatrick, 132
Savan, Leslie, 267-69, 562-64
Schrag, Robert L., 237
Schweitzer, Mary, 615
Seinfeld, 366-69
Sherman, Cindy, 311-13
sign, 322
Smith, Danielle, 133
Smythe, Dallas, 388
Sontag, Susan, 309, 334
speech genres, 184-85
sponsor, 63
stages of writing process, 80
Stafford, William, 86
Star Trek, 122-29
Stein, Ed, 42
stereotypes, 418
stories, 25
    and news, 143-45
    and stereotypes, 147
    Christian Science Monitor stories and page locations,
        162, 165
    ads made of stories, 227
storytelling in ads, 258-59
Straney, Lisa, 472-74

strategies
  for reading media, 52-54
  and tactics for revision, 493, 502-508
style
  and TV news, 90
  bad advice, 535
  as ornament, 537
  as clarity, 542
  classical division of style, 537
  fixation on correctness, 547-49
  as constitutive, 555-59
  as interaction between subject, persona, and audience, 557-58
  and hegemony, 559-69
  as display, 566
subject
  of photo and power relations, 339-40
  audience named as subjects, 463
"Swinging on a Star", 397-99, 555

tabloid news, 173
taboos, 451-53
talk groups—titles, 599
talk shows—topics (pause), 176
taste, 391-97
technical events, 246-49
television
  audiences segmented, 42
  conventions, 62-65
  and illusion of participation, 301
  "toaster with pictures", 347-48
  as-if reality, 436
text, 6
  presumes audience, 8
  texts divide into genres, 83-84
  and image in print ads, 241-46
theme—basis of unity in news stories, 145
Thoreau, Henry David, 44

Time magazine and cyberporn, 625
Tom Tomorrow, 164, 434
tourism
  exempts us from experiencing what is seen, 310
  and photography, 336
trademarks and public usage, 234-35
Turpin, Paul, 620
Twitchell, James, 395

vectors about public issue, 499-502
visual, 291-94
  elements on TV news, 168
  added to verbal image, 240-41
  phrases (pause), 293-94
  and descriptive writing, 330
  and the Other, 334-35
vulgar, 395

Weltner, Linda, 130
White, E. B., 543-45
Williams, Joseph, 549
Williams, Raymond, 29, 40
Wilson, John K., 481
words and style, 572-75
writing
  three stages in process, 80
  as extension of voice, 81
  in genres, 85
  application of news to college writing, 150-51
  difference in genres between news and college writing, 268
  advice to "show, don't tell", 304
  recursive nature, 496
  calls audience into existence as audience, 571

Yon, Seth, 14

Zwerdling, Daniel, 562-64